Classical and Modern Social Theory

Classical and Modern Social Theory

Edited by

Heine Andersen and Lars Bo Kaspersen

BLACKWELL
Publishers

Copyright © Hans Reitzels Forlag A/S 1996; copyright © editorial arrangement and introduction
Heine Andersen and Lars Bo Kaspersen 1996; 2000

First published in Danish as *Klassisk og Moderne Samfundsteori* by Hans Reitzels Forlag A/S,
Copenhagen, 1996

First published in English 2000

2 4 6 8 10 9 7 5 3 1

Blackwell Publishers Inc.
350 Main Street
Malden, Massachusetts 02148
USA

Blackwell Publishers Ltd
108 Cowley Road
Oxford OX4 1JF
UK

Library of Congress Cataloging-in-Publication Data
Klassik og moderne samfundsteori. English.
    Classical and modern social theory / edited by Heine Andersen and Lars Bo Kaspersen.
        p.   cm.
    Includes bibliographical references and indexes.
    ISBN 0-631-21287-6 (hc. : alk. paper) — ISBN 0-631-21288-4 (pbk. : alk. paper)
    1. Sociology—Philosophy.   2. Sociology—Philosophy—History.   I. Andersen, Heine,
    1945–   II. Kaspersen, Lars Bo.

    HM606.D36 K53 2000
    301′.01—dc21

                                                                              99-058779

British Library Cataloguing in Publication Data
A CIP catalogue record for this book is available from the British Library.

Typeset in 10 on 12 pt Times New Roman
by Ace Filmsetting Ltd, Frome, Somerset
Printed in Great Britain by MPG Books, Bodmin, Cornwall

This book is printed on acid-free paper.

Contents

Part III: Contemporary Challenges to Classical and Modern Social Theory   391

Contributors

Heine Andersen is an associate professor in the Department of Sociology at the University of Copenhagen, Denmark. His research interests include social theory, the philosophy of social science, and the sociology of science. He was one of three authors of "Contemporary Sociology in Denmark" in the *International Handbook of Contemporary Developments in Sociology*, edited by R. P. Mohan and S. Wilke (1994).

Margareta Bertilsson was educated at the Universities of California (Santa Barbara) and Lund, Sweden, and has been professor of sociology at the University of Copenhagen since 1994. She is also an associate editor of the *European Journal of Social Theory*, and she is specially interested in the relation between social theory, law and morality, and the sociology of knowledge. Her recent publications include "The Balkan Tragedy: A Universal or a Particular Issue" in *European Societies*, edited by T. Boje and others (1999).

Tom Broch is an associate professor in the Department of Sociology at the University of Copenhagen. The subjects of his research include communication, semiotic theory, and the foundations of social theory.

Staf Callewaert was educated at the Universities of Louvain, Belgium, and Lund, Sweden, and is now a professor in the Department of Education, Philosophy, and Rhetoric at the University of Copenhagen. His main interests include education in the Third World, and the sociology of culture and education, and his recent publications include "Philosophy of Education, Frankfurter Critical Theory, and the Sociology of Pierre Bourdieu" in *Critical Theories in Education*, edited by I. Popkewitz and L. Fendler (1999).

Jørn Falk was once a craftsman and now works on the sociology of work, social movements, communities, and civil society, mainly in Denmark.

Halvor Fauske is an associate professor at Lillehammer College, Norway. His current research focuses on the sociology of youth, child care, and social work, and he has recently published a selection of Jürgen Habermas's writing on modernity and youth in the 1990s.

Willy Guneriussen is a professor in the Department of Sociology at the University of Tromsø, Norway, following an earlier training in philosophy. His main areas of research include the philosophy of science, and theoretical traditions in social science, as well as discourses of modernity.

Roar Hagen is an associate professor in the Department of Sociology, University of Tromsø, where his main interest is the theory of collective action. Recent publications include "Rational Solidarity and Functional Differentiation" in *Acta Sociologica* (2000).

Gorm Harste was educated at the Universities of Louvain, Belgium, and Aarhus, Denmark, where he now is an associate professor of sociology in the Department of Political Science. He is especially interested in social and political theories, European state-building, and modernity, and he was coordinator of the Nordic network for a contemporary diagnosis of modernity from 1987 to 1997.

Lars Bo Kaspersen was educated at the Universities of Copenhagen and Aarhus in Denmark and Sussex in the United Kingdom, and he is now an associate professor in the Department of Sociology at the University of Copenhagen. His interests include state formation in early modern Europe, the welfare state, and globalization, and recent publications include "State and Citizenship under Transformation in Western Europe" in *Public Rights, Public Rules*, edited by Connie McNeely (1998) and *Anthony Giddens: An Introduction to a Social Theorist* (2000).

Sven-Åke Lindgren is an associate professor of sociology at the University of Gothenburg, Sweden, where his interests include the sociology of knowledge, cultural sociology, and criminology.

Nils Mortensen is an associate professor of sociology, Aarhus University, Denmark. Subjects of his research include the organization of work, technological change, and family life, as well as social exclusion and inclusion. He is editor of *Social Integration and Marginalization* (1995).

Per Månson is an associate professor sociology at the University of Gothenburg, Sweden, where his areas of interest include social psychology and Marx and Marxism. Among his recent publications are "Back in the USSR" in *History Today* (October 1997) and "State, Nation, and Nationalism in Russia: A Historical Perspective" in *Nationalism in Diaspora* (1997).

Gunnar Olofsson is a professor of sociology at the University of Växjö, Sweden, and has recently, with Ian Gough, edited *Capitalism and Social Cohesion: Essays on Exclusion and Integration* (1999). The subjects of his research include social movements and labor market policy.

Henrik Ørnstrup, works on the history of ideas about the individual and society, as well as classical German sociology from Georg Simmel to Theodor Geiger.

Dag Østerberg is an emeritus professor of sociology at the University of Oslo and a member of the Norwegian Academy of Science. He has published extensively on general and social philosophy, as well as urban sociology and the sociology of culture, including *Metasociology: An Inquiry into the Origins and Validity of Social Thought* (1989).

Uffe Østegaard is the Jean Monnet professor of European civilization and integration in the Center for European Cultural Studies at the University of Aarhus, Denmark. His publications in various languages deal with national identity, national political cultures, and nation-states in Europe.

William Outhwaite studied at the Universities of Oxford and Sussex, where he has taught since 1973 and is now professor of sociology in the School of European Studies. He is currently working on post-communism and contemporary Europe. His recent books include *The Habermas Reader* (1996), *The Blackwell Dictionary of Twentieth-Century Social Thought* (with Tom Bottomore, 1993), and *The Sociology of Politics* (with Luke Martell, 1998).

Poul Poder Pedersen is a research fellow in the Department of Sociology, University of Copenhagen, where his interests include postmodernity and power. With Timo Cantell, he has contributed "Postmodernity and Ethics: An Interview with Zygmunt Bauman" to *A Bauman Reader*, edited by Peter Bilharz (in the press).

Anders Ramsay has taught sociology at the University of Lund and the University Colleges of Kristianstad and Halmstad, Sweden, and has published work on the critique of political economy, political theory, and the sociology of health and the environment. He is a founder and a member of the editorial board of the Swedish journal *Res Publica*.

Pål Strandbakken is a research fellow at the National Institute for Consumer Research in Lysaker, Norway, where his interests include sustainable consumption, green consumer advice, and product durability. His earlier research concerned the sociology of religion and future studies.

Jens Peter Frølund Thomsen is an associate professor in the Department of Political Science, University of Aarhus, Denmark, where the subjects of his research include political theory and public policy. Recent publications include *State, Economy, and Society* (with Bertramsen and Torfing, 1990) and *British Politics and Trade Unions in the 1980s: Governing Against Pressure* (1996).

Karin Widerberg is a professor of sociology in the Department of Sociology and Human Geography, University of Oslo, Norway. She has published books and articles on the feminist theory of science and methodology, understandings of gender, sexual violence, and law from a feminist perspective. She is currently working on a project on "The Sociality of Tiredness."

Preface

An important purpose of social theory is to provide concepts for understanding social interactions and social structures, and stability and change in social life. The origins of social theory are in ancient Greece, but in its modern form it first developed during the eighteenth century as a child of the Enlightenment, industrialization, the emergence of capitalism, and the creation of nation-states in Western Europe.

Interest in social theory has oscillated with changing political and intellectual conjunctures, and in recent years more and more people have shown an increasing concern about social theory in general. The experience of a rapidly changing world is undoubtedly one of the reasons for this growing interest.

Scientific theories of society are not an easy matter. Many students regard social theory as a difficult area which can only be approached with painstaking efforts; still, it is not always easily accessible. Very few textbooks have been intended to introduce the broad scope of social theories emerging in the nineteenth century and also the most recent developments.

The purpose of this book is to provide a first introduction to the different traditions and concepts within social theory in such a way that a basic knowledge and a general view can be created before the reader proceeds to the primary literature itself. The book consists of three parts: classical social theory, modern social theory, and contemporary challenges to classical and modern social theory. The tradition, the basic idea, and the fundamental concepts of each theory are presented, and each chapter contains brief biographical information about the originators of the theories. Each chapter includes a short list of key concepts and definitions, and a comprehensive bibliography with the titles of original works and the most important secondary literature. Books and articles are listed with the intention of facilitating the search for additional literature and further reading. Each bibliography is divided into primary and secondary sections (the only exemptions are the thematic chapters). The primary bibliographies list works by the major theorists discussed in the chapters; the titles are in English or in the original language where no translations could be found. The secondary bibliographies are lists of the major introductions and commentaries, and the additional literature mentioned in the chapters. An asterisk * indicates that a title is recommended as introductory reading.

The book is aimed primarily at students in at higher and further education (including universities, business schools, teacher-training colleges, schools for social workers and nurses) but A-level or high-school students specializing in sociology could also benefit from several chapters in the book. The book is a useful work of reference to clarify key concepts and also a tool to find relevant literature.

Social theory is a wide subject and a number of other theorists and theories could have been included. When selecting theories we have favoured those of a sociological character, and the book does not include theories with a special focus on the political or economic dimensions of social life. Furthermore, with the exception of the last chapter we have limited the book to theories developed after about 1850.

The genesis of the book was slow. From preliminary ideas in 1993 to the first edition, which came out in Danish in 1996 and Swedish in 1999, we went through a long process. From the very beginning it was thought of as a Scandinavian project. The first outline was discussed with teachers and scholars from Norway, Sweden, and Denmark, and many problems were cleared away in the first phase. We are grateful to these Scandinavian colleagues who participated in meetings during the first phase of the project. Later on the authors agreed to start all over again to prepare an English edition, and many corrections and changes were made. Consequently, we are grateful to all the authors who, without grumbling or complaints, did an enormous amount of work to finish this version. Lastly we would like to thank Ole Gammeltoft and Hans Reitzels Publishers, Copenhagen, for their excellent cooperation and for believing in our ideas in the first place. Many thanks to Susan Rabinowitz from Blackwell Publishers too for helping us through to the English edition.

Heine Andersen
Lars Bo Kaspersen
January 2000

Acknowledgements

We would like to thank a number of people for translating some chapters into English. The chapters not mentioned here have been translated by the authors themselves. Marianne Risberg, chapters 3, 21, 27; Marilyn Piety, chapter 4; Annette Andersen, chapters 7, 8, 12, 24, 25; Anders Ramsay and Chris Mathieu, chapter 10; Annette Andersen and Marianne Risberg, chapter 11; Mark Hebsgaard, chapters 15, 26; Margaret Wold, chapter 17; Billy O'Shea, chapter 18; Karen Margrete Wiin Larsen, chapter 20; Lennart Nygren, chapter 23; Mark Hebsgaard, chapter 26; Steve Sampson, chapter 28; Brendan Sweeney, chapter 30.

part **I**

Classical Social Theories

chapter 1

Classical and Modern Social Theory

William Outhwaite

This book is planned as an introduction to Classical and Modern Social Theory, and the present chapter is therefore in many ways an introduction to an introduction. I shall first address the question of what is understood by social theory, and then sketch out what I take to be the main lines of development within social theory, its relationship to sociology, social anthropology, and the other social sciences, as well as to literary and cultural theory and the changing relations between what one can call classical and modern social theory. As we shall see, it is not just a matter of some theories which were once "modern" coming to acquire the status of "classics"; it is also the case that "classical" theories can be and have been reconsidered and incorporated into current theorizing.

More speculatively, and I shall return to this theme later, it can be argued that the very idea of theorizing about *society* (as opposed to, say, "the world," the natural order, or the state or polity) is modern by definition, in that it is inextricably bound up with the form of life which we call modernity. This developed in Europe and North America around the eighteenth century and was exported from there more or less systematically to the rest of the world. In other words, to think of human societies not just as aspects of a natural and/or divinely sanctioned order, but also not just as human contrivances, such as political constitutions, which can be modified more or less at will as a result of human decisions, presupposes that we live in or can appeal to a society characterized by what we take to be modern conceptions of individualism, democracy, and citizenship. And if we take this view of social theory, it carries a very substantial set of presuppositions which some present-day theorists, especially those associated with the idea that we are now in a condition of "*post*-modernity," would see as too heavy to bear.

What is Social Theory?

The term "social theory" is increasingly used in course descriptions, publishers' catalogues, journal rubrics, and so forth. The reason, I think, is that we need a very broad term of this kind to refer to work which does not fall squarely within the boundaries of sociology or the other social sciences, or of philosophy or any other single academic discipline. Although sociologists have the most prominent place in this volume, it would clearly have been imperialistic to hijack not just Marxism but also such thinkers as the philosopher, Jean-Paul Sartre (1905–80) or the historian of ideas, Michel Foucault (1926–84) into the camp of *sociological* theory. At the same time, any account of contemporary sociology which did not address the contributions of such thinkers as these would be seriously incomplete (cf. Skinner 1985; Outhwaite 1987).

Sociologists as diverse as the Frankfurt School's main thinker, Theodor Adorno (1903–69) and the leading contemporary British sociologist, Anthony Giddens (b. 1938) have therefore tended to prefer broader terms such as *Theorie der Gesellschaft* or social theory (Giddens 1979) In Giddens's case, this was partly because he saw sociology as too closely identified with a particular cluster of theories modelled on the natural sciences of the nineteenth century and focused on *industrial* society. This interpretation can be questioned, especially in the light of changes in sociology in the past couple of decades; more important, I think, is the fact that both our conceptions of sociology and our ideas about the nature of scientific theory have changed in important ways over the course of the twentieth century.

Classical and Modern Theory

That such changes should have taken place in the course of such a long period is hardly surprising. What *is* surprising, however, is that we seem to have experienced something of a circular movement. What is normally called classical sociology includes Herbert Spencer (1820–1903) and Karl Marx (1818–83), and sometimes Auguste Comte (1798–1857), who invented the name sociology. It centres around the work of a small number of approximate contemporaries writing in the late nineteenth and early twentieth centuries;, Ferdinand Tönnies (1855–1936), Max Weber (1864–1920), Emile Durkheim (1858–1917), Vilfredo Pareto (1848–1923), and Georg Simmel (1858–1918). These latter thinkers, even when, like Durkheim, they were desperately concerned to establish sociology as an independent academic discipline (Clark 1973), were also active in adjacent disciplines such as philosophy. Their image of sociology, in other words, was an inclusive one, and this is perhaps best expressed by Simmel in his image of sociology as a second-order science which incorporates the more specialized contributions of history and other social sciences. This is an image which has persisted to the present, when sociologists are often seen as magpies, snatching fragments from economics, legal theory, linguistics, history, or wherever and, to change the metaphor, mixing them up into a heady and sometimes dangerous cocktail.

The other point to make about the classical writers is that their conception of theory is as a means of explaining concrete social processes such as suicide, the division of labour, the emergence of capitalism, or other processes of social modernization. What happens to these theories in retrospect is that they are of interest to subsequent generations not so much for their substantive claims as for their status as what the American historian of science, Thomas Kuhn (1962), called paradigms or exemplars which show us how we might wish ourselves to theorize about social phenomena. Only specialists, for example, are passionately concerned with assessing just how great was the contribution of Protestant Christianity to the changes in values which helped to make early capitalism possible, but Weber's ideas about the way in which one might explain such processes, in particular the idea that causal explanations in the social sciences are incomplete until they are complemented by interpretative understanding (*Verstehen*), remains one of the cornerstones of modern social theory.

Historians of social thought often criticize the selective and present-focused history which pervades accounts of classical social theory. Such accounts tend to portray Max Weber, for example, as part of a trinitarian system of oppositions with the ghost of Karl Marx on one hand and the work of his contemporary, Emile Durkheim, on the other. In fact, of course, although the first of these relationships was indeed very important for Weber (he once said that the seriousness of a modern scholar could be measured by how seriously he took Marx and Nietzsche (1844–1900)), he was also drawing from and criticizing a huge range of contemporaries who are nowadays mostly known only from the mentions of them in Weber's texts. Our accounts of the "classics," and even of the more recent history of social thought, are, however, inevitably selective and partial. To put it another way: they fit the model of interpretation proposed in Hans-Georg Gadamer's (b. 1900) existentialist hermeneutics, in which we are concerned with the practical meaning of a text *for us today*, rather than the more traditional ideal of merely understanding the text in its own terms and its own historical context.

Shifting borderlines between classical and modern

The borderline between "classical" and "modern" social theory, which most accounts locate in roughly the same place as this volume, is of course historically relative and shifting. The classical theorists did not appear like Chianti bottles with *classico* labels freshly attached to them, and the retrospective attachment of the classical label stretches further into the twentieth century as we move into the twenty-first. The early functionalist anthropologists, Bronislaw Malinowski (1884–1942) and A. R. Radcliffe-Brown (1881–1955), along with Talcott Parsons (1902–79) and Robert Merton (b. 1910), could easily be assigned now to the classical category, and contemporary social theorists often place intellectual bets on which of them will enjoy classical status a hundred years from now.

Parsons is, however, a pivotal figure in more than this historically relative sense. His first major work, *The Structure of Social Action*, published in 1937, was the concrete embodiment of a particular conception of the history of sociological theory which was dominant in the middle years of the twentieth century and continues to enjoy widespread support. In Parsons's version, the classics (his holy trinity is composed of Durkheim, Weber, and Pareto) can be seen to converge on a general theory of social action which Parsons spelled out here and in his subsequent works. This theory could be systematized according to some at least of the prescriptions of mid-twentieth-century philosophy of science and was in principle open, Parsons thought, to empirical testing and confirmation.

On this model, then, Parsons was the midwife of *modern* sociology as well as its leading exponent. Even sociologists who did not accept Parsons's particular blend of action theory and functionalist system theory tended, in the middle decades of the twentieth century, to accept something like this periodization, also stressing, for example, the advances in empirical research techniques or the massive expansion in the numbers of people working in the social sciences in the period after World War II. Whatever the future might hold for sociology and the other social sciences, it seemed that they had definitely come of age. Marx, Weber, Durkheim, and the other founding fathers were, as the B-movie gangsters say, "history."

This triumphalist vision was called into question in the late 1960s. First, the revival of social conflicts in many of the advanced capitalist countries eroded the credibility of the dominant sociological paradigm, US structural functionalism, which stressed the integration and value consensus of societies. It also encouraged a revival of Marxist social theory, which had been marginalized in the "free world" with the beginning of the Cold War and perverted into the official state doctrines of Marxism-Leninism and "scientific communism" in the socialist countries. Marxism came back in a variety of forms, ranging from dogmatic orthodoxy to the Neomarxism of Yugoslav "praxis philosophy" or Frankfurt School "critical theory." Other classical social theorists benefited from a resurgence of interest in the history of social thought, marked in the English-speaking countries by Giddens's very influential *Capitalism and Modern Social Theory* (1971), with its very detailed discussion of Marx, Weber, and Durkheim.

Contemporary sociological theory also became more ambitious and speculative, with a shift of hegemony from the US to continental Europe and an explosion of interest in Althusserian Marxism, Frankfurt critical theory, British Wittgensteinian philosophy, French structuralism, and the work of Michel Foucault, Pierre Bourdieu (b. 1930), and others. What the British historian of political thought, Quentin Skinner, later called *The Return of Grand Theory in the Human Sciences*, in an edited volume in 1985 which documented this shift, meant that "the classics" seemed less like remote ancestors and more like older contemporaries. This was particularly true of the Marxist literature, which was almost always concerned to stress that the contemporary interpretation was in any case what Marx really meant (at least in his better moments). But it was also hard to read Foucault's account of surveillance and punishment, for example, without thinking of Max Weber's sociology of *Herrschaft* (domination) and rationalization.

Social theory – past and present

Generally, then, the time-perspective of sociology changed. Just as its substantive concerns once again became a little more historical, in a partial reversal of what the great historical sociologist, Norbert Elias (1897–1990) attacked in 1983 as "The Retreat of Sociologists into the Present" – in other words, their excessive concentration on contemporary social phenomena (Smith 1991), so its sense of its own past shifted. Giddens had attacked, in an influential article in 1972, the "myth of the great divide" between the more or less unformed or chaotic prehistory of sociology and the subject in its modern "scientific" form. This, as Giddens showed, involved a lack of sensitivity to the work of the classics and an undue degree of confidence in the scientific credentials of "our" social thought.

Giddens's more nuanced account of the continuities and discontinuities in social theory came to be recognized as a more adequate one. Substantively, sociology shifted its theoretical focus from "industrialism" or "industrial society" to "capitalism" or at least *Spätkapitalismus*, and then to a broader focus on "modernity," in which it addressed dimensions of power and culture which had previously been somewhat marginal to its concerns. Giddens (1990), for example, sees industrialism and capitalism as two of the central points on the compass of modernity, but he adds the two further points of surveillance, in Foucault's sense of the term, and military power, which had been curiously neglected by most of his immediate predecessors and contemporaries in sociology, who had tended to see conflict in intrasocietal terms (e.g. class conflict and/or industrial conflict), even at the height of the Cold War and the anti-colonial independence movements.

Social Sciences and Natural Sciences

This process of a return to earlier traditions in social theory or, to put it another way, the partial retraditionalization of sociological theory, can of course be evaluated in very different ways. Many sociologists and other social scientists would see it as at best a diversion from, and at worst a threat to, the pursuit of genuinely scientific knowledge of society which would be disciplined, systematic, verifiable, and cumulative. It will readily be seen that such divergent evaluations reflect not just different conceptions of the proper role of sociology and the other social sciences, but differing conceptions of the way in which we can come to know social phenomena and even of their very nature.

To address these issues is to venture into two of the principal domains of philosophy: ontology, which is concerned with the nature of things or, even more broadly, with the nature of Being itself, and epistemology, the theory of knowledge. A systematic discussion of these issues is beyond the scope of this introductory chapter, but we can boil them down to a single pair of questions:

1 Are human social processes radically different from those encountered in the (rest of the) natural world?
2 Is our knowledge of such processes radically different from our knowledge of (other) natural processes?

The model of unitary science and empiricism

The negative answer to these questions runs something like this. Science, at least as it has
been understood since the seventeenth-century revolution in natural scientific thinking, is
essentially a unitary enterprise of recording facts about the world, ordering them, and explaining them by means of theories. Scientists are more likely to succeed in this enterprise
if they are open-minded and detached in their approach to the phenomena which they study;
the preconceptions of common sense are likely to be a source of error. (It is obvious, is it
not, that the sun rises in the east, passes over the earth's surface, and sets in the west, that
heavy bodies always fall faster than light ones, and so on?)

On this view, the important distinction is that between science and non-science or common sense. There are no radical differences of principle between the social sciences and the
other sciences. No doubt the study of human societies will turn out to look more like animal
biology than like physics or astronomy, but there is no reason except favouritism to study
human beings in a radically different way from other animals. Most people who take this
view of the unity of the natural and the social sciences concede that our preconceptions and
prejudices are likely to be stronger when we study ourselves and our societies, but we can
and should overcome this with discipline and training, and should not pay much attention to
our own prescientific intuitions about society or those of its other members. The difficulties
of overcoming these preconceptions, along perhaps with the greater complexity of human
social processes, may mean that the social sciences will take longer to achieve reliable or
positive knowledge, but we will get there in the end. Auguste Comte, who, as we noted
earlier, invented the term sociology, also developed the idea of a gradual ascent of all the
sciences to what he called the "positive" stage.

Comte's multi-volume treatises had come to seem a little quaint by the end of the nineteenth century, but the idea of positive, scientific knowledge was developed in a less speculative way by Ernst Mach (1838–1916) and by the logical empiricists of the Vienna Circle
from the end of World War I. An empiricist is someone who believes that all our knowledge
comes from experience; the logical empiricists combined this principle with modern mathematical logic in a philosophical analysis of the language of science conceived as a unitary
enterprise (unified science). Just as the eighteenth-century Scottish empiricist, David Hume
(1711–76) had rejected any so-called knowledge which does not consist in relations of
ideas (e.g. mathematics) or matters of fact, so the logical empiricists held that all our knowledge is exhausted by necessary truths, such as $2 + 2 = 4$ or "bachelors are unmarried," and
by verifiable statements about matters of fact. Anything else was not just false but meaningless. The Austrian-British philosopher, Karl Popper (1902–94) rejected many of the detailed views of the logical empiricists but propounded an influential variant of his own in
his *Logic of Scientific Discovery* (1934) and subsequent works.

Something like this conception of testable empirical knowledge of both nature and society spread to the English-speaking countries and Scandinavia, reinforcing existing traditions and becoming dominant in the middle decades of the twentieth century. It provided a
kind of charter for the developing social sciences in the postwar period. Even natural scientists, who tend to pay less attention than social scientists to the philosophy of science, could
be found to use Popper's ideas for polemical purposes (Gilbert and Mulkay 1984) or even
explicitly to defend them (Medawar 1969).

The critique of positivism

This positivistic conception, sometimes also called naturalist because it upheld the idea of the essential unity of natural and social science, did not offer much by way of a philosophy of *social* science. Books on the philosophy of social science tended to consist of a number of chapters expounding general philosophy of science followed by a rather sad coda on the obstacles confronting the social sciences and how far they had to go to attain the standards of the natural sciences. In the 1960s and 1970s this conception of science came under attack from two directions: philosophy and history.

W. V. O. Quine (b. 1908) in the US and Mary Hesse (b. 1924) in Britain developed a philosophical critique of the idea of theory-independent facts which could arbitrate between competing theories. As Quine (1953: 41–2) puts it, "our statements about the external world confront the tribunal of sense experience not individually but only as a corporate body . . . The unit of empirical significance is the whole of science." In a less extreme but similarly striking formulation, Hesse suggested that theories are related to empirical reality rather like nets which are anchored to the ground at only a limited number of points. This drift in philosophy towards a more holistic conception of theories can lead, as it did for Quine, to the position known as conventionalism, that science involves more or less ungrounded choices between theories which can at best aim to be compatible with or to "save" the phenomena observed.

This move in philosophy converged with the historical demonstration by Kuhn (1962) that scientists were in practice much more the contented prisoners of their theories than philosophers of science had liked to believe. Solving "puzzles" within established paradigms or disciplinary matrices, scientists tended not to abandon an established theory until the counter-evidence was really massive *and* an alternative theory was available. Theory change, on this conception, became not unlike processes of political or social revolution, not just in the degree of commitment and passion involved but also in requiring not just the decay of the old order but also the availability of an emergent alternative.

Alternatives to conventionalism can be roughly divided into rationalist attempts to ground science in logical necessity, with the claim that, if scientific theories are true, they are necessarily true and realist accounts which assert that science aims to describe and explain real objects and processes in the world which exist independently of our descriptions of them but which we may with luck manage to describe reasonably adequately. As Roy Bhaskar (1978: 250) puts it, "Science . . . is the systematic attempt to express in thought the structures and ways of acting of things that exist and act independently of thought."

Hermeneutics and phenomenology

Positivist naturalism, in both its nineteenth- and twentieth-century forms, has always attracted an anti-naturalist response. The late nineteenth-century and early twentieth-century critiques of positivist social science in the name of interpretive understanding (*Verstehen*) are echoed by later followers of the Austrian-American phenomenologist, Alfred Schütz (1899–1959) or the British philosopher, Peter Winch (1926–99). Here again there is a continuity among those who stress that human actions and human societies can be understood from the inside, in a way which has no parallel in the study of nature. To come to understand a society, on this view, is in some ways like learning a language (as Winch argues and as anthropologists, who often do both together, will confirm); to understand the "point," the meaning or purpose of what is said or done is distinct from being able to explain it as a quasi-natural process. A sophisticated computer program could predict how often I am likely to use certain words in the rest of this chapter, or even (again on a probabilistic basis) complete my words as I begin to write them. (The disabled astrophysicist, Stephen Hawking, has a machine of this kind.) But no computer of the kinds we know at present would be able to guess what points I want to make in the rest of this chapter, nor how I will choose to make them.

Generalizable causal explanations and interpretation of meaning

Such a conception of history and the other social sciences may sustain a radical anti-naturalism, as in the work of Wilhelm Dilthey (1833–1911), where the sciences of *Geist*, grounded in the understanding of expressions (*Ausdrücke*), are sharply differentiated from the sciences of nature, concerned as they are with generalizable causal explanations. Less radically, one can argue, as Max Weber did, for an integration of the two approaches: explanations in the social sciences, and the theories which underpin them, must be both causally adequate, in that they fit the observable sequence of events, and meaningfully adequate, in that we can understand why other human beings more or less like ourselves might have acted in the ways described.

In his classic work on the Protestant Ethic, for example, Weber identifies what looks like one causal factor among others contributing to capitalist economic innovation in early modern Europe, namely certain variants of Protestant Christianity. To have a prima facie causally adequate explanation, it may be enough to show that otherwise similar countries or regions were indeed more innovative, the greater the prevalence of ascetic Protestantism. But to obtain a meaningfully adequate explanation, Weber has to show what it was in ascetic Protestantism, and specifically in the Calvinist doctrine of predestination (the doctrine that everything that happens in this world and the next was pre-ordained by God from the beginning of time) that might encourage disciplined and dedicated work in one's calling. His suggestion involves conjecture about *what it was like* to be a Calvinist: the inner loneliness left by the absent god created an anxiety which could be mitigated by success at a godly calling within the world.

What concerns us here is not the validity of this explanation but its structure, in which, as Weber put it rather later, "sociology attempts an interpretive understanding of action in order *thereby* to explain its course and consequences." This explanatory structure is one which we arguably also find in Emile Durkheim's slightly earlier study of *Suicide* (1897). Durkheim had argued in *The Rules of Sociological Method* (1895), only two years prior to this study, in quite a Comtean way, that there were such things as social facts which could only be explained by other social facts and not by states of the individual consciousness. Stressing the difference between sociology and common sense, he had warned against invoking the inaccessible domain of personal motives. Yet in *Suicide* we find a strong, if implicit, appeal to intuitions about *what it is like* to be a Protestant, or divorced, or living through an epoch of economic crisis, and so forth. In this conception, *pace* Durkheim's formal methodological structures, we already know a good deal about the fine texture of social life by being members of human societies.

For Weber, at least, the social sciences remain distinct from the natural sciences because of this possibility of understanding the meaning of the processes under investigation – something which in the case of nature could not be done outside the realm of metaphysics. Yet this does not make them in principle any less scientific or objective. A number of subsequent social theorists radicalized Weber's *Verstehen* thesis in such a way as to widen the gap again between the social and the natural sciences. Alfred Schütz, drawing on Edmund Husserl's (1859–1938) phenomenological philosophy, and in particular his ideas about what is taken for granted in the pre-scientific "natural attitude," stresses the continuity between ordinary "typifications" in everyday life, as when we walk into a store and can usually distinguish the attendants from the other shoppers, and the more formal types constructed by the social scientist. Somewhat later, Peter Winch and the critical theorist, Karl-Otto Apel (b. 1922) showed how the analysis of language by the Austrian philosopher, Ludwig Wittgenstein, paralleled many of the insights of the older hermeneutic tradition. For Winch, the upshot was that social science, if it can be called that, is an essentially philosophical endeavor to understand the concepts used by members of the society one is studying. Apel, with his close ally Jürgen Habermas (b. 1929), argued that this was not enough, that the presence of power relations in human societies required the fusion of interpretive and explanatory approaches in a potentially emancipatory form of social science. (Habermas argued in *Knowledge and Human Interests* (1971) that Freudian psychoanalytic theory and the Marxist critique of ideology were examples of such emancipatory sciences.) A position of this kind is often described as critical hermeneutics.

Are causal laws "real"?

The debates between these various conceptions of the philosophical status of social theory and the social sciences continue to rage. Realist philosophers of science such as Rom Harré (b. 1927) and Roy Bhaskar (b. 1944), reworking earlier scientific realist claims against the background of the mutation of positivism into conventionalism, have offered some clarification by providing a rather different model of science as a whole, in which causal laws are analyzed not as universally true *statements* but as references to the natures and powers of things which exist independently of our descriptions of them. The tendencies built into things may conflict and neutralize one another, so that there is nothing for the eager empiricist to observe. Here on Earth, for example, the balance between gravitational attraction and the centrifugal force produced by the Earth's rotation means that we are neither pinned to the ground nor flying off into space. Similarly, it can be argued, when we observe someone trying to give up smoking the interplay between rational considerations of health and economy on one hand, and habit and physical addiction on the other, may produce a similar stalemate in which the addict goes on smoking. Realists can accept that social processes are partly a result of our concepts and partly of cruder processes of power and exploitation, which are conceptually mediated but not reducible to relations between concepts. Theories of ideology have frequently addressed these issues (see, for example, Therborn 1980).

Our knowledge and its open-ended character

As I and others have argued more fully elsewhere (see, for example, Outhwaite 1987; Half-penny 1982), the history of positivist philosophy of science is the history of its disintegration. The original idea of the piecemeal verification of empirical propositions gives way to a sloppier competition between alternative theories which wrap up the empirical data so thoroughly in their own packages of concepts and models that the idea of directly comparing their degree of empirical support seems misplaced. In the case of the social sciences, things are even messier. Marxists, functionalists, ethnomethodologists, and others can all find abundant supportive material for their respective contentions; none can be subjected to a crucial test or experiment. Faced with this situation, which finds its theoretical expression in so-called conventionalist conceptions of science, some theorists have adopted a rationalist strategy which stresses the a priori truth of successful theories. We do not need, for example, to test whether certain chess-moves are better than others; we know it from first principles. Something similar applies to forms of market behaviour, where what is manifestly the best strategy serves as a kind of standard by which we can measure deviations from pure economic rationality. The alternative, realist approach stresses the fallibility and open-ended character of our knowledge but insists that there are states of affairs in nature or the social world which are as they are independent of our descriptions of them, and about which we in principle know ourselves to have been right or wrong.

I have argued elsewhere for a significant convergence in the philosophy of social science around a realist philosophy of science and a conception of social science oriented to critical hermeneutics. We need, I think, a realist philosophy of science (including social science) in order to sustain the notion of a social world which exists in relative independence of the specific descriptions which we may give of it. This is not only a pragmatic presupposition which gives meaning to scientific activity and disagreement; it is also a necessary condition of our existence as human beings extending over time and space. We need to take on board the insights of the hermeneutic tradition if we are to give an adequate account of the complexities of our access to social reality and our prescientific understanding of it. And we need a *critical* hermeneutics because, as Habermas and others have rightly insisted, meanings and the understanding of meanings cannot be dissociated from relations of power and domination and the attempt to transcend them.

In such a conception, which draws on and combines the strengths of positions which have often been seen as irreconcilably opposed to one another, many of the longstanding oppositions between holism and individualism, structure and agency, materialism and idealism can be seen not as fundamental metatheoretical choices to be made once and for all at the beginning of inquiry but as posing issues to be argued out in concrete terms, in relation to specific social situations located in time and space. Some social structures, for example, though of course conceptually mediated, may be relatively impervious to redefinitions by individual actors, while others may appear to be largely made up of actors' individual or collective interpretations. Individualist explanations of governmental decisions may compete with, but may also complement, more structural and long-term explanations. Here, metatheory and the more abstract forms of theory appear as outline frameworks to be filled with substantive content. The most promising path for social theory is between the two extremes of old-fashioned philosophical legislation and a purely opportunistic pragmatism of performativity – something which was already clear to the founding fathers of the social sciences at the beginning of the twentieth century.

Convergence and Fragmentation

The past 25 years have seen, then, a parallel and convergent process in both the philosophy of social science and the social sciences themselves, in which the somewhat simplified scientistic conceptions which were prevalent in the middle decades of the twentieth century have been replaced by conceptions which are more sophisticated yet at the same time closer in many ways to those found in the early decades of the twentieth century. Max Weber would, I think, have felt more at home, though probably no less irritated, in many recent debates in English-language philosophy of social science than in, say, 1953, the year of his brother Alfred's death. In the remaining pages of this chapter I shall offer some thoughts about where we may be heading in the coming century.

The social sciences worldwide (and they have become increasingly global in their orientation and dissemination) are marked by tendencies toward both unification and division. In the preceding pages I have emphasized the trends toward the flexible cooperation between philosophy and the social sciences and between individual social science disciplines, so far as these still remain distinct. The revival of the classics and the seminal influence of a number of social theorists across a wide range of disciplines has been an important unifying force, as has the rise of social theory itself. Running against this trend, however, are pressures toward specialization and the division of labour familiar from the example of the natural sciences and similarly reinforced by funding opportunities and by disciplinary structures petrified along the obsolete divisions between academic departments. It is not just that that ambitious social scientists may prefer to be large fish in small ponds, presiding over a strictly limited area of inquiry; they will tend to find it easier to obtain funds for clearly circumscribed projects. The relation to the past remains ambivalent: many social scientists, not just empirical researchers but even sophisticated and original theorists such as Niklas Luhmann (1927–98), deplore the frequent reference back to the classics and to traditional problematics. What C. Wright Mills (1916–62) denounced as the coexistence of grand theory and abstracted empiricism remains an equally possible future for the social sciences in the twenty-first century.

Pluralism in social theory

At the "grand theory" end of the playing field, albeit ostensibly in opposition to grand theory, are a number of skeptical trends of which the most recent go under the labels of poststructuralism, postmodernism or, for the more sophisticated, antifoundationalism. Echoing the critique by the French philosopher, Jean-François Lyotard, of the "grand narratives" of traditional political theory (Lyotard 1984 [1979]), these critics have accused the social sciences of overlooking "difference" and diversity in their hubristic efforts to construct excessively general theories. As I have argued elsewhere in more detail, such conceptions do not offer a very convincing picture of social scientific reality. Some social theorists *have* adopted a strident and even arrogant tone, Durkheim's *Rules* being a good example, but they have not been as one-sided as their polemical provocations might suggest. On the whole, as many who have tried in vain to apply Kuhn's paradigm concept to the social sciences have been forced to accept, the image of social theory as a whole, and of most of the individual social sciences, is one of a remarkable diversity of shifting affiliations. And though social theory was generally slow to address issues of race and gender, and international conflict or the environment, it has responded promptly to the theoretical and practical challenges posed by ethnic minority, feminist, peace, and environmentalist movements in the last third of the century, just as social theory in the late nineteenth century and more recently responded to the rise of socialist and communist movements.

Conclusion

This suggests a more general conclusion. To paraphrase a remark by the German philosopher, Johann Gottlieb Fichte (1762–1814), what kind of social sciences we choose to have depends primarily on what sort of societies we are. Societies which want, and which want their universities to want, social science departments whose output and social utility are as quantifiable as that of departments of applied science will derive less benefit, I suspect, than those which allow social theory to develop in relative freedom from institutional constraints, free to address what it, rather than its paymasters, identifies as important issues for investigation. The greatest threat to this approach lies, perhaps, in the attempts to revive and enforce conceptions of specialized academic professionalism and performance in a half-baked extension of a science policy developed in relation to "big science" and of dubious application in the domain of the social sciences.

Bibliography

Apel, Karl-Otto. 1967: *Analytic Philosophy of Language and the Geisteswissenschaften*. Dordrecht: Reidel.
Bhaskar, Roy. 1978 [1975]: *A Realist Theory of Science*. 2nd edn. Brighton: Harvester.
—— 1979: *The Possibility of Naturalism*. Brighton: Harvester.
Clark, T. N. 1973: *Prophets and Patrons: The French University and the Emergence of the Social Sciences*. Cambridge, MA: Harvard University Press.
Durkheim, E. 1952 [1897]: *Suicide*. London: Routledge & Kegan Paul.
—— 1982 [1895]: *The Rules of Sociological Method*. London: Macmillan.
Elias, Norbert. 1987 [1983]: The Retreat of Sociologists into the Present. *Theory, Culture and Society*, 4/2–3, 223–47.
Elster, Jon (ed.) 1986: *Rational Choice*. Oxford: Blackwell.
Giddens, Anthony. 1971: *Capitalism and Modern Social Theory*. Cambridge: Cambridge University Press.
—— 1972: Four Myths in the History of Social Thought. *Economy and Society*, 1, 357ff. (Reprinted in: Giddens, 1977, *Studies in Social and Political Theory*. London: Hutchinson.)
—— 1979: *Central Problems in Social Theory*. London: Macmillan.
—— 1990: *The Consequences of Modernity*. Cambridge: Polity Press.
Gilbert, Nigel, and Mulkay, Michael. 1984: *Opening Pandora's Box: A Sociological Analysis of Scientists' Discourse*. Cambridge: Cambridge University Press.
Habermas, Jürgen. 1971 [1968]: *Knowledge and Human Interests*. London: Heineman.
Halfpenny, Peter. 1982: *Positivism and Sociology: Explaining Social Life*. London: Allen & Unwin.

Harré, Rom. 1986: *Varieties of Realism*. Oxford: Blackwell.

Keat, Russell. 1971: Social Scientific Knowledge and the Problem of Naturalism. *Journal for the Theory of Social Behaviour*, 1.

Kuhn, Thomas. 1962: *The Structure of Scientific Revolutions*. Chicago: University of Chicago Press.

Lyotard, Jean-François. 1982 [1979]: *The Postmodern Condition. A Report on Knowledge*. Manchester: Manchester University Press.

Medawar, Peter. 1969: *Induction and Intuition in Scientific Thought*. London: Methuen.

Outhwaite, William. 1987: *New Philosophies of Social Science*. London: Macmillan.

Parsons, Talcott. 1968 [1937]: *The Structure of Social Action*. New York: Free Press.

Popper, Karl. 1971 [1934]: *Logik der Forschung*. Tübingen: J. C. B. Mohr.

Quine, W. V. O. 1953: Two Dogmas of Empiricism. In Quine, 1953, *From a Logical Point of View*. Cambridge, MA: Harvard University Press.

Schutz, Alfred. 1972 [1932]: *The Phenomenology of the Social World*. London: Heinemann.

Skinner, Quentin (ed.) 1985: *The Return of Grand Theory in the Human Sciences*. Cambridge: Cambridge University Press.

Smith, Dennis. 1991: *The Rise of Historical Sociology*. Cambridge: Polity Press.

Therborn, Göran. 1980: *The Ideology of Power and the Power of Ideology*. London: Verso.

Winch, Peter. 1958: *The Idea of a Social Science and its Relation to Philosophy*. London: Routledge.

chapter 2

Karl Marx

Per Månson

KEY CONCEPTS

ALIENATION – estrangement.

CAPITAL – A relationship between bourgeois society's main classes, the bourgeoisie and the proletariat, which is the dominant production structure in bourgeois society.

MATERIALISTIC CONCEPTION OF HISTORY – the foundation of history and of the study of history is the productive sphere of society. Politico-legal forms and people's consciousness are to be understood in relation to the economic base.

MODE OF PRODUCTION – the manner in which a certain society (in a certain epoch) has organized its material production, including its scientific, technical, and organizational level.

PRODUCTIVE FORCES – the collective capacity of society's ability to extract and produce necessities from nature.

RELATIONS OF PRODUCTION – the social and economic conditions that prevail among people and classes in society's material production.

SURPLUS VALUE – That part of the value created in production that does not go to the reproduction of the wage laborer.

Biography: *Karl Marx*

Karl Marx was born on May 18, 1818, in Trier in western Germany, where his father was a lawyer. After completing secondary school in 1835, Marx studied in Bonn and Berlin. In Berlin he was swept into the young Hegelian movement. He took his doctoral degree with a dissertation on Greek natural philosophy in Jena in 1841 and then he became editor of the liberal newspaper *Rheinische Zeitung* in Cologne.

In 1844 Marx moved to Paris with his wife, Jenny von Westfahlen, published *Deutsch-Französische Jarhbücher*, and came into contact with Friedrich Engels. Marx also worked on a book that was published in 1932 under the title of *The Economic and Philosophic Manuscripts*.

From 1845 to 1848 Marx lived in Brussels, where he organized the *Communist League* together with Engels and wrote the *Communist Manifesto*. Just prior to that, he had published *The Holy Family* (1845) and *The Poverty of Philosophy* (1847). Another book, *The German Ideology*, was written in 1845–6, but was not published until 1932.

During the revolution of 1848–9 Marx was living in Cologne, where he published a newspaper called *Neue Rheinische Zeitung*. After the revolution Marx found his way to London, where he lived for the rest of his life. In London the Marx family lived for a long time in extreme poverty and three of their six children died. Marx worked mainly on developing his theory of the capitalist mode of production, which led to the 1867 publication of the first book of *Capital*. In 1857–8 he wrote a "preliminary work" to *Capital*, published in 1939–41 (1953 in Berlin) under the title *Grundrisse der Kritik der Politischen Ökonomie*. He published *A Contribution to a Critique of Political Economy* in 1859 and the polemical *Herr Vogt* in 1860. Marx also wrote a number of newspaper articles during these years.

From 1864 to 1872 Marx worked with the First International, which was filled with strife and in which various anarchists, in particular, were opposed to Marx. Marx quit the organization after writing *The Paris Commune*, following the fall of the Paris Commune in 1871. During his last years Marx was in extremely poor health. His wife died in 1881 and one of his daughters died in January 1883, Marx himself passed away on March 14, 1883 and was buried in Highgate Cemetery in London.

Historical and Intellectual Background

Karl Marx's life coincided with the beginning of a change in the European countries from agrarian to industrial societies. It was in England, particularly, in the late eighteenth century that the Industrial Revolution began a concentration of the new working class into factories and housing areas; and Marx obtained most of his basic empirical data for his theory of the development of capitalism from England. Just as important to Marx's theory, however, was the French Revolution of 1789 with its abolition of feudal conditions, the growth of a bourgeois society, and the appearance of an anti-bourgeois socialist left.

When Marx appeared on the scene, Germany, compared to England and France, was still a feudal country that was not united until 1871. The direct intellectual background for Marx's theories involved Germany's chances of catching up with more developed countries, and this debate was carried on by the radical successors of the philosopher G. W. F. Hegel (1771–1831). With his grand philosophical system, Hegel had attempted to show that human history had a goal, the most salient features of which were the creation of a reasonable state and the realization of the concept of freedom. Since Hegel believed that the Prussian state of his time had made the greatest advances toward realizing freedom and reason, as a professor in Berlin he became somewhat of a "state philosopher" for Prussia.

The radicals among Hegel's followers, the young Hegelians, objected to this and criticized the dominant position of religion in Prussia. Marx belonged to the young Hegelian movement for a time, but he soon came to criticize its belief that philosophical analysis would lead to change in and liberation of Germany. Instead, he was more influenced by Hegel's historical method in which development and change through *dialectic contradictions* are the primary components, although he rejected Hegel's emphasis on spiritual forces in history. In contrast, Marx stressed human social conditions, particularly their material production, as crucial to historical development.

Another important source of inspiration for Marx was the French socialist tradition that arose during the French Revolution of 1789 and continued through the revolutions of 1830 and 1848. The most important aspect of this tradition was the idea and goal of a new and more radical revolution than that of 1789. In the coming revolution the new class, the industrial workers or proletariat, would take power and abolish all classes. Beside these revolutionaries who were oriented toward class struggle, there were more reform-oriented socialists such as the "utopian socialists," Claude Henri Saint-Simon (1760–1825) and Charles Fourier (1772–1837). Like the Englishman, Robert Owen (1771–1858), they wanted to build a socialist society through state reforms or by creating small local societies in which the division of labour was abolished and people lived in harmony with one another and with nature. Although Marx was critical of these socialists and based his thinking more on the "theory of class struggle," he incorporated some of their criticism of the modern capitalist industrial society into his own theories.

A third tradition of importance in Marx's scientific work was British political economy, with names such as Adam Smith (1723–90) and David Ricardo (1772–1823). They had analyzed the new capitalist market economy and Marx continued their analyses, although to a great extent he reached different conclusions. Of particular importance was the fact that Marx took up their *labor theory of value*, the idea that the value of a commodity is determined by the quantity of work put into it. Other socialists also took up this tradition, particularly the so-called *Ricardian socialists*, who tried to demonstrate the injustice of a system in which the workers created all value but received only part of it for themselves. Marx objected to their moral criticism of the distribution of value and in his own theory of surplus value he tried to explain why the workers received only a part of the value they created.

These three traditions – German philosophy and Hegel in particular, French socialism, and British political economy – form the most important intellectual background for the theories of Marx. Which of them is most important depends on what perspective one has on Marx, whether we see him primarily as a philosopher, a revolutionary, or a scientist. Whatever the case, we may say that all three traditions are present in Marx's lifework and that this work is characterized by the special way in which he synthesized these (and other) traditions.

Theories

During his life Marx developed numerous theories and analyses, all of which dealt with the origin and development of industrial capitalism. These theories and analyses are complemented by a general understanding of history that includes precapitalist conditions, but Marx did not make a deep analysis of either pre- or postcapitalist social conditions. He wrote very little about the socialist society that, according to him, was to succeed capitalist society. Instead, he concentrated on the foundations and mode of operation of capitalist economy, the importance of class conflict between the bourgeoisie and the proletariat that is inherent in the economy, and the possibility that this conflict may lead to a socialist revolution.

Of all the theories Marx presented, three appear to be most important. The first theory is presented in an unfinished form in the incomplete work, *Economic and Philosophic Manuscripts* from 1844, and deals primarily with *alienation of the wage worker*. Then follows a presentation of what Marx himself called the "materialistic conception of history," later shortened to *historical materialism*. This view of history was developed as a criticism of Hegel's philosophy of history and of the young Hegelians' views. Finally, during his many years of struggle with "the economy," Marx created what was perhaps his most important theory, the *theory of capital*, which was based on what Marx himself thought to be his main contribution to science: the *theory of surplus value*. Other theoretical contributions such as the theory of revolution, class, and the state can be seen as parts of these three comprehensive theories. Consequently, we will examine the theory of alienation, the materialistic conception of history, and the theory of capital, and take up the other subsidiary theories toward the end.

The Theory of Alienation

Marx himself never developed a comprehensive theory of alienated labor, but what later came to be called the *theory of alienation* is presented on a few pages of the *Economic and Philosophic Manuscripts*. These manuscripts can be seen as a criticism of Hegel's philosophy and that of the young Hegelians with the help of political economy, but it is also a criticism of the economy with the help of philosophy. In his own analysis of the alienation of labor – *estrangement* – in the modern capitalist industrial society, Marx builds on two assumptions: that labour expresses man's species being and that labor is performed as wage labor.

The first assumption is based, in turn, on Hegel's idea that labor is a process in which man shapes both himself and the world. Thus, labor is tantamount to human self-creation. At the same time, however, Marx criticizes Hegel's focus on abstract intellectual work and, instead, stresses work in material production.

The other assumption is based on the idea that material production has been carried out under various social conditions throughout history. Before industrial capitalism there were serfs and before that material labor was carried out by slaves. Under capitalism, the means of production are the private property of a special class and productive labor is carried out by people without property, *wage laborers*, who sell their labor power in order to survive. According to Marx, when these two assumptions are combined the result is the alienation of labor.

Hegel's and Feuerbach's theory of alienation

Before Marx, Hegel and the materialistic young Hegelian, Ludwig Feuerbach (1804–72), used the term alienation. Hegel links the term alienation (*Entfremdung*) to the terms estrangement (*Entäusserung*) and objectification (*Vergegenständlichung*) in his theory of development of the human mind. In labor, man is alienated from his humanity and becomes an object for himself. Thus, he becomes estranged from the social world he has created. At the same time, however, this estrangement and objectification are necessary elements for the mind to learn to know itself by becoming something else, and man can abolish this alienation if he sees himself in his own objectification. Here, in his analysis of alienation, Marx takes up Hegel's theory of the importance of human labor, but he rejects the idea of the existence of a superhuman spirit and the process of its development.

Several years before Marx wrote about alienated labor, Ludwig Feuerbach published *The Essence of Christianity* (1841). In this book Feuerbach not only criticized religion (as did most of the young Hegelians, including Marx and Engels), but he went a step further and tried to explain why it exists. Feuerbach bases religion in man's worldly existence and believes that, in religion, man expresses his dream of a different and better world. It is not God who has created man, as religion teaches, but it is man who has created (the concept of) God. Man has objectified his own being in God and then provided his creation with a creative force of his own. In this way the object, the concept of God which is created by man, has become the subject and the true subject, man, has made himself an object. In this way, man has become estranged – alienated – from himself and, according to Feuerbach, religion expresses this alienation of man from himself.

Marx's theory of alienation

Marx, who, like most radicals, was influenced by Feuerbach's book, links his own analysis of alienation to the basic idea and Feuerbach's theory that man as subject has created an object which, by a dialectic reversal, becomes subject, so that man makes himself the object. But Marx believes this process is not a matter of religion or consciousness, but of the basis of human existence in the world: labor.

In his analysis of the alienation of labor, Marx also criticizes the economists for viewing private property as something that is natural; he says, instead, that it must be viewed as a historical phenomenon. Similarly, the form of labor – wage labor – that is private property's opposite and complement is a historical form of labor and not anything "natural." As in Feuerbach's analysis of religion, the wage laborer is alienated from his own creation, and the product of his labor becomes a commodity. At the same time, wage labor means that the worker also becomes a commodity. In this way, the wage laborer becomes a slave to his own product: "the object which labour produces – labour's product – confronts it as something *alien*, as a *power independent* of its producer" ("Economic and Philosophic Manuscripts," in *Marx–Engels Collected Works*, vol. 3: 272).

Because the product of labor does not belong to the wage laborer, but rather to the private owner, the wage laborer is separated from his product which becomes an alien force. This, in turn, means that labor is seen as something external and forced upon him, something that the wage laborer flees as soon as possible.

Since, according to the first condition above, it is labor, or more precisely man's free productive activity, in which man expresses his special "essence," wage labor means that what separates man from animals disappears. In labor, the wage laborer becomes an animal, while during his free time, when he is not at work, he tries to realize himself as a man. Since, like all other animals, man must eat, rest, sleep, and relax, and since under wage-labor conditions he can do this only during his free time, the wage laborer becomes a man in his animal functions, while in his human functions he becomes an animal. Thus, according to Marx, the result of wage labor is that:

> man (the worker) only feels himself freely active in his animal functions – eating, drinking, procreating, or at most in his dwelling and in dressing-up, etc.; and in his human functions he no longer feels himself to be anything but an animal. What is animal becomes human and what is human becomes animal. (*Marx–Engels Collected Works*, vol. 3: 274ff)

In addition to the fact that wage labor alienates man from his product and his productive activity, which distinguishes him from animals, he also becomes alienated from his species. After all, according to Marx (and Hegel) his "species-being" is determined by his conscious productive activity, which is also a goal in itself. Under conditions of wage labor, however, labor is not a goal in itself, but only a means of maintaining life. This too means that what distinguishes man from animals, the free, conscious activity of life, disappears.

The form of wage labor also means social alienation, and the alienation of people from one another. This, according to Marx, is a result of the three other forms of alienation. Thus, wage labor and its counterpart, private ownership, cause man's "species-being," conscious free life activity under social forms, to become an "animal" and individualistic life activity.

Consequently, man ultimately becomes alienated from that which is a product of his actions: society. As in the case of Feuerbach's concept of God, society becomes estranged from the individual and directed against him. "Society" then becomes a force that lives its own life over which no one has control.

As mentioned above, the theory of alienation was unknown until the 1930s but, particularly since the 1960s, it has become extremely important and much discussed and used in so-called humanistic Marxism. It was used to criticize the "affluent society" of the Western world, but it was also used by many opposition figures in Eastern Europe who analyzed and criticized "actually existing socialism." It was also harshly criticized by certain Marxists, particularly the Althusser school (chapter 9), which believed that the theory of alienation, with its talk of the "human species-being," was not a part of Marx's scientific contribution, but that the theory belonged to Marx's "bourgeois humanistic period."

The Materialistic Conception of History

The materialistic view of history, or historical materialism as it was later called, is never presented in detail or in a comprehensive manner in any of Marx's works. Marx developed his view of history in his critique of Hegel and the young Hegelians, particularly in *The Holy Family* and *The German Ideology*. The *Communist Manifesto* contains a nucleus of the concept and the introduction to his *Contribution to a Critique of Political Economy* contains perhaps the most famous account. Finally, Marx used his materialistic method in his analyses of contemporary political developments, particularly the events of the revolution of 1848 and later in *Class Struggles in France, 1848–50* and *The Eighteenth Brumaire of Louis Bonaparte* (originally written as articles) and *The Paris Commune*.

The materialistic *conception of history*

As initially presented, the materialistic understanding of history is primarily a critique of the idealistic view of history held by Hegel and the young Hegelians. Marx stresses the importance man's production of his own necessities of life has for historical development and ridicules the Germans' emphasis on the "intellect" or "self-consciousness." Instead of beginning a study of human history with intellectual or political conditions, Marx believes that in order to make history at all men must live, first and foremost. Human life requires food and drink, clothing and shelter, so that the production of these material needs is the initial precondition for all history and thus for all history writing. As a result, any attempt to analyze and explain history must be based on this fact. Other social phenomena, such as social conditions, politics, and thought, must be seen in the light of this fact.

Productive forces, relations of production, and mode of production

Marx strongly stresses that this is a general view of history that "by no means affords a recipe or schema, as does philosophy, for neatly trimming the epochs of history." The materialistic view of history does not involve using an abstract scheme that is to be forced onto reality and "viewed apart from real history, these abstractions have in themselves no value whatsoever" (Marx 1970a: 48). The most important abstractions or concepts that Marx uses are *productive forces*, *relations of production*, and *mode of production*. Most simply, productive forces may be said to be man's relationship to nature, that is, the level of knowledge and technology and the form of organization humanity has developed in its processing of nature. Relations of production refer to the socioeconomic relations between various classes (for example, feudal lords and serfs, or private property and wage laborers), and mode of production expresses the totality, or the synthesis, of productive forces and relations of production. Furthermore, Marx uses a metaphor of the "base" of society, its economic groundwork, and a politico-legal and ideological "superstructure" to stress that the mode of production is fundamental in every society and that its political, legal, moral, and intellectual relationships must be understood with this "base" in mind.

Social revolution

The materialistic concept of history also includes the theory that the conditions of production can favor or oppose further development of the productive forces. According to Marx, when the conditions of production hinder further development, a period of social revolution begins. In his introduction to *Contribution to a Critique of Political Economy*, in which Marx summarizes his own intellectual development in his study of Hegel and the young Hegelians, he states that people are born into an existing production structure and that this objective production structure determines both the legal and the political relationships that represent the predominant thinking in society. When the relations of production no longer generate the productive forces, but are transformed into "fetters" for them, a period of social revolution begins and the entire social order undergoes an upheaval.

Thus, according to Marx, a social revolution occurs when the two "parts" of the mode of production, the productive forces and the relations of production, come into conflict with each other, such as when feudal relations of production prevented further development of the productive forces and the bourgeois revolution in England and later in France took place. Marx also believes that it is possible to distinguish four different modes of production in history – the Asian, antique, feudal, and modern bourgeois modes of production – each of which has its own special features and its special relationships between those who control the means of production and the immediate producers.

The materialistic conception of history

The materialistic concept of history also contains a critique of a nonhistorical mechanism of materialism (primarily that of Feuerbach) and thus it can be seen as *historical* materialism and not just as historical *materialism*. In several brief aphorisms Marx wrote before beginning *The German Ideology*, he stresses the subjective and active side of historical development and states that people are not merely passive and observing beings in the world, but that they are active and intervening. This subjective side has been developed by idealism, but only in the abstract, since idealism is not based on material reality.

Marx also indirectly criticizes the "Utopian socialists" and their idea that socialism can be brought about by "educating" people. But, Marx said, the educators must also be educated and, if this is the case, who will educate them? Marx believed instead that people change themselves and that socialism is prepared by practical action in a revolution. This revolution is needed not only to bring down the old class, but also "because the class *over-throwing* it can only in a revolution succeed in ridding itself of all the muck of ages and become fitted to found society anew" (Marx 1970a: 95). Consequently, Marx concentrated on political work, and it is in the light of this that his famous Eleventh Thesis on Feuerbach must be seen: "The philosophers have only *interpreted* the world, in various ways; the point is to change it" (Marx 1970a: 123).

Theory of Capital

Marx's most important scientific contribution was his work on political economy, which dominated his life. Marx himself believed he had developed a theory of the "laws of motion of capitalist society," with emphasis on laws of *motion*. As a dialectician, he tried to find contradictions and developmental trends that were inherent in the basic structure of the capitalist economy, but he also attempted to discern the problems that would ultimately abolish this mode of production.

Capitalism as a historical phenomenon

For Marx capitalism was always a historical phenomenon, that is, a social formation that has a beginning, a development, and an end. Thus, large portions of his theory of capital deal with the origin of capitalism, but more important is his theory of its mode of operation and, particularly, his explanation of the capitalist company's profits. However, his theory contains very little on what future society, socialist society, will look like. As antagonistic as he was toward the utopian socialists, he refused to "write recipes for the soup kitchen of the future." Moreover, the trends he saw in capitalism were opposed by other tendencies and actual developments are always determined by the actual practical actions of people.

Nor is his analysis of the capitalist mode of production based on a moral critique of those who possess capital. Even though he could be highly critical of them and their supporters in politics or science, he always viewed their actions as a result of their position in the economic structure. The entrepreneur "must" act as he does, given the economic laws that are in effect. For this reason, it was impossible within the framework of capitalism to carry out reforms that would abolish this mode of production. The only thing that could abolish the laws of motion of capital was abolition of the system itself.

Relationship of capital

The basis of capitalism is the actual relationship of capital, the relationship between the administrator of capital, who is supposed to multiply (increase) capital, and the wage laborer who, with his labor, creates this increase. For Marx, capital is never fundamentally a thing, machines, or even money. It is a social relationship. In its social movement, however, it sometimes appears as money, sometimes as commodities, and sometimes as factories and machines. Marx speaks all along of the movement of *value*, for under capitalism the whole point of production is to increase the value of that which is produced. This is done by producing *commodities* that have a greater value than that of the commodities (raw materials, machines, labor power, etc.) that are used to produce them.

The historical prerequisite for capitalism

The historical prerequisites for capitalism are, first, that capital has accumulated in private hands and become private property and, secondly, that a "free" class of wage workers has arisen that has nothing but its capacity to work to sell in order to survive. The first condition involved the spread of trade, the discovery of new continents, and the monopolizing of the means of production, which began in the fifteenth century. The other condition involves the "liberation" of peasants and craftsmen from their ability to survive on their farms and in their guilds. When this privately owned capital and this "free" worker meet, the conditions arise for a capitalist mode of production. This mode of production made its actual breakthrough in the Industrial Revolution in England in the late 1700s and it captured one country after the other.

Use value and exchange value

In his abstract theory of a capitalist mode of operation, Marx distinguishes between the *use value* and the *exchange value* of a commodity. The use value is a thing's usefulness, which depends on its qualitative properties. The use value of a coat is that it can protect against the cold, that of a car is that it can be driven, etc. The exchange value, on the other hand, refers to the quantity of goods (or money) for which a particular commodity can be exchanged and, in accordance with the labor theory of value, it is based on the quantity of labor invested in its production. This labor refers not to the actual work that was done, but to the time required for the commodity to be produced, regardless of the actual work that was done, that is, it refers to the abstract work.

Surplus value

In the capitalist system, with its focus on the production of goods, abstract labor is constantly exchanged for other abstract labor, but where does the increase in value come from? Marx calls this necessary increase in value the "law of motion of capital" and it is expressed by the formula M-C-M', where M means money (money capital), C means commodities (commodity capital), and M' means more money, i.e. M' > M. This law of motion of capital is the very foundation of the capitalist mode of production and the scientific task at hand is to explain how it works.

Marx rejects all theories that claim the increase in value (which appears in the form of profits for the individual company) can be explained by the efficiency of the division of labor, that "society" gives up a part of this value to the capitalists or that the workers are paid too little for their work. Instead, he believes that the capitalist system is based on the existence of a special commodity "whose use-value possesses the peculiar property of being a source of value." This remarkable commodity can be purchased on the market by those who have money: "the capacity for labour, in other words labour-power" (Marx 1976a: 270).

Thus, under capitalism, man's ability to work has become a commodity that can be bought and sold on a labor market. Like all other commodities, the value of labor power is determined by the quantity of work that goes into its production, in this case the quantity of work involved in the production of "food, clothing, shelter, etc.," that goes into the sustenance of the wage labor. This is the exchange value of labor power and it corresponds to the wages the worker receives when he or she sells his or her labor capacity to the capitalist. But the use value of the labor power is the value the wage worker can create during a certain time and the difference between the use value and the exchange value of labor power is equal to the surplus value that is created in production and is the basis of profits.

Thus, according to Marx, capitalism's unprecedented ability to increase value and thus to accumulate capital is based on the systematic extraction of a higher value of labor power than the value used for its own production. This *surplus labor* is nothing new in history. During slavery the slave had to work more than what was needed to provide for himself and his family. Otherwise there would be no point in owning slaves. The system of having serfs also makes use of people's ability to work more than is needed for themselves. In this case, it was even possible to distinguish between the days the serf worked on "his own" farm and the days he worked on his master's. Marx believes that capitalism works on the same basic principle, but that this is concealed by the fact that labor is converted to value and that, on the surface, the wage worker is paid for his entire working day. In reality, he is paid only for the time required to produce the value of the things he himself needs to survive and the rest of the day he produces surplus value for capital.

Absolute and relative surplus value

This "insatiable lust for surplus value" of capitalism is behind the system's unprecedented potential for development which, according to Marx, was also a precondition for the "higher social relationships" of socialism. Capital constantly tries to increase the size of the surplus value, initially by increasing the *absolute surplus value*, i.e. by increasing the length of the working day in exchange for a certain wage (a certain value). In the early days of capitalism, 14- and 16-hour working days were common, but since labor capacity "resides in" living people, the working day cannot be increased without a limit.

Thus, in the course of events, the *relative surplus value* becomes more and more important. This involves reducing the share of the working day that is required to produce the value of the labor power or, in other words, to make less expensive those goods the wage worker needs in order to survive. If the value of these goods drops, then the wage worker spends a lower and lower portion of his working day creating the value of his own wage, so that the share that creates surplus value can become larger and larger. Thus, in the history of capitalism there is an unprecedented development of the productive force of labor that helps to increase the amount of surplus value.

The time of circulation of capital

Another important factor in increasing surplus value is reducing the time of circulation of capital. This is based on the idea that a company has a certain amount of money capital, M. This money purchases goods (raw materials, machines, labour power, etc.), and sets in motion the production of new goods that are then sent to market for sale. Once they have been sold and the money, M' (more money), is returned to the company, the process begins again and the time expired between when the money leaves and when (more) money returns is called the time of circulation. If this time is one year, for example, then 1 million pounds at 20 percent profit becomes 1.2 million in a year. If the time of circulation can be reduced by half, then the capital will become 1.2 million after just half a year and in one year it will become 1.44 million. Thus, the profit will become 0.44 million per year instead of 0.2 million if the time of circulation is reduced by half.

The idea is to produce raw materials and transport them to the factory faster and faster, but also to produce new goods, get them on the market, sell them, and return the money to the company faster and faster, and this is seen in reality by the development of transportation, marketing, or credit. Thus, capitalism can be seen as an incredible chase after time. After all, as the saying goes, time is money under capitalism.

The contradictions of capitalism

Thus the capitalist economy is an extremely productive and effective economy, but it also contains inherent contradictions. One of these is the problem of *realizing surplus value*: where does the value come from that is to be exchanged for the newly created value? According to Marx, there is always a potential risk of a *crisis of overproduction* in capitalism, a crisis that is based on the fact that more is produced then the amount of value available in society to purchase it.

Another such problem is the "law of the falling tendency of the rate of profit." During its development, capitalism increasingly replaces living labor with nonliving labor, materialized labor (machines). But since only living labor can create new value (machines and raw materials simply transfer the value that has gone into their production), there is always a risk that surplus value will decline in relation to total capital invested, thereby reducing the profit rate. There are counter-tendencies to this, such as an increase in the degree of exploitation of labor (lengthening the working day or intensifying labor), reducing wages to below their value, reducing fixed capital, etc.

These and other inherent contradictions in capitalism mean that the system cannot survive in the long term, but capitalist development itself creates the conditions for its own demise. This occurs because capital is centralized and concentrated, but mainly because it also creates the social and political conditions for the emergence of the class – the proletariat – that will bring the system down. The workers' struggle develops through history from opposition in the beginning against the new machines that have taken their jobs from them (for example the Luddites in England), to the struggle against the individual capitalist, to collective organization, first at the individual factory and then as a class. Instead of a struggle against the manifestations or individual representatives of capitalism, a struggle develops against the entire system of private capital and unpropertied wage workers. It is this struggle of the working class, according to Marx, that is the precondition for the rise of socialism and not, as the utopian socialists thought, the existence of well-meaning intellectuals to "educate" the proletariat.

Other Theories

During his long intellectual work, Marx analyzed a number of historical and social conditions that are now a part of more specialized theories, such as the theory of class, state, or revolution. These "partial theories" are part of Marx's overall view of history or his analysis of the economic laws of motion of bourgeois society. Although Marx speaks extensively of classes, for example, he never presents a systematic theory of class. It is symptomatic that at the end of the third book of *Capital*, where he finally takes up the subject of classes, the manuscript stops after a page and a half.

Class theory

Despite this, we can reconstruct Marx's view of classes in bourgeois society, based on a number of other analyses he made. The most important point is that Marx defines classes on the basis of their relationship to production and their source of income, and that this (objective) relationship means that they have different interests for which to fight. Under capitalism, the bourgeoisie (capital owners) and the proletariat (wage workers) are the most important classes. In addition, during Marx's time, there were landowners who based their position in society on the ownership of land, the petty bourgeoisie (who owned their means of production and worked themselves at their business) as well as technicians, foremen, and civil servants. In his concrete political analyses (such as *The Eighteenth Brumaire of Louis Bonaparte*) Marx attempts to explain events with reference to the actions of the various classes or class factions, based on their own interests.

State theory

Marx also discusses the state, particularly the bourgeois state, in several different publications, perhaps most importantly in *The Paris Commune*. His general view is that under bourgeois conditions it expresses the interests of the bourgeoisie and that, as a result, it must fundamentally be transformed in the transition to a future socialist society. He also viewed the commune as the precursor of a future state form, as the "political form at last discovered under which to work out the economical emancipation of labour" (*Marx–Engels Collected works*, vol. 22: 334). In his critique of the German Social Democratic Party's proposed platform of 1875 he also mentions the term "dictatorship of the proletariat" as a transitional form, but otherwise this concept plays a minor role in his writings.

Theory of revolution

It is also difficult to find a comprehensive presentation of his theory of revolution, particularly since Marx changed some of his views during his life, mainly on the basis of actual events. Nevertheless, the proletariat is always the revolutionary class; as the labor movement emerges, its organization becomes more and more important in his theories. In his youth he linked the proletariat to philosophy, in the Communist League he saw the avant-garde as important, but an aging (and hardened) Marx placed his greatest hope in the class's own movement and organization.

Marx focuses more and more on the idea (particularly after the publication of *Capital*) that the revolution is a protracted process based on capitalism's own development, while, paradoxically enough, he was more hopeful of a revolution in the near future in his youth. Toward the end of his life, he even said that the working class in certain countries with a developed democracy (he mentions Holland, England, and the United States) could come to power by parliamentary means, but as an overall theme he always presents class struggle as the driving force of the socialist revolution.

Method

Marx's social-science method was long viewed as relatively unproblematic, but with the "rediscovery" of Marx during the 1960s, this side of Marx also came to be examined and discussed. Interest in Marx's method in *Capital* increased, particularly after the publication of Roman Rosdolsky's book *The Making of Marx's "Capital"* (1989, originally 1968). Rosdolsky had undertaken a thorough reading of the *Grundrisse* (the "preliminary study" for *Capital*) and, among other things, he discusses the changes Marx made in his plans to present the theory of capital. According to Rosdolsky, the various books of *Capital* are on different levels of abstraction: the first book deals with "capital in general," while the second and third books (published by Engels in 1885 and 1894 respectively) deal with "capital in its concrete appearance."

Marx himself wrote very little about his method but, based on what he did write, we can conclude that he viewed the human brain's capacity for abstraction (that is, disregarding the less important in order to reach the "deep," the "essential," or the "inner relationship" in what is being analyzed) as important. He also distinguishes between the research aspect and the presentation aspect of the investigation, where the former must reach the most important relationships through abstraction and the latter must make concrete and incorporate the relationships that are left outside the abstract analysis.

He also writes that, based on his dialectical method, he sees movement and change in the phenomena he analyzes and that, as a result, no social phenomenon is eternal. In the theory of capital he says that the most fundamental relationship under capitalism is that material production occurs in the form of the production of commodities and that it is this production of commodities, which focuses on increasing value, that is the most profound secret of capitalism. Consequently, he also begins his presentation of the theory of capital on this most abstract level and then continues toward an increasingly concrete and complex reality.

Conclusion

The life of Karl Marx is intimately linked to the epoch between the French Revolution and the Russian Revolution. He was born 29 years after the French Revolution and died 34 years before the Russian Revolution, and he was an important source of inspiration to Russian Social Democracy and the faction, the Bolsheviks, which seized power in 1917. The most important event of this epoch was the rise and breakthrough of capitalist industrial society, first in northwestern Europe, then in more and more countries of the world. Inspiration from the French Revolution is most clearly noticeable in the young revolutionary Marx. Whereas the older Marx certainly still considered himself a revolutionary, he saw the social revolution more as a long-term class movement.

Initially, developments in Germany were his central theme. Then he shifted his focus to France and its revolutionary traditions. Then, in conjunction with his work on the economy, he became more interested in England. Toward the end he returned to Germany – and in part Russia – as countries of interest for a possible socialist revolution: Germany because a social democratic labour movement developed there first and Russia because it was there he first gained revolutionary supporters.

During his lifetime, Marx was known primarily within radical circles and it was only decades after his death that his name became more generally known. It was precisely the events in Germany and Russia that had an important hand in this, and in 1891 what was then by far the largest labor party in the world, the German party, adopted Marxism as its official ideology. Since then Marx has been one of the most discussed persons in the twentieth century, particularly since the Russian Revolution was followed by other revolutions carried out in his name. Before the fall of Eastern European communism and the dissolution of the Soviet Union in 1989–91, more than one-third of the people on earth lived under regimes that claimed they intended to implement the theories of Marx. Consequently, Marx is far more important in the twentieth century than he was in the nineteenth, so that the acceptance and development of his theories deals primarily with the further development of Marxism.

Marx and academic science

Marx himself never saw the academic scientific world take him seriously. Only after Marxism had become the official ideology of the German Social Democratic Party and the Second International (founded in 1889) were his theories discussed in scientific circles. In 1896 the Austrian economist, Eugen Böhm-Bawerk, published *Zum Abschluss des Marxschen System* (Böhm-Bawerk 1898), in which he criticized Marx's theory of value, his theory of the falling rate of profit, and his theory of breakdown. A number of other academics also criticized various parts of the theories of Marx (or frequently those of the Marxists) and, before his death in 1895, Engels himself criticized the fad of "flirting" with a simplified and dogmatic Marxism that swept through the university world in the early 1890s.

For a long time, established science viewed Marx as a "socialist prophet" whose "prophecies" must be rejected. Particularly after the Russian Revolution and Stalin's takeover,

Marx was linked to dictatorship and slavery. This was expressed well by the philosopher of science, Karl Popper, who published *The Open Society and its Enemies* (1945) after World War II, in which he criticizes what he calls the historicism of Marx (and Hegel). By this Popper means that history has a goal and that everything must be seen in the light of this goal.

Later, in the 1950s, Marx again appeared in academic discussions and the "writings of his youth" became better-known and were used to criticize conditions both in the capitalist world and in "actually existing socialism." Also of importance was the criticism of Talcott Parson's sociology, with its focus on society's community of values and its view of conflicts as dysfunctions (chapter 14). In comparison, social researchers such as C. Wright Mills and Ralph Dahrendorf used Marx as a conflict sociologist (chapter 16).

During the latter part of the 1960s Marx returned to the university with full force. At that time many of the Marxist theoretical traditions that had long remained outside science were discovered while, at the same time, many new ones arose. Marx was read, reread, and reconstructed, stimulated by other intellectual traditions such as structuralism and phenomenology, and for a decade or so there were almost as many Marxist tendencies as there are tendencies in the social sciences. Even in the 1980s new directions in Marxism arose, and today it goes without saying that the theories of Marx are a part of our legacy of knowledge in the social sciences.

Bibliography

Primary

A complete bibliography of works by Marx and Engels can be found in:
Draper, Hal. 1985: *The Marx-Engels Register* (vol. 2 of the *Marx-Engels Cyclopedia*). New York: Schocken Books.

There are four different editions of collected works by Marx and Engels:
Marx-Engels Gesamtausgabe (MEGA), published 1927–35, covering the time until 1848.
Marx-Engels Werke (MEW), published in the DDR in 39 volumes, 1956–68.
Marx-Engels Collected Works (MECW), an English translation in 50 volumes, 1975–95.
Gesamtausgabe (MEGA), a new edition, started in 1975, and expected to be approximately 100 volumes.

Works and selected writings by Marx and Engels are published in many editions. A selection follows:
Marx, Karl. 1954: *The Eighteenth Brumaire of Louis Bonaparte*. London: Lawrence & Wishart.
——— 1956: *The Holy Family, or, Critique of a Critical Critique*. Moscow: Foreign Languages Publishers.
——— 1960: *Critique of Hegel's 'Philosophy of Right'*. London: Cambridge University Press.
——— 1963: *The Poverty of Philosophy*. New York: International Publishers.
——— 1964a: *Pre-Capitalist Economic Foundations*. London: Lawrence & Wishart.
——— 1964b: *On Religion; Selections*. New York: Schocken Books.
——— 1965: *Selected Correspondence*. Moscow: Progress Publisher.
——— 1969: *Theories of Surplus Value: Parts 1–3*. Moscow: Progress Publishers.
——— 1970a: *The German Ideology*. London: Lawrence & Wishart.
——— 1970b: *A Contribution to the Critique of Political Economy*. New York: International Publishers.

—— 1971a: *Revolution and Counterrevolution*. London: Unwin Books.

—— 1971b: *The Paris Commune, 1871*. London: Sidgwick and Jackson.

—— 1971c: *Critique of the Gotha Programme*. Moscow: Progress Publihers.

—— 1971d: *On Revolution*. New York: McGraw-Hill.

—— 1971e: *The Cologne Communist Trial*. London: Lawrence & Wishart.

—— 1971f: *Ireland and the Irish Question*. Moscow: Progress Publishers.

—— 1972a: *The Class Struggle in France, 1848 to 1850*. Moscow: Progress Publishers.

—— 1972b: *Articles from the Neue Rheinische Zeitung 1848–49*. Moscow: Progress Publishers.

—— 1973a: *Grundrisse: Foundations of the Critique of Political Economy* [rough draft]. New York: Random House.

—— 1973b: *Feuerbach: Opposition of the Materialist and Idealist Outlook*. London: Lawrence & Wishart.

—— 1974a: *The First International and After*. Harmondsworth, Middlesex: Penguin Books.

—— 1974b: *The Communist Manifesto*. Belmont, MA: American Opinion.

—— 1974c: *Economic and Philosophic Manuscripts of 1844*. Moscow: Progress Publishers.

—— 1976a: *Capital: A Critique of a Political Economy*, vol.1. Harmondsworth, Middlesex: Penguin Books.

—— 1976b: *Wage-Labour and Capital and Value, Price and Profit*. New York: International Publishers.

—— 1976c: *On Literature and Art*. Moscow: Progress Publishers.

—— 1978: *The Revolution of 1848*. Harmondsworth, Middlesex: Penguin Books.

—— 1987: *On Historical Materialism*. Moscow: Progress Publisher.

Marx, Karl, and Engels, Friedrich. 1938: *The Civil War in the United States*. London: Lawrence & Wishart.

—— 1968: *On Colonialism*. London: Lawrence & Wishart.

Cristman, H. M. (ed.) 1966: *The American Journalism of Marx and Engels; a Selection from the New York Daily Tribune*. New York: New American Library.

Secondary

Bottomore, Tom (ed.) 1979: *Karl Marx*. Oxford: Blackwell.

Bottomore, Tom. 1981: *Modern Interpretations of Marx*. Oxford: Blackwell.

Böhm-Bawerk, Eugen. 1898: *Karl Marx and the Close of His System*. London: T. F. Unwin.

Carver, Terrell. 1983: *Marx and Engels: The Intellectual Relationship*. Bloomington: Indiana University Press.

Cohen, G. A. 1978: *Karl Marx's Theory of History*. Oxford: Clarendon Press.

Foner, Philip S. 1983: *Karl Marx Remembered*. San Francisco, CA: Synthesis Publications.

Geras, Norman. 1983: *Marx and Human Nature*. London: Verso.

Gouldner, Alvin W. 1980: *The Two Marxisms: Contradictions and Anomalies in the Development of Theory*. London: Macmillan.

Hobsbawm, Eric (ed.) 1982: *The History of Marxism*. Vol. 1: *Marxism in Marx's Days*. Brighton: Harvester.

Hook, Sidney. 1968: *From Hegel to Marx: Studies in the Intellectual Development of Karl Marx*. Ann Arbor, MI: University of Michigan Press.

McLellan, David. 1971: *The Thought of Karl Marx: An Introduction*. London: Macmillan.

—— 1980: *Marx Before Marxism*. London: Macmillan.

—— 1981: *Karl Marx: His Life and Thought*. London: Granada Publishing.

—— (ed.) 1983: *Marx: The First Hundred Years*. London: Pinter.

Mandel, Ernest. 1971: *The Formation of the Economic Thought of Karl Marx*. New York and London: Monthly Review Press.

Mészáros, István. 1978: *Marx's Theory of Alienation*. London: Merlin.

Morrison, Ken. 1995: *Marx, Durkheim, Weber: Formations of Modern Social Thought*. London: Sage.

Murray, Patrick. 1990: *Marx's Theory of Scientific Knowledge*. London: Humanities Press International.

Nicolaus, Martin. 1968: The Unknown Marx. *New Left Review*, 48, 41–61.

Ollman, Bertell. 1976: *Alienation: Marx' Conception of Man in Capitalist Society*. Cambridge: Cambridge University Press.

Padover, Saul K. 1985: *Karl Marx: An Intimate Biography*. New York: Meridian.

Parkinson, G. H. R. (ed.) 1982: *Marx and Marxism*. Cambridge: Cambridge University Press.

Popper, K. R. 1945: *The Open Society and its Enemies*. London: Routledge and Kegan Paul.

Rosdolsky, Roman. 1989: *The Making of Marx's "Capital"*. London: Pluto Press.

Schmidt, Alfred. 1971:*The Concept of Nature in Marx*. London: New Left Books.

Schmitt, Richard. 1997: *Introduction to Marx and Engels: A Critical Reconstruction*. Oxford: Westview.

Seigel, Jerrold. 1978: *Marx' Fate: The Shaper of a Life*. Princeton, NJ: Princeton University Press.

Sweezy, Paul M. 1968: *The Theory of Capitalist Development*. New York: Monthly Review Press.

Tucker, Robert C. 1972: *Philosophy and Myth in Karl Marx*. Cambridge: Cambridge University Press.

Wood, Allen W. 1981: *Karl Marx*. London: Routledge & Kegan Paul.

chapter **3**

Herbert Spencer

Heine Andersen

KEY CONCEPTS

EVOLUTION – a process characterizing all things in the universe, according to Spencer. This process consists of aggregating elements into more complex structures, from the more uncertain, incoherent, and homogeneous to the more certain, integrated, and heterogeneous.

INSTITUTION – lasting elements in a social structure, regulating and controlling action, and hence handling basic functions.

ORGANISM ANALOGY – the assumption that properties of biological organisms are able to be retraced in society. Spencer claimed the existence of the following identical features: (1) growth; (2) increasing differentiation and complexity; (3) increasing functional interdependency (integration) between the parts; and (4) the life of the whole spanning the individual parts. The important difference is that all individuals in society have tactile senses, as opposed to the individual cells in an organism.

SOCIAL FUNCTION – what the individual elements in a social structure contribute in order to sustain this structure.

SURVIVAL OF THE FITTEST – the principle that the struggle for survival ensures the development of properties that best fit into the demands of the environment.

Biography: *Herbert Spencer*

Herbert Spencer was born in the Midlands of England, in the industrial city of Derby, in 1820, and he died in 1903. His father, who was a schoolmaster, imposed few restriction on him during his childhood, but never gave him an academic education. At 17, Spencer got a job in a railway construction firm, where he received a practical education as an engineer while simultaneously studying in his spare time, in particular, modern biological theories; phrenology also aroused his interest. Gradually, he was affected by the radical, liberal, and nonconformist ideas of that time, and in the early 1840s he published articles in the Unitarian journal, *Nonconformist*. In 1848 through his uncle, he got a job as a writer on the leading mouthpiece of laissez-faire ideology, *The Economist*, working with prominent economists, such as Nassau William Senior (1790-1864). This work introduced him to London's leading radical, intellectual circles.

   Herbert Spencer never married, and society sometimes found his eccentric personality and increasing self-centredness annoying. However, being a man of fortune (Spencer inherited property several times during his lifetime), he was in a position to devote himself to his studies and writing about what he viewed as his life's work, figuring out a comprehensive philosophical system based on the idea of evolution. From around 1870, his articles yielded an increasing income, enabling him to employ assistants for collecting vast amounts of empirical data. Throughout his entire life Spencer loathed established academic life, which he viewed as much too conservative, and he declined several offers from universities, as well as academic honours.

Herbert Spencer belongs to the category of thinkers who gained a large reputation and influence in their lifetime, but who have since almost been forgotten. He is one of the most outstanding representatives of the radical-liberal belief in progress and evolutionary thinking, which emerged during the eighteenth century and strongly affected the world view.

Spencer's life and intellectual development were also quite special. His thinking and research was both encyclopedic and synthesizing, transgressing all existing boundaries between academic disciplines. For more than 50 years, from the 1840s till the end of the 1890s, Spencer worked on developing a theory, which was both political and cosmopolitan, addressing fundamental philosophical issues and political theory as a synthesis of empirical knowledge about the different aspects of human life, viewed through the perspectives of biology, psychology, anthropology, and sociology. Spencer's ideas represented a fusion of evolutionary theory, inspired by the natural sciences of that time (especially biologists and geologists, such as Jean Baptiste de Lamarck (1744–1829), Karl Ernst von Baer (1792–1876), and Charles Lyell (1797–1875)), with naturalism and empiricism in understanding man and society, and a very radical, almost anarchistic political liberalism and individualism. He was strongly engaged in the radical philosophical and unorthodox circles in England which had emerged as a result of utilitarian moral philosophy and perception of society (two of the great figures were Jeremy Bentham (1748–1832) and James Mill (1773–1836)). But Spencer was also critical of the utilitarian idea that the overall welfare of society should govern moral judgements, political goals, and legislation, fearing that this might threaten the freedom of the individual.

Spencer did not draw much inspiration from orthodox, liberal economic theory, even though he subscribed to and advocated economic laissez-faire liberalism. He studied closely (and criticized) Thomas Malthus's (1766–1834) book on population theory, *Essay of the Principle of Population* (1798), which strongly affected his understanding of the struggle for survival as the driving force behind social development. Especially on the basis of this idea, he elaborated on the principle of "survival of the fittest" (before Charles Darwin (1809–82) published *The Origin of Species* in 1859).

The Idea of Evolution and the Structure of Spencer's System

Although Spencer's thinking was synthesizing and interdisciplinary, it can be divided into elements which, in part, reflect the chronology he himself followed. From the early 1840s till the end of the early 1850s, his work focused on issues pertaining to social policy and morality, which he increasingly viewed from the perspective of evolution. One early result of this approach was the book *Social Statics* from 1850. By the mid-1850s he was engaged on a very ambitious, systematic plan called "A System of Synthetic Philosophy" the outcome of which was a 10-volume series, including *First Principles* (philosophical foundation), *Principles of Biology, Principles of Psychology, Principles of Sociology, Principles of Morality*. By and large, Herbert Spencer realized his plan before his death in 1903. The most important aspects of these works are the idea of evolution, and the related ideas of politics and moral philosophy, as well as sociological issues.

Evolution, individualism, and liberalism

Late in life, in 1879, Spencer wrote that right from the beginning "my ultimate purpose lying behind all proximate purposes, has been that of finding for the principles of right and wrong in conduct at large, a scientific basis" (Spencer 1890: vii). One of his ambitions was to develop an individualist ethical and political theory in keeping with knowledge of the natural sciences. Today we would define his perception as a form of *ethical naturalism* (chapter 27), implying that one can take a stand on ethical issues as right or wrong, good or evil, based on actual conditions, such as the order of nature (this perception is criticized below). For Spencer, these conditions concerned basic features of nature and the evolution of social life. Just as individual biological organisms (in ontogenesis) and species (in phylogenesis) developed from simple, uniform, and undifferentiated forms into complex, heterogeneous, and differentiated entities, all other spheres of the universe developed according to similar basic principles. On the basis of this perception, Spencer derived three universal principles for all evolution: (1) evolution as concentration (or integration); (2) evolution as differentiation, change from the homogeneous to the heterogeneous and complex; and (3) evolution as movement from the indefinite, toward something ever more definite and ordered. Ethically right conduct should build on insight into, and be in keeping with, these principles.

In his early years, Spencer used in particular the idea of evolution in his theories on politics and morality, summarized in his first great work, *Social Statics* (1850). The primary idea was that morality was an inherent human property, evolving continuously even in the sense of moral perfection. The basic view was consequential and extreme individualism. In order for the laws of evolution to be effective, thus enabling man to develop and perfect his capabilities and morals, it would require the greatest possible amount of individual freedom: "Every man has freedom to do all he will, provided he infringes not the equal freedom of any other man" (Spencer 1954: 95). Spencer specifies this principle in a series of rights, all of which imply minimizing state regulation. One of his most provocative views was that the right to freedom could justify the right to *ignore the state*.

According to Spencer, the natural evolution of a society, characterized by the greatest possible freedom, would strive toward a balance in which moral properties, such as the sense of justice and philanthropy, would become still more perfected. Several forces would drive this development, such as the struggle for survival (survival of the fittest) and a form of cultural learning (inspired by Lamarck). If the necessary freedom were to exist, morally right properties would develop and strengthen through usage.

One central and illustrative example was Spencer's argument against the poor laws. He argued that these were detrimental to private benevolence and obstructed philanthropy. Not only should suffering be considered unavoidable, it is also desirable in an evolutionary perspective:

> It seems hard that widows and orphans should be left to struggle for life or death. Nevertheless, when regarded not separately, but in connection with the interest of universal humanity, these harsh fatalities are seen to be full of the highest beneficence – the same beneficence which brings to early graves the children and diseased parents and singles out the low-spirited, the intemperate, and the debilitated as the victims of an epidemic. (Spencer 1954: 289)

The assumption is that, when viewing the struggle for survival from the perspective of the evolution of mankind, suffering is useful and ethically right because it leads to perfect balance and adaptation. Such a perception contains several serious problems, both as a theory of historical development and as a theory of ethics. These problems will be discussed after Spencer's sociological theory.

Spencer's Sociology

In his sociological theories and studies, Spencer formulated his evolutionary doctrine in detail, and these works have gained lasting influence. His application of concepts, such as social institutions, differentiation, complexity, integration, and social structure, in many ways anticipated later thought on functionalism, systems theory in sociology, and anthropology, despite subsequent criticism and rejections of his work. Supported by his assistants, he collected extensive data and systematized existing empirical data on different societies, their family structures, institutions, religions, and forms of government, especially concerning pre-industrial societies. His major works are *The Study of Sociology* (1873), *Principles of Sociology* (three volumes, 1876–96), and *Descriptive Sociology* (1873–1934, publication continued posthumously).

The analogy of organisms and types of societies

One of the ideas guiding Spencer's perception of society and his approach was the analogy he constructed between society as an entity and biological organisms. The analogy in itself was not new. Since Plato, social thinkers have found inspiration in biological organisms. However, inspired by contemporary biological theories, Spencer attempted to utilize this idea more concretely, to analyze the evolution of different types of societies as moving from lower, simple, and fairly uncomplex communities to progressively more complex, differentiated, and hence integrated ones. True to his empirical scientific understanding, he also used this analogy to claim (just as Emile Durkheim did later; see chapter 5) that society must be studied as a thing, an entity existing in itself, which is not merely the aggregate of individuals (Spencer 1893, vol. I: 436). According to Spencer, it was possible to draw analogies between certain sectors or institutions in society and organs in biological systems: the supply system (production sector) in society corresponds to digestive organs, the distribution system (transport and distribution) corresponds to the distributive organs (e.g. blood circulation), and the regulating system, that is, political, controlling institutions, corresponds to sensory and motor organs. Even though Spencer used the analogy of organisms literally, he admitted basic differences between society and biological organisms, the most important being that the single elements of society (individuals) are sensory, whereas this is only the case with specific biological tissues.

It is not easy to see how Spencer's holistic conception of organisms is compatible with his basic individualist view and his idea about the struggle for survival being the driving force behind evolution. Organicism, which is often associated with conservative ideology, usually means that individual acts are explicable in terms of collective traditions and institutions, which leads easily to collective needs being given priority over individual ones (see below). Spencer's application of the analogy is thus not very consistent. Nevertheless, the analogy of organisms guided Spencer's analyses of the evolution of different types of societies, which he placed in a progressive framework. This framework is not unequivocal, since Spencer actually elaborated two typologies, the interrelationship of which is not quite clear. In one of these, the criterion for typification was the degree of complexity. This criterion governs the data analysis in *Descriptive Sociology*. Here, the development of the political system determined how great, differentiated, and complex societies could become. This resulted in five categories: (1) simple societies with no heads (hunter and gatherer societies); (2) simple societies with heads (primitive agricultural societies); (3) compounded societies (more complex agricultural societies); (4) doubly compounded societies; and (5) triple compounded societies (industrial societies). The types differ systematically from one another in terms of the development stage of the supply system, the distributive system, and the regulating system.

But Spencer also used another, more abstract typology. This was bifurcated in militant and industrial societies (this distinction was quite common in the eighteenth century; cf. Peel 1971: 192). He claimed that wars and conquests had been of fundamental importance for the creation of larger, more complex societies characterized by division of labor. Societies capable of subjugating others, thus expanding, had been based on a centralized state power, a strong military class, and a fixed hierarchy. The division of labor had been based on coercion so that those in power and the military could be sustained by the productive class (Spencer 1893, vol. II: 602). In contrast, the industrial society is based on voluntary social relations, more decentralized power structures, and a division of labor based on functions rather than a power hierarchy. The two types of society will also encourage different personality features. Military societies encourage virtues, such as courage, strength, obedience to authority, and vindictiveness. The most typical characteristics of industrial societies are independence, resistance to coercion, honesty, truthfulness, kindness, less orthodoxy, and a higher regard for others' individuality (Spencer 1893, vol. II: 638ff). This characteristic of the two types of societies, especially their personality types, links Spencer's political and moral philosophical understanding of evolution to an implied progress in the sense of morality.

The Evolution of Social Institutions

In his major work on sociology, *Principles of Sociology*, Spencer unfolded and analyzed how social systems within the three subsystems mentioned could be described and explained according to the hypothesis of evolution. Among other things, these analyses included kinship relations, ceremonial institutions, political institutions, religious institutions, professional institutions (medicine, art, law, science, etc.), and industrial institutions. His approach was to examine how these institutions evolved from their most primitive forms, an almost animal stage, into increasingly complex, differentiated, and functional forms. However, Spencer described the "genealogical tree" of present forms rather than explaining the evolutionary mechanisms. For example, he viewed primitive forms of war trophies as an institution, which served to regulate relationships between the conquerors and the conquered after a war. These war trophies were the "forefathers" of the more developed societies' use of emblems, decorations, uniforms, and clothes symbolizing power and place in hierarchies in order to stabilize the latter. He assumed that in a future, fully developed industrial society, the need for hierarchy and hence these types of symbols would disappear. Spencer applied this evolutionary-functionalist method to analyze all the different types of societies. Two of these, family forms and political institutions, are addressed below.

Family institutions

Spencer viewed the family as the basic institution, the originating form of relatively stable communities, and biological reproduction as a most basic human need. Originally, rules and norms tied to family and kinship served to ensure stable environments for raising children, social integration, authority relationships, and regulation of religious ceremonies. The construction and development of these norms are profoundly affected by the struggle for survival. Societies that have had time to develop functional norms have an advantage over those that have not. For instance, fixed matrimonial rules are an evolutionary advantage over promiscuity, because they provide more stable conditions for raising children and prevent internal conflicts in society. Consequently, such societies are more capable of providing a wall of strength against the outside world, and are thus more formidable during wars and conflicts. More complex systems of kinship rules about marriage, descent, mutual obligations, etc., offer further advantages, because they provide larger entities of social ties and constitute the basis for more complex power hierarchies, which again can be used in production and war.

Spencer assumed an evolution from promiscuity over monogamy, polyandry, polygyny, and then back to monogamy. Originally, polyandry and polygyny offered advantages over monogamy (and promiscuity), because these resulted in larger family units and a greater number of social ties. At an even higher level of development, monogamy may again prove advantageous, in part because the integrative and organizing function is taken over by other institutions (political or economic) which gradually become established, and in part because wars play a less important role in the development of industrial society. By and large, however, this description of the evolution of family forms as a process progressing along a single line has been contradicted by later anthropological and ethnographic research (one should bear in mind that Spencer had access to a limited amount of data). However, Spencer's analytical approach has played an important role in many later theories, influencing the view of development as that which yields functional advantages under selection pressure from the environment.

Political institutions and class division

For Spencer, the decisive stage in development toward the complex and strongly differentiated industrial society was the creation of centralized political institutions. Here too, the pressure on society from its surroundings played a leading part, first and foremost in the form of wars. Original societies that had succeeded in organizing military leadership, for example, with a ruler and a war council with governing power and authority, were the ones to survive, expanding and increasing in population. Evolution has been an upward spiral, beginning with simple political organizing, then war, conquest, inclusion of other populations, more complex political reorganization, new wars, etc. As societies grow in size and population, various control functions become specialized, such as a professional military, or a military class, administration, a legal system, a system for collecting taxes, and systems of representation.

Spencer viewed class division, social inequality, and growth in hierarchical political institutions as the functional response to wars. Examples of this are the distinctions between conquerors and conquered, the establishment of slave systems, the internal hierarchies of the political system, the monopoly of owning land, and the political elite's use of coercion to increase its own and future descendants' wealth. However, it is surprising that Spencer expected this inclination toward increased centralism, power concentration, and inequality would be broken at a certain stage in development, when societies would begin to assume the nature of the industrial type. According to Spencer, the very growth of a society's overall wealth, and the interdependence caused by expanded trade, would enable individuals to accumulate wealth relatively independent of the politically determined hierarchy. In this way, a decentralized power base would emerge which could compete with the political elite. This would promote individualism and create pressure for greater political equality and the abolition of politically rooted monopolies. Spencer claimed that this helped to explain why the importance of wars would gradually decline. Originally, wars played a positive role in evolution. "Warfare among men, like warfare among animals, has had a large share in raising their organizations to a higher stage" (Spencer 1969: 174). The following quotation serves to illustrate Spencer's perception of the role of wars in evolution and his explanation of their decreasing positive influence:

> Severe and bloody as the process is, the killing-off of inferior races and inferior individuals, leaves a balance of benefit to mankind during phases of progress in which the moral development is low . . . But as there arise higher societies, implying individual characters fitted for

closer co-operation, the destructive activities exercised by such higher societies have injurious re-active effects on the moral natures of their members . . . After this stage has been reached, the purifying process, continuing still an important one, remains to be carried on by industrial war – by a competition of societies during which the best, physically, emotionally, and intellectually, spread most, and leave the least capable to disappear gradually, from failing to leave a sufficiently-numerous posterity. (Spencer 1969: 180)

Influence and Critique

In view of the marginal position ascribed to Spencer in the history of ideas, and the justified criticism to which his theories have been subjected, it is difficult to form a valid picture of his impact. The fact is, however, that his works and ideas gained enormous ground during his lifetime, especially from 1870 onward. His works were translated into several languages and sold in hundreds of thousands of copies. When travelling around the world, he was celebrated and offered academic positions, honours, and honorary posts (which he declined on grounds of principle). No doubt, one reason was that his belief in progress based on "survival of the fittest" was in keeping with the strongly competitive and laissez-faire business climate of that time.

Spencer also had a strong impact on early American sociologists (especially William G. Summer (1840–1910) and Franklin H. Giddings (1855–1931) who used his books in their teaching). But since his ideas were highly controversial, both politically and religiously, he also encountered considerable opposition, including attempts at censorship by conservative and ecclesiastical circles.

Criticism of Spencer touches upon three specific issues of fundamental importance. The first concerns the inherent conflict between his individualist perception of man and that of society as an organism. Emile Durkheim's critique of Spencer in his book *The Division of Labour in Society (De la division du travail social*, 1893) has had a lasting impact. Durkheim's major critique was that a theory which assumes man to be driven exclusively by calculations of self-interest will never be able to explain the integration of society. Norms and rules, the basic pillars of social order, cannot be based exclusively on mutual advantages. Then several decades later, the American sociologist Talcott Parsons advanced an almost identical critique in his book *The Structure of Social Action* (1937), pointing out the difficulties of solving the classical problem of social order by applying a purely individualist and utilitarian theory of action (chapter 14). If one assumes that individuals act in a purely utilitarian manner toward goals which they choose independently of one another, it will be difficult to understand how relatively stable social institutions are ever established at all.

The second issue concerns the relationship between Spencer's doctrine of evolution as a theory of evolution in nature, biology, and society, and his ethical and political understanding. As mentioned earlier, this is an example of ethical naturalism, the conception that what is ethically right can be derived from universal laws assumed to be effective in the real world. The problem with Spencer's theory was that he wanted to deduce that being fitter for survival would develop into a sense of morality. Ethical naturalism, including Spencer's version, was subject to strong criticism early in this century, and rejected as "the naturalist fallacy" by the philosopher George E. Moore (Moore 1971, chapter 27). This criticism of ethical naturalism was widely accepted, and contributed strongly toward undermining Spencer's theory. (One of Spencer's contemporaries, the biologist Thomas Henry Huxley (1825–95), had already advanced a similar critique: the ethically right requires transgressing the order of nature.)

The third issue of criticism concerns the methodological problems of transferring an explanatory principle inspired by biology, such as "survival of the fittest," to social conditions. This critique was formulated stringently only later in criticism of functionalism in anthropology and sociology. According to this critique, it is not plausible to consider "natural selection" and "survival of the fittest" as evolutionary mechanisms for social development, because analogies with biological concepts, such as genes, reproduction, death, organisms, and population cannot be applied to the social and cultural spheres of life (see Elster 1983; van Parijs 1981).

There is no doubt that one of the reasons why posterity has taken a negative stand on Spencer is his association with social Darwinism. This political-ideological theory, which was also linked to theories of eugenics and was used to defend colonial wars, flourished from the end of the nineteenth century and continued into the interwar period, especially in the USA and Germany, and was also supported by industrial and financial magnates (see Bannister 1979; Hofstadter 1964). Even though Spencer inspired social Darwinism, he did attempt to distance himself from this ideological application of the theory. He subscribed to the equal rights of races, and in his view states should keep aloof from colonial administration. He was also deeply depressed about the growing number of wars, which he witnessed in the last decades of his life, and which he referred to as a "period of social cannibalism" (Duncan 1908: 410). This state of affairs also contradicted his theory that the inherent tendency of industrialism was to evolve toward more peaceful conditions. Still, despite these major critical points, some contemporary theorists are attempting to revive the principles of survival of the fittest and natural selection to explain social phenomena. These include areas within so-called sociobiology, economics, and game theory (chapter 13).

Bibliography

Primary:

Perrin, Robert G. 1993: *Herbert Spencer: A Primary and Secondary Bibliography*. London: Garland.
Spencer, Herbert. 1855: *The Principles of Psychology*. 2 vols. London: Williams and Norgate.
—— 1862: *First Principles*. London: Williams and Norgate.
—— 1868–74: *Essays: Scientific, Political, and Speculative*. 3 vols. London: Williams and Norgate.
—— 1873–1934: *Descriptive Sociology*. 14 vols. London: Williams and Norgate.
—— 1893–6 [1876–96]: *The Principles of Sociology*. 3 vols. London: Williams and Norgate.
—— 1884: *The Man versus the State*. London: Williams and Norgate.
—— 1890 [1879]: *The Data of Ethics*. London: Williams and Norgate.
—— 1904: *An Autobiography*. 2 vols. London: Williams and Norgate.
—— 1954 [1850]: *Social Statics*. New York: Robert Schalkenback Foundation.
—— 1969 [1873]: *The Study of Sociology*. Ann Arbor, MI: University of Michigan Press.
—— 1972: *On Social Evolution. Selected Writings*, ed. J. D. Y. Peel. Chicago: University of Chicago Press.

Secondary:

Andreski, Stanislav. 1972: *Herbert Spencer: Structure, Function and Evolution*. London: Nelson.

Bannister, Robert C. 1979: *Social Darwinism. Science and Myth in Anglo-American Thought.* Philadelphia: Temple University Press.

Carneiro, Robert L. 1981: Herbert Spencer as an Anthropologist. *Journal of Libertarian Studies,* Spring, 153–210.

Duncan, David. 1908: *Life and Letters of Herbert Spencer.* London: Methuen.

Elliot, Hugh. 1917: *Herbert Spencer.* London: Constable.

Elster, Jon. 1983: *Explaining Technical Change.* Cambridge: Cambridge University Press.

Gray, Tim. 1996: *The Political Philosophy of Herbert Spencer: Individualism and Organicism.* Brookfield, VT: Avebury.

Green, J. Reynolds. 1906: *Herbert Spencer.* London: J. M. Dent.

Hofstadter, Richard. 1964 [1944]: *Social Darwinism in American Thought.* Boston: The Beacon Press.

Hudson, William Henry. 1996: *An Introduction to the Philosophy of Herbert Spencer.* London: Routledge/Thoemmes Press.

Moore, George Edward. 1971 [1903]: *Principia Ethica.* Cambridge: Cambridge University Press.

Peel, J. D. Y. 1971: *Herbert Spencer: The Evolution of a Sociologist.* London: Heinemann.

Rumney, Jay. 1966 [1937]: *Herbert Spencer's Sociology.* New York: Atherton Press.

Taylor, Michael W. (ed.) 1996a: *Herbert Spencer: Contemporary Assesments.* London: Routledge/Thoemmes Press.

—— 1996b: *Herbert Spencer and the Limits of the State: the Late Nineteenth-Century Debate Between Individualism and Collectivism.* Bristol: Thoemmes.

Turner, Jonathan H. 1985: *Herbert Spencer.* Beverly Hills, CA: Sage.

Van Parijs, Philip. 1981: *Evolutionary Explanation in the Social Sciences.* Totowa, NJ: Rowman and Littlefield.

Webb, Beatrice. 1979 [1906]: *My Apprenticeship.* Cambridge: Cambridge University Press.

Weinstein, David. 1998: *Equal Freedom and Utility: Herbert Spencer's Liberal Utilitarianism.* Cambridge: Cambridge University Press.

Wiltshire, David. 1978: *The Social and Political Thought of Herbert Spencer.* Oxford: Oxford University Press.

chapter **4**

Ferdinand Tönnies

Jørn Falk

KEY CONCEPTS

ARBITRARY WILL – A will that is subject to thought; corresponds to Gesellschaft and refers to premeditated actions and the separation of means and ends.

ESSENTIAL WILL – thought that is subject to the will; corresponds to Gemeinschaft and refers to unreflective actions, driven by the emotions, custom, or conscience.

GEMEINSCHAFT – denotes the internal bonds between people united by a common language, custom, or religious denomination.

GESELLSCHAFT – denotes the external bonds that are established when people meet as conscious partners in trade and interest.

NORMAL TYPE – an analytical construct; a heuristic, interrogative tool that is used to describe the formation of social groups (cf. Weber's concept of an *ideal type*).

Biography: *Ferdinand Tönnies*

Ferdinand Tönnies was born on July 26, 1855, in Oldenwort parish on the Ejdersted peninsula near Husum in the duchy of Schleswig. He started his wandering years and scholarly pursuits in 1872 with studies in Strasbourg, Jena, Bonn, Leipzig, and Tübingen; in 1877, he received his doctorate in classical philology. Henceforth, he conducted private studies in Berlin and in London, laying the ground work for the *magnum opus* of his younger years, *Gemeinschaft und Gesellschaft*. This early work became his so-called *Habilitationsschrift*, that is, it constituted his licence to teach, and he proceeded to teach as a *Privatdozent* at the University of Kiel, during which time he was an assiduous contributor not only to scholarly journals, but to political and socio-ethical periodicals as well. He travelled extensively, even to America. *Gemeinschaft und Gesellschaft* was published in 1887, but did not lead to tenure immediately. Not until 1913, the year following the second printing, did he become professor of economic and political science at Kiel, and he left the position again in 1916. From 1920, he finally began to teach sociology at Kiel, as an emeritus professor. In 1909, together with Simmel, Weber, and others, he founded the *Deutsche Gesellschaft für Soziologie*, which elected him president in 1922. He was twice awarded honorary doctorates and became an honorary member of several foreign sociological associations, as the *Altmeister der Soziologie* of the Weimar Republic. Immediately after the Nazis came to power in 1933, he was dismissed without a pension. Tönnies died on April 11, 1936, at Kiel – not very far from Ejdersted, his birthplace.

Intellectual Background and Foundation.

Ferdinand Tönnies was born in the year the Danish government adopted a joint constitution in a vain attempt to keep the duchies within the Danish monarchy. In the following years Schleswig-Holstein was absorbed into the German *Reich*, the consolidation of which was energetically pursued by Otto von Bismarck ("with blood and iron"). This transformed *das Land der Dichter und Denker* from a relatively nonpolitical *Kulturnation* to a *Kulturstaat* (Bleicher 1990). The concept of culture is here associated with a *Bildungsbürgertum* that had a common language and literature, but only later, if at all, felt the need for a common state.

The term *Kultur* in German intellectual history was the social antithesis of the concept of *Zivilisation* (Elias 1978), which is here associated with soulless, mechanistic processes, and which forms the starting point of the critique of modern industrial society. *Kultur* was originally a universal notion. Romantic ideas of a *Volk* with common "roots," language, and fate changed this concept in the direction of a particularistic, national antithesis that focused on the lived life of ordinary people and emphasized emotions rather than cold reason; the natural and organic rather than the affected and artificial; the languages of the people rather than a French-influenced cosmopolitan *Zivilisation*. But after a while, the very same ideas made a large part of the German cultural elite "useful idiots" for the authoritarian-monarchist empire of Kaiser Wilhelm that evolved in the second half of the nineteenth century. The social critique inherent in the idea of *Kultur* was lost here in unabashed praise of the *Reich*.

Sociological Thought as Consciousness of Crisis

Tönnies was *not* one of these useful idiots, and this eventually affected his academic career to such an extent that he never had one. Luckily, he had a well-to-do father, who was a marshland farmer, descended from a long line of farmers, and a stock-market speculator who prospered by investing in beef cattle sold to England. It was through his mother, who came from a distinguished Lutheran family, that he belonged to *das Bildungsbürgertum*. The seven children in the family had a private tutor. Later the family moved to Husum, and young Tönnies's mentor there was Theodor Storm (1817–88), a poetic realist, who, in a series of lyrical and melancholy novels, described the Frisian people and landscape. The question arises of whether one can therefore read Tönnies's early work as an elegy – although of an academic sort – over the loss of the joys of Ejdersted, the *Gemeinschaft* of the land of his childhood. This possibilty will be discussed below.

Elegiac or not, modern German sociology originated from a consciousness of crisis among a handful of scholars around the turn of the previous century. They were all – Tönnies, Simmel, Weber, and others – confronted with an empire that, although it had achieved a superficial political unity, was deeply divided by class, religious, and regional differences. They all saw these problems from the rather dilatory perspective of the cultural elite, which gives an indication of the complex nature of their social and cultural habitude. They all came from comfortable middle-class families which could support them economically, if necessary. They were all "cultured," they had trod the academic path from *Abitur* and *Dissertation* to *Habilitation* and were consequently certified members of the cultural elite (Liebersohn 1989). And they all attempted, each in their own way, to solve the problem of instability within the empire. Tönnies was the first of them to begin to speculate on what it is that binds people together in society.

Early Work of Lasting Importance

In view of the fact that Tönnies published over 800 titles, it is, of course, absurd to claim that he only really wrote only one book: *Gemeinschaft und Gesellschaft*. This early work would in retrospect – because recognition came later – signal the beginning of a new epoch in the history of sociology: it laid the foundations of sociology as a discipline in its own right in Germany. It has been called a bridge between the nineteenth century's all-encompassing sociological doctrines and the twentieth century's analytical sociology (Szaki 1979: 339).

Tönnies drew from a variety of sources: the seventeenth century's natural-rights philosophers, especially Thomas Hobbes (1588–1679), as well as Baruch Spinoza (1632–77) and Adam Ferguson (1723–1816); positivist sociology such as that of Auguste Comte (1798–1857) and Herbert Spencer; Arthur Schopenhauer (1788–1860), especially his concept of the will, and in addition a touch of Friedrich Nietzsche (1844–1900); various socialist theorists, especially Marx, as well as the evolutionary theorists J. J. Bachofen (1815–87), Lewis H. Morgan (1818–81), Henry Maine (1822–88), and others (Heberle 1968).

Tönnies, unlike Spencer (see chapter 3), considered it useless to speculate about amoebas, insects, and other animal "communities," because the objects studied by sociology are defined by will and thought. With regard to the human will he adopted Schopenhauer's view of *die Welt als Wille und Vorstellung*, although Tönnies also distanced himself from Schopenhauer by considering the will as specifically human – not necessarily as something irrational.

All social relations, according to Tönnies, can be deduced from the will of the individuals who enter into such relations. He thus sided with the natural-rights philosophers, despite criticizing them for completely identifying the will with the rational will, which separates the end of an act from its means. By identifying social relations with willed relations, Tönnies also distanced himself from all variations of positivist organicism (as well as the behaviourism of a future age), which makes society independent of the human will.

Gemeinschaft and Gesellschaft or Community and Society

That which binds people together is, according to Tönnies, based on reciprocity, on the interrelationship of demands and services that constitutes the group as a social system. The relationship and also the resulting association itself can now be understood in two ways, either as real and organic life, as the essence of the *community* (*das Wesen der Gemeinschaft*), or as ideal and mechanical structure, as the concept of *society* (*der Begriff der Gesellschaft*). Tönnies gives a quite plastic description of the difference between the two relations:

> All intimate, familiar, exclusive living together, so we discover, is understood as life in community (*Gemeinschaft*). Society (*Gesellschaft*) is public life, is the world itself. When in community with one's own, one finds oneself from birth connected through good and bad fortune; one goes into society as into a foreign country. The youth is warned against "bad company" (*Gesellschaft*), the expression "bad community," however, rings false. (Tönnies 1972: 3–4)

The difference between German *Gemeinschaft* and *Gesellschaft* is difficult to express in the English language. The usual translations are "community" and "society," but in ordinary language no sharp distinction is found. The meaning of the German *Gemeinschaft* (community) is clear, however, when Tönnies discuss a *Gemeinschaft* of language, of custom, and of faith; in contrast, the meaning of *Gesellschaft* (society) in fact is best illustrated by words which are not usually translated as "society," for example, German compound words like *Aktiengesellschaft* (joint-stock company) *Abendgesellschaft* (dinner party), or *Reisegesellschaft* (travelling companions). In this case the etymology is also misleading, because the words *Gemeinschaft* and *Gesellschaft* mean more or less the same thing. Tönnies's valid, if slightly laboured, argument is that *Gemeinschaft* is an old word, *Gesellschaft* is new. The Gothic word *Ga-mainz* (just like the Latin word *com-munis*) means "shared provisions," while *Ge-sell* comes from the Old Norse *salr* which means shared living space. And humans were nomadic hunter-gatherers long before they settled down and became farmers. They shared food for millennia before they began to build houses for common use. Only much later did *Gesellschaft* become the craftsman's community, that between master and apprentice, *Ge-sell*: housemate (Otnes 1991: 293).

Normal Types

But apart from the semantic implications, what analytical significance does the distinction between Gemeinschaft and Gesellschaft have for Tönnies? Gemeinschaft and Gesellschaft denote what he calls "normal types," between which actual life moves. Thus, the "normal type" corresponds to what Weber (later, but with greater impact) called an "ideal type," that is, a theoretical construct that has no immediate, empirical, classificatory correspondence to actuality. Gemeinschaft, as a normal type, denotes the internal bonds between people: kinship (the bond of blood), neighborhood (the bond of place, based on custom), and friendship (the relatedness of sentiment). The outward forms of Gemeinschaft are, for example, house, village (commonage), and country town (*die Stadt*). Its general concept is the people, united by internal bonds of language, custom, beliefs, as well as the (in principle, universal) bond of religious community (cf. the communion of saints).

Gesellschaft, on the other hand, denotes the external bonds in which people meet as partners in trade and interest. Gesellschaft is more highly concentrated in larger cities, but it can be seen in varying degrees everywhere in society. While the integrative aspect is strongly represented in Gemeinschaft, the agonistic aspect dominates Gesellschaft. The latent, disintegrative conflicts are reined in, however, not by custom, conscience, or religion, but by conventions, agreement, politics, and public debate. The difference between Gemeinschaft and Gesellschaft can be formulated as the difference between sharing versus trading in which the starting point is things or wares, rather than emotions, which are shared or traded.

Essential Will and Arbitrary Will

Gemeinschaft and Gesellschaft, as an analytical dichotomy, have an objective as well as a subjective dimension. These dimensions consist partly of a materialistic theory (based on Hobbes, Marx, and others) of an evolution from primitive communism to modern, capitalist society, and partly of a theory of the will (inspired by Schopenhauer and Nietzsche), in which external social transformation is seen as a result of an underlying transition from a condition of the organic unity of the will to a condition of the individualization of the will. The *sociological* concept must therefore be a *psychological* concept as well. The concept of the human will and thought must likewise be understood as having a dual, dichotomous character.

Tönnies distinguishes between thought that is subject to the will and a will that is subject to thought. Each concept produces a coherent whole, "in which the multiplicity of the emotions, instincts and drives forms a unity," but one in which the unity of the first concept "must be understood as real and natural and the unity of the other as ideal and artificial" (Tönnies 1972: 87). Tönnies calls the first sense of the human will the essential will (*Wesenwille*) and the second sense the arbitrary will (*Kürwille*).

Corresponding to the three levels of Gemeinschaft (kinship, neighborhood, and friendship) are the three forms of essential will, namely pleasure, custom, and recollection. Pleasure is the animal form of the essential will: the will to breathe, to eat and drink, and to reproduce. Custom is the disposition toward certain things and activities, acquired by experience and practice, cultivation. Recollection is the community's spiritual form, in which the idea of a people has its basis in a collective, mythic memory, potentially communicated through art.

Likewise, the arbitrary will corresponds to Gesellschaft and involves the purpose of an action, an *end* to achieve, in which certain external *means* are considered and chosen. Following the Tönniesian tripartite division (which marks increasing degrees of refinement), we find aspiration, calculation, and consciousness. To Gesellschaft belong, consequently, the economic, the political, and the scientific man, all of whom are "choice-making" types. Its general concept is not the people, but the nation, the state, the nation-state.

Types of Action

In other words, we are dealing with two types of action. One type is driven by emotions, custom, or conscience and acts unreflectingly, in accordance with these inner urges. The other type is premeditated and seeks to actualize an idea, regardless of whether it conflicts with these internal urges or not. Essential will therefore refers to the types of action in Gemeinschaft, in which means and ends make up an essential whole (cf. "the *essence* of community"). The arbitrary will, on the other hand, denotes the types of actions in Gesellschaft in which the ends and means are separated in thought, translated into concepts (cf. "the *concept* of society"). All social bonds, according to Tönnies, are shaped by both types of will and are thus analogous to chemical elements that can be combined in different proportions. Both the essential will and the arbitrary will contain rational action. Tönnies could later on, in reference to Weber's four types of action (see chapter 6), emphasize that the value-rational type of action, as well as the affective and the traditional types, belongs to the concept of essential will (Tönnies 1931: 6).

A Gemeinschaft Romantic?

Tönnies has occasionally been accused of romanticizing Gemeinschaft. It has been argued that the analytical dichotomy which, according to Tönnies, exists between Gemeinschaft and Gesellschaft contains a fundamental bias, "as if *Gemeinschaft* were presented as something good and *Gesellschaft* as something bad" (Tönnies 1931: VI). Nothing could be further from the truth. One could argue, however, that the very way Tönnies formulated the theme of his investigation afforded the grounds for certain misinterpretations. Under §1 in *Gemeinschaft und Gesellschaft*, Tönnies states the principle that the effect of the relations between individuals can be either affirmative or negative.

But Tönnies has already made his choice (as his purpose was to do away with the divisions in the empire) when he says that the theory and the object of the investigation "will be focused exclusively on relations of mutual affirmation" (Tönnies 1972: 3). Unruly and negative wills are thus defined out of the field of inquiry. Such a positive position could well be called idyllic, in that Gemeinschaft actually involves hidebound paternalism, devoted submission, extreme violence, and rebellion.

The axe-murder of kin, which we know from the tradition of blood vengeance in *Njal's Saga*, may exemplify the ultimate form of violence in Gemeinschaft, whereas the violence in Gesellschaft is exemplified in Glauber Rochas's suggestive film about hegemonic violence in rural districts of Brazil by the instrumental, impersonal, hired assassin, *Antonio the Killer*. This example suggests that the most extreme form of violence in Gesellschaft is not necessarily an urban phenomenon, although an example of this is found in the loathsome, callous, psychopathic killer, Mack the Knife, from Bertolt Brecht's *Threepenny Opera*.

The above examples are, in a sense, inspired by Tönnies because even "antisocial" relations were accounted for in his sociological system. He published, for example, a series of empirical studies of the Hamburg strike of 1896–7 (Tönnies 1896, 1897, 1898). He was thus in possession of substantial (and controversial) knowledge concerning the living and working conditions of seamen and dockworkers. Although this kind of knowledge seldom figured in his theoretical works, it made him a controversial person in public. He was, in fact, known as the "Strike Professor" (he was a titular professor, that is, one without a chair, after 1891) because of the frequency with which he spoke on issues of social ethics and reforms. As a result, the Prussian Ministry of Culture suspected him of being a social democrat, or even worse. No chair for that *Kerl*!

Malefactors and Crooks

Late in life, Tönnies published a series of statistical works on serious crime among men in Schleswig-Holstein (Tönnies 1929a; b; Bellebaum 1976: 251–2). Here he states that there is a distinction between the type and frequency of crime in urban and rural areas. Two "normal" types of criminal emerge in these works: malefactors (*Frevlern*), i.e. arsonists, thugs, and sex offenders (found primarily in rural areas) and crooks (*Gaunern*), i.e. thieves, burglars, and swindlers (found primarily in urban areas).

Tönnies had distinguished, in his early work, between hostility that is the result of the weakening, or severing, of pre-existing social bonds and hostility that is the result of alienation, ignorance, and suspicion. In Gemeinschaft hostility usually expresses itself as acute anger, hatred, and ill will, whereas hostility in Gesellschaft usually expresses itself as chronic fear, loathing, and aversion. (Tönnies 1972: 155–6). Thus the theory corresponds to his later interest in the two types of criminal referred to above. Malefactors act with a spontaneous passion that springs from a brutal, unreflective, or immediate egoism. Here we are dealing with a coarser kind of mentality. Crooks, on the other hand, act with premeditation. They have a clear consciousness of their objective (that is, to appropriate to themselves goods belonging to others) and their activity is the means (distinguished from the end) for the attainment of that end. Crooks are thus characterized by a more refined form of egoism than are malefactors.

Thus one looks in vain here for any idealizing of Gemeinschaft along the lines of rural romanticism: the coarse malefactors are found primarily in rural districts. Some existential homesickness is clearly, in Tönnies's case, distinguished from a nostalgic desire to return to the land.

Philosophy of Culture and Pure Sociology

The question, however, is whether it is possible, keeping the analytical dichotomies in mind, to speak – as has so often been done – of a *transition* from Gemeinschaft to Gesellschaft? The first edition of *Gemeinschaft und Gesellschaft* was published in 1887 with the subtitle, *Abhandlung des Communismus und des Sozialismus als empirischer Culturformen*. Tönnies asserts here in a supplement entitled "Results and Outlook," that "two *ages* (*Zeitalter*) confront each other in the great cultural developments: an *age* of society follows an *age* of community" (Tönnies 1972: 251). The italics are Tönnies's own and accentuate the problem of the relationship between these two "ages."

Thus the two ages seem both to confront each other (systematically) and to follow, one from the other (irreversibly). The first relation corresponds to the analytical dichotomies referred to above. The second relation may be interpreted developmentally, in either the revolutionary sense (as is the case with Marx) or the evolutionary sense (as is the case with Tönnies). Tönnies had earlier indicated how Gesellschaft through education, newspapers, etc. bred class consciousness and, consequently, apocalyptic class struggles.

> The Class struggle may destroy both society and the state which it wishes to transform. Since the entire culture has been transformed into a civilization of state and *Gesellschaft*, the culture itself, in this transformation, is drawing towards its own end; unless its scattered seeds survive and again bring forth the essence and idea of community, thus secretly fostering a new culture amidst the decaying one. (Tönnies 1972: 251)

The subtitle of the 1887 edition echoes the schema of a historical materialism in which civilization evolves from primitive communism to modern socialism as "empirical forms of culture," as a comparative cultural philosophy. A draft of *Gemeinschaft und Gesellschaft* from 1880–1 was, in fact, subtitled *Theorem der Cultur-Philosophie*. But when Tönnies describes the whole affair as a result of the fact that culture has changed into a civilization, it echoes the philosophical dichotomy of German idealism between *Kultur* and *Zivilisation*, where culture is a product of Gemeinschaft and *Zivilisation* a product of Gesellschaft, where "*Gemeinschaft* is understood as a living organism and *Gesellschaft* as a mechanistic aggregate or artefact" (Tönnies 1972: 5).

A Shift in Emphasis

In 1887, when Tönnies is on the point of proclaiming the evolutionary necessity of socialism, it can therefore be interpreted as a practical, political reinvestment in *Kultur* as the critical antithesis of a capitalistic *Zivilisation*. Tönnies was no useful idiot to the German empire. All his life he supported various social and ethical reforms, including the establishment of trade unions, cooperative societies, etc., in order to make the emergence of the new culture, the scattered seeds of which were already beginning to unfold in the lap of capitalistic civilization, more conspicuous. For Tönnies "Gemeinschaft is the genuine and enduring expression of common life, Gesellschaft is merely a temporary incarnation" (Tönnies 1972: 5).

Here Tönnies is somewhat ambiguous. If Gesellschaft is merely a temporary phenomenon, a transition, then such an evolutionary claim would appear to conflict with the systematic view that Gemeinschaft and Gesellschaft represent polarities that, in principle, can never be done away with, but which express something fundamental about the human condition. If this view is correct, then there can be no transition from Gemeinschaft to Gesellschaft (nor, for that matter, from Gesellschaft to Gemeinschaft). The one can be more or less dominant, however, in relation to the other, but that is a different story altogether.

When the second edition of Tönnies's early work appeared in 1912, its subtitle was *Grundbegriffe der reinen Soziologie*. A quarter of a century had passed between the two editions and the new subtitle (retained in subsequent editions) exhibits Tönnies's later efforts to divide sociology into a number of subdisciplines. He distinguishes, at this point, between general sociology and special sociology, with the latter being further subdivided – as, for example in *Einführung in die Soziologie* – into pure sociology, applied sociology, and empirical sociology (Tönnies 1931: 5–6).

This represents a shifting of the theoretical centre of Tönnies's early work. Where the subtitle of the 1887 edition of *Gemeinschaft und Gesellschaft* emphasizes the historical interpretation of these phenomena and the politically and ethically useful story of communism and socialism as empirical forms of culture (applied sociology), the subtitle of the 1912 edition emphasizes ontological determinations, or the construction of fundamental sociological concepts (pure sociology). This categorical distinction between theoretical research, interpretation, and *sociography* based on statistical material (empirical sociology) would eventually – despite the fact that Tönnies himself emphasized the fundamental unity of theory and empirical methods – result, on one hand, in extremely abstract, theoretical constructions (*á la* Talcott Parsons, cf. chapter 14) and, on the other, in a monumental accumulation of data (*á la* Paul Lazarsfeld, cf. chapter 16). It is perhaps because of this that a sharp distinction between theory and practice has been abandoned by contemporary sociologists.

Tönnies's Audience in America and Elsewhere

The subtitles mentioned above designate two possible interpretations of Tönnies's ideas: either as a cultural philosophy based on evolutionary theory (this view was most prevalent around the printing of the first edition of *Gemeinschaft und Gesellschaft,* and is therefore less favored today) or as pure sociology. Maybe the most accurate interpretation of Tönnies is, after all, that he was a philosopher whose main concerns were ontological, but who spoke through the mask of sociology (König 1987: 196). In this case, the analytical dichotomy he posited between Gemeinschaft and Gesellschaft is his most important contribution to sociology.

But these interpretative options have not really dominated the reading of Tönnies, which has tended to establish an evolutionary either/or between Gemeinschaft and Gesellschaft, where Tönnies himself (all ambiguities aside) stresses a more or less close relationship between them. Textbooks often lump him together with Comte and Spencer as advocating a positive theory of stages, or conflate his Gemeinschaft with Durkheim's mechanical solidarity (see chapter 5), despite the fact that Durkheim's concept describes a stage in an evolutionary sequence, whereas Gemeinschaft (and Gesellschaft) denotes an aspect of every possible society, and despite the fact that mechanical solidarity describes the objective structure of a society, whereas Gemeinschaft is based on relations of will.

Tönnies gave a lecture on the topic of "The Present Problems of Social Structure" at a sociology congress at the 1904 World's Fair in St. Louis (Tönnies 1905). His efforts in America did not immediately bear fruit, but he gradually achieved a small scattering of disciples there. It seems likely, however, that he was more praised than he was actually known (Cahnman 1981: 103).

Chicago School researchers, Park, Wirth, Redfield, and others, knew him quite well, but they had a tendency to transform his concept pairing into spatial categories, that is, they tended to interpret Gemeinschaft as the rural, agricultural form of life, and Gesellschaft as existence in large urban settings (this view can be traced back to Simmel in his work, *Die*

Grossstädte und das Geistesleben, which can be seen as an exclusively methodological investment in the concept of Gesellschaft, which is here the equivalent of metropolitan life). In 1921, Sorokin and Zimmerman introduced their notion of the rural-urban continuum, which viewed the huge wave of (im)migration to America as one continuous movement from countryside to city, or, taking an evolutionary perspective of Tönnies's dichotomy, from Gemeinschaft to Gesellschaft. Tönnies's transhistorical normal types, which are valid with respect to any part of society, are reduced, in this way, to a rural and an urban sociology respectively.

Last but not least, Parsons's detailed references to Tönnies in *The Structure of Social Action* contributed to Tönnies's renown. Thus Parsons's famous "pattern variables" can be viewed as a useful commentary on the Gemeinschaft–Gesellschaft dichotomy, but hardly as a theoretical advance (Cahnman 1981: 102).

Scandinavian Friends and Questionable Disciples

Tönnies also traveled in Scandinavia. In the introduction to the Norwegian translation of *Einführung in die Soziologie* (Tönnies 1932: III), he greets his expanded circle of readers with the words, "to my Scandinavian friends and all those who value and promote sociology." The translation was the work of Tönnies's pupil and later colleague at Kiel, Ewald Bosse. Tönnies's Scandinavian readership continued to be primarily Norwegian, centered around the Oslo school of sociology (Høgsnes 1986; Otnes 1990, 1991; Østerberg 1988; also the Swede Asplund 1991).

Why Tönnies's Danish readership is so small is a bit of a mystery. The old connections between the universities at Kiel and Copenhagen were at least partly intact, despite the battle at Dybbøl. Tönnies had dedicated the second edition of *Gemeinschaft und Gesellschaft* to his good friend, the Danish professor of philosophy, Harald Høffding (1843–1931), who is mentioned several times in connection with the reception of the early work. Høffding had referred (somewhat unjustly) to Tönnies's project as one of social pessimism, but he also praised the work, devoid as it was of "the passion of Rousseau or Schopenhauer," for its objectivity (Høffding 1899: 142–57) which he called its *uforstyrrethed*, its imperturbability (Tönnies 1931: VII).

Futhermore the sociologically trained Danish philosopher Christian Petersen (1893–1983) (who was later awarded the degree of Doctor of Philosophy for his work on Emile Durkheim) wrote on Tönnies's ideas, as did Theodor Geiger (1891–1952), epecially before his exile in Denmark (Geiger 1927; Geiger 1931).

It is possible that Tönnies's imperturbability extended to the reception of his ideas around the turn of the century by the German *Jugendbewegung*, which had naively taken his concept of Gemeinschaft and turned it into an "organic" and "genuine" alternative to the varied strains of modern rationalism and individualism. But when, in 1933, he was one of all too few university instructors who took public exception to anti-Semitic student excesses at the University of Breslau, it seems that his imperturbability was beginning to give way (König 1981). As a social-liberal, he had in 1931 put his confidence in "the internationalism of national labour movements" (Tönnies 1931: IX) and became a member of the SPD. Another acronym had by that time, however, taken control: NSDAP.

The National Socialist interpretation of Tönnies's ideas was the most ignominious of them all. The stubborn anti-Nazi had to stand helplessly on the sidelines as new "useful idiots" introduced the "brown" synthesis: the *Aufhebung* of the analytical dichotomy between Gemeinschaft and Gesellschaft to the Nazi concept *"Volksgemeinschaft."* In contrast to many other colleagues – Theodor Geiger, for example – Tönnies chose internal exile. He had become an old man.

Bibliography

Primary:

Bibliographies (all incomplete):
Bellebaum, Alfred. 1976: Werkverzeichnis. In Dirk Käsler (ed.): *Klassiker des soziologischen Denkens*, 386–94. Munich: Verlag C. H. Beck.
Brenke, Else. 1936: Verzeichnis der Schriften von Ferdinand Tönnies aus den Jahren 1875 bis 1935. In *Reine und angewandte Soziologie. Eine Festschrift für Ferdinand Tönnies zu seinem achtzigsten Geburtstag am 26. Juli 1935*, pp. 383–403. Leipzig: Buske.

Difficulties in publishing the huge amount of work are also discussed in: Wassner, Rainer. 1985. Überlegungen zu einer Tönnies-Werkausgabe. In Lars Clausen et al. (eds): *Tönnies heute*. Hamburg: W.G. Mühlau Verlag.

Tönnies, Ferdinand. 1887: *Gemeinschaft und Gesellschaft. Abhandlung des Communismus und des Sosialismus als empirischer Culturformen*. Leipzig: Fues's Verlag. (*Community and Association*, translated and supplemented by Charles P. Loomis. London: Routledge 1955).
—— 1896: Zum Hamburger Streik. Ethische Kultur. *Wochenschrift zur Verbreitung ethischer Bestrebungen*, 4, 409ff.
—— 1897a: Hafenarbeiter und Seeleute in Hamburg vor dem Streik 1896/97; Der Hamburger Streik von 1896/97. *Archiv für Soziale Gesetzgebung und Statistik*, 10, 173ff.
—— 1897b: Das Ende des Streiks; Streik-Terrorismus. *Ethische Kultur*, 5, 9–6.
—— 1897c: *Thomas Hobbes Leben und Lehre*. Stuttgart: Frommann.
—— 1898: Die Enquête über Zustände der Arbeit im Hamburger Hafen. *Archiv für Soziale Gesetzgebung und Statistik*, 12, 303ff.
—— 1905a: The Present Problems of Social Structure. *American Journal of Sociology*, 10, 569–88.
—— 1905b: *Schiller als Zeitbürger und Politiker*. Berlin-Schöneberg.
—— 1905c: *Strafrechtsreform*. Berlin.
—— 1906: *Philosophische terminologie in psychologisch-soziologischer ansicht*. Leipzig: Thomas.
—— 1907: *Das Wesen der Soziologie: Vortrag gehalten in der Gehe-Stiftung zu Dresden am 12. Januar 1907*. Dresden.
—— 1914: *Die Gesetzmässigkeit in der Bewegung der Bevölkerung*. Tübingen: Mohr.
—— 1915: *Englische weltpolitik in Englischer beleuchtung*. Berlin: Springer.
—— 1918: *Menschheit und Volk*. Graz.
—— 1919: *Die Entwicklung der sozialen Frage bis zum Weltkriege*. Berlin: Vereinigung wissenschaftlicher Verleger.
—— 1921: *Marx Leben und Lehre*. Jena: Erich Lichtenstein.
—— 1922: *Kritik der öffentlichen Meinung*. Berlin: Springer.
—— 1923: *Verhandlung des 3. Deutschen Soziologentages am 24. Und 25. Sept. in Jena. Reden und Vortraege von Ferdinand Tönnies (u.a.) und Debatten ueber das Wesen der Revolution*. (Deutsche Gesellschaft für Soziologie. Schriften. Serie 1, Bd 3). Tübingen: Mohr.
—— 1925–29: *Soziologische Studien und Kritiken I–III*. Jena: Gustav Fischer.

—— 1926a: *Fortschritt und soziale Entwicklung: Geschichtsphilosophische Ansichten*. Karlsruhe: Braun.

—— 1926b: *Das Eigentum*. Wien.

—— 1927: *Der Selbstmord in Schleswig-Holstein: eine statistisch-soziologische Studie*. Breslau.

—— 1929a: Ortsherkunft von Verbrechern in Schleswig-Holstein. *Deutsche Statistisches Zentralblatt*, 21, 146ff.

—— 1929b: Die schwere Kriminalität von Männers in Schleswig-Holstein in den Jahren 1899–1914. *Zeitschrift für Völkerpsychologie und Soziologie*, 5, 26ff.

—— 1929c: *Der Kampf um das Sozialistengesetz 1878*. Berlin: Springer.

—— 1931: *Einführung in die Soziologie*. Stuttgart: Ferdinand Enke.

—— 1935: *Geist der Neuzeit*. Leipzig: Buske.

—— 1961: *Custom: An Essay on Social Codes*. New York: Free Press.

—— 1972 [1912]: *Gemeinschaft und Gesellschaft. Grundbegriffe der reinen Soziologie*. Darmstadt: Wissenschaftliche Buchgesellschaft.

—— 1974a: *On Social Ideas and Ideologies*. New York: Harper & Row.

—— 1974b: *Karl Marx, His Life and Teachings*. East Lansing: Michigan State University Press.

—— 1975: *Studien zur Philosophie und Gesellschaftslehre im 17. Jahrhundert*. Stuttgart-Bad Cannstatt: Frommann-Holzboog.

—— 1982: *Die Tatsache des Wollens*. Berlin: Duncker & Humblot.

—— 1989: *Ferdinand Tönnies, Harald Höffding: Briefwechsel*, ed. Cornelius Bickel and Rolf Fechner. Berlin: Duncker & Humblot.

—— 1990: *Die Nietzsche-Kultus: Eine Kritik*. Berlin: Akademie-Verlag.

Secondary:

Asplund, Johan. 1991: *Essä om Gemeinschaft och Gesellschaft*. Göteborg: Korpen.

Bellebaum, Alfred. 1976: Ferdinand Tönnies. In Dirk Käsler (ed.), *Klassiker des soziologischen Denkens*. Munich: Verlag C. H. Beck.

Bleicher, Josef. 1990: Struggling with Kultur. *Theory, Culture and Society*, 7, 97–106.

Cahnman, Werner J. (ed.) 1973: *Ferdinand Toennies. A New Evaluation. Essays and Documents*. Leiden: E. J. Brill.

—— 1981: Tönnies in Amerika. In Wolf Lepenies (ed.), *Geschichte der Soziologie*, 4, 82–114. Frankfurt am Main: Suhrkamp.

Cahnman, Werner, and Heberle, Rudolph (eds) 1971: *Ferdinand Toennies. On Sociology: Pure, Applied, and Empirical*. Chicago: University of Chicago Press.

Clausen, Lars, et al. (eds) 1981: *Ankunft bei Tönnies*. Hamburg: W. G. Mühlau.

—— (ed.) 1985: *Tönnies heute*. Hamburg: W. G. Mühlau.

Durkheim, Emile. 1889: [Review of Gemeinschaft und Gesellschaft.] *Revue philosophique de la France et de l'Etranger*, 27, 416ff.

Elias, Norbert. 1978: *The Civilizing Process*. vol. 1: *The History of Manners*. Oxford: Basil Blackwell.

Fechner, Rolf. 1991: Treue Freundschaft. Die Bedeutung des Briefwechsels zwischen Ferdinand Tönnies und Harald Höffding für die Interpretation von Tönnies' Werk. In Lars Clausen et al. (eds), *Ausdauer, Geduld und Ruhe*, Hamburg: Rolf Fechner.

Geiger, Theodor. 1927: Die Gruppe und die Kategorien Gemeinschaft und Gesellschaft. *Archiv für Sozialwissenschaft und Sozialpolitik*, 58, 338–75.

—— 1931: Gemeinschaft. Gesellschaft. In Alfred Vierkandt (ed.), *Handwörter buch der Soziologie*, 173–80, 201–11. Stuttgart (1959).

Heberle, Rudolph. 1937: The Sociology of Ferdinand Tönnies. *American Sociological Review*, 2, 9ff.

—— 1948: The Sociological System of Ferdinand Tönnies: Community and Society. In Harry F. Barnes (ed.), *An Introduction to the History of Sociology*, 227–48. Chicago: University of Chicago Press.

——— 1955: Das soziologische System von Ferdinand Tönnies. Zum 100. Geburtstag des grossen deutschen Soziologen. In *Schmollers Jahrbuch*, 75, 385ff.

——— 1968: Toennies, Ferdinand. In *International Encyclopedia of the Social Sciences*, 98–103. New York.

Høffding, Harald. 1899: Social Pessimisme. In *Mindre Arbejder*. København: Det Nordiske Forlag.

Høgsnes, Geir. 1986: Ferdinand Tönnies og dikotomien »Gemeinschaft und Gesellschaft«. In *Sosiologi i dag*, 4, 33–53.

Joas, Hans. 1996: *The Creativity of Action*. Chicago, IL: University of Chicago Press.

König, René. 1955: Die Begriffe Gemeinschaft und Gesellschaft bei Ferdinand Tönnies. *Kölner Zeitschrift für Soziologie und Sozialpsykologie*, 3, 348–421.

——— 1981: Die Situation der emigrerten deutschen Soziologen in Europa. In Wolf Lepenies (ed.), *Geschichte der Soziologie,* 4, 115–58. Frankfurt am Main: Suhrkamp.

——— 1987: *Soziologie in Deutschland*. Munich and Vienna: Verlag C. H. Beck.

Liebersohn, Harry. 1989: Lukács and the Concept of Work in German Sociology. In Judith Marcus and Zoltán Tarr (eds), *Georg Lukács: Theory, Culture, and Politics,* New Brunswick and Oxford: Transaction.

Østerberg, Dag. 1988: *Metasociology: An inquiry into the Origins and Validity of Social Thought.* Oslo: Universitetsforlaget.

Otnes, Per. 1990: Das Ende der Gemeinschaft? In Carsten Schlüter (ed.), *Renaissance der Gemeinschaft?* Würtsburg: Königshausen & Neumann.

——— 1991: Renessanse for Gemeinschaft? *Tidsskrift for samfunnsforskning*, 1, 291–311.

Shils, Edward. 1995: The Value of Community. In Tomasi Luigi (ed.), *Values and Post-Soviet Youth: The Problem of Transition*. Chicago: University of Chicago Press.

Szaki, Jerzy. 1979: *History of Sociological Thought*. London: Aldwych Press.

Wirth, Louis. 1926/7: The Sociology of Ferdinand Tönnies. *American Journal of Sociology*, 32, 412ff.

chapter 5

Emile Durkheim

Willy Guneriussen

KEY CONCEPTS

ANOMIE – Social situations characterized by the absence of or unclear norms, causing uncertainty and frustration (anomic suicide).

CONSCIENCE COLLECTIVE – a system of collective ideas (religious, moral, empirical) characteristic of a society, which shapes the perceptions of individuals.

FUNCTION – the notion that, e.g., a custom is maintained because it has positive consequences for (parts of) society (feedback between consequences and causes).

HOLISM – the idea that society comprises a whole or organized system with its own laws or functions. The whole – the social reality – exists independently of individuals and exerts an influence on them.

MECHANICAL SOLIDARITY – The form of solidarity found in primitive societies characterized by equality – "attraction through similarity."

ORGANIC SOLIDARITY – the form of solidarity found in complex societies based on mutual dependency between specialized activities.

Biography: *Emile Durkheim*

Emile Durkheim was born in 1858, in Epinal, France. He grew up in a traditional, orthodox Jewish family. His father was a rabbi (as his grandfather and great-grandfather had been). The family was quite poor. The plan was that Emile too should become a rabbi, but he changed his mind, and later on he rejected the Jewish faith. He remained a nonbeliever for the rest of his life. In 1879 he became a student at the most prestigious postgraduate school of higher education, the Ecole Normale Supérieure in Paris. He graduated in 1882 and worked for a few years as a teacher of philosophy in a grammar school. In 1887 he got a position in the faculty of the humanities at the University of Bordeaux. He was responsible for teaching social science and pedagogics. He married the same year.

During the years in Bordeaux (until 1902) Durkheim was very productive and wrote three of his most important books. His students and friends described him as very disciplined, serious, and stern. Together with some of his collegues he founded the influential journal *L'Année Sociologique* in 1896, and he remained its most important contributor until the war in 1914 when journal was closed. He made a great contribution to reforming the educational system in France. The social sciences (particularly sociology) were given a central position in higher education and research. Durkheim wanted empirical studies of society to be given more priority, and felt that too much weight had been attached to philosophy and the humanities within the universities. He was also engaged in political debate and activities (particularly during the Dreyfus affair), and expressed left-liberal and social-democratic sympathies.

In 1902 he was appointed a professor in pedagogics at the Sorbonne University in Paris. Durkheim wanted it to be a position in sociology, but it was not until 1913 that it was redefined to include sociology. He published his last main work (on religion) in 1912. During World War I he was involved in writing and publication concerning the war, criticizing German aggression and also German culture. Durkheim died at the age of 59 in 1917.

To a considerable extent, the great classical theories are influenced by, and expressions of, the political and moral conflicts, economic processes, and ideological movements of the nineteenth century. Durkheim's sociology too is characterized by this tension between science and morality, politics and ideology. Much of his scientific work displays an interest in promoting moral reform. His general sociological aim was to define the necessary conditions for a stable, smoothly functioning, modern society. On this foundation, he thought it possible to formulate "correct," scientific solutions to the most pressing problems of his age. Durkheim was also involved in the greatest political conflicts of his time (Lukes 1973). He was in favour of a liberal, democratic constitution, the development of the welfare state, and the regulation of the capitalist economy. He aligned himself with reformist socialism, but was also influenced by *conservative* ideas on the importance of morality, the family, religion, and tradition (Nisbet 1975, 1980).

The roots of Durkheim's sociology reach deep into the history and intellectual life of France. His theory of the foundation and progress of modern society is based on ideas first clearly formulated during the dramatic social changes that came about from the end of the eighteenth century onwards (see chapter 1). Durkheim's most significant predecessor was Auguste Comte (1798–1857), the founder of French *positivism*. Comte was the first to use the term "sociology" to identify the new social science, and his was one of the first attempts to establish an autonomous basis for the scientific study of society. Science was to be something other than philosophical "speculation."

The Foundations of Sociology: Methodology and Social Reality

A particular inspiration for Durkheim was Comte's notion that sociology studied a peculiar objective reality. Comte argued that reality is hierarchically structured into distinct levels of organization, each level being governed by its own specific laws and forces. The biological level ranks higher than the physical but lower than the social level, with its autonomous laws. "Social reality" is a collective reality distinct from the physical, biological, and psychological; it could neither be reduced to, nor explained by, these other levels.

Durkheim was especially keen to combat all kinds of individualistic theories, criticizing the French sociologist, Gabriel Trade (1843–1904) in particular. Such theories usually claim that social processes, conditions, and structures result solely from the qualities of individuals, and the interaction of individual actions. This applied, for instance, to liberal and utilitarian economists, such as Adam Smith (1723–90), who had dominated economic thinking for over 100 years (if we disregard Marxism). Consequently, Durkheim makes repeated attempts to prove that social structures and institutions cannot be explained solely in terms of the qualities and psychological dispositions of individuals. He maintained, for example, that the rate of suicide in a given society could not be regarded as a result, or the sum, of the emotions, motives, and decisions of a number of individuals. Rather, there are supra-individual social causes or forces which affect the propensity to commit suicide in different societies.

Another important example of Durkheim's holism is his analysis of voluntary *contracts*, for example, financial arrangements (Durkheim 1893, vol. I: chapter VII). Since an increasing number of relations between individuals in modern society were contract-based, many theorists argued that modern society was a product of the interests and actions of individu-

als (for example, Herbert Spencer; see chapter 3). But Durkheim argued that contracts between individuals rested on given social and collective conditions. A number of institutional structures, laws, and informal rules exist that lay down the conditions for making and
keeping contracts. The conditions for making contracts, their content and consequences,
are determined by supra-individual social circumstances, laws, and norms. This he terms
the *non-contractual foundation of contracts*. Durkheim's striking holism, and his insistent
denial that the acts, ideas, and motives of individuals could explain any social processes and
patterns, have given rise to a lot of debate (and criticism), both in his own time and since.

The Methodology of Sociology

Durkheim wrote on methodological issues throughout his entire *oeuvre*. In 1895 he published a considerable monograph on methodology: *Les Règles de la méthode sociologique*
(The Rules of Sociological Method) (Durkheim 1895). This is the second of his four major
works. The aim of the book was to establish procedures for revealing general, supra-
individual, social laws, structures, and functional connections. It has since come to be regarded as an example of positivist, anti-individualist social science, and has come in for
much criticism from both critics of positivism and theorists who take more individualist
positions. Here, Durkheim asserts quite unambiguously that sociology ought to study only
collective social facts in its search for chains of causality and function. The understanding,
perceptions, and motives of individual social actors have no place in a program of this kind.
Society is to be studied "from the outside," as an object, rather than "from the inside," based
on actors' subjective views. Science must discard all the prejudices, lack of clarity, and
misconceptions that often characterize lay perceptions (Durkheim 1895: chapter 2).

   In his own studies of various types of social phenomena, Durkheim does not always
follow his own methodological instructions. This is most evident in his later studies of
religion. Indeed, there he often starts from the experiences, feelings, and perceptions of
actors, before proceeding "upwards" to a more supra-individual, structural level. Evidently,
Durkheim is not always as unambiguously positivistic as his textbook on method would
have it. At times he seems to shift away from a causal, deterministic perspective toward a
more interpretive perspective in social science.

Social facts

Perhaps the best-known principle of Durkheim's sociology is the following one, taken from
"Rules" (Durkheim 1895): *consider social facts as things existing outside, or independent
of, individuals, and imposing constraints on them*. This dense formulation expresses the
essence of Durkheim's theory of social reality. The reason why Durkheim thinks social
facts should be *regarded* as things . . . is that they *have* some of the characteristics of things
– in a way they *are* things. The issue is not only a matter of an appropriate methodological
recipe, but also an ontological assumption (an assumption regarding the nature of existence).

   In other words, social facts have concrete or objective existence – they constitute an
inert, stable order, consisting of laws, functions, and causal relations. This means that soci-

ologists may discover the structure and laws of social order by methods similar to those used by physicists to discover the laws of nature. Durkheim incorporates various kinds of social facts. Among others, he deals with the most crystallized "morphological" aspects of society – the fundamental social structure. Fixed patterns of behaviour (for example, suicide rates in different societies) he also regards as a central category of facts. Beyond this, he includes laws, values, norms, and finally, received ideas and "currents of opinion." Structures are located at the most stable or crystallized end of the scale, while the currents of opinion are at the most fluid end. Here it might be suggested that, whereas Durkheim in his early career was particularly interested in the morphological or structural aspects of society, he later began to emphasize the more "ideal" aspects: morality, values, and ideas. According to Durkheim, statistical surveys and analyses provided the most suitable method for the study of social structures and fixed patterns of behaviour.

The objectivity of social reality is further underlined when Durkheim argues that it exists beyond, or independent of, individuals. This implies that the social is not to be understood as a psychological phenomenon. To be sure, Durkheim takes the view that society cannot exist without individuals and their ideas, emotions, and moral points of view. Nonetheless, society is much more than just the sum of all these individual qualities and ideas. Thus, he sometimes describes the social as a "synthesis," by which he means that the social is constituted as a new form through the interactions of the (intended and unintended) consequences of all actors. The totality of interaction between individuals will result in an independent, objective order that goes beyond the individual level and adheres to its own supra-individual principles.

Social constraint

This line of thought contains a refutation of subjectivist and idealistic social theories. It is not the ideas and conceptions of individuals that determine how society functions. The supra-individual social order is primary, while individuals' actions and ideas are derived from, or are an effect of, this primary structure. This is the third element of Durkheim's methodological recipe: social facts impose constraint on individuals. Social constraint is not defined by Durkheim as an unfortunate restriction on individual freedom. Constraint is the very basis of stable social life. Without such constraint, society would be no more than a chaotic struggle between selfish individuals. Each individual can only achieve security, happiness, and some degree of freedom if the actions of all are simultaneously regulated by a supra-individual force.

Often it seem both sensible and reasonable to speak of individuals acting in accordance with social constraints. A fall in commodity prices may cause involuntary or undesirable changes in behaviour. Structures of social authority may constrain individuals to behave in ways they would otherwise find undesirable. Laws (and associated sanctions) may be perceived as constraints. Some actors may have physical means of coercion at their disposal and further their own interests by prevailing upon others to act in particular ways. However, in other contexts it seems unreasonable to speak of constraint. People feel they are acting freely, in accordance with their own wishes and judgements. They do not directly feel any constraint. They choose, for example, to marry "their heart's desire." They visit kin, help friends, give presents, and teach their children "proper manners," without feeling forced to do so. But Durkheim insists that even in all these domains, in which we feel no form of constraint and believe we are acting of our own free will, our actions are really the result of various forms of social constraint. The constraint may often be imperceptible and invisible, but it is constraint nevertheless. This he illustrates as follows: although we are not normally conscious of the fact that all our physical activity is subject to the force of gravity, it is nonetheless a constant physical constraint that is of fundamental significance for our behavior.

The various meanings of "social constraint"

What is meant by "social constraint"? Durkheim assumes that one form of constraint in society is a function of the number of people (volume) and the extent of contact between them in a given area (density). As the number of people and the frequency of contact increase, pressure is exerted on each individual. Durkheim uses this mechanism to explain, for instance, the emergence of the division of labor and professional specialization in a given population. He also assumes that the material structures of society affect individual behavior. Technological change, new means of communication, and changes in settlement patterns (for example, urbanization) have consequences for modes of action, even though this may not have been the actors' original intention. In all these cases, social constraint is of a *material* nature, influencing the decisions and actions of individuals in the shape of external conditions which individuals must consider and adapt to. This constitutes a materialist element in Durkheim's sociology. However, as we shall see, for him this element was not the most important, and nonmaterial determinants assumed increasing importance in his later theories.

Second, we may speak of *structural* constraints: the organization of society into hierarchical patterns, distinct groups, kinship and family networks, and various activities, forms an outer social framework that affects all behavior. Individuals must take account of these given external social structures in the same way as they must take material conditions into account. Well-adjusted individuals will not always feel themselves subject to constraints. Subjectively, they may feel they are acting on their own free will. But the social structure constitutes a significant external force that will be felt particularly strongly in cases of deviancy when the norms laid down by the structure are broken. The straightforward example of marriage may illustrate the significance of social structures. Statistical surveys often reveal clear relations between group membership, social status, and marriage. Even if many individuals feel they have married freely and for love, in Durkheim's view such group-level regularities are an indication that behavior is affected by supra-individual structural "forces."

Socialization and constraint

Third, we must deal with moral or *normative* constraints, and this is one of the most central concepts in Durkheim's sociology. These constraints function in a substantially different manner from all external material conditions and forces, because it operates through *actors' perceptions, emotions, and motivations*. We are constrained because we feel respect for other individuals, authorities, institutions, etc., and because we feel obliged to act in accordance with received norms. A sense of respect and a feeling of obligation arise in human beings as a consequence of *socialization*. By socialization is meant the formation of personality as a result of the demands and expectations encountered in our social environment. Whereas in childhood we act on primitive emotions of pleasure and pain, without regard to moral norms, as adults we will be capable of distinguishing right from wrong, and we will also be motivated to act in accordance with moral expectations. For Durkheim this means that the values and norms of the environment have been internalized in our personality. The (originally) external constraint has become an internal one, in the shape of subjective needs and motives.

This idea of internalization of social constraint is the very key to understanding Durkheim's theory of social integration, and it clearly distinguishes his sociology from, for example, Marx. Whereas Marx stressed the material forces that constrain individuals, and regarded moral motivation as a secondary phenomenon, for Durkheim the material is only one (secondary) aspect. It is only through the combination of external and internal social constraints that society can be integrated into a stable social order.

Finally, we may also speak of a *cultural* or cognitive constraint in Durkheim. He regards human ideas, concepts, representations – perceptions of reality – as the result of social or cultural influences. He points to language as a supra-individual structure. As they mature within a language community, individuals also acquire a collective, received mode of thinking and constructing categories. He also maintains that there is a connection between social structure and the categorization of reality through language.

In connection with this latter form of social constraint, it is easy to see that constraint is not to be regarded as primarily restricting or oppressing individuals. Collectively imposed modes of thought are what enable individuals to acquire a sense of ordered reality in the first place. This constraint is primarily creative rather than restrictive.

Modes of Explanation

Durkheim's thoughts on explanation in sociology have had a profound significance for subsequent social science, particularly functionalism (see chapter 14).

A common type of explanation is what is termed *intentional explanation*. We say that someone waves their hand in order to greet an acquaintance, they take out their wallet to pay for goods in a shop, or write their name to sign a contract. In all these examples, in other words, we are explaining individual actions in relation to the intentional aim the actors seek to achieve. Among the classics of social science, Max Weber (see chapter 6) was notable for seeking to award this kind of explanation definitive methodological prominence.

It is clear that, for Durkheim, intentional explanations are of little significance. From the outset he rejected the view that society could be understood in terms of the subjective consciousness and goals of actors. Society is a supra-individual objective reality, a force which influences the behavior of individuals, independent of their subjective goals and intentions. At best, we may sometimes offer intentional explanations of isolated individual actions. Nevertheless, we cannot explain general regularities in behavior and social institutions in this way. The fact that everyone buys goods from shops, that we "choose" to pay with money, and that the shopkeeper accepts money as a means of payment, is a social – that is, institutional – reality that affects our behavior and intentions. And the "subjective" goals which I, as an individual, wish to realize are often the result of social influences or socialization.

Thus the social sciences must, like the natural sciences, offer *causal explanations*. It is important to seek regular causal relations between factors or events over a certain period, independent of actors' intentions and ideas. In this way, Durkheim sought to discover, for example, a connection between religion and patterns of suicide in different societies, and between legal reform and the development of the division of labor. However, it was difficult in sociology to establish exceptionless laws similar to those of physics. Sociology normally has to be content with *statistical* relations between variables. Still, for Durkheim universal determinism is a scientific ideal toward which sociology too must strive.

Functionalism

However, Durkheim regards ordinary causal explanations as sociologically inadequate. Sociology must explain the complex interactions and mutual influences between the distinct elements of a whole or, to be more precise, within a *self-regulating system*. This requires *functional explanations*. Here we have some of the most characteristic elements of Durkheim's sociology. He explicitly employs a biological analogy, comparing society to an organism or an organic system. (There were many in Durkheim's day, for instance Herbert Spencer, who used the organism as a model of society.) In an organism, we cannot understand isolated relations between cause and effect independent of the organized whole of which they form part. For example, when the heart pumps blood around the body, it has the effect of providing cells with energy and removing waste products. And as physical activity intensifies, so does the heart rate (a deficiency of energy in the cells triggers signals to the heart and lungs, which then increase the intensity of their action), and the result is faster blood circulation and increased energy supply. To this extent, there is an ordinary cause-and-effect relationship. However, the point is that the *function* of the heart is to pump blood in order to provide cells with energy, etc.. That the heart has such effects is an explanation of its activity – in a sense, the effect explains the cause. This is often termed causal "feedback." The more general function of the heart is to help to sustain the organism. This occurs through the interaction of the activities of the heart and the other organs of the body. The organism as a whole emerges as a self-regulating system, in which changes in one part trigger, and are checked by, changes elsewhere, and in which all the organs appear to act in combination to maintain the fully functional organism.

According to Durkheim, society actually functions in the same way. The institutions of society have functions equivalent to the organs of a living organism. One function of the family is the socialization of children in such a way that they acquire the social skills demanded by society, and it is this need for socialization that contributes to the maintenance of the family. The (most important) function of religion is, in Durkheim's view, its contribution to social integration, and if religious traditions have such positive social effects, they will also be preserved as a result of these effects (more on this later). The thoughts and intentions of individuals are not decisive factors.

Nonetheless, Durkheim's functionalism is limited: he claims that an institution, norm, tradition, or whatever, will be *maintained* as a result of positive social effects. But this function cannot explain how the institution emerged in the first place. In reconstructing the history of an institution, we have to use ordinary causal explanations. Furthermore, Durkheim rejects the view that everything that exists in a given society must necessarily have a positive function. Many customs may have emerged as a result of historical accidents, and persist without having any demonstrably positive effects.

In spite of the fact that Durkheim draws an analogy between organisms and society, in his view sociology must also be clearly distinguished from biology. Society, of course, has institutions rather than organs. And society possesses a kind of awareness, or conscience collective, which ordinary biological organisms do not have. Moreover, society's most elementary units – individuals (who may be equated with the cells of an organism) – also possess a conscience.

The use of functional explanations is controversial in sociology, and is normally accepted only by theorists who adopt a holistic perspective.

Solidarity and Social Order

In his first major work (*La Division du travail social*, [The Division of Labour in Society], 1893), Durkheim attempted to describe the fundamental characteristics of modern society. In the nineteenth century it was a common (and fairly romantic) notion among intellectuals that "primitive," or premodern, societies were often very stable and harmonious. Because these societies were so simple, "natural," and transparent, many thought they were not as exposed to conflict and confusion as the modern, or "complex," society. To a large extent, Durkheim shared this view, but he rejected the idea that harmonious integration was possible only in simple, premodern societies. His aim was to reveal what he perceived as a peculiarly *modern* form of integration and solidarity.

The most typical trait of primitive societies is their *segmentary* nature (Durkheim 1893: chapter vi). Such societies consist of clearly delimited collectivities or clans, characterized by homogeneity and equality between individuals within these collectivities. Role specialization and division of labor are rudimentary – with the exception of some authority figures. Individuals have little or no autonomy within the group, and individuality is so rudimentary that even the need for freedom and independence is barely present.

Mechanical solidarity

The similarity and proximity between individuals in such primitive societies function as social "glue" or "mortar." People are attracted to others who are similar to themselves; *mechanical solidarity* is the term Durkheim uses for the association of actors that emerges here. This is the dominant foundation of cohesion in simple societies where there is little differentiation. People may be similar in many respects – in terms of housing, occupation and the use of tools, clothing, customs, cuisine and lifestyle; they may be equal with regard to power; experience the same emotions, needs, and ideas, and hold similar moral and religious attitudes. The more primitive a society, the more similarity will there be on all these dimensions, and the more conspicuous is its mechanical solidarity. Such societies are characterized by collectivism.

We may note that Durkheim takes both material and nonmaterial aspects into account –

shared ideas are as important as equality in material living conditions in primitive societies. A comprehensive, strong *conscience collective* is an essential characteristic of any primitive society. The French word *conscience* means both knowledge (sense of reality, theories, ideas) and conscience (moral sense and feelings). The conscience collective is basically religious in primitive societies. By religious Durkheim means possessing a strong sense of right and wrong, of what is sacred, and this is manifest in the form of all the various rules, rituals, and ceremonies that must be observed to show respect for the sacred.

As a result of equality in material living conditions and customs, the intimacy of social life and the continuous reciprocal "surveillance" of behavior, and the intense conscience collective which demands respect for rules and all that is held sacred, there will be a strong reaction to any form of deviancy in primitive societies. Deviancy is often regarded as a religious offence.

Solidarity in modern societies

There is a comprehensive division of labor in modern societies. Individuals engage in different, often highly specialized occupations. They are no longer so closely bound to groups marked by a large degree of internal equality and homogeneity. They can move within and between several social groups or circles, and no single group has the kind of irresistible power – typical of collectivities in primitive societies – to rigidly impose a particular way of life on the individual. This is the primary reason why individuals in modern societies necessarily develop in different directions. Differences of many kinds emerge between individuals, just as differences also emerge between professions and trades. And because so many differences emerge between individuals, groups, and occupations, many theorists in Durkheim's day thought that high levels of conflict were inevitable in modern societies. Solidarity or a sense of collectivity would be weakened as a result of the numerous conflicts of interest resulting from all the differences.

Durkheim thought a specifically modern form of solidarity would emerge: *organic solidarity*. In primitive societies solidarity is a manifestation of "attraction through similarity." What type of attraction could possibly exist between people when similarity is replaced by numerous differences? Will these differences not rather give rise to conflict? Durkheim seeks to demonstrate that the many differences that develop as a corollary of modernization take a specific form: through occupational specialization, a large number of differences necessarily arise, but at the same time comprehensive *mutual dependency* is created between the many kinds of labor, and between individuals. The shoemaker dedicates all his working hours to making shoes, and thus simultaneously becomes dependent on others who produce the commodities he needs – clothes, tools, food, etc.. All producers are dependent on each other's products, and thus a complex dependency emerges. They complement one another, participating in a differentiated, coherent system, just as specialized organs function in a living organism (hence the term *organic* solidarity). For this reason, Durkheim also states that modern societies are "functionally integrated."

If this theory was correct, modern society would normally have evolved relatively free of conflict. But Durkheim himself was aware of the fact that antagonisms and powerful conflicts were commonplace in the nineteenth century. He put this down to the fact that development had not occurred along "normal" lines, and attempted to explain this anomaly *why some conflict does exist*

(Durkheim 1893: Book III). He thought this was partly due to the persistence into modern society of some old disparities of power and wealth – from feudalism, for instance – which were incompatible with the new order. He also argued that very rapid changes and adjustments in any given period do not allow the various elements of society time to adjust to one another.

Individualism

In his early work, Durkheim argued that the conscience collective and religion would become less and less significant in a functionally differentiated society, due to the differences between people. With increasing differentiation in working and social life, as well as the weakening of the conscience collective as a binding force, modern society would be characterized by *individualism*. When individualism gains too much strength, it has the effect of destroying solidarity. To avoid total disruption, individualism must be counteracted through the development of new institutional bonds between people. There is some uncertainty on this point in Durkheim's theory. Because he views society as a self-regulating system, he assumes that such a correction of individualism will emerge naturally and spontaneously. On the other hand, however, he is also interested in finding practical measures that might restrain rampant individualism. He thought the family had too limited an importance in modern society to constitute an effective counterweight. Nor did he believe in the socialist notion that a powerful state would be adequate. According to Durkheim, the state was too distant from everyday social life to be capable of having any decisive moral effect on the collectivity. In several works after 1893 he suggested certain measures: for instance, he advocated establishing new types of organization in the economic sector – so-called corporations, which had certain similarities with the medieval guild system. The point was that those involved in a certain kind of occupation, employers and employees alike, should unite in a national organization. He thought this would lead to the development of solidarity between actors, and thus counteract the tendencies toward ruthless competition and individualism. He also thought school reforms, in the shape of new syllabuses and modes of cooperation, might restrain individualism. If children were educated in the spirit of solidarity at school, they would develop social habits that would also be important in adulthood. He also suggested restrictions on the right to divorce.

to stop the break down of solidarity

Changes in Durkheim's Thinking

Many commentators have pointed to a tendency in the development of Durkheim's theories: early in his career, he expressed a strong belief in society's ability to develop solidarity and unity spontaneously. Later, he came to accentuate more and more the need for active political and moral regulation of social life, especially in the economic sphere. Eventually, he concluded that the basic principles of the modern market economy largely nurtured competition and egoism, and that the economy therefore had to be actively regulated in order to ensure widespread solidarity. We could not just wait for solidarity to evolve "naturally."

Later, Durkheim also modified his previously negative judgement of individualism. He reached the perception that individualism was not necessarily the same as egoism and the

contradictions/modifications

radical destruction of social bonds. It became clear to him that modern societies could not be based on a strictly collectivist ethos. The problems associated with the division of functions and specialization in modern societies could be solved only by assuming values and relations that took a high level of individualism for granted. He thought a more positive and more valuable type of individualism, one distinct from egoism, was in the process of emerging. This he termed *moral individualism*. The autonomy of the individual is fundamental, but this autonomy also involves the capacity for moral reflection, and moral obligations. Given the correct form of socialization and the development of social relations, *modern* individualists would be able to strike a balance between individual independence and social bonding. Durkheim places some emphasis on the fact that individualism is not "natural." It is predicated on modern ways of life and institutions. In primitive societies collectivism is the "natural" condition.

Suicide and Society

In his third major work, *Le Suicide* (Suicide, 1897), Durkheim concentrates primarily on the tendency toward crisis in modern societies. The optimistic belief in a spontaneous emergence of solidarity that we find in his first book is here eclipsed by a deep concern with the course of contemporary social development.

At first glance, suicide appears to be the most extreme act of individual behavior imaginable: the individual severs all social ties completely. Typically, however, Durkheim seeks out the collective – supra-individual – forces that also influence this extreme "deviancy." Every suicide is, of course, characterized by individual motives. Yet, clearly, there is a stable pattern of suicide in any society, and in Durkheim's view this must ensue from social conditions and forces. Moreover, each individual's motives are marked by attitudes and emotions characteristic of the social environment within which the individual grows up and functions. Thus suicide is regarded as a kind of "exaggeration of social habits." Any given society has a "natural" rate of suicide that is the result of social causes or dominant social forces within this society.

Altruistic and egoistic suicide

Durkheim distinguishes three categories of suicide: altruistic, egoistic, and anomic. He argues that *altruistic suicide* is typical of premodern societies that are characterized by collectivism. The individual is strictly subject to the collectivity, and we have to do with mechanical solidarity. Strong collectivities provide individuals with a profound sense of social belonging. In itself this is a life-giving force. Nonetheless, such integration means that the individual is of little significance in relation to the value of the collectivity or group as such. The needs, expectations, and values of the group always take priority over individual wishes and demands, and individuals cannot protect themselves against the demands of their environment. In certain situations this means that individuals must often make sacrifices in deference to group aims and values. Suicide may also result from the importance attached by the group to "honor" – for example, among officers, or the honor of a family. Someone who loses honor may have to sacrifice his life. The traditional Hindu custom of burning widows is another example of altruistic suicide. Durkheim's general claim is that a high rate of altruistic suicide is an indication that social integration is too strong. The individual has too little independence vis-à-vis the group. (Relevant examples are mass suicides among extreme religious sects.)

In modern societies the situation is often quite the opposite: many suicides are the result of very weak social integration. This is what Durkheim terms *egoistic suicide*. The bonds between people are so weak that for many the fundamental social needs of belonging and community will not be satisfied. This deficiency may reduce the desire to live. Furthermore, when social networks and group identity are weak, many will not receive sufficient support from others when they run into problems. Isolation increases the probability of suicide as a reaction to personal problems and crises. Durkheim found family size significant, for example. Suicide was more frequent among members of small families than members of large ones. He also found that women had a lower tendency to commit suicide than men, and that the rate was lower the more children they had. His explanation was that women were more closely tied to family and kin than men. He also demonstrated that Protestant regions or countries had a higher suicide rate than Catholic ones. This difference he attributed to the the fact that Protestantism promotes a more individualistic ethos and less participation in communal religious practice.

According to Durkheim, altruistic suicide may be viewed as a result of something good and highly valued – strong social solidarity in close collectivities. It is "only" an extreme variant of such "virtues," something to be expected in large groups marked by this way of life. Likewise, a certain rate of egoistic suicide may be viewed as a result (or a natural exaggeration) of another highly valued way of life: modern individualism. A major problem is determining what is a "natural" rate. But Durkheim thought the strong increase among certain groups and in certain regions an obvious symptom of disease – a sign of the drastic weakening of important forms of social collectivity. This was something that struck the urban, industrial, and thus most modern, parts of society in particular. The extent of altruistic and egoistic suicide is an indicator of the strength of social integration.

Anomic suicide

There is, however, another important cause of suicide that has nothing to do with the direct relations between people, but rather with the way norms and rules exert control over, or determine, human behavior. Some human needs have biologically conditioned "saturation points," for example, the need for food and drink. But a number of socially conditioned needs have no natural saturation point. There are no biological mechanisms that signal to us that we have enough money, influence, status, power, luxury, or refinement. According to Durkheim, there must be social standards and rules to indicate the "correct" levels for the satisfaction of such needs. For example, within a certain profession, there might be a general salary scale which is considered fair and reasonable by members (and other groups). This will lead individuals to regard receipt of this salary as satisfactory. Each individual's expectations are marked by existing norms and practices. In the absence of such stable social norms, individuals will have no means of assessing their expectations.

Durkheim also assumes individuals to be incapable of limiting their own demands and aspirations, unless the environment imposes clear norms. This might easily result in confusion, exaggerated expectations, and widespread frustration, if large numbers of people start striving to reach ever-higher levels, with no clear notion of an appropriate limit. Durkheim terms such conditions *anomic*. The word literally means "lawless" or "normless," and he employs the term *anomic suicide* to describe suicide arising from frustration created by ambiguous norms or their total absence. He points to an increase in suicide rates during periods of economic fluctuation. It was acknowledged that economic crises were accompanied by an increase in the suicide rate. But Durkheim also found a growing suicide rate in periods of strong economic growth. In both cases, the outcome is that customary, fixed expectations as regards income and rewards are disturbed as a result of change. Individuals lose control of their desires and expectations, and this results in increasing frustration. A modern economy is generally characterized by dynamism, change, and sudden fluctuations. This sector is also dominated by a strong ideology of achievement. Anomie is therefore a relatively chronic condition. This is part of the reason why Durkheim strongly advocated the comprehensive regulation of economic activity in modern societies.

The concept of anomie is also used in analyses of other sectors besides the economy. In general, great social changes, reorganization, and mobility are always marked by anomie. Anomie has become one of the central concepts of the social sciences.

Durkheim's analysis has had an enormous influence on all subsequent research into suicide, and many aspects of his theory have been confirmed by a number of studies, although many of these have also served to modify the original theory. Bearing in mind that many of the statistical techniques commonly used today had not been developed at the time, his statistical approach was very advanced. Still, he has been criticized for methodological weaknesses, for example, using public statistics without checking the reliability of the official records.

Religion and Social Integration

In his last major study of religion (Durkheim 1912), he examines in detail religious customs and myths among Australian Aborigines. Durkheim's analysis was exclusively based on other researchers' fieldwork. But the book also has a more general aim: to explore some fundamental religious elements found in all societies, modern society included. Durkheim's theory is controversial, but his understanding of the functions of religion, and his analysis of rituals and symbols, have exerted enormous influence on the subsequent sociology of religion.

A universal feature of religion is that it is an *organized collectivity* or, as he puts it, a "church." Religion is always collective in nature. Furthermore, religion also comprises a shared sense of reality or *belief*. This need not be a belief in personified gods, but in all religions there are notions of special *powers* that influence human beings, and a clear distinction between the *sacred* and the *profane*. The sacred, whether it be persons, places, times (holy days), institutions, or symbols, is the very incarnation of the special power to which believers feel they relate. Consequently, respect for the sacred is the most typical religious feeling. Disgust, shame, and fear connected with violations of the sacred (sacrilege and profanity) are other characteristic emotions.

Two further central features of religious life are *symbols* and *rituals*. It is a characteristic expression of the power of the sacred, and respect for it, that there evolves a system of rituals and ceremonies connected with worship. The rituals may function to remind believers of significant events (for example, Christmas and Easter). Their function may be to give believers strength in times of crisis and loss (for example, funerals). Or they may be important markers of changes in social status (for example, confirmation and weddings). There may also emerge (a system of) collective symbols, which are concentrated meaningful expressions of the sacred (for example, the totem in primitive societies or the crucifix in Christianity).

The more general function of religion is to be found in its contribution to social integration. Shared faith and feelings, shared use of symbols, participation in ceremonies and ritual practices within an organized collective framework, all reinforce or renew the sense of collectivity and the bonds between believers. And because actors find strength through participation in religious activity, their trust in religious ideas is maintained. This understanding of function was, of course, at odds with Christians' own understanding of their religion. In their view salvation, rather than social functions, was most important. But Durkheim rejected such objections, saying that science could not build on the religious notions of believers. Rather, it had to be content to study objectively observable effects. Since it is only of concern in matters of belief, the issue of salvation was excluded.

The sacred and the social

There is an even more controversial side to Durkheim's theory of religion. He claimed that when believers worshiped their gods or sacred sites and objects through ritual and symbols, it was really *society* that was the object of adoration. Conceptions of god(s) and the sacred were only a distorted expression of society as a real force. While Christians, for example, feel or experience a relationship to an almighty god, Durkheim argues that they are, in fact, simply under the influence of a social force. He argued that Christians were not "totally" mistaken in their belief in an almighty god. They *were* influenced by a real force. Their error is "only" their belief that this is a transcendent or otherworldly force. In science, according to Durkheim, we cannot take such nonempirical forces into account. Rather, science must look to the empirical, and religious customs can then be explained only by assuming that society is a moral force which imposes feelings of respect and notions of the sacred upon individuals. Of course, Christian critics of Durkheim reacted strongly to this theory.

For Durkheim, ritual practices, symbolism, the whole panoply of organized collective religious worship, is dubbed the *practical* dimension, and this is for him of greater importance than the intellectual dimension, that is, the specific content of belief. He thought the sense of reality in traditional religion would gradually give way to rational scientific knowledge. But at the same time he argued that there would in all societies be a notion or a sense of something sacred. There would also be elements of collective cult activity, in the shape of rituals and symbols. This would persist because for individuals society always functions as a moral force. This is also in part a critique of modern notions that morality can be constructed on a purely rational foundation for individuals. Morality will always have a nonrational foundation, in the form of emotions and ideas produced by social powers, rather than intellectual arguments (alone).

In his conclusion, Durkheim suggests some criteria for a modern sense of religion, which can no longer be based on belief in supernatural gods. He refers to the intense political life of the French Revolution after 1789. During this period a large number of new ceremonies, rituals, and symbols emerged which had nothing to do with traditional gods. People gathered for festivities in which they praised the nation, new institutions, the ideas of individual liberty, and the universal rights of man. Durkheim argued that such a "political cult" could constitute a vital form of religion under modern conditions, concluding that many of the crises of his own time were the result of a lack of sufficient "religious" enthusiasm. He suggested elsewhere that the workers' movement might power the development of a new, modern, sense of the "religious."

Durkheim's Significance

As mentioned several times in this chapter, Durkheim has exerted a great influence on the social sciences, especially the functionalist and structuralist schools of anthropology and sociology. His was the dominant theory of social science in France from the beginning of this century. After his death in 1917, many of his students refined his core ideas, but in the 1930s his dominance was broken.

In anthropology, central theorists like Radcliffe-Brown (1952; cf. chapter 14) and Lévi-Strauss (1969; cf. chapter 19) have built on the Durkheimian inheritance. Radcliffe-Brown continued the more "materialist" approach of Durkheim's first major work, while Lévi-Strauss was more inspired by his later theory of symbols and religion. In sociology, the structural functionalist Talcott Parsons (see chapter 14) refined many of Durkheim's ideas. Parsons's central role in sociology from World War II until the 1970s contributed to maintaining an interest in Durkheim, and Parsons's heirs still consider Durkheim an important forerunner (Alexander 1982: chapter 15).

Durkheim's theories have also been subjected to harsh criticism by later social scientists. Most of his most important ideas (for example, those on social facts and holism) have been rejected by many supporters of individualist positions, such as rational choice theory, exchange theory, symbolic interactionism, and ethnomethodology. And his belief in integration and consensus, and his lack of concern with problems of power, have been criticized by supporters of more conflict-oriented theory, for example, Marxists.

Bibliography

Primary

Durkheim, Emile. 1893: *De la division du travail social*. Paris: Libraire Felix Alcan, (4th edn, 1922; translated as *The Division of Labour in Society*. London: Macmillan, 1984).
—— 1895: *Les Règles de la méthode sociologique*. Paris: Presses Universitaires de France (14th edn, 1960; translated as *The Rules of Sociological Method*. London: Macmillan, 1982).
—— 1897a: *Le Suicide. Etude de Sociologie*. Paris: Presses Universitaires de France (new edn, 1960; translated as *Suicide. A Study in Sociology*. London: Routledge and Kegan Paul, 1952).
—— 1897b: La prohibition de l'inceste et ses origines. *L'Année Sociologique*, 1. (*Incest: the Nature and Origin of the Taboo*. New York: Lyle Stuart, 1963).
—— 1898: L'Individualisme et les Intellectuels. *Revue Bleue 4e série*, X, 7–13. Reprinted in Durkheim 1970: *La Science Sociale et L'Action*. Paris: Presses Universitaires de France.

—— 1903 (with Marcel Mauss): De quelques formes primitives de classification: contribution a l'étude des représentations collectives. *L'Année sociologique*, 6, 1–72. (*Primitive Classification*. Chicago: University of Chicago Press, 1963)

—— 1912: *Les Formes élémentaires de la vie religieuse*. Paris: Libraire Felix Alcan (2nd edn, 1925; translated as *The Elementary Forms of the Religious Life*. London: Allen & Unwin, 1915).

—— 1922: *Education et sociologie*. Paris: Libraire Felix Alcan. (Translated as *Education and Sociology*. Glencoe, IL: Free Press, 1956).

—— 1924: *Sociologie et philosophie*. Paris: Librairie Felix Alcan. (Translated as *Sociology and Philosophy*. Glencoe, IL: Free Press, 1953).

—— 1925: *L'Education morale*. Paris: Librairie Felix Alcan. (Translated as *Moral Education*. Glencoe, IL: Free Press, 1961).

—— 1928: *Le Socialism: sa définition, ses débuts, la doctrine Saint Simonienne*. Paris: Presses Universitaires de France. (Translated as *Socialism and Saint-Simon*. London: Routledge & Kegan Paul, 1959).

—— 1938: *L'Evolution pédagogique en France*. Paris: Libraire Felix Alcan. (Translated as *The Evolution of Educational Thought*. London: Routledge & Kegan Paul, 1977).

—— 1950: *Leçons de Sociologie: physique de meurs et du droit*. Istanbul: L'Université d'Istanbul and Paris: Presses Universitaires de France. (Translated as *Professional Ethics and Civil Morals*. London: Routledge & Kegan Paul, 1957).

—— 1960a: *Montesquieu and Rousseau*. Ann Arbor: University of Michigan Press.

—— 1960b: *Emile Durkheim 1858–1917: A Collection of Essays*, ed. Kurt Wolff, Columbus: Ohio State University Press.

—— 1969: *Journal Sociologique*. Paris: Presses Universitaires de France.

—— 1970: *La Science sociale et l'action*. Paris: Presses Universitaires de France.

—— 1975: *Textes I–III*. Paris: Les Editions de Minuit.

—— 1983: *Pragmatism and Sociology*. Cambridge: Cambridge University Press.

—— 1992: *Lettres à tous les Français*. Paris: A. Colin.

Works published only in English:

Durkheim, Emile. 1915: *"Germany above All": the German Mental Attitude and the War*. Paris: Colin.

—— 1979: *Durkheim: Essays on Morals and Education*, ed. W. S. F. Pickering. London: Routledge.

—— 1983: *Durkheim and the Law*, ed. Steven Lukes and Andrew Scull. Oxford: Robertson.

—— 1986: *Durkheim on Politics and the State*, ed. Anthony Giddens. Stanford, CA: Stanford University Press.

—— 1994: *On Institutional Analysis*, ed. M. Traugott. University of Chicago Press.

Secondary:

Alexander, Jeffrey. 1982: *Theoretical Logic in Sociology. Vol. 2: The Antinomies of Classical Thought: Marx and Durkheim*. Los Angeles: University of California Press.

Aron, Raymond. 1990: *Main Currents in Sociological Thought*. London: Penguin Books.

Giddens, Anthony. 1978: *Durkheim*. Glasgow: Fontana.

LaCapra, Dominick. 1972: *Emile Durkheim: Sociologist and Philosopher*. Ithaca, NY: Cornell University Press.

Lévi-Strauss, Claude. 1969 [1962]: *Totemismen*. Uppsala: Argos.

Lukes, Steven. 1973: *Emile Durkheim. His Life and Work: A Historical and Critical Study*. New York: Harper & Row.

Nisbet, Robert. 1975: *The Sociology of Emile Durkheim*. London: Heinemann.

—— 1980: *The Sociological Tradition*. London: Heinemann.
Parsons, Talcott. 1968: *The Structure of Social Action. Vol. 1: Marshall, Pareto, Durkheim*. New York: Free Press.
Radcliffe-Brown, A. R. 1952: *Structure and Function in Primitive Society*. London: Routledge & Kegan Paul.
Taylor, Steve. 1982: *Durkheim and the Study of Suicide*. London: Macmillan.

chapter 6

Max Weber

Per Månson

KEY CONCEPTS

BUREAUCRACY – an ideal type of organizational form characterized, among other things, by impersonal rules, separate spheres of competence, and a formalized promotion process.

CHARISMA – a "gift of grace" or an extraordinary quality that a leader has or is believed to have by his followers.

IDEAL TYPE – an analytical construct produced by an investigator which stresses certain properties at the expense of others. It is used in research for comparative purposes.

LEGITIMACY – the leader or ruler is believed to have the right to exercise his leadership or his dominance over his subordinates or subjects.

MEANING – the subjective content a concrete individual puts in his action or a theoretically constructed content in a hypothetically constructed individual.

POWER – the probability that an individual will be able to carry out his will in a social relationship.

RATIONALITY – the relationship between means and ends. With value rationality the value that is embraced determines what actions are to be carried out. With purposive rationality the actors calculate what means will most effectively lead to the goal that has been set.

SOCIAL ACTION – an action that, with regard to its subjective meaning, relates itself to the actions of others and orients itself in accordance with these.

STATE – a political institution whose administrative staff successfully maintains its right to a monopoly over legitimate means of physical force within a geographic area.

VERSTEHEN – a method in social and cultural sciences based on understanding an action. A direct observational understanding perceives immediately, based on knowledge of rules or intuitive understanding, the meaning of an action. An explanatory understanding explains an action by the motives, conscious or unconscious, the actors have for their action.

Biography: *Max Weber*

Max Weber was born on April 21, 1864, in Erfurt, Thuringia. When he was 5 years old his family moved to Berlin. His father was an attorney and his mother a religiously pious and well-educated woman who devoted herself to charity.

After completing secondary school in 1882, Weber studied in Heidelberg, Strasbourg, and Berlin, where he defended a dissertation in 1889 and presented his *Habilitationsschrift* (postdoctoral dissertation) in 1892. In 1893 Weber married Marianne Schnitger. In 1894 Weber became professor of economics at Freiburg and in 1896 at Heidelberg. His father died in 1897 following a bitter quarrel with his son. After this, Weber suffered several mental breakdowns and he resigned his professorship. In the following years Weber wrote several methodological works and in 1905 he published *The Protestant Ethic and the Spirit of Capitalism*. Up until World War I Weber worked on his sociology of religion, work that was published after his death in *Wirtschaft und Gesellschaft*.

In 1916 Weber published works on Hinduism and Buddhism and in 1917 one on ancient

Judaism. In 1918 he became professor of political economy in Vienna. After invitations from students in Munich, Weber lectured on "Science as a Vocation" and "Politics as a Vocation" in November 1917 and January 1919.

Toward the end of his life Weber was drawn into politics. He became active in the DDP (German Democratic Party), wrote on constitutional issues, and was appointed a member of the Heidelberg Workers' and Soldiers' Council. In the spring of 1919 he was part of the German peace delegation at Versailles.

In 1919 Weber became a professor at Munich. In October 1919 his mother died and in June 1920 his sister Lili committed suicide. Max Weber suddenly became ill himself and died on June 14, 1920.

Historical and Intellectual Background

Weber's scientific contribution is intimately connected to the issues that dominated the political and intellectual scene in Germany during the decades surrounding the turn of the century. Politically, the unification of Germany in 1871, Chancellor Otto von Bismarck's strong position, and the vacuum he left behind in German domestic politics with his departure in 1890, particularly the country's belated development toward modern mass democracy, were some of the questions to which Weber directed his attention.

Intellectually, Weber belonged to the "founding generation" of sociology, although his professorship did not include this subject until a year before his death. His development of the "science of social action" occurred mainly in conjunction with the debate between the German historical movement called historicism and the rising movement of positivism, particularly on the question of the specificity of the cultural sciences with respect to natural science and on the possibility of a value-free social science. Weber also commented on the modern philosophy of science and as an economic historian he was influenced by the modern economic theory that appeared toward the end of the nineteenth century. Of particular importance to Weber was the great methodological battle between the Austrian Carl Menger (1840–1921), who maintained that abstract models were important in economics, and Gustav von Schmoller (1838–1917), who saw economics as a historical science.

Theories

Weber did not produce any simple theories; rather, his entire lifework was a struggle to determine what factors were behind the unique development of the West that had led to modern capitalism. Weber was particularly interested in the importance of religion in various cultures and in his sociology of religion he planned to analyze and write about the six great religions of the world. Weber also wrote about methods in the social sciences and on political relations, especially German and, after the 1905 revolution, Russian political relations. Thus his collected contribution can be divided into methodology, the sociology of religion, and political sociology. This division should not hide the fact that all these parts come together and that the distinguishing factor is emphasis on the various topics.

Methodology

Weber participated in the debate that took place around the turn of the century between the historicists and the advancing positivists. Particularly in Neo-Kantianism (a movement within modern scientific theory that borrowed extensively from Kant), numerous scholars had attempted to point out the differences between the social and cultural sciences and natural science. The hermeneuticist Wilhelm Dilthey (1833–1911) believed that since cultural science studied acting individuals with ideas and intentions, a special method of understanding (*Verstehen*) was required, while natural science studied soulless things and, consequently, it did not need to understand its objects. Wilhelm Windelband (1848–1915) believed that the difference between the natural and the cultural sciences was that the natural sciences strove to find universal laws (nomothetic sciences), while the cultural sciences were individualizing (ideographic) sciences. Heinrich Rickert (1863–1936) believed that it was method that distinguished the sciences. Cultural phenomena can be studied by the methods of natural science, to be sure, but in this case the investigator never arrives at the specific nature of the phenomenon.

In the late nineteenth century there arose, in opposition to this, a movement in economics using abstract models based on assumptions of human rational behavior. While the historicist Gustav von Schmoller viewed economics as a historical science that should study historical development using the customary source criticism and creative methods, the rising marginalist movement and its representatives believed that economics was a deductive science that, on the basis of certain assumptions, could predict economic behavior. Weber took something of an intermediate position in these debates and incorporated views from both sides into his own theory of science.

The relationship of science to values

According to Weber, social and historical reality consists of manifold actions and interests. When the investigator studies this "chaos of facts" he does so from certain points of view. The statement of the problem and the selection of facts that the researcher makes are always related, consciously or unconsciously, to "cultural values." He studies what is important for him to study. Thus, according to Weber, there can never be any objective scientific analysis of cultural life, since the investigator always ascribes cultural significance to the phenomena he studies. Attempts to write an objective history are also based on certain cultural values. The problem, then, is that this also opens the door for various other kinds of value judgements.

The value-neutrality of science

While social science is value-relevant, it must also be value-neutral, according to Weber. Science can speak only of facts, never of values. Weber strongly stresses that there is a fundamental difference between ""existential knowledge," that is, knowledge of what "is," and "normative knowledge," that is, what "should be" (Weber 1949: 51). Every person has his values and the choice of these values is always subjective. Consequently, science can never state an opinion on "true" values, but must rather limit itself to analyzing the effects of various actions. But it can never say what actions should be chosen. There is always an insurmountable chasm between empirical knowledge and value judgements. This difference between "is" and "ought" must prevent the scientist from using his prestige and knowledge to assert his own values at the expense of others.

The ideal type

To solve the problem of the relationship of science to values and the value-neutrality of science, Weber developed his ideal-type methodology. In part he took the notion of ideal types from modern economics, which he believed worked with ideal types, for example, when it speaks of the ideal type "market."

An ideal type is a mental construct – a mental picture – that the investigator uses to approach the complex reality. The ideal type has nothing to do with "ideals," but is ideal only in a purely logical sense. The investigator can create ideal types of anything and none of them assesses any value. The ideal type is an instrument for the investigator to use as he attempts to capture the manifold nature of reality, and its utility lies in its "success in revealing concrete cultural phenomena in their interdependence, their causal conditions and their *significance*" (Weber 1949: 92). The investigator arrives at the ideal type through "the one-sided *accentuation* of one or more points of view and by the synthesis of a great many diffuse, discrete, more or less present and occasionally absent concrete individual phenomena, which are arranged according to those one-sidedly emphasized viewpoints into a unified *analytical* construct" (Weber 1949: 90).

Weber uses his ideal-type methodology in part to reject the idea that science can capture reality "as it is objectively." As a Neo-Kantian, Weber was a nominalist, that is, he believed that concepts (ideal types) are always creations of human reason that never have a counterpart in reality. This also applies to the "laws" investigators believe they find in social reality. According to Weber, these laws too are ideal types and, thus, knowledge of social laws is never knowledge of reality, but simply a means with which we can gain knowledge of reality. For example, when Weber discusses Marx he says the laws Marx and the Marxists thought they had found in history and in bourgeois society were actually nothing but ideal types. As ideal types, they have a very important significance if they are used in a comparison with reality, but according to Weber they are actually dangerous if we believe they are empirically valid or express actual forces in reality.

Verstehen

A fourth aspect of Weber's doctrine of science is his *Verstehen* method. This expression is taken from Dilthey, but Weber used it in a somewhat different sense. Weber distinguishes between direct observational understanding (*aktuelles Verstehen*) and explanatory understanding (*erklärendes Verstehen*). Direct observational understanding is obtained directly, either because one knows the rules for a certain behavior (in church, for example) or by empathy when someone expresses his feelings. We understand most everyday events in this intuitive manner.

We gain an explanatory understanding when we know the motives behind a person's actions. In this case, the action is explained precisely by the intent behind it: what the person wanted to achieve with the action. It is this type of explanatory understanding that science should work with, according to Weber. Although many believe he makes use of empathetic faculties in his method of understanding, Weber clearly bases his methodology on a rationally founded explanatory understanding. In this respect Weber criticizes Dilthey, who built his method of understanding on a psychology of understanding, and thus Weber was closer to the abstract economic model of *Homo economicus*. This man is always economically rational and can be seen as an ideal type in the Weberian sense, which is a manner of looking at man from a certain standpoint that exaggerates certain qualities and ignores others. Economic behaviour can be explained with the help of this *Homo economicus*, who always strives for maximum returns on a minimum investment and who also has complete knowledge of prices and goods on the market.

Philosophy of value

Weber's theory of science is another step in the direction of "God's death," an idea which had emerged since the Enlightenment. Since religion began to release its grip on people's minds, other values such as "nation," "development," "human rights," and "science" have been cherished in modern society. Weber believes that these values must also be freely chosen by people. This means a "disenchantment" of the world, which is a result of the rationalization of man and of the world that has occurred throughout history. This is the deepest topic in Weber's analysis of historical development and, as a result of this development, man has lost his meaning and must choose his values. As a researcher, Weber himself contributed to this development which, as a private individual, he regretted deeply.

The Sociological Ideal Types

In accordance with his methodological teaching, Weber developed ideal types for his substantial sociology. These ideal types are based on the four ideal types of action. This is important, since according to Weber sociology is "a science concerning itself with the interpretative understandning of social action and thereby with a causal explanation of its course and consequences" (Weber 1978a: 4). This methodological individualism means that sociology should be able to trace its analyses back to the actions of the individual. This also applies to more abstract concepts such as state, class, or organization. Thus, these types of action are fundamental and other ideal types can be traced to them.

Ideal types of social action

Weber distinguishes four different ideal types of action:

1   Traditional action, i.e. actions that are controlled by tradition or deeply rooted habits.
2   Affectual actions, i.e. actions that are determined by the actors' specific affections and emotional state.
3   Value rational, i.e. actions that are determined by a conscious belief in the inherent ethical, esthetic, religious, etc. value of a type of behavior, regardless of its effects.
4   Purposive rational, i.e. actions that are carried out to achieve a certain goal. In this action

the actor calculates which actions will lead in the best and most effective manner to the achievement of the goal that has been set.

In all these cases it is possible to gain an explanatory understanding of the action if we know the traditions, affects, values, or goals behind the action. However, traditional and affectual action often lie outside the scope of meaningful social behavior, since the actor himself may not be aware of the link between the action and the driving force behind it. Unlike the last two ideal types, these actions are irrational, since they are controlled by tradition or emotions.

The difference between an affectual action and a value-rational action oriented toward a value is that in the latter action the ultimate goals of the action are clear and consciously formulated, while the former is guided by an emotional stimulus. The difference between value rational and purposive rational action is that the actor acting toward a value feels that the value places requirements on a certain action, while the actor acting toward an end consciously calculates which action to choose in order to achieve his end. In the former case the action is carried out so that the actor will live up to the cause, regardless of the consequences of his actions, while in the latter case it is precisely the consequences of a certain action that are of interest. Here the action is seen solely as a means toward achieving the end.

It is important to realize that these ideal types are precisely that – ideal types – and that they do not exist in their "pure form" in reality. They can only "formulate in conceptually pure form certain sociologically important types to which actual action is more or less approximated or, the more common case, which constitutes its elements" (Weber 1978a: 26).

Ideal types of legitimacy

Some of Weber's most important concepts are his ideal types of the legitimate exercise of power. Since many of the actions an individual performs are part of an organizational or institutional order, "action, especially social action which involves a social relationship, may be guided by the belief in the existence of a legitimate order" (Weber 1978a: 31). The question here is why an individual sees an order as legitimate and why he voluntarily subjugates himself to the exercise of power. As in the question of the types of action, Weber presents four ideal types for the basis of legitimacy. An individual can see a social order as legitimate:

1 because of tradition; it has always been legitimate (traditional legitimacy);
2 because of an emotionally based belief in an ideal, a revelation, or an example (charismatic legitimacy);
3 because of a rational belief in the validity of an absolute value (value-rational legitimacy);
4 because the rules or laws of the order are seen by the actor as legitimate (purposive rational legitimacy). This legitimacy, in turn, can be of two kinds: (a) it is legitimate because it is a joint agreement by the actors, and (b) the rules or laws have been enacted by an authority that the actors see as legitimate and therefore they consent.

These four ideal types of legitimacy correspond to the four types of actions. Here we see how Weber himself bases his various ideal types on social action, in accordance with his own methodological recommendations. Later, in *Economy and Society*, speaking of various ideal types of organizations, Weber returns to these ideal types, but this time he calls them "pure types of legitimate authority" and he has also reduced their number to three. Weber discusses the types of pure authority that can occur within an organization and what reasons a member may have for seeing those in power as legitimate:

1 Traditional reasons involve a view that the old traditions are sacred and that the one who, in accordance with the tradition, has a right to exercise authority is legitimate.
2 Charismatic reasons involve reverence toward a person's exceptional qualities, such as holiness, courage, or leadership. The actor is a "supporter" of his leader and sees this leader as legitimate on the grounds of his qualities.
3 Rational reasons involve the legality of a prescribed order and the belief that those who, in accordance with this order, have the right to exercise power are legitimate.

As we see, it is the value-rational legitimacy that has disappeared, presumably because when Weber takes up the ideal types of organization he discusses only three, which correspond to the three types of authority indicated above. An organization that is held together only by belief in a certain value is probably not possible without a leader who, in this case, obtains his legitimacy on charismatic grounds.

It is important to stress that the charismatic leader need not possess the qualities his supporters ascribe to him or her. The important thing is that the supporters believe in him or ascribe these properties to their leader, and that they express some emotionally founded hope or concept of change. Thus, according to Weber, charisma is a revolutionary force in history.

Ideal types of organizations

Weber distinguishes three different ideal types of organizations, based on what type of action and what legitimate authority are predominant:

1 In traditional organizations actions are dominated by traditional action and authority by traditional legitimacy.
2 In charismatic movements the action is dominated by affectual action and the authority by charismatic legitimacy.
3 In bureaucratic administrative staffs the action is dominated by purposive rational action and the authority by purposive rational legitimacy.

The bureaucratic administrative staff, or "bureaucracy," is perhaps Weber's best-known ideal type. He believes that it has a number of characteristics, seen from the standpoint of the ideal type. Weber divides these characteristics into three groups, the first of which deals with the general and mutual concepts found in a bureaucracy. There are five of these:

1 The rules are determined by agreement or imposition and these rules are to be followed at least by the members of the organization.
2 The legal system consists of a comprehensive system of abstract rules and the administration of justice consists of the application of these rules in individual cases.

3   The typical person of legal authority is the "superior" ("the boss"), who makes decisions in the capacity of the office he holds, but he must also follow the impersonal order.
4   Those who comply with the authority do so in their capacity as members of the organization.
5   Members do not obey the authority as an individual, but they obey the impersonal order.

The second group deals with bureaucracy as a rational system of authority with the following characteristics: continuous exercise of official duties in accordance with set rules; various spheres of competence; a hierarchical order; the rules are technical rules or norms; the administrative staff is separate from the ownership of the means that are required for administration or production; an office holder does not have ownership rights to his office; the administration's actions are confirmed in written documents; and the system can assume various forms.

According to Weber, bureaucratic administration is the exercise of legal authority in its purest form. He describes in ten points how this most rational organization is constructed (note that "rational" here means in the sense of a "rational ideal type"; in reality, a bureaucracy can be quite irrational). The administrative staff and the official comply with the following criteria:

1   They are personally free and subject to obedience only with regard to impersonal duties in office.
2   They are organized in a strict hierarchy of official positions.
3   Each position has its own clearly defined sphere of competence.
4   The officeholder holds his office in virtue of a contract, i.e. in principle, in accordance with a free selection due to . . .
5   Professional qualifications, which have been demonstrated in rational action by tests or confirmed by a diploma. He is employed (not elected) to his position.
6   Officeholders are compensated with fixed monetary salaries. Salaries are graduated primarily in accordance with rank in the hierarchy, then according to the responsibility that comes with the position, and, in general, according to the social prestige that comes with the position.
7   The office is seen by its holder as his only or main occupation.
8   The officeholder has a career before him. There is a system of "promotion" based on time of service or performance or both. Promotion is dependent on the opinion of the superior.
9   The official cannot own the means of administration and cannot appropriate his position.
10 The official is subject to strict and systematic discipline and control while carrying out his duties.

According to Weber, this organizational form and its legal authority is from the technical standpoint superior to other forms of organization because of its precision, stability, discipline, and reliability. Thus, to a great extent, it is possible to predict the results by both the superiors and other actors. It is used in "church, state, armies, political parties, economic enterprises, interest groups, endowments, clubs, and many other" organizations. The development of bureaucracy is particularly important since it is the "root of the modern Western state" (Weber 1978a: 223).

The ideal types of classes and status groups

Weber's "class analysis," like his other substantial analyses, is based on various categories of ideal types that, in principle, can be traced to the acting individual. With regard to social stratification, Weber defines a class as all the people who are in the same class situation. The class situation is defined on the basis of material provisions, external social position, and inner life, which is based on the control the individual has over material things or performance capability and how this control can result in income in a given economic order.

Weber distinguishes an owner class which is defined on the basis of ownership of the means of production, an occupational class defined on the basis of the ability to sell goods and services on the market, and a social class which is defined as the totality of class situations between which individual or generational mobility can occur. Weber also introduces the concept of a status group, which is defined on the basis of the individual's lifestyle, formal education, and origin or profession.

As we see, Weber's category of the owner class is similar to Marx's class concept (see chapter 2). But Weber's other class categories point toward a more complex class analysis that includes subjective factors as well. Weber's class categories have been used extensively in modern sociology, particularly in the United States.

Power and state

With regard to the possibility one person has to exercise influence over another person, Weber distinguishes between power, authority, and discipline. Weber also defines these concepts on an individual level, where power *(Macht)* is the "probability that one actor within a social relationship will be in a position to carry out his own will despite resistance." Authority *(Herrschaft)* is "the probability that a command with a given specific content will be obeyed by a given group of persons." Finally, discipline is "the probability that by virtue of habitation a command will recieve promt and automatic obedience in sterotyped forms, on the part of a given group of persons" (Weber 1978a: 53).

Weber defines a political organization as an authoritative organization whose order is continuously guaranteed by the threat or the use of force by the administrative staff. In this way, the state becomes a political institution whose administrative staff, within a given geographical region, successfully maintains the right to a monopoly on legitimate physical compulsion in order to maintain a certain social order.

Sociology of Religion

In his sociology of religion, Weber used his ideal types to try to answer his fundamental question: Why was it in Europe that capitalism had its breakthrough and later became a dominant force in the world? This question cannot be answered as the Marxists did, simply by pointing to the initial accumulation of capital and the creation of a "free" class of wage laborers. Even though these institutional factors were important to the origin of capitalism, they do not explain why certain people in history began to act in a capitalist manner. After all, according to Weber, any explanation of a historical phenomenon must be traced back to human social action and, thus, the investigator must try to gain an explanatory understanding of why certain people acted as they did, based on those people's own conditions. It was this that Weber attempted to do in his famous study on the connection between the Protestant ethic and the spirit of capitalism.

The Protestant ethic and the spirit of capitalism

Early capitalism emerged in a part of Europe that had also undergone a religious reformation. What meaningful link was there between Protestantism and the appearance of capitalism?

Weber created two ideal types, the Protestant ethic and the spirit of capitalism, to examine this question. He constructs the former ideal type on the basis of the Swiss reformer Jean Calvin's (1509–64) doctrine of faith. It was based on Luther, but Calvin developed a predestination doctrine of his own in which God, in his omnipotence, has determined the fate of every man long before that man is born. Thus God has decided which people will gain salvation and which are condemned to eternal damnation. For those people who embraced this belief, the question of whether they were sentenced to eternal life or eternal death led to psychological uncertainty. This led to a sense of inner loneliness in the individual who had to walk the path toward his fate, which had already been decided an eternity ago. Weber believed that this created an ascetic attitude toward life and a denial of the physical among believers. It was demanded of the Christian that he live his entire life to the glory of God. In this situation, people looked for signs indicating that they were among the chosen ones and, by succeeding in a hard and laborious life, a person could at least believe he was chosen for salvation.

Weber constructs the other ideal type, the spirit of capitalism, on the book *Advice to a Young Tradesman* written in 1748 by Benjamin Franklin (1706–90). In this book Franklin offers advice to those who would like to succeed in business. He believes they must remember that time is money, that credit is money, and that money, with hard work, can produce more money. This focus on the multiplication of money is also linked to a call for a moral and ascetic life in which those who have provided credit would rather hear the sound of a hammer at five o'clock in the morning then see the borrower at the pool table.

Weber believes that even though the content of the two cultures, the Protestant ethic and the spirit of capitalism, were different and based on different assumptions, they lead to similar actions. Protestant action was value-rational action, that is, it attempted to live up to the value of being saved and to find signs of salvation. Capitalist action is purposive rational action, that is, it attempts to find effective means of achieving an end, the multiplication of money. To the Protestant, the ascetic life and diligence were part of a life lived in the glory of God and were not directed toward the multiplication of money. Despite this, however, it broke with what Weber calls the "feudal spirit," which contained an irrational use of wealth in the form of a life of luxury. In order for capitalism to rise, this form of the luxurious use of wealth had to give way to an accumulation and reinvestment of accumulated money. The Protestant ethic played a key role in this transition.

Weber did not believe that Protestantism "caused" capitalism or that the early Protestants _i.e / the world contantly + didn't socialise !_

were cynical money-worshipers (although there were isolated examples of this). Instead, using his fundamental methodology, he attempted to understand acting people so that, on the basis of this knowledge, he could explain historical events. Once capitalism had become established, it no longer needed this value-based foundation as a criterion for action. It was sufficient that purposive rational action had become institutionalized, as it was in the modern capitalist company. But in the transition from precapitalist to capitalist action, some justification was needed for the first capitalist to begin acting in an ascetic and world-oriented manner. According to Weber, the Protestant ethic contributed just this kind of strong force that could make people begin acting differently and not simply on the basis of tradition.

The economic ethic of the world religions

In addition to analyzing the role of Protestantism in the rise of early capitalism, Weber also worked on a major comparative study of world religions. This study did not deal with the metaphysical "essence" of the various religions, rather Weber analyzed the importance religion had for the "the conditions and effects of a particular type of social action" (Weber 1978a: 399). Weber was particularly interested in how various religions hindered or promoted a special sort of economic rationality and, in this sense, the study of world religions was part of Weber's overall investigation of what specific factors led to the rational capitalism of the Western world.

Weber analyzed Confucianism and Taoism in China, Hinduism and Buddhism in India, and finally ancient Judaism. He also planned, but was unable to complete, studies on Islam, Talmudic Judaism, early Christianity, and various religious sects within the Reformation. The studies Weber carried out deal with the various social conditions in which the different religions operated, the social stratification, the links of various groups to different religions, and the importance of various religious leaders.

Weber summarized his results in a brief introduction when his collected studies on religion were published. The fundamental question he asks is "to what combination of circumstances the fact should be attributed that in Western civilization, and in Western civilization only, cultural phenomena have appeared which (as we like to think) lie in a line of development having universal significance and value" (Weber 1978b: 13). As a result of his analysis of the various religions of the world and their respective social conditions, Weber distinguished a number of factors that separated the West from other societies. These factors are:

1   Science. To be sure, empirical knowledge, consideration of the problems of the world and of life, and philosophical and ideological wisdom have developed in other cultures as well, but they lack the systematic development of knowledge based on natural science and experimentation that is found in the West. The West has also developed systematic forms of thought and rational concepts within historical research and law.

2   Art. In music the West has developed a rational harmony-based music with counterpoint and chordal harmony, a notation system that allows the composition and performance of modern musical works, and a number of instruments such as the organ, piano, violin, etc. In architecture, only the West has developed a rational use of the Gothic arch to distribute

weight and to reach over all kinds of rooms. Only in the West has a printing art appeared that is aimed solely at literature.

3   Administration. Although other cultures have also had institutions of higher learning similar on the surface to the Western university, it is only here that there is a rational, systematic, and specialized practice of science by trained experts. This has led to the development of professionally trained organizations of officials and to the fact that the "most important functions of the everyday life of society have come to be in the hands of technically, commercially, and above all legally trained goverment officials" (Weber 1978b: 16).

4   The state. Of course, there is a form of "state" in all cultures, but "the State itself, in the sense of a political association with a rational, written constitution, rationally ordained law, and an administration bound to rational rules or laws, administrated by trained officials, is known, in this combination of characteristics, only in the Occident" (Weber 1978b: 16f).

5 Economics. In all cultures and in all groups there is and has always been a "lust for money" and it is not this that distinguishes Western capitalism from the economies of other cultures. Rather, it is the rational bridling of this irrational impulse that makes possible the appearance of a rational capitalism. This capitalism is based on the "expectation of profit by utilization of opportunities for exchange, that is on (formally) peaceful chances of profit" (Weber 1978b: 17). In addition, it is only here that the specifically capitalist organization of labor has developed with rational calculation, based on a free labor force. Only here has the economy developed a systematic use of technology and, moreover, "modern rational capitalism needs . . . a calculable legal system and administration in terms of formal rules" (Weber 1978b: 25).

The final result of this comparative sociology of religion is that the specific nature of Western development is that there is a "specific and peculiar rationalism of Western culture" (Weber 1978b: 26). Thus, according to Weber, the basis of this unique Western development is not to be found in the economy, but in its unique rationalization process. Capitalism is simply an expression of this rationalization, just as the modern state with its administration and armies, bureaucracy, legitimization of power, science, and art all are. It is the discovery of this rationalization process that is perhaps Weber's most important contribution to social science.

Political Sociology

Weber's political sociology consists of two parts: a great number of analyses of and comments on German political developments, in particular, and comparative historical studies on the "sociology of domination" in *Economy and Society*. In his inaugural address on becoming a professor at Freiburg in 1894, Weber paints a bleak picture of the political culture of Germany following the departure of Bismarck in 1890. The Junker class, which supported both the state bureaucracy and the corps of officers, acted mostly out of egoistical class interest and the bourgeois class was far too weak and underdeveloped, with its apolitical cultural *Schwärmerei*, to lead Germany toward a modern mass democracy. Nor were the labor leaders spared by Weber. He also hated Kaiser Wilhelm II, particularly for his fitful and capricious foreign policy.

Much later, when Wilhelm II was gone and Germany was about to write a new constitution, Weber advocated a form of parliamentary government he called plebiscitary leadership democracy, in which the president is directly elected by the people and, by virtue of his position, he could go over the head of parliament and turn directly to the people. The president would base his legitimacy in part on charisma. This led to an extensive debate in Germany as to whether Weber advocated the form of leader that Hitler later came to be.

The sociology of domination

In his political analyses in *Economy and Society* Weber applies his ideal types of organization and legitimacy and their importance to various forms of power and domination. He presents a lengthy discussion of the "essence, conditions, and development of bureaucracy," the traditional forms of organization (which he divides into patriarchal and patrimonial dominance and feudalism), and "charismatic dominance and its transformations."

These three forms of political organization and power differ from one another. Bureaucracy and patriarchalism are opposites in many respects, since bureaucracy is based on rational rule and legal or rational authority, while patriarchalism is based on traditional rules and traditional authority. However, both have in common the fact that they have continuity and predictability as their most important properties and that they are "everyday" in nature, that is, they are part of everyday routines.

The charismatic movement and its routinization

The charismatic movement, with its charismatic authority, differs on several important points from both traditional organizations and bureaucracies. Charisma is a force that is fundamentally outside everyday life and, whether it be religious or political charisma, it is a revolutionary force in history that is capable of breaking down both traditional and rational patterns of living; but charismatic domination is unstable in nature. The authority of the charismatic leader stems from "the supernatural, superhuman, or, at least, specifically exceptional powers" he possesses, at least in the eyes of his followers (Weber 1947: 358). This force lies outside the routines of everyday life, and the problem arises when this extraordinary force is to be incorporated into a routine everyday life.

Weber calls this process the "routinization of charisma," which means that the leader (or if his is dead, his successor) and the followers want to make "it possible to participate in normal family relations or at least to enjoy a secure social position." When this happens, the charismatic message is changed into dogma, doctrine, regulations, law, or rigid tradition. The charismatic movement develops into either a traditional or a bureaucratic organization, "or a combination of both" (Weber 1947: 364).

Bureaucracy and democracy

The bureaucratic organization is also a transforming force in history, but in a more long-term manner. It spreads particularly in modern Western society, where the state administration, the capitalist company, political parties, and other interest-based organizations utilize the bureaucratic form of organization. Weber also believes that this bureaucratization must increase in state administration with the spread of political democracy, since direct democratic administration ("direct democracy") cannot solve the fundamental problems predictably, such as equal treatment of citizens and an abstract system of rules. Consequently, democratization of a state also means bureaucratization, particularly since modern political parties themselves are developing more and more into bureaucratic organizations.

Patriarchal and patrimonial domination

Of the traditional, prebureaucratic forms of organization and authority, the patriarchal structure of dominance is the most important in history. It is not based on the duty to obey an impersonal, objective goal or abstract norm, but it is based on personal relationships of loyalty and personal subjugation to a ruler. The original model for this domination is founded in the master's authority in the household. When a master or a patriarchal ruler dies, the authority passes to the new master or patriarchal ruler, who then takes his authority from tradition.

When the patriarchal domination has developed by having certain subordinate sons of the patriarch or other dependents take over land and authority from the ruler, Weber calls this patrimonial domination and a patrimonial state can develop from it. In the patrimonial state, such as Egypt under the Pharaohs, ancient China, the Inca state, the Jesuit state in Paraguay, or Russia under the czars, the ruler controls his country like a giant princely estate. The master exercises unlimited power over his subjects, the military force, and the legal system. Patrimonial dominance is a typical example of the traditional exercise of power in which the legitimacy of the ruler and the relationships between him and his subjects are derived from tradition.

Feudalism

The ideal types of patriarchal and patrimonial domination should be distinguished from that of feudalism, particularly as it developed in Western Europe. The feudal structure of domination was based on a system of enfeoffing vassals who were subjects of the ruler, while it had also developed a system of mutual rights and duties between the ruler and the vassals. Thus, this class of land-owning vassals was subordinate to the highest authority, but was above the mass of free citizens and formed a unit. In Russia, for example, even the highest nobleman had no rights whatsoever vis-à-vis the czar, while in Western Europe a system of mutual rights and duties between ruler and vassals developed. This later developed into a struggle among various noble families over the nature of these contract-based individual rights and duties. This struggle forms an important background to the rise of the Western state, with its impersonal and eventually bureaucratic legal system. From the "subjective" rights under feudalism there developed an "objective" legal order under capitalism.

The Fateful Topic of Rationality

Weber's search for the causes behind the origin of modern Western capitalism led him to the conclusion that its specific nature was found in its unique *rationality*. It is not the actual urge to create more money that distinguishes capitalism from other economic systems, but the fact that the increase in money occurs in rational forms, where the calculability, predictability, civil legal system, and the systematic use of science and technology in production are the most important elements. For this reason, Weber looked at the development of this rationality in history, which is called Weber's thesis of the rationalization tendency in history.

The rationalization tendency in history

The rationalization tendency means that man's actions move more and more from the traditional to the affective and value-rational, and on to purposive rational action. Similarly, the legitimization of power moves from traditional and charismatic legitimacy to legal rational legitimacy, and traditional organizations and charismatic movements become bureaucratic forms of organization. The rationalization tendency is found at various levels, in human thought, actions, and the legitimization of power, and in social organizations.

The rationalization of thought involves a "disenchantment of the world" (*Entzauberung der Welt*), expressed mainly in the spread of science. Modern science makes the world systematically calculable and predictable, thus creating a totally new picture of the world, compared to the previous nonscientific picture. A large part of Weber's investigation of the sociology of religion deals with the contribution of the various religions to this "disenchantment of the world" and how action has been directed more and more toward intervention in this world, rather than toward the beyond. The world has become less and less magic and more and more possible to calculate rationally toward an end.

This rationalization tendency has permeated modern Western culture and, because of its economic, technical, and administrative efficiency, it will continue to spread. Even in the society that the German Social Democrats were fighting for, a democratic socialist society, Weber believed that rationalization and bureaucratization would increase. This is because in a planned economy the role of the bureaucracy increases of necessity and all life is subjugated to calculation and planning.

The ethic of responsibility and the ethic of conviction

According to Weber, the development toward increased rationality has led to a number of problems for man in modern society. After the demise of traditions and the disappearance of high ideals, modern man himself must take responsibility for his actions. We can no longer act in accordance with the "ethic of conviction," based on the idea that "the Christian does what is right and leaves the consequences of his action to God." Instead, we must act in accordance with the "ethic of responsibility" and "answer for the foreseeable consequences of our actions." But the requirement that modern man act in accordance with the ethic of responsibility is a difficult one and, time and again, he flees, saying that responsibility for his actions lies not on himself, but on "the world, people's stupidity, or still, will blame God who has created such people" (Weber 1989b: 55).

Thus, the ethic of responsibility corresponds to purposive rational thought and actions, while the ethic of conviction corresponds to value-rational thought and action, although the ethic of conviction must also morally judge the means with which man hopes to achieve his high objective. Weber takes as an example the revolutionary socialists during World War I, who would rather have seen many years of war and then a revolution than peace without a revolution. Thus, to achieve their goal – a revolution that was not even socialist, but antifeudal – they would continue the war with its millions of casualties. Consequently, the advocate of the ethic of responsibility must also take a position on the moral justification of the means to achieve his ends. According to Weber, "it is perfectly ridiculous on their part to condemn the 'power politicians' of the old regime in the name of morality, because they themselves resort to the same means, however fully justified the rejection of their ends might be" (Weber 1989b: 56).

The rational iron cage

Weber regrets the loss of high ideals and of meaning in existence that have resulted from rationalization. The paradox and tragedy of our time is that rationalization has taught people to master nature, to develop technology for producing the means of survival, and to create administrative bureaucratic systems for regulating social life, while the existential basis of life – the choice of values and ideals and the search for meaning beyond soulless calculation of effective means for achieving a certain goal – is disappearing more and more. Modern man is trapped in a rational "iron cage of commodities and regulations" and he has lost his humanity. At the same time, he believes he has achieved the highest stage of development:

> No one knows who will live in this cage in the future, or whether at the end of this tremendous development entirely new prophets will arise, or there will be a great rebirth of old ideas and ideals, or, if neither, mechanizes petrification, embellished with a sort of convulsive self-importance. For of the last stage of this cultural development, it might well be truly said: "Specialists without spirit, sensualists without heart; this nullity imagines that it has attained a level of civilization never before achieved." (Weber 1968b: 182)

Weber's Significance as a Classic of Sociology

Even though Weber was active during the growth of German sociology – he was among the founders of the German Sociological Society in 1909 – he had no direct bearing on early sociology. His importance was more indirect, particularly through a circle of intellectual friends who came together every Sunday at his home in Heidelberg. These included the young Georg Lukács (see chapter 9) and, through him, Weber's arguments spread to the Frankfurt School (see chapter 10). Weber also had a certain indirect influence on the classical German sociology of knowledge, including names such as Max Scheler (1874–1928) and Karl Mannheim (see chapter 27).

Weber's importance as a classical sociologist did not begin until Talcott Parsons introduced him to the American public (see chapter 14). Parsons himself studied and defended a dissertation in Heidelberg during the latter half of the 1920s, and in 1930 he translated *The Protestant Ethic and the Spirit of Capitalism* into English. Parsons later based much of his book *The Structure of Social Action* (1937) on Weber, and as Parsons's influence grew in American and later in international sociology, Weber also gained more and more status as a classic.

Another important influence Weber had on modern sociology was via the advancing movement of phenomenology, in which the Austrian Alfred Schütz (see chapter 12) developed Weber's theory of action and *Verstehen* methodology in his book *Der sinnhafte Aufbau der sozialen Welt* (1932). Through a book by Schütz's followers Peter Berger and Thomas Luckman, *The Social Construction of Reality* (1966), Weber came to be seen as one of the founders of a "subjectivist" and phenomenological sociology.

A third path may be followed from Weber's interest in empirical social research (Weber himself conducted several industrial sociological studies) to the empirical social research program of Paul Lazarsfeld and Anthony Oberschall. They were primarily involved in developing his empirical methods and not so much the metascientific and comparative history analyses. Apart from this, Weber's class categories have also inspired a number of studies and trends.

Finally, Weber also inspired several historical sociologists, such as C. Wright Mills (see chapter 16), Raymond Aron (1905–83), Reinhard Bendix (1916–91), Charles Tilly, and Barrington Moore, Jr. These people, who are unlike one another and certainly do not form a "school," stress Weber's extensive historical and comparative emphasis.

Today Weber is a well-established classical sociologist whose works are still read, discussed, and taken as a starting point for a number of works (e.g. Jürgen Habermas's theory of communicative action [see chapter 21] or Anthony Giddens's structuration theory [see chapter 24]). His collected works are being published and there are both Weber societies and Weber conferences. During the past decade, in particular, with its debate over "postmodernism," Weber's critique of blind faith in science and rationality seems to have appealed to many. Thus, he is not just an early predecessor of modern sociology and social science, but he is definitely present, participating in the debate over the problems of modern society.

Bibliography

Primary:

Bibliographies:

Seyfarth, Constance, and Schmidt, Gert. 1982: *Max Weber Bibliographie: Eine Dokumentation der Sekundärlitteratur.* Stuttgart: F. Enke.
Kivisto, Peter, and Swatos, William H. Jr. 1988: *Max Weber. A Bio-Bibliography.* New York, Westport, CT, and London: Greenwood Press.
Murvar, Vatro. 1983: *Max Weber Today: An Introduction to a Living Legacy: Selected Bibliography.* Brookfield: Max Weber Colloquia.

Collected works:

Max Weber Gesamtausgabe (MWG) (collected works) is in the process of being published. It is expected to reach a total of 35 volumes; so far 12 have been published. Previous collected works were edited and published by Marianne Weber.

Weber, Max. 1920–1: *Gesammelte Aufsätze zur Religionssoziologie*. Band I–III. Tübingen: J.C.B. Mohr (Paul Siebeck).
—— 1921: *Gesammelte Politische Schriften*. München: Drei-Masken Verlag. 1958. 2nd enlarged edn, ed. Johannes Winkelmann. Tübingen: J. C. B. Mohr (Paul Siebeck). (3rd and 4th eds 1971 and 1980.)
—— 1924: *Gesammelte Aufsätze zur Sozial- und Wirtschaftsgeschichte*. Tübingen: J. C. B. Mohr (Paul Siebeck).
—— 1924: *Gesammelte Aufsätze zur Soziologie und sozialpolitik*. Tübingen: J. C. B. Mohr (Paul Siebeck).

Works published in English:

Weber, Max. 1947: *The Theory of Social and Economic Organization*. New York: Free Press.
—— 1949: *The Methodology of the Social Sciences*. New York: Free Press.
—— 1952: *Ancient Judaism*. Glencoe, IL: Free Press.
—— 1958a: *The Rational and Social Foundation of Music*. London; Amsterdam: Feffer and Simons.
—— 1958b: *The City*. New York: Free Press.
—— 1961: *General Economic History*. New York: Collier-Macmillan.
—— 1963: *Basic Concepts in Sociology*. New York: Citadel Press.
—— 1964: *The Religion of China*. New York: Collier-Macmillan.
—— 1965: *The Sociology of Religions*. London: Methuen.
—— 1967a: *The Religion of India*. New York: Free Press.
—— 1967b: *Max Weber: Essays in Sociology*. London: Routledge & Kegan Paul.
—— 1968a: *On Charisma and Institution Building*. Chicago: University of Chicago Press.
—— 1968b: *The Protestant Ethic and the Spirit of Capitalism*. London: Unwin University Books.
—— 1970: *From Max Weber: Essays in Sociology*. London: Routledge & Kegan Paul.
—— 1974: *On Universities: The Power of the State and the Dignity of the Academic Calling in the Imperial Germany*. Chicago: University of Chicago Press.
—— 1975: *Roscher and Knies: The Logical Problems of Historical Economics*. New York: Free Press.
—— 1976: *The Agrarian Sociology of Ancient Civilizations*. London: New Left Books.
—— 1977: *Critique of Stammler*. New York: Free Press.
—— 1978a: *Economy & Society*. Berkeley: University of California Press.
—— 1978b: *Selections in Translation*. Cambridge: Cambridge University Press.
—— 1989a: *Max Weber's 'Science as a Vocation'*, ed. Peter Lassman and Irving Velody. London: Unwin Hyman.
—— 1989b: *The Profession of Politics*. Washington, DC: Plutarch Press.
—— 1994a: *Political Writings*. Cambridge; New York: Cambridge University Press.
—— 1994b: *The Russian Revolution*. Cambridge: Polity Press.

Secondary:

Albrow, Martin. 1990: *Max Weber's Construction of Social Theory*. London: Macmillan.
Alexander, Jeffrey C. 1983: *Theoretical Logic in Sociology*. Vol. 3: *The Classical Attempt at Theoretical Synthesis: Max Weber*. London: Routledge & Kegan Paul.

Antonio, Robert J., and Glassman, Ronald M. 1985: *A Marx-Weber Dialogue*. Lawren ce, KS: University Press of Kansas.
Beetham, D. 1985: *Max Weber and the Theory of Modern Politics*. 2nd edn. Cambridge: Polity Press.
*Bendix, Reinhard. 1962: *Max Weber: An Intellectual Portrait*. London: Heinemann.
Bendix, Reinhard, and Roth, Guenther. 1971: *Scholarship and Partisanship: Essays on Max Weber*. Berkeley: University of California Press.
Breiner, Peter. 1996: *Max Weber and Democratic Politics*. Ithaca, NY: Cornell University Press.
Brubaker, Rogers. 1984: *The Limits of Rationality: An Essay on the Social and Moral Thought of Max Weber*. London: Allen & Unwin.
Bruun, H. H. 1972: *Science, Values and Politics in Max Weber's Methodology*. Copenhagen: Munksgaard.
Burger, Thomas. 1976: *Max Weber's Theory of Concept Formation: History, Laws and Ideal Types*. Durham, NC: Duke University Press.
Cahnman, Werner J. 1995: *Weber & Toennies: Contemporary Sociology in Historical Perspective*. New Brunswick: Transaction.
*Collins, Randall. 1986a: *Max Weber. A Skeleton Key*. Beverly Hills, CA and London: Sage.
—— 1986b: *Weberian Sociological Theory*. Cambridge: Cambridge University Press.
Dronberger, Ilse. 1971: *The Political Thought of Max Weber. In Quest of Statesmanship*. New York: Appleton-Century-Crofts.
Eldridge, John E. T. (ed.) 1972: *Max Weber: The Interpretation of Social Reality*. London: Nelson.
Eliœson, Sven. 1990: Max Weber and his Critics. *International Journal of Politics, Culture and Society*, 3, 513–37.
—— 1991: Between Ratio and Charisma. Max Weber's Views on Plebiscitary Leadership Democracy. *Statsvetenskaplig Tidskrift*, 94, 317–39.
Ferrarotti, Franco. 1982: *Max Weber and the Destiny of Reason*. New York: Sharpe.
Germain, Gilbert G. 1994: Max Weber and the Modern State. In Asher Horowitz and Terry Maley (eds), *The Barbarism of Reason: Max Weber and the Twilight of Enlightenment*, Toronto: University of Toronto Press.
Giddens, Anthony. 1972: *Politics and Sociology in the Thought of Max Weber*. London: Macmillan.
Glassman, Ronald M., and Murvar, Vatro (eds) 1984: *Max Weber's Political Sociology. A Pessimistic Vision of a Rationalized World*. Westport, CT and London: Greenwood Press.
Green, Robert W. (ed.) 1959: *Protestantism and Capitalism. The Weber Thesis and Its Critics*. Boston: Heath.
Hekman, Susan J. 1983: *Weber, the Ideal Type and Contemporary Social Theory*. Notre Dame, IN: University of Notre Dame Press.
Hennis, Wilhelm. 1983: Max Weber's 'Central Question'. *Economy and Society*, 12, 135–80.
—— 1987: *Max Weber. Essays in Reconstruction*. London: Allen & Unwin.
Heydebrand, Wolf, et al. 1994: *Max Weber: Sociological Writings*. New York: Continuum.
Honigsheim, Paul. 1968: *On Max Weber*. New York and London: Free Press and Macmillan.
Kalberg, Stephen. 1980: Max Weber's Types of Rationality: Cornerstones for the Analysis of Rationalization Processes in History. *American Journal of Sociology*, 85, 1145–79.
—— 1994: *Max Weber's Comparative-Historical Sociology*. Oxford: Polity Press.
Kocka, Jürgen, and Gneuss, Christopher (eds) 1968: *Max Weber. Ein Symposion*. Munich: DTV.
*Käsler, Dirk. 1988: *Max Weber: An Introduction to his Life and Work*. Cambridge: Polity Press.
Lachman, Ludwig. 1970: *The Legacy of Max Weber*. Berkeley, CA: Glendessory Press.
Lash, Scott, and Whimster, Sam (eds) 1987: *Max Weber. Rationality and Modernity*. London: Allen & Unwin.
Lassman, Peter, and Velody, Irving (eds) 1989: *Max Weber's "Science as a Vocation"*. London: Unwin Hyman.
Lemann, Hartmut, and Roth, Guenther. 1993: *Weber's "Protestant Ethic": Origins, Evidence, Context*. Washington, DC: German Historical Institute.

Lenhardt, Christian. 1994: Max Weber and the Legacy of Critical Idealism. In Asher Horowitz and Terry Maley (eds), *The Barbarism of Reason: Max Weber and the Twilight of Enlightenment,* Toronto: University of Toronto Press.

MacRae, Donald G. 1974: *Weber.* London: Fontana.

Mitzman, Arthur. 1985: *The Iron Cage: A Historical Interpretation of Max Weber.* New York: Alfred A. Knopf.

Mommsen, Wolfgang J. 1984: *Max Weber and German Politics 1890–1920.* Chicago: University of Chicago Press.

—— 1989: *The Political and Social Theory of Max Weber.* Chicago and Cambridge: University of Chicago Press and Polity Press.

Mommsen, W. and Osterhammel, J. (eds) 1987: *Max Weber and his Contemporaries.* London: Allen & Unwin.

Oakes, G. 1988: *Weber and Rickert. Concept Formation in the Cultural Sciences.* Cambridge, MA: MIT.

Parkin, Frank. 1982: *Max Weber.* London: Tavistock.

Ringer, Fritz. 1997: *Max Weber's Methodology: The Unification of the Cultural and Social Sciences.* Cambridge, MA: Harvard University Press.

Roth, Guenther. 1976: History and Sociology in the Work of Max Weber. *British Journal of Sociology,* 27, 306–18.

Roth, Guenther, and Schluchter, Wolfgang. 1979: *Max Weber's Vision of History. Ethics and Methods.* Berkeley: University of California Press.

Sahay, Arun (ed.) 1971: *Max Weber and Modern Sociology.* London: Routledge & Kegan Paul.

Scaff, Lawrence A. 1989: *Fleeing the Iron Cage. Culture, Politics and Modernity in the Thought of Max Weber.* Berkeley: University of California Press.

Schluchter, W. 1981: *The Rise of Western Rationalism: Max Weber's Developmental History.* Berkeley: University of California Press.

—— 1988: *Rationalism, Religion and Domination. A Weberian Perspective.* Berkeley: University of California Press.

Schmidt, Gert. 1976: Max Weber and Modern Industrial Sociology: A Comment on Some Recent Anglo-Saxon Interpretations. *Sociological Analysis and Theory,* 6, 47–73.

Shroeter, Gert. 1980: Max Weber as an Outsider: His Nominal Influence on German Sociology in the 20s. *Journal of the History of the Behavioural Sciences,* 16, 317–32.

Sica, A. 1988: *Weber, Irrationality and Social Order.* Berkeley: University of California Press.

Swedberg, Richard. 1998: *Max Weber and the Idea of Economic Sociology.* Princeton, NJ: Princeton University Press.

Tenbruck, Friedrich. 1975: Das Werk Max Webers. *Kölner Zeitschrift für Soziologie und Sozialpsychologie,* 27, 663–702.

—— 1980: The Problem of Thematic Unity in the Work of Max Weber. *British Journal of Sociology,* 31, 313–51.

Turner, Bryan S. 1981: *For Weber: Essays on the Sociology of Fate.* London: Routledge & Kegan Paul.

Turner, Stephen P., and Factor, Regis 1984: *Max Weber and the Dispute over Reason and Value.* London: Routledge & Kegan Paul.

—— 1994: *Max Weber: The Lawyer as Social Thinker.* London: Routledge.

Weber, Marianne. 1975: *Max Weber: A Biography.* New York: Wiley.

Whimster, Sam (ed.) 1998: *Max Weber and the Culture of Anarchy.* Basingstoke: Macmillan.

Wiley, Norbert (ed.) 1987: *The Marx-Weber Debate.* Beverly Hills, CA and London: Sage.

Willer, David. 1967: Max Weber's Missing Authority Type. *Sociological Inquiry,* 37, 231–9.

Wolin, Sheldon S. 1994: Max Weber: Legitimation, Method and the Politics of Theory. In Asher Horowitz and Terry Maley (eds), *The Barbarism of Reason: Max Weber and the Twilight of Enlightenment,* Toronto: University of Toronto Press.

Wrong, Dennis (ed.) 1970: *Max Weber.* Englewood Cliffs, NJ: Prentice Hall.

chapter **7**

Georg Simmel

Henrik Ørnstrup*

KEY CONCEPTS

DIFFERENTIATION – because of division of labor and specialization, society is differentiated, which makes originally homogenous groups heterogeneous. Society becomes more complex and confused, but at the same time capable of carrying out much more varied functions.

---

* All quotations from German are translated by the author unless otherwise stated.

INDIVIDUALITY – modern social development creates modern individuality, which has a dual character. On one hand, it produces liberty (see "Personality"), and on the other, the individual is released into a roaring societal machine that threatens the individual with anonymity and alienation.

PERSONALITY – is to Simmel both a utopian and a tragic conception of genuineness, honesty, and originality in the modern world. Personality as such is a product of the modern world, but so is its erasure.

SOCIALIZATION (*Vergesellschaftung*) – society is an event in which individuals participate in interaction based on certain interests and goals (also described as "contents," e.g., hunger, love, economy). Sociology must deal with the forms of social interaction (e.g., division of labor, flirtation, competition) and not the contents.

Biography: *Georg Simmel*

Georg Simmel was born on March 1, 1858, at the corner of Friedrichstrasse and Leipzigstrasse in the heart of Berlin, the youngest of seven children. When Simmel's father died in 1874, the rich music publisher Julius Friedländer became his guardian. Simmel later inherited part of Friedländer's fortune, which enabled him to pursue an academic career. This resulted in a professorship only four years before his death.

Simmel first studied history with Theodor Mommsen, switched to ethnopsychology – a type of ethnology – and finally arrived at the faculty of philosophy where, in 1884, he wrote a doctoral thesis about Immanuel Kant. In 1890 he married Gertrud Kinel, who, under the pseudonym Enckendorf, was a successful writer on topics such as philosophy of religion and sexuality.

Simmel became a very popular lecturer in Berlin, but this success did not earn him a salaried position. After 14 years as an unpaid lecturer he was appointed an "extraordinary professor." In the following years Simmel tried to get professorships elsewhere in Germany, with help from, among others, his friend Max Weber. Not until 1914 did he succeed at Strasburg, which at the time did not have a good reputation.

In Berlin, Simmel opened his home once a week to an exclusive group of intellectuals, among others Georg Lukács, Ernst Bloch, and Max Weber. Most of them were fascinated by Simmel. He possessed a mixture of seriousness and polite irony, something coquettishly double-edged. These traits are also evident in his writings, a patchwork quilt of theses and observations which often make it difficult to determine his presonal point of view. Simmel died in 1918.

Today Georg Simmel is considered one of the founding fathers of modern sociology, along with his German contemporaries Max Weber (1864–1920; see chapter 6) and Ferdinand Tönnies (1855–1936; see chapter 4). None of them were sociologists, for the simple reason that sociology did not exist as a subject or profession. Political and institutional forces, especially in Germany, did not accept it as an independent scientific discipline. In fact, the founders themselves doubted whether it was possible and meaningful to develop a distinct scientific discipline called sociology.

Georg Simmel's production of manifesto articles and epistemological analyses that aimed at an actual definition of sociology is larger than both Weber's and Tönnies's. Besides, he is the best example of the fundamental ambiguity that characterizes modern, classical sociology. A look at his production reveals that sociology occupies only a minor part of Simmel's fields of interest, and this is where the ambiguity comes out. In *practice*, Simmel – and Weber and Tönnies – did not regard sociology as a science in the modern sense, but as a certain way to look at the world. In this sense, sociology was a perspective that Simmel used whether he wrote about Rembrandt, the Alps, or Schopenhauer. Sociology as a certain viewpoint, as an element that, in principle, can be integrated in any analysis – that is the ambiguous legacy of Georg Simmel's work.

The Three Phases of Simmel's Work

Simmel's production is traditionally divided into three phases, which illustrate how much he was influenced by contemporary thought. At the beginning of his career, Simmel was a positivist and was influenced by Herbert Spencer's evolutionism. He would only deal with what could be observed or described as a relation between known causes and effects.

In the book *Über sociale Differenzierung* (On Social Differentiation) from 1890, Simmel claims to be able to reduce various human ideas and values to a product of society. He continues this path in *Einleitung in die Moralwissenschaft* (Introduction to Moral Science) by reducing morality to a useful social regulator, but at the same time he discusses epistemological issues that later become fixtures throughout his production. The young Simmel was, in general, a skeptical relativist, a label that stuck to him for a long time. In Germany, sociology became almost synonymous with subversion of values, if not subversion of society.

Just before the turn of the century, Simmel wrote a vast number of essays and prepared the great work that establishes his name as one of the most original thinkers of his time. *Philosophie des Geldes* (*Philosophy of Money*) from 1900 (1978) is Simmel's main work but also a crossroads for his thinking. Things had changed since the early 1890s, and although there are traces of positivistic evolutionism, the book leaves no doubt that Simmel's perspective has expanded drastically.

He started to focus on problems of modern society from the individual's point of view. Earlier, Simmel did not hesitate to reduce the individual to a product of society, but he now started to see how the modern lifestyle was entangled in a number of painful conflicts in relation to the individual personality.

In 1908 he published a collection of distinctly sociological articles and essays entitled *Soziologie – Untersuchungen über die Formen der Vergesellschaftung* (Sociology – Treatises on Social Forms and Sociation). This great work concluded the second phase of Simmel's production, and in a way it was also the conclusion of Simmel's struggle with the more basic problems within sociological theory. The sociological aspect is still there, but now simply as part of a more general philosophy of life and culture which remained Simmel's main concern until his death. His essay collection *Philosophische Kultur* (Philosophical Culture) from 1911 is the best expression of this fact. It is also his most accomplished piece of work, presenting sociological analyses of topics ranging from coquetry to metaphysical profundities. Shortly before his death, Simmel collected a number of long articles in *Lebensanschauung – Vier methaphysische Kapitel* (Outlook on Life – Four Metaphysical

Chapters). The title alone says something about his paradoxical development from positivistic criticism of metaphysics to declared philosophical metaphysics on his deathbed.

This contrast is only apparent, however, and gives a false picture of his work which, in reality, did not change significantly after the turn of the century. For example, his philosophy of life and culture were already fully developed in the concluding chapters of *Philosophy of Money*.

Simmel's Foundation of Sociology

The two manifesto articles *Das Problem der Soziologie* (The Problem of Sociology, originally published in Simmel 1908) and *Das Gebiet der Soziologie* (The Object of Sociology, published in Simmel 1917), presented Simmel's definition of sociology as an independent science. At the turn of the century, sociology had a bad reputation and was not at all accepted as a science in Germany. In the early 1800s, Auguste Comte had defined sociology as a noble science, an encyclopedic science in an enormous hierarchical system of sciences. This definition was now considered almost ridiculous, and because of it, the name itself, sociology, was regarded as derogatory. The name also created misunderstanding, because some people thought that it was somehow related to the dreaded socialism. So Simmel had plenty of reason to attempt to found a new, modern sociology that would clearly distance itself from earlier attempts.

Sociology and social development

Simmel saw the emergence of sociology as a product of social development. A science about society had become necessary, because modern society was becoming more and more complex and confused. It was no longer possible to explain culture, religion, or economy, in other words society, with a point of departure in the single individual. Isolated contributions or heroic acts by single individuals could no longer explain history and social development. And the alternative – referring to metaphysical forces or God – was no longer acceptable. Consequently, there was a need for a science or descriptive method to analyze the complexity and fundamental dynamics of modern society across the existing descriptive methods.

One example is language. We cannot understand this phenomenon by referring to individual geniuses or God. Simmel claimed that different phenomena could be understood as outcomes of interaction between single individuals: "based on the sum and sublimation of countless single contributions, the embodiment of the social energies in structures that exist and develop beyond the individual" (Simmel 1908: 3). In other words, nobody "invented" language, and sociology could be *the* science to analyze phenomena that are outcomes of a number of different, complex processes that are not controlled by a tangible subject.

Sociology – a method without an object

Consequently, instead of pointing out an object, Simmel wanted to identify sociology by means of a certain viewpoint, a certain method. Just as induction in its day spread to all sciences, sociology now offered itself as a new research principle within the humanities.

Man should be considered a social creature, but exactly this point of view made it impossible for sociology to become an independent science. In the nineteenth century, sciences were defined and delimited according to their object. But sociology's problem, that is, society, is its object. Sociology has a method, but no object. The purpose of Simmel's manifesto articles was therefore to construct an object that could make sociology a valid, independent science. This would be realized by an analysis of a concept of society that, in principle, is very simple, but has far-reaching consequences.

Society as forms of interaction (Wechselwirkung)

Simmel saw society as the product of interaction, and the concept of interaction is an attempt to label the most significant characteristics of society, perhaps especially of modern society. Society is not a thing, not a tangible subject, but it is clearly the objective of sociological science. Therefore, Simmel could use the concept of interaction to describe society as an object or a unit that is not a thing or a metaphysical entity: "We describe each object as a unit, provided that the relation between its components is reciprocal and dynamic" (Simmel 1890: 129). In other words, since it is the reciprocal, dynamic interaction between the components that creates a unit, interaction is a crucial concept to Simmel, not just for understanding society, but for understanding the entire world. He viewed interaction as a basic principle, which, among other things, means "that everything interacts with everything in some form; that there are relations between each point in the world and all other forces" (Simmel 1890: 129).

Simmel thus claims that society "exists where several individuals participate in interaction" (Simmel 1908: 4). But society is more than just interaction, which in itself cannot explain society as a phenomenon. There is always a driving force behind interaction, always a purpose, and Simmel adds that, "this interaction is always based on certain drives or certain purposes" (Simmel 1908: 4). Society is not a machine, a blind and aimless mechanism. According to Simmel, people ultimately drive society's development. These are real individuals with needs, interests, instincts, and goals which they satisfy through different forms of social interaction. These drives (which are *not* Freudian) can be religious, erotic, political, social, etc. Interests can be economic, educational, etc. "Due to these interactions, a unit, or rather a 'society' emerges, based on the bearers of these drives and purposes" (Simmel 1908: 4). Simmel calls this unit *Vergesellschaftung*, which can be translated as sociation. Depending on the character of interaction, the outcome is different sociological entities such as a walk, a family, a nation-state, etc.

Simmel describes everything that works as an incentive for the individual (drive, purpose, intention, interests, etc.) as *contents*, which are the substance of society, the catalysts. But Simmel's central point is that these contents are not of a social nature.

> Neither love nor hunger, neither work nor piety, neither technology nor the functions or results of intelligence imply, as they appear or are given sociation (*Vergesellschaftung*). (Simmel 1908: 5)

These "contents" really cause the reciprocal process. In other words, sociation is the form in which individual interests, drives, or intentions are realized:

> These are then, in reality, inseparable elements in all social being and events: an interest, purpose, a motive and a form or kind of interaction between individuals, through which or in the shape of which that content reaches social reality. (Simmel 1908: 5)

It is important to realize that Simmel's very simple and elegant analysis is not a reflection of reality. In reality, we cannot separate contents and form in this way. For example, we cannot imagine social interaction or sociation as expressions of a conscious choice by an individual. We are always caught up in interaction. Loneliness is thus also a sociological concept, a form of interaction. Society or "the others" always take part in the loneliness, as experienced in the crowd. Simmel uses loneliness to characterize the way different societies structure groups according to whether they produce room for loneliness (Simmel 1908: 55). His distinction between form and contents is therefore exclusively a theoretical technical maneuver that enables him to define sociology as an independent science, "a science with society and nothing else as its object can only consist in examining these interactions, these forms of sociation" (Simmel 1908: 7).

Simmel's definition of sociology

Simmel has thus secured his sociology definition against a reductionistic view that reduces everything that happens in society to a pure product of the very same society. Sociology will deal with the societal aspect of society. All the things that, strictly speaking, do exist within society are not society as such. Sociology must concentrate on forms of sociation, as they are the social aspects of society, society as such.

Simmel claims that he can prove that the distinction between contents and form in the concept of society is meaningful, because the same form of interaction is found in relation to different contents, and different forms realize the same contents. Competition, imitation, division of labor, and party formation are examples of different forms of interaction in criminal gangs, corporations, families, and art styles. Conversely, content-related interests can be realized in different forms. Economic interests may, for instance, result in competition or monopolies.

The result of Simmel's analysis of the social concept is a conception of society as the *sum of forms of relationship*, and this is the perspective sociology should apply. In other words, sociology is the science of forms of social interaction or *Vergesellschaftung*. Simmel's concept of society is not an abstract general concept, but a dynamic concept that aims to maintain that society is not static, not a container for actions. Society constantly emerges in forms of interaction. We can say that society is constantly produced in events. It is not predetermined and forms of sociation should not be perceived as causing the existence of society. Forms of interaction are society. If we do away with all interaction, there is nothing left. Then again, interaction by itself is also unthinkable. Interaction is always a concrete event, an "occurrence" (*Geschehen*), where individual drives are involved in certain forms of interaction.

Differentiation

What is strange about Simmel's foundation of sociology is that he himself never systematically applied its inherent method and program. He wrote his two manifesto articles and then
continued in different directions without considering or referring to these fundamental articles again. In practice, they amount to a parenthesis.

Simmel still studied forms of interaction, but the crucial theme in his production – as we
shall see below – is not embedded in his theory of science, which was related to his original
foundation of sociology.

Division of labor and specialization

Division of labour and specialization are two forms of social interaction that occupied Simmel
throughout his work. Here, in the struggle between these two categories, he found his theme:
character, conditions, and the fate of individuality in modern society.

Differentiation has been a sociological key concept in the description of the evolution of
modern society, since Herbert Spencer (see chapter 3) developed his evolution theory in the
1850s and 1860s. Differentiation means that a social phenomenon is separated into various
parts that are either similar or different in type or function. Sociology characterizes such a
state or process as differentiation, not as disintegration, because the social phenomenon
does not disappear or disintegrate in the process. Even if society is disintegrated or differentiated, it survives as a "system."

Simmel's first book, which deals with differentiation, established his significance for
sociology by introducing a number of problem areas and conflict potentials that were not
originally considered in the concept and which differ from Spencer's and Durkheim's perceptions. Spencer described society as a superorganism that develops through progressive
integration and differentiation. The development moves from a state of coherent homogeneity to a state of coherent heterogeneity. Durkheim (see chapter 5), who also contributed
decisively to the concept of differentiation, calls the two states mechanic and organic solidarity, while modern sociology often uses the concepts of segmented and functional differentiation. Both Spencer and Durkheim perceived social development, via the concept of
differentiation, as progress. Society became still better at adapting itself, and differentiation
was, in broad terms, the process that ensured progress.

Originally, Simmel agreed with Spencer and Durkheim. As a young man he saw differentiation as relatively unproblematic, and in his view, society developed as an organism
through continued integration and differentiation. The development was based on rationality and biology, as the social organism or the system constantly improved its efficiency and
ability to adapt. So differentiation is positive, progress is automatic, development is heading in the right direction, and ultimately nature guarantees social progress. A hundred years
ago there were plenty of good reasons to be positive about differentiation. Increasing specialization, division of labor, the simultaneous explosive population growth and technological development seem to affirm the statement. As progress ruled, society became a
better and better society, so to speak.

In his early writings, Simmel used the energy-saving aspect of division of labor and specialization to point out the increasing differentiation. Differentiation is an evolutionary advantage, because the social body saves energy that can then be invested elsewhere. Simmel thus at the same time sets a quantitative goal for progress and development via differentiation:

> Each being is more perfect if it can reach the same goal with less effort. All culture strives to not only make more of the subhuman nature's energy useful for our purposes, but also to do it in still more energy-saving ways. (Simmel 1890: 258)

In other words, modern society is more perfect than earlier societies, because specialization and division of labor enable it to produce more goods faster. Society as an organism therefore saves energy. Nobody cared to look at this from nature's point of view, and parameters like resources and sustainability only became issues several generations later.

Individuality and Differentiation

Individuality can be described as a product of social differentiation. Historical development from the stable feudal society of the Middle Ages to modern, market-oriented, urban life is a story about how individuals, through trade, population growth, division of labor, and specialization, differentiated themselves from each other to a much larger extent than before. Sociologically, Simmel describes this development as follows.

According to Simmel's thesis, there is a close correlation between individuality and the size of the group the individual belongs to. If we imagine two groups, M and N, that are very different, but each consisting of similar and closely related persons, then a quantitative expansion of the group – for example, population growth – will increase differentiation. The original, insignificant differences within the groups will now become more pronounced, and the individuals will differentiate from each other. This process, historically expressed in the division of labor, produces or radicalizes individuality.

Simmel now assumes that the humanly possible forms of differentiation are limited and he is therefore able to conclude that the larger the differentiation within groups M and N, the larger the probability that the forms of differentiation in the two groups resemble each other. The apparently paradoxical point is then that differentiation has a dual character: no matter how different groups M and N are to begin with, the differentiation process will increase their resemblance as groups. This is why we talk about a paradoxical identity between differentiation and levelling. On one hand, each group produces individuality, but on the other hand, the group as such loses individuality as it is levelled in relation to other groups.

The role of the individual

From the individual's point of view, this process obviously implies increased personal freedom. In the tight medieval group, individual freedom was strictly regulated, but the group the individual belongs to was strongly individualized in relation to other groups. Differentiation may, for example, mean that the local capitalist and worker are estranged in relation to each other within the local group. Worker and capitalist have to find their peers outside the local group, which creates new, crossover groupings that loosen the bonds to those who are close and establish new relations with remote groups.

Thus, we can conclude that *from the individual's point of view* differentiation is not unproblematic. Along with the differentiation of traditional society emerges a specific, modern form of individuality, first and foremost characterized by a significantly increasing individual freedom. But simultaneously, society itself turns into a huge machine, threatening to crush the individual. In contrast to Spencer and Durkheim, Simmel focused more and more on this relationship. Before, the perspective of social development was rationality and progress, but they are being replaced by a crisis consciousness that maps contradictions and conflicts from the individual's perspective. Is the individual's new-found freedom only "freedom" to enter the still more complex structure and rationality of modern society?

Individuality and Modernity

The relation between the individual's desire to actualize itself authentically and autonomously and society's "wish" to put the individual in a specific box to perform a specific function is an issue that increasingly occupied Simmel. He saw the modern city as an example of this conflict which confronts the individual with enormous performance demands, loneliness, and alienation. His famous essay, "The Metropolis and Mental Life," analyzes the mentality that characterizes life in the city. First he notes that the city bombards the individual with impressions – crowds of people, incidents, and accidents, everything at high speed. To survive this inferno of external influence, urban people develop a mental shield; they interpret impressions intellectually and are guided by cold calculation, in contrast to villages, where individuals react naturally or emotionally.

In this connection, Simmel saw a parallel to the all-important role of money in the cities. There are few personal relations in the city, the most important things are time and money, quantitative units that ensure precision and impersonal objectivity in human relations. This is the logic or rationality that controls everyday life.

Urban life mentality

How does this affect character or mentality? First of all, Simmel saw the city dweller as blasé and reserved, experiencing most phenomena negatively, and unable to appreciate the uniqueness of things and people. Everything and everybody is equally important in a constant flow of money, everything and everybody is at the same level. Quantity, not quality, is the only difference, that is, how much each item or person costs.

Paradoxically, the result of this indifference is that individuals in the cities seek out the extreme. The extravagant and the bizarre thrive in big cities because it is the only way to get noticed. Encounters are fleeting and superficial, and therefore it is important to "appear 'to the point,' to appear concentrated and strikingly characteristic" (Simmel 1950: 421). Again this is in contrast to the village, where contacts are frequent and lasting.

As we have seen, Simmel's analysis of the metropolis reveals a number of problems in connection with the modern division of labor and specialization that has become the result of the differentiation process. To Simmel, the city is the symbol of these problems that all concern the fate of the individual. Individuals in the cities are differentiated, they have their function or role in the great clockwork, but in Simmel's words, this is only a "quantitative individuality." The qualitative individuality, personality, is levelled.

It could also be described as the difference between the external and internal. In the city, the personality is doomed to an external life dominated by the tough logic and rationality of the money economy. In the traditional village, life is more internal and emotional, but then individual freedom is more limited

The conflict between individual and society

Simmel had no solution to the classical conflict as it took place between the individual and society at the turn of the century. He concluded his analysis laconically, noting that it was not his task to accuse or apologize, only to understand. However, there is no doubt that Simmel's optimism from the 1890s yielded to a more pessimistic view of the future:

> To be sure, unlimited competition and individual specialization through division of labour have affected individual culture in a way that shows them not to be its most suitable promoters . . . I should prefer to believe, however, that the ideas of free personality as such and of unique personality as such, are not the last word of individualism. I should like to think that the efforts of mankind will produce ever more numerous and varied forms for human personality to affirm itself and to demonstrate the value of its existence. (Simmel 1950: 84)

Modernity as tragedy

Simmel never finished with this issue. The closest he got to a solution was to consider it tragically inevitable, which is the same as saying that the problem, by definition, is insoluble. In other words, it is inherent in its development logic that modern society simultaneously produces and destroys individuality.

Personality is a specifically modern phenomenon, but so is its obliteration. This is Simmel's tragic conclusion:

> a tragic fate . . . is, I suppose, how we describe the fact that the destructive forces that turn on a being spring from the deepest layers of the being itself; that its destruction fulfils its inherent destiny, and in a way is the logical development of the structure by which this being built its own positivity. (Simmel 1911: 146)

Simmel's Significance

The fact that Simmel gave up trying to solve the problem of individuality in modernity has not deterred more recent research. Simmel has inspired many social theorists in the twentieth century. The influence of classical German sociology and Simmel is today more obvious among cross-disciplinary social theorists than professional sociologists. Simmel was in a way the Anthony Giddens (see chapter 24), Niklas Luhmann (see chapter 22), or Jürgen

Habermas (see chapter 21) of his day. The most important legacy from Simmel is not his manifesto, but more his way of practicing sociology: crossover, multidimensional, social analysis taking its point of departure from contemporary problems.

Simmel's critical attitude and keen observations inspired the so-called Frankfurt School (see chapter 10) especially Walter Benjamin (1892–1940) and Theodor Adorno (1903–69), and he thus paved the way for the socially critical essay which, based on a small, isolated social phenomenon, set out to say something universal about modern society. Simmel strongly influenced the young Georg Lukács (1885–1971; see chapter 9). However, Lukács in his old age distanced himself from his mentor. Both the title and the style of Lukács's first book, the collected essays *Soul and Form* (originally Lukács 1911) are very much influenced by Simmel.

After World War II, Leopold von Wiese (1876–1969) adopted Simmel's definition of sociology into his so-called formal sociology, in reality a misunderstanding of Simmel's concept of form. Because of this interpretation, Simmel was for a long time seen as a strict, form-fixated sociologist who catalogued different social forms of interaction, a perception far from the purpose of Simmel's distinction between form and contents.

Since the early 1980s, Simmel has had a renaissance. An important contribution to this revival was David Frisby's *Sociological Impressionism* (Frisby 1981), a book that challenged the worst prejudices about Simmel's work, prejudices that thrived because nobody bothered to read the man's writings. Frisby's and others' re-evaluation of Simmel has sparked a renewed interest in his writings in Germany.

Bibliography

Primary:

Georg Simmel *Gesamtausgabe* (collected works) is in the process of being published by Suhrkamp and is expected to reach a total of 24 volumes. So far the following volumes have been published: 2 (1989), 3 (1989), 4 (1991), 5 (1992), 6 (1989), 8 (1993), 9 (1993), 10 (1994), 11 (1992), 7 (1995), and 14 (1996).

Simmel, Georg. 1890: *Über sociale Differenzierung*. Leipzig: Duncker & Humblot.
—— 1892: *Die Probleme der Geschichtsphilosophie*. Leipzig: Duncker & Humblot. (Translated as *The Problems of the Philosophy of History*. New York: Free Press 1977).
—— 1892–3: *Einleitung in die Moralwissenschaft 1–2*. Berlin: Hertz.
—— 1904: *Kant. 16 Vorlesungen*. Leipzig: Duncker & Humblot.
—— 1906: *Kant und Goethe*. Berlin: Bardt, Marquardt.
—— 1907: *Schopenhauer und Nietzsche*. Leipzig: Duncker & Humblot. (Translated as *Schopenhauer and Nietzsche*. Amherst: University of Massachusetts Press, 1986).
—— 1908: *Soziologie*. Leipzig: Duncker & Humblot.
—— 1910: *Hauptprobleme der Philosophie*. Leipzig: Göschen.
—— 1911: *Philosophische Kultur*. Leipzig: Klinkhardt.
—— 1913: *Goethe*. Leipzig: Klinkhardt & Biermann.
—— 1916: *Rembrandt*. Leipzig: Kurt Wolf.
—— 1917: *Grundfragen der Soziologie*. Berlin: Göschen.
—— 1918: *Lebensanschauung*. Leipzig: Duncker & Humblot.
—— Kurt Wolff (ed.) 1950: *The Sociology of Georg Simmel*. Glencoe, IL: Free Press.
—— 1955: *Conflict. The Web of Group Affiliations*. Glencoe, Ill: Free Press.

—— 1959a: *Essays on Sociology, Philosophy and Aesthetics*, ed. Kurt Wolff. Colombus: Ohio State University Press.

—— 1959b: *Georg Simmel 1858–1918: A Collection of Essays with Translations and a Bibliography*, ed. Kurt Wolff. Columbus: Ohio State University Press.

—— 1959c: *Sociology of Religion*. New York: Philosophical Library.

—— 1968: *The Conflict in Modern Culture, and Other Essays*. New York: Teachers College Press.

—— 1971: *On Individuality and Social Forms: Selected Writings*, ed. Donald N. Devine. Chicago: University of Chicago Press.

—— 1976: *George Simmel: Sociologist and European*, translated by D. E. Jenkinson et al. Sunbury, Middlesex: Nelson.

—— 1978 [1900]: *The Philosophy of Money*. Boston: Routledge & Kegan Paul.

—— 1980: *Essays on Interpretation in the Social Sciences*, ed. Guy Oakes. Manchester: Manchester University Press.

—— 1983: *Schriften zur Soziologie*, ed. H. Dahme and O. Rammstedt. Frankfurt am Main: Suhrkamp.

—— 1984a: *Georg Simmel on Women, Sexuality, and Love*, ed. Guy Oakes. New Haven: Yale University Press.

—— 1984b: *Das Individuum und die Freiheit*. Berlin: Klaus Wagenbach.

—— 1985: *Schriften zur Philosophie und Soziologie der Geschlechter*, ed. H. Dahme and Köhnke, Frankfurt am Main: Suhrkamp.

—— 1987: *Das Individuelle Gesetz*, ed. M. Landmann. Frankfurt am Main: Suhrkamp.

—— 1996: *Essays on Religion*, ed. Horst Jürgen Helle with Ludwig Nieder. New Haven: Yale University Press.

—— 1997: *Simmel on Culture: Selected Writings*, ed. David Frisby and Mike Featherstone. London: Sage.

Secondary:

Adorno, T. 1974: Der Essay als Form. In *Gesammelte Schriften*, vol. 11. Frankfurt am Main: Suhrkamp.

Corser, Lewis A. 1971: 'Georg Simmel'. In Lewis A. Corser, *Masters of Sociological Thought*. New York: Harcourt Brace Jovanovich.

Dahme, H.-J. (ed.) 1984: *Georg Simmel und die Moderne*. Frankfurt am Main: Suhrkamp.

Dörr-Backes, Felicitas, and Nieder, Ludwig. 1995: *Georg Simmel: Between Modernity and Postmodernity*. Würzburg: Königshausen und Neumann.

Frisby, David. 1981: *Sociological Impressionism*. London: Routledge and Kegan Paul.

*Frisby, David (ed.) 1994: *Georg Simmel: Critical Assesments*. London: Routledge.

Helle, H.-J. 1988: *Soziologie und Erkenntnistheorie bei Georg Simmel*. Darmstadt: Wissenschaftliche Buchgesellschaft.

Kracauer, S. 1920–1: Georg Simmel. In *LOGOS 1920–21*. Tübingen: J.C.B. Mohr.

Levine, D. N. 1980: *Simmel and Parsons: Two Approaches to the Study of Society*. New York: Arno Press.

Mayntz, Renate. 1968: Simmel. In D. L. Sills (ed.), *International Encyclopedia of the Social Sciences*, vol. 14. New York: Macmillan and Free Press.

Poggi, Gianfranco. 1996: Three Aspects of Modernity in Simmel's Philosophie des Geldes: Its Epiphanic Significance, the Centrality of Money and the Prevalence of Alienation. In Richard Kilminster and Ian Varcoe (eds), *Culture, Modernity and Revolution: Essays in Honour of Zygmunt Bauman*, London: Routledge.

Sellerberg, Ann-Mari. 1994: *A Blend of Contradictions: Georg Simmel in Theory and Practice*. New Brunswick: Transaction Publishers.

Smelser, Neil J. 1997: *Problematics of Sociology: The Georg Simmel Lectures, 1995*. Berkeley: University of California Press.

Spykman, N. J. 1966 (1925): *The Social Theory of Georg Simmel*. New York: Atherton Press.

Susman, M. 1959: *Die geistige Gehalt Georg Simmels*. Tübingen: J.C.B. Mohr.

Weingartner, R. H. 1962: *Experience and Culture: The Philosophy of Georg Simmel*. Middletown, CT: Wesleyan University Press.

Wolff, Kurt H. 1974: Georg Simmel. In Kurt H. Wolff, *Trying Sociology*. New York and London: John Wiley.

chapter 8

American Pragmatism

Nils Mortensen

KEY CONCEPTS

THE GENERALIZED OTHER – represents the common norms and values in a group or society. The individual develops an idea of the generalized other by abstracting from its identification with specific roles to the role of "anybody" (Mead).

THE LOOKING-GLASS SELF – expresses the thesis that people develop a self-image by using the perceptions and judgements of others as a mirror (Cooley).

PRAGMATISM – a philosophical view founded by Peirce, James and Dewey. It implies that understanding the meaning of concepts and statements must be based on the collective relationship of actions of which they are part.

PRIMARY GROUP – Cooley's concept refers to groups characterized by intimate face-to-face contact, cooperation, and "we-feelings."

ROLE-TAKING the ability to put oneself in someone else's place and imagine how others will react to one's behavior.

Historical Context

American sociology was developed early, but names like George Herbert Mead and Charles Horton Cooley are rarely counted among the "real" classics such as Emile Durkheim (see chapter 5) or Max Weber (see chapter 6). One reason may be that American pragmatism can be seen as primarily philosophical or social-psychological rather than a sociological theory.

However, there are strong arguments for including American pragmatism in a review of classical sociological theory. It has played a decisive role in the development of the microsociological branch of sociology. Basic concepts like "primary group" and "role-taking" originated with Cooley and Mead. Moreover, sociological pragmatism was closely related to contemporary philosophical pragmatism, which sought the foundation of philosophical issues in a theory of social action. This pragmatic action theory is today considered a central contribution to sociological theory on social action.

According to Hans Joas (1993: 18ff), philosophical pragmatism challenges especially philosophies that are based on the concept of a "lonely ego" facing the world. Two examples of a "lonely ego" are utilitarianism and the epistemology of the French philosopher, René Descartes (1596–1650). Utilitarianism operates with a "lonely actor" who rationally pursues his own goals and interests. Descartes's philosophy is based on the fact, obvious to him, that we can doubt everything except the fact that we can doubt. This is translated into the famous maxim: I think, therefore I am (*cogito ergo sum*).

The keywords in the pragmatic alternative are action and collectivity. Thought and cognition are understood pragmatically, that is, as part of a collective relationship of actions. According to the philosopher, Charles Sanders Peirce (1839–1914), Descartes's doubt is self-delusion and not real doubt, because we are always entangled in prejudices. At some point we may start to doubt what we originally believed in, but that is because we find positive reasons to doubt, and not because of Descartes's maxim. Descartes's lonely cognitive ego is replaced by social interaction among people who are trying to handle the real problems they encounter during the flow of actions (Joas 1993: 19).

Peirce is today considered the sharpest and most original of the pragmatic philosophers, but the single most influential contemporary work was probably William James's *The Principles of Psychology* of 1890. This work indicates an interest in what in broad terms could be called psychological phenomena as central in pragmatism. A good example of pragmatism's analysis of psychological issues is the analysis by the philosopher John Dewey (1859–1952) of the connection between consciousness and action.

Dewey criticizes yet another example of the idea of "the lonely ego," namely behaviorism, which analyzes actions by means of the so-called reflex arc: an external stimulus followed by the individual's inner processing of this stimulus, and finally action. Dewey turns this idea upside down: The action determines which stimuli are considered important in a given context. Action should not be understood as a delimited single occurrence: Action must be seen in the light of a totality of continuous actions. Similarly, he criticizes the notion that actions are guided by single purposes. Many purposes and plans unfold simultaneously. If in a situation it proves impossible to pursue all the different impulses or limitations that are at stake in the flow of actions, selection of a dominating motive can occur (Joas 1993: 21).

Pragmatism is vulnerable to a critique that says that it is simply a new type of utilitarianism in disguise: If an idea "works," it is true. If we take this literally, it would mean, for example, that the ideas of Nazism were true because they worked. This is a misunderstanding of pragmatism. The point is, at a basic level, to look for an understanding of thought and consciousness in the collective action processes in which they are embedded. Pragmatism's ideas of "purpose" and about "what works" must be seen in the light of a broad idea of collective problem-solving that includes completely different action projects ranging from common practical tasks, or political conflicts, to philosophical reflections on what truth is.

But there are several further basic elements in pragmatism: Echoes of the philosopher G. W. F. Hegel play a central role, which is apparent in how significant the concept of consciousness or "Mind" is to Cooley and Mead. Also Charles Darwin's theory of evolution is a strong source of inspiration, not least because of his thorough comparative observations. Pragmatism sees itself as a scientific theory in a strict sense, with claims about avoiding speculative concepts and documenting statements with empirical references.

Biography: *Charles Horton Cooley*

Charles Horton Cooley (1864-1929) was born in Ann Arbor, Michigan. Initially he studied engineering, but he switched to economics and wrote a Ph.D. thesis on *The Theory of Transportation* (1894). Cooley had been attracted to sociology for some time, because it represented a break with the rampant individualism in contemporary American society. In the early 1890s he became affiliated with the University of Michigan at Ann Arbor at the same time as George H. Mead and John Dewey, and was a professor of sociology there from 1904 until his death. Cooley is described as a shy person who preferred a quiet life as a family man and university professor. However, he did accept election as president of the American Association of Sociology in 1918. Cooley's main works are *Human Nature and the Social Order* (1902), *Social Organization* (1909), and *Social Process* (1918). Elegant language was very important to Cooley. Frequent references to, for example, Shakespeare and Goethe, and a spacious and reform-oriented view of society are evidence of the humanism which permeates his work. At a time when attempts to organize the American working class were systematically repressed, Cooley thought that organization of workers and class struggles were natural aspects of the social process of organization.

Charles H. Cooley

Cooley has entered sociological history especially as the father of two concepts, *the primary group* and *the looking-glass self*. The concept of *the looking-glass self* has been displaced by Mead's far more precise elaboration of concepts about role-taking, whereas the primary group has remained a key concept in sociology. However, these two concepts play a minor role in Cooley's general holistic sociological view, which has not had any lasting influence on sociological theory, but which is an interesting, early, theoretical attempt to get away from seeing the individual and society as contradictions.

The primary group and the looking-glass self

Cooley criticizes Descartes's individually cognizing ego for being an expression of a limited, abnormal introspection by "a self-absorbed philosopher doing his best to isolate himself from other people and from all simple and natural conditions of life" (Cooley 1962: 6). First, self-consciousness belongs to a developmental phase that a child does not reach until it is 2 years old, and second, it is a mistake to see the I-aspect of the consciousness as subordinated to its we-aspect: They are equally original. Individual and society are two sides of the same coin.

What ties the two aspects together is first of all the primary group. "By primary groups I mean those characterized by intimate face-to-face association and coöperation" (Cooley 1962: 23). The main examples of primary groups are families, children's play groups, and neighbourhood groups. The primary group is primary because it is fundamental in forming the individual's social nature, but it is also the primary social or collective formation.

According to Cooley, the primary group leads to a kind of fusion of the individualities into a common entity that is best described as a *we*. There may be internal differentiation and competition in a primary group, but selfish passions "are socialized by sympathy, and come, or tend to come, under the discipline of a common spirit" (Cooley 1962: 23). However, the ability to sympathize, which the individual learns in the primary group, functions not only in face-to-face relations. It is the actual basis for more general social formations such as organizations, institutions, and democracy. In many ways, the concept of sympathy, seen as a factor of social cohesion, as central to Cooley's sociology as the concept of solidarity is to Durkheim.

Cooley uses the concept of the looking-glass self to analyze the process in which the individual is socialized. He uses the mirror as a metaphor: Others are your mirror. You are not really an individual or a self until you can see your reflection in others: Just as we see our face and body in a mirror and are satisfied or dissatisfied depending on whether the reflection lives up to our expectations, we see an opinion about our looks, intentions, actions, etc. in the imagination of someone else's consciousness. There are three components in this social mirroring process: (1) imagining that our behavior is registered by someone else; (2) imagining how the other judges us; and (3) self-esteem, such as pride or humility (Cooley 1902: 184). Cooley's study of his own children is one basis of his theories about the development of the self, and he published the results in an article about how children use the word *I*.

Cooley's organic holism

A major theme in Cooley's sociology is the idea that society is an organic, mental, and vital whole in continual development. Cooley uses the concept organic in the general sense that influences are transferred from one part to another, so that all parts are tied together in an interdependent whole. This is actually a very vague concept of an organic whole. Unlike theorists who, for example, saw money as analogous with blood cells in the blood stream, Cooley resists drawing an exact parallel between society and an organism. The organism is a metaphor. The whole can also be described as an organization, which again means reciprocal influences and causal relations between parts, and it contains contradictions in the form of a dramatic process of thrusts and counterthrusts.

To Cooley, the character of society is above all mental. Thus the first sentence in Cooley's book *Social Organization* is: "Mind is an organic whole made up of coöperating individualities, in somewhat the same way that the music of an orchestra is made up of divergent but related sounds" (Cooley 1962: 3). This mind has two phases: the social mind and the individual mind. The argument for emphasizing "mind" is that the mental character of social life is what distinguishes it from animal life. Despite this mental focus, Cooley still acknowledged phenomena such as power and economic interests, which he proves in his straightforward and comprehensive analysis of classes, poverty, and social disorganization in *Social Organization*.

Cooley talks about the whole being under continual development. A vital impulse of unknown origin seems to be present, working ahead in numerous directions and variations. There seems to be some kind of adaptive growth taking place, which means that in the different social forms of life we see – for example, institutions, conventions, theories, ideals – the growth of each takes place in contact and interaction with the growth of the others (Cooley 1918: 8). Development is seen as tentative processes in which social institutions or phenomena are subjected to a pragmatic test resulting in the selection of certain institutions and phenomena.

The organic holistic view permeates Cooley's work. One question that comes to mind is that if Cooley is right, then why is it so common to see the individual as the point of departure? Cooley's answer is the "naive individualism of the thought," according to which individuals are easier to recognize, while society is more diffuse. Therefore individuals seem to come before society.

Biography: *George Herbert Mead*

George Herbert Mead was born in 1863 in South Hadley, Massachusetts, as a preacher's son. He first studied at Oberlin College, Ohio, a liberal institution and the first American college where women could get a bachelor's degree. He worked for a couple of years as a schoolteacher and in railway construction. From 1887 to 1888, he studied psychology and philosophy at Harvard University where he especially followed the Hegel-inspired theologian Josiah Royce. He worked simultaneously as a private tutor to the children of the philosopher William James. Mead spent the years 1888 to 1891 in Germany - first a year in Leipzig and then two years in Berlin, where he became interested in the psychologist Wilhelm Wundt's attempts to build psychology on a physiological basis. He was also influenced by Darwin's theory of evolution and cogent comparative scientific methods. However, Mead never got an academic degree.

Back in the USA, he was offered a position as a psychology and philosophy teacher at the University of Michigan at Ann Arbor. Here he became a close friend of the philosopher John Dewey, and when Dewey was offered a position as a professor of philosophy at University of Chicago, Mead went with him to be his assistant. He stayed at the University of Chicago, and at the time of his death he was head of the department of philosophy.

Mead was a popular and influential lecturer. He covered a wide field of philosophy and the history of ideas, but he also discussed other topics, for example, Einstein's theory of relativity, and tried to incorporate them in his own thinking. Mead participated actively in social reform movements in Chicago. He published many articles, but did not write books. After his death in 1931, four books based on students' notes from his lectures were published. One of these books, *Mind, Self, and Society* (1934), places itself unconditionally as one of the classics in sociology.

George H. Mead

Communication

A good place to start a review of Mead's sociology is his critique of two positions he rejected. After Cooley's death, Mead published an article about Cooley's significance, in which he criticized Cooley for using mind or consciousness as a basic concept (Mead 1930). The first point of criticism was, in simple terms, that Cooley saw communication as originating in the consciousness. Mead argued that it is the other way around, that consciousness develops gradually as a result of communication, and especially through language. The other point of Mead's criticism was radical behaviorism, represented by the psychologist, John B. Watson, a former student of Mead's. Watson's argument was that consciousness is an inner, unobservable, psychological phenomenon and that consequently scientific psychology must be based solely on the observable behavior of individuals. Mead argues, however, that phenomena such as the individual's meaning or motivation must be included in the study of actions.

By some kind of introspection, Cooley wanted to understand the other's mind. Watson wanted to dismiss altogether a study of inner states of consciousness. Mead chooses a third way. He argues for a *social behaviorism* concentrating on communication between people. Social behaviorism

> is able to deal with the field of communication in a way which neither Watson nor the introspectionists can do. We want to approach language not from the standpoint of inner meanings to be expressed, but in its larger context of co-operation in the group taking place by means of signals and gestures. Meaning appears within that process. Our behaviorism is a social behaviorism. (Mead 1934: 6)

The interchange of various gestures, ranging from body language to complicated linguistic utterances, plays a major role in Mead's theory. A gesture is any sound or movement an individual uses to stimulate action in another individual. It is fundamental that social action consists of two or more parties influencing each other through gestures. Interchange of gesture and response could be a dog showing its teeth followed by another dog growling, or someone asking to borrow a match and receiving one. Both examples include gesture, but the first example is what Mead calls a *nonsignificant gesture* and the second one is a *significant symbol*.

Nonsignificant gestures are part of communication between two organisms, but it is communication without reflection, consisting of biologically based responses. In contrast, a significant symbol is addressed to the self and to another at the same time. Significant symbols thus depend on a common interpretation of meaning.

Role-taking and the generalized other

According to Mead, human communication implies a basic ability to "be another to one-self": Addressing someone requires an ability to put oneself in the other's place. Mead calls this mechanism *role-taking*, and by this he means more than just learning the role of mother, police officer, waitress, etc. Role-taking implies a fundamental ability to mentally project how others will react to one's actions.

Individuals in face-to-face interaction can take the specific other's role. In larger groups, the individual must imagine the group's general reaction, and this is what Mead calls taking *the generalized other's role*, that is, imagining the reactions of a group, community, or society. In the early phases of socialization, role-taking occurs in specific role-plays in which the child learns the basics of being someone else for itself. Here Mead distinguishes between play and game. A child can play alone, but a game requires team-work. In the game, the role-taking process is developed, because one must be ready to take on the role of any other player. Later on, the individual acquires the ability to take on the role of the generalized other, which corresponds to the common norms and values of society.

Being a self implies that the individual is neither merely an object that is pushed around by nature nor a totally free subject. Before an individual can become a subject for its own actions, it must first become an object for itself. Mead calls this objective side of the self the *me*.

> And it is due to the individual's ability to take the attitudes of these others in so far as they can be organized that he gets self-consciousness. The taking of all those organized sets of attitudes gives him his "me"; that is the self he is aware of. (Mead 1934: 175)

The "me" is the known, conscious, and reflected aspect of the self-process. The "me" is the person's perception of who he or she is, and it contains experiences from various roles, situations, other individuals, and social values. But even though the "me" is a product of society, it has an individual aspect. Each person represents the generalized other in its own unique style. Mead uses the concept "I" about the creative and imaginative side of the self that can suggest new reactions and create surprises. It comes out spontaneously and offers suggestions that allow the individual to adapt its behavior to new circumstances, conflicts, and disturbances in its interaction with others.

Mead operates with a notion that societal evolution tends toward a growing differentiation; however, the generalized other develops simultaneously. His theory about the development of the generalized other is somewhat vague, but certain elements may provide an answer. First of all, the concept of emergence plays an important role in Mead's thinking. He sees it as a fundamental trait of development, and not only social development. "Emergence involves a reorganization, but the reorganization brings in something that was not there before" (Mead 1934: 198). For example, consciousness and identity (the self) can be seen as emerging from social communication processes, and to continue this line of thought, new structures could emerge in the evolution of the generalized other. In this connection, Mead mentions somewhere an ideal community of communication. He says that there is established *a universe of discourse which transcends the specific order* within which the members of the community, in a specific conflict, place themselves outside of the community order as it exists . . . it is *a social order that includes any rational being who is or may be in any way implicated in the situation with which thought deals*. (Mead according to Habermas 1981, vol. 2: 144–5)

This imagined community of communication may be a new, emerging quality that gradually develops in the generalized other. Moreover, he does not see the fact that modern man takes on many different roles as a sign of superficiality and disintegration, but rather as a sign of a more differentiated ability for role-taking.

Action

Whereas the primary core of Weber's concept of action was the individual's actions in which others were then somehow implicated, the centre of Mead's concept of action is the intersubjective. In fact, he substitutes a concept of interaction for a concept of action. To Mead, social action implies two or more persons, not just the actions of one individual. Social action implies a continuous, reciprocal role-taking process, it is flexible and adapts to the demands of changing situations. Social interaction is also dependent on other parties besides those directly involved. The participants share a common perspective because they are able to take on the role of the generalized other. This broadens the context of social interaction. In other words, we do not only consider that special other we are involved with; we also see our actions in the light of the generalized other, that is, according to what we think the general expectations, norms, and values are in an imagined collectivity.

Social action can furthermore be seen as containing two action relationships. On one hand it is a fragment of a broad social process. Teamwork situations at work are an example of a broad organization process. On the other hand, an action is an episode in the lives of the involved individuals.

Mead sees thought and reflection as a mediating function between a social stimulus and a behavioral reaction. However, as he respects the view that human behavior is a form of higher-level animal behavior, he says that thought must primarily be seen as behavior that is provoked by the interruption of an action process. In other words, thought originates from action and not the other way around. People pause and reflect about the meaning of stimuli, and this delay gives them time to take on another's role, to formulate possible actions and evaluate them in relation to other responses and the relevance for goal attainment.

Thoughts start with reference to objects that have obstructed or impeded one's behavior, and they end with an action plan for handling and manipulating objects. An object can be a physical thing, an individual, a social role, an idea, or oneself. Consciousness is understood as an inner discourse, a prevocal linguistic communication. Consciousness and thought contain a paradox: it is a completely private experience and yet thought is communicated through language. According to Mead, language consists primarily of so-called significant symbols, that is, symbols with a common meaning, which therefore represent the generalized other's standpoint. The meaning of objects should not be seen as metaphysical or as references to underlying essences. It varies according to prior knowledge and current purpose and is formed in the common, practical interaction of individuals:

> Meaning is thus not to be conceived, fundamentally, as a state of consciousness, or as a set of organized relations existing or subsisting mentally outside the field of experience into which they enter; on the contrary, it should be conceived objectively, as having its existence entirely within this field itself. (Mead 1934: 78)

The Significance of Sociological Pragmatism

Hans Joas, probably the modern sociologist who has the deepest knowledge of American pragmatism, credits Cooley with the first attempt to develop pragmatism in a sociological direction and a pragmatic theory of the self. However, Joas also criticizes Cooley: his theory of the self is not sufficiently unfolded, he is generally theoretically inconsistent, and he overemphasizes emotional aspects (Joas 1993). Others share this criticism (Angell 1968; Asplund 1967a).

Cooley is trapped by his language. He uses many suggestive metaphors, for example, comparing society to a football team, but the effect is often accomplished at the expense of convincing, well-developed concepts. The basic concepts of organization, social whole, and "mind" overlap, and they are all expressions of a vague idea that everything is connected to everything else.

There are no sharp edges in Cooley's sociology – as shown in the lack of precise concepts, and in his optimistic – and perhaps naive – belief in sympathy as a fundamental part of human social nature. Cooley's concept of sympathy is, however, rather complex. The immediate association to the word "sympathy" is kindness, but in Cooley's terminology it often means the ability to feel empathy and to put oneself in someone else's place (Angell 1968). One way to develop Cooley's sociology could therefore be to see "the ability to put oneself in someone else's place" as the central category. First of all, this is the basic mechanism of socialization through which the self is formed. Second, "putting oneself in someone else's place" is the basis of Cooley's perception of public opinion and democracy. Instead of emphasizing consensus, he emphasizes a more basic – so to speak methodological – readiness to accept that adversaries are entitled to their own points of view.

A typical point of criticism against Mead's theories is that they underemphasize the macro aspects of society. His macro aspects are significantly less detailed and less precise than his micro aspects (Baldwin 1986: 152). Mead does not have the structural macro concepts of Marx, Durkheim, or Weber, but then again, he is not trying to develop what we understand by sociological theory. He is primarily a philosopher and should be judged by the sociological fruitfulness of his theory of action. In this respect Mead is original, because he does not start from "individual" or "society," but from linguistic communication, which is a far more precise point of departure than Cooley's concepts of primary group and sympathy.

As a theorist, Mead is more convincing than Cooley, but their work shares a basic optimism. Mead's central theory of communication as a continual process of role-taking may be seen as underestimating conflicts. We all know countless examples of social situations that do not work out because the participants are unable to "take on the other's role." But first of all, Mead's communication theory is not a descriptive theory about communication, but a theory about what constitutes social actions, and that actions, to the extent they are social, must imply role-taking. Second, "the generalized other" comprises a multitude of symbolizations of successful as well as unsuccessful communication.

As a lecturer, Mead had a great influence on the so-called Chicago School, which counts William I. Thomas and Robert E. Park among its most prominent figures (Joas 1993: 26–43). It is difficult to find a common denominator for the works of the Chicago School, but one characteristic trait seems to be thorough empirical studies, motivated by the desire to find possible social reforms in the dramatic social turmoil of the city. In fact, Max Weber witnessed the upheaval in Chicago. During a visit in 1904, he described the city "like a man whose skin has been peeled off and whose entrails one sees at work" (Weber according to Schwartz 1989: 53).

An explicitly sociological theory based on pragmatism, the so-called symbolic interactionism, was later developed by Herbert Blumer (see chapter 12), but for a long time, pragmatism had no influence on the dominating theoretical development in sociology. Thus, Talcott Parsons's (1937: chapter 14) theory building did not include pragmatists among the classical sociologists, and according to Robert Nisbet's *The Sociological Tradition* (1966), establishing the basic themes of sociology was a purely European matter. However, social psychology has for a long time considered Mead a central theorist.

Recently, Mead's role in sociological theory has been emphasized, primarily because of the Germans Hans Joas and Jürgen Habermas (see chapter 21). Due to Joas's work (Joas 1980), Mead's theory about intersubjective communication became a significant element in Habermas's theory about communicative action (Habermas 1981).

Bibliography

Primary:

Cooley, Charles H. 1902: *Human Nature and the Social Order*. New York: Charles Scribner.
—— 1918: *Social Process*. New York: Charles Scribner.
—— 1962 [1909]: *Social Organization*. New York: Schocken Books.
—— 1969: *Sociological Theory and Social Research*. New York: A. M. Kelley
—— 1998: *On Self and Social Organization*, ed. Hans-Joachim Schubert. Chicago: University of Chicago Press.
Mead, George H. 1930: Cooley's Contribution to American Social Thought. *American Journal of Sociology*, 35, 693–706.
—— 1932: *The Philosophy of the Present*. Chicago: University of Chicago Press.
—— 1934: *Mind, Self, and Society*. Chicago: University of Chicago Press.
—— 1936: *Movements of Thought in the Nineteenth Century*. Chicago: University of Chicago Press.
—— 1938: *The Philosophy of the Act*. Chicago: University of Chicago Press.
—— 1977: *On Social Psychology: Selected Papers*. Chicago: University of Chicago Press.
—— 1982: *The Individual and the Social Self*. London: University of Chicago Press.

Secondary:

Aboulafia, Mitchell. 1991: *Philosophy, Social Theory, and the Thought of George Herbert Mead*. Albany: State University of New York.
Angell, Robert C. 1968. Charles H. Cooley. In David L. Sills (ed.), *International Encyclopedia of the Social Sciences*, vol. 3. New York: Macmillan and Free Press.
Asplund, Johan. 1967a. Charles H. Cooley. In Johan Asplund (ed.), *Sociologiska teorier*. Stockholm:

Almqvist & Wiksell.

Baldwin, John D. 1986: *George Herbert Mead: A Unifying Theory for Sociology.* Newbury Park: Sage.

Cohen, Marshall J. 1982: *Charles Hoorton Cooley and the Social Self in American Thought.* New York: Garland.

Cook, Gary A. 1993: *George Herbert Mead: The Making of a Social Pragmatist.* Urbana: University of Illinois Press.

Conk, G. 1987: *The Philosophical Anthropology of George Herbert Mead.* New York: P. Lang.

Habermas, Jürgen. 1981: *Theorie des kommunikativen Handelns.* Frankfurt am Main: Suhrkamp.

Hamilton, Peter. 1992: *George Herbert Mead: Critical Assesments.* London: Routledge.

James, William. 1962 [1890]: *The Principles of Psychology.* 2 vols. New York: Smith.

Jandy, Edward Clarence. 1969: *Charles Horton Cooley, His Life and Social Theory.* New York: Octagon Books.

Joas, Hans. 1980: *Praktische Intersubjektivität. Die Entwicklung des Werks von G. H. Mead.* Frankfurt am Main: Suhrkamp.

—— 1993: *Pragmatism and Social Theory.* Chicago: University of Chicago Press.

—— 1997: *G. H. Mead: A Contemporary Re-Examination of His Thought.* Cambridge, MA: MIT Press.

Lewis, David, and Smith, Richard L. 1980: *American Sociology and Pragmatism: Mead, Chicago Sociology, and Symbolic Interaction.* Chicago: University of Chicago Press.

Nisbet, Robert A. 1970 [1966]: *The Sociological Tradition.* London: Heinemann.

Miller, David L. 1980: *George Herbert Mead: Self, Language, and the World.* Chicago: University of Chicago Press.

Parsons, Talcott. 1937: *The Structure of Social Action.* 2 vols. New York: Free Press.

Reiss, Albert J. Jr. (ed.) 1968: *Cooley and Social Analysis.* Ann Arbor: University of Michigan Press.

Rosenthal, Sandra B., Hausman, Carl R., and Anderson, Douglas R. 1999: *Classical American Pragmatism: Its Contemporary Vitality.* Urbana: University of Illinois Press.

Schwartz, Jonathan M. 1989: Towards a History of the Melting Pot, or Why there is a Chicago School of Sociology but not a Detroit School. In Jonathan M. Schwartz, *In Defense of Homesickness,* Copenhagen: Akademisk Forlag.

Stuhr, John J. 1999: *Pragmatism and Classical American Philosophy: Essential Readings and Interpretive Essays.* New York: Oxford University Press.

White, Morton. 1973: *Pragmatism and the American Mind: Essays and Reviews in Philosophy and Intellectual History.* New York: Oxford University Press.

Winterer, Caroline. 1994: A Happy Medium: The Sociology of Charles Horton Cooley. *Journal of the Behavioral Sciences,* 30/1, 19–27.

Wundt, Wilhelm. 1973: *The Language of Gestures.* The Hague: Mouton.

chapter 9

Marxism

Per Månson

Marxism During the 1900s: A Survey

Marxism was one of the most important currents of thought in the twentieth century. Its significance has been primarily political and ideological, but in recent decades it has also been incorporated into modern social science. Before the fall of communism in Eastern Europe in 1989–91, one-third of the earth's people lived in countries in which the regimes considered themselves Marxist, and in many other countries there were parties and groups that based their politics and worldview on some form of Marxism.

Marxism entered the universities after the student revolt of 1968 and many students and teachers saw it as an alternative to "bourgeois" social science, which was predominant. In the subsequent years, Marxism was developed and came to be used in both theory development and empirical research. After playing an important and distinctive role during those years, Marxist-oriented theories are now part of a general education in the social sciences.

Marxism has been far from unified during the twentieth century. In political Marxism there are various directions, such as Leninism, Luxemburgism, Stalinism, Trotskyism, Maoism, etc. They have frequently waged a bitter political and ideological struggle not only against their "main enemy," capital, but also against one another. In academic Marxism, much of the development has involved combining Marxism with other views, and structuralist, historical, phenomenological, and Hegelian Marxism have been developed.

During the decades around the turn of the century, Marxism was gathered into the Social Democratic Second International. The Marxism predominant at that time was called *orthodox Marxism*. Around 1900 there arose some challengers to the domination of this type of Marxism, linked to names such as Eduard Bernstein (1850–1932), V. I. Lenin (1870–1924), and Rosa Luxemburg (1871–1919). One of these challengers, *Bolshevism*, came to power in Russia in 1917 and another challenger, Bernstein's so-called *revisionism*, took governmental power in the German Revolution of 1918.

After 1920 the international labour movement was divided into communism and social democracy. While communism was based on a new state ideology called *Marxism-Leninism*, social democracy began to lose interest in Marxism. For a long time Marxism was identical to Marxism-Leninism in the eyes of many, and it was not until 1968 that a different Marxism gained broader support.

In the early 1920s several currents appeared that were outside both Russian Marxism-Leninism and Western social democracy. One of these appeared in Austria and is called *Austro-Marxism*. It is mainly politically oriented, but it had some theoretical innovations as well. At the same time, several theoreticians appeared on the scene who, although they differed in many ways, came to develop a Marxism that was called *Western Marxism*. It was mainly theoretical, lacked contact with the organized labor movement, and found its first institutional base in the Frankfurt School (see chapter 10). During the following decades a number of philosophically and social-science-oriented Marxists appeared, in part because several previously unknown works by Marx were published during the 1930s and 1940s (see chapter 2).

Parallel with this, there developed primarily in China, but later in other nonindustrialized nations as well, a Marxism for developing nations that attempted to find a revolutionary strategy for countries where the people were primarily peasants subjected to colonial and imperialist forces. Its foremost representative was the Chinese leader Mao Zedong (1893–1976) and consequently the body of this Marxism is called *Maoism*. Like *Trotskyism* (after Leon Trotsky, 1879–1940), *Stalinism* (after Joseph Stalin, 1879–1953), and *Luxemburgism*, Maoism experienced a certain upswing in connection with the student revolt and the appearance of revolutionary leftist groups in the Western world. During the 1980s these different tendencies declined in importance and today they are found mainly in various guerrilla movements in developing countries.

Orthodox Marxism

When Karl Marx (see chapter 2) died in 1883, there was no generally accepted Marxism. One version was created, however, during the 1880s, primarily by Karl Kautsky (1854–1938) and Eduard Bernstein who, in the first Marxist theoretical journal *Die Neue Zeit* (1883–1917), presented the theories of Marx as a unified proletarian worldview. Also of great importance was Marx's longtime friend and comrade in arms Friedrich Engels who, until his death, served as the primary authority within orthodox Marxism. When the German Social Democratic Party adopted Marxism as its official ideology at its congress in Erfurt in 1891, it was a breakthrough for this theoretician, and until the collapse of the Second International when war broke out in 1914, Marxism was the incontrovertible ideology of the international social democratic labor movement.

In Russia too a kind of Marxism developed at an early stage. Marx's *Capital* had been published there in 1872 and, after the previously dominant revolutionary populism (which directed its agitation toward the peasants) had suffered several defeats during the 1870s, the "Father of Russian Marxism" Grigory V. Plechanov (1856–1918) developed his theories from a Marxist perspective. Plechanov chose to direct his agitation toward the growing class of industrial workers, and he tried to show that capitalism was making a breakthrough in Russia. The populists believed Russia could jump over the "capitalist stage" and go directly from feudalism to socialism because, since time immemorial, the peasants had had a village structure with collective ownership and decision-making. Initially the Russian Marxists worked alongside the Liberals and both maintained that capitalism was the strongest force in the country. Their ways soon parted when the Marxists became more and more radical.

The Marxism that was developed by Kautsky, Bernstein, Plechanov, and others viewed Marx's theories as a whole. The philosophical foundation, *dialectical materialism*, was based on Engels's influential book, *Anti-Düring* (1878, English translation 1966) and his *dialectic of nature*. The dialectic of nature states that reality ultimately consists of material and that progress is driven by contradictions. The "three laws of dialectics," the "unity and conflict of opposites," the "transition of quantity into quality," and the triad thesis–antithesis–synthesis, were seen as laws of nature, history, and human thought.

Orthodox Marxism also had a theory of history, *historical materialism*, where the interplay between productive forces and the relations of production (see chapter 2) were seen as crucial to the structure of a society and to historical development. It also had a *theory of capitalist development* that was based on Marx's theory of capital, and finally a *theory of revolution* which also generated a policy based on *class struggle* in capitalist society. In orthodox Marxism it was assumed that Marx had demonstrated that capitalism would, of natural necessity, be replaced by socialism, due to historical and economic laws.

Bernstein's revisionism

In Germany around the turn of the century, Bernstein maintained that social democracy had to reject some parts of Marxist theory, particularly the entire theory of class struggle and the theory of unavoidable revolution. Instead, social democracy should openly show itself to be what it was in actual practice, a party that was oriented toward parliamentary elections and social reform. Socialism was more a matter of improving the living conditions of the broad masses rather then taking power through revolution, which was summarized in Bernstein's famous statement, "The ultimate goal of socialism is unimportant, the movement toward it is everything" (*Die Neue Zeit*, vol. 16:1, 1897: 556). Thus, Bernstein's revision of Marxism can be seen as the origin of modern social democracy.

Luxemburg's "spontaneism"

Bernstein's revisionism was criticized both by Kautsky and by the leftist leader Rosa Luxemburg. Luxemburg, who was also an economic and theoretical Marxist and published *The Accumulation of Capital* in 1913, saw the revolutionary potential of developing the spontaneous class-consciousness of the proletariat and, consequently, she advocated the general strike as a political method. She soon came into conflict with the party leadership for her criticism of the party's bureaucratization, formed her own party during the war, and was murdered during the January revolt of 1919 after the Social Democrats formed a government.

Marxism–Leninism

Bernstein was also criticized in Russia, as well as domestic "revisionism," which Lenin called "economism." The economists wanted to leave the political struggle to the liberals, since the coming anti-czarist revolution was a bourgeois one. In addition, a conflict broke out within Russian social democracy over what the nature of the party should be. One wing wanted to create a broad labor party similar to the German one, while another wing wanted to create an underground party of professional revolutionaries. At a congress in 1903 the party split into Mensheviks (the minority) and Bolsheviks (the majority). Lenin, who was the leader of the Bolsheviks, led a relentless struggle against his political opponents and, in practice, there were two parties after 1912. During the Russian Revolution of 1917 the Mensheviks cooperated with the Social Revolutionaries (populists) and with the bourgeois left, but after the Bolsheviks assumed power all other parties were banned.

After Lenin's death in 1924 a struggle for leadership broke out and there was an extensive discussion over which direction the new Soviet state should take. Joseph Stalin became the sole leader in the late 1920s. Under his leadership there was a fierce collectivization of agriculture and intensive industrialization with an emphasis on heavy industry. There were also a number of purges within the party and a new doctrine, Marxism–Leninism, was developed. This doctrine was based on the writings of Marx, Engels, and Lenin, but since Stalin was the highest authority in the field it was primarily his ideas that dominated. After a philosophical struggle on whether natural science should be founded on Marxism, Stalin declared that all knowledge must be subjugated to the leading role of the party. Not just philosophy and science, but also art, literature, music, architecture, and the new film art were to be used to build the "socialist society," and other ideas were banned and castigated.

Marxism–Leninism as molded by Stalin became a dogmatic, catechistic doctrine based on the dialectical and historical materialism of orthodox Marxism, combined with Lenin's uncompromising battle against those who deviated in politics or thought. Since practically all the leaders in the Bolsheviks' old guard were sentenced to death in various trials, Stalin came to stand for the highest guarantee of Marxism until his death. The Third Communist International, which was created in 1919 and abolished in 1943, subjugated all the communist parties of the world to Moscow. Although Marxist–Leninist ideology underwent certain changes before the fall of the Soviet Union, it retained its fundamental dogmatic characteristic.

The Rise of Western Marxism

After the defeat of revolutions in Germany, Hungary, and Italy the revolutionary socialists found themselves in a difficult situation. The new regime in Russia was moving more and more clearly toward dictatorship and Western social democracy had actively helped to put down the revolts. In this situation, several radical Marxists undertook a thorough reevaluation of the entire socialist tradition, which gave rise to Western Marxism.

The Hungarian György (Georg) Lukács (1885–1971), the German Karl Korsch (1886–1961), and the Italian Antonio Gramsci (1891–1937) were all revolutionary socialists who had participated in the revolts in their respective countries. Lukács was an art and literature critic who was converted to communism in 1918 and a year later was appointed education minister in the short-lived council government of Béla Kuns in Budapest. After its fall, Lukács fled to Moscow in 1929 where he remained until 1945, when he returned to Hungary. In 1956 he joined the Hungarian revolt without abandoning his Marxist convictions and he later founded a special Budapest School of Marxism.

Korsch, who studied philosophy in London, joined the leftist German party USPD during the war and then actively participated in the workers' and soldiers' council movement during the German revolution. He later joined the German Communist Party, KPD, and in 1923 was appointed justice minister in the coalition government between the Social Democrats and Communists in the state of Thuringia. In 1933 Korsch was forced by Hitler's government to flee the country and he did not return to Germany until 1956. Seriously ill, he went back to the United States, where he died.

Gramsci was born in a poor family in Sardinia and while studying history and linguistics at the University of Turin he came into contact with socialism. After joining the Italian Socialist Party in 1913 he wrote for the party's paper *Avanti* and later participated in the revolutionary factory council movement in Turin in 1919–20. In 1921 he was one of the founders of the Italian Communist Party, the PCI, and he became its leader in 1926. That same year Gramsci was arrested by Mussolini's regime and sentenced to 20 years in prison. He was released in 1937 while critically ill and died shortly thereafter.

György (Georg) Lukács

In *History and Class Consciousness*, published in 1923, Lukács criticized the theory of the dialectic of nature and maintained that dialectics applied only to the human world. Based on Marx's analysis of commodity fetishism in *Capital*, Lukács states that bourgeois society and bourgeois science see only isolated portions of social reality, but not how these parts go together. The specialization of labor and the atomization of modern society have concealed society in its totality. People have become objects that are controlled by objective laws that they can do nothing about. Lukács calls this reification or "objectification," which means that man's humanity has disappeared.

According to Lukács, the proletariat is the only class that can grasp society as a totality. Even though under capitalism the working class is seen and treated as an object, the class can develop a consciousness of itself as subject in the historical process of change. What had been missing in the Western European revolutions and what made them fail was precisely this developed class consciousness among the proletariat. Even if the individual worker does not possess this class consciousness and sees himself as both subject and object, the class *per se* can possess this consciousness in the form of a party. Lukács saw Lenin's Bolsheviks as such a party and it was for this reason that he supported Russian communism despite its dictatorship and dogmatism.

When *History and Class Consciousness* was published it was subjected to harsh criticism by the communists and the book was censured by the Third International in 1924. Lukács himself repudiated the book and returned to literary criticism and esthetic theory during his exile in the Soviet Union. Much later he returned to fundamental problems in his work on ontology, where he analyzed and discussed the views of Hegel, Marx, and others.

Lukács's major significance is found in the fact that he stressed the importance to Marxism of Hegel's subject–object dialectic. He was the first to call attention to the problem of alienation which he reconstructed from the brief pages in *Capital* dealing with commodity fetishism, and he incorporated non-Marxist views into his Marxism, primarily Weber's theory of rationality (see chapter 6). There is also a direct line between Lukács and the Frankfurt School (see chapter 10), which continued to develop the importance of Hegel to Marx.

Karl Korsch

In his 1923 book *Marxism and Philosophy* Karl Korsch also criticized orthodox Marxism and its dialectical materialism. In this book Korsch tried to use Marxism to analyze its own development which, according to him, had occurred in three stages. During the first stage, 1843–8, which was a revolutionary period, Marx had developed the revolutionary dialectic in which the concept of practice played an important role. The second stage began with the crushing of the June revolt in France in 1848 and continued until the turn of the century. During this phase, which included a capitalist upswing and the crushing of the dreams of liberation of the previous phase, Marxism was developed – by Marx and Engels, among others – into a positivist science that under the Second International became a dogmatic and scholastic theory devoid of contact with revolutionary practice.

Korsch believed that "scientific socialism" had been reduced to a scientific theory on the laws of motion of society and that Marxism had been separated from revolutionary practice: "Thus the materialistic conception of history, which in Marx and Engels was essentially a dialectical one, eventually become something quite undialectical in their epogones" and reduced to a "kind of heuristic principle of specialized theoretical investigation" or a "number of theoretical formulations about the causal interconnection of historical phenomena in different areas of society" (Korsch 1970: 62).

The third phase began in the early 1900s when socialist revolution was again on the agenda and this phase was represented by Luxemburg and Lenin. According to Korsch, Marxism once again became revolutionary because the practical issue of the dictatorship of the proletariat was once more on the agenda after a long phase of reformism. This Marxism was expressed by the Third International, but it had become just as dogmatic as the Marxism of the Second International on what Korsch believed to be the main question, the relationship between Marxism and philosophy. In his philosophical work Lenin had built on dialectical materialism but, according to Korsch, he had never analyzed the basic problem itself, which the philosophy of Marxism was actually based upon. Like the theoreticians of the Second International, Lenin had adopted the naive materialism that Engels had expressed in *Anti-Düring*, while the revolutionary materialistic dialectic that Marx had developed during the first phase of Marxism, and which was expressed in the "Theses on Feuerbach" (which was the only one of the philosophical writings of Marx's youth that had been published at the time) had not been incorporated into the Third International. Korsch himself maintained that Marxism as a theoretical system must always be in intimate contact with practical revolutionary activity and that this was the true meaning of materialistic dialectics.

Like Lukács, Korsch was subjected to harsh criticism by both social democrats and communists. The social democrats condemned the book as "communist heresy" and the communists condemned it as "revisionist heresy" (Korsch 1970: 100). In his book Korsch stated that he agreed in principle with Lukács in his criticism of both the Second and Third International's Marxism. Here we see what was perhaps the most important element in the tradition of Western Marxism as presented by these works, namely the attempt to find a "genuine" Marxism outside the scholastic and dogmatic Marxism that had developed in the organized labor movement and later under the communism of Marxism–Leninism.

Antonio Gramsci

Gramsci also criticized the Marxism of the Second International for its dogmatic belief in a mechanical development and he based his view on the more Hegel-inspired dialectics of early Marx. One difference between Lukács and Korsch, on one hand, and Gramsci on the other is that the former two left active politics after participating in revolts in their own countries, while Gramsci founded and became the leader of his country's communist party. As an active politician he was more interested in questions of political strategy, although his long prison sentence prevented him from developing this further.

His experiences of the factory council movement in Turin in 1919–20 led Gramsci to lean toward council communism in which the workers' own mass organizations are seen as the foundation of both the struggle against the bourgeois state and the new socialist society. Gramsci praised the Soviets in the Russian Revolution, but after the defeat in Italy he stressed the importance of a unified revolutionary party. The newly founded PCI joined the Comintern, and Gramsci stated that the party consists of three levels: the *captains* who guide it and develop political strategy and the *corporals* who relate the leadership's orders to the *soldiers*, who lack creativity and organizational skills. In this respect he was close to Lenin, but Gramsci always emphasized what he called an "organic centralism" (in contrast to the "democratic socialism" of the Bolsheviks), which meant that there must always be a dialectic between the leaders and those who are led.

Gramsci's great significance as one of the originators of Western Marxism is found primarily in the notebooks he wrote during his long prison term. Although the prosecutor said at his trial that "We must prevent this brain from operating for 20 years," Gramsci managed to write 33 notebooks while in prison, around 2,500 printed pages (Joll 1979: 70). Because of the censorship in prison, he could not say directly what he thought in his notebooks, but was forced to use code words. He called Marxism the "philosophy of practice," Lenin was "Il'ich," and Trotsky was "Bronstein." The expression the "philosophy of practice" was well chosen, since Gramsci totally rejects the positivistic and evolutionistic view of Marxism that dominated the Second International.

For Gramsci, historical materialism was primarily *historical* materialism. He thought it was wrong to mix Marx's materialistic view of history with Engels's dialectic of nature and he was particularly opposed to the "vulgar materialism" of Plechanov. Influenced by the Italian idealistic philosopher of history, Benedetto Croce (1866–1952), Gramsci often stressed the subjective side of the problem in his analyses and he was more interested in the role of ideology and politics than the importance of the economy in the development of society and revolutionary strategy. Consequently, Gramsci has been called the "superstructure theoretician" of Marxism.

Gramsci analyzed, in particular, the role of the intellectual in society and in revolutionary strategy. In one sense, of course, every person is an intellectual, but according to Gramsci not all people have a social role as an intellectual. Gramsci distinguishes between "traditional" and "organic" intellectuals, where the former belong to traditional groups such as writers, artists, philosophers, and, especially in Italy, spokesmen for the Church. This type of intellectual believes he is independent of the rest of society. Organic intellectuals, on the other hand, are part of an organic link to the class whose collective consciousness they express. This does not mean that there is a direct link, for example, between the workers and the intellectuals who express the interests and worldview of the workers. The intellectuals belong to the "superstructure," and it is here that they find their main task.

Gramsci used the distinction between traditional and organic intellectuals in historical analyses of France, England, and the United States, but also in discussions on the role of the intellectual in the struggle for socialism. According to Gramsci, there was a dialectical relationship between socialist intellectuals and the working class: the intellectuals obtained their material from the experiences of the working class and, in return, they gave this class an overall theoretical consciousness. Within the communist party are organized the "collective intellectuals" and Gramsci calls this party (with reference to the Italian thinker Niccoló Machiavelli [1469–1527]) the "modern prince." According to Gramsci, the most important role of the intellectual is to develop an ideology that is capable of challenging the dominant bourgeois ideology and to help the working class gain hegemony.

Hegemony and civil society

The term "hegemony" is probably Gramsci's best-known contribution to Marxism. In the Marxism of that time, it usually referred to the *political* supremacy of the working class over other classes, but Gramsci used it primarily as an *ideological* concept. The task of the working class's intellectuals was to try and develop an ideology that could be presented as valid for the entire society. It was this that bourgeois society had managed to do and, consequently, in most cases, the capitalist state did not need to use violence to maintain the rule of capital. The struggle for ideological hegemony is carried out primarily in civil society, a term Gramsci used to describe a cultural sphere between the economic and political spheres of society.

Because of his long prison sentence, it was difficult for Gramsci to follow developments within the world communist movement and, unlike Lukács and Korsch, he avoided public condemnation for his views. When the so-called Eurocommunism appeared during the 1960s, Gramsci was one of its most important ideologists, particularly due to his concept of the "historical bloc" which came to be used in the Italian Communist Party to legitimize its cooperation with the dominant Christian Democratic Party. Thus, Gramsci's political importance during the twentieth century is much greater than that of Lukács and Korsch. On the theoretical level, however, all three contributed to the development of Western Marxism.

Praxis Marxism

During the 1950s and 1960s a current appeared in several Eastern European states that was given the name Praxis Marxism. The term comes in part from Marx's concept of practice and in part from a journal of that name that came out in Yugoslavia in 1964. After Marx's *Economic and Philosophical Manuscripts* were published in 1932, it became possible for many philosophers and social thinkers to challenge the Soviet version of Marxism and to find support for this challenge in the writings of Marx. This was seen first in France where Jean-Paul Sartre, among others, developed a phenomenologically based Marxism in which Marx's more humanistic views in his early works played an important role (see chapter 17).

The background to the origin of this Praxis Marxism was the conflict between Stalin and the Yugoslav communist leader, Tito (1892–1980) and the expulsion of Yugoslavia from the Comintern in 1948. During the 1950s a group of philosophers developed a "Yugoslavian Marxism" that stood in opposition to Soviet Marxism–Leninism. The idea of the workers' councils and self-rule played an important role in this Marxism of practice, which was in agreement with both the young Marx's emphasis on the role of human activity and the Yugoslavian Communist Party's attempt to develop a "socialist market economy" with workers' control of companies. This Marxism was supported by the Yugoslavian authorities until the late 1960s, but after extensive student unrest in 1968 the group was accused of having inspired it. The journal was banned in 1974 and the most prominent philosophers were exiled.

The Marxism of practice also spread to other Eastern countries where the so-called Petofi Circle in Budapest, inspired by Lukács and others, developed a humanistic Marxism that was highly critical of the way in which "actually existing socialism" met "human needs" and analyzed "everyday life." After the death of Lukács in 1971 it became more and more difficult for the group to work, and most of its leading thinkers, including Agnes Heller (b. 1929), Ferenc Fehér (b. 1928), András Hegedüs (b. 1922), and György Markus (b. 1934), were exiled. In Czechoslovakia humanistic Marxism formed an important theoretical and ideological background to the creation of "socialism with a human face," which was crushed by the Warsaw Pact invasion of 1968. *The Dialectics of the Concrete* (1976, orginally 1963) by Karel Kosik (b. 1926) played an important role. In Poland too there was a current that stressed humanistic Marxism in which existing socialism was criticized by the philosopher Leszek Kolakowski (b. 1927) in his book *Man without Alternatives* (1960) and the economist Oscar Lange (1904–65) in a number of books.

Structural Marxism

Structural Marxism appeared in the 1960s, led by the French philosopher Louis Althusser (1918–90), in opposition to humanistic Marxism. Structural Marxism arose in criticism of earlier Western Marxism's focus on the acting subject, and during the 1970s it came to be the dominant Marxist current at many Western universities. In contrast to humanistic Marxism, Althusser stressed Marxism as a *science* that examined objective structures and he believed that humanistic, historicistic, and phenomenological Marxism, which was based on Marx's early works, was caught in a "pre-scientific humanistic ideology."

Louis Althusser

Louis Althusser was born in Algeria and studied philosophy at the elite Ecole Normale Supérieure in Paris, where he also taught for many years. He joined the Communist Party in 1948, and during the 1970s he advocated a Maoist-inspired anti-authoritarian line in discussions on renewal of the party. In his private life Althusser was a manic depressive and he killed his wife during an attack of this illness in 1980. Althusser spent the next ten years of his life, until his death, in mental institutions.

Althusser's structural Marxism was part of a structural tradition that can be traced back to the French sociologist Emile Durkheim (see chapter 5). In linguistics, Ferdinand de Saussure and Roman Jakobson (1896–1982) developed structuralist theories, as did Claude Lévi-Strauss (see chapter 18) in social anthropology. In psychoanalysis, Jacques Lacan (see chapter 18), and in research on historical mentalities Michel Foucault (see chapter 19) came out with structuralistically inspired views. Like Althusser, they all maintained that the conscious activities of human actors were unable to explain the appearance and historical development of society. Rather, it is the task of science to reveal unconscious and deeply rooted structures in both language and social life in order to explain empirical phenomena.

Althusser believed that Marx, with his historical materialism, had created a new science. As Althusser put it, he had opened up "a new 'continent', that of history – just as Thales opened up the 'continent' of mathematics for scientific knowledge, and Galileo opened up the 'continent' of physical nature for scientific knowledge" (Althusser 1993: 14). Marx had created this science of history through an "epistemological break" (an expression Althusser took from the French philosopher of science, Gaston Bachelard (1884–1962), which means that a researcher breaks with old ideas and constructs a new "problematic" within an area). This occurred in 1845/6 when, in *The German Ideology*, Marx broke with the young Hegelian humanistic ideas of man's species-being and human alienation and began to examine society and its history as based in a structure of productive forces and relations of production. According to Althusser, how deep and important this break by Marx was is indicated by the fact that even in *Capital* Marx sometimes lapses back into an ideological problematic. Thus, this most important of Marx's books must be read *symptomatically*, that is, one must read it critically, see what is not in it, and try to find in it the deeper structure.

The creation of a science means that the researcher constitutes an area as a scientific object. This constituted scientific object differs from the actual object in that theoretical practice produces its concepts from ideological "raw material." In this regard, Althusser also criticizes those forms of empiricism that maintain that to "know is to abstract from the real object its essence" (Althusser and Balibar 1997: 35f). Their knowledge of the object becomes a part of the object itself, while for Althusser scientific knowledge is based on production of those concepts that are a precondition for knowledge.

Althusser also criticizes an economic interpretation of Marxism, in which all social phenomena are reduced to "economy" and he believes that society is a structure in which the three levels – the economic, the political, and the ideological – all have "relative autonomy" with their own specific development. The economy is merely "determinant in the final instance" (an expression Althusser took from Engels). This means that the economy is the instance in the social structure that is able to explain why different substructures have the place and function they do in the totality. But the various structures and the contradictions found in them are all "overdetermined" by the structure as a whole. Like all structuralists, Althusser asserts that the totality comes first and that it is more than the sum of its parts (holism).

Althusser also introduces a fourth level of society, which he calls the theoretical level. Like the other levels, it possesses relative autonomy. Production occurs on this level too, although here it is scientific knowledge that is produced. This is done in that ideological concepts and facts (what Althusser calls *Generality I*), with the help of *Generality II* (a set of concepts), converts these ideological ideas into scientific knowledge (*Generality III*). With his epistemological break, Marx had also developed a new causal concept in his historical science, structural causality. This causal concept is based on the philosophy of Baruch Spinoza (1632–77) and differs from both the concept of "linear causality" (a cause is followed by an effect) found in natural science and that of Hegel (and the romantics) called "expressive causality," where the "essence" of the totality is expressed in its various parts. Structural causality determines "the elements of a structure, and the structural relations between those elements, and all the effects of those relations, by the effectivity of that structure" (Althusser and Balibar 1997: 186). Thus it is the organization and appearance of the structure itself that explain both the mode of operation and the position of the parts in the whole.

Etienne Balibar

Althusser's symptomatic reading of Marx was primarily a reconstruction of a Marxist philosophy that was mainly unstated in the works of Marx himself. What this meant for historical materialism was developed by Althusser's co-worker Etienne Balibar (b. 1942). According to Balibar, the various modes of production in history differ from one another in the way in which they combine three invariable elements: the worker, the means of production (the objects of labor and the means of labor), and the nonworker. These can be related to one another either as an ownership relationship or a true or material acquisition relationship. Thus, a mode of production is a certain structure in which the elements of that structure are combined in a certain special way. Various modes of production found in history

(Asiatic, antique, feudal, capitalist, and communist) differ from one another precisely in the manner in which they combine the fundamental elements to form an ordered structure.

The concept of the mode of production is an unhistorical concept that refers to the relationships between the invariant elements in direct material production, but also to the relationships among the various levels of society. Under capitalism, for example, we find exploitation of the direct producer in time and space while, at the same time, the producer creates the means of his own reproduction. Consequently, there is no need for extra-economic means in capitalist production. Under feudalism, however, the production necessary for the producer was separate in time and space from the additional labor exploited by the feudal lord. Thus, under feudalism extra-economic structures intervened in the direct production.

Each concrete society is a *social formation* in which various modes of production can exist side by side. For example, in Russia around the turn of the century there were both feudal and capitalist modes of production. While the concept of the mode of production is an abstract structural one that contains no historical development, but indicates the structural causality and the overdeterminations of the contradictions found in the structure, the concept of social formation tries to take up the problem of the transition between different modes of production. When the contradictions at the various levels of a mode of production or the dominant contradictions of the various modes of production coincide, then society faces a revolution. Thus it is not human actors or even classes that "make" a revolution, but rather it comes about as a result of structural relationships.

Nicos Poulantzas

Althusser's structural Marxism was also developed for state and class theory, particularly by Nicos Poulantzas (1936–79) in the book, *Political Power and Social Classes* (1975, first published in 1968). The most important part of his class analysis is based on Althusser's idea that each concrete social formation is a combination of various modes of production and that the levels in the capitalist mode of production possess "relative autonomy." Thus, under capitalism class relationships are far more complex than indicated by an economistic reduction to material production with its classes of the bourgeoisie and the proletariat. Classes are not just objective phenomena that can be defined on the basis of the capitalist economy, but "the concept of class covers the unity of class practices (class 'struggle'), of social relations as effects of the unity of the *levels* of structures" (Poulantzas 1975: 75). The classes constitute themselves conceptually in class struggle and in this way Poulantzas rejects the traditional view of classes as either an objective "class in itself" or a subjective "class for itself." They are effects of social practice at all levels.

The structural Marxists developed new theories with regard to the state as well. Since economic exploitation under capitalism occurs directly in production without extra-economic intervention, the capitalist state holds a relatively autonomous position with respect to the main classes in society. The task of the state is to guarantee the conditions under which production and reproduction can occur, and it cannot be reduced simply to an expression of the ruling class. Since there are also a number of different classes from various modes of production and different class factions in the capitalist mode of production, Poulantzas states that there is a "power bloc" consisting of various classes and class factions that hold "hegemony" in the state. This power bloc is able to rule because the state, particularly through political and ideological practices, can break the unity of the ruling classes, for example, by treating people in the lower classes like isolated individuals, each one of which has a vote.

Capital Logic

Around 1970 another current of Western Marxism appeared, called the logic of capital. It is called this because the people concerned did not wish to use the concept of dialectics to designate Marx's method, but believed that in his critique of political economy Marx had exposed the logic of capital. This logic is expressed in the law of motion of capital, M–C–M', where M stands for money, C stands for commodities, and M' stands for more money (M' > M), and it is the laws of, or logic in, this increase in value found in capitalism that is Marx's most important discovery, according to the logic of capital.

This emphasis on *Capital* (and its "preliminary work" *Grundrisse*) distinguishes capital logic from the Althusser School, which believed that Marx's most important contribution was the "science of history," historical materialism. Thus, while the Althusser School sets the year 1845/6 (when Marx developed the history of materialism in *The German Ideology*) as a crucial turning point in the theoretical development of Marx, the representatives of capital logic tend to see 1857/8 as such a turning point. It was then that Marx wrote his major manuscript *Grundrisse*, which was meant to present his critique of political economy, but which was impossible to publish because of its unstructured and, in part, completely chaotic nature. While working on *Grundrisse* or somewhat later, Marx solved the problem of capital's increase in value, that is, he discovered the origin of surplus value in the production process. Consequently, he was able to develop his theory by solving this puzzle and he published it in 1867 after thoroughly processing the material.

Traditionally, Marxism has held that the relationship between historical materialism and the theory of capital is such that the theory of history provides the general historical laws of motion, while the theory of capital provides the specific laws of motion for capitalism. This was the view of both orthodox Marxism and Marxism–Leninism. Althusser too saw the relationship this way, but with the important difference that, instead of accepting traditional dialectic materialism, he tried to reconstruct Marxist philosophy on the basis of Marx's break with the young Hegelians. This changes historical materialism as well as the theory of capital. Few in the Althusser School analyzed economic questions, however. Most studied sociological or political relationships such as class, party, or state.

The basic idea behind capital logic is expressed by its claim that Marx's theoretical "break" came in connection with his work with the economy. Marx's critique of political economy is not a continuation or concretization of historical materialism, but rather *a completely different theory*. According to the logic of capital, historical materialism is not a theory in the true meaning of the word, but rather, as Marx himself wrote, it is a guide for further studies. It is rather the theory of capital that is Marx's greatest discovery and essentially it deals with capital's subsumption (subordination) of reality to itself. Consequently, the concepts in *Capital* (commodity, use and exchange value, surplus value, capital, etc.) are not pure economic terms. They are, particularly under advanced capitalism, concepts of social theory, and the "logic of capital" subjugates more and more areas of social reality under itself. But it is primarily the forms of this subordination that capital logic studies, analyzes, and tries to explain.

The capital logic movement developed primarily in West Germany, but it also had a certain amount of influence in other countries, particularly Denmark. Unlike the Althusser School, capital logic had no individual as its theoretical inspiration, but some of the key people were Roman Rosdolsky (1898–1967), Helmuth Reichelt (b. 1939), and Elmar Altvater (b. 1938).

The levels of abstraction of capital: Roman Rosdolsky

In his book *The Making of Marx's "Capital,"* Roman Rosdolsky examines how *Capital* came into being, as the title suggests. After a thorough reading of *Grundrisse* and Marx's own plans and manuscripts, Rosdolsky concluded that Marx's theory of capital was something completely different from what had been previously believed. The most important thing Rosdolsky discovered is Hegel's great importance to Marx's theory, particularly the dialectic between essence and appearance. Here Rosdolsky (and capital logic) differ completely from the Althusser School, which wanted to purge Hegel from Marxism.

Another important discovery is that *Capital* is written on various levels of abstraction. In the first book, Marx analyzes "capital in general," which deals with the "formal logical determination of all value elements and their forms of development in a capitalist mode of production," without any concrete attributes such as competition or different kinds of capital in other countries. The other books, particularly the third, analyze "capital in its reality in general," which deals with the "general conditions for individual capitals, their relationship to one another under development of the capitalist mode of production," how capital moves when there are markets, competition, monopolies, etc. In addition, it is possible to discern a third level, "capital in its reality," where concrete individual capital exists that is determined by a number of other noneconomic factors.

The distinction between the underlying nature of capitalism and its surface manifestations and between the levels of abstraction in the development of the concept of capitalism imply a crucial methodological assumption, namely that there is a deeper inherent logic in capital that actually controls it, but that can be seen only in a distorted and deceptive guise in what can be observed directly on the surface. This assumption plays an important role in capital logic's understanding of both the dynamics of capitalism and its historical origin.

Capital, which appears under capitalist conditions in the relationship between those who use capital and wage laborers, has a basic structure, a "nature" which involves increasing value. This increase in value did not arise under capitalism. It existed in all trade even a thousand years ago. Money was used to buy goods that were then sold for more money. Under capitalism, however, the law of surplus value has also subsumed material production that is necessary for human survival. M–C–M' is the principle that controls not only the trade of commodities that are produced outside this principle, but during the course of capitalism's development this "logic" has penetrated every nook and cranny of society.

Capital as an all-encompassing subject

The essential part of the logic of capitalism is its inherent compulsion to expand, its constant increase in surplus value, and its compulsion toward accumulation. In his book *Zur logischen Struktur des Kapitalbegriffs bei Karl Marx* (The Logical Structure of the Concept of Capital in Karl Marx, 1970), Helmuth Reichelt formulates the idea that all previous historical development can be seen as a process in which the logic of capitalism has gradually expanded and unfolded from its germinal form in the very first exchange of commodities, and as its (temporary) culmination it has assumed the controlling role, the role of an all-encompassing subject under the capitalism of today.

The logic of capital does not end with its economic laws of motion. The logic continues by acting on the living conditions of wage laborers outside production as well. The logic of capital comes through in the state, in organizations and education, in child care and care for the aged, even in human relations and love. Consequently, many analyses of the logic of capital deal with the state's involvement in increasing value, with education and socialization, or with sociopsychological or psychological relationships under capitalism.

Reichelt believes that in this regard history can be seen as a process of the increasing alienation of labor. While the human species has gradually liberated itself from the constraints of nature by developing productive forces, it has become more and more alienated, with respect both to nature and to itself, by coming under the abstract logic of capital, which operates totally in the dark, behind people's backs, and beyond their control. The logic of capital continues to expand and reaches its culmination under capitalism, the ultimate level of alienation.

The logic of capital also placed great emphasis on the inherent tendency of capitalism to collapse. Capitalism's logic of expansion also contains its own contradictions, barriers, and tendencies to collapse. Eventually its possibilities for expansion are exhausted and the living labor, which is the source of surplus value, is replaced more and more by machines and capital-intensive technology. Many proponents of the logic of capital stressed the "law of the falling tendency of profit rates" as an expression of this inherent contradiction and tendency toward collapse. To survive the competition, capitalists are constantly forced to introduce more advanced technology to reduce costs. But when living workers are replaced with machines, the capitalist also reduces that which is the source of surplus value. The result is increasing impoverishment of the labor force, unemployment, and economic crises.

This is particularly important with regard to their view of the capitalist state. In the theory of "state-interventionist capitalism" (STINCAP), the basic view is that increasing intervention by the state – particularly since the crisis of the 1930s – is determined by the need to accumulate capital and to ward off some of the inherent contradictions in the logic of capital (Altvater 1972; Braunmühl et al. 1973; Mattick 1971). This applies not only to economic policy and industrial policy in the narrow sense, but also, for example, to labor-market policy, social policy, and educational policy. Social policy and labor-market policy, for example, can meet the need of maintaining surplus labor power and conversion to different conditions of production, while educational policy can meet the need for socialization and training of the labor force to participate in production. (Analyses of education and socialization include Altvater and Huisken 1971; Krovoza 1976.)

There are also limitations on the state's ability to eliminate the inherent contradictions of capitalism. Proponents of the logic of capital (such as Altvater et al. 1972 and Cogoy in Braunmühl et al. 1973) build on the assumption that state expenditure (predominantly, at least) is unproductive and reduces the total surplus value. Thus, in the long term, they must limit the possibility of capital accumulation.

Conclusion: Marxism in the 1980s and 1990s

The influence of the Althusser School was greatest in France, but it had followers in England and other countries as well. In Denmark it had an impact on state theory, class analysis, and research on developing countries.

In the mid-1970s structural Marxism dominated academic Marxism in many places, but it was also sharply criticized by many for its abstract character, its reduction of class struggle to "structural effects," and for its sharp distinction between reality and scientifically constituted research objects. It was criticized, in particular, by English historical Marxists, such as Eric Hobsbawm, E. P. Thompson, Dona Torr, and Christopher Hill.

The logic of capital was also subjected to harsh criticism, beginning in the mid-seventies. It was attacked on methodological grounds for being a closed, speculative, and dogmatic system of thought. With regard to its actual content, the main criticism was that it had a tendency to deduce everything from what benefited the accumulation of capital. Its use of the "law of the falling tendency of profit rates" and its assumption that state expenditure basically hindered the accumulation of capital were also criticized (Andersen et al. 1975; Hellesnes 1977).

Since the late seventies the positions of both the logic of capital and the Althusser School have been eroded as distinct theoretical movements and new ones have arisen to take their place. In England the Althusserians Paul Hirst and Barry Hindess continued a theoretical development of historical materialism (Hindess and Hirst 1977). Class analyses inspired by Poulantzas were further developed by Erik Olin Wright (1978, 1979, 1985) and his analytical model also led to a Nordic project with a comparative class analysis (see chapter 11). Other new currents from the eighties are Neo-Gramscianism and analytical Marxism (taken up in chapter 11).

Since the dissolution of the Soviet Union, orthodox Marxism and Marxism–Leninism have basically disappeared. In recent years many Marxists have analyzed the rise and fall of the Soviet Union. In addition, Marxists who are more interested in the cultural forms of late capitalism have appeared, such as the American literary historian, Fredric Jameson, who analyzes postmodernism from a Marxist perspective (Jameson 1991). In political Marxism, writers such as E. Laclau and C. Mouffe (see chapter 11) and H. Wainwright (1994) have tried to develop a political strategy that takes into account the appearance of new social movements in recent decades. Like everything else, Marxism changes over the course of time and "postcommunist Marxism" is facing new challenges, the main one of which may be to develop an alternative to the neoliberal ideology that has been predominant for over a decade.

Bibliography

Althusser, Louis. 1965: *Pour Marx*. Paris: Maspero.

—— 1969a: *Lénine et la philosophie*. Paris: Maspero.

—— 1970: Idéologie et appareils idéologiques d'etat. *La Pensée*, 151, 3–38.

—— 1972: Reply to John Lewis. *Marxism Today*, Oct.–Nov.

—— 1974a [1967]: *Philosophie et philosophie spontanée des savants*. Paris: Maspero.

—— 1976 [1974]: *Essays in Self-criticism*. London: New Left Book.

—— 1990: *Philosophy and the Spontaneous Philosophy of the Scientists & Other Essays*, ed. Gregory Elliott. London: Verso.

—— 1993: *For Marx*. New York: Verso.

Althusser, Louis, and Balibar, Etienne. 1997 [1965]: *Reading Capital*. New York; London: Verso.

Altvater, Elmar. 1972: Zu einige Probleme des Staatsinterventionismus. *Probleme des Klassekampfs*, 3, 1–53.

Altvater, Elmar, and Huisken, Freerk (eds) 1971: *Materialien zur politischen Ökonomie des Ausbildungssektors*. Erlangen: Politladen GMBH.

Andersen, Heine, Groth, Chr., Koch, Carsten, and Olsen, Ole Jess. 1975: *Kritik af kapitallogikken*. Copenhagen: Demos.

Anderson, Perry. 1976: *Considerations on Western Marxism*. London: NBL.

Balibar, Etienne. 1974: *Cinq études du matérialisme historique*. Paris: Maspero.

—— 1977: *On the Dictatorship of the Proletariat*. London: NBL.

Benton, Ted. 1984: *The Rise and Fall of Structural Marxism*. London: Macmillan.

Braunmühl, Claudia von, Funken, Klaus, Cogoy, Mario, and Hirsh, Joachim. 1973: *Probleme einer materialistichen Staatstheori*. Frankfurt am Main: Suhrkamp Verlag.

Callincos, Alex. 1976: *Althusser's Marxism*. London: Macmillan.

Cammett, John M. 1967: *Antonio Gramsci and the Origins of Italian Communism*. Stanford: Stanford University Press.

Cutler, A., Hindess, B., Hirst, P. Q., and Hussain, A. 1971/8: *Marx's Capital and Capitalism Today I-II*. London: Routledge & Kegan Paul.

Dunne, Raul (ed.) 1991: *Quantitative Marxism*. Cambridge: Polity Press.

Elliott, Gregory. 1987: *Althusser. The Detour of Theory*. London: Verso.

Engels, Friedrich. 1966 [1878]: *Herr Eugen Dühring's Revolution in Science*. New York: International Publishers.

Fehér, F., Heller, A., and Márkus, G. 1983: *Dictatorship over Needs*. Oxford: Blackwell.

Good, Patrick. 1979: *Karl Korsch. A Study in Western Marxism*. London: Macmillan.

Gramsci, Antonio. 1978: *Selections from political writings (1921–1926)*, translated and edited by Quintin Hoare. New York: International Publishers.

—— 1985: *Selections from Cultural Wri tings*, ed. D. Forgacs and G. Nowell-Smith. Cambridge, MA: Harvard University Press.

—— 1992: *Prison Notebooks*, ed. Joseph A. Buttigieg. New York: Columbia University Press.

Heller, Agnes. 1984: *A Radical Philosophy*. Oxford: Blackwell.

Hilferding, Rudolf. 1968: *Das Finanzkapital. Eine Studie über die jüngste Entwicklung des Kapitalismus*. Frankfurt am Main: Europäische Verlagsanstalt.

Hellesnes, Jon. 1977: Den kapitallogiske marxismen og dogmatismens bakveje. *Norsk filosofisk Tidsskrift*, 2, 109–26.

Hindess, Barry. 1983: *Parliamentary Democracy and Socialist Politics*. London: Routledge.

—— 1987a: *Freedom, Equality and the Market*. London: Tavistock.

—— 1987b: *Politics and Class Analysis*. Oxford: Blackwell.

Hindess, Barry, and Hirst, Paul Q. 1975: *Pre-Capitalist Modes of Production*. London: Routledge & Kegan Paul.

—— 1977: *Mode of Production and Social Formation: An Auto-Critique of Pre-Capitalist Modes of Production*. London: Macmillan.

Hirst, Paul Q. 1979: *On Law and Ideology*. London: Macmillan.

—— 1985: *Marxism and Historical Writing*. London: Routledge & Kegan Paul.

—— 1986: *Law, Socialism and Democracy*. London: Allen & Unwin.

Howard, Dick, and Clare, Karl E. (eds) 1972: *The Unknown Dimension. European Marxism since Lenin*. New York and London: Basic Books.

Hunt, Ian. 1993: *Analytical and Dialectical Marxism*. Aldershot: Routledge & Kegan Paul.

Jacoby, Russel. 1981: *Dialectic of Defeat. Contours of Western Marxism*. Cambridge: Cambridge University Press.

Jameson, Fredric. 1991: *Postmodernism, or, the Cultural Logic of Late Capitalism*. London: Verso.

Jay, Martin. 1982: *Marxism and Totality. The Adventures of a Concept from Lukács to Habermas*. Cambridge: Polity Press.

Joll, James. 1977: *Gramsci*. Glasgow: Fontana/Collins.

Jones, Gareth Stedman, et al. 1977: *Western Marxism. A Critical Reader*. London: New Left Books.

Kaye, Harvey J. 1984: *The British Marxist Historians*. Cambridge: Polity Press.

Kolakowski, Leszek. 1960: *Der Mensch ohne Alternative*. Munich: R. Piper.

—— 1978: *Main Currents of Marxism*. 3 vols. Oxford: Clarendon Press.

Korsch, Karl. 1970: *Marxism and Philosophy*. New York and London: New Left Books.

Kosik, Karel. 1976: *Dialectics of the Concrete: A Study on Problems of Man and World*. Dordrecht: Boston Studies in the Philosophy of Science.

Krovoza, Alfred. 1976: *Produktion und Sozialisation*. Cologne: EVA.

Kusin, V. V. 1971: *The Intellectual Origins of the Prague Spring. The Development of Reformist Ideas in Czechoslovakia 1956–1967*. Cambridge: Cambridge University Press.

Lenin, Vladimir Ilich. 1969 [1902]: *What Is to Be Done? Burning Questions of our Movement*. New York: International Publishers.

Levi, Margaret (ed.) 1991: *Marxism*. 2 vols. Aldershot and Brookfield, VT: Edward Elgar.

Lichtheim, George. 1964: *Marxism. A Historical and Critical Study*. London: Routledge & Keagan Paul Ltd.

Lukács, Georg. 1971: *Lenin: A Study on the Unity of His Thought*. Cambridge, MA.

—— 1971: *History and Class Consciousness: Studies in Marxist Dialectics*. London: Merlin.

—— 1978: *The Ontology of Social Being. 1. Hegel's False and his Genuine Ontology*. London: Merlin Press.

Lunn, Eugene. 1982: *Marxism and Modernism. An Historical Study of Lukács, Brecht, Benjamin, and Adorno*. Berkeley: University of California Press.

Luxemburg, Rosa. 1969: *The Crisis in German Social-Democracy*. New York: H. Fertig.

—— 1973: *The Accumulation of Capital – an Anti-Critique*, ed. with an introduction by Kenneth J. Tarbuck. New York: Monthly Review Press.

—— 1989: *Reform or Revolution*. London: Bookmarks Publication.

Mattick, Paul. 1971: *Marx and Keynes: the Limits of the Mixed Economy*. London: Merlin Press.

McLellan, David. 1980: *Marxism after Marx. An Introduction*. London: Macmillan.

Merquior, J. G. 1986: *Western Marxism*. London: Granada.

Nordquist, Joan. 1987: *Antonio Gramsci*. Santa Cruz: Reference & Research Services.

Pike, Sherley R. 1986: *Marxism and Phenomenology. Theories of Crisis and their Synthesis*. London and Sydney: Croom Helm.

Poster, Mark. 1977: *Existential Marxism in Postwar France. From Sartre to Althusser*. Princeton, NJ: Princeton University Press.

Poulantzas, Nicos. 1965: *Nature des choses et droit. Essai sur la dialectique du fait et de la valeur*. Paris: Bibliothèque de philosophie du droit, vol. 5.

—— 1970: *Fascisme et dictature. La IIIe internationale face au fascisme*. Paris: Seuil.

—— 1975a [1968]: *Political Power and Social Classes*. London: NBL.

—— 1975b [1974]: *Classes in Contemporary Capitalism*. London: NBL.

—— 1976 [1975]: *The Crisis of the Dictatorships: Portugal, Greece, Spain*. London: NBL.

—— 1978: *State, Power, Socialism*. London: NBL.

—— 1980: *Repéres: hier et aujourd'hui*. Paris: Maspero.

Reichelt, Helmuth. 1970: *Zur logischen Struktur des Kapitalbegriffs bei Karl Marx*. Frankfurt am Main: Europäische Verlagsanstalt.

Riechers, Christian. 1970: *Antonio Gramsci – Marxismus in Italien*. Frankfurt am Main: Europäische Verlagsanstalt.

Rosdolsky, Roman. 1989: *The Making of Marx's "Capital"*. London : Pluto Press.

Scanlon, James P. 1985: *Marxism in the USSR. A Critical Survey of Current Soviet Thought*. Ithaca, NY, and London: Cornell University Press.

Schaff, Adam. 1974: *Structuralism and Marxism*. Oxford: Pergamon Press.

Schmidt, Alfred. 1971: *The Concept of Nature in Marx*. London: New Left Books.

Sheehan, Helena. 1985: *Marxism and the Philosophy of Science. A Critical History*. Atlantic Highlands, NJ: Humanities Press.

Sher, Gerson S. 1977: *Praxis. Marxists Criticism and Dissent in Socialist Yugoslavia*. Bloomington: Indiana University Press.

Smith, Tony. 1993: *Dialectical Social Theory and its Critics. From Hegel to Analytical Marxism and Postmodernism*. Albany: State University of New York Press.

Therborn, Göran. 1978: *What Does the Ruling Class Do When it Rules*. London: NLB.

Thompson, E. P. 1978: *The Poverty of Theory*. London: Merlin Press.

Van Parijs, Philippe. 1993: *Marxism Recycled*. Cambridge: Cambridge University Press.

Wainwright, Hilary. 1994: *Argument for a New Left: Answering the Free-Market Right*. Oxford: Blackwell.

Worsley, Peter. 1982: *Marx and Marxism*. London; New York: Tavistock Publications.

Wright, Erik Olin. 1978: *Class, Crisis and the State*. London: NLB.

—— 1979: *Class Structure and Income Determination*. New York: Academic Press.

—— 1985: *Classes*. London: Verso.

chapter 10

The Frankfurt School

Anders Ramsay*

---

* Quotations from German are translated by the anthor.

KEY CONCEPTS

ANAL CHARACTER – alludes to the second phase of the child's development according to Freudian psychoanalysis, the anal-sadistic phase. A character which is fixated in this phase acquires a high level of self-control.

CRITICAL THEORY – a theory that at the same time is both critical of society and critical of theories concerning this society and scientific methods to approach it. As far as the theories and the methods contribute to concealing relations of oppression and exploitation, they are criticized as ideological.

THE ENLIGHTENMENT – the period in European history (ca. 1650–1800) characterized by the liberation of the bourgeoisie from despotic monarchy. The philosophy of enlightenment questioned all faith in authority and confinement to tradition under the influence of the natural scientific worldview. The Frankfurt School uses the concept of enlightenment in a more comprehensive sense.

EXISTENTIAL PHILOSOPHY – philosophy which examines the condition of individual human existence, not the abstract subject of knowledge. The philosophy of existence emanates from Søren Kierkegaard and its most famous representatives in Germany between the wars were Martin Heidegger and Karl Jaspers.

INSTRUMENTAL REASON – reason that exclusively contemplates the world as an object of technical manipulation. The most effective means are employed to reach a given end, while the end in itself, on the contrary, is not the object of any discussion.

METAPHYSICS – the branch of philosophy which has the task of determining the basic structures of what is or may exist. Often used synonymously with ontology.

MYTH – a symbolic narrative about events that have occurred which explains why the world is as it is and always must be. Myth structures the image of the world in so-called primitive or archaic societies.

SPHERE OF CIRCULATION – the market sphere, the economic sphere where commodities and labor power are exchanged for money and economic subjects compete with each other. According to Marx, this sphere conceals and distorts the real circumstances behind economic intercourse, which consists of the exploitation of the commodity labor power in the sphere of production.

SUPEREGO – according to Freud, the instance in the psychic structure which can be compared to a judge and which is formed through the internalization of the parental authority.

The Frankfurt School primarily refers to the group of social researchers and philosophers who worked together from the beginning of the thirties under the directorship of Max Horkheimer (1895–1973) at the Institut für Sozialforschung (the Institute of Social Research, IfS), in Frankfurt am Main and, after the Nazis' seizure of power in 1933, in Geneva, New York, and Los Angeles. Their work was above all theoretically grounded in Marxism and psychoanalysis. It aimed at elaborating a theory on the relation between the economy, psychology, and culture of contemporary capitalist society through interdisciplinary cooperation within a shared theoretical framework. Horkheimer formulated both the aims of the group's research and the theoretical frame of the work. To begin with, this approach was simply called materialistic, later on the label *critical theory* or *critical theory of society* was coined within the group. Critical theory was a code word for Marxism, a Marxism, however, which was not identical with any orthodox brand. The name "Frankfurt School" first came into public use during the sixties, when the work of the IfS was rediscovered by the radical German student movement.

Biography: *Theodor W. Adorno*

Theodor W. Adorno was born in Frankfurt am Main in 1903 as Theodor Wiesengrund-Adorno. His father, a well-to-do wine merchant, was Jewish but at the time of his son's birth had converted to Protestantism. His Catholic mother and aunt were both musicians and greatly influenced his childhood. While still a schoolboy he studied music. From 1921 to 1924 he studied philosophy, sociology, psychology, and the science of music at the University of Frankfurt and met Max Horkheimer and Walter Benjamin. After his graduation in philosophy he studied composition for six months under Alban Berg in Vienna. During the twenties he made a name for himself as a music critic and published about a hundred articles on music before his first independent philosophical work. In 1931 he took his doctor's degree (*Habilitation*) with a thesis on Søren Kierkegaard. From 1934 to 1938 he studied at Oxford and was in close contact with Benjamin in Paris and Horkheimer in New York. After his return to Germany from the USA in 1949 he became an ordinary professor of philosophy in 1956 and led the IfS after Horkheimer's retirement in 1959. Adorno gradually became a well-known figure in the postwar Federal Republic, especially as a cultural critic and philosopher of music. The last years of his life were characterized by increasingly violent conflicts with gradually more militant radical students. When he died in August 1969 he was in the middle of writing his large *Aesthetic Theory* (1984).

The most famous names which have given the Frankfurt School its reputation are those of the philosopher and sociologist, Theodor W. Adorno (1903–69), the literary critic and philosopher, Walter Benjamin (1892–1940), the philosopher, Herbert Marcuse (1898–1979), and the psychologist, Erich Fromm (1900–80). Horkheimer's right hand in the administration of the affairs of the IfS was the economist, Friedrich Pollock (1894–1970). Pollock belonged to the Institute from its establishment in 1923. The literary sociologist, Leo Löwenthal (1900–93) functioned as managing editor of the scientific journal of IfS, *Zeitschrift für Sozialforschung*, which was published between 1932 and 1941 (from the last issue of 1940 as *Studies in Philosophy and Social Science*). The journal was, during its period of publication, the center of the Institute's activities. It published almost all the important works of the collaborators. The founder of the institute was the economist, Felix Weil (1898–1975), who never had a prominent position as a scientist, but continually, in the capacity of initiator and Maecenas, took an active part in the work of the IfS.

All these individuals did not, however, work together at the Institute simultaneously and there are marked differences between their individual theoretical positions. Neither Benjamin nor Marcuse worked in Frankfurt before 1933. After Hitler's seizure of power, Benjamin lived in Paris and never took part directly in the collective work. Adorno did not become an official member of IfS until 1938 in New York, about the same time as Fromm left. Adorno, however, did take part in the collective work during the preceding years through intensive contact by mail with Horkheimer from his exile in England. During the twenties and thirties Adorno and

Benjamin to a certain extent represented a position of their own, which did not influence the work of the IfS until later. Marcuse joined the Institute just as it left Germany. He was initially influenced by the existential philosophy of his teacher, Martin Heidegger (1889–1976), which was emphatically rejected by Adorno, and later by the writings of the young Karl Marx, the so-called *Economic and Philosophical Manuscripts*, which were published in the early thirties. Pollock, on the other hand, was less philosophically inclined than many of the others.

While each one of the scholars attached to the Institute belongs to a school of thought, they were also individual, original thinkers, representing their own version of critical theory. Other associates of the IfS, such as the lawyers and political scientists, Franz Neumann (1900–54) and Otto Kirchheimer (1905–65), were even further removed from Horkheimer's critical theory. At the same time, however, the Frankfurt School during its first ten years shows all the characteristics of a scientific school: an institutional basis, a joint organ of publication, and, in the person of Horkheimer, a typical science manager who formulated a scientific paradigm and held the administrative leadership in his hands.

Horkheimer and his associates were active during a dramatic period of twentieth-century European history, the era of National Socialism, Stalinism and World War II. Almost every one of them was of Jewish origin and all of them were politically oriented to the left, but with a few exceptions none was politically active to any notable extent. They were, above all, social scientists and philosophers, and they took a distanced and gradually more critical position toward both the social democratic and communist wings of the labor movement. Their exile during the reign of German National Socialism and a certain degree of political disillusionment came to influence their work.

The Historical Setting of the Frankfurt School

Felix Weil, the founder of the IfS, was the son of a multimillionaire, Hermann Weil (1868–1927), who made his fortune as a grain merchant in Argentina. In his student days, the younger Weil became involved in the revolutionary events following World War I. Hermann Weil supported, on his son's initiative, the founding of an institute for social scientific research. The many attacks during the years immediately after the war from right-wing groups against prominent Jewish politicians and businessmen probably made the conservative and assimilated Weil conscious of the danger of antisemitism and contributed to his generosity. The formulation of the research goals of the IfS included, among other things, "antisemitism as a sociological problem " (van Reijen and Schmid Noerr 1988: 165). It was not, however, until the beginning of the forties that antisemitism seriously became part of the research agenda of the IfS.

The first years of the IfS

The activities of the IfS began with a meeting sponsored by Felix Weil, "The First Marxist Work Week," an eight-day seminar held in May 1923. Some 20 persons participated, including, besides Weil himself, Friedrich Pollock and the historian, Karl August Wittfogel (1896–1988) who was the only non-Jew in the inner circle of the IfS during the thirties. The seminar discussed problems in Marxist theory in connection with two recent works, Georg Lukács's (1885–1971) *History and Class Consciousness* (see chapter 9) and Karl Korsch's

(1886– 1961) then unpublished *Marxism and Philosophy* (see chapter 9). Both authors took part in the seminar and gave accounts of their respective books. Common to these works, in distinction from a traditional Marxist notion with its stress on the importance of the objective historical process for the socialist revolution, was their emphasis on the subjective moment in Marxism and their advocacy of the necessity of a self-conscious, active proletariat to carry through the revolution. This conception would also become very important in the theory of the Frankfurt School, as the self-consciousness of the proletariat would be problematized and a subject of research for the IfS.

The first director of the Institute was the Austrian historian and economist, Carl Grünberg (1861–1940), a distinguished representative of Austro-Marxism (see chapter 9). The research of the IfS during Grünberg's period as director was mainly historically oriented and centered on the labor movement, socialism, and economics. A joint project was launched with the Marx-Engels Institute in Moscow, from the outset a prototype for Weil, on the publication of the collected works of Marx and Engels. Pollock wrote a dissertation on the problems of the planned economy in the Soviet experiment. The majority of collaborators and doctoral students at the IfS during the Grünberg period were communists or belonged to various splinter groups of the German Communist Party (KPD).

Horkheimer's entrance

Grünberg led the IfS until 1928, when he suffered a stroke. Horkheimer, who had been Pollock's friend since their youth, was appointed to the directorship, since he was considered less politically controversial than Grünberg's former assistants. In January 1931 Horkheimer delivered his inaugural lecture as both director of the IfS and a professor of social philosophy.

Since 1929 the IfS's building had also housed the Frankfurt Psychoanalytic Institute, in the establishment of which Horkheimer took an active part. Since its opening, Erich Fromm, who was to become one of the most important collaborators with the IfS during the first years of Horkheimer's directorship, worked there as a *Dozent*. Horkheimer, however, functioned as director of the IfS in Frankfurt for less than two years. Thanks to the establishment of a branch of the Institute in Geneva and the transfer of their economic resources, by the time of the seizure of power by the National Socialists, the members of the Institute were able to go into exile in Switzerland. In 1934 the IfS was established at Columbia University in New York City, to which it formally belonged until 1950.

Biography: *Max Horkheimer*

Max Horkheimer was born in Stuttgart in 1895 as the son of a Jewish textile manufacturer. He first studied to become a merchant to take over his father's business. At 16 he made the acquaintance of Friedrich Pollock, one year older, with whom he entered into a lifelong pact of friendship. A series of literary attempts from his adolescent years were later published as *Aus der Pubertät*. In 1917 Horkeimer was conscripted as a soldier. After the war he took his matriculation examination together with Pollock in Munich and witnessed from a distance with sympathy the short lived socialist council-republic. He then studied philosophy, psychology, and economics in Munich, Freiburg, and Frankfurt. He graduated under Hans Cornelius in Frankfurt and became his assistant. In 1925 he took his doctor's degree (*Habilitation*) and lectured until 1930 as a *Privatdozent*. During his years in the USA he was head of the research department of the American Jewish Committee from 1943 to 1944. From 1951 to 1953 he was Vice-Chancellor of the University of Frankfurt, the first refugee from National Socialism ever to hold that position at a German university. From 1954 to 1959 he was a guest professor at the University of Chicago. He died in 1973.

The Materialist Research Program

In his opening speech, Horkheimer formulated his interdisciplinary, materialist, social-research program, which signalled a new direction for the IfS. It was Horkheimer's premise that the tasks of classical social philosophy, the study of man in his social relationships, could be posed today only in a community of researchers from various disciplines united by a shared basic theoretical view. Philosophy should live on as theory and not, as in positivism, the scientific philosophy of science, be reduced to a formal logic of research. All researchers should be theoreticians as well as specialists in their own areas. Social research *(Sozialforschung)*, which takes upon itself the cloak of social philosophy, should further a theory of contemporary society. It is, however, as far from theoretical constructions without any empirical substance as it is from descriptions of pure facts. The theoretical and the empirical should mutually inspire and penetrate each other, which is what critical theorists call dialectics. Social research is not the same as sociology, but it is occupied with many of the same problems and issues (Horkheimer 1932: II).

Horkheimer's critique of Lukács

Horkheimer claimed that it is not possible to rehabilitate the earlier sovereign position of philosophy as metaphysics, that is, the instance that gives final answers independent of science. He stressed the belief that knowledge is always incomplete and represents an antimetaphysical materialism. It has often been claimed that Horkheimer took his position from *History and Class Consciousness*, a fashionable Marxist work of the twenties (cf. Jay 1973; Therborn 1977). However, Lukács's Hegelian idea that reality possesses a structure which can be immediately grasped by the knowing subject was understood by Horkheimer as metaphysical. In Hegel, the subject finally, after several roundabout ways, reached full knowledge of the object. A complete identity then prevails between subject and object and together they constitute the totality of reality. In Lukács the knowing subject is the revolutionary proletariat. When the proletariat reaches insight into its situation in capitalist production and moves on to revolutionary action, it has reached insight in social totality. Thus, the proletariat would be the identical subject–object of history, and absolute knowledge and revolutionary action coincide (cf. Korthals 1985).

Against this conception Horkheimer put his understanding of knowledge as always being incomplete. Theory and reality stand facing each other in a tense relationship and knowledge has a character of what today we would call "trial and error." Horkheimer's position can to a certain extent be traced back to that of his teacher, Hans Cornelius (1863–1947), emphasizing interdisciplinary research. While the Frankfurt School has become well-known for its critique of positivism, in the sense that all research should be undertaken with natural science as its prototype, it is actually possible, during the early phase of the Frankfurt School, to talk about Horkheimer's positivism, in the sense of empirical research. The positivism Horkheimer adhered to never meant reducing reality to physically measurable entities, only that all results should be tested against experience. Another important inspiration for Horkheimer was his reading of Hegel's foremost contemporary critic, Arthur Schopenhauer, who sharpened his eye for the particular and the concrete. Suffering and injustice always befalls individuals and can never, as in Hegel and the Hegelian Lukács, be redeemed by being inscribed into a superior historical meaning.

Political doubts

There was also a more immediate historical and political cause for Horkheimer's skepticism. In 1923 Weil and his friends could easily be fascinated by Lukács's idea of the proletariat as the identical subject–object of history, as long as they carried fresh memories of the revolutionary attempts of 1918–19 and had seen the possibility of a politically active proletariat seizing power. Things looked different in 1930, with the experience of the political chaos of the Weimar Republic, with the rise of National Socialism, and the political impotence of the labor movement. More and more, it seemed unlikely that history would turn out the way it was foreseen by philosophy.

Horkheimer now looked for the aid of psychology and sociology. In his introductory lecture he announced a research project which would pose the questions of social philosophy anew:

> which connections can be demonstrated between the economic role of a specific social group in a specific era in specific countries, the transformation of the psychic structure of its individual members, and the ideas and institutions as a whole that influence them and that they created? (Horkheimer 1993: 12)

Capitalism and Psychological Changes

What Horkheimer had in mind was a broadly conceived project which, with the help of modern sociological methods of research and psychoanalytic theory would investigate the relationship between social development and psychic structure among German workers and employers. Thus a theme was struck, the idea of fundamental psychological or anthropological (psychology and anthropology were used as synonyms by Horkheimer and his co-workers) changes in the transition from competitive to monopolistic capitalism, which from now on would remain central to the Frankfurt School.

This project had actually started already in 1929, under the leadership of Fromm. The investigation was never finished (a reconstruction was made much later, cf. Fromm 1984), because, among other reasons, about half of the material was lost during the flight into exile in 1933. Some of the results from the questionnaires were used in the next large IfS project,

Studien über Autorität und Familie (Horkheimer 1936). Here, instead of investigating a distinct social group, the task shifted to changes in family structure during a severe economic crisis. In Fromm's original investigation of workers and employees, an attempt was made for the first time to find a relationship between personality traits and political views. Because direct interviews, according to the psychoanalytic model, were not possible to carry through, seemingly harmless questions were inserted, intended to reveal personality traits and attitudes which would not show up in other more direct questions concerning politics, childrearing, women's conditions, etc. The results were politically alarming. Only 15 per cent of the workers who were members of KPD (the Communist Party) or SPD (the Social Democratic Party) showed themselves unambiguously radical, while 25 per cent had authoritarian tendencies or were outright authoritarians. The rest of the population investigated was ambivalent. The authoritarian character or personality, which was introduced here for the first time by Fromm, would later be an object for further investigations by the IfS in the USA.

The breakdown of the liberal era

The relationship between the development of society and psychological-anthropological changes was estimated in the mid-thirties by the Frankfurt School on the basis of the results presented in *Studien über Autorität und Familie*; it seemed to be such that capitalism had left the liberal era with free-market competition and entered a monopolistic phase in which the ownership of the means of production was concentrated into fewer hands. Different psychological characteristics correspond to these phases. The independent economic subject of the liberal era is typified by an anal character with a desire for collecting and saving. In monopoly capitalism larger trusts and organizations are developed, on which the individual becomes dependent for his survival. Each person instead finds himself in a hierarchic order of dependence upwards and downwards. This promotes the sadomasochistic character which reacts with subservience toward the stronger and contempt towards the weaker. A gloomy perspective opens up: In economic crisis the fatherly authority in the patriarchal nuclear family of class society is weakened. But this does not open the road to a freer individual or a more matriarchal structure, but an increasingly authoritarian society acquires direct influence over individuals.

Fascism and Stalinism

With the transition of liberal capitalism into monopoly capitalism the road is open to authoritarian regimes, such as German National Socialism. Therefore Horkheimer concluded in "Die Juden und Europa" ("The Jews and Europe"), a totally pessimistic text, finished just before the outbreak of war in September 1939, that "he who does not wish to speak of capitalism, should also be silent about fascism" (Horkheimer 1939: 115). Horkheimer ruthlessly criticized all factions of the refugees from Nazi Germany. He opposed those refugees who in exile praised the capitalistic order of old Germany, while at the same time condemning the Marxist critique of capitalism, which Horkheimer held to be the only theory that foresaw fascism.

> The totalitarian order is nothing but its predecessor liberated from all inhibitions. Just like old people sometimes become just as vicious as they actually always were, at the end of the epoch class domination takes the form of *Volksgemeinschaft* [national community] . . . Fascism is the truth of modern society, which theory caught at first. Fascism fixes the extreme differences finally produced by the law of value. (Horkheimer 1939: 116)

Neither can Horkheimer share the hopes of the communist refugees that fascism will collapse and be succeeded by socialism, since the workers' movement has been betrayed by its own leaders through the Stalin–Hitler pact.

Here, for the first time, antisemitism is brought up. The Jews are also criticized by Horkheimer for idealizing the liberal order in which they were better off. They are persecuted, Horkheimer claims, because they are a reminder of the economic sphere of circulation, which has lost its meaning in the age of monopolies. They are no longer needed as agents of the sphere of circulation and therefore become the first victims. The consequence of antisemitism is the totalitarian order, and the struggle against this order must therefore be the struggle against antisemitism and its social basis. Or, as he emphatically expressed himself: "Liberalism can not be re-established" (Horkheimer 1939: 121).

The authoritarian state

The fascist state is for Horkheimer a variant of what he calls the authoritarian state (Horkheimer 1978a). This state means in part a return to the beginning of the epoch of the bourgeoisie, where its prehistory can be found in absolutism. In this perspective, the liberal state appears as a parenthesis. In his own time, Horkheimer distinguishes three variants of the authoritarian state: integral statism or state socialism, fascism, and reformism. Both of the latter ones are, using a term introduced by Pollock, denoted as state capitalistic. In state capitalism, in fascism as well as in reformism (which is the name given to democratic states) bureaucracy has the economic mechanism in its hand and distributes the surplus value. Market and private property persist, but the mechanisms of competition are dispensed with. Integral statism or state socialism – Horkheimer, of course, had in his mind the Soviet Union under Stalin – is, on the other hand, the most obvious form of the authoritarian state, since it has made itself completely independent of private capital. Compared to the other two, fascism is just a mixed form.

The Dialectic of Enlightenment

Between 1942 and 1944 Horkheimer and Adorno, now both living in Los Angeles, together wrote what would become the most famous and noteworthy work of the Frankfurt School, *The Dialectic of Enlightenment*. Horkheimer and Adorno pose themselves the question "why mankind, instead of entering into a truly human condition, is sinking into a new kind of barbarism" (Horkheimer and Adorno 1979 [1947]: xi). They look for the answer in contradictions within enlightenment, the very movement which was supposed to lead to a condition of true humanity. However, they redefine this concept from encompassing only a period in intellectual history to a universal attempt of humanity as a whole to understand and control the world. Therefore, it is said that myth is already enlightenment.

Myth and enlightenment

The dialectic of enlightenment means that enlightenment has reverted to its opposite and has become a myth. The world of myth is tied to the cyclical character of nature, "the eternal return" and therefore the retreat into myth is a new imprisonment in nature. "Eternal return" and "new imprisonment in nature" signal a new influence on critical theory from the discussions of Adorno and Benjamin during the thirties. To Horkheimer and Adorno the repetition of the cycle of nature reappears in the power of mathematical formalism over thinking, in the compulsory action of the neurotic and in the compulsion of the capitalist economy to perpetually repeat the circulation process of commodity exchange. Just like the exchange of commodities, enlightenment makes everything alike, erases all particular qualities, and finally turns against itself in that it forbids every thought which does not simply reproduce what is. Here we are back in the critique of the idea of identity between thought and reality, which Horkheimer once opposed in Lukács, but the object of critique is now the demand of positivism for conceptual clarity.

The dialectic of enlightenment also means that the only way out lies in enlightenment itself. Horkheimer and Adorno do not want to be mistaken for presenting either a conservative criticism of culture or existential philosophy. Despite their irreconcilability with enlightenment, going as far as calling it totalitarian, they still share the strivings of enlightenment towards free thinking, and "man's emergence from his self-incurred immaturity" (Horkheimer and Adorno 1979: 81 in the famous words of Immanuel Kant):

> Its [enlightenment's] untruth does not consist in what its romantic enemies have always reproached it for: analytical method, return to elements, dissolution through reflective thought; but instead in the fact that for enlightenment the process is always decided from the start. (Horkheimer and Adorno 1979: 24)

The self-reflection of enlightenment

Read from a philosophical angle, *The Dialectic of Enlightenment* is a critique of reason, but a critique of reason with its own means, a self-reflection of enlightenment. The development of the human being into a reasonable being means that it increasingly masters the natural environment in the form of the development of the forces of production. Simultaneously it also increasingly masters his own inner nature, as it has been described by Sigmund Freud (1856–1939), through the frustration of the satisfaction of immediate drives and the development of the superego. The critique is directed against this mastering reason or the narrowing of reason to *instrumental* reason, as it is called in a later book by Horkheimer (Horkheimer 1947). Simultaneously, *The Dialectic of Enlightenment* is a plea for a more comprehensive, reflexive reason, as envisioned by philosophy from Kant to Hegel, the period in the history of philosophy which, particularly for Adorno, constituted the climax of thinking. From the point of view of social theory the book can be read as an extension of both the analysis of the occidental process of rationalization, as presented by Max Weber (see chapter 6), and of Marx's analysis of the reduction of the commodity to exchange-value (see chapter 2) as a process with consequences for society and culture as a whole.

The book has an oddly fragmentary and unfinished form. The title first given to it by Horkheimer and Adorno, "Philosophical Fragments," is actually the most appropriate. An introductory conceptual qualification of about 50 pages is followed by two lengthy digressions. The first one, "Odysseus or Myth and Enlightenment," is a reading of Homer's epic on the homecoming of Odysseus as the story of the birth of the bourgeois individual in the struggle with the world of myth. To outwit the dangers lurking on his way, Odysseus trained the ability of cunning and self-control demanded by modern man. When he allows himself to be tied to the mast, in order not to be tempted by the songs of the sirens, he anticipates the disciplined enjoyment of the concert audience of later times. The proletarians, the oarsmen, whose ears he plugs with wax to prevent them from being enticed, are not allowed enjoyment but must work. The second digression, "Juliette or Enlightenment and Morality," deals with how all the moral values which the enlightenment advocates are hollowed out by the demands of consequence and system. This is followed by a chapter on "The Culture Industry: Enlightenment as Mass Deception," in which modern mass culture is criticized for fitting culture into the circulation of commodities. The last chapter (except for a number of "Notes and Drafts," bringing the book to an end), "Elements of Anti-Semitism," presents the theory behind the project on antisemitism, which would be the last great research project of the IfS in exile.

The Authoritarian Personality

In the beginning of the forties the IfS managed to establish contact with the American Jewish Committee as an external financier, which led to the breakthrough of the Frankfurt School to a broader scientific public with probably their most successful attempt ever to combine social theory and empirical research. The project, called *Studies in Prejudice*, resulted in five larger studies, mainly centered on psychological and historical aspects of antisemitism. Adorno was one of four co-authors of the most famous of the studies, *The Authoritarian Personality* (Adorno et al. 1950).

This study combined several methodological approaches. It is above all famous for the various scale-models which were constructed to measure different attitudes of the persons interviewed: antisemitism (the A–S scale), ethnocentrism (E scale), politico-economic conservatism (PEC scale) and antidemocratic trends (F scale, where F stands for fascism). These scales were constructed with the aid of questionnaires. The study also employed psychological picture tests and qualitative analyses of interviews conducted by professional psychologists.

Prejudice and personality structure

The idea of the book was to investigate socio-psychological presuppositions for the totalitarian delusion, which, according to the study, to a certain extent had been shown to be independent of economic, political, and geographical circumstances. The old idea from

Fromm's investigation of German workers about the connection between political ideology and psychic constitution was tried here in a new context. The point, however, was not to explain the emergence of totalitarian systems in a reductionistic manner derived from psychology alone. Psychological changes were understood only as results of social changes that also were realized in the individual. Interest was rather directed towards this social-psychological force field between individual and society.

The questionnaires distributed posed explicit questions concerning opinions on current political and economic issues and on attitudes toward ethnic and religious minorities. Moreover, questions were posed, as in Fromm's investigation, concerning private views and behavior which were not directly related to politics or prejudice. These questions concerned youth, sexuality, friendship, superstition, work, education, literature, criminality, etc. Through studying patterns in the totality of the answers to these types of questions it was claimed that it is possible to access underlying traits of personality that revealed authoritarian tendencies. The results showed a higher correlation between psychologically motivated inclinations and explicit prejudices than between political convictions and conscious prejudices. That is to say, the personality structure is a stronger determinant as to whether a person is inclined to fall victim to hateful propaganda and persecute weaker groups, than if he or she has conservative or even reactionary views. Through choosing a number of individuals on the extreme ends of the scales for in-depth interviews, i.e. one group of extremely prejudiced and one of relatively unprejudiced persons, it was possible to control the results.

The authoritarian type of personality shows a stiff, unchanging, psychic structure. He recognizes unreservedly everything and everybody who possesses power, he emphasizes in an irrational way conventional values, correct outward behavior, success, industriousness, health, and physical cleanliness. His conventionalism expresses itself in uncritical attitudes and hierarchical thinking. He relates submissively to the idealized moral authority in the group he considers himself belonging to, while at the same time he is constantly prepared to condemn those who do not belong or whom he considers of less worth. The authoritarian personality lacks a spontaneous and vivid relationship to other human beings. Behind this negative attitude to everything that does not concern oneself or one's own group lies a weakened self, in a psychoanalytical sense. Adorno is well aware that the division "prejudiced" and "unprejudiced" is in itself a stereotype of the kind shown by the authoritarian personality. The schematic thinking characterizing the authoritarian personality can, however, also be found among the unprejudiced, which is explained by Adorno as a general cultural pattern in consequence of increasing mechanization and bureaucratization.

The Frankfurt School after the War

After 1950, when Adorno and Horkheimer had returned to Germany, Adorno became the one who personified the critical theory of society and influenced several generations of students. The radical generation of students of the sixties, in particular, embraced critical theory as a current within Western, non-Stalinist Marxism. Simultaneously Herbert Marcuse experienced a late popularity, above all in the USA, as the philosopher of the student revolt and its elder spokesman, particularly with his study of *One-Dimensional Man*, a critique of consumer society, typical of its time. Many in the sixties generation gradually oriented themselves toward more orthodox brands of Marxism and criticized what was understood as a pessimistic tone in the critical theory of Horkheimer and Adorno, which led them to reject revolutionary political practice.

The Frankfurt School and Aesthetics

It is possible to trace how "splinters" of the Frankfurt School, after its dissolution, have been used in a multitude of productive ways within social theory, methodology, theory of socialization, social psychology, pedagogics, etc. (Brunkhorst 1986). During the eighties and the nineties Adorno's and above all Benjamin's works have found several new readers, particularly within the humanities. It is within aesthetics and cultural theory that Adorno and Benjamin, with their respective, posthumous, unfinished *Aesthetic Theory* (Adorno 1997) and *Das Passagen-Werk* (Benjamin 1982), have left the most lasting imprints. Benjamin searches for the original history (*Urgeschichte*) of modernity during the nineteenth century in the world of commodities in the market arcades of Paris. This work presents all the peculiarities of Benjamin: his delight in fragments and quotations, his eye for detail, and his collector's nature. The book, which occupied him until his death, is to a large extent an enormous collection of quotations which he put together during his studies in the National Library of Paris, concerning such widely varied subjects as fashion, railways, the *flâneur*, architecture, Karl Marx, Saint-Simon, the Paris Commune, etc.

Adorno's aesthetic theory attempts to show the social content in all art, even the most advanced art which seems to turn away entirely from society. A common reading of Adorno is that he ultimately can not see any other critical instance than art. "Art is the social antithesis of society" (Adorno 1997: 8). Adorno deals above all with modernist art, particularly modern music. Authentic art is the carrier of a truth which may be interpreted by philosophy. It is characterized by a development of the material where the artist, though striving toward being as advanced as possible, or "absolutely modern," unintentionally expresses social contradictions. While culture as a whole is subsumed under the commodity form and thus becomes ideology, only the most advanced art, which is simultaneously the most inaccessible for the audience, remains as the only instance capable of expressing any truth at all about the condition of society. Thus Adorno claims that, for instance, the atonal music of Arnold Schönberg anticipated the sufferings of the victims in the concentration camps.

Obviously, this theory of art can no longer be fully valid after the dissolution of modernism. In the postmodern condition art no longer searches ahead, but moves backwards, quotes, paraphrases, and spreads in different directions. The entirety of everyday life is aestheticized, simultaneously as the borders between, for instance, art and advertisement are erased. In this situation, however, Adorno's quest for the truth and social content of art is still a challenge for critical aesthetics (Billing 1994).

Bibliography

Primary:

Bibliographies:

A general bibliography of the Frankfurt School can be found in Wiggershaus, Rolf. 1994: *The Frankfurt School. Its History, Theories and Political Significance*. Cambridge: Polity Press.

Adorno:

Görtzen, René. 1983: Theodor W. Adorno. Vorläufige Bibliographie seiner Schriften und der Sekundärlitteratur. In Ludwig von Friedeburg and Jürgen Habermas (eds), *Adorno- Konferenz 1983*. Frankfurt am Main: Suhrkamp.

Nordquist, Joan. 1994: *Theodor Adorno (II): A Bibliography*. Santa Cruz: Reference and Research Service.

Schultz, Klaus. 1971: Vorläufige Bibliographie der Schriften Th. W. Adornos. In Hermann Schweppenhäuser (ed.), *Th. W. Adorno zum Gedächtnis. Eine Sammlung*. Frankfurt am Main: Suhrkamp.

Benjamin:

Benjamin, Walter. 1989: *Gesammelte Schriften*, ed. Rolf Tiedemann and Hermann Schweppenhäuser, bd. 7, vol. 2. Frankfurt am Main: Suhrkamp.

Tiedemann, Rolf. 1972: Bibliographie der Erstdrucke von Benjamins Schriften. In Siegfried Unseld (ed.), *Zur Aktualität Walter Benjamins,* Frankfurt am Main: Suhrkamp.

Fromm:

Funk, Rainer. 1981: Gesamtverzeichnis der Schriften Fromms. In *Erich Fromm. Gesamtausgabe,* ed. Rainer Funk, vol. X, Register. Stuttgart: Deutsche Verlags- Anstalt.

Horkheimer:

Schmid Noerr, Gunzelin. 1986: Bibliographie der Erstveröffentlichungen Max Horkheimers. In Alfred Schmidt and Norbert Altwicker (eds), *Max Horkheimer heute: Werk und Wirkung,* Frankfurt am Main: Fischer.

Marcuse:

Kellner, Douglas. 1984: Bibliography. In *Herbert Marcuse and the Crisis of Marxism*. London: Macmillan.

Collected works:

Adorno, Theodor W. 1970–86: *Gesammelte Schriften*, ed. Rolf Tiedemann. 20 vols. Frankfurt am Main: Suhrkamp.

Benjamin, Walter. 1972–89: *Gesammelte Schriften*, ed. Rolf Tiedemann und Hermann Schweppenhäuser. Frankfurt am Main: Suhrkamp.

Fromm, Erich. 1980–1: *Gesamtausgabe*, ed. Rainer Funk. Stuttgart: Deutsche Verlags-Anstalt.

Horkheimer, Max. 1985–96: *Gesammelte Schriften*, ed. Alfred Schmidt, and Gunzelin Schmid Noerr. 19 vols. Frankfurt am Main: Fischer.

Marcuse, Herbert. 1978–87: *Schriften*. 9 vols. Frankfurt am Main: Suhrkamp.

Works:

Adorno, Theodor W. 1950: *The Authoritarian Personality*, (with Else Frenkel-Brunswik, Daniel J. Levinson, and R. Nevitt Sanford). New York: Harper.

—— 1967 [1955]: *Prisms*. London: Spearman.

—— 1969: *Stichworte. Kritische Modelle 2*. Frankfurt am Main: Suhrkamp.

Berkeley: University of California Press.

Marcuse, Herbert. 1987 [1932]: *Hegel's Ontology and the Theory of Historicity.* Cambridge, MA: MIT Press.

—— 1932: Neue Quellen zur Grundlegung des Historischen Materialismus. *Die Gesellschaft,* 9, 136–74.

—— 1933: Über die philosophischen Grundlagen des wirtschaftswissenshaftlichen Arbeitsbegriffs. *Archiv für Sozialwissenschaft und Sozialpolitik,* 257–92.

—— 1934: Der Kampf gegen den Liberalismus in der totalitären Staatsauffassung. *Zeitschrift für Sozialforschung,* 3/2, 161–95.

—— 1937: Über den affirmativen Charakter der Kultur. *Zeitschrift für Sozialfor schung,* 6/1, 54–94.

—— 1941: *Reason and Revolution: Hegel and the Rise of Social Theory.* New York: Oxford University Press.

—— 1955: *Eros and Civilization: A Philosophical Inquiry into Freud.* Boston: Beacon Press.

—— 1964: *One Dimensional Man. Studies in the Ideology of Advanced Industrial Society.* London: Routledge & Kegan Paul.

—— 1965: *Kultur und Gesellschaft.* 2 vols. Frankfurt am Main: Suhrkamp.

—— 1968a: *Protest, Demonstrations, Revolt.* Stockholm: Aldus and Bonnier.

—— 1968b: *Negations. Essays in Critical Theory.* Boston: Beacon Press.

—— 1970: *Five Lectures: Psychoanalysis, Politics, and Utopia.* London: Allan Lane.

—— 1972a: *Counterrevolution and Revolt.* Boston: Beacon Press.

—— 1972b: *An Essay on Liberation.* Harmondsworth, Middlesex: Penguin Books.

—— 1972c: *Studies in Critical Philosophy.* London: NBL.

—— 1978: *The Aesthetic Dimension. Toward a Critique of Marxist Aesthetics.* Boston: Beacon Press.

—— 1983: *From Luther to Popper.* London: Verso.

—— 1985: *Soviet Marxism: A Critical Analysis.* New York: Columbia University Press.

—— 1998: *Technology, War and Fascism.* London: Routledge.

Zeitschrift für Sozialforschung, Jahrgang I–IX, ed. Max Horkheimer. Mit einer Einleitung von Alfred Schmidt. Reprint, 1980. München: Deutscher Taschenbuch Verlag. [Articles and reviews by Adorno, Benjamin, Fromm, Horkheimer, Marcuse, and others. Primarily in German, but also in English and French.]

Neumann, Franz. 1966 (1957): *The Democratic and the Authoritarian State: Essays in Political and Legal Theory.* London: Collier-Macmillan.

Secondary:

Alway, Joan. 1995: *Critical Theory and Political Possibilities: Conceptions of Emancipatory Politics in the Works of Horkheimer, Adorno, Marcuse, and Habermas.* Westport, CT: Greenwood Press.

Andrew, Benjamin (ed.) 1989: *The Problems of Modernity. Adorno and Benjamin.* London and New York: Routledge.

Bernstein, Jay. 1994: *The Frankfurt School: Critical Assesments.* London: Routledge.

Billing, Björn. 1994: Estetiken efter Adorno. *Häften för kritiska studier,* 27/2–3, 20–38.

Bonss, Wolfgang. 1982: *Die Einübung des Tatsachenblicks. Zur Struktur und Verän derung empirisher Sozialforschung.* Frankfurt am Main: Suhrkamp.

Bonss, Wolfgang, and Axel Honneth (eds) 1982: *Sozialforschung als Kritik. Zum Sozialwissen schaftlichen Potential der Kritischen Theorie.* Frankfurt am Main: Suhrkamp.

Bottomore, Tom. 1984: *The Frankfurt School.* London: Routledge.

Brodersen, Momme. 1996: *Walter Benjamin: A Biography.* London: Verso.

Brunkhorst, Hauke. 1983: Paradigmakern und Theoriendynamik der Kritischen Theorie der Gesellschaft. *Soziale Welt,* 3.

—— 1986: Soziologie und Kritische Theorie. Zur Bedeutung der Frankfurter Schule für die Nachkriegssoziologie. In Josef Hülsdünker and Rolf Schellhase (eds), *Soziologiegeschichte. Identität und Krisen einer 'engagierten' Disziplin*. Berlin: Duncker & Humblot.

Buck-Morss, Susan. 1977: *The Origin of Negative Dialectics: Theodor W. Adorno, Walter Benjamin and the Frankfurt Institute*. Hassocks, Sussex: Harvester.

—— 1989: *The Dialetics of Seeing. Walter Benjamin and the Arcades Project*. Cambridge, MA: MIT Press.

Cook, Deborah. 1996: *The Culture Industry Revisited*. Lanham, MD: Rowman & Littlefield.

Christie, Richard, and Jahoda, Marie (eds) 1954: *Studies in the Scope and Method of 'The Authoritarian Personality'*. Glencoe, IL: Free Press.

Dahms, Hans-Joachim. 1994: *Positivismusstreit. Die Auseinandersetzungen der Frankfurter Schule mit dem logischen Positivismus, dem amerikanischen Pragmatismus und dem kritischen Rationalismus*. Frankfurt am Main: Suhrkamp.

Dubiel, Helmut. 1985: *Theory and Politics*. Cambridge, MA: MIT Press.

Eyerman, Ron. 1981: *False Consciousness and Ideology in Marxist Theory*. Stockholm: Almquist & Wiksell.

Fischer, Gerhard (ed.) 1996: *"With the Sharpened Axe of Reason": Approaches to Walter Benjamin*. Oxford: Berg.

Friedeburg, Ludwig von, and Habermas, Jürgen (eds) 1983: *Adorno-Konferenz 1983*. Frankfurt am Main: Suhrkamp.

Fuld, Werner. 1979: *Walter Benjamin. Zwischen den Stühlen. Eine Biographie*. Munich: Hanser.

*Held, David. 1980: *Introduction to Critical Theory: From Horkheimer to Habermas*. London: Hutchinson.

Honneth, Axel. 1991: *The Critique of Power*. Cambridge, MA: MIT Press.

Jameson, Fredric. 1990: *Late Marxism. Adorno, or The Persistence of the Dialectic*. London and New York: Verso.

Jarvis, Simon. 1998: *Adorno: A Critical Introduction*. Cambridge: Polity Press.

Jay, Martin. 1973: *The Dialectical Imagination: A History of the Frankfurt School and the Institute of Social Research, 1923–1950*. London: Heinemann.

—— 1984: *Adorno*. London: Fontana.

*Kellner, Douglas. 1984: *Herbert Marcuse and the Crisis of Marxism*. London: Macmillan.

Korthals, Michiel. 1985: Die kritische Gesellschaftstheorie der frühen Horkheimer. Missverständnisse über das Verhältnis von Horkheimer, Lukács und dem Positivismus. *Zeitschrift für Soziologie*, 14/4, 315–29.

Migdal, Ulrike. 1981: *Die Frühgeschichte des Frankfurter Instituts für Sozialforschung*. Frankfurt am Main: Campus.

Missac, Pierre. 1995: *Walter Benjamin's Passages*. Cambridge, MA: MIT Press.

Nicholson, Shierry Weber. 1997: *Exact Imagination, Late Work: On Adorno's Aesthetics*. Cambridge, MA: MIT Press.

Reijen, Willem van, and Schmid Noerr, Gunzelin (eds) 1988: *Grand Hotel Abgrund. Eine Photobiographie der Kritischen Theorie*. Hamburg: Junius Verlag.

Rose, Gillian. 1978: *The Melancholy Science: An Introduction to the Thought of Theodor W. Adorno*. London: Macmillan.

Therborn, Göran. 1977: The Frankfurt School. In *Western Marxism: A Critical Reader*. London: New Left Books.

*Wiggershaus, Rolf. 1994: *The Frankfurt School. Its History, Theories and Political Significance*. Cambridge: Polity Press.

Witkin, Robert. 1998: *Adorno on Music*. London: Routledge.

Wolin, Richard. 1994: *Walter Benjamin: An Aesthetic of Redemption*. Berkeley: University of California Press.

Zenit 1993: 1 (119).

chapter 11

Neo-Marxist Theories

Jens Peter Frølund Thomsen and Heine Andersen

KEY CONCEPTS

ANTAGONISM – a state of conflict and oppression between two groups, in which the relation modifies the ideal interests of each group.

CLASSES – refers to individuals' position in the social division of labor. Classes consist of a sum of individuals that carry out the same functions in the social division of labor.

DISCOURSE – a horizon of meaning and action, i.e., a certain segment of the social reality that is organized by interpretations and forms of actions derived from these interpretations.

DISLOCATION – refers to the fact that structures should not be seen as pure limitations to political action. Structures embody contradictory processes and are therefore incapable of determining actions and developments in any direct and predictable manner.

EXPLOITATION – a social relationship in which one group gains welfare advantages from another group's labor. Analytical Marxism explains exploitation as differences in the possession of productive resources.

HEGEMONY – defined by Gramsci as ideological leadership based on broad social acceptance; in discourse analysis a broad alliance of groups that dominate the groups that are not part of this alliance.

HISTORICAL MATERIALISM – a theory of historical development, originally advanced by Karl Marx. Gerald A. Cohen formulates the theory as a technological, functionalist theory. Economic structures rise and fall according to that which benefits or impedes the development of productive forces. Legal, political, and ideological structures are conditioned by the economic structure.

PROPERTY RELATIONS – ownership of productive resources. Analytical Marxism operates with the following types of resources: capital, labor, and productive capabilities and skills.

UNDECIDABILITY – social relations become undecidable because they are dislocated. In other words, conflicts are conjunctural phenomena, but phenomena that are embedded in social relations and structures. Dislocation and undecidability are features that make transformative practices possible.

By the late 1970s, several Marxist scholars had reached the conclusion that classical Marxism was in a process of crisis, and they found it hard to use it as a tool with which to analyze modern society. This led to the development of two new approaches within the Marxist tradition: Neo-Gramscian theory or discourse analysis; and analytical Marxism. These two approaches developed at the same time and share the declared purpose of renewing Marxist theory by bringing in insights from other traditions. They both share the view that the classic texts of Marxism should be approached in an undogmatic manner. The approaches have nothing else in common, but they do highlight some general epistemological issues with relevance for theory construction within the social sciences. Analytical Marxism is clearly influenced by certain strands of positivism, which means that social theory is defined as a deductive-nomological system. Analytical Marxism sees it as strictly necessary to derive causal hypotheses from a set of strong assumptions about the nature of social relations and human beings. In contrast, discourse analysis accepts a hermeneutic conception of theory according to which there is no need to explain and predict within the social sciences. The key focus for discourse analysis is to analyze social relations and human beings as historical products, an endeavor that makes it entirely irrelevant to make strong assumptions as a starting point. Therefore these two approaches touch upon major epistemological issues within the social sciences. In particular, they represent two different ways of defining the concept of social theory.

Neo-Gramscian Theory: Discourse Analysis

At the end of the 1970s, the attempt to renew Marxist theory drew attention to the importance of the writings of the Italian Marxist and strategist, Antonio Gramsci (see chapter 9). Some argued that Gramsci's work could underpin a new left-wing project because he insisted that a democratization process need not involve a direct confrontation between classes. The Gramscian conception of democracy allows for the possibility that elements of bourgeois-liberal democracy can play a positive role in the construction of a socialist society (Jessop 1980; Laclau and Mouffe 1985: 149–93; Mouffe 1979; Sassoon 1980). As such, Gramsci rejects the Leninist view that bourgeois institutions necessarily have to be completely destroyed because they have no relevance for working-class ideology.

Gramsci was crucial in the development of a new approach to social analysis, an approach reflected in British discourse analysis. Gramscian analysis is more relevant when analyzing modern societies than classical Marxism, primarily because Gramscian concepts allow for greater complexity and because they are not direct derivatives of rigid class analysis.

Discourse analysis was introduced in the mid-1980s and has been developed by the Argentinean-English philosopher and political scientist, Ernesto Laclau (b. 1935), and the Belgian-English philosopher, Chantal Mouffe (b. 1937), who together agreed to establish a new approach to social analysis by utilizing Gramscian insights. Of course, Gramscian texts only serve as a starting point for discourse analysis which, as the name implies, forms part of the linguistic turn within the social sciences. According to Laclau and Mouffe, discourse analysis involves an effort to apply linguistic tools to social and political phenomena. In this respect, their project represents one of the most original contributions to political science within the last ten years.

Discourse analysis combines strands of linguistic philosophy, such as structuralism, analytical philosophy, and poststructuralism (see chapter 18). Its epistemological foundation involves a deliberate rejection of rationalism, objectivism, and deterministic notions of causation. In this view, traditional attempts to reveal the inner rationality of social developments by invoking strong assumptions about "rational behaviour," "profit maximization," and "class behavior" are untenable because they ignore the composite character of modern society. According to discourse analysis, modern societies embody both changing and competing forms of behavior. As a consequence, modern societies do not show the kind of stability and transparency that are often taken for granted in traditional models of causation. In terms of causation, discourse analysis sees historical configurations of variables as causally significant. In effect, discourse analysis strives for neither parsimony nor the generation of law-like statements.

Discourse analysis is stimulating because it takes issue with some of the key tenets of much social science. First, discourse analysis asserts that ideology, language, and symbols are just as important as material relations when explaining historical development. Second, it insists that material relations cannot be understood in isolation from their linguistic and ideological conditions of existence. The third claim is that language and symbols represent the tools with which reality is constructed. Finally, discourse analysis claims that political conflict and dominance engender structural changes in social organization.

Discourse analysis is a subjectivist approach which regards language, symbols, and ideological consciousness as the origins of human action. However, as we shall see later, these aspects are not necessarily emphasized at the expense of the material and structural aspects of the social organization. Discourse analysis is simply subjectivist in its basic perspective.

Historical Background

Discourse analysis borrows certain ideas from Karl Marx (see chapter 2), but the influence of Antonio Gramsci is far more significant. Discourse analysis rejects Marx's class analysis and fully accepts Gramsci's view that non-class-based forces can also play an important role in historical development (Laclau and Mouffe 1985: 65–88). A brief discussion of the difference between Marx and Gramsci according to discourse analysis is necessary here.

Marx strives to understand social dynamics while also maintaining that society constitutes a stable order rooted in class relations. Discourse analysis fully accepts the attempt to create a dynamic theory, but rejects Marx's attempt to define modern society in terms of stable class structures. Discourse analysis holds that one cannot have it both ways if the real aim is to generate a theory capable of illuminating different social dynamics. Furthermore, discourse analysis also argues that modern society cannot possibly be reduced to one political conflict (Laclau and Mouffe 1985: 83–5).

This attempt to understand society in more complex terms is what makes Gramsci particularly attractive. Compared with Marx, Gramsci's analyses were always historically specific and developed in the context of an analysis of Italian history, a context which was entirely different from the historical characteristics of Western Europe which fuelled Marx's thinking. Given the history of Italy, and its delayed unification, Gramsci draws attention to very different, yet equally important, political lines of conflict within Italian society. Gramsci underlines how religious, cultural, and ideological issues as well as economic issues lead to important dimensions of conflict in the social order (Gramsci 1982: 294–313). He does not reject class struggle as the basic conflict, but the distinctive thing about Gramsci's analyses is that he emphasizes other dimensions of conflict which are not necessarily reducible to class conflict (Gramsci 1982: 57–8, 130, 133, 181, 222).

However, discourse analysis is both post-Marxist and post-Gramscian and does not accept Gramsci's insistence on the primacy of class struggle. Instead, Laclau and Mouffe want to draw out the full implications of the pluralistic line of thought which is implicit in Gramscian analysis. Political plurality, social dynamics, and their mutual interaction represent crucial ingredients in the discourse analytical approach. The full implications of these claims will be described below, but put briefly, the aim of discourse analysis is to pave the way for a new, postmodern understanding of politics.

Discourse Analysis

In contrast to mainstream political and sociological theory, British discourse analysis is strongly influenced by French and Anglo-Saxon language philosophy, especially by the French philosopher, Jacques Derrida (b. 1930), and the Austrian language philosopher, Ludwig Wittgenstein (1889–1951). Using the work of these two philosophers, discourse analysis advances its main proposition that social reality is – and can only be – discursively constituted.

In philosophical terms, discourse analysis seeks to go beyond that distinction which is often made between language and reality. The gap between language and reality is just one of countless dichotomies in social science, but probably the most basic one. In a social science context, this dichotomy is important because it tends to build upon the further assertion that linguistic, that is, nonmaterial, phenomena are less significant than material phenomena. This materialistic view is most clearly expressed in Marx's insistence that the material reality works behind the backs of social actors and therefore exerts a decisive influence on their linguistic and ideological consciousness (see chapter 2).

Discourse analysis does not accept this materialistic view of history because it differentiates between consciousness and materiality and it reduces language and consciousness to secondary phenomena compared to material relations. In a novel attempt to construe consciousness and material reality as different aspects of the same social reality, discourse analysis introduces the concept of discourse. This concept rejects any ontological distinction between language and reality and any a priori hierarchy of explanatory principles.

Discourse as social practice

The concept of "discourse" refers to the social world as a linguistic reality. However, the central idea is that a discourse is not equivalent to the notion of language. British discourse analysis strives to define the concept of discourse as certain forms of practice through which language, actors, and types of behavior connect to one another (Laclau and Mouffe 1985: 108). By emphasizing discourse as a practice, discourse analysis insists that discourse includes nonlinguistic as well as linguistic elements. Discourse can specifically be defined as an actively constructed horizon of meaning and action, that is, as referring to concrete relations established among certain objects, language codes, and types of behavior (Laclau and Mouffe 1985: 105–8; 1987: 64–92).

In other words, the major ontological claim of discourse analysis is that discourse is coextensive with the social; that what is true for discourse is also true for reality. Discourses operate at all levels of society because all social interaction between human beings requires a frame of meaning and the existence of particular language codes. The organization of the family, the workplace, or the activities of the state cannot take place unless a common discursive framework exists within these spheres. In other words: if one denies the existence of social and political discourses, one simply makes the social world unintelligible.

We illustrate the implications of the concept of discourse by considering the pollution and environmental imbalances which cause considerable problems almost everywhere. Discourse analysis would approach this problem by raising two sets of questions: Has this conspicuous, global problem automatically become the first priority on national political agendas? Why didn't the environment become a crucial political issue until the end of the 1960s, given that pollution has existed since the origins of industrialism? The answers that discourse analysis would give to those questions would emphasize that very little, if anything, follows from the real existence of a given problem. Environmental problems do not by themselves lead to environmental regulation. Environmental regulation results from the imposition of a green discourse into social reality.

To the discourse analyst it is important to recognize that the environmentalist discourse establishes only one possible horizon of meaning; there is a struggle between discourses.

So the owners of capital insist that the very same ecological imbalances should be conceptualized in an entirely different manner. First, the capitalists disagree with the environmentalists about the size of the problem. Second, they do not support the same policy recommendations, since their discourse emphasizes that environmental regulation should be subordinated to the demands of market profitability .

This is a clash between two discourses. Neither is more true than the other and they both present reality, but they are different versions of reality. The two discourses also produce different constructions of meaning about the same problem in the so-called "real world," which is no more real than it allows for different interpretations. Hence, language and reality not only coincide, the linguistic dimension actively – and causally – also constructs the real world. In effect, discourse analysis tries to substantiate how these constructions of the real world are deeply political in character. Politics operates in and through discursive practices.

The Discourse Analytical Conception of Politics

Discourse analysis argues that some ontological issues have to be critically examined in order to generate a new conception of politics (Laclau 1989: 63–6; 1992: 121–37). As a consequence it is necessary to pose the fundamental question: What kind of assumptions have to be introduced in order to understand politics as a distinct category with independent effects on society?

In an attempt to produce a more satisfactory theory of politics, discourse analysis makes two important assumptions with respect to the nature of social agents and social structures. First, with respect to agents, it is assumed that there is no necessary causal relation between the structural location of agents and their specific identity or interests (Laclau 1990: 18–25, 103–12). Agents occupying similar structural locations can take on totally different identities. Second, it is assumed that social structures often embody a constitutive conflict (dislocation) between a set of dominating processes and a set of competing processes (Laclau 1990: 39–55). Structures are never fully constituted as they always encompass contradictory processes and, therefore, inherent potentials for their own transformation.

Social undecidability

These two ontological assumptions imply that social relations should always be conceived as *undecidable* with regard to the identity of social actors and the specific construction of social structures (Laclau 1990: 36–41). The identity of social agents and the future course of structural developments are contingent and highly unpredictable. Social identities and structures develop in and through historical processes and should always be analyzed in close relation to their specific, historical conditions of existence. Thus, Laclau's principle of undecidability necessitates dynamic, historical analysis and rejects attempts to predict social identities and structural developments from abstract, theoretical models.

Laclau's explicit purpose is to provide a social model which leaves genuine room for historical change and political intervention. There is no doubt that Laclau is motivated by the shortcomings of Marxism: that is, its inability to understand change within the capitalist order. Yet discourse analysis also wants to understand how a minimum of organizational and political coherence is imposed upon society. These forms of practice which create change as well as stability in the social order constitute the core of the discourse analytical conception of politics (Laclau 1990: 33–5).

Discourse analysis claims that political activities should not be defined by institutional criteria, that is, by their institutional origin or localization (Laclau and Mouffe 1985: 153). Political activities have no origin in an ontological sense, which means recognizing that politics pays no respect to institutional borders in modern society (Laclau and Mouffe 1985: 153). Institutional criteria, therefore, have no relevance when assessing to what extent a certain social practice qualifies as a political practice. Moreover, an attempt to define politics in terms of particular agents, for example, social classes, is no solution either. Social classes are not by definition irrelevant, but the dominant political discourses at particular points of time may not have any relation to classes. Hence, no compelling reasons exist for accepting the notion of class struggle as an adequate definition of politics.

Politics and antagonisms

Discourse analysis sees politics as the very condition for the construction of the social order. It is political activities which account for the very nature of the social order. Accordingly, discourse analysis defines politics as antagonistic and hegemonic struggles taking place in the context of dislocated structures (Laclau 1990: 61). Politics is defined by three central concepts: antagonisms, hegemony, and dislocation. Politics refers to conflicts of interest, authority founded in dominance and consensus, and structural changes in society. These elements deserve to be examined in more detail.

It is the concept of antagonism which leads discourse analysis to conclude that society does not exist, or that it exists only as a number of partial orders (Laclau and Mouffe 1985: 113). An antagonism specifies a relation of conflict between two opposite social groups. Although the conflict can be about religion, economy, gender, race, or other things, we are dealing with a specific type of conflict. An antagonism exists when opposite groups actively strive to block one another's identity. Antagonisms operate through the use of two complementary linguistic tactics. The antagonizer makes a "chain of difference" in relation to the particular group it wishes to dominate. This results in a line of demarcation between two political camps: one representing "us" and the other representing "them." The next step for the antagonizer is to establish a "chain of equivalence" by the use of an ideological language that makes different, antagonized groups symbolize a common identity. If, for instance, a national majority argues that all immigrants and refugees are criminals and scroungers, a chain of equivalence has been established which deprives all these groups of their distinct characteristics.

Chains of difference represent the origin of conflict, whereas chains of equivalence amplify the conflictual character by not respecting "objective" differences. However, it should be emphasized that an antagonism involves a reciprocal process; the antagonizer is never totally dominant, as the antagonized groups strive to do exactly the same thing in order to avoid further loss of identity. Antagonisms involve domination, but also active resistance.

An antagonism engenders particular effects. Interests do not exist prior to the political process, but are strictly relational. The ideal interests and preferences a given actor group might have can never be fully realized because of the existence of antagonizing groups. In effect, antagonisms establish a basic negativity in the social world, because if a structure is antagonistic, no one group can fully realize its identity. As such, the ultimate effect of antagonistic constructions is that a given social order cannot be established as a complete order (Laclau and Mouffe 1985: 122–34).

If we return to our example, the antagonism established by demands for a green economy means that capital owners can no longer fully pursue their original role, because they have been deprived of their traditional identity, that is, their freedom to base production exclusively on profit maximization. Thus, because of the existence of antagonizing green groups, the capitalist class has not only been pressurized into a new situation, but also into an entirely new process of identification. As a result of this political pressure, capital owners have to reshape their identity. Similarly, when the environmentalists articulate their interests, they are confronted by a capitalist class which constantly tries to prevent the initiation of radical reforms to the capitalist economy. Accordingly, the basic logic is that relations of power and resistance, in a reciprocal process, continuously modify social interests and their structural underpinnings.

Politics and hegemony

Discourse analysis does not claim that every social relation can be changed at any time. The political field does not consist of conflictual relations among more or less equal groups. Discourse analysis does not agree with classical pluralism in regarding the political system as a system of "checks and balances," but rather conceives of it as a system of "checks and imbalances," a system that relies heavily on politically dominating coalitions (Laclau and Mouffe 1985: 142). The concept of hegemony refers to the existence of politically dominating coalitions of actors in any society.

Discourse analysis tries to substantiate this approach by a further elaboration of the Gramscian concept of hegemony (Laclau 1990: 94). Hegemony is thus another type of political activity. This does not mean that hegemony is unrelated to antagonistic conflict; rather, antagonisms always constitute the core of a hegemonic project (Laclau and Mouffe 1985: 135).

The starting point of hegemonic struggle is the construction of antagonistic relations. Yet hegemony also involves an effort to establish a society-wide, political authority on the basis of a common discursive interest This means recognizing that hegemonic constructions base themselves on a "policy of exclusion" and a "policy of inclusion." Hegemonic construction involves the conscious exclusion of competing groups and discourses (Laclau and Mouffe 1985: 134–45). In order to achieve a particular identity, a hegemonic discourse points out its distinctive foes, those which have to be marginalized in order to pave the way for hegemonic domination. Subsequently, a hegemonic construction points out its friends, which involves a particular attempt to establish a broad alliance based on an agreed policy discourse. The policy of inclusion provides a common identity uniting different groups around a particular discursive understanding of social reality. As an example, the capitalist economy and the organization of the European Union are still maintained by hegemonic alliances, but it is also a fact that both hegemonic projects essentially coexist with environmentalists and social movements opposing further European integration.

In terms of authority, the concept of hegemony does not refer to formal authority, but to that type of authority which originates from dominance and from general social and political support. Therefore, the concept of politics in discourse analysis has no problem analyzing the breakdown of the Eastern Bloc, where national-popular movements gained hegemonic domination over existing authorities in the communist state apparatus. The result was the establishment of another formal authority through pure political intervention.

In theoretical terms, hegemony constructs antagonistic cleavages (frontiers) in the social order, where certain groups achieve dominance and authority in relation to those groups whose alternative, opposing demands are excluded (Laclau and Mouffe 1985: 136). However, it is crucial to emphasize that the operation of antagonisms also has implications for the structural levels of society. Antagonisms are not agency-centered as such. Antagonisms affect structural parameters as well; an antagonistic struggle is often a battle about selecting those values and organizing principles which are supposed to direct the future course of structural and institutional development. The antagonistic conflicts over the construction of environmental regulation and European Union institutions are paradigmatic in this respect.

Neo-Marxist Critiques

British discourse analysis has been criticized by Marxist scholars in particular. One of the strongest objections comes from two Neo-Marxists, Bob Jessop (1990) and Norman Geras (1987, 1988). In their view, the concept of discourse is unable to address the central axis of modern sociological and Marxist theory, that is, the fundamental relation between the social structures and social actors. Hence it is argued that discourse analysis fails to offer a solution to the structure-agency problem in the social sciences. Indeed, it is often suggested that discourse analysis exaggerates the free will of actors at the expense of the structural constraints within which they operate. According to Neo-Marxists, this is a key weakness because structural and institutional factors put limits to what is discursively possible (Geras, 1987, 1988; Jessop 1990: 294–301).

In response, discourse analysis would argue that this conception of social structures is misleading. In order to avoid classic problems it is necessary to see structures as ontologically open-ended, because this allows for the emergence of different and competing discourses. If the social world is completely structured, there is no room for agency or for that matter political intervention. Thus, discourse analysis rejects structural determinism because such a notion is incompatible with the view that the world is open for different and changing discursive interpretations.

Discourse analysis has received considerable attention in both negative and positive terms. Within an Anglo-American context, one should refer to loyal presentations by Daly (1991) and especially Dallmayr (1989) who delivers a competent, philosophically oriented description of discourse analysis. For very critical reviews (or outright rejections), readers should consult the British journal *New Left Review*, especially contributions by Norman Geras (1987, 1988) and Nicos Mouzelis (1988).

Analytical Marxism

Another Neo-Marxist school emerging around 1980 was analytical Marxism. The central founding figures were the Norwegian Jon Elster (b. 1940), the Canadian-British philosopher, Gerald A. Cohen (b. 1941), and the Americans, Adam Przeworski, John E. Roemer

(b. 1945), and Erik Olin Wright (b. 1947). This school is sometimes referred to as either "rational choice Marxism" or "neo-classical Marxism," pertaining to inspiration from rational choice theory and modern, so-called neoclassical economic theory (see chapter 13).

Analytical Marxism is defined neither by a certain theory nor by any mutual set of key assumptions. Rather, it is centered around certain themes and guiding principles concerning approaches and methodological ideals. Jon E. Roemer (1986: 1ff) and Erik Olin Wright (1994: 178–98) have offered a description of these. They strongly emphasize (like Laclau and Mouffe) that analytical Marxism relates freely and undogmatically to Marx's theory (see chapter 2) and is even extremely critical at certain points. They call into question many key elements of Marx's economic theory, especially the labor theory of value, and the assumption about the inherent tendencies of capitalism to break down as a result of the so-called law of falling rate of profit. Analytical Marxism also takes a critical stand on orthodox interpretations of Marx's theory of historical development and class theory.

Nevertheless, this school maintains the term Marxism because it takes as its point of departure traditional themes from Marxism, such as class, exploitation, the development of productive forces and historical change, the role of the state and politics, and revolutions. But analytical Marxism also raises a series of new questions which have traditionally been neglected. For example, how can classes behave as collective actors (and can they behave collectively at all)? Why (if at all) is exploitation wrong (morally)? Does the working class under modern capitalism have an interest in socialism? Is a socialist revolution possible? Does exploitation exist in (the now dissolved) socialist societies? Are there any morally justifiable reasons for the demand for equality?

The word analytical was chosen in order to stress methodological cogency, rigorousness, and linguistic clarity, inspired by analytical philosophy, modern mathematics, and other methods used by contemporary "bourgeois" science. Analytical Marxists, such as Roemer and Przeworski, and in particular Jon Elster (1985), further stress the assumption of individual, egocentric rationality and methodological individualism. Rational choice theory and game theory are also incorporated (see chapter 13).

During the fifteen years that analytical Marxism has existed, a wide variety of analyses have appeared, ranging from theoretical to empirical and historical to moral philosophical. The most central, which are addressed below, deal with the theory of history, class and exploitation, politics, revolutions, and moral theory (see Mayer 1994 for a detailed description and critical analysis).

Cohen's Defense of Historical Materialism

In 1978 Gerald A. Cohen published his book, *Karl Marx's Theory of History: A Defense*. Even though this book has been subject to severe criticism, it deserves mentioning. In a nutshell, Marx's understanding of history was that changes were brought about by growth in productive forces, and that relations of production could either promote or impede the development of productive forces, affecting the development of class structure. When relations of production obstruct the development of productive forces this may lead to revolution, which changes the economic foundation. The political-ideological superstructure then adapts to the new conditions (see chapter 2).

One of the most frequently discussed issues in Marxism has always been the precise contents of these assumptions and their scientific status. Rather than searching for the "original meaning" intended by Marx in the texts, Cohen constructs his own version of the theory, based on those elements from Marx which best comply with the methodological principles of cogency, clarity, and empirical validity. Cohen's result is an unadulterated technological and functionalist version of historical materialism. It contains three major principles: (1) Productive forces have an inherent tendency for continuous development throughout the entire course of history; (2) The development of productive forces explains the relations of production; (3) The structure of the economic foundation explains institutions in the political-ideological superstructure.

Cohen energetically sets out to justify and defend these three clear and very bold theses. In the first thesis, which has a solid empirical foundation, he justifies man's rationality, used in the struggle against shortage and material distress. Functionalism is used to validate the second and third theses. The second thesis, on the primacy of productive forces, is explained by a historical mechanism, or axiom, ensuring that relations of production become optimal for the development of productive forces. Relations of production have a predisposed disposition to develop in a way that makes them beneficial to the productive forces. For example, feudalism was overthrown and replaced with capitalism when the former hampered the development of modern industrial production.

In a similar way, the thesis about superstructure (3) is explained by the tendency of political institutions, legal systems, and ideological conceptions to adapt in a way which makes them functional and useful for sustaining and developing the economic basis. This theory has been subject to the same methodological criticism that can be used against any functionalist theory (see chapter 14; Elster 1982). Another type of criticism has been that, in emphasizing productive forces and technology, the theory leaves too little room for variations in class relations or the relative strength between classes (Levine and Wright 1980).

Nevertheless, this book in general has been given great importance, probably due to its methodological qualities. It is composed clearly and cogently, and analyzes a series of assumptions which have played key roles in the history of Marxism, but which were often formulated vaguely, making them difficult to analyze and evaluate.

Classes and Exploitation

The most important contributions concerning class and exploitation draw on different sources, and come from John E. Roemer (especially Roemer 1982; 1986b; 1988) and Erik Ohlin Wright (especially Wright 1985, 1994, 1997).

John E. Roemer

Like other analytical Marxists, Roemer thoroughly rejects Marx's labor theory of value. Instead, Roemer applies assumptions and methods from modern economic theory and game theory, though most Marxists have found such bourgeois theories incompatible with concepts of exploitation and class. Roemer claims that property relations to the resources and assets necessary for production are decisive in explaining exploitation. These may be capital, labor, or productive capabilities and skills. His basic idea is that exploitation exists if some agents work more than it takes to produce what they themselves consume. Equally, if a group exists which can appropriate a larger share of the production result than what they themselves produce, exploitation exists. Roemer demonstrates that, if this is the case, the exploited class might gain welfare improvements if existing property relations were changed. In this scenario, the exploited class withdraws from the form of production defined by existing property relations, taking with them their share of productive resources and establishing new property relations. From this perspective, revolutions throughout history are perceived as successive eliminations of forms of exploitation.

Roemer's results are remarkable in that he reconstructs a series of Marx's theses based on this modern theory. Apart from the types of exploitation addressed by Marx, such as the slave economy of Antiquity, and feudalist and capitalist production forms, Roemer also defines socialist exploitation. This is the type of exploitation found in socialist societies with collective ownership of the means of the production and division of production outcome according to the principle of how much the individual contributes. Furthermore, Roemer demonstrates that asymmetric property relations in product and credit markets may cause exploitation, such as that between developed and less developed countries.

Erik Olin Wright

While Roemer's contribution was purely theoretical, others have attempted to bridge theoretical and empirical analyses of the class structure in modern capitalist society, first and foremost Erik Olin Wright. From the perspective of orthodox Marxist theory, the emergence of a new bourgeois class (typically wage-earners employed in nonmanual jobs, such as services, business, and public institutions) is particularly difficult to explain. Inspired by Louis Althusser and Nicos Poulantzas (see chapter 9), Wright advanced (prior to the emergence of analytical Marxism) a class theory more complex than the traditional one, emphasizing the concept of contradictory class locations (Wright 1978). However, influenced by Roemer, Wright later modified his theory (Wright 1985).

Wright operates with three forms of exploitation: (1) exploitation based on capital; (2) exploitation based on organizational control; and (3) exploitation based on the possession of productive capabilities and skills. Different positions in society have various degrees of access to each of these elements. People working in managerial positions typically possess productive capabilities and skills necessary for managerial positions as well as organizational control, but they do not possess the capital. Therefore, these people are both exploiters and the exploited. In conclusion, it should be mentioned that this theory has been applied to several extensive empirical studies, comparing different countries, including Scandinavia (Wright 1985; Ahrne and Wright 1983; Ahrne et al. 1985; Hoff and Andersen 1989).

Politics and Revolutions

One fundamental problem with orthodox Marxist theory is explaining political action in general and revolutions in particular: how and when can classes appear as collective actors? This is known as the problem of collective action (which is also related to the problem of

collective goods; see for example, Hardin 1982). Marx distinguished between two conditions or states of consciousness: the class *in itself* (*die Klasse an sich*), and the class *for itself*
(*die Klasse für sich*). As a class in itself, its members do not recognize that they share class
interests and therefore cannot act in accordance with them. In contrast, as a class for itself,
the members have gained insights upon which they can act collectively.

This problem is central in the analyses of class conflicts, political action, and revolutions
made by Adam Przeworski (1985a), Jon Elster (1985), and others. In applying rational
choice theory and game theory, one can demonstrate certain results regarding interests and
rational action, which at first may seem almost paradoxical. Even though everybody may
benefit from a certain action, such as a revolution, this may not prove rational to the individual actor (viewed from a game theoretical perspective, the problem is a prisoner's dilemma; see chapter 13). As a result, exploitation continues, although the exploited would
be better off if they acted collectively and carried out a revolution.

Przeworski, however, takes his analyses further and demonstrates that in capitalist societies, political systems, to a great extent, provide subordinate classes with possibilities for
improving their material living conditions. Theoretically, a labour-friendly government can
reallocate resources through the tax system to the benefit of those badly in need, and simultaneously maintain both financial stability and capitalist ownership of businesses (Przeworski
1985a). Further, economic development has led to a numerical reduction of the working
class, and it is no longer in the majority, which places socialist parties in a tactical dilemma.
In combination, according to Przeworski (and others), this explains why revolution is not a
rational, attractive alternative action in modern capitalist societies, even though exploitation exists.

Justice and Freedom

Is exploitation unjust? The very name indicates that it is. But a condition is not made more
or less just simply by giving it a certain name. Marxism has always been characterized by
an equivocal and inconclusive stand on ethical concepts such as justice and freedom (Lukes
1987; Wood 1981; 1986). On one hand, concepts such as exploitation, oppression, and
liberation clearly indicate moral engagement. On the other hand, Marxism contains no explicit account of the moral principles (if any) on which this engagement is based. Quite the
contrary; morality has usually been rejected as a form of ideology or an illusion. Marxism
has always been skeptical toward attempt to advance universal, ahistorical, moral principles. (Naturally, this especially includes principles such as the sacredness of private property.)

In terms of exploitation, the fundamental question is whether the issue can be subject to
moral judgement at all. If exploitation is the result of blind universal laws of which no one
is in control, moral judgement seems pointless. Traditionally, many liberalists claim the
only thing that counts morally is individual actions, that is, whether one has acquired one's
income and fortune legally. No one can be responsible for the distribution, which occurs as
a spontaneous result.

Cohen's book actually seems to contain this type of fatalism. Nevertheless, he has tried
to formulate a theory of justice (Cohen 1981). Here he points to the dilemma between the
long-term development of productive forces and the immediate limitation of exploitation.

In some phases, exploitation is a functional condition for continuous development of the productive forces, which will benefit future generations in their liberation and ensure them a higher degree of equality. The open question is whether this can be called unjust. And when exploitation no longer benefits productive forces, relations of production will change, according to Cohen's theory. Cohen has not reached a final solution to this problem.

Nor does Roemer find exploitation unjust by definition; "socially necessary exploitation" may occur (Roemer 1982: 278ff). But he attempts to go a step further and offers moral justification for this type of exploitation, which serves productive forces. His answer is tied to another Marxian idea, self-realization, the unfolding of man's full capacities, such as creative powers, needs, and knowledge, etc. However, Roemer has not solved the problem, but analytical Marxism has at least contributed to a clearer formulation. The dilemma between whatever can increase production in the long term, and the principles of just distribution at a given point in time, is universal and still extremely urgent.

Influence and Critique

By throwing some of the untenable elements of orthodox Marxism overboard and simultaneously drawing on methods from modern social-science traditions, analytical Marxism has infused new vitality into Marxist theory, which has caused considerable interest even outside this field. Other themes that have been subject to analysis from this perspective are: gender inequality, preindustrial societies, the revolutions in East Europe, and many others issues (see bibliography).

But analytical Marxists have also been subject to extensive criticism. One such criticism has been that analytical Marxism is not Marxist at all, but reformist or outright bourgeois (Kieve 1986; Lebowitz 1988; Wood 1989). Other critics have claimed that applying rational choice and methodological individualism lead to an overemphasis on individual economic motives, and to atomism, the application of general and abstract basic assumptions resulting in a static and ahistorical theory.

Bibliography

Primary:

Ahrne, Göran, Ekerwald, M., and Leiulfsrud, H. 1985: *Klassamhällets förändring*. Lund: Arkiv Förlag.
Ahrne, Göran, and Wright, Erik Olin. 1983: Classes in the United States and Sweden: a Comparison. *Acta Sociologica*, 26/3, 211–35.
Aston, T. H., and Philpin, C. H. E. (eds) 1985: *The Brenner Debate: Agrarian Class Structure and Economic Development in Pre-industrial Europe*. Cambridge: Cambridge University Press.
Bowles, Samuel, and Gintis, Herbert. 1986: *Democracy and Capitalism: Property, Community, and the Contradictions of Modern Thought*. New York: Basic Books.
Carling, Alan. 1986: Rational Choice Marxism. *New Left Review*, 160, 24–62.
—— 1991: *Social Division*. London: Verso.
Cohen, Gerald A. 1978: *Karl Marx's Theory of History. A Defence*. Princeton, NJ: Princeton University Press
—— 1981: Freedom, Justice and Capitalism. *New Left Review*, 126, 3–16.
—— 1986: Forces and Relations of Production. In John E. Roemer (ed.), *Analytical Marxism*. Cambridge: Cambridge University Press.

—— 1995: *Self-ownership, Freedom, and Equality*. Cambridge: Cambridge University Press.

Elster, Jon. 1982: Marxism, Functionalism and Game Theory. *Theory and Society*, 11/4, 453–82.

—— 1985: *Making Sense of Marx*. Cambridge: Cambridge University Press.

—— 1988: *An Introduction to Karl Marx*. Cambridge: Cambridge University Press.

Hoff, Jens, and Andersen, Jørgen Goul. 1989: The Comparative Project on Class Structure and Class Consciousness: An Overview. *Acta Sociologica*, 32/1, 23–49.

Laclau, Ernesto. 1977: *Politics and Ideology in Marxist Theory*. London: Verso.

—— 1989: Politics and the Limits of Modernity. In Andrew Ross (ed.), *Universal Abandon?* Edinburgh: Edinburgh University Press.

—— 1990: *New Reflections on the Revolution of Our Time*. London: Verso.

—— 1992: Beyond Emancipation. In Jan Nederveen Pieterse (ed.), *Emancipations, Modern and Postmodern,* London: Sage Publications.

—— 1994: *The Making of Political Identities*. London: Verso.

Laclau, Ernesto, and Mouffe, Chantal. 1985: *Hegemony and Socialist Strategy*. London: Verso.

—— 1987: Post-Marxism Without Apologies. *New Left Review*, 166, 79–106.

Levine, Andrew, Sober, Elliott, and Wright, Erik Olin. 1987: Marx and Methodological Individualism. *New Left Review*, 162, 67–84.

Levine, Andrew, and Wright, Erik Olin. 1980: Rationality and Class Struggle. *New Left Review*, 123, 47–79.

Miller, Richard W. 1984: *Analyzing Marx: Morality, Power and History*. Princeton NJ: Princeton University Press.

Mouffe, Chantal. 1979: Hegemony and Ideology in Gramsci. In Chantal Mouffe (ed.), *Gramsci and Marxist Theory,* London: Routledge & Kegan Paul.

—— 1993: *The Return of the Political*. London: Verso.

Przeworski, Adam. 1985a: *Capitalism and Social Democracy*. Cambridge: Cambridge University Press.

—— 1985b: Marxism and Rational Choice. *Politics and Society*, 14/3, 379–409.

—— 1990: *The State and the Economy under Capitalism*. Chur, Switzerland: Harwood Academic Publishers.

—— 1991: *Democracy and the Market: Political and Economic Reforms in Eastern Europe and Latin America*. Cambridge: Cambridge University Press.

Roemer, John E. 1981: *Analytical Foundations of Marxian Economic Theory*. Cambridge: Cambridge University Press.

—— 1982: *A General Theory of Exploitation and Class*. Cambridge, MA: Harvard University Press.

—— 1985: Should Marxists be Interested in Exploitation? *Philosophy and Public Affairs*, 14/1, 30–65.

—— 1986a: An Historical Materialist Alternative to Welfarism. In Jon Elster and Aanund Hylland (eds), *Foundations of Social Choice Theory*. Cambridge: Cambridge University Press.

—— (ed.) 1986b: *Analytical Marxism*. Cambridge: Cambridge University Press.

—— 1988: *Free to Lose. An Introduction to Marxist Economic Philosophy*. Cambridge, MA: Harvard University Press.

—— (ed.) 1994a: *Foundations of Analytical Marxism*. Aldershot: Edward Elgar.

—— 1994b: *A Future for Socialism*. London: Verso.

—— 1994c: *Egalitarian Perspectives: Essays in Philosophical Economics*. Cambridge: Cambridge University Press.

Van Parijs, Philippe (ed.) 1992: *Arguing for Basic Income*. London: Verso.

Wood, Allen W. 1981: *Karl Marx*. London: Routledge & Kegan Paul.

—— 1986: Marx and Equality. In John E. Roemer (ed.), *Analytical Marxism*. Cambridge: Cambridge University Press.

Wright, Erik Olin. 1978: *Class, Crisis and the State*. London: New Left Books.

—— 1979: *Class Structure and Income Determination*. New York: Academic Press.

—— 1985: *Classes*. London: Verso.

—— 1994: *Interrogating Inequality. Essays on Class Analysis, Socialism and Marxism*. London: Verso.

—— 1997: *Class Counts: Comparative Studies in Class Analysis*. New York: Cambridge University Press.

Wright, Erik Olin, Becker, U., et al. 1989: *The Debate on Classes*. London: Verso.

Wright, Erik Olin, Levine, Andrew, and Sober, Elliott. 1992: *Reconstructing Marxism: Essays on Explanation and the Theory of History*. London: Verso.

Secondary:

Anderson, W. H. Locke, and Thompson, Frank W. 1988: Neoclassical Marxism. *Science and Society*, 52/2, 215–28.

Dallmayr, Fred. 1989: *Margins of Political Discourse*. New York: State University of New York Press.

Daly, Glyn. 1991: The Discursive Construction of Economic Space: Logics of Organization and Disorganization. *Economy and Society*, 20/1, 79–102.

Geras, Norman. 1987: Post-Marxism? *New Left Review*, 163, 40–82.

—— 1988: Ex-Marxism Without Substance: Being a Real Reply to Laclau and Mouffe. *New Left Review*, 169, 34–61.

Gramsci, Antonio. 1982: *Selections from the Prison Notebooks*. London: Lawrence & Wishart.

Hardin, Russell. 1982: *The Logic of Collective Action*. Baltimore, MD: Johns Hopkins University Press.

Hirst, Paul Q. 1984: Economic Classes and Politics. In Alan Hunt (ed.), *Class and Class Structure*. London: Lawrence and Wishart.

Inquiry. 1986: 29/1 [articles about Jon Elster's book: *Making Sense of Marx*].

Jessop, Bob. 1980: The Political Indeterminacy of Democracy. In Alan Hunt (ed.), *Marxism and Democracy,* London: Lawrence and Wishart.

—— 1990: *State Theory*. Oxford: Polity Press.

Kieve, Ronald A. 1986: From Necessary Illusion to Rational Choice? A Critique of Neo-Marxist Rational Choice Theory. *Theory and Society*, 15, 557–82.

Lebowitz, Michael A. 1988: Is "Analytical Marxism" Marxism? *Science and Society*, 52/2, 191–214.

Lukes, Steven. 1987: *Marxism and Morality*. Oxford: Oxford University Press.

Mayer, Tom. 1994: *Analytical Marxism*. London: Sage.

Mouzelis, Nicos. 1988: Marxism and Post-Marxism? *New Left Review*, 167, 107–23.

Petersen, Trond. 1984: Class and Exploitation: Description and Ethics. Notes on John Roemer's "A General Theory of Exploitation and Class." *Acta Sociologica*, 27/4, 323–37.

Sassoon, Anne S. 1980: Gramsci: A New Concept of Politics and the Expansion of Democracy. In Alan Hunt (ed.), *Marxism and Democracy*. London: Lawrence and Wishart.

Wood, Ellen M. 1989: Rational Choice Marxism: Is the Game Worth the Candle? *New Left Review*, 177, 41–88.

chapter 12

Social Interaction Theories

Gorm Harste and Nils Mortensen

KEY CONCEPTS

ACCOUNTABILITY – a concept used by Garfinkel to describe the ability of actors to express themselves in their acts in ways that make sense and that are acceptable to others.

COMMON SENSE – the intersubjective typified knowledge we take for granted in all situations.

EXPECTATION – expectations are not psychological, but social and reciprocal, as the individual expects that others expect something of it and that it can expect sanctions from others if it does not act as expected.

FACE-TO-FACE INTERACTION – interaction among people who are present at the same time and place.

INDEXICALITY – a concept used by Garfinkel to describe how many expressions, especially expressions such as "well," "and so on," etc. have meaning by pointing to implied intersubjective contexts.

LIFE-WORLD – a concept introduced by Husserl about the horizon of the common symbolic context of meaning that is presupposed by actors.

NORM – the set of expectations according to which individuals are presumed to act in all situations.

RATIONALITY – in contrast to usual conceptions about formal or means–end rationality, many interaction theorists, especially Schütz and Garfinkel, emphasize that there are many different types of inexplicit "rationality" in actions.

SELF – According to Blumer, the fact that a person is an object for itself. Furthermore, the self is a process, not a structure.

STAGE/BACK STAGE – Goffman's concepts for how we attempt to act presentably in the part (the stage) of our lives that is visible to others, while the back stage is less controlled by this requirement.

SOCIAL REALITY – Berger and Luckmann's concept that describes how individuals live in an objectively predetermined but manmade social order.

SYMBOLIC INTERACTION – Blumer's basic concept that all interaction occurs by way of common symbols.

TYPIFICATION – Schütz's concept for how we interpret events and what we do, based on learned ideas and concepts through which we select what seems relevant to us.

A common perception today is that anything goes, that it is up to the individual to find meaning in life, or that meaning is simply impossible in a reality created by the media. In a social theoretical context, this view is most strongly expressed by so-called postmodern authors like Jean-François Lyotard and Jean Baudrillard (see chapter 26) and by culture-sociological skeptics like Christopher Lasch and Richard Sennett (see chapter 25). The breakdown of social norms and the loss of meaning are, however, classical themes in sociology. In his book about suicide first published in 1897, Emile Durkheim (see chapter 5), pointed out that modern societies create what he called "anomie," and Max Weber (see chapter 6) thought that meaning was lost in the "iron cage of rationality" in the modern organization society.

When we consider issues like decay of norms and loss of meaning, we must examine *what* social norms and meanings we have and *how* we can study them methodologically, especially the latter. A thorough examination of how to study norms and meaning was the purpose of several American sociological trends in the 1950s. The common method of these trends, which are philosophically inspired by American pragmatism and German phenomenology, is a study of norms and meaning based on face-to-face relations among people. Different schools formed in this field, notably symbolic interactionism and ethnomethodology, but many theorists do not fit into these categories. For the sake of simplicity, we can gather these different analytical trends together under the term "interaction theories."

Interaction theories show that social life contains an infinite number of explicit as well as implicit norms and meanings. They document layer upon layer of rules and meanings in social behavior: There are rules about and interpretations of how to walk down the street, about not bumping into other people, what to do when it almost happens anyway, about courtesy, conversation, quarrels, intrigues, cooperation, etc. An important point in interaction theory is that "society" is not only where we officially think it is – in political dramas, financial transactions, or public administration decision-making processes. A large part of social life happens "between the lines" in people's completely unnoticed daily interactions.

This chapter will start with Herbert Blumer, who translated George H. Mead's philosophy (see chapter 8) into an explicit sociological school. Next, we will introduce the philosophical phenomenology that Alfred Schütz developed in a sociological direction by combining it with inspiration from American pragmatism. From Schütz we will draw a connection, first to Peter Berger and Thomas Luckmann's theory of the social construction of reality and then to Harold Garfinkel's ethnomethodology. Finally, the chapter will discuss Erving Goffman's original analyses of human interaction.

Blumer and Symbolic Interactionism

Herbert Blumer's symbolic interactionism is a direct continuation of Mead, whose lectures he had followed. The primary difference between Blumer and Mead is that Blumer deals with sociological issues and tries to argue for the Mead-inspired theory as superior to other schools in sociology. He is polemical, especially in relation to Parsons's functionalism.

Blumer (1900–87) was active in many contexts, for example, as an editor of journals, a public mediator in labor conflicts, and in the American Sociology Association. Like Mead, he was an excellent lecturer. His production is limited, and his most important articles from the 1930s and 1950s are published in the book *Symbolic Interactionism* (1969).

Here we will briefly review Blumer's sociological formulations of Mead's thoughts about the self and social interaction. A positive evaluation of Blumer is that he develops Mead's theory further. A more critical evaluation is that he simply popularizes Mead, and that *Symbolic Interactionism* contains very few and simple, but often repeated points.

Blumer says about the self that a human being is an organism with a self. This implies above all that a human being is an isolated object that can recognize itself, act in relation to itself, and even communicate with itself. The self is a process, not a specific structure, and the central point is that the self is "a mechanism of self-interaction with which to meet the world" (Blumer 1969: 62). According to Blumer, other concepts of the self as, for example, a collection of needs and motives, or a structure of internalized norms and values, miss the central point that the self is a reflexive process. The core of the self's consciousness is *indication*.

Everything of which a person is conscious is something it indicates to itself. For example, there is a difference between physical hunger and the idea or "indication" of hunger.

On this basis, Blumer formulates an action theory centered on the indication process.

> What he takes into account are the things that he indicates to himself. They cover such matters as his wants, his feelings, his goals, the actions of others, the expectations and demands of others, the rules of his group, his situation, his conceptions of himself, his recollections, and his images of prospective lines of conduct . . . He is not in the mere recipient position of responding to such matters; he stands over against them and has to handle them. (Blumer 1969: 64)

Blumer repeatedly takes exception to the view that social interaction simply expresses or represents the participating actors' inner conditions and motives or an external cultural or structural order. In other words, Blumer sees social interaction as a fundamental formative process. Participants in social interaction must build their own action projects through a constant interpretation of each other's action projects, and this occurs in a continuous process. Psychological conditions and social organization are relevant only as long as they are part of the interpretation process.

Blumer's approach to social interaction also stresses the inherent element of change: Given norms and structures are not just reproduced; redefinition and transformation of human relations are always possible.

Compared to Mead, Blumer is much more programmatic and concerned with defining a particular sociological school. He is, for example, very programmatic in his rejection of culturalistic or structuralistic views of society. He could legitimately be accused of reducing society to interactions, and he is consequently unable to analyze societal phenomena such as economic and political processes, which imply types of communication that transcend face-to-face interaction, such as communication by means of symbolically generalized media (Parsons: chapter 14).

The Phenomenological Inspiration

More than anyone, Schütz has managed to include philosophical phenomenology in social theory. To Max Weber (see chapter 6), understanding and interpretation of contexts of meaning were the most important methods for analyzing social actions, and it was these methods and their consequences for the field of sociology that Schütz decided to examine. Phenomenology and the related method, hermeneutics, were developed in the first third of the 1900s in Germany and in France by philosophers such as Edmund Husserl (1859–1938) and Henri Bergson (1859–1941). When Schütz had finished his first major book, *Der sinnhafte Aufbau der sozialen Welt*, in 1932, Husserl offered him a job as an assistant. However, because of Nazism, the job never materialized, but the job offer testifies to the importance of Schütz's work.

Husserl's theory of intentionality had shown that all knowledge and consciousness contain the dual aspect *consciousness of* and *consciousness that*. But we cannot understand our knowledge if we do not know that we *categorize* and *typify* it as knowledge. We must be able to place what we know as meaningful in relation to something we do not know as much about. Knowledge is subjected to what Husserl calls a "phenomenological reduction," in the sense that all phenomena, experiences, and thoughts can only be identified if they are a *subject's* knowledge: When I look out the window at the house across the street, I possess a knowledge directed not only at my own observations; I also know that there is something on the other side of the house. I know that I can look in other directions, that the trees next to the house are placed in a context, and that the signs that constitute the experience of the house are categorized and typified in relation to many other signs, most of which are absent in my immediate observation.

However, Husserl's theory of knowledge has difficulties interpreting how we can have a *common* social consciousness. I know something, you know something, but how can we be sure we know the same thing? Is logical inference from subjectivity to intersubjectivity possible?

Husserl's own solution to the intersubjectivity problem is threefold: First, all experience and knowledge are bodily experiences that are not only simultaneous with the experience but the very precondition of this simultaneity. This bodily experience is at the same time an experience of one's placement in relation to the surroundings and thus in relation to other people. Second, knowledge is tied to signs and symbols which we have been given intersubjectively, for example, we have learned a common language. Third, our knowledge and symbols can be something we "have," but primarily it is an implied precondition that is hidden in everything we do and know. It constitutes our *lifeworld* (Husserl 1986), the implied horizon of our experiences.

The Sociology of Everyday Life: Alfred Schütz

There are two basic themes in Alfred Schütz's theories. The first is the issue of intersubjectivity, an area where he criticized both Weber and Husserl's early writings. Meaning is not some inner subjective state. Meaning is constituted from the start in the common social world. The other theme is rationality. Schütz was originally inspired by Weber's ideal types of rationality, but he wanted to go even further and investigate in what sense actions are rational, not in the sense of ideals of rationality but in relation to whether actions in some sense could be rational according to their own criteria (*Eigenrationalität*).

Biography: *Alfred Schütz*

Alfred Schütz (1899-1959) was born in Vienna. He studied philosophy, economics, and law, and graduated from law school in 1921. For most of his life, he lived a double life, making his living as a lawyer and legal consultant in banking, and spending most of his energy on philosophy and sociology. After the Nazi occupation, he emigrated to Paris and in 1939 to New York. From 1943 he was associated with the New School of Social Research in New York, but not until 1956 did he concentrate on his work as a professor at the New School. Schütz was, from the beginning of his studies, preoccupied with clarifying the fundamental methodological problems concerning the concept of meaning. In the US, he studied American pragmatism and his last writings are clearly influenced by George H. Mead, John Dewey, and William James. Schütz's works were written in German and English and they are published as a compilation entitled *Collected Papers*.

The common-sense world

Husserl's concept of lifeworld is concretized by Schütz as a common-sense world which is the background of the many "special worlds," for example, the world of agriculture, university, school, football, family life. This conceptual development from "lifeworld" to "common-sense world" is influenced by Schütz's readings of American pragmatism. The different worlds are influenced by specific *typifications* and *relevance systems*. The concrete typification is experienced in a fellowship with others in a so-called "consociate relationship." This "we relationship" is not necessarily intimate like Cooley's primary groups (see chapter 8). Our actions are imbued with meaning by a *social rationality* in each special world, including the world of science.

In the study of the common-sense world it is, according to Schütz, important to understand two things: First, methodologically, any scientific description of a phenomenon is an abstraction in relation to our presupposed understanding of phenomena and problems in our lives. In this connection, Schütz talks about *first-order concepts*. The objectifying descriptions of science are *second-order concepts*, selected and reconstructed on the basis of the implied, primary context of life and meaning. Second, this context of life and meaning is already presupposed and preinterpreted as a social, *intersubjective* relationship. These two conditions are expressed in a quotation from Schütz's thesis of 1932:

> Thus, any science that deals with the meaning of the social world refers to the meaningful actions in the life of the social world, to our daily experience of other people and to our understanding of implied meanings and of newly created meaningful behavior. (Schütz 1974: 18)

The common-sense life is, according to Schütz, the paramount reality. Everybody can have their own personal dreams, fantasies, interests, and special knowledge, but we share a common, "real," pragmatic everyday which is a world of work, a world consisting of projects like getting up in the morning, taking the bus, painting the ceiling, picking up our kids, etc. And only in this everyday common-sense world of "work" are we "wide awake."

The implied knowledge and common sense of everyday life contain what Schütz calls a "natural inclination." This natural inclination gives us certain reference systems that we can base our interpretations on, but it is also connected to a perspective of a common world which enables us to overcome our "finite provinces of meaning," that is, our personal, subjective part of the world (Schütz 1973: 230f). We are always able to move beyond what Schütz calls the communication paradox between our subjective inclination and our intersubjective, common symbol world. This ability is due to the fact that a natural inclination constitutes a coherent world that is connected to the world of others. Poetically, we can say that all islands meet under the sea: From person to person everyday life is an expression of the same type of everyday and parallel lives (Schütz 1973: 258f). However, this does not mean that individual, more or less clear typifications are harmoniously coherent. They can be full of contradictions, just as the typifications of different individuals can conflict. Typifications in scientific observation are based on requirements of consistency and absence of contradiction, but that is precisely because contradictions must be revealed and explained in science. In contrast, in the pragmatism of everyday life, temporary and apparent contradictions are more or less easily managed, and the implied consensus in the lifeworld is not challenged.

Rationality in everyday life

Schütz points out that there are different forms of rationality in the lifeworld. Therefore, rationality does not only concern planning, science, and formal goal orientation as Weber's concept of means-end rationality claimed, nor is it as subjective as his concept of value rationality suggests. Social sciences and especially sociology must assume that a social rationality is connected with the life contexts that are being researched, and that researchers, science, its concepts, way of thinking, and institutions belong to themselves.

The basic rationality of the lifeworld is its commonality. Even though our motives can be subjective, they can only be maintained and connected to action if they point to a socially constructed context of implied meanings. That is why Schütz does not accept a separation of individual and society. He writes, for example, that "the life-world is neither my private world nor your private world, nor is it my and your world added together, but the world of our common experience" (Schütz and Luckmann 1979: 98). The meaning of our actions is not just subjective. For instance, we often experience our actions and expressions being given a meaning which we did not intend, but which we still have to account for. In other words, we cannot just subjectively ascribe any meaning to our actions.

Actions are not instrumental effects of motives in consciousness. This is a clear parallel to John Dewey's theory of motives (see chapter 8). Phenomenologically, motives are intentional, which means that they are conceived with an action in mind. Motives do not come before actions as a cause before an effect, and in this connection Schütz distinguishes "in order to" motives from "because" motives. "In order to" motives are inseparable from the relationship of actions. "Because" motives emerge after the action and are a sort of rationalization of why we acted as we did.

Schütz makes a methodological demand on sociology that its concepts must be *adequate*. The interpretations of sociology must, in principle, be equivalent to the observed subjects' own interpretations of their actions, or at least interpretations the subjects would approve. As the sociologist Anthony Giddens (see chapter 24) has often pointed out, this demand criticizes Freudian and structuralist sociology as well as Marxist and behavioralist sociology. We could say that the first two types assume *too* complex, underlying motives for actions and the last two assume *too* simple motives.

Ultimately we can explain what we mean only by referring to what has meaning and what is typified and made "relevant" in our common everyday life. In this way, Schütz demonstrates that strangers who meet very often and very quickly try to establish a mutual common sense of implied, common knowledge, which they can then elaborate and, in case of disagreement, draw upon. Thus, when sociologists want to interpret what is going on in everyday life, the sociological observers must keep a constant dialogue going between the knowledge and the meanings that can be interpreted by understanding them at a participant level and at a scientific, distancing, observer level. Researchers must not exclude themselves from the meaning that participants in everyday life attribute to their actions, but they must seize the opportunity to be participants and to activate their existing knowledge. On the other hand, the researchers cannot just hold to the implicit and presupposed meanings and rationalities that are embedded in the observed everyday life and in the researchers' own everyday lives. They must try to make the underlying, common-sense meanings explicit, and by some kind of rationalizing procedure construct a second-order concept derived from those meanings.

Schütz's theory is, among other things, a comment on the difficulties connected with intercultural communication. Schütz lived in involuntary exile in the US and his reflections are often marked by almost endless interpretation of small and large cultural differences. His theory demonstrates how difficult it is for individuals of different backgrounds to reach identical interpretations, but also that it is possible to be open to others. We have an indisputable ability to orient ourselves toward a common, prior knowledge and to reconstruct and express this common, implied knowledge in words. If necessary, it is easy to establish common references, even among people from totally different cultures. Thus, our everyday knowledge is not only a fixed structure embedded in the "natural inclination"; it is continuously developed and created in socializing processes.

Berger and Luckmann on the Social Construction of Reality

In 1966 two of Schütz's most prominent students, the German Thomas Luckmann (b. 1927) and the American Peter Berger (b. 1929 in Austria) wrote their famous and easily read book, *The Social Construction of Reality*, in which they elaborated Schütz's theories and expanded them into a more historical orientation and in the direction of including more macrosocial problems. The basic views from Schütz are combined with more recent sociological insights, as well as classical theory elements from Marx, Durkheim, and Weber. In many ways, *The Social Construction of Reality* was an impetus toward a broader sociological interest in Schütz.

In addition to the book he wrote with Berger, Thomas Luckmann has collected and edited Alfred Schütz's posthumous papers in two volumes, published as *Strukturen der Lebenswelt* (1984). Peter Berger, who is a declared Christian sociologist, has published a good deal, among other things, two instructive introductions, *Invitation to Sociology* (1963), and in 1981 *Sociology Reinterpreted: An Essay on Method and Vocation*, with Hansfried Kellner. In 1967 he published *The Sacred Canopy*, in which he applies the theory of the social construction of reality to understanding the social meaning of religion. The theme is Christianity's role in the development of a long series of other traits of the modern social order, for example, individualization, adaptation to the loss of meaning, and secularization. Berger concludes that we need interpretations that can help "maintain the world," or, in other words, encompassing interpretations of the cosmos we live in. These interpretations must be able to handle the fact that we can control only a small part of the world in which we move around and see ourselves as parts.

Berger's multifaceted production can be illustrated by the article "New York 1976 – a Signal of Transcendence" from his book, *Facing up to Modernity* (1979). Big cities are often seen as centers of rationality, but Berger points out that we also live our lives in big cities, move around in their enormous chaos, and interpret it. And as a city, New York is a "center of magic." Big cities not only rationalize life in a strictly instrumental way; they can also make it magic. People use metaphors like jungle and wilderness about New York. But New York is also a melting pot of an abundance of cultures, and as such it can be a symbol of "the holy city," where all contrasts of human life find their resolution.

The reality of the social construction of reality

To Blumer and, as we shall see, Harold Garfinkel can be ascribed a kind of idealism in which social reality is seen as depending on the meaning that people attribute to it. In contrast, Berger and Luckmann offer a social theory in a more realistic perspective: Social reality is created by society, it is constructed but it is also a reality, it is real. Its meaning and the types of knowledge that are attached to it are real and cannot be interpreted as one wishes. Consequently, social reality consists of objective, socially created interpretations and patterns of interpretations. Berger and Luckmann formulate their sociology as a "sociology of knowledge":

> the sociology of knowledge must concern itself with whatever passes for "knowledge" in a society, regardless of the ultimate validity or invalidity (by whatever criteria) of such "knowledge." And in so far as all human "knowledge" is developed, transmitted and maintained in social situations, the sociology of knowledge must seek to understand the processes by which this is done in such a way that a taken-for-granted "reality" congeals for the man in the street. In other words, we contend that *the sociology of knowledge is concerned with the analysis of the social construction of reality*. (Berger and Luckmann 1966: 15)

Berger and Luckmann attempt to combine phenomenological and interactionist inspiration with thoughts from Marx and Weber. From Weber they continue the tradition of value-free science. The social reality is real, and the researcher must stand in an observing position. As a normal "everyday" person and as part of scientific institutions, he participates in changing and developing the social reality. But research is subject to a reality perspective. Researchers must take cognizance of society instead of trying to change it, which would threaten the recognition of society's objectivity. Berger, especially in line with Weber, presents this so-called value relativism (Berger and Kellner 1981: 18–23).

That part of the theory that emphasizes the creation of society is inspired by Marx. Berger and Luckmann are especially influenced by the *Ökonomisch-Philosophische Manuskripte* from 1843–5 in which the young Marx expresses a humanistic anthropological view inspired by Hegel and Feuerbach (see chapter 2). Marx is working with a theory about subjective action (*Tätigkeit*) which is seen as concrete labor. This subjective action is then externalized (*entäussert*) and objectified into products of labor. But this process leads to alienation (*Entfremdung*), experienced by the workers when they face these objective consequences of their own production.

Berger and Luckmann hold on to this point of departure, but de-emphasize the alienation aspect. They translate Marx's concepts into three basic societal processes: (1) externalization, that is, society is a human creation; (2) objectification, that is, society as an objective reality; (3) internalization, that is, society becomes internalized in individuals via the socialization process. Social reality has emerged as a regulated and institutionalized reality and is developed in a dialectic relationship that corresponds to Marx's analysis:

> man . . . and his social world interact with each other. The product acts back upon the producer. Externalization and objectivation are moments in a continuing dialectical process. The third moment in this process, which is internalization (by which the objectivated social world is retrojected into consciousness in the course of socialization) . . . *Society is a human product. Society is an objective reality. Man is a social product.* (Berger and Luckmann 1966: 78–9)

Institutions and socialization

In connection with the objectification process, Berger and Luckmann use the concept of *institution*, a broad concept that includes all kinds of temporally, spatially, and socially fixed action patterns, from family, school, and religion to, for example, trips to the beach in the summer as an annual, repeated, and well-established institution. Social reality may be objective, but it is manmade and an expression of conscious knowledge and actions embedded in meaning. This gives it a theoretical touch which permits Berger and Luckmann to include Durkheim's understanding of social relations as an irrefutable fact without ending up with a functionalist view of the institutions of society. The reality of society is not found in the functional reality but in the significance of institutions in the maintenance of the everyday world. In the introduction to their book, they write, "the central question for sociological theory can then be put as follows: How is it possible that subjective meanings *become* objective facticities?" (Berger and Luckmann 1966: 30).

Social institutions are created historically and developed historically, but they are constantly tested by socialization when they will be taken over and legitimized by new generations. Thus, institutions are created consecutively. Everyday life and institutions therefore contribute to sustaining each other's world or universe. Without the repetition of everyday life and the maintenance of institutional patterns, institutions disappear, be they family traditions, going to church, or military discipline. The groups of everyday life, like its primary socialization of children into adults and its secondary socialization of individuals into new groups and norm formations, are crucial for the objective social reality. Objectivity is thus found not so much in abstract formations of symbols, power, or systems as in their repeated reproduction of the concrete everyday life. A person's life is first and foremost maintained through its everyday life and the symbolic reality construction embedded there.

Berger and Luckmann do not employ any strong or complicated language theory, but they still point out that people become social individuals through language and that countless norms in the social order have a linguistic character. Linguistic norms and rules become the rules of social life. "Language originates in and has its primary reference to everyday life" (Berger and Luckmann 1966: 53). Still, language has the "capacity to transcend the 'here and now' . . . through language an entire world can be actualized at any moment" (Berger and Luckmann 1966: 54). Therefore everyday life as well as institutions is sustained by the way we use language as well as symbols.

Garfinkel and Ethnomethodology

Although Harold Garfinkel mentions Schütz as his main inspiration, he analyzes meaning in the context of action and uses almost none of Schütz's terminology. His analyses concentrate on social action, which places them in a strong pragmatic tradition. Garfinkel's sociology and the branch he called "ethnomethodology" have a strong empirical foundation. Most of the basic concepts originate from empirical studies of everyday conversations. There are also empirical examples in Blumer's, Schütz's, and Berger's analyses, but empirical studies do not have the same crucial importance as in ethnomethodology.

The name "ethnomethodology" is also empirically founded. In 1945 Garfinkel was involved in a study of jurors, or in his own words "how jurors knew what they were doing in doing the work of jurors" (Garfinkel 1974: 15). He was struck by how the jurors' practice could be compared to subjects like ethnobotany or ethnomedicine. The jurors had not studied law, but still tried to think in legal terms. Their practice was an expression of people's use of method, hence the name ethnomethodology.

Biography: *Harold Garfinkel*

Harold Garfinkel was born in 1917. From 1946 he studied sociology under Talcott Parsons at Harvard University. He read phenomenologists like Husserl, Aaron Gurwitsch, and Schütz and was already interested in everyday "definitions of situations," for example, in his first article, published in 1949.

In 1952 he finished his Ph.D. thesis on *The Perception of the Other*. The fact that his published work mostly consists of articles is symptomatic of his interest in details, situations, and individual norms.

From 1954 he worked at the University of California in Los Angeles, where he started out in the department studying mental illness. At the end of the 1950s he started working with Aaron Cicourel, whose work *Method and Measurement in Sociology* (1964) strongly criticizes the ability of quantitative methods to understand a social reality and at the same time defends qualitative methods. In the mid-1960s Garfinkel and Cicourel organized seminars at Berkeley and Los Angeles, featuring, among others, Harvey Sacks, Emanuel Schegloff, and Roy Turner. This marked the beginning of ethnomethodology as an influential school of sociology with many researchers in the US as well as Europe.

Garfinkel's production is very limited and he has not written any monographs. His most important, early articles are collected in the book *Studies in Ethnomethodology* (1967). The articles demand great patience from the reader, because they are written in a more or less convoluted manner – probably so that the reader would not understand them in too simplistic a way.

Garfinkel's methodology and basic concepts

Garfinkel generalizes the idea of the popular use of method. Everybody constantly tries to use methods in their everyday lives. This is a continuation of Schütz's thesis that we are all in a certain sense social researchers who interpret meaning. He actually says that ethnomethodology studies people who make sociology. The point that the methods people use say a lot about the fundamental traits of social order is central in ethnomethodology. We could say that ethnomethodology claims that social order is a continuous, practical result of people's "methodical" everyday lives.

So the central object of study is the methodical character of everyday life. In a continuation of the phenomenological tradition, ethnomethodology shows that all people incessantly typify and classify themselves, other people's statements, events, etc. But the central point for ethnomethodology is the typification *processes* or the *methods* for classification. It is difficult to reconstruct people's methods, and the rules and typifications we use are first and foremost valid because they are used. In an important sense, we can say that Garfinkel, like Ludwig Wittgenstein, claims that rules manifest themselves through use.

For example, there are rules for eating nicely: One rule is not to take food with your hands. But the point is that sometimes this rule can be broken and nobody would see it as bad table manners. At the end of a meal, it might be all right to pick up a piece of vegetable with your fingers, because one has demonstrated, almost imperceptibly, that one is about to break a rule. In other words, rules for good table manners are constructed as they are being used.

Garfinkel's central concepts clearly express both the methodical and inexplicit nature of people's use of methods. It should be mentioned that Garfinkel prefers to demonstrate people's use of method in favor of constructing abstracts concepts for it. One concept is *accountability*: The meaning of an activity is tied to one's ability to account for it, which can be done by demonstrating the meaning to others through language or body language, etc.

Indexicality is another central concept. An index in a book is a list of keywords that refer to a detailed description. *Index* is also the Latin word for index finger. Garfinkel's indexical expressions are expressions that shorten the contextual relation by simply referring to "this," "that," "etc.," or "like." Through such expressions, we constantly refer to implied relations, to presupposed knowledge, to earlier examples of "the same," to the situation in which the conversation takes place, or the context of the interaction. Linguistic expressions thus sustain meaning through rules that are above all implicit.

Elements of the concepts of *accountability* and *indexicality* can be traced back to Husserl's concept of "phenomenological reduction," because one point is that all understanding depends on some form of reduction that presupposes implied common understanding. It would, for example, be impossible to write an introductory textbook of sociology if all social knowledge had to be explained from scratch. Narration, understanding, accountability, and indexicality depend on reciprocity. People operate on the assumption that it is possible to account for what they and others do.

Examples from Garfinkel's analyses

Garfinkel wanted to demonstrate how "phenomenological reduction" works in practice. For example, he asked his students to report a common conversation by writing in one column what was actually said and in another column explicate what they and their partners understood by what they said. The result could be like this (Garfinkel 1967: 25).

HUSBAND:	Dana succeeded in putting a penny in a parking meter today without being picked up.	This afternoon as I was bringing Dana, our four-year-son, home from the nursery school, he succeeded in reaching high enough to put a penny in a parking meter when we parked in a meter parking zone, whereas before he has always had to be picked up to reach that high.
WIFE:	Did you take him to the record store?	Since he put a penny in a meter that means that you stopped while he was with you. I know that you stopped at the record store either on the way back. Was it on the way back, so that he was with you or did you stop there on the way to get him and somewhere else on the way back?

HUSBAND: No, to the shoe repair shop.   No, I stopped at the record store on the way to
                                                           get him and stopped at the shoe repair shop on
                                                           the way home when he was with me.

If we take the example literally, it shows that there is an implicit and implied meaning in what is said and that it can be difficult for outsiders to understand a conversation in a group they do not belong to. But Garfinkel also uses the example to demonstrate that it is impossible to make the implicit explicit. When he asked his students for an exhaustive and literal report of what was actually said, the students gave up because the task was impossible (Garfinkel 1967: 26). He concludes that the problem is not just the relationship between what was said and what was meant, but also *how it was said* (Garfinkel 1967: 27). Maybe the reported conversation did not even concern what was said, but, because of the tone of voice and gestures, it was the introduction to a marital fight.

Another way to analyze the implicit rules of interaction is observing what happens when rules are broken. In this connection, Garfinkel uses provocation as a sociological method. Attempts to break everyday norms can be used methodologically. A so-called *breaching* reveals the strength of rules and the limits when deviance is sanctioned. Garfinkel demonstrated, for example, that to insist that others explain exactly what they mean is very upsetting: "What do you mean, 'What do you mean?' A flat tire is a flat tire. That is what I meant. Nothing special. What a crazy question!" (Garfinkel 1967: 42).

A famous example is when he instructed his students to go home to their families, act as if they were renting a room in their house, and exhibit common courtesy, for example, knock on the door before entering, ask permission to sit down, etc. The students' families reacted very strongly to this breaking of the common family order. Several students were accused of incredible rudeness, ungratefulness to their family, being fresh, causing trouble, etc. Others were suspected of being overstressed, sick, or having problems with their love life, etc.

These examples indirectly confirm some of Durkheim's methodological rules. First, Garfinkel reformulates Durkheim's theory that morality is a social fact. Garfinkel's social fact becomes a question of how rules of interaction are reproduced as a fact in language. Second, the methodological trick of breaching norms demonstrates Durkheim's thesis that social norms are identified by the sanctioning of breaches of them (Durkheim 1982: 97–101).

Developments in ethnomethodology

Part of ethnomethodology has developed so-called conversation analysis, which is also strongly influenced by Erving Goffman and by Ludwig Wittgenstein's philosophy of everyday language. A normal conversation, for example, contains rules for turn-taking, breaks and interruptions, beginning and ending, for how a conversation turns serious and how it turns pleasant, when to deal with problems that need to be discussed again, etc. If we include nonverbal aspects, there is an almost endless number of rules that are used and developed in each conversation.

Likewise, it is possible to analyze conversations where certain common aspects are excluded, for example, telephone conversations in which it is important to express continuously that one is still present. Breaks in telephone conversations are almost impossible and are therefore filled with small talk. This so-called phatic communication which assures the other that "I'm still here" is not only a large part of conversation. It is also a very important part of the content of interaction because it stabilizes the social order among the participants. Conversation analysis has thus been used to interpret communication in organizations, and it turned out that small talk played an important part. It greases the wheels and makes it easier to deal with complicated matters.

An analysis of turn-taking in dialogues (Sacks, Schlegoff, and Jefferson 1974) showed that dialogues often function as straitjackets, because turn-taking between the participants requires adherence to very specific rules. Therefore some interaction participants are difficult to interrupt and others too easy. Similarly, there seem to be surprisingly objective rules for starting laughter, ending a dialogue (even if others still want to say something), and for how to present a statement as criticism, support, or rejection. John Heritage and David Greatbach (1986) conducted a study of how political rhetoric presents itself in practice and they discovered that clever orators can often evoke thundering applause, not because of what they say but because of the way it is introduced, contrasted, or presented as the last of three points, the way they raise their voice, or enunciate the end, etc.

Goffman and the Social Stage

Goffman is often categorized as a symbolic interactionist, and his ties to the tradition from Mead and Blumer are obvious in many of his works that focus on how the identity or the self is actually maintained and functions in the interactions of modern society. But Goffman is also influenced by anthropology. He is like an anthropologist from another planet studying the strange habits of modern, Western men. Although he uses several ideas from symbolic interactionism, Goffman develops his own, original analyses. Like Garfinkel, he is above all an empiricist and his concepts are always linked to observations. He is probably sociology's most sensitive observer of social interaction, and for him even the smallest detail is significant.

Biography: *Erving Goffman*

Erving Goffman (1922-82) was born in Alberta, Canada. After studying at the University of Toronto, he studied sociology at the University of Chicago. In connection with an affiliation with the University of Edinburgh, he carried out fieldwork on the Shetland Islands. In the 1950s he worked for the American National Institute of Mental Health and did one year of participant observation at a psychiatric hospital. From 1958 to 1968, he worked at the University of California, Berkeley. From 1968 until his death he was professor of anthropology and sociology at the University of Pennsylvania. Goffman wrote numerous articles and books, all original, thorough, often a little ironic, but always fascinating studies of human interaction. However, it is impossible to point to a certain *main* work in his production. Shortly before his death, Goffman was elected president of the American Sociology Association, but because of serious illness, he was unable to give the traditional lecture at the Association's annual congress in 1982.

Maintaining the self

A central perspective in Goffman's work is how we try, with very sophisticated means, to maintain our self-image vis-à-vis others. A typical example is how we say "oops" when we trip on a staircase, thus signaling to others that we are usually in full control (Goffman 1981: 99). We shall give three examples of Goffman's analyses of self-maintenance.

In his first and very influential book, *The Presentation of Self in Everyday Life* (1959), Goffman uses theater as a metaphor of social interaction. One of the main concepts is impression management, that is, managing the impression we hope others will get of us. The stage, as the obvious part of a person's appearance, is another concept of the theatrical model, including, of course, front stage and back stage. One's choice of furniture and clothes are settings and props. One's clothes, status symbols, way of talking, etc. make up the personal front. On the front stage, we show off; back stage we hide from the audience. A laundromat is an example of front stage and back stage behavior. It is a public space, but also a place where it is hard to hide one's dirty laundry, so impression management at a laundromat requires a careful performance. Rather than trying to impress others, we want to be as anonymous as possible and do not want others to look at our laundry.

Face-work is another example of Goffman's analysis, found in *Interaction Ritual* (1972). Keeping the right face in front of others is very important and is connected with strong emotions. We can be in a "wrong face" if we happen to present information that does not fit in with the picture that usually works in that situation. Or we can be "out of face" if we do not have a face ready that is normally expected from us in a certain situation. We can also overdo the performance, go into aggressive face-work, and try to make ourselves look better at someone else's expense. The risk is that, while others apparently express approval of the aggressive self-promoter, they may secretly be gathering ammunition for revenge. We can also underplay our face and thus force others to make compensating remarks: A hostess who belittles her cooking in front of her guests makes the guests praise the meal.

The third example of how one tries to protect and preserve one's social self is Goffman's description of the territories of the self and the violations of these territories in *Relations in Public* (1971). The most important territory is the *personal space* around the body. If others get too close, even without touching one, it will, under normal circumstances, make one feel that one's space has been invaded. Other territories are *temporary* or *situational*, for example, movie theater seats or park benches. The *use space* is the area we need around us to do what we have to do and which is respected by others. The *information preserve* is personal facts and information of a more intimate nature. A person engaged in conversation with a group of people claims a right to have control over such facts and information.

Goffman's analyses of violations of the territories of the self demonstrate his sensitivity to trivial phenomena that few people seem to notice. He writes about behavior in elevators and about the embarrassment people feel when an elevator is emptied: the passengers are caught between contradicting impulses. They want to keep a maximum distance from the others, but are hesitant because evasive maneuvers could insult the others. Even the slightest thing does not escape Goffman's attention. He describes how a person who borrows a sweater from someone else may feel a slight discomfort if the sweater is still warm from the owner, and he notices now nudists try hard not to look as if they are checking out other people's private parts. This last example has inspired one of his many rules for etiquette one may find in modern life: "When bodies are naked, glances are clothed" (Goffman 1971: 46).

These observations give Goffman detailed insight into the encompassing cooperation that is involved in self-maintenance. A member of a group is expected to be very flexible to save the face and feelings presented by others, and to do this willingly and spontaneously because of emotional identification with others and their emotions (Goffman 1972: 10). Politely, we disregard small gaffes in others' face-work or pretend they are insignificant coincidences: "Thus poise is one important type of face-work, for through poise the person controls his embarrassment and hence the embarrassment that he and others might have over his embarrassment" (Goffmann 1972: 12–13).

The book *Stigma* (1963) points out that not only stigmatized people can be embarrassed. Those people the stigmatized meet are also embarrassed: We do our best to pretend not to notice, even if the person in front of us has a disfiguring birthmark. Reciprocal impression management can also become grotesque, as when two people who want to go through the same door stand around for a long time because neither of them wants to be pushy.

Discussion of Goffman

Two issues seem to be important in the debate about Goffman's work. One is his concept of the self, the other is his work as a sociological theorist.

Goffman's analyses pose the question, what is the self? On one hand, Goffman can be read as a cynical observer of interaction among modern people who want to gain as many advantages as possible. He says, for example, that the self is partly an image pieced together of impressions we make in the process of actions, and partly the player in an ongoing play that handles others' judgments honorably or dishonorably (Goffman 1972: 31–2). In this connection he has been credited as a "postmodern" theorist, according to whom all ideas of a deep or essential self behind the various role-plays is fiction (Tseëlon 1992).

But other examples in Goffman's analyses demonstrate that he respects the ability of individuals to "be themselves" in spite of surroundings and the necessity of role-playing. He has studied creativity among deviants and stigmatized persons who have managed to maintain their feeling of self against all odds. In *Asylums* (1961), he says: The feeling of "being someone" comes from being included in large social contexts, while the feeling of "oneself" comes from all those apparently insignificant ways in which we withstand this pressure. Our status is backed up by the solid, physical buildings of the world, but the feeling of personal identity is mostly found in the cracks.

Concerning Goffman's status as theorist, it is interesting that his books are compilations of essays rather than theoretic presentations. As Giddens remarks, the reader can dip in almost anywhere in any of his books and immediately pick up the flow of Goffman's reasoning (Giddens 1987: 110). Reading his work does not require an introduction to his "theory." But could there still be a general theoretic contribution in his production? It was mentioned above that he talks about maintaining dignity in a *ritual play*. Here the concept of ritual is essential. One's face is sacred, and therefore the order of expressions that are needed to maintain it is a ritual. It is remarkable how often he returns to Durkheim's concepts of rituals in which the central point is that the ritual institutes a separation between something "sacred" and something "profane" (Goffman 1971, 1972).

In *Asylums*, Goffman describes how sports events and dances at psychiatric hospitals could be seen as ceremonies that functioned to unite a community that would otherwise be separated into patients and staff. His analysis of the territories of the self shows that part of common behavior among modern people can be analyzed as religious rituals. In modern society, the traditional, "big" rituals have been displaced by "small" ones in everyday interpersonal rituals: "What remains are brief rituals one individual performs for and to another, attesting to civility and good will on the performer's part and to the recipient's possession of a small patrimony of sacredness" (Goffman 1971: 63). At one point, Goffman agrees with Durkheim's view of the moral order as an external, compelling fact in relation to the individual. Universal human nature is not especially human, he says. To acquire it, a person has to become a construct, "built up not from inner psychic propensities but from moral rules that are impressed upon him from without" (Goffman 1972: 45).

Finally, we should mention that his last article is entitled "The Interaction Order" (1983). Goffman's main thesis as a theorist is, then, that all the apparently insignificant incidents in people's daily interaction and conversations are subject to an order. This order is not characterized by one big overall principle, but consists of an endless number of different examples of something that can be seen as forms of ritual behavior.

The Significance of Social Interaction Theory

The social interaction analyses presented here seem to document, almost to overflowing, something everybody already knows, namely everyday life in its most routinized form. This knowledge about little everyday incidents that we think are trivial is exactly what the social interaction theory analyses pay most attention to. There are a number of main points in these analyses.

First, they show that we often think we do one thing, but we actually do something else. When we talk, we normally think that what we say is ordered and structured, more or less like a written text. That is not the case. Even when scientific and legal discussions are transcribed from a tape, for example, they often turn out to contain lots of ums and ahs, terrible sentence constructions, interruptions, and odd references.

Second, the many small, seemingly insignificant details combine to form a larger network of meanings in everyday life. Each everyday expression is a part of the everyday whole. Tiny changes in everyday norms tell us a lot about radical social changes in social interaction and power relations between different status layers, which is something Norbert Elias (1976: chapter 23) has analyzed.

Third, interaction analysis can help us understand the character of problems in the social integration of immigrants and refugees in companies, organizations, neighborhoods, problems among young and old, among different professions and cultures. Goffman's work and ethnomethodological studies have had an impact on reforms in psychiatric institutions and on the development of communication processes in organizations (Silverman 1970; Frost et al. 1985; Putnam and Pacanowsky 1983).

Finally, a few critical comments. A central point of criticism is that interaction theory ignores historical and cultural contexts. Much of what is said about everyday interaction, the taken-for-granted nature of everyday coexistence, etc. is analyzed in a modern, Western context. Blumer's and Schütz's theories are formulated as universal theories that apply to consciousness, language, social actions, and social life, regardless of historical and cultural contexts. Garfinkel is not interested in what areas of validity his analyses apply to, while Goffman is conscious that his analyses of the interaction play apply to a vaguely defined, modern, Western context. But interaction and everyday life in Europe have changed a lot over many centuries. Norbert Elias (see chapter 23) and later Niklas Luhmann (see chapter 22) have demonstrated how the codes of interaction and everyday norms have been developed through modification and universalization of aristocratic interaction norms as they were adopted by the bourgeoisie and later by other social classes (Elias 1976; Luhmann 1980–95).

Of course, other cultures have other relevance systems and typifications, and on this point Jürgen Habermas (1970 and 1981: chapter 21) and Anthony Giddens (1976: chapter 24) have criticized the view of action and meaning in interaction theory as being too narrow. It tends to focus only on the immediate context of a given situation, which is the case in Blumer's, Garfinkel's, and Goffman's analyses. But interactions draw on a broader social context and enter into larger social structures. Although the meaning of social actions always refers to or presupposes contexts, communicative contexts can go beyond contexts and change them. Many social actions are meant to change contexts or act across contexts, for example, in what Habermas calls common action coordination, which is seen in political actions. With Durkheim (1964) in mind, we can also ask how it is possible that highly differentiated social orders (big cities or large organizations) can be integrated if intercourse cannot be coordinated across contexts. Such action coordination depends on a development of certain types of interaction that operate with communication across the immediate contexts and face-to-face relations of the actors.

Too much focus on the immediate action context is the reason that interaction analysis is unable to create theories and analyses of more macrosocial phenomena. These theories do not have much to say when large amounts of empirical data are processed, or when large, complex institutions such as states or entire cultures are analyzed. Social microrelations are the main stage of the analysis. In view of this criticism, it is interesting that Habermas and Giddens have adopted and developed a number of the concepts of these theories in their own analyses. They link their analysis of the formation of norms and meaning in human face-to-face communication with analyses of more comprehensive, even global, social structures and processes (Habermas 1981; Giddens 1984).

Bibliography

Primary:

Berger, Peter. 1966 [1963]: *Invitation to Sociology*. Harmondsworth, Middlesex: Penguin Books.
—— 1967: *The Sacred Canopy: Elements of a Sociological Theory of Religion*. New York: Doubleday.
—— 1979: *Facing up to Modernity*. Harmondsworth, Middlesex: Penguin Books.
—— 1990: *A Rumor of Angels: Modern Society and the Rediscovery of the Supernatural*. New York: Anchor Books.
—— 1993: *A Far Glory: The Quest for Faith in an Age of Credulity*. New York: Anchor Books.
—— 1997: *Redeeming Laughter: The Economic Dimension of Human Experience*. Berlin: Walter de Gruyter.
—— (ed.) 1998: *The Limits of Social Cohesion: Conflict and Mediation in Pluralist Societies*. Oxford: Westview.

Berger, Peter, & Luckmann, Thomas. 1966: *The Social Construction of Reality*. New York: Doubleday.

Berger, Peter, and Kellner, H. 1981: *Sociology Reinterpreted: An Essay on Method and Vocation*. Garden City, NY: Anchor Press.

Berger, Peter, and Luckmann, Thomas. 1995: *Modernity, Pluralism and the Crisis of Meaning: The Orientations of the Modern Man*. Gütersloh: Bertelsmann Foundations.

Berger, Peter, Neuhaus, Richard John, and Novak, Michael (eds) 1996: *To Empower People: From State to Civil Society*. Washington, DC: American Enterprise Institute.

Berger, Peter, and Bernstein, Ann (eds) 1998: *Business and Democracy: Cohabitation or Contradiction?* London: Pinter.

Blumer, H. 1937: Social Psychology. In E. P. Schmidt, *Man and Society*, New York: Prentice Hall.

—— 1939: Collective Behaviour. In Alfred McClung Lee (ed.), *Principles of Sociology*. New York: Barnes and Noble.

—— 1954: What's Wrong with Social Theory? *American Sociological Review*, 19.

—— 1956: Sociological Analysis and the Variable. *American Sociological Review*, 21.

—— 1969: *Symbolic Interactionism – Perspective and Method*. Englewood Cliffs, NJ: Prentice-Hall.

Garfinkel, H. 1956: Conditions of Succesful Degradation Ceremonies. *American Journal of Sociology*, 61, 420–4.

—— 1963: A Conception of, and Experiments with, "Trust" as a Condition of Stable Concerted Actions. In O. J. Harvey (ed.), *Motivation in Social Interaction*, New York: Ronald Press.

—— 1967: *Studies in Ethnomethodology*, Englewood Cliffs: Prentice Hall.

—— 1974: The Origin of the Term 'Ethnomethodology'. In Roy Turner (ed.), *Ethnomethodology. Selected Readings*, Harmondsworth, Middlesex: Penguin Books, 15–18.

—— 1991: Respecification: Evidence for Locally Produced, Naturally Accountable Phenomena of Order, Logic, Reason, Meaning, Method, etc., in and as of the Essential Haecceity of Immortal Ordinary Society. (I) An Announcement of Studies. In G. Button (ed.), *Ethnomethodology and the Human Sciences*, Cambridge: Cambridge University Press.

Garfinkel, H., and Sacks, Harvey. 1970: On Formal Structures of Practical Action. In J. C. McKinney and E. Tiryakian (eds), *Theoretical Sociology: Perspectives and Developments*. New York: Appleton-Century-Crofts.

Garfinkel, H., Lynch, M., and Livingston, E. 1981: The Work of a Discovering Science Construed with Materials from the Optically Discovered Pulsar. *Philosophy of the Social Sciences*, 11, 131–58.

Garfinkel, H., and Wieder, D. Lawrence. 1991: Two Incommensurable, Asymmetrically Alternate Technologies of Social Analysis. In G. Watson and R. Seiler (eds), *Text in Context: Contributions to Ethnomethodology*. London and Beverly Hills, CA: Sage.

Goffman, Erving. 1959: *The Presentation of Self in Everyday Life*. Garden City, N.: Doubleday.

—— 1961a: *Encounters: Two Studies in the Sociology of Interaction*. Indianapolis: Bobbs-Merrill.

—— 1961b: *Asylums: Essays on the Social Situation of Mental Patients and other Inmates*. Garden City, NY: Anchor Books.

—— 1963a: *Behavior in Public Places, Notes on the Organization of Gatherings*. New York: Free Press.

—— 1963b: *Stigma. Notes on the Management of Spoiled Identity*. Harmondsworth, Middlesex: Penguin Books.

—— 1969: *Strategic Interaction*. Philadelphia: University of Pennsylvania Press.

—— 1971: *Relations in Public. Microstudies of the Public Order*. New York: Harper & Row.

—— 1972 [1967]: *Interaction Ritual. Essays on Face-to-Face Behaviour*. Harmondsworth, Middlesex: Penguin Books.

—— 1974: *Frame Analysis. An Essay on the Organization of Experience*. New York: Harper.

—— 1975: *Replies and Responses*. Urbino, Italy: Università di Urbino.

—— 1979: *Gender Advertisements*. London: Macmillan.

—— 1981: *Forms of Talk*. Oxford: Basil Blackwell.

—— 1983: The Interaction Order. *American Sociological Review*, 48, 1–17.

Schütz, Alfred. 1973: *Collected Papers*. Vol. 1. The Hague: Martinus Nijhoff.

—— 1974 [1932]: *Der sinnhafte Aufbau der sozialen Welt*. Frankfurt am Main: Suhrkamp.

—— Grathoff, Richard (ed.) 1978: *The Theory of Social Action: The Correspondence of Alfred Schutz and Talcott Parsons*. Bloomington: Indiana University Press.

—— 1981 [1924–8]: *Theorie der Lebensformen*. Frankfurt am Main: Suhrkamp.

—— 1982a [1970]: *Reflections on the Problem of Relevance*. Westport, CT: Greenwood Press.

—— 1982b: *Life Forms and Meaning Structure*. London: Routledge & Kegan Paul.

Schütz, Alfred, and Luckmann, Thomas. 1979–84: *Strukturen der Lebenswelt, I–II*. Frankfurt am Main: Suhrkamp.

Schütz, Alfred, and Gurwitsch, Aron. 1989: *Philosophers in Exile: The Correspondence of Alfred Schutz and Aron Gurwitsch*, ed. Richard Grathoff. Bloomington: Indiana University Press.

Secondary:

Burns, Tom. 1992: *Erving Goffman*. London: Routledge.

Charon, Joel M. 1998: *Symbolic Interactionism: An Introduction, An Intepretation, An Integration*. Upper Saddle River, NJ: Prentice Hall.

Cicourel, Aaron. 1964: *Method and Measurement in Sociology*. New York: Free Press.

—— 1968: *The Social Organization of Juvenile Justice*. New York: Wiley.

Dilthey, Wilhelm. 1970 [1908]: *Der Aufbau der geschichtlichen Welt in den Geisteswissenschaften*. Frankfurt am Main: Surhkamp.

Drew, Paul, and Wootton, Anthony (eds) 1988: *Erving Goffman: Exploring the Interaction of Order*. Boston: Northeastern University Press.

Durkheim, Emile. 1964 [1893]: *The Division of Labor in Society*. New York: Free Press.

—— 1982: *The Rules of Sociological Method and Selected Texts on Sociology and its Methods*, ed. Steven Lukes. London: Macmillan.

Elias, Norbert. 1976 [1939]: *Über den Prozeß der Zivilisation, Bd. 1*. Frankfurt am Main: Suhrkamp.

Embre, Lester (ed.) 1988: *Wordly Phenomenology: The Continuing Influence of Alfred Schütz on American Human Science*. Washington, DC: University Press of America.

Frost, Peter et al. (eds) 1985: *Organizational Culture*. London: Sage.

Gadamer, Hans-Georg. 1975 [1960]: *Wahrheit und Methode*. Tübingen: J.C.B. Mohr.

Giddens, Anthony. 1976: *New Rules of Sociological Method*. London: Hutchinson.

—— 1984: *The Constitution of Society*. London: Polity Press.

—— 1987: Erving Goffman as a Systematic Social Theorist. In Anthony Giddens, *Social Theory and Modern Sociology*. Cambridge: Polity Press.

Gorman, Robert A. 1977: *The Dual Vision: Alfred Schütz and the Myth of Phenomenological Social Science*. London: Routledge & Kegan Paul.

Habermas, Jürgen. 1970: *Zur Logik der Sozialwissenschaften*. Frankfurt am Main: Suhrkamp.

—— 1981: *Theorie des kommunikativen Handelns Bd. 2*. Frankfurt am Main: Suhrkamp.

Heritage, John. 1984: *Garfinkel and Ethnomethodology*. Oxford: Polity Press.

Heritage, John, and Greatbach, David. 1986: Generating Applause: A Study of Rhetoric and Response in Party Political Conferences. *American Journal of Sociology*, 92, 110–57.

Husserl, Edmund. 1986: *Phänomenologie der Lebenswelt*. Stuttgart: Reclam.

Koev, Kolyo (ed.) 1990: *Phenomenology as a Dialogue: Dedicated to the 90th Anniversary of Alfred Schütz*. Sofia, Bulgaria: Critique and Humanism.

Luhmann, Niklas. 1980–95: *Gesellschaftsstruktur und Semantik Band*. 4 vols. Frankfurt am Main: Suhrkamp.

Manning, Phil. 1992: *Erving Goffman and Modern Sociology*. Cambridge: Polity Press.

Marx, Karl. 1966: Ökonomisch-philosophische Manuskripte. In *Karl Marx und Friedrich Engels Studienausgabe, Band II,* Frankfurt am Main: Fischer Verlag.

Putnam, Linda, and Pacanowsky, Michael. 1983: *Communication and Organizations. An Interpretative Approach.* London: Sage.

Sacks, Harvey. 1963: Sociological Description. *Berkeley Journal of Sociology*, 8, 1–16.

—— 1972: An Initial Investigation of the Usability of Conversational Data for Doing Sociology. In D. Sudnow (ed.), *Studies in Social Interaction.* New York: Free Press.

—— 1987: On the Preference for Agreement and Continuity in Sequences in Conversation. In G. Button and J. R. E. Lee (eds), *Talk and Social Organization,* Clevedon, UK: Multilingual Matters.

—— 1992: *Lectures on Conversation*, ed. G. Jefferson 2 vols. Oxford: Blackwell.

Sacks, Harvey, Schegloff, Emanuel A., and Jefferson, G. 1974: A Simplest Systematics for the Organization of Turn-taking in Conversation. *Language*, 50, 696–735.

Silverman, David. 1970: *The Theory of Organizations.* London: Heinemann.

Thomason, Burke C. 1982: *Making Sense of Reification: Alfred Schütz and Constructionist Theory.* Atlantic Highlands, NJ: Humanities Press.

Tseëlon, Efrat. 1992: Is the Presented Self Sincere? Goffman, Impression Management and the Postmodern Self. *Theory, Culture & Society*, 9/2, 115–28.

Turner, Roy (ed.) 1974: *Ethnomethodology.* Harmondsworth, Middlesex: Penguin Books.

Wagner, Helmuth R. 1983: *Alfred Schütz: An Intellectual Biography.* Chicago: University of Chicago Press.

Wolff, Kurt H. (ed.) 1984: *Alfred Schütz: Appraisals and Developments.* Dordrecht and Boston: M. Nijhoff.

chapter 13

Rational Choice

Roar Hagen

When faced with several courses of action,
people usually do what they believe is to
have the best overall outcome. This
deceptively simple sentence summarizes the
theory of rational choice.

(Elster 1989a: 22)

KEY CONCEPTS

COLLECTIVE GOODS – goods of such a nature that if one person gains benefits from them, they also benefit others.

GAME THEORY – is interested in the interaction between rational maximizing actors with fully or partly conflicting interests. Games are situations in which the outcome of an individual's choice is also dependent on the decisions of others. Each actor must attempt to predict others' choices in order to determine his or her own strategy. Game theory distinguishes between constant sum (also called zero-sum) games, in which one's gain is the other's loss, and variable sum (non-zero-sum) games, in which both may gain from certain combinations of strategies.

METHODOLOGICAL INDIVIDUALISM – the view that society consists of individuals and actions, and that social phenomena should be explained as resulting from individual decisions and actions.

NORMATIVE ACTIONS – are defined as the opposite of rational actions, in which actors are not oriented toward the consequences of their actions, but toward social rules and values for their own sake.

RATIONAL ACTION – minimally implies consistent, future-oriented, and instrumentally efficient action. Rational choice theory assumes that actors *optimize* or *maximize* utility, i.e., that actors, in addition to gaining an overall view of possible alternative actions, also calculate the advantages and disadvantages of the various alternatives, and choose the most beneficial one.

Over the last two decades, the influence of rational choice theory has spread in sociology. This development arouses strong feelings in many people. Proponents see in rational choice a new, unifying paradigm for the social sciences, while opponents characterize this departure as a retreat to positions that sociology had long since abandoned, and a reduction of sociology to economics (Østerberg 1988; Smelser 1992; Friedman 1996; Udehn 1996). A third group regard rational choice as a fruitful supplement to more traditional sociological perspectives (Therborn 1991).

The struggle between proponents and opponents of rational choice fall into one of the long lines of conflicts in the field of sociology. We might distinguish between two major directions in philosophical and social science thinking about how individuals relate to one another and to society. One view assumes that individuals contract relations with one another on the basis of utility considerations; the other explains how individuals construct societies by means of concepts that reveal some form of shared meaning, such as culture, collective values, or social norms. Rational choice is a continuation of utility-based thinking about interindividual relations, and it has taken shape as a departure from the consensus view of society proposed in particular by Talcott Parsons (see chapter 14).

Proponents of rational choice raise several objections to Parsons's systems theory. Coleman and Fararo (1992) argue that Parsons's theoretical system eventually became so comprehensive and complex that it became incomprehensible to other sociologists. Moreover, Parsons operated with supra-individual entities which had their own needs and objectives, just as he developed a concept of subordinated, norm-driven actors. In contrast, rational choice is intended to be based on simple, easy-to-grasp premises and models. It rejects the existence of collective entities "over ," and independent of, individuals. The fundamental unit in society is individual human action. This view, often termed *methodological individualism*, does not preclude the use of concepts of, for example, social systems, but the explanation of social institutions and social change presupposes the ability to demonstrate how they are created through the actions of, and interaction between, individuals.

Rational choice is also distinct from purely descriptive and causal modes of sociological explanation (Coleman 1986). Extensive research based on questionnaire survey data is limited to providing causal explanations of behavior, in which the causes are either the characteristics of individuals or their environment – so-called background variables, such as sex and class – without the researcher introducing the actor in any active role. Goal and intention have not necessarily disappeared entirely from the analysis, but are present as "*post*

hoc rationalizations ," which provide only intuitive explanations as to why the causal structure is the way it is. Both this type of statistical correlation or causal analysis, and Parsonian
systems theory, lack a fully developed concept of the intentional, calculating actor.

Rational Action

Rational choice is a program for generating theory, models, or mechanisms based on a
small number of simple assumptions about individuals (Abell 1991):

- Assume actors are rational, and that they maximize their own interests, given their objective resources and preferences.
- Demonstrate in the model the structure of mutual dependencies existing between actors,
  such that the outcome for all is determined by what each individual does. Every individual
  must therefore attempt to take into account the actions of others when deciding between
  courses of action.
- On the basis of these two assumptions, the model defines alternative actions for each individual actor.
- The model's predictions can then be tested against the description of the empirical outcomes of the action to be explained.

If this simple model fails, new models can be constructed by altering the conditions:

- Replace the self-interest condition with a richer set of utility/preference conditions, for
  example, altruism, evil, indifference, jealousy, etc.
- Replace the condition relating to objective resource calculations with subjective conceptions of resources.
- Replace the conditions regarding objective calculations of possible actions with subjective
  conceptions of potential actions.
- Reorganize the structure of mutual dependencies.

The central factor in the construction of the model is an actor with control over his or her
own actions. It is assumed that actors opt for those actions that have the greatest utility.
Rational choice might therefore also be termed "the theory of rational man ," the "rational
action model" or the "theory of economic" or even "selfish man ."

Within the social sciences there are many different notions of rationality, and from the
points above it can be inferred that rational choice operates within a thin theory of rationality. It takes preferences as given and relates them to outcomes. The broad theory is not
limited to formal considerations of consistency, but concerns itself with the substance of
the actor's beliefs and desires (Elster 1985a). Within a broader approach we could also
point to different concepts of rationality as value-rationality (Weber, see chapter 6), communicative rationality (Habermas, see chapter 21) and system rationality (Luhmann, see
chapter 22) which relate actions to values, to social norms, and to system operations.

However, scientific assumptions on utility maximization do not necessarily entail a view
of human beings as rational and selfish. Rational choice theory provides a method. The
reason for making the rational actor the foundation for the construction of the model is
heuristic. The assumption that actors are rational has greater explanatory power than the

opposite point of view. In the light of the rationality model, it becomes easier to spot deviations, which we can then attempt to explain by modifying our assumptions about rationality.

Exchange Theory

George C. Homans (1910–89), Peter M. Blau, and Richard Emerson are the immediate sociological forerunners of rational choice theory. Homans (1958; 1961) was unhappy with Parsons's systems theory and structural functionalism (see chapter 14). His aim was to put the intentional actor back into sociological analysis. Homans claimed that the human yearning for recognition is a universal motivation, and that social behavior should be regarded as acts of exchange. He attempted to combine this exchange perspective with B. F. Skinner's behavioral psychology: actions which the individual regards as positive are reinforced, while actions and interactions regarded as negative are avoided.

The exchange model became a kind of stimulus–response pattern, and the concept of goal-oriented action gave way to a reductionism which did not differ much from the conditioned reactions Skinner demonstrated in his experiments with pigeons. His association with Skinner did not win Homans much sympathy among sociologists. Moreover, Homans wished to develop a sociology of small groups, while rational choice theorists are today more concerned with macrorelations, and with relations between micro and macro levels. Blau's and Emerson's interests took this macroanalytical direction, but although exchange theory stands in close proximity to rational choice theory, its current blossoming is inspired to a greater extent by theories of economics and political science. Gary Becker, the winner of the 1992 Nobel Prize for economics, is in this respect a more important source of inspiration than Homans and Blau.

Gary Becker

Gary Becker (b. 1930) employs basic economic principles in his treatment of sociological themes like education, crime and punishment, marriage, the family, friendship, altruism, etc. Becker (1964) was one of the first to develop a concept of "human capital" as a parallel to physical capital. Why do people choose to pursue further education? Becker's point of departure is the utility maximization model; he says that variations in educational patterns between social groups, countries, and types of education vary with the "rewards." This way of approaching social phenomena appears strange to most sociologists, perhaps even more so when it comes to issues like criminality, choice of spouse, and whether to have children.

In contrast to a normative viewpoint, which states that crime must be combated because it is wrong, Becker begins with a social calculation, asking how much crime society should tolerate. In this equation, he not only includes the losses criminals inflict on society, but also the costs of investigating, trying, and punishing them. Just as society ought to choose courses of action on the basis of utility evaluations, Becker assumes that crime too is based on a calculation. Likewise, it is assumed that a person remains single until he or she finds it more profitable to marry. When a number of people enter the marriage stakes, a market for marriage partners is formed, and supply-and-demand mechanisms operate. Demographic change is explained on the basis of an assumption that parents regard children as an investment. The division of labor between men and women in the home is a combined effect of natural differences, such as women's propensity to bear children, and the desire to maximize the family income. Profitability and efficiency explain the sex-specific division of labor, rather than the male domination of the female, as feminist theory would have it. The models generate falsifiable hypotheses. When more women choose to take higher education than might be expected in view of the fact that they receive a lower return on their investment than men, we must seek other utility effects than income to explain the difference.

Becker introduces an economic mode of thinking about activities that sociologists have been accustomed to regarding as noneconomic. He offers explanations in terms of rational calculations where sociologists have traditionally referred to background, internalization of norms, values, and culture. In several of these spheres – in particular, in criminology and demography – Becker has successfully challenged sociological conventions and gained support and influence. With his consistent application of an economic approach to the study of social phenomena, Becker represents one extreme of rational choice theory, but he also serves as a scientific ideal for James S. Coleman (1993).

James S. Coleman

James S. Coleman (1926–95) is the central figure in the current rational choice movement. Coleman trained as a chemical engineer before taking a doctorate in sociology at Columbia University. He was for a long time employed at Johns Hopkins University, before becoming professor of sociology at Chicago University in 1973. In 1990, in spite of considerable opposition, Coleman was elected president of the American Sociological Association.

In Coleman's comprehensive production, we may distinguish two paradigms of what sociology is all about. One analyzes how social structure creates individual actions and causal social processes. This perspective guides most of Coleman's empirical research in many areas, of which the best-known are probably his studies of educational processes and institutions. His most important theoretical contribution here is *Introduction to Mathematical Sociology* (1964). The second paradigm is founded in action theory, and seeks to explain how social systems and structures are a result of the choices and actions of individuals. The most important outcome here is the monumental thousand-page work *Foundations of Social Theory* (1990), in which he attempts to do as the title says: to establish a theoretical foundation for sociological analysis which can also inform social change.

In a 1986 article, Coleman combines the need for a theory of rational choice with a critique of Talcott Parsons's systems theory. Parsons does not keep the promise made in *The Structure of Social Action* (1937) to develop a *voluntaristic theory of action*. Parsons remains on the macroanalytical level, while Coleman emphasizes the need to combine the micro and macro levels in social analysis. Pure macro-to-macro analyses demonstrate how one system affects another, for example, how the Protestant ethic as a macrosystem of religious doctrine created a capitalist economic system.

Such methodological holism is unsatisfactory because, among other things, we lack sufficient data for comparative studies. There is too little inter- and intrasystemic variation over time to test the relationship empirically. Moreover, the emergence of the system remains unexplained in such an approach.

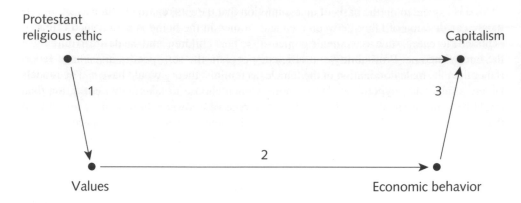

Figure 13.1   Macro and micro level choices: the religious ethic's influence on economic organization.

An alternative strategy might be to go from the macro level to the level of individual actions (1) and then back again (2 and 3). This is the program of methodological individualism. We find the reduction from the macro level to individual actions in, for instance, Max Weber, who showed how Protestant doctrine affected the values of individuals (see chapter 6). Weber, however, did not carry through the last step in the analysis: he did not show whether individual orientations combined to create the structure of economic organization which we call capitalism, and if so, how. It is the third relationship that has proved the greatest intellectual challenge for theory and empirical research which seeks to analyze macrorelations along the lines of methodological individualism.

The central theoretical problem for a sociological theory which builds on a concept of individual action is thus double-edged. We must show how the combined effect of actors' goal-oriented actions has the effect of creating a particular behavior at the systemic level, and moreover, how these goal-oriented actions are in turn shaped by the system (Coleman 1986). However, the system's shaping of individual actions is never total. There is at least a "millimeter" of space for maneuver between actor and structure, and actors select among the possibilities present in this space. This selection should not be explained by values to which the actors themselves give expression, as sociologists and anthropologists often do. Instead our explanations should make reference to the *utility functions* for actors.

Rational Choice in Scandinavia

Rational choice is a largely American phenomenon. It is represented in many sociology departments there, and has an especially strong position at the University of Chicago, where both James Coleman and Jon Elster taught, in Arizona through, for instance, Michael Hechter, and in Washington. In Europe, rational choice is associated with names like Sigwart Lindenberg and Reinhard Wippler in Holland, Karl Dieter Opp and Hartmut Esser in Germany, and Peter Abell in England. Rational choice theory has also gained some prominence in Scandinavia, most notably perhaps in Norway, where we will take a closer look at it.

As early as the mid-1960s, the social anthropologist, Fredrik Barth (b. 1928), introduced a perspective informed by transaction theory. Observable patterns of action should not be explained as expressions of normative structures, but vice versa; normative structures and values are viewed as the outcomes of transactions (Barth 1981). An actor contracts exchange relationships with other actors in order to increase, or at least maintain, his or her values. This is the main point of *the analysis of generative processes* which has been an inspiration for many other anthropologists and sociologists.

The Norwegian sociologist, Ottar Brox (b. 1932), sets out to show in his work how local adaptations ("custom"), which society at large regards as traditional or traditionalistic, have a rational base (1964). Brox's analysis of the institution of the "pot-fish " (1984) is illustrative. Along the coast of northern Norway it was once customary for many people to go out on the fjords and fish for their dinner; they said they were "taking one for the pot." Often the fisherman would catch more fresh fish in a short time than he himself could use, and the surplus would be given away to neighbors, friends, and acquaintances. However, such "generosity " was not a manifestation of altruistic values, but an exchange in a barter economy. At a later date, the donor would himself receive fish, other goods, or be helped out in other ways when he needed it. Such systems of exchange relations are supported by custom and social norms. With the coming of the refrigerator, however, it became more profitable to keep the fish than "give it away." Such new latent modes of action are exploited by persons who are willing to break norms and are less sensitive to sanctions. They can thus function as entrepreneurs, changing the existing system of mutual dependencies.

Gudmund Hernes

Gudmund Hernes (b. 1941), who studied with Coleman, has taken an interest in education and inequality, applying rational choice theory to analyses of power and powerlessness. He initiated and led the large-scale public inquiry into power relations in modern Norwegian society, appointed and funded by the Norwegian government. Among other things, the aim was to develop a holistic understanding of the functioning of political and economic systems, in order to be able to analyse better the distribution of resources in post-Keynsian economies. For this purpose, Hernes has developed a model for the analysis of the processes of the negotiated economy and mixed administration (Nielsen and Pedersen 1988; 1993).

The three central concepts in Hernes's model are *power, interest*, and *exchange*. Actor A has power over B to the extent that A controls something of interest to B, and vice versa. This mutual dependence forms the basis of exchange, because actors can make decisions vis-à-vis one another. Actors may relinquish control over something of less interest to themselves, in favor of obtaining control over something of greater value. Hernes summarizes the parties' mutual dependency, power, and negotiating strength in the following formula:

A's direct power over B = A's control over item X • B's interest in item X = B's direct dependence on A (Hernes 1982: 14; 1993).

A and B are not necessarily individual persons, but rational actors cooperating in groups for their own benefit. Parliamentarians pass laws and may therefore contract exchange relations with those who are affected by parliamentary votes. Farmers control foodstuff production and thus have a lever on authorities and consumers. Unions may exercise power by striking. Henry Milner (1994) has undertaken to explore further the relationship between social democratic policies and rational choice theory.

Jon Elster

The Norwegian philosopher and social scientist, Jon Elster, has a prominent international position within the rational choice school, but many others have also found his contributions significant and interesting; for instance, Elster has contributed to the renewal of the critique of functional explanations in sociology.

According to Elster (1979a; 1982; 1983; 1985a), a large amount of sociological literature is based on an implicitly regulative idea that if a given pattern can be demonstrated to have unintended, unacknowledged beneficial effects, then we have also explained why it exists and is maintained. An institution or behavioral pattern often has consequences that are of benefit to a dominant economic or political structure, even though these consequences are both unintended by the actors and unacknowledged by those who receive the benefits. The revelation of such connections is an important task for social science. But problems arise when the word "consequence" is replaced by "function" and the benefits are used to explain the institution or pattern of behavior. Functionalism postulates an end without an intentional actor – in grammatical terms, a predicate without a subject. Elster finds examples of this mode of explanation in the work of many sociologists. For instance, Pierre Bourdieu (see chapter 20) and Michel Foucault (see chapter 19) tend to view all social actions as part of a systematic universal apparatus of oppression. Elster aims his critique in particular at Robert Merton's concept of latent functions (see chapter 14) and the Marxist theory of the state (see chapters 2 and 9).

Marxists have a tendency to see all aspects of bourgeois society as means to an end which aims to secure the potential of capital to exploit the working class. The function of the state for capital not only consists in being a direct means of oppression, and combating strikes and revolutions with violence; it also secures the control of capital over the means of production by promoting the bourgeois ideology in the school system. Similarly, the welfare state can be presented as part of the "conspiracy" of capital against the working class. The bourgeois state will often act in direct opposition to the interests of individual capitalists, for example, by introducing laws regulating the working environment, which place limits on exploitation. When state actions of this kind are explained in terms of their serving the capitalist system as a whole, Marxists render themselves invulnerable to empirical falsification. It has also often been said, or implied, that the bourgeoisie use the state, but as a rule, *how* they do so is never demonstrated.

In Elster's view, functional explanations must be abandoned and replaced by a combination of intentional and causal explanations. Instead of postulating classes as collective actors, we must analyze the ways in which rational individuals combine to act in order to achieve common goals. *Game theory* is, according to Elster, an appropriate tool for giving Marxist macro theories a micro foundation.

Maximization

Statements of the type that the basic element of society is individual action, or that actors do what they believe is best for themselves, are, according to Elster (1989a), "trivially true" and "seductively simple." They appear immediately comprehensible and reasonable. When we have to choose between courses of action, of course we select what is probably the best means of achieving the goal we have set ourselves. Furthermore, most sociologists nowadays advocate action theory in one form or another, that is, they hold that society consists of individual human actions. However, rational choice theory differs from almost all other sociological theories in assuming that the rational actor *maximizes* the difference between costs and benefits. This is what lends rational choice theory its strength: it compares actions with regard to expected outcomes for actors, and postulates that actors will select the course of action that leads to the best outcome for them. At its most explicit, rational choice requires the specification of costs and benefits for all actions, and then predicts that actors will select the optimal course of action (Coleman and Fararo 1992).

However, putting this rigorous program into practice is not so simple. First, the actor must be able to consider all possible alternative actions and their consequences. This will often prove to be impossible, and besides, it requires the calculation of costs that are difficult to assess. The value of information cannot be calculated in advance, and actors cannot therefore rationally decide when they have sufficient information. Second, having acquired such an overall view, actors must *evaluate* the consequences and *rank* the alternatives with regard to their utility. Expressions like *optimal choice* and *maximization* easily create the impression of a scale which actors can use to compare the consequences of alternative courses of action.

The concept of utility associated with names like Jeremy Bentham (1748–1832), John Stuart Mill (1806–73), and William Stanley Jevons (1835–82) became a central concept in English economic and philosophical thought from the end of the eighteenth century onward. The early utilitarians understood utility as a quality of objects that could be measured in terms of "utils." Francis Y. Edgeworth (1845–1926) thought it possible to construct a "hedonometer " for utility in the same way that we use a thermometer to measure temperature. However, individuals derive varying satisfaction from the same object, depending on the circumstances; when we have eaten one steak, we do not get the same pleasure from eating a second. Nor is utility the same as money; it is reasonable to imagine that the value of every shilling falls as we accumulate more of them. Nor do different people derive the same pleasure or utility from a particular object. Eventually, the aim of constructing a scale to measure utility was abandoned, and today the theory of rational choice is based on a concept of *expected subjective utility* (Luce and Raiffa 1957).

Participants in experimental situations are asked to rank certain specified alternatives, administered as paired comparisons. Actors have to indicate whether they prefer one alternative over the other, or are "neutral." When this has been done for all possible combinations, we have a list of actors' preferences. We can then mathematically convert preferences into utility functions, which are a way of awarding numerical values to choices, so that the more highly preferred alternatives receive higher values. We can then say that people *maximize* utility, so long as we note that this means only that actors opt for the highest preference. One alternative has more utility than another because it is preferred, not vice versa.

This type of experimentally defined utility function does not correspond to real social situations and choices. In real life there are always alternatives that are not considered, and empirical investigations show that actors are far from consistent in their choices. Rational choice theory has been criticized for overlooking the problem of information and overestimating actors' ability to calculate. Herbert A. Simon (1954; 1982) assumes that actors do not choose optimal solutions, but rather *satisfactory* ones. They do not seek the best alternative, but one they find good enough. Amitai Etzioni (1988) argues that choices are made against a background of normative and affective factors. Raymond Boudon (1989) goes even further, suggesting a concept of *subjective rationality*, by which even actions based on values and trust are characterized as rational choices. This involves such a powerful extension of the concept of rationality that any conscious action is necessarily rational, seen from the actor's point of view.

When subjected to theoretical reflection, apparently simple and obvious statements like "the best alternative " and "maximization " turn out to be extremely complex, problematical, theoretical constructions.

Collective Action

Rational choice theory is concerned with situations in which actors are mutually dependent on one another, so that the outcome for any one individual is also determined by what the others do, and furthermore, actors realize, and take into account, the mutual dependency that exists between them when selecting between courses of action. Another term for this is strategic interaction – the individual actor seeks to anticipate others' reactions to his own actions. An important form of strategic interaction is collective action, where actors are dependent on one another in such a way that they must coordinate their plans of action in order to produce collective goods for themselves. When the rational actor model underlies the explanation of collective actions, we not only encounter problems, but also paradoxes.

Mancur Olson (1965) mounted an attack on those social science theories that regarded it as self-evident that self-interest could explain how rational actors solve collective problems or combine to act for their own benefit. Such theories are typically based on an assumption that what is beneficial for the group is also beneficial for each individual member. But in a consistent rational choice perspective, costs and benefits must be associated with each individual actor. And here Olson demonstrates that it is certainly beneficial to cooperate for the attainment of collective goods, but it is even more beneficial to opt for the free-rider strategy, to sponge on the collective efforts of others. Since it is in the nature of collective goods that they also benefit those who do not pay for them, rational, maximizing actors will necessarily choose to be free-riders, betraying the collectivity. But if everyone chooses to act selfishly, the collective good will not be realized.

Game theory

Game theory is an important part of rational choice theory. It was originally developed by the mathematician, John von Neumann, in cooperation with Oskar Morgenstern, but since then this method of analysis has been extended to other fields, like economics and politics (e.g., Rapoport 1960; 1992; Schelling 1960). Game theory is particularly suited to providing formal analyses of strategic interaction which may be checked experimentally. A game has at least two players or actors. Each actor chooses a course of action, and when participants have selected their strategies, each draws benefits which are dependent on their own and others' decisions. A distinction is drawn between *cooperative games* where the actors can make binding and enforceable agreements with each other, and *noncooperative games* where this is not the case. In noncooperative games the solution to the game is determined by its *equilibrium point*, that is, the combination of strategies where every player's strategy is a best reply to all other players' strategies. A strategy is called dominant, or a best replay, to the other player's strategies if it maximizes this player's payoff so long as the other player's strategies are kept constant. The solution emerges spontaneously as the result of anticipation of what others players will do and is self-stabilizing. Among noncooperative games the one known as the *prisoner's dilemma* has aroused particular research interest and debate. This game also provides a formal representation of the underlying structure of collective action (Hardin 1982).

Two players meet in a situation in which each has two possible strategies. The actors select independently of one another, so that the game has four possible outcomes. The outcomes are represented by paired scores, so that if the outcome is the upper right-hand corner, the first value, −1, is awarded to A, while B is awarded the other value, 3. In a prisoner's dilemma game involving two players, both may choose between the strategies of cooperation and defection. If both cooperate, they receive positive payoffs of 1 each. If both defect, they receive payoffs off 0 each. If one cooperates and the other defects, the cooperator receives an even worse payoff of −1, while the defector does very well with a positive payoff of 3. There is, consequently, a strong incentive not to cooperate. Defection is the *dominant* strategy in the game, since it gives the best outcome for each player, regardless of which strategy the opponent chooses. Mutual defection is the equilibrium point.

The solution is, however, *individually rational*, but *collectively irrational*. It is collectively deficient because there is at least one other outcome in which all players are better off, namely that which results from mutual cooperation. This is the logic of collective action from the perspective of rational choice theory. *It may be in everyone's individual interest not to cooperate in a collective effort, even though everyone would be better off if everyone cooperated* (Barry and Hardin 1982: 25). It may appear paradoxical that an irrational result follows logically from reasonable and rational premises, but the conclusion seems to be that nonrational players are more likely to acquire collective goods than rational ones (Rapport 1960).

The situation changes if the players in the prisoner's dilemma game are participants in an

		B	
		Cooperate	Defect
A	Cooperate	1,1	−1, 3
	Defect	3, −1	0, 0

Figure 13.2   The prisoner's dilemma

Bibliography

Primary:

Axelrod, Robert. 1984: *The Evolution of Cooperation*. New York: Basic Books.
Barth, Fredrik. 1971: *Socialantropologiska problem*. Venersborg: Prisma.
—— 1981: *Process and Form in Social Life. Selected Essays of Fredrik Barth*. London: Routledge & Kegan Paul.
Becker, Gary S. 1957: *The Economics of Discrimination*. Chicago: University of Chicago Press.
—— 1964: *Human Capital*. New York: Colombia University Press.
—— 1976: *The Economic Approach to Human Behavior*. Chicago: University of Chicago Press.
—— 1981: *A Treatise on the Family*. Cambridge, MA: Harvard University Press.
—— 1996: *Accounting for Tastes*. Cambridge, MA: Harvard University Press.
Becker, Gary S., and Becker, Guity Nashat. 1997: *The Economies of Life: From Baseball to Affirmative Action to Immigration, How Real-World Issues Affect our Everyday Life*. London: McGraw-Hill.
Blau, Peter M. 1964: *Exchange and Power in Social Life*. New York: Wiley.
Brox, Ottar 1964: "Avvisning av storsamfunnet" som økonomisk tilpasningsform. *Tidsskrift for samfunnsforskning*, 5, 167–78.
Brox, Ottar, and Gunneriussen, Willy. 1984: *En polemikk om kokfisk*. (Stencil) Tromsø: Institutt for Samfunnsvitenskap.
Coleman, James S. 1964: *Introduction to Mathematical Sociology*. New York: Free Press.
—— 1986: Social Theory, Social Research, and a Theory of Action. *American Journal of Sociology*, 91/6, 1309–13.
—— 1990: *Foundations of Social Theory*. Cambridge, MA: The Belknap Press of Harvard University Press.
—— 1993: The Impact of Gary Beckers Work on Sociology. *Acta Sociologica*, 36/3, 169–78.
—— 1996: *James S. Coleman*, ed. Jon Clark. London: Falmer Press.
Coleman, James S., and Fararo, Thomas J. 1992: Introduction. In James S. Coleman and Thomas Fararo (eds), *Rational Choice Theory. Advocacy and Critique*, Newbury Park, CA: Sage.
Elster, Jon. 1979a: *Forklaring og dialektikk*. Oslo: Pax.
—— 1979b: *Ulysses and the Sirens*. Cambridge: Cambridge University Press.
—— 1982: Marxism, Functionalism and Game Theory. *Theory and Society*, 11, 453–82.
—— 1983: *Explaining Technical Change*. Cambridge: Cambridge University Press.
—— 1985a: *Making Sense of Marx*. Cambridge: Cambridge University Press.
—— 1985b: *Sour Grapes*. Cambridge: Cambridge University Press.
—— 1989a: *Nuts and Bolts for the Social Sciences*. Cambridge: Cambridge University Press.
—— 1989b: *The Cement of Society*. New York: Cambridge University Press.
—— 1989c: *Solomonic Judgements*. Cambridge: Cambridge University Press.
—— 1993: Some Unresolved Problems in the Theory of Rational Behaviour. *Acta Sociologica*, 36/3, 179–90.
Emerson, Richard M. 1987: *Toward a Theory of Value on Social Exchange*. Newbury Park, CA: Sage.
Hardin, R. 1982: *Collective Action*. Baltimore, MD and London: Johns Hopkins University Press.
Hechter, Michael. 1987: *Principles of Group Solidarity*. Berkeley: University of California Press.
Hernes, Gudmund, et al. 1982: *Maktutredningen*. Sluttrapport. NOU: 3.
Homans, George C. 1958: Social Behavior as Exchange. *American Journal of Sociology*, 63, 597–606.
—— 1961: *Social Behavior. Its Elementary Forms*. New York: Harcourt, Brace and World.
—— 1964: Bringing Men Back In. *American Sociological Review*, 29/5, 809–18.

Luce, R. D., and Raiffa, H. 1957: *Games and Decisions*. New York: Wiley.

Midgaard, Knut. 1970: *Communication and Strategy*. Oslo: Universitetsforlaget.

—— 1980: On the Significance of Language and a Richer Concept of Rationality. In L. Lewin and E. Vedung (eds), *Politics as Rational Action*. Dordrecht: Reidel.

Olson, Mancur. 1965: *The Logic of Collective Action. Public Goods and the Theory of Groups*. Cambridge, MA: Harvard University Press.

Philipson, Tomas, and Becker, Gary S. 1996: *Mortality Contingent Claims, Health Care, and Social Insurance*. Cambridge, MA.

Rapoport, Anatol. 1960: *Fights, Games and Debates*. Ann Arbor, MI: Michigan University Press.

Schelling, Thomas. 1960: *The Strategy of Conflict*. Cambridge, MA: Harvard University Press.

Taylor, Michael. 1987: *The Possibility of Cooperation*. London, New York, and Oslo: Cambridge University Press and Universitetsforlaget.

Secondary:

Abell, Peter (ed.) 1991: *Rational Choice Theory*. Upleadon: Elgar.

Acta Sociologica 1993: Special Issue on Rational Choice Theory, 36/3.

Andersen, Heine. 1993: Rationelle valg - en ny strømning i sociologisk teori. *Dansk Sociologi*, 4/3, 4–21.

Barry, Brian, and Hardin, Russel. 1982: *Rational Man and Irrational Society? An Introduction and Sourcebook*. London: Sage.

Blossfeld, Hans-Peter, and Prein, Gerald. 1998: *Rational Choice Theory and Large-Scale Data Analysis*. Boulder, CO: Westview.

Boudon, Raymond. 1989: Subjective Rationality and the Explanation of Social Behaviour. *Rationality and Society*, 1/2, 173–96.

Coleman, James, and Fararo, Thomas J. (eds) 1992: *Rational Choice Theory*. Newbury Park, CA: Sage.

Elster, Jon (ed.) 1986: *Rational Choice*. Oxford: Basil Blackwell.

Etzioni, Amitai. 1988: *The Moral Dimension: Toward a New Economics*. New York: Free Press.

Friedman, Jeffrey (ed.) 1996: *The Rational Choice Controversy: Economic Models of Politics Reconsidered*. New Haven: Yale University Press.

Harris, Michael, and Kelly, Gavin. 1996: *Rethinking Preferences in Rational Choice*. Political Economy Working Papers, no. 5. Sheffield: Political Economy Research Centre.

Hedström, Peter, and Swedberg, Richard. 1996: *Rational Choice, Empirical Research, and the Sociological Tradition*. Stockholm: Universitet, Sociologiska Institutionen.

Hernes, Gudmund. 1993: Hobbes and Coleman. In A. Sørensen and S. Spillman (eds), *Social Theory and Social Policy. Essays in Honor of James S. Coleman*. Westport, CT: Praeger.

Lindenberg, Siegwart. 1997: *Rational Choice and Solidarity*. London: Sage.

Milner, Henry. 1994: *Social Democracy and Rational Choice: The Scandinavian Experience and Beyond*. London and New York: Routledge.

Nielsen, Klaus, and Pedersen, Ove K. 1988: The Negotiated Economy: Ideal and History. *Scandinavian Political Studies*, 11/1, 79–102.

—— 1993: The Negotiated Economy: General Features and Theoretical Perspectives. In J. Hausner, N. Jessop, and K. Nielsen (eds), *Institutional Frameworks of Market Economics*. Aldershot: Averbury.

Moser, Paul K. (ed.) 1990: *Rationality in Action*. Cambridge: Cambridge University Press.

Østerberg, Dag. 1988: *Metasociology*. Oslo: Universitetsforlaget.

Parsons, Talcott. 1937: *The Structure of Social Action*. Glencoe, IL: Free Press.

Rakner, Lise. 1996: *Rational Choice and the Problem of Institutions: A Rational Choice Institutionalism and its Application by Robert Bates*. Bergen: Chr. Michelsen Institute.

Rapoport, Anatol. 1992: Game Theory Defined: What it is and is Not. *Rationality and Society*, 4/1, 74–82. [This issue is devoted to the Use of Game Theory in the Social Sciences.]

Rovira, Juan R. 1995: *Foundations of Rational Choice*. Manchester: University of Manchester.

Schmidtz, David. 1995: *Rational Choice and Moral Agency*. Princeton, NJ; Chichester: Princeton University Press.

Shepsle, Kenneth A., and Bonchek, Mark S. 1997: *Analyzing Politics: Rationality, Behaviour and Institutions*. London: W. W. Norton.

Simon, Herbert A. 1954: *Administrative Behavior*. New York: Macmillan.

—— 1982: *Models of Bounded Rationality*. Cambridge, MA: MIT Press.

Smelser, Neil. 1992: The Rational Choice Perspective: A Theoretical Assessment. *Rationality and Society*, 4/4, 381–411. [This issue is devoted to the Rational Choice Perspective.]

Sobel, Jordan Howard. 1994: *Taking Chances: Essays on Rational Choice*. Cambridge: Cambridge University Press.

Therborn, Göran. 1991: Cultural Belonging, Structural Location and Human Action. Explaining in Sociology and in Social Science. *Acta Sociologica*, 34/3, 177–91.

Udehn, Lars. 1996: *The Limits of Public Choice. A Sociological Critique of the Economic Theory of Politics*. London and New York: Routledge.

Young, Lawrence A. (ed.) 1997: *Rational Choice and Religion*. New York: Routledge.

Zey, Mary (ed.) 1992: *Decision Making: Alternatives to Rational Choice*. Newbury Park, CA: Sage.

chapter 14

Functionalism

Heine Andersen

KEY CONCEPTS

AGIL SCHEME – acronym for the four functional prerequisites in Parsons's theory: adaptation (to environment), goal attainment (organizing collective efforts to realize goals), integration (of societal community), and latency, or latent pattern maintenance, such as reproduction of commitment to beliefs, values, expressive symbols, and meaning.

DYSFUNCTION – harmful consequences of a recurrent social or cultural form for society as a whole or for a social system of which it is a part.

FUNCTION – the beneficial consequences of a recurrent social or cultural form for society as a whole or for a social system of which it is a part. It is a task that a social or cultural form performs within a larger system.

LATENT FUNCTIONS – functions that are neither intended nor recognized.

MANIFEST FUNCTIONS – functions that are intended and recognized.

SOCIAL STRUCTURE – recurrent parts of a social system and their functional interrelations at a given point in time. Components of structure can be norms, roles, values, collectivities, social strata, and institutions.

SOCIAL SYSTEM – a plurality of individual actors interacting with each other.

UNIT ACT – the smallest unit of an action system. According to Parsons, it includes four elements: an actor, an end, the situation (divided into conditions and means), and a normative orientation.

Functionalism in social theory is part of a broad stream of ideas developed since the late nineteenth century, a set of beliefs and values that underlines utility and functional relations. Literally, "function" (from Latin *fungi, functio* to effect, perform, execute) means "to perform" or "to serve" (a purpose). The meaning is known from architecture as a philosophy of design, holding that form should be adapted to usage and material. It has developed also into pragmatic thinking in areas such as politics and management, where what matters is getting things to work, piecing together elements of society or organizations.

In modern social theory, functionalism emerged as a distinct school, first in social anthropology early in this century, and later in sociology, beginning in the 1930s. Its roots, however, are as ancient as the analogy of the organism, used in the philosophy of Antiquity by Plato (BC 428/7–348/7) and Aristotle (BC 384–322), and found throughout the history of ideas in several later variations, as in Thomas Hobbes's metaphorical representation of society as the monster figure *Leviathan* (1651). The person who gave the name "sociology" to that field, Auguste Comte, also made use of the analogy of society as an organism.

The idea of perceiving something as determined by a purpose or an end goes back to Aristotle's reference to the *telos* (purpose) of things as their *final cause*, as distinct from the antecedent, mechanical *efficient cause* (see chapter 30), when explaining motions or states of affairs. The same principle can be discerned in the method of twentieth-century functionalism, such as when explaining the existence of social norms and institutions by demonstrating their beneficial effects on the reproduction and survival of society. The idea of a latent *telos* is also found in late eighteenth-century classical political economics, illustrated by Adam Smith's metaphor of the "invisible hand" as the automatic mechanism that maximizes wealth, individual welfare, and economic efficiency through the increase in division of labor and self-interested competition in the spontaneous order of capitalist market economies. Teleology (from *telos*) is also widespread in the nineteenth-century philosophy of history, for example, in G. F. W. Hegel's philosophical system, where history is understood as a large universal process, moved by the Absolute Spirit coming to knowledge of itself as spirit.

In sociology, the immediate forerunner of functionalism and source of inspiration was Emile Durkheim (see chapter 5), but Herbert Spencer's evolutionism (see chapter 3) also played a role. For all their theoretical differences, both shared an organic perception of society. With Spencer, the organism analogy was elaborated on in detail and quite literally (somewhat in contradiction to his general individualistic position), whereas with Durkheim it occurs only in a more metaphorical sense. Both share the reference to the beneficial consequences of elements in the social structure. This is reminiscent of Spencer's analysis of the succession of different forms of family in societal evolution, or Durkheim's account of the (collective) beneficial effects of punishment for crime. Both also shared a common problem perspective, that of integration under conditions of increasing differentiation (division of labor) and complexity in modern industrial societies.

From these early sources to its peak in the decades after World War II in the theories of Talcott Parsons and Robert K. Merton, the development of functionalism passed through studies within the field of social anthropology.

Functionalism in Social Anthropology

When Talcott Parsons went to London as a student in 1924, he attended lectures by the Polish-British social anthropologist, Bronislaw Malinowski (1884–1942), lectures that probably influenced the direction of Parsons's later intellectual development. Partly in opposition to earlier evolutionists and diffusionists, functionalism in early twentieth-century social anthropology became a link between these forerunners and the functionalism found later in sociology. Much of the terminology of functionalism, including the very term "functionalism," stems from Malinowski and his contemporary, the British anthropologist Alfred Reginald Radcliffe-Brown (1881–1955).

Functions as explanations

The guiding principle of functionalism in anthropology is made clear in Malinowski's claim that functional analysis "aims at the explanation of anthropological facts at all levels of development by their function, by the part which they play within the integral system of culture" (Malinowski 1926: 132, cited in Merton 1968: 76). The meaning of function is shown in his definition of functionalism, namely the assumption that:

> in every civilization every custom, material object, idea and belief fulfills some vital function, has some task to accomplish, represents an indispensable part within a working whole. (Malinowski 1926: 132–3, cited in Merton 1968: 86)

Some additional and important elements in this kind of functionalism are spelled out in Radcliffe-Brown's definition of function in an influential article from 1935:

> The *function* of any recurrent activity such as the punishment of a crime, or a funeral ceremony, is the part it plays in the social life as a whole and therefore the contribution it makes to the maintenance of the structural continuity. The concept of function as here defined thus involves the notion of a *structure* consisting of a *set of relations* amongst *unit entities*, the *continuity* of the structure being maintained by a *life-process* made up of the activities of the constituent units. (Radcliffe-Brown 1965: 180)

These statements indicate: (1) an holistic perception of society, (2) based on an assumption that all parts of the structure are related to one another and work together in such a way, that (3) the structure is maintained by the actions performed by people in the structure, in such a way that the needs of the individual are also met. Further, it becomes clear that what is explained – the *explanandum* – is certain persistent social or cultural traits: customs, material objects, ideas, beliefs, and recurrent activities.

Controversy over functions of magic

An illuminating example can be found in Malinowski's analysis of magic in his famous study of the Trobriand islanders, which also gained paradigmatic status because of its fieldwork method, using careful long-term participant observation. In his view, magical rituals are standardized, permanent, and traditional forms, originating from people's spontaneous ways of coping with anxiety caused by uncertainty and danger. The function of magic – the explanation of its purpose – is the confidence and certainty it provides to people, which they need to perform productive work, thus maintaining continuity of the social structure (Malinowski 1948, first published in 1925). This example shows one further peculiarity of functional explanation: its neglect of the account given by the actors themselves (that the rite brings good luck, or the like), which is discounted by the anthropologist as myth, from later rationalization. Notice also that Malinowski's explanation refers to *individual* needs and psychological mechanisms. Rites, customs, beliefs, etc., are seen as being functional responses to basic individual needs: organic, physiological, and psychological. Individuals for their part behave so as to reproduce these cultural and social elements.

Assigning this much importance to individual needs as determinants of functions provoked controversy and opposition from Radcliffe-Brown. In accordance with his more Durkheimian leanings, he wanted to reverse the order of determination by giving primacy to social structure and social relations. In his analysis of magic and rituals (with rituals surrounding childbirth as an example, based on studies in the Andaman Islands; Radcliffe-Brown 1948, first published in 1922) he stated precisely the opposite of Malinowski: these rites – or more correctly, the fear of not performing these rites properly – produced strong individual sentiments. Sentiments are instrumental to maintaining social structure, not the opposite. The real function of the rite is its contribution to the survival of social relations by vitalizing the societal importance of childbirth (Radcliffe-Brown 1965, first published in 1939). This controversy is reminiscent of the problem that was later labeled "actor-structure" or "micro-macro," a problem that became still more visible and acute as structural functionalism took form in the work of Talcott Parsons and his collaborators in the following decades.

Talcott Parsons

> **Biography:** *Talcott Parsons*
>
> Talcott Parsons was born in 1902 in Colorado Springs and grew up under conditions that may be characterized as Protestant religious, liberal, and intellectual. In 1920 he went to the rather conservative Amherst College in Massachusetts and moved to Europe in 1924, first to the London School of Economics, where he attended lectures by the social anthropologist Bronislaw Malinowski, and studied economics. The following year he went to Heidelberg, where Max Weber had been a professor until 1918. Besides Max Weber, Parsons became acquainted here with the then contemporary debates in German philosophy and economic history, and wrote his doctoral thesis on *The Concept of Capitalism in Recent German Literature*.
>
> In 1926 Parsons went back and became an instructor in economics and sociology, first at Amherst and then at Harvard, where he stayed until his death in 1979. In his earlier years he played an important role in making Weber (and other European classical sociologists) known to English-language audiences, partly by translating Max Weber's *The Protestant Ethic and the Spirit of Capitalism* (1930). Parsons moved to the new Department of Sociology at Harvard, created in 1931 with P. Sorokin as its head. In 1937 he published his first major work, *The Structure of Social Action*.
>
> Beyond this, especially after World War II, his academic standing grew rapidly, and it is no exaggeration to say that during the following two decades he became one of the dominant figures in postwar sociology in the United States (though, in spite of US world dominance in sociology at that time, Parsons never did gain similar influence in Europe). In 1946 he became the head of the new, multidisciplinary Harvard Department of Social Relations, from which emanated an impressive list of publications during the next ten years, and in which "structural functionalism" was constructed and articulated. Most of Parsons's later work can be seen as elaborations, corrections, and reactions to criticism of his theoretical constructions from that period.
>
> From the late 1960s, however, Parsons witnessed the decline of structural functionalism, but he energetically continued his scholarship after retirement in 1973. He died in 1979 in Germany, on a visit taking part in celebrations in Heidelberg of the fiftieth anniversary of his own doctoral degree (Hamilton 1983: 31-55).

The functionalism of the 1950s, or structural functionalism, as it is now called, became almost synonymous with the name of Talcott Parsons. When Parsons started working out his theory in the 1930s, however, his point of departure was in no way functionalism as described above, related neither to Spencer, Durkheim, nor the social anthropologists. His first major work, *The Structure of Social Action* (1937), began with the sentence: "Who now reads Spencer?" (implying "nobody"), and though Durkheim's work played an important role, the functional aspects of his approach did not.

Parsons's starting point, on the contrary, was an attempt to explore, clarify, and reconstruct a theoretical and methodological basis for understanding *social action* as voluntary, nonreductionist and antipositivist. Important influences at that time were German idealist philosophy, especially Neo-Kantian, and Max Weber, which he studied when he was in Heidelberg in the 1920s (see the biographical sketch), as well as the model of action he found in economic theory. In doing so, Parsons ignored or opposed several leading schools in American social science, including Chicago sociology, pragmatism, and behaviorism (see chapters 8 and 12). Parsons also excluded the work of the founder of his own department at Harvard, Pitirim A. Sorokin (1889–1968).

Only later, beginning in the early fifties, was the concept of social system and the functional perspective introduced, making the influence of earlier functionalism visible. Familiar standard concepts from functionalism now came into play, such as functional system imperatives (also called functional prerequisites), structure, status roles, socialization and internalization, social control and steering media. He continued, however, to talk about social systems as a specific kind of action system, and much of his later work can be seen as endeavors to overcome the opposition between his early voluntaristic actor perspective and the sneaking and unintended implications of his structural functionalism, like reification of culture, determinism, and a static view on social systems.

The following description will take as a leitmotif the "problem of social order," which played an important part in much of Parsons's work. In a broad sense it is a basic problem in all sociological theories, and here it should not be taken in a normative sense (meaning that existing social order should be preserved), but just as a catchword, designating the problem, if and how we can explain the existence of recurrent patterns of norms, institutions, and coordination of action, etc.

Parsons's Theory of Social Action

The first exposition of Parsons's theoretical scheme for the analysis of social action is found in his more than 800-page book of 1937, *The Structure of Social Action*. Distinctive and in some ways strange, the focus of this volume is a comprehensive scrutiny of four social theories, namely those of the economist Alfred Marshall (1842–1924), the economist and sociologist Vilfredo Pareto, and the sociologists Max Weber (see chapter 6) and Emile Durkheim (see chapter 5). The book became the starting point for a new theoretical movement in American sociology.

The guiding principle of the book, clearly influenced by the teachings of Max Weber and his method of (hermeneutic) *Verstehen*, was the idea that sociology should be the study of (subjectively) *meaningful social action*. It had to be built upon a *voluntaristic* perception of social action, that is, the assumption that action is the result of what people voluntarily choose to do. By this, he wanted to distance himself from every kind of reductionism, whether material, biological, psychological, behaviorist, or any other nonsocial factor.

Since the Renaissance, the voluntaristic perception of human action in social theory and social philosophy has been linked to the individualistic and utilitarian traditions, from Thomas Hobbes, John Locke (1632–1704), Jeremy Bentham, Adam Smith, and Herbert Spencer to neoclassical economics (and the later rational choice theory). However, these traditions also make more acute the fundamental and very obstinate problem of *social order*, a classical problem in social thinking with both normative and explanatory aspects.

The problem of social order

The explanatory problem Parsons confronted was how to explain the existence of relatively ordered patterns of social actions and recurring social institutions from individualistic premises, implying that people independently choose what they want to do. In *Leviathan* (1651) Thomas Hobbes, and many others since, used the idea of man in a presocial "crude state of nature," where man is selfish, aggressive, greedy, and jealous, thrust into a "solitary, poor, nasty, brutish, and short" life. The only solution for Hobbes was the force of a sovereign, installed through a contract, who by the sword could compel people into obedience to law and order.

This type of solution Parsons considered flawed. Like Durkheim, he did not believe in sheer fear of punishment as sufficient to secure social order. Parsons's main objection was the perception of human action underlying the individualist theories, and especially the utilitarian model of human action, which was also associated with a positivistic epistemology. Typical of the utilitarian model is the perception that all action is rational in the sense of purposive (means–end) rational, taking for granted the ends (or preferences in the terminology of modern economics) which actors pursue. Today, this model is well-known from standard elementary economic and rational choice theory. The problem of action is reduced to (1) choosing the most efficient strategies when (2) the end (goal) is given and (3) the situational conditions are known. Rationality simply refers to collecting data about situational conditions and causal laws in order to predict consequences of feasible action, and then calculating optimal action.

The defect in this model is defined under the label "the utilitarian dilemma." The dilemma, according to Parsons, emanates from the indeterminate status given to the *ends* in the utilitarian model of action. In this model, there exist only two possible answers to the question of how ends are determined. One, in accordance with the positivist understanding, is that ends are determined by situational conditions. In this case, ends as a distinct category are actually eliminated from the model, and the actor has no choice concerning ends. Alternatively, ends can be considered completely "random," not determined by anything intelligible, neither as seen from the subjective perspective of the actor, nor from the explanatory perspective of the observer. In this case, ends are just to be taken as empirical phenomena, which cannot be explained.

Because of the rooted and widespread influence of utilitarian ideas in modern thinking, Parsons's critique of utilitarian models of action is still relevant, for example, concerning modern economic theory, rational choice theory, and certain offshoots of Marxian theory. Parsons wanted to avoid the idealist pitfalls of the hermeneutic, Neo-Kantian tradition of Rickert and Dilthey, which were also visible in the work of Max Weber, Georg Simmel, and others. Here he found a tendency toward allowing material situational conditions to disappear so that actions and their products could be understood as the "externalization of spirit," that is, actions, norms, social institutions, and cultural product are seen as external, objectified products of ideas, intentions, and other subjective factors.

The unit act

Parsons found the solution to the problem in *Structure of Social Action* when he discovered certain distinct "residual categories," which had a tendency toward mutual convergence in the four theories he analyzed (Marshall, Pareto, Weber, and Durkheim). Residual categories are concepts with an ad hoc character that play an important role in a theory, but are not fully or explicitly integrated into its framework. In Marshall's theory, for example, Parsons found nonutilitarian assumptions about human character, like industriousness, frugality, honesty, and entrepreneurship.

These observations were used by Parsons as a kind of justification for the main conclusion of the whole investigation in *Structure of Social Action* (already presented in chapter 2), the specification of the abstract analytical components of the basic unit of any social act. (Parsons somewhat misleadingly called these observations "empirical verification.") The *unit act*, according to Parsons, consists of the following four elements:

1 The actor;
2 An end, i.e. a future state of affairs toward which the process of action is oriented;
3 The situation. This is divided into:
    3.1 The conditions of action. These are the factors that cannot be altered by the actor, and;
    3.2 The means of action. These are the factors that the actor can control;
4 The actor's subjective orientation toward these elements, which is expressed in his choice of action, called the normative orientation. (Parsons 1968a: 44)

Parsons's claim is that these are necessary analytical elements, which are a priori categories (in a sense akin to Kant's pure forms of sensibility and understanding, like time, space, and causality), indispensable in every kind of empirical analysis. As one can see, the innovation compared to the utilitarian model is the fourth element, which is also the determining factor related to the opening problem, that of the social order. Normative orientation, including norms, values, beliefs, etc., is supposed to guide and limit the choice of ends, as well as means, in the course of action.

Normative and conditional order

The basis for this idea of a normative order first of all goes back to Durkheim's notions of solidarity and collective consciousness behind moral order. But Parsons blames Durkheim for his "subjective" positivism, implying a tendency to conflate reality with ideas and values, causing certain material conditions to disappear if they were obstacles to the realization of values (Parsons 1968a: 446). What Parsons wanted was an action model that was able to handle the "state of tension between two different orders of elements, the normative and the conditional" ("conditional" referring to the elements in the situation that cannot be altered or controlled by the actor; Parsons 1968a: 732). This is the same tension as that between purposive rationality and value rationality in Weber, and Parsons is sympathetic to Weber's idea that subjective values are realized in personal ways of life, and in a legitimate, valid order (which he mentions as Weber's "direct equivalent of Durkheim's rules possessing moral authority"; Parsons 1968a: 717). The outcome is thus a perception of norms and social institutions as a kind of compromise between Kant and Spencer, between ideal, *ultimate values* and what can be realized under factual situational conditions and material needs.

Returning to the problem of social order, the solution of which Parsons considered to be a precondition for a satisfactory theory of social action, this outcome obviously fostered a new question: Where do these ultimate values originate from, and how do they become common values? Parsons frankly talked about "common value systems," but does not explain how values become common in social action systems. After all, Parsons's unit of analysis in *Structure of Social Action* remained the individual actor. What was needed was an elaboration on the properties of actors in interaction with other actors, and on the properties of the social systems constituted by these interactions. This indicates the shift in Parsons to the perspective of social systems.

Action Systems and the Social System

The shift to the system perspective does not imply an abandonment of the action perspective. Parsons persistently talked about "action systems," and the social system is just one of four action systems, which besides the social system include culture, personality, and behavioral organism (behavioral organism was added later than the three others; Parsons 1951: 6; Parsons and Shils 1951: 8, 54ff; Parsons 1964: 81). Nevertheless, it means that Parsons increasingly shifted his focus to the problem of how action systems are integrated in supra-individual structures, and how such structures are maintained, reproduced, and changed.

The four action systems

The separation of a social system from culture, personality, and behavioral organism should not be interpreted empirically. It is purely an analytical and conceptual distinction to be used in analyses of empirical situations involving social actions. Here it can be asked how actions relate to culture, how they relate to other actors, to the actor's own personality, and to her/his (biological) organism. In the real world, the different systems interpenetrate each other, as when cultural norms are internalized in personality.

Culture is defined as a system of signs and symbols, including "ideas or beliefs, expressive symbols or value patterns" (Parsons 1951: 4). Thus, culture was originally divided into three parts: (1) cognitive ideas and beliefs (including scientific knowledge); (2) expressive symbols, such as art, aesthetic forms and styles, and; (3) value systems, including ethical values (meaning culture consists of symbols related to "truth, goodness, and beauty"). Parsons later added a fourth component, which he called "constitutive symbolization," concerned with the most basic existential questions of human life, the problems of *meaning* underlying the major religious and philosophical systems. Constitutive symbolization makes the link to what Parsons calls *the ultimate reality* (see below).

Personality is perceived mainly within a Freudian reference, as an energy system, giving the actor motivation as well as guidelines for orientation of action (Parsons and Shils 1951:

17–33, 61–88; Parsons et al. 1953: 13–29; Parsons 1954: 336–47). He uses Freud's three-layered model of personality, consisting of the *id* dominated by instinctual energy, the *ego*, which rationally adapts irrational impulses to conditions of reality, and the *superego*, the conscience, setting the ideal standards of action and (internally) punishing failure with a sense of guilt. From other parts of psychology, Parsons made the assumption that actors are basically motivated by need-dispositions and a tendency toward optimizations of gratification. Behavioral organism simply refers to man as a biological being, underlying and conditioning the other systems of action.

The social system

Of greatest importance to the development of structural functionalism was, of course, the conceptual framework connected to the last of the four action system in Parsons's scheme, the social system. In the simplest terms, "a social system is a plurality of individual actors interacting with each other" (Parsons 1951: 5). Like Durkheim, Parsons claimed social systems to be a reality *sui generis*, not reducible to properties of individual actors. Further, he held the view that we must clarify a frame of reference concerning structural properties of social systems before addressing their dynamic aspects. By *structure,* he referred to the analytical relevant parts of the system and their functional interrelations in a given state, a kind of snapshot of the system at a given moment. Relevance here means functional significance regarding, for example, stability, change, integration, or disruption of the system.

This strategy explains an emphasis on well-known structural concepts, like status, role, institution, norm, and value pattern. Parsons later summed up the main components of social structure as roles, collectivities, values, and norms. Originally, the most fundamental was the pair status–role (Parsons 1951: 25–6). *Status* is the position within a social system where an actor is located, and *role* is how actors from a particular status are expected to behave. Roles are thus backed by internalized mutual normative expectations concerning what are considered proper actions in particular situations, furthered by mechanisms of social control. Subjective meaning and legitimacy of role expectations are derived from the value pattern, and supported up by institutionalized systems of sanctions. Thus, although culture is separate from its social system, cultural values interpenetrate the social system by setting normative standards for evaluating role performance. Roles are also distinguished from personality. A person is *not* a bundle of roles (as some critics have said), but roles represent the *interpenetration* between social system and personality, where interpenetration results from processes of socialization, internalization of norms and values, and social control.

It should be obvious how these concepts and assumptions influence the problem of social order, also known as the problem of "double contingency." In every interaction, the outcome for each actor is dependent not only upon her or his own choices, but upon those of other actors as well. Thus, social order becomes a problem of coordination, focusing attention on how harmony can be achieved between personalities from differentiated role systems, each with their own internalized norms, expectations, value orientations, and sets of moral standards. The key element, according to Parsons, is culture. Internalization of common cultural values in the personality's superego is basic to norms and evaluative standards that bring about coordination of action orientations and motivation, and thereby the harmonious functioning of the social system.

A tendency toward reifying culture can be observed here, which later became one of the main targets of criticism of Parsons. This tendency, however, ran counter to his own intention, according to which culture "is on one hand the product of, on the other hand a determinant to, systems of human action" (Parsons 1951: 15). Nevertheless, if culture were to secure the solution to the problem of social order, it seems Parsons was then compelled to give primacy and a high degree of autonomy to culture, on a level beyond mere beliefs and symbolic expressions of individual actors.

The pattern variables

This ambivalence concerning the relationship between action and culture can be illustrated by looking at the famous pattern variables. These pattern variables consist of four or five dichotomies, the number depending on the context, which according to Parsons represent basic values or types of action orientation between which actors have to choose in every action situation. He touched upon them in his earlier work, *Structure of Social Action*, but elaborated on them more fully in *Social System* and later works.

The five pattern variables are (Parsons and Shils 1951: 77):

1   Affectivity – affective neutrality;
2   Universalism – particularism;
3   Ascription – achievement;
4   Specificity – diffuseness;
5   Self-orientation – collective-orientation.

As can be seen, these pattern variables are linked to a number of traditional, fundamental questions and concepts in social theory and moral philosophy. Parsons considered the pattern variables to be a kind of specification of Ferdinand Tönnics's *Gemeinschaft and Gesellschaft* (see chapter 4), but they can also be connected with Max Weber's ideal types of action and authority, related to traditional versus modern societies (see chapter 6). The dichotomy ascribed or achieved was used earlier by Ralph Linton to characterize status in social structure. The claim now is that any actor, in order to make an action situation meaningful in subjective terms, has to start by defining the situation. To do this, the actor must choose one of the extremes in each of precisely these dichotomies.

One way to look at these concepts is purely analytically. They provide a conceptual framework, which in an illuminating way can be used to analyze and classify a wide range of phenomena, such as single and concrete everyday situations (e.g. buying something), a role (e.g. father), an organization (e.g. bureaucracy), or a type of society (e.g. modern capitalist societies).

These pattern variables, however, are not just meant to be tools for describing. They also serve an important role in explaining the ordered functioning of social systems. They "are organizers which define and integrate whole systems of action" (Parsons and Shils 1951: 170). Clearly, these pattern variables refer to dilemmas concerning basic cultural values, like the scope of universal human rights (universalism versus particularism), personal morals (for example, self-orientation versus collective-orientation), or obligations concerning care for particular categories of persons, for example, close relatives (affectivity versus affective neutrality). Typical of the pattern variables is the combination of that which is determinated, and that which is not. Certain predetermined alternatives, from among which a selection is to be made, present "a very general set of categories which comprise all the possible ways of relating the personality processes . . . [to] cultural standards on one hand and social object on the other" (Parsons and Shils 1951: 170). It is the *selection* of a given alternative, however, that is not determined. Thus, it is the actor's choices which do the work of translating these abstract values into role expectations and role performances within social systems.

This conceptual framework, however, contains no explanation for the existence of either the pattern variables themselves, or the values they express. Obviously, these pattern variables should not be taken as empirical generalizations. They should be considered as having a kind of a priori status, existing before any cultural traditions or symbolic expressions. Further, this distinctive status of culture opens the possibility for conflicts between the logic immanent in culture and the functional imperatives of social systems. Culture is not supposed to be derived from either psychological properties of personalities or from functional imperatives of social systems. On the contrary, culture follows its own obstinate logic of coherence, consistency and meaningful congruity. This makes the relationship between culture and the other action systems crucial, especially the social system, which became topical in the AGIL scheme, where Parsons tried to identify the principal functional imperatives of action systems and their interrelations.

The AGIL Scheme

"AGIL" is an abbreviation of *adaptation, goal attainment, integration,* and *latent pattern maintenance* (or latency), which are the four functional characteristics Parsons found common in all action systems. The idea originated from studies of small-group behavior, conducted by some of Parsons's collaborators (Robert F. Bales and Edward Shils) in the early 1950s. In studies of interaction processes Bales had observed a tendency toward regularity in the way groups worked when asked to solve any task (Bales 1950: chapter V). As a rule, they always passed through the same four phases, the first of which was an instrumental orientation toward given external tasks (adaptation). They would then shift attention to problems concerning internal control and coordination of group-member performance (goal attainment). This would be followed by attending to the inevitable critical development of problems involving solidarity and group cohesion (integration). Finally, they would move on to a kind of relaxing phase (latency), where sentiments and tensions were expressed and managed.

This phase model of group processes is then (courageously, one might say) transformed and generalized into a universal typology of functions in action systems and social systems. The claim now is that all human systems need to accomplish exactly these four functions in order to survive. In the general scheme of things (and in more mature terms) the four functional imperatives mean (Parsons 1965: 38–41; 1971: 4–28; and Platt 1974: 13–15):

> *Adaptation*: the providing of disposable facilities and resources from the system's external environment;
> *Goal attainment*: selection and coordination of goals according to importance, mobilization of motivation, and organizing efforts of actors;
> *Integration*: mutual adjustment of units and subsystems from the perspective of their contribu-

tion to the effective functioning of the system as a whole;
Pattern maintenance: maintaining the stability of institutionalized culture, which includes maintenance of the pattern itself and of the actor's motivational commitment to the pattern.

The next step is to connect each of these four functions to the four action systems. In accordance with the supposed presence of the four functional imperatives in all human systems, Parsons further identified subsystems corresponding to AGIL in all systems and subsystems, resulting in a structure like a nest of Chinese boxes. Thus, at the general level of action theory, the function of adaptation is performed by the behavioral organism (here referring to the basic functions concerning relations to physical environment, such as manual work, sensory activities), goal attainment is performed by the personality (mobilization of energy from organisms, etc.), integration of units by the social system, and pattern maintenance, of course, by the cultural system. In a similar way, the social system contains four subsystems, shown in figure 14.1.

As can be seen at the level of social systems, the four subsystems performing the AGIL functions are called the *fiduciary system,* the *societal community,* the *polity,* and the *economy.* "Fiduciary system" is the name that Parsons preferred for the social subsystem that performs the pattern-maintaining function of reproducing, legitimizing, and maintaining commitment to beliefs, moral values, and expressive symbols. Its primary link is to the cultural action system (Parsons thus avoids speaking of culture as a part of the social system). The societal community is reminiscent of Tönnies's *Gemeinschaft,* which was a subsystem in which solidarity, unity, cohesiveness, and loyalty to norms and institutions were produced.

Ultimate reality

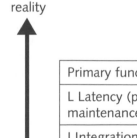

Primary function	Action system		Social system
L Latency (pattern maintenance)	Cultural system		Fiduciary system
I Integration	Social system		Societal community
G Goal attainment	Personality		Polity
A Adaptation	Behavioral organism		The economy

Conditions
Physical-organic
environment

Figure 14.1 The AGIL scheme at the levels of action systems and social systems

Polity, or the political subsystem, deals with selecting and coordinating collective goals, and organizing and coordinating collective efforts to realize these goals by enforcing compliance to the normative order, making it *binding*. Finally, the economy handles the job of producing and distributing goods, thus procuring the material preconditions for the functioning of the whole system. The economy represents the interface between the social system and the physical environment.

The cybernetic hierarchy of control and steering media

The idea now is that between all these subsystems there are mutual interchanges, each subsystem thus supplying the other with something of functional importance. Since there are four subsystems, there are six relationships of mutual interchange, but there is insufficient room in this chapter to present them all in detail. We can, however, describe the main principle of the interchange as two opposing flows (Parsons 1965: 38; 1967: 207–10; Parsons and Platt 1974: 30–2, 426–34). The first one goes from bottom to top in figure 14.1, transporting energy and material from the physical environment, extracted via the behavioral organism and the economy, and distributed from there to the other subsystems. The reverse flow consists of information, extracted from the "ultimate reality," and sent out to the other social subsystems via the cultural and fiduciary subsystems.

To explain how the social subsystems and their interchange work, and how the functional control is mediated, Parsons introduced his concept of *generalized symbolic media of interchange*. This idea was fostered by his studies in the fifties, together with Neil Smelser, of the economic subsystem (Parsons and Smelser 1956), where he dealt with the functions of *money* as a symbolic medium, carrying information on needs (as purchasing power) from potential buyers to potential sellers, thus allocating productive efforts according to purchase power in the economy. Money symbolizes economic goods. By looking in the other subsystems for analogies to money as a steering medium in the economic subsystem, he constructed three other symbolic media, characteristic of each of the other subsystems. In the polity, the medium of interchange is *power* (Parsons 1967: 297–354), in the societal community, the medium is *influence* (Parsons 1967: 355–82), and in the fiduciary system, the medium is *value commitment* (Parsons 1968b).

Thus, power is seen as a generalized symbolic medium in the sense that a power position in an institutional structure implies entitlement to make certain decisions that are binding and obligatory on the collectivity and its members. Under representative democratic rule, it can be said that voters exchange their votes for expected benefits from a political system, implying an obligation, enforced by law, to obedience to legitimate decisions made by government. Power symbolizes a capacity for instrumentally effective and organized, collective efforts. By analogy, influence means a capacity to bring about desired decisions in the interest of collectivities, though in this case by persuasion and appealing to loyalty on behalf of common interests, based on position in a prestige hierarchy in a societal community. Influence thus symbolizes the will to act according to principles of solidarity. Finally, the generalized medium of *value commitment* operates through a general conviction of legitimacy of norms and moral values, and a readiness to implement them into action. Thus, value commitment appeals to concepts of moral duty, honor, and guilt.

Parsons's assumption then, was that the hierarchy of control works by means of these steering media. They make it possible for the second flow, that of information going top to bottom, from culture to economy, to hold the controlling function of the system as a whole. "Hierarchy of control" is here used in the cybernetic sense (cybernetics: general theory of automatic control, working by means of flows of information, for example, the nervous system and mechanical-electrical communication systems), where the functions of the whole social system and its adaptation to external given conditions of scarcity are formed by the constraints and guidelines given in the basic systems of moral values, beliefs, expressive symbols, and meaning-constitutive codes in culture.

Social change and social evolution

This model of how basic cultural patterns control and shape the adaptation of social systems to environmental conditions is the basis of Parsons's theory of social change, which he dealt with in several works, beginning in the middle of the sixties (Parsons 1966; Parsons 1971). The theory is evolutionary. The initial idea is that social systems change in functional response to disturbances in the balance between the two opposite flows in the hierarchy of control (information and energy). The most general and significant characteristic is an increasing differentiation *between* and *within* the action systems and their subsystems, thus resulting in higher degrees of subsystem specialization and autonomy. The direction of differentiation is defined by the phenomena that cause increase in the capacity for adaptation and the management of complexity. A precondition is the development of new mechanisms of integration. One example was the invention of money, a symbolic medium of interchange. The diffusion of money as a generalized symbolic medium has meant an enormous increase in the capacity to coordinate larger systems of economic actors, and has thus increased the capacity to adapt.

Through this emphasis on differentiation, Parsons followed ideas established in earlier analyses of the evolution of modernity, such as those of Spencer, Durkheim, and Weber. Regarding the development of modern, Western societies, Parsons understood the (capitalist) *industrial revolution* as an increase in differentiation *between* the economy and other subsystems (primarily leading to greater autonomy from the polity and societal community), as well as differentiation *within* the economy (division of labor). The *democratic revolution* basically meant greater differentiation between the polity and the societal community (between the state and civil society), and within the political system (for example, separation of executive, judicial, and legislative powers). The third important revolution, according to Parsons, is the *educational revolution*, the significance of which above all consists of a differentiation between culture and societal community, and between different aspects of culture, expanding capacities of rationality (science, technology, professions, etc.). Greater autonomy of culture vis-á-vis societal community also implies more universal and abstract value patterns.

Cultural patterns, evolution, and social order

Social change, according to Parsons, means an evolutionary process of differentiation, integration and complexity, whereas cultural patterns are gradually articulated in still more differentiated forms of social life, adapted to external conditions. Returning now to the problem of social order, the question is raised of how cultural patterns are able to bring together these manifold forms under such conditions of increasing diversity in institutional settings and role patterns, etc., which also means an increasing diversity of life conditions and greater plurality in societal communities.

First, it should be kept in mind that the kind of cybernetic control function ascribed to culture does not imply either cultural determinism or idealist reductionism (for example, that a social institution is an "objectified spirit"). The controlling function obviously implies that cultural patterns exert a heavy influence on the shaping of social structure, including norms, roles, identity and boundaries of collectivities, and political and economic institutions. It should be noted, however, that cultural patterns are certainly not the only influence.

A more important and much more stubborn problem is how the autonomous, nearly transcendental, status of cultural patterns can be explained. As mentioned above, Parsons initially intended some sort of dialectical relationship between culture and individual action, where culture is created by individuals, but also determines individual action. But Parsons carefully abstained from making culture a part of the social system, purporting that it creates a reality of its own apart from what individual actors do, believe, or judge. If culture were simply to be taken as the sum of individual beliefs and value commitments, why should we then expect these individual cultures to work together?

This view on culture raises fundamental philosophical questions concerning the ontological status (ontology: theory about the nature of being) of levels of reality and regarding how human beings can recognize these levels, questions that Parsons increasingly dealt with. As far back as when he wrote *Structure of Social Action,* he used the phrase "ultimate values." Later, he introduced the model of a cybernetic hierarchy of control, and placed "ultimate reality" opposite and not-reducible to the material (physical-organic) environment. His idea was that codes of meaning can be extracted from this nonempirical reality by that part of the cultural pattern that he named "constitutive symbolization." Thus, concerning Parsons, the world is dualistic, consisting of two levels of reality, conditions (physical-organic reality) and the ultimate reality.

The fundamental philosophical question arising from this dualistic ontology and its epistemological counterpart, (which was how we can come to know anything about an ultimate, nonempirical reality), was treated by Parsons only in some of his late works, beginning in the 1970s. Even here, he made only a few sketchy reflections. He always kept his distance from philosophy, and never systematically confronted his main arguments from the perspective of history of philosophy, which contains extensive discussions of these problems. The one exception was his last work, where he explicitly referred to the transcendental philosophy of Immanuel Kant. He also tried to invoke purely empirical arguments, most importantly by pointing out the teleological (goal-seeking) character of living systems and their evolution, as well as their open-ended character. He argued that it appeared as if there were some direction or goal, but that this "goal-seeking (was simultaneously) not wholly determined by some factor operating . . . from the outside." An additional empirical argument was the tendency in the evolution of living systems to increasing adaptive capacity (Parsons and Platt 1974: 31).

Regarding *how* culture interchanges with this ultimate reality, Parsons often referred to religion:

It is primarily in the religious context that throughout so much of cultural history belief in some kind of "reality" of the non-empirical world has figured prominently. With full recognition of the philosophical difficulties of defining the nature of that reality, we wish to affirm our sharing the age-old belief in its existence. (Parsons 1978: 356)

I do not know how literally these statements should be taken. In any case, they show the depth and dimensions of the problems involved. In the end, we cannot say that Parsons ever managed to conclude his search for a synthesis of voluntary action theory and structural functional theory of social systems.

Robert K. Merton

Biography: *Robert K. Merton*

Robert King Merton was born in Philadelphia in 1910. After earning a BA from Temple University, he continued his studies at Harvard in 1931, where some of his most important teachers were Pitirim A. Sorokin and the young Talcott Parsons. His early interests were mainly in the social contexts of modern science and technology, which resulted in his 1938 dissertation about science in seventeenth-century England. In 1941 he came to Columbia University, where he spent most of his teaching and research career and is now professor emeritus. Early in his career he broke with the "grand theory" strategy, typical of Parsons. His most important contribution originates from his study of structural functionalism as an empirical oriented program, based on "middle range theory." He and many followers made this program fruitful through studies covering a wide range of substantial social phenomena, from science to deviant behavior, bureaucracy, and self-fulfilling prophecies.

Another school of structural functionalism, originating in the early postwar years, is linked to Robert K. Merton, who for a while was part of Parsons's circle in the 1930s. However, over the years, Merton became increasingly skeptical of the "grand theory," which reflected Parsons's ambition to find an all-compassing, unified theory before beginning empirical studies of social reality. His own suggestion, first put forward in a critical comment to Parsons in 1947, and later in a more elaborate form in his article "On Sociological Theories of the Middle Range" (Merton 1968: 39–72), was to start instead by working out mid-level theories, covering only delimited aspects of social phenomena, such as groups, social mobility, or role conflict. Merton himself conducted several studies of this type, dealing with phenomena like reference group theory, anomie, self-fulfilling prophecy, and unintended consequences of social action, role conflicts, bureaucracy, deviance, norms, and stratification in science.

Partly because of this middle range strategy, the kind of functionalism typical of Merton's approach became quite different from that of Parsons. One implication was the abandonment of the idea in Parsons and earlier functionalism that one should try to set up a system of functional prerequisites, valid for all social systems. He also rejected the core idea of earlier functionalism (Malinowski and Radcliffe-Brown) that recurrent social phenomena should be explained by their functions, such as their benefits to society as a whole. In his very influential criticism, *Manifest and Latent Functions* (Merton 1968: 73–138, first published in 1948), he summarized in three (rejectable) postulates what he thought was flawed in earlier functionalism:

1 Postulate of the functional unity of society, the assumption that what matters is the contribution of some social element to the *whole* system, thus presupposing that there is such a unity.
2 Postulate of universal functionalism, the claim that *all* social or cultural forms have some (positive) function.
3 Postulate of indispensability, that the function performed by a social or cultural form (or this form itself) is an *indispensable* precondition for the survival of the social system.

Merton argued that none of these postulates was empirically justifiable, and that certain important concepts were unclear. Instead, he constructed a program of functional analyses, built on a typology of *different kinds of functions,* thus leaving it to empirical investigation to determine which of these types would be fitted into which particular social forms. The typology was based on two dichotomies:

1 A distinction between *manifest* and *latent* functions. Manifest functions of a social item are the consequences that are intended, or of which the participants are aware. Latent functions are unintended and unrecognized consequences. As can be seen, Merton actually used two criteria, intentionality and awareness, thus opening up a more complex typology, with four types (intended and recognized, intended but not recognized, unintended but recognized later, unintended and not recognized). This distinction opens an interesting area for analysis and empirical study concerning the relationship between intended and unintended consequences, and concerning processes triggered when hitherto latent functions become manifest.
2 A distinction between *functions* (beneficial consequences) and *dysfunctions* (harmful consequences). This is derived from the rejection of the a priori assumption of universal functionality. In advance, we can expect all social forms to have some mix of functions and dysfunctions, implying that the estimate of the net balance will become an empirical question.

An important implication of this modification to functionalism is a defection against the claim that functionalism contains one, and only one, particular mode of *explanation*. Of the four types covered by Merton's typology, functionalism of the Malinowski/Radcliffe-Brown school included only one, *latent functions*, which according to Merton was of course an arbitrary narrowing of the field. For him it became an empirical task to decide if particular social forms were of this specific type, or if they belonged to another. Nobody, of course, would argue that dysfunctions exist because of their harmful consequences. As regards manifest functions, matters are a little more complicated, because of Merton's combination of two criteria within his definition. If it is supposed that the manifest functions of certain items are always intended, these items must be explicable as intentional and actor-based, such as an item being brought about by some actor who wanted to produce that function. If it is supposed that the manifest function was not intended, but recognized later, then the origin cannot be explained as intentional, meaning that some other explanation must be found.

Consequently, structural functionalism in the form Merton gave it became a conceptual framework and a set of guidelines to be used in empirical research, rather than a theory with general explanatory claims (examples are shown in Coser [ed.] 1975). As such, it became a very useful tool, and it is much easier to use in conducting empirical research than the general and abstract theory of Parsons.

Influence and Criticism

During the 1950s and 1960s, particularly in the USA, functionalism gained a very prominent position in sociology. One can ask, however, to what degree key figures like Parsons and Merton should be considered originators, as opposed to mere exponents, of a generally very common way of thinking, which spread out into industrialized societies during the middle decades of the twentieth century (cf. my introductory remarks). Because of this, it can be difficult to measure their influence. Many sociologists, as well as people from other academic disciplines, or even politicians and managers, continue to use some kind of functional approach and perspective, without necessarily being influenced by, or even knowing about, Parsons or Merton. Thus, when Parsons is sometimes described as *the* overall dominant figure in sociology during that period, it appears to be exaggerated, especially as seen from a European point of view. In Scandinavia and other European countries, Parsons never gained that much influence, but also when looking at American sociology from this position it seems to be an exaggeration, perhaps originating from the extensive network of personal contacts that Parsons is said to have had.

Criticism

A similar kind of illusion occurs, perhaps, concerning the later and present influences in sociology of structural functionalism, which is often declared to have withered completely away. This impression is the result of the extensive criticism that structural functionalism received from the late 1960s onward, when Parsons's functionalism was met with increasing and overwhelming criticism, sometimes going to almost shrill heights of intensity. The target of criticism was primarily his structural functional theories of social systems, rather than his early theory of social action.

Many considered the theory initially put forward in *Social System* to be a departure from the initial action theory approach (Robertson and Turner 1991 [eds]: 8ff, with references; Giddens 1982: 95ff; Habermas 1987: 725–34). One main point in the criticism was that the theory implied the elimination of human agency, of living, acting individuals. Human beings were reduced to "cultural dopes" or, in the words of Dennis Wrong (1961) conceived as "over-socialized."

Related to this criticism was the accusation of a tendency toward reification of culture and of cultural determinism, as touched on above. Some also found this to imply an a priori assumption of consensus on cultural patterns, thus making the theory blind, or at least insensible, to conflicts in moral values and norms. Ralf Dahrendorf (1968: 107–28; 1974: 59–112; chapter 16 in this book) characterized the theory as "utopian," in the sense that it was a description of some fictionally harmonious and smoothly functioning society, rather than the real world. The emphasis on integration and stability also motivated criticism for being unable to deal with social change. This is connected to the next criticism, based on empiricist methodology, that a grand theory of this type could not stand up to the criteria of empirical testability. Parsons himself assigned an analytical status to most of his conceptual frameworks, the cognitive utility of which should be demonstrated by its analytical power.

This bring us to another, and probably more obstinate methodological criticism, which concerns the methodology of explanation in functionalism, originating from its teleological character (Stinchcombe 1968: 80–101; Elster 1983: 49–68). In functional explanation, (beneficial) *consequences* (Y), such as integration, are used to explain a certain social item (X), for example, a social role pattern. X is claimed to exist *because* it produces Y, meaning Y explains X. This method obviously creates serious problems, the most grave of which concerns the chronological sequence. Ordinarily, we would expect that what explains something should come before what is to be explained. That would not be the case, however, if we were to say that a role pattern exists because it produces integration. The usual strategy to escape from this difficulty is to say that functional explanations only deal with recurrent, relatively persistent forms (not individual occurrences). The consequences referred to are, thus not future consequences of the role pattern as it is today, but consequences today of the same role pattern as it was yesterday. This strategy solves the time sequence problem, but is still not sufficient, because in addition we need a way to account for how the integrating effects of yesterday's role pattern cause the role pattern to continue to exist today. In other words, a mechanism is needed to account for the feedback loop between consequences and their originator. The debate shows that such a generally working feedback mechanism does not seem plausible in social life. Of course, this criticism only affects functionalism which has generally explanatory pretensions, and therefore does not apply to much of Mertonian functionalism.

Actually, criticism of the Mertonian type of functionalism has been not so much his approach in general as specific issues, such as his sociology of science. Parsons's theory, and structural functionalism in general, was charged with the allegation of being ideologically biased, a conservative defense of the status quo as the best possible world (Mills 1959; Moore 1963; Gouldner 1971). In his polemic (and entertaining) book *The Sociological Imagination*, C. Wright Mills parodied Parsons's academic prose (which is often indisputably stilted and unnecessarily complicated) to show that much of what Parsons said was common-sense knowledge. Some criticism entailed misrepresentations, as well as properties which were incomplete due to the theory's unfinished status, but other criticism addressed serious problems in structural functionalism. As shown, Parsons was seriously aware of the problems concerning agency (or voluntary actions theory, in Parsons's own terms) and concerning the treatment of social change. The criticism of conservative bias being necessarily immanent in functionalism is, however, probably misleading (see chapter 27).

It would also be misleading to think that these criticisms have totally eliminated the influence of functionalism (Colomy 1990: xiii–lxii). Although certain core assumptions have been abandoned, especially from Parsons's theory, it should not be forgotten that several basic core concepts, like role, norm, and institution, are still standard furniture in sociology, heavily carved by functionalist thinking. Even at the level of general theory, there are influential trends which include ideas and concepts from structural functionalism. Besides the neofunctionalist program that emerged in the 1980s (see chapter 15), the theory of system and life world by Jürgen Habermas (see chapter 20), and the system theory by Niklas Luhmann (see chapter 22) are sociological positions that draw on Parsons. Functionalist theory has even been used in attempts to reconstruct Marx's historical materialism (see chapter 11). Regarding Merton's program, there is an interesting kinship with elements in the critical theory of Habermas, such as the uncovering of hidden (latent) dysfunctions of, for example, power structures, aiming to make them visible (manifest) and thus accessible to reflection. Jon Elster (1985) has used the idea of unintended consequences to clarify aspects of Marx's theory of alienation. Thus, in spite of its drawbacks, functionalism continues to influence the development of modern sociology.

Bibliography

Primary:

Merton, Robert K. 1948: Discussion. *American Sociological Review,* 13, 164–8.
—— 1967: *On Theoretical Sociology.* New York: Free Press.
—— 1968: *Social Theory and Social Structure.* Enlarged edn. New York: Free Press.
—— 1970: *Science, Technology and Society in Seventeenth Century England.* New York: Harper & Row.
—— 1973: *The Sociology of Science: Theoretical and Empirical Investigations,* ed. and with an introduction by Norman W. Storer. Chicago: University of Chicago Press.
—— 1976: *Sociological Ambivalence and Other Essays.* New York: Free Press.
—— 1979: *The Sociology of Science: an Episodic Memoir.* Carbondale: Southern Illinois University Press.
—— 1985: *On the Shoulders of Giants: A Shadean Postscript.* San Diego: Harcourt Brace Jovanovich.
—— 1994: *A Life of Learning: Charles Homer Haskins Lecture.* New York: American Council of Learned Societies.
—— 1996: *On Social Structure and Science.* Chicago: University of Chicago Press.
Merton, Robert K., and Gaston J. 1977: *The Sociology of Science in Europe.* Carbondale: University of Southern Illinois Press.
Merton, Robert K., and Blau, P. 1981: *Continuities of Structural Inquiry.* London: Sage.
Merton, Robert K., Fiske, Marjorie, and Kendall, Patricia L. 1956: *The Focused Interview: a Manual of Problems and Procedures.* Glencoe, IL: Free Press.
Merton, Robert K., Reader, K., and Kendall. P. L. (eds) 1957: *The Student Physician. Introductory Studies in the Sociology of Medical Education.* Cambridge, MA: Harvard University Press.
Parsons, Talcott. 1951: *The Social System.* London: Routledge & Kegan Paul.
—— 1954: *Essays in Sociological Theory.* Rev. edn. New York: Free Press.
—— 1964: *Social Structure and Personality.* New York: Free Press.
—— 1965: An Outline of the Social System. In T. Parsons, E. Shils, Kasper D. Naegle, and J. R. Pitts: *Theories of Society: Foundations of Modern Sociological Theory.* New York: Free Press.
—— 1966: *Societies. Evolutionary and Comparative Perspectives.* Englewood Cliffs, NJ: Prentice-Hall.
—— 1967: *Sociological Theory and Modern Society.* New York: Free Press.
—— 1968a [1937]: *The Structure of Social Action.* New York: Free Press.
—— 1968b: On the Concept of Value-Commitments. *Sociological Inquiry,* 38, 135–60.
—— 1971: *The System of Modern Societies.* Englewood Cliffs, NJ: Prentice-Hall.
—— 1977: *Social Systems and the Evolution of Action Theory.* New York: Free Press.
—— 1978: *Action Theory and the Human Condition.* New York: Free Press.
—— 1991: *The Early Essays.* Edited and with an introduction by Charles Camic. Chicago: Univer-

sity of Chicago Press.

Parsons, Talcott, and Shils, E. A. (eds) 1951: *Toward a General Theory of Action*. Cambridge, MA: Harvard University Press.

Parsons, Talcott, Bales, R. F., and Shils, E. A. 1953: *Working Papers in the Theory of Action*. Westport, CT: Greenwood Press.

Parsons, Talcott, Bales, R. F., Shils, E. A., Olds, J., Zelditch, M., and Slater, P. E. 1955: *Family, Socialization and Interaction Process*. New York: Free Press.

Parsons, Talcott, and Smelser, N. 1956: *Economy and Society*. New York: Free Press.

Parsons, Talcott, and Platt, G. M. 1974: *The American University*. Cambridge, MA: Harvard University Press.

Secondary:

Bales, R. F. 1950: *Interaction Process Analysis*. Cambridge, MA: Harvard University Press.

Clark, J., Modgil, C., and Modgil, S. 1990: *Robert K. Merton. Consensus and Controversy*. Basingstoke: Falmer Press.

Coser, Lewis A. (ed.) 1975: *The Idea of Social Structure. Papers in Honor of Robert K. Merton*. New York: Harcourt Brace Jovanovich.

Colomy, Paul. (ed.) 1990: *Functionalist Sociology*. Aldershot: Elgar.

Dahrendorf, R. 1968: *Essays on the Theory of Society*. London: Routledge & Kegan Paul.

—— 1974: *Pfade aus Utopia : Arbeiten zur Theorie und Methode der Soziologie*. Munich: R. Piper.

Elster, Jon. 1983: *Explaining Technical Change*. Cambridge: Cambridge University Press.

—— 1985: *Making Sense of Marx*. Cambridge: Cambridge University Press.

Giddens, Anthony. 1982: *New Rules of Sociological Method*. London: Hutchinson.

Gouldner, A. W. 1971: *The Coming Crisis of Western Sociology*. London: Heinemann.

Habermas, Jürgen. 1987: *Theory of Communicative Action*. Vol. 2. Boston: Beacon Press and Cambridge: Polity Press..

Hamilton. P. 1983: *Talcott Parsons*. London: Routledge & Kegan Paul.

Holmwood, John. 1996: *Founding Sociology? Talcott Parsons and the Idea of a General Theory*. London: Longman.

Linton, R. 1936: *The Study of Man*. New York: Appleton-Century Crofts.

Malinowski, B. 1926: Anthropology. *Encyclopedia Britannica*. First Supplementary Volume.

—— 1948: *Magic, Science and Religion and Other Essays*. Chicago: Chicago University Press.

Mills, C. Wright. 1959: *The Sociological Imagination*. London: Penguin Books.

Mongardini, Carlo, and Tabboni, Simonetta (eds) 1997: *Robert K. Merton and Contemporary Sociology*. New Brunswick, NJ and London: Transaction.

Moore, B. 1963: Strategy and Choice in Social Science. In M. Stein and A. Vidich (eds), *Sociology on Trial*. Englewood Cliffs, NJ: Prentice-Hall.

Radcliffe-Brown, A. R. 1948: *The Andaman Islanders*. Glencoe, IL: Free Press.

—— 1957: *A Natural Science of Society*. New York: Free Press.

—— 1965: *Structure and Function in Primitive Society*. London: Cohen & West.

Robertson, R., and Turner, B. S. (eds) 1991: *Talcott Parsons. Theorist of Modernity*. London: Sage.

Sklair, L. 1970: The Fate of the Functional Requisites. *British Journal of Sociology*, 21, 30–42.

Smelser, N. J. 1959: *Social Change in the Industrial Revolution*. Chicago: University of Chicago Press.

Stinchcombe, A. L. 1968: *Constructing Social Theories*. New York: Harcourt, Brace & World.

Sztompka, P. 1986: *Robert K. Merton. An Intellectual Profile*. London: Macmillan.

Turner, J. H. 1974: *The Structure of Sociological Theory*. Homewood: Dorsey Press.

Wrong, D. 1961: The Oversocialized Conception of Man in Modern Sociology. *American Sociological Review*, 26, 1180–1201.

chapter 15

Neofunctionalism

Halvor Fauske

KEY CONCEPTS

ACTION CONTINGENCY – describes action as a choice between many possible alternatives in order to avoid oversimplification and determinism.

MUTLIDIMENSIONAL SOCIOLOGY – sociology combining elements from different metatheoretical and theoretical approaches; it is nonreductionist, i.e., it does not reduce action to instrumental or normative action and does not explain social order by involving values and consensus, or outside coercion.

NEOFUNCTIONALISM – a reconstruction of sociology based on a new interpretation of the functionalistic tradition. More descriptive of a tendency or movement than of a theoretical position.

POST-POSITIVISM – a position within the theory of science putting equal emphasis on theoretical and empirical elements. No sharp distinction between theory and fact is upheld. Empirical data are always to a certain degree determined by the theory chosen – which also indicates that empirical tests will not suffice to reject a theory. In the final analysis, the bases for any scientific statement are pragmatic criteria such as prediction and control in the natural sciences, and political or moral criteria in the social sciences.

SYMBOL COMPLEXITY – symbols refer to action and are important for interpretation and understanding. Symbols provide a space for explication and association. Symbol complexity refers to the profusion of symbols from which options of action can be interpreted.

During the seventies, functionalism became less significant, no longer constituting a point of reference for criticism and the development of theory. The attempts made by Talcott Parsons to merge theories based on action with those based on structures in order to appease the feuding factions within theoretical social sciences seemed more or less to have failed (see chapter 14). Within micro- as well as macrosociology, new and radical approaches were advanced; challenging, within both fields, the basic assumptions lying behind functionalism and contributing to the compartmentalization of sociology into divergent and more or less incompatible schools. It would appear that Anthony Giddens was right in his assessment, namely that the battle over functionalism was over and that the combatants had left the battlefield. Almost nobody was preoccupied with discussing functionalism any longer. New theories and approaches had attracted major attention and became the focal point of the prevailing sociological debate (Giddens 1976). Sociology seemed to have entered a post-Parsonian phase (Tiryakian 1979/80).

Gradually, however, there was a "rediscovery" of Parsons – initially in Europe, later to be followed up in the US. In the mid-eighties, Jeffrey C. Alexander introduced the term "neofunctionalism" (1985) in order to stress that this rediscovery constituted a reconstruction as well as a revision of Parsons's theory. The implicit reference to Neo-Marxism is deliberate. First of all, this comprises a critique of the fundamentals inherent in the original theory. In the second place, these new approaches seek to integrate elements from mutually conflicting theoretical traditions. Thirdly, neofunctionalism tends to manifest itself in multifarious variants rather than in one single unveiling. For that reason, Alexander emphasizes how neofunctionalism should primarily be understood as a wide-ranging intellectual tendency or movement; and only to a lesser extent as a theory per se. The two sociologists responsible for the most all-embracing reconstructions of Parsons's sociology are Richard Münch and Jeffrey C. Alexander.

The Rediscovery of Parsons in German Sociology

Parsons died in May 1979 during a visit to Germany, where he had just participated in a seminar organized by the University of Heidelberg in celebration of the fiftieth anniversary of the award of a doctoral degree to Parsons. Prominent German sociologists like Niklas Luhmann (see chapter 22), Jürgen Habermas (see chapter 21), and Wolfgang Schluchter gave lectures, all thematically linked to Parsons's sociology. This celebration was indicative of the blossoming European interest in Parsons's work.

To be sure, German sociology had for a long time been influenced by Parsons's thought as imparted via Luhmann´s systems theory. Luhmann studied under Parsons in the early sixties without in any way becoming an imitator. Rather, Luhmann's systems theory should really be considered a revision of Parsons's functionalism. The problem, as Luhmann describes it, is that Parsons postulates certain theoretical systems structures as a prerequisite for functional analysis. Thus this analysis becomes limited to examining how these structures are maintained. Luhmann emphasizes that his functional analysis centers on investigating which mechanisms or structures function toward reducing complexity. The objection he raises against structural functionalism is that functional analysis becomes subserviant to structural description. In his own approach functional analysis receives priority, which is why he calls his own *systems theory functional-structural.*

As it turned out, Luhmann's revised functionalism, incorporating systems theory, was to exert considerable influence upon young German sociologists. In the early seventies, his famed exchange with Jürgen Habermas on systems theory as well as critical theory further stimulated academic interest in Parsons (Habermas et al. 1971). Later on, Habermas gradually adopted key elements from Parsons´s analyses of economic and political systems (see chapter 21). In the two-volume work *Theorie des kommunikativen Handelns* (Theory of Communicative Action) he ranks Parsons among the classics, "theoreticians who continue to have something to teach us" (Habermas 1981, vol. 1: 8f). Although Habermas does indeed criticize Parsonian sociology, it still remains a fundamental underpinning of the theory of communicative action. Furthermore, Habermas generalizes his own theoretical strategy by maintaining that any social theory claiming serious consideration cannot avoid dealing with Parsons's sociology (Habermas 1981, vol. 2: 297).

Richard Münch and the Reconstruction of the Theory of Action

Biography: *Richard Münch*

Richard Münch was born in 1945 in Niefern, near Pforzheim. After studying sociology, psychology, and philosophy at the University of Heidelberg from 1965 to 1970, he became a research assistant at Augsburg. From 1974 to 1976, he was a research counsellor and professor at the University of Cologne. In 1977 he became professor of social sciences at the University of Düsseldorf, a position he has held ever since. His fields of research are sociological theory, historical-comparative sociology, and political sociology.

Unlike Habermas, Richard Münch is very keen to develop Parsons's sociology, while letting it rest firmly on its own premises. In 1976 he published the book *Theorie sozialer Systeme* (The Theory of Social Systems) in which he attempted to develop a theory filling the lacunae in the works of Luhmann and Parsons. His strategy centered on combining an empirical systems concept with social action as the fundamental principle. Thus he employed an empirical systems concept like Luhmann, while also centering on the principle of social action, as does Parsons in his theory. The result is an approximation, lying somewhere between Parsons's analytical systems theory and Luhmann's empirical systems theory, the latter built on the fundamental notion of "meaning."

In successive steps, Münch changes strategy. His work becomes more specifically concerned with evolving Parsons's theory along the lines of what he calls the voluntaristic theory of action redefined, and the theory of a voluntaristic order. In the main, however, it would appear that Münch concedes to Parsons's theory. Like Habermas, Münch bases his reasoning upon Parsons's work in its entirety, not upon hand-picked tidbits of his theory or select phases of his theoretical development, as has frequently been the case. According to Münch, Parsons's critics have fallen prey to the lack of an institutionalized, adequate, and comprehensive understanding of the complete work (a so-called *Werkverständnis*) (Münch 1980: 45).

The reinterpretation of Parsons's sociology

In two separate articles, Münch attempts to reinterpret the Parsonian line of reasoning. He claims that the key to reading Parsons is to see him in the light of the philosophy of Immanuel Kant (1724–1804). His view is that Parsons's sociology is unintelligible without recourse to Kant´s critique of theoretical (pure) and practical reason (1979: 388f). The idea broached in *The Structure of Social Action* (1937) is that the basic assumptions of sociology lie not in data about sociological problems, but in the categories we use to grasp the entire social order. Consequently, the book offers a useful conceptual analysis that helps to provide a satisfactory interpretation of the most important question sociology must tackle: How is social order possible? As Münch sees it, Parsons's first great work is the "sociological equivalent" of Kant's moral philosophy.

Like Kant´s, Parsons´s thought proceeds along two levels: empirical knowledge and categories, the application of which are essential for interpretation and understanding. These two levels are intrinsically connected. Categories remain a necessary component of our knowledge of the world – and, all the while, our empirical experiences constitute the raw material, the stuff that our interpretation and comprehension is made of. According to Kant and Parsons alike, these two levels partially overlap.

In order to clarify the relationship existing between these two levels, Münch seizes a concept used by Parsons to describe the correlation between the subsystems of the action systems, making this idea a cornerstone in his reinterpretation of Parsons. That idea is interpenetration, signifying a reciprocal relationship of systems as they penetrate each other. This concept implies that the systems concerned partially coincide and partially differ. Thus, interpenetration is a zone where two systems merge, be they theoretical, empirical, or systems of action. For example, institutionalization may be understood as the interpenetration between the cultural system and the social system, while internalization may be understood as an interpenetration between the personality system and the social system.

Through the intercession of interpenetrational zones, the primary functions of the subsystems are strengthened and extended. For example, institutionalization and internalization tend to strengthen the coercive powers inherent in the prevailing norms. At the same time, systems governing culture and personality are also reinforced, since institutionalization constitutes a specification of values, while internalization really means a universalization of expectations. Thus, the cultural system acquires a more specific relevance for the social system, while the personality system is endowed with a general capacity to transfer expectations from concrete interactions to similar interactions. This makes the normative culture more consistent, the institutionalization within the various social systems becomes more specific, individuals become more strongly attached to the normative culture, while the personality per se is given more autonomy because individuals are less tied to specific situations.

According to Münch, it is precisely the linkage between these two levels that has proved fruitful in Parsons's sociology. This type of duality is a prerequisite for developing a voluntaristic theory of action. Münch points out the fact that while Dennis Wrong's article (1961) criticizing Parsons for employing an oversocialized concept of "actors" is widely known, few are familiar with Parsons's reply (1962). In his rebuttal, Parsons repudiates the notion that socialization and internalization imply that the individual is necessarily subjugated under societal norms. The precondition for developing individuality lies in the internalization of cultural – as opposed to societal – norms; norms that amount to more than what society has institutionalized. Thus the individual becomes more strongly tied to normative culture, yet at the same time less dependent upon particular ties (Münch 1982: 72). As indicated by Münch, this places Parsons in agreement with Kant's comments on human freedom – a standpoint which also influenced Durkheim and Simmel.

The reconstruction of the AGIL diagram

Münch sees in the AGIL diagram the only theoretical starting point with the potential to deliver an adequate analysis of social development as such. Previously, he maintained that Luhmann's empirically based systems concept was superior to Parsons's analytical systems concept. He has later considered this critique of Parsons as fallacious (Münch 1980: 32) – his conclusion being that any further developments of the theory of action will have to be based precisely on an analytic systems concept. What remains particularly useful about the AGIL diagram is its discrimination between ruling and dynamic subsystems. By ordering the system of action within a cybernetic hierarchy, Parsons is able to offer a characterization of the ruling and dynamic factors at work whenever new variants of the old social order arise, and whenever a new order replaces the old after a social upheaval has taken place.

Starting with the fact that action can always be interpreted as based on symbols, Münch establishes how these symbolic systems may be more or less complex, leading to a variety of interpretations and actions. By linking action and symbol, defined as above, Münch redefines the AGIL diagram along the axes of *action contingency* and *symbol complexity*.

The symbolic systems may vary from the highest degree of complexity to the highest degree of order while actions may vary from the highest degree of contingency (uncertainty) to the highest degree of predictability. Viewed from this perspective, four distinct, analytic fields of action unfold, each field representing a specific aspect of the social order.

A high degree of symbol complexity as well as contingency of action indicates that many means and many objectives are gauged from the principle of optimum goal realization. When a concrete goal has been chosen, the situation may be described as displaying low action contingency, while at the same time, symbol complexity is high. Low action contingency alongside low symbol complexity betokens a state of affairs where the realization of goals proceeds ac-

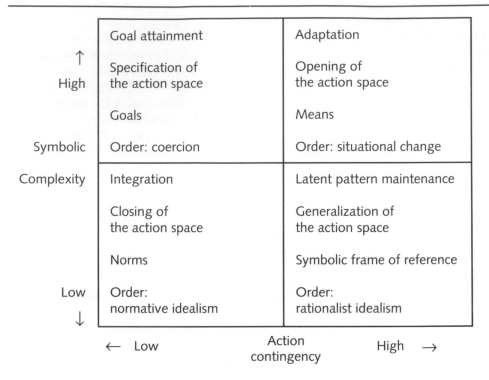

	Goal attainment	Adaptation
↑ High	Specification of the action space	Opening of the action space
	Goals	Means
Symbolic	Order: coercion	Order: situational change
Complexity	Integration	Latent pattern maintenance
	Closing of the action space	Generalization of the action space
	Norms	Symbolic frame of reference
Low ↓	Order: normative idealism	Order: rationalist idealism

← Low   Action contingency   High →

Figure 15.1   Reconstruction of the action system

cording to certain norms, that is, each action and its interpretation become more unequivocal. In this case, the action sphere diminishes, contributing to the integration of actors into the prevailing system. Low symbol complexity combined with high action contingency indicates a state of generalized value systems where many different actions can be assigned to one single principle (like, for instance, "love your neighbour as you love yourself").

A nonfunctionalistic action theory

In the restructured AGIL diagram, action is analyzed as an uninterrupted generalization and specification, an opening and closing of the action sphere. This represents Münch's attempt at formulating a process-centered theory, emphasizing contingency, development, and change rather than continuity, stability, and equilibrium. He does not see this as a departure from Parsons; if anything, he regards it as a rehabilitation of the core concepts underpinning Parsons's sociology as a theory of production and reproduction of structures. For this same reason, he does not believe that Giddens's and Bourdieu's theories of structuration (see chapters 20 and 24) could represent anything new in relation to the tradition in sociology which has centered on *social ordering* (processes producing and reproducing social order) (Münch 1989: 102).

By defining social order in relation to all the subsystems in the action system, Münch launches a multidimensional concept of order. In addition to the normative order which interested Parsons the most, Münch operates with an order produced by economic processes, political processes, and rational arguments (Münch 1989: 107f).

Thus, an institutional change is integrated into the action theory while the AGIL diagram concurrently becomes an overarching paradigm for variegated theoretical approaches to understanding social order as such. The exchange theory may be localized within the subsystem for adaptation, being as it is a domain charged with conflicts of interest as well as communities based on utilitarian principles. The theory of conflict is especially bound up with the subsystem of goal attainment – power and coercion being crucial elements. The normativistic life-world sociology may be understood as a subsystem of integration, while the subsystem for latent pattern maintenance may form the basis for rationalist theories of culture since this is where we find the sphere of rational arguments. Münch points out that – taken separately – each of the theories described above is too limited to be expected to provide adequate explanations, which is why they must be combined in an integrated paradigm of interpenetrating subsystems.

Münch denies that the purpose of the AGIL diagram is to provide a functionalistic explanation. The diagram can be used to analyze a cross section of reality viewed as a convergence of dynamizing and controlling systems. Furthermore, he asserts that Parsons's argument was not intended as a functionalistic one either. The difference between Parsons's theory of action and Luhmann's systems functionalism is that Parsons's theory is analytic, not empirical. In other words, it merely describes aspects of reality and thus cannot be seen as a model of how social systems actually work empirically. Since the Parsonian model is nonfunctionalistic, methodological problems of functionalism are irrevelant (Münch 1980: 33). Münch also has his reservations concerning the launching of the term "neofunctionalism." This term is seen as having too many unfortunate connotations; instead, he suggests replacing it with the designation "theory of action" (Münch 1989: 235).

Jeffrey Alexander's Reconstruction of Classic Sociology

> **Biography:** *Jeffrey C. Alexander*
>
> Jeffrey C. Alexander was born in 1947. As an undergraduate he studied at Harvard University where he was introduced to Parsons's sociology. He earned his Ph.D. at the University of California, Berkeley, under the guidance of Robert Bellah and Neil J. Smelser. He is currently professor of sociology at the University of California, Los Angeles. His publications include works in the fields of social theory, cultural studies, mass media studies, and studies of social change.

Jeffrey Alexander's works have played an important role in the reinterpretation of Parsons's sociology. The foundations for the renewal of functionalism were laid with his four-volume *Theoretical Logic in Sociology*, published in 1982–3. These books contain an elaboration of the conclusion drawn by the author in an article, published some years previously, in which Alexander had argued that Parsons had created a theoretical framework potentially capable of overcoming the contradictions inherent in classical sociological theory; though neither Parsons nor his collaborators had taken full advantage of the intrinsic possibilities in this theory. So, Alexander claimed, the fundamental discovery made by Parsons was as yet unknown (Alexander 1978: 193ff). Alexander sees it as his task to further cultivate the theoretical approaches he finds incipient in the work of Parsons.

On the face of it, *Theoretical Logic in Sociology* does have a good deal in common with Parsons's first major work *The Structure of Social Action*. Alexander confronts positivism's excessive reliance on empirical data, arguing in favor of the need for a general theory, as does Parsons. By and large, he chooses to include the same classics as Parsons, except for the fact that Marx is reinstated fully among these classics while Pareto and Marshall are excluded. Like Parsons, Alexander analyzes the classics, employing a dialectical model where contradictions are resolved into a synthesis.

According to Alexander, the salient contradiction prevailing in classical sociology is one between idealism and materialism, represented by the theories of Durkheim and Marx. Weber's works are seen as an attempt to arrive at a synthesis between idealism and materialism, while Parsons's efforts are classified as the modern reconstruction of classical thinking, aiming at a multidimensional sociology. Although Alexander's method has many traits in common with Parsons's, the contents of their analyses differ significantly. Be this as it may, outward likenesses may well have contributed to the work being understood more narrowly as a recapitulation of Parsons's sociology (Holmwood 1982).

Sociology based on post-positivism

As a beginning, Alexander suggests, sociology should be based on a post-positivistic understanding of science, the chief point in this understanding being that the driving forces in scientific development should be understood as much through theoretical as through empirical explanations. This view is in opposition to positivism, which reduces theory to empirical data. The main tenets in positivism are that a sharp distinction exists between empirical observations and nonempirical propositions; and furthermore, that nonempirical propositions constitute philosophy and metaphysics and, as such, deserve no place in empirically based science.

Alexander retorts with the following argument: all scientific theories are located in an interrelationship, situated within a specific metaphysical and empirical habitat, meaning that, in other words, scientific explanations may be assigned to different locations within a continuum demarcated by that particular habitat. This continuum is distended from general axioms by way of models, concepts, definitions, classifications, rules, hypotheses, correlations, and methodological assumptions to actual observations (Alexander 1982a: 2–5). The analytical components or levels are partially dependent and partially independent of one another. Thus, even if a particular scientific endeavor concentrates on one level, there will nevertheless be correlations to other levels.

The dismissal of the positivistic tradition does not lead Alexander to reject the fact that the social sciences can indeed deliver valid knowledge. On the contrary – he seeks to establish foundations for reasoning based on "post-postivistic standards for rational knowledge"

(Alexander 1982a: 114). In this context, he refers to the requirements Habermas places on validity as an example of such a standard for rational cognition (see chapter 21).

A new theoretical logic

Alexander's attempts at constructing a new theoretical logic for sociology are also meant to strengthen and reinvigorate the discipline. Of fundamental importance for such a construction are the concepts of action and order; according to Alexander, these concepts constitute "the true presuppositions of sociological debate" (1982a: 65). These two concepts possess qualities that can be related to all levels in the scientific continuum. Therefore, taken together, they are well suited as a frame of reference for any debate regarding the theoretical logic of sociology. It is, however, important that the concepts remain distinct from each other so as not to simplify the complexity of sociological theories. Both concepts have an inherent dilemma: you may choose to interpret action in a normative or instrumental manner, while order may be explained as an internal, subjective, and value-based order – or as an external, objective, and coercive order.

In other words, action may be understood either as being guided by norms or as utilitarian, and social order may be construed as a result of either a consensus prevailing between the society's members or of coercion from the outside. These two choices amount to dilemmas in the sense that, at the extreme ends of the spectrum, are choices between two evils. On one hand, you can emphasize the rational actors, integrated by coercion from without; on the other hand, you can perceive these actors as led by norms and integrated by a consensus concerning certain fundamental values. Adherence to either of these two positions is viewed by Alexander as reductionist, or one-dimensional sociology, because resulting analyses become narrowed down to merely one aspect of action and social order. There are, however, ways of transcending these two positions – which we may dub sociological materialism and sociological idealism respectively – although none of the attempts made thus far has been entirely satisfactory.

Parsons remains the one who has come closest to providing a satisfactory solution to this dilemma. His attempt to transcend, dialectically, the dilemmas of individualism versus collectivism, and positivism versus idealism is a good place to start and a bona fide alternative to theories based on only one dimension. The development from the analysis of action in *The Structure of Social Action* to the AGIL diagram clearly illustrates Parsons's multidimensional concept of action. Action takes place in a continuum, embracing preconditions and unequivocal values, along the dimensions of adaptation, goal attainment, integration, and latent pattern maintenance (legitimizing). In this fashion, Parsons incorporates elements from several other models and theories of action. The diagram's means/goals aspect is culled from rational theories of action; the idea that the specific goals are tethered to a value consensus is derived from idealism; while the focus on action as a way of adapting to external conditions is a trait characteristic of positivism. As far as the AGIL diagram is concerned, relationships existing between the particular elements are always specific in nature. According to this line of reasoning, each subsystem must be understood as partially autonomous and partially dependent upon the other subsystems. The reciprocal interaction occurring between the subsystems is arranged within a cybernetic hierarchy, structured in such a manner that the subsystems simultaneously determine and rule over the exchange going on between them (see chapter 14).

Like Parsons, Alexander suggests that the inherent dilemmas in social theory can be transcended through specific negation in the sense used by G. W. F. Hegel (1770–1831). Thus, the positions are negated while elements from each of the positions are incorporated in the synthesis:

> Applying this dialectical notion to theoretical logic, I propose that action should be conceived not as either instrumental or normative, but as both. Furthermore, this action should be conceived as ordered both through internal and external structures. (Alexander 1982a: 123)

Alexander calls this – his understanding of action and order as a question of synthesis rather than of two opposites – a multidimensional approach. In this context, multi-dimensionality should be construed as the post-positivistic standard used by Alexander to evaluate theoretical logic as he finds it expounded in the works of Marx, Durkheim, Weber, and Parsons.

Alexander focuses on Karl Marx's and Emile Durkheim's theories in order to epitomize the inherent contradiction between sociological materialism and idealism, and in order to spell out the intrinsic deficiencies in the two positions. Like Parsons, he considers the sociology of Max Weber an attempt to transcend materialism as well as idealism. Alexander ranks Parsons as a successor to Max Weber in his attempt to resolve the contradictions in social theory; yet although Parsons gains most headway in these attempts, he does not manage to present a satisfactory multi-dimensional theory, measured by the standard held by Alexander (Alexander 1983a: 135). Unlike Weber, Parsons does not provide merely one-sided analyses of rationality and instrumental actions, but in Alexander's estimation he does overemphasize values and consensus.

Even though Alexander does join in the critique of Parsons in certain respects, he does not side entirely with these critics. He prefers to distance himself from the debate between Parsons and his critics by developing a standard "broad enough to include the concerns of critics and defenders alike" (Alexander 1983b: 309). Such a multidimensional approach opens up the possibility of a more loosely defined, less sectarian version of functionalism (Alexander 1983b: 287). So he does not reject functionalism like Münch; rather, he envisions the possibilities lying in a type of functionalism which appears to be rather different from traditional versions.

Neofunctionalism: Unity Resting on Slender Foundations?

In his introduction to the book *Neofunctionalism*, Alexander discusses suitable terminology. Neofunctionalism, he writes, is not quite functionalism, yet somewhat related to that concept. Besides, he also adds, "functionalism" was never really an appropriate term to describe Parsons's sociology (1985: 8). Alexander goes on to provide a short historical survey of functionalism, pointing out that this -ism has always been a byword for a wide range of variegated ideological, empirical, and theoretical approaches. Parsons himself tried to break free of the appellation and its static connotations in the mid-sixties. His associates and students began to call the theory action theory. Furthermore, beginning in the late seventies, there seemed to be a tendency among those who had been critically disposed toward Parsons's functionalism to view this term as misleading (Therborn 1980).

Indeed, Parsons chose to discard the term "structural functionalism," although he knew that the term would probably continue to cling to him. Alexander considers it a certainty that "functionalism" will endure as a term for the sociological approach developed by Parsons. Thus it remains rather futile to declare the term "functionalism" no longer valid. Better, Alexander maintains, to grab the bull by the horns and hang on to "functionalism" as a term, yet at the same time redefine the concept to denote merely a theoretical tradition. "Functionalism" is too imprecise to be a conceptual framework, a method, a model, or an ideology. Functionalism, then, may live on as tradition, and that is all. According to Alexander, this tradition is characterized as follows (1985: 10):

1   An open and pluralistic description of society as a whole.
2   An even-handed apportionment when it comes to action vs. structure.
3   Integration is viewed as a possibility; deviance and social control are considered realities.
4   Discernment between personality, culture, and society.
5   Differentiation is viewed as the central driving force producing social change.
6   The development of concepts and theory is considered to be independent of all the other levels involved in sociologic analysis.

Alexander is well aware that this exposition amounts to a break with the preponderant view shared by sociologists. Functionalism has been associated with anti-individualism, opposition against social change, conservatism, idealism, and a lack of empirical foundation. In this context, Alexander points out how a conflict-oriented, radical functionalism has developed since the early seventies. This turn also derives from a new approach to reading Parsons, resulting in his not being placed in a conservative tradition, but in the democratic and humanistic tradition of Kant or in the tradition of social democratic welfare as represented by T. H. Marshall (1893–1982) (Bershady 1973; Münch 1982; Alexander 1983b; Nielsen 1991).

Some confusion has arisen as a result of the rejection of elements hitherto considered crucial to functionalism. For example, Hans Joas points out how Giddens's critique of functionalism is no longer accurate – not because his aim is poor, but because the bull's eye has moved (Joas 1990: 100). As Joas demonstrates, the crux of the problem lies in the fact that Alexander's account of the functionalistic tradition is extremely vague. It is difficult to establish whether continuity exists between functionalism and neofunctionalism, because functionalism has acquired new substance while, at the same time, neofunctionalism seems to include everything functionalism has been criticized as lacking. If anything, the theoretical and empirical work produced by neofunctionalists in the eighties and later seems more influenced by elements from the critique of Parsons than by the elements supposedly so crucial to functionalism. As indeed indicated by Alexander himself, the contributions to the book *Neofunctionalism* have about them a collective air of ideological criticism, materialistic orientation, an angle of controversy, and interactionist approaches.

The Evolution of Neofunctionalism

In his book on Parsons, as well as in his introduction to the collection of essays on neofunctionalism, Alexander airs his doubts as to whether or not there is a future for Parsons's sociology. Conjecture allows him to envision several possibilities: neofunctionalism might set out to establish itself as a veritable school of thought, or it might develop into one among several sociological approaches. It still remains an unanswered question whether neofunctionalism is old wine in new bottles, or whether it is truly a new brew, as Alexander chooses to phrase it (1985: 16). In the ten years that have passed since Alexander wrote this, an assortment of theoreticians, considering themselves to be representatives of neofunctionalism, have each provided their contribution toward making neofunctionalism an inclusive term describing a certain type of sociological approach and analysis.

Paul Colomy is one of the younger American sociologists who has contributed as a chronicler and interpreter of tradition as well as a supplier of theoretical and empirical work on social change. His work has proven pivotal in developing the theory of differentiation which was formulated as a reply to criticism inveighing against functionalism's lack of a theory of social changes and conflicts. When Parsons and his collaborators launched this theory, a new round of criticism ensued. Adversaries claimed that, historically and empirically, the theory of differentiation was not specific enough; that actors and social groups were nonexistent in the analyses, and that integration was prioritized at the expense of power and conflict.

As part of his revision of the theory, Colomy integrates parts of this critique; for example, he strongly accentuates that there will always remain less differentiated structures deviating from the trends that dominate current developments. These structures may in fact be a hotbed of criticism and renewal. To the extent that this criticism gains a following, such criticism may contribute either to higher levels of differentiation, or toward the opposite: de-differentiation. Furthermore, Colomy makes a case against merely combining structural elements as a means of sufficiently explaining social change; also called for is an analysis of what he calls voluntaristic elements, which give developments heading and form. This is his way of involving social movements and actors in the theory (Colomy 1985; 1990a; 1990b).

Within political sociology, David Sciulli has developed a theory about societal constitutionalism, using empirical criteria in the evaluation of democratization. According to Sciulli, oligarchies and submissive citizens pose a hazard to modern, industrialized society. He finds the forces to counterbalance this tendency in the type of autonomous, collegiate organizations described by Parsons. From here, he reconstructs Parsons's vision of a liberal society emanating from a more critical analysis of societal development (Sciulli 1986; 1990; 1991). Mark Gould proceeds in an even more critical manner, developing a theory about social crises through a combination of Karl Marx, Talcott Parsons, and Jean Piaget (1896– 1980). As an added boon, still according to Gould, such a theory would – if fully expanded – provide the insight into social organization and political practice needed to transcend capitalism (Gould 1985; 1987). Several works building on a neofunctionalist approach have also been published within fields like professionalization, social inequality, sociology of culture, and feminist sociology.

What is the Significance of Neofunctionalism at Present?

Neofunctionalism may be viewed as "a self-conscious intellectual movement," as Colomy chooses to put it. In his view, neofunctionalism has played a prominent role in the attempt to create a general theory and establish a metatheoretical synthesis; it has shed light on the importance of ideological persuasion and placed functionalism to the left in the political landscape, all the while refining analysis of social systems by incorporating dynamics and conflicts. Furthermore, he posits that functionalism has formulated a post-positivist basis for sociological analysis (1990c; 1992: 24). This assessment should be viewed in the context of the US, where functionalism "lost" the battle to positivist empiricism (Turner 1991: 234ff). From this perspective, neofunctionalism's contribution is different than when it is viewed from a European point of view.

Indeed, notes Hans Joas, as a general approach, neofunctionalism may seem focused on the US as to which theoreticians representatives of the movement refer to, as well as in its choice of how to present the problems at hand. As an example of this, Joas points to the absence of recent European social theoreticians in Alexander's publications (Joas 1988: 492). This does not quite hold true when you look at Alexander's latest works, in which he does indeed deal with more current social theory (1992; 1995), but there is still no denying that neofunctionalism needs to be understood in an American context. It is possible that the neofunctionalists, having further consolidated their position, will begin to refer to up-to-date European social theorists; indeed signs are apparent that this is in process.

As one might expect from the above line of reasoning, neofunctionalism has been regarded differently in the US and Europe. In the US, Alexander's projected reconstruction of sociology was met with great expectations right from the outset. This may have been part of the reason for the mixed reviews his books received (Collins 1985). Among other things, criticism has been directed in part at the conceptual framework employed by Alexander. For instance, Walter S. Wallace has countered that a pivotal concept such as "theoretical logic" is only flimsily described. The same holds true for the concept of "multidimensionality" (Wallace 1984: 641f). According to Donald L. Levine, however, Alexander makes the same mistake which he denounces in the work of other theoreticians. Operating within a flawed conceptual framework, he ends up ignoring dichotomies such as materialism versus idealism, instrumentalism versus goal orientation, rationality versus emotionality, etc. (Levine 1986: 1238f). This censure is levied against Alexander's metatheoretical works, making it an objection raised against the foundations of neofunctionalism as well.

As mentioned above, neofunctionalism has been met in Europe with perplexity as to what it is and what it is not. The designation would seem to be so all-inclusive that the connection to the "original" functionalism becomes unclear, as do the demarcation lines separating neofunctionalism from other approaches. Furthermore, Europe has quite a few examples of theories involving syntheses, with scholars like Niklas Luhmann, Jürgen Habermas, Pierre Bourdieu, Norbert Elias, and Anthony Giddens, to name only some, who have produced wide-ranging and substantial contributions toward the reconstruction of societal theory.

Nor is it to be expected that neofunctionalism will rise to the same importance as that enjoyed by functionalism in its heyday. As George Ritzer emphasizes, these new theoretical syntheses are essentially different from Parsons's attempt at reaching an overarching theory for all the social sciences (Ritzer 1990: 2). But if neofunctionalism is to become more than just a stateside phenomenon it may be necessary, as pointed out by Bryan S. Turner, that it evolves in a multicultural as well as a multidimensional direction (Turner 1991: 248).

Bibliography

Primary:

Alexander, Jeffrey C. 1978: Formal and Substantive Voluntarism in the Work of Talcott Parsons: A
    Theoretical and Methodological Reinterpretation. *American Sociological Review*, 43, 177–98.
—— 1982a: *Positivism, Presuppositions and Current Controversies. Theoretical Logic in Sociology.*
    Vol. 1. Berkeley: University of California Press.
—— 1982b: *The Antinomies of Classical Thought: Marx and Durkheim. Theoretical Logic in Sociol-*
    ogy. Vol. 2. Berkeley: University of California Press.
—— 1983a: *The Classical Attempt at Theoretical Synthesis: Max Weber. Theoretical Logic in Soci-*
    ology. Vol. 3. Berkeley: University of California Press.
—— 1983b: *The Modern Reconstruction of Classical Thought: Talcott Parsons. Theoretical Logic in*
    Sociology. Vol. 4. Berkeley: University of California Press.
—— (ed.) 1985: *Neofunctionalism.* Beverley Hills, CA: Sage.
—— 1988a: *Action and Environments: Towards a New Synthesis.* New York: Columbia University
    Press.
—— 1988b: *Durkheimian Sociology: Cultural Studies.* Cambridge: Cambridge University Press.
—— 1988c: The New Theoretical Movement. In N. J. Smelser (ed.), *Handbook of Sociology.* Lon-
    don: Sage.
—— 1992: General Theory in the Postpositivist Mode: The 'Epistemological Dilemma' and the Search
    for Present Reason. In S. Seidman and D. G. Wagner (eds), *Postmodernism and Social Theory.*
    Cambridge: Polity Press.
—— 1995: *Fin de Siècle Social Theory: Relativism, Reduction, and the Problem of Reason.* London:
    Verso.
—— (ed.) 1998: *Real Civil Societies: Dilemmas of Institutionalization.* London: Sage.
Alexander, Jeffrey C., Giessen, B., and Smelser, N. J. 1987: *The Micro-Macro Link.* Berkeley: Uni-
    versity of California Press.
Alexander, Jeffrey C., and Colomy, P. 1990: *Differentiation Theory and Social Change. Comparative*
    and Historical Perspectives. New York: Columbia University Press.
Boudon, Raymond, Cherkaoui, Mohamed, and Alexander, Jeffrey C. (eds) 1994: *The Classical Tra-*
    dition in Sociology: The European Tradition. London: Sage.
Münch, Richard. 1976: *Theorie sozialer Systeme. Eine Einführung in Grundbegriffe, Grundannahmen*
    und logische Struktur. Opladen: Westdeutscher Verlag.
—— 1979: Talcott Parsons und die Theorie des Handelns I: Die Konstitution des Kantianischen
    Kerns. *Soziale Welt*, 30, 385–409.
—— 1980: Talcott Parsons und die Theorie des Handelns II: Die Kontinuität der Entwicklung. *Soziale*
    Welt, 31, 3–47.
—— 1982: *Theorie des Handelns. Zur Rekonstruktion der Beiträge von Talcott Parsons, Emile*
    Durkheim und Max Weber. Frankfurt am Main: Suhrkamp.
—— 1985: Commentary: Differentiation, Consensus and Conflict: Some Comments on Smelser,
    Colomy, Lechner and Smelser. In J. C. Alexander and J. Turner (eds), *Neofunctionalism,* Newbury
    Park, CA: Sage.
—— 1987a: Parsonian Theory Today: In Search of a New Synthesis. In A. Giddens and J. Turner
    (eds), *Social Theory Today,* Cambridge: Polity Press.
—— 1987b: *Theory of Action: Towards a New Synthesis Going Beyond Parsons.* London: Routledge
    & Kegan Paul.
—— 1988: *Understanding Modernity: Toward a New Perspective Going Beyond Durkheim and Weber.*
    London: Routledge & Kegan Paul.
—— 1989: Code, Structure and Action: Building a Theory of Structuration from a Parsonian Point of

View. In J. H. Turner (ed.), *Theory Building in Sociology. Assessing Theoretical Cumulation*, London: Sage.

—— 1991: *Dialektik der Kommunikationsgesellschaft*. Frankfurt am Main: Suhrkamp.

—— 1994: *Sociological Theory*. 3 vols. Chicago: Nelson Hall.

Secondary:

Bershady, H. J. 1973: *Ideology and Social Knowledge*. Oxford: Basil Blackwell.

Collins, R. 1985: Jeffrey Alexander and the Search for a Multi-dimensional Theory. *Theory and Society,* 14, 863–76.

Colomy, P. 1985: Uneven Structural Differentiation: Toward a Comparative Approach. In J. C. Alexander and J. Turner (eds), *Neofunctionalism*, London: Sage.

—— 1990a: Uneven Differentiation and Incomplete Institutionalization: Political Change and Continuity in the Early American Nation. In J. C. Alexander and P. Colomy (eds), *Differentiation Theory and Social Change. Comparative and Historical Perspectives*. New York: Columbia University Press.

—— 1990b: Strategic Groups and Political Differentiation in the Antebellum United States. In J. C. Alexander and P. Colomy (eds), *Differentiation Theory and Social Change. Comparative and Historical Perspectives*. New York: Columbia University Press.

—— 1990c: *Neofunctionalist Sociology*. Aldershot: Edward Elgar.

—— 1992: *The Dynamics of Social Systems*. London: Sage.

Giddens, A. 1976: Functionalism: après la lutte. *Social Research*, 43, 325–66.

Gould, M. 1985: Prolegomena to any Future Theory of Societal Crisis. In J. C. Alexander and J. Turner (eds), *Neofunctionalism,* London: Sage.

Habermas, J. 1981: *Theorie des Kommunikativen Handelns*. 2 vols. Frankfurt am Main: Suhrkamp.

Habermas, J., and Luhmann, N. 1971: *Theorie der Gesellschaft oder Sozialtechnologie*. Frankfurt am Main: Suhrkamp.

Holmwood, J. 1982: Review of Alexander, Theoretical Logic in Sociology, vol. 1. *Sociology*, 16, 599–601.

Joas, H. 1988: The Antinomies of Neofunctionalism: A Critical Essay on Jeffrey Alexander. *Inquiry*, 31, 471–94.

—— 1990: Giddens' Critique of Functionalism. In J. Clark, C. Modgil, and S. Modgil (eds), *Anthony Giddens. Consensus and Controversy,* Basingstoke: Palmer Press.

Levine, D. L. 1986: Review of Theoretical Logic in Sociology. Volume 3: The Classical Attempt at Theoretical Synthesis: Max Weber. *American Journal of Sociology*, 91, 1237–9.

Nielsen, J. K. 1991: The Political Orientation of Talcott Parsons: The Second World War and its Aftermath. In R. Robertson and B. S. Turner (eds), *Talcott Parsons. Theorist of Modernity*. London: Sage.

Parsons, T. 1962: Individual Autonomy and Social Pressure: An Answer to Dennis H. Wrong. *Psychoanalysis and Psychoanalytic Review,* 49, 70–80.

Ritzer, George. 1990: *Frontiers of Social Theory. The New Synthesis*. New York: Columbia University Press.

Sciulli, D. 1986: Voluntaristic Action. *American Sociological Review*, 51, 743–67.

—— 1990: Differentiation and Collegial Formations: Implications of Social Constitutionalism. In J. C. Alexander and P. Colomy (eds), *Differentiation Theory and Social Change. Comparative and Historical Perspectives,* New York: Columbia University Press.

—— 1991: *Theory of Societal Constitutionalism: Foundations of a non-Marxist Critical Theory*. Cambridge: Cambridge University Press.

Tiryakian, E. A. 1979/80: Post-Parsonian Sociology. *Humbolt Journal of Social Relations*, 7, 17–32.

Turner, B. S. 1991: Neofunctionalism and the 'New Theoretical Movement': Post-Parsonian

Reapproachment between Germany and America. In R. Robertson and B. S. Turner (eds), *Talcott Parsons. Theorist of Modernity*, London: Sage.

Turner, J. 1987: *Revolution in the Development of Capitalism*. Berkeley: University of California Press.

Wallace, Walter S. 1984: Alexandrian Sociology. *American Journal of Sociology*, 90, 640–53.

Wrong, D. H. 1961: The Oversocialized Conception of Man in Modern Sociology. *American Sociological Review*, 26, 183–93.

chapter 16

Conflict Theory: An Alternative to Functionalism?

Pål Strandbakken

KEY CONCEPTS

CONFLICT THEORY – a theory of society that presupposes a conflict of interest between individuals; that humans strive for resources, prestige, and power and that this produces winners and losers. Social order is explained by force. Dahrendorf uses *coercion theory* rather than conflict theory.

CONSENSUS THEORY – a theory of society that presupposes that people have – and realize – common interests; that harmony should prevail. Social order is explained by common interests. Dahrendorf prefers the term *integration theory* for consensus theory.

POST-CAPITALIST SOCIETY – Dahrendorf's term for Western societies after the blurring of the opposition between labor and capital due to the separation of ownership and control, the separation that is thought to transcend Marx's claim that relations of authority in the last resort are always relations of property.

RADICAL SOCIOLOGY – a very imprecise term for political and disciplinary opposition to the sociological mainstream (meaning Parsons), used to describe Mills's work, as well as numerous contributions from student activists and young scholars in the sixties.

The main focus of this chapter is *one aspect* of the critique directed at structural functionalism (see chapters 5 and 14) in the late fifties and early sixties. *Functionalism was attacked for being a theory of consensus.* The two concepts of functionalism and structural functionalism are more or less used as synonyms, but the correct usage probably is to view "functionalism" as a more general notion than "structural functionalism," which should be reserved for the Parsons tradition (see chapter 14).

The discussion concentrates on two works of principal importance, both coincidentally published in 1959: Ralf Dahrendorf's (b. 1929) *Class and Class Conflict in an Industrial Society* and C. Wright Mills's (1916–62) *The Sociological Imagination.* Even important aspects of Mills's critique of functionalism are left out, as irrelevant in this context, and to a degree we limit our review of the controversy to the situation around 1960. The conflict versus consensus debate is largely treated as *an episode* in the history of sociology, where the main arguments are present from the beginning.

The Intellectual Background

In the transition from pre to post World War II American sociology changed focus, parallel to a changed geographical location of the most prestigious institutions. Before World War II the University of Chicago (see chapter 8) was the power center of North American sociology. Chicago sociologists were the offspring of the European heritage, most notably Max Weber (see chapter 6) and Georg Simmel (see chapter 7), and they developed the study of modern urban life using fieldwork and life-history approaches (Faris 1970). The most influential sociological work in this period – the model study – was Thomas and Znaniecki's *magnum opus, The Polish Peasant in Europe and America*, published in 1918–20, a work that builds on content analyses of immigrant letters as well as biographical material. Another example of this vital interwar years' sociology is the work of Thorstein B. Veblen (1857–1929), particularly *The Engineers and the Price System* of 1921, in which Veblen anticipates many of the modern debates over meritocracy and "new middle classes."

From Chicago to Harvard

After 1945 this rich and original tradition becomes almost invisible. Geographical hegemony moved eastward, to Harvard and Columbia, and the discipline's leading figures from now on are Talcott Parsons (see chapter 14) and Paul Lazarsfeld (1901–76). This really implies a double break; away from genuine American research traditions, and away from the Chicago version of the European tradition as well. After World War II, Parsons, who had been a student in Heidelberg, became the leading carrier and interpreter of European sociological traditions in North America.

In the fifties, Parsons's theoretical approach – called structural functionalism – seemed to be quite unopposed in the US and in the parts of the world that were heavily influenced by American politics, economy, and culture. This hegemony does not, however, necessarily mean that American sociologists worked with the theory of structural functionalism. Just as today, most of the social scientists probably worked with empirical studies of society. What it does mean is rather that those who did engage in social theory usually did it from inside a functionalist paradigm.

The perspective of functionalism

The starting point of functionalism is the view that society is a social system made up of a number of mutually dependent parts or elements in an equilibrium. Changes in one part necessarily lead to changes in other parts, so that the totality of change can be said to occur inside an overreaching order. For functionalist thinkers, social change has tended to be something that is always gradual or incremental.

Earlier, more extreme versions of functionalism tended toward presupposing that all structures and events were functional for the system as a whole, that the mere existence of a structure or an event was a proof of its indispensability for the maintenance of the system. Even if this extreme functionalism was not accepted theoretically, it might still have survived as a kind of general orientation. This is the root of the alleged conservatism of functionalism. This orientation somehow forces functionalist sociology to look for positive "functions" of war, poverty, or racism on the system level. The focus on the re-establishment of system equilibrium tends to obscure possibilities for meaningful social change with reference to normative orientations like justice, equality, etc.

Since the theme here is the conflict-theory alternative, we will not discuss functionalism any further, though it is indirectly treated through the description of its adversaries. Before discussing Dahrendorf and Mills it is, however, necessary to offer two more general comments:

1   The conservative bias or tendency of functionalism does not mean that American sociology in the period should be described as right-wing. In an American context most of them would probably be labelled "liberal." Their view of science, which was rooted in the logical positivism of the interwar years, was insisting on research as value-neutral. This really was a response to the irrationality of the European right.

2   Critics of functionalism tend to overlook elements of self-criticism in the functional-

ist movement, like the important contributions from Robert K. Merton (see chapter 14). Mills is especially guilty of this; he clearly prefers to attack Talcott Parsons, and in Parsons's body of work he chooses to criticize the quite abstract *Social System* (1951) rather than, for example, *The Structure of Social Action* (1937). Mills makes it easy for himself. Unlike Mills, Dahrendorf comments on Merton's work, but he too concentrates on criticizing Parsons. Sadly, lesser critics usually follow Mills's and Dahrendorf's bad examples here.

Ralf Dahrendorf's Conflict-Theory Alternative

> ### Biography: *Ralf Dahrendorf*
>
> A German sociologist, born in 1929, as the son of a rather important social-democratic politician. He joined the SPD at the age of 18. Through his work *Class and Class Conflict in an Industrial Society* (1959), he reintroduced the class theory of Karl Marx into sociology, and thereby gained significance as a theoretician. Increasingly influenced by liberal thought, he left the Social Democrats (SPD) in 1967 and joined the Free Democrats (FPD). In the years when "all" intellectuals went to the left, Dahrendorf went right. He made a career in the FDP as a representative in the German Parliament, as Secretary of State in the German Foreign Office, and as an EU Commissioner. After that he had a mainly academic career in England, among other posts as the director of the London School of Economics. Among his other publications are *Essays in the Theory of Society* (1968), *Homo Sociologicus* (1973), *The New Liberty* (1975), *Die Chancen der Krise* (1983), and *Fragmente eines neuen Liberalismus* (1987).

Ralf Dahrendorf's *Soziale Klassen und Klassenkonflikt in der Industrielle Gesellschaft* was published in West Germany in 1957. Two years later the revised English-language edition, *Class and Class Conflict in an Industrial Society*, was published. Through this work conflict theory entered modern sociology. A key word here is "modern," because the conflict–consensus dichotomy is obviously present in European intellectual controversies long before 1959, a point that Dahrendorf also emphasizes. His point of departure is Karl Marx (see chapter 2), more precisely the unfinished class theory in *Capital*, volume III. Dahrendorf "completes" or reconstructs the chapter by trying to use Marx's logic, and by digging out what Marx had written about classes and class conflicts in other connections.

The class theory

The central point for Dahrendorf is that *class theory is something fundamentally different from theories of stratification*. While theories of stratification are empirical and descriptive, concerned with income inequalities, status differences, and different consumption patterns, class theory is analytical, concerned with societal antagonism and driving historical forces.

Here – in the extension of class theory – lies an important departure from the period's orthodox structural functionalistic theory of change. For Marx and Dahrendorf, structural change means that the system as a whole may change or even perish, that new groups might come into being while old groups disappear, that the relations between classes might change completely and that new institutions might replace old ones.

In Parsons's perspective, social change will typically mean that social groups increase or decrease in size over time and that different social roles change their relative importance. Dahrendorf follows Marx's view that the structure as a whole may change, and that one conflict will tend to dominate in a society at a given time. This conflict will point to the structure of society, and can often be explained with reference to a dichotomous model of class. It is assumed that one class in a conflict tends to defend the present state of affairs (the status quo), while the other seeks change. Contrary to Marx, however, Dahrendorf does not claim that all potentially structure-changing conflicts are necessarily class conflicts.

Coercion and integration

Dahrendorf's use of concepts is surprising. It is not coincidental that for the title of his book he uses the term "industrial society." According to him, the separation of ownership and control, the creation of a group of managers without ownership and a group of owners without responsibility for business management, has changed society from "capitalist" to "post-capitalist." *Industrial society* then, is a concept covering Western post-capitalist societies, *and* the "socialist" societies in the Soviet camp, where the link between ownership and control that Marx presupposes was blurred as well. An even more surprising choice of concepts is that he largely avoids the terms conflict and consensus when he characterizes the differences between Parsons's theory and his own. He prefers to emphasize the difference between an "integration theory of society" and a "coercion theory of society" (Dahrendorf 1959/1972: 159).

The Janus-headed society

Actually, Dahrendorf's project is not to *replace* integration theory, later to be known as consensus theory, or simply functionalism. He offers a supplementary or complementary theory; his coercion or conflict theoretical perspective is showing us the other side of society's Janus face.

He understands the relation between the two perspectives as an extension of the controversies between utopians, following Jean-Jacques Rousseau (1712–78; see chapter 1), and rationalists following Thomas Hobbes (see chapter 1), the discourse over relations between the common will and egoism. According to Dahrendorf, we have to chose between Rousseau's "utopian" vision of an almost stateless society where inhabitants take care of things through unselfish debate based on a general consensus of values, and Hobbes's "rationalist" vision of a society where people act like wolves towards each other, and have to be constrained by a strong government.

> There is one large and distinguished school of thought according to which social order results from a general agreement of values, a consensus omnium or volonté générale which outweighs

all possible or actual differences of opinion and interest. There is another equally distinguished school of thought which holds that coherence and order in society are founded on force and constraint, on the domination of some and the subjection of others. (Dahrendorf 1959/1972: 157)

The linking of the conflict–consensus controversy to this discourse between two major traditions in the study of politics and society reduces the impression of it being a mere episode in recent intellectual history.

So Dahrendorf does not claim that his own view should replace or could transcend the perspective of consensus theory. He asserts that neither perspective should plead exclusive validity. Consensus/integration and conflict/coercion imply complementary images of society and its parts. Both perspectives are valid, that is they are both illuminating and necessary for social analysis. So they should really be criticized only when they claim primacy, when they reach for total explanatory power. Obviously, it is here that Talcott Parsons is most vulnerable.

This actually means that the title of this chapter is slightly misleading when it refers to Dahrendorf's work: "Coercion theory" is not aimed at replacing functionalism, because it is not an alternative theory, it is a complementary one. The choice of one over the other is a matter of what question one wants to answer:

> We have to chose between them only for the explanation of specific problems; but in the conceptual arsenal of sociological analysis they exist side by side. (Dahrendorf 1959/1972: 163)

The chapter's title is misleading in another respect as well. "Conflict theory" should not be opposed to "functionalism" because these are concepts on a different level. Dahrendorf is criticizing Parsons and the other functionalists for their insistence on integration and consensus, not for their functionalism. Dahrendorf might be just as functionalist in his explanations as Parsons, but he is a "conflict functionalist" rather than a "harmony functionalist."

> Dahrendorf's emphasis on such things as systems (imperatively co-ordinated associations), positions, and roles links him directly to structural functionalism. As a result, his theory suffers from many of the same inadequacies as structural functionalism. (Ritzer 1992: 266)

So Dahrendorf really does not attack functionalism; he is rather opposing postwar structural functionalistm for its bias toward the study of integration, harmony, and consensus. In his view the study of social harmony is necessary but not sufficient.

C. Wright Mills's Critique and Alternative

Biography: *C. Wright Mills*

An American sociologist and leftist intellectual, born in Waco, Texas, in 1916. Mills was trained at the Universities of Texas and Wisconsin, but he spent most of his professional life in New York, where he worked at the Bureau of Applied Social Research and later at

Columbia University. He was a very controversial person who made a lot of enemies. From the middle fifties, following the publication of *The Power Elite* (1956), until his death in 1962, he was more or less drifting away from academic sociology, developing a role of a prophet, publishing political pamphlets. In this period, however, he also wrote his sociological masterpiece, *The Sociological Imagination* (1959). Other important books include *White Collar: The American Middle Classes* (1951) and *The New Men of Power: America's Labor Leaders* (1948) plus two books written in collaboration with Hans Gerth, *Character and Social Structure* (1953) and *From Max Weber: Essays in Sociology* (1946).

While Dahrendorf's contribution to conflict theory in 1959 was limited to just one book, Mills at the same time had been a practicing social scientist for fifteen years; he had published four extensive empirical studies and some other books prior to the publication of *The Sociological Imagination*. Mills's criticism of contemporary sociology was more comprehensive than Dahrendorf's opposition to the structural functionalists' consensus models, and his polemic was much more hostile and hurtful.

Today, *The Sociological Imagination* is probably best known for its second chapter, "Grand Theory," where Mills ridicules the prose of Talcott Parsons. His translation of Parsons into "straightforward English" remains one of sociology's most worthwhile murders.

At the time of publishing, however, it was his attack on "Abstracted Empiricism" that caused the greatest stir. It was controversial for two reasons: First, he hurt more people here. The number of "high theoreticians" was after all quite small, while his descriptions of the activities of abstract empiricism were unpleasantly close to the daily activities of most sociologists and political scientists. Second, his caricature of empiricism was aimed at an identified colleague at Mills's own institution. This colleague, Paul F. Lazarsfeld, had even been his supervisor at the Bureau of Applied Social Research when Mills wrote *The Puerto Rican Journey: New York's Newest Migrants* (Mills 1950).

The controversies that followed this rude breach of etiquette largely obscured Mills's alternative and destroyed his real project, which was to reconstruct a tradition where the social sciences were "attempts to help us understand biography and history, and the connexions of the two in a variety of social structures" (Mills 1980 [1959]: 40). Mills's critique of mainstream sociology was primarily pointing to its alleged failing quality and lack of societal relevance. According to him, contemporary sociology had failed its mission because it did not fulfill the "promise" of classical sociology. Among other things it lacked "sociological imagination." In addition, Mills delivered a surprisingly modern epistemological critique of the self-image of empiricism and of structural functionalism, it is not, however, these interesting and important aspects of Mills's work that reserve a place for him in this context.

Mills as a conflict sociologist

The rationale for putting Mills together with Dahrendorf is his *political* critique of the conservatism of structural functionalism, conservatism disguised as value neutrality, and his disciplinary concern – or rather obsession – with *power*.

Mills wanted to study history and our "history-making," and he states that Parsons's terms and perspective make it difficult to formulate the idea of conflict in an effective way (Mills 1980 [1959]: 52). He was not very interested in the condition of working classes; for instance, in his "class trilogy" he is rather studying the power elite of the working class in *The New Men of Power: America's Labor Leaders* (Mills 1948).

His controversial political pamphlets from the late fifties and early sixties are based on his study of *The Power Elite* (1956). That work's main thesis is that American federal politics had been turned into a project for the top leaders of defence, business, and the political parties, and that these groups were about to develop into a coherent power elite, aided by intermarriage and career shifts, etc. Ironically, Mills's vision seems to have much in common with the message in Eisenhower's farewell speech, where the outgoing president warned of the undue influence of what he called "the military-industrial complex." *The Power Elite* caused a great stir in the US; Mills was accused of oversimplification and of delivering a political statement rather than a sociological analysis. Talcott Parsons and Daniel Bell (see chapter 25) were among critics that opposed the work for reasons of disciplinary quality, but they could not prevent the book from being a political success. It sold very well and it was translated into a lot of languages. It even made its author famous. The power elite thesis was further developed and expanded in the political pamphlet *The Causes of World War Three* (1958), in which Mills wrote about the "community" between the elites of US and the Soviet Union; he was toying with the idea of an international power elite with a "functional" unity of interests, in spite of their different ideologies (Horowitz 1983: 287). With this publication we might say that Mills had exchanged his role as a sociologist for a role as a political prophet.

In between the publication of *The New Men of Power: America's Labor Leaders* and *The Power Elite* he published *White Collar: The American Middle Classes* (1951). The middle classes were "new" because they did not any longer consist of independent owners of small businesses, but were made up of employees in the large corporations. These middle classes were about to become the largest social class. If Mills ever wrote a book that most social scientists agree to call a modern classic, *White Collar* is that book. Its main focus is more on alienation and class culture than on power, but "middle class boredom and conventionality" (Horowitz 1983: 228) is not the only message, it is also concerned with questions of the class's diminishing power because of a gradual loss of economic independence, the middle classes' lack of will and ability to unionize and so on, leading to their being squeezed between a wealthy upper class and a politically conscious working class. So the concerns of *White Collar* do fall within Mills's usual preoccupations.

The leitmotif of Mills's sociological work is the ambition to study politics and history – often focusing on the identification of decision-makers – in such a way that common people might understand their own historical situation, the forces they are exposed to, constraints on individual action, etc. He claimed that this was achieved in classical sociology, that the classics had interpreted society and history for their contemporaries and made it understandable for them.

Mills's contribution did not have an immediate influence on academic sociology in the US. Even as the most famous leftist intellectual in North America, he was so completely alienated from academic sociology in the period that only student activists and foreigners seemed to be able to read him in a fairly unprejudiced way (or with other sets of prejudice than his contemporary sociological colleagues).

The Development of the Conflict–Consensus Debate

In a 10- to fifteen-year period following 1960 disagreements over questions of conflict and consensus seemed to be *the* important sociological discourse. Dahrendorf's emphasis on coercion and social classes, and his references to Marx – not much read by sociologists at the time – allowed conflict theory to take a position as the politically radical alternative, sympathetic to student unrest, race riots, civil rights activism, antinuclear weapons campaigns, and "the new (noncommunist) left." Political development in the sixties could be (and indeed was) interpreted as a kind of falsification of the work of Talcott Parsons, maybe even as a negation of the ideological foundation of society at large. The critique of sociology and the critique of society appeared to be closely related, and it became rather common for social scientists to engage in politics.

A sociologist who sought a political career – and succeeded – was Ralf Dahrendorf. Ironically, he did not join the left, but – from 1967, when he left the Social Democrats – he was active in the small German liberal party, the FPD (the Free Democrats). He was elected to the Bundestag, he became Parliamentary Secretary for the German Foreign Minister, and he later became a Commissioner for the European Union. Mills also tried to develop a kind of political role or praxis, based on attempts at implementing enlightenment ideas about freedom and reason in the masses through the medium of the paperback book. But he died in 1962, before the sixties had really started.

It is not easy to detect any substantial development of the discourse between integration and coercion in the sixties and seventies. The key works of Mills and Dahrendorf supply most of the disciplinary scope. What happened in the sixties was that more and more newly educated sociologists – especially outside the US – adapted their perspectives. In a comment, Lipset and Smelser complain that:

> In any article discussing major trends in American sociology designed for publication in England it is clearly necessary to discuss C. Wright Mills for he seems to have become an intellectual hero to a youthful section of the British political community. It must be reported, however, that he has little importance for contemporary American sociology, although his books are best-sellers outside the field and are widely hailed in certain political circles. (Lipset and Smelser 1961)

Those who had not had to relate to *the person* C. Wright Mills seemed to be more willing and able to detect the qualities of (parts of) his contribution.

Even though Mills was an academic pariah in his milieu, and Dahrendorf was a well-respected and integrated member of his, we might have to conclude that Mills's perspective is more valuable, mainly because it contains potential for development. Dahrendorf's picture of the two faces of society is kind of static; for him a combination of conflict theory and consensus theory is simply not possible, while Mills's politically and historically conscious sociology appears as an adequate modernization of classical theory.

An unintended consequence of these controversies might be an increased awareness of older theory, and of the history of the social sciences, among sociologists. When disciplinary disagreement again and again was framed as a discourse of intellectual history, referring to classical sociology and social philosophy, it became evident that the study of society presupposed a certain level of philosophical refinement.

For a period is was quite common to hear leftist sociologists criticizing empirical – particularly quantitative – sociology for being ahistorical and unreflected, and this is probably a result of the way Mills and Dahrendorf undermined parts of the mainstream's foundation.

New controversies, new perspectives

As indicated, the conflict-consensus dichotomy came to be more or less identified with the left-right antagonism that dominated universities in the sixties. At the same time, however, sociology was also split along the positivism/antipositivism dimension. We are not treating the theory of science discourse here, but it is worth mentioning that this debate too – at least in its early stages – seemed to replicate the left–right divide. But in their relation to positivism we would have to place Dahrendorf together with Parsons, Merton, and Lasarzfeld, while Mills, under the influence of Horkheimer and Adorno (see chapter 10), had actually acquired much of the perspective of this "new" critique of science.

The end of the debate

That Alwin W. Gouldner (1920–81) wrote his preface to *The Coming Crisis of Western Sociology* in January 1970 seems like a piece of good timing: a kind of staged farewell to one decade and an introduction to another. This book, more than any other, sums up the sociology of the sixties, the sociology of "the movement" in its American version.

There is really not much conflict theory left in Gouldner's book. Keywords like "conflict" and "coercion" are not included in the index, "Dahrendorf" is mentioned only once, "Mills" appears eight times, while "power" and "Marxism" are still important. *The Coming Crisis* was in many ways a study of how sociology was influenced by "the new left." The new left, in 1970, was not much interested in the concerns of Dahrendorf, and it was interested only in certain parts of Mills's work. It is not just a matter of Mills's and Dahrendorf's thoughts being internalized, and therefore not mentioned. Questions of driving forces behind social and historical change had almost disappeared from the focus of radical sociology at this point, largely to be replaced by cultural criticism and concern with individual freedom and freedom from conformity.

On the other hand, Parsons himself tried to accept the challenge of treating theories of change and historically aware sociology, in works like *Societies* (1966) and *The System of Modern Societies* (1971). His complete answer to his (sixties) critics was not completed until 1977, when he published *The Evolution of Societies*, a contribution that came too late – and was really not good enough – in a debate that actually had ended.

A more recent and rather ambitious attempt at formulating the future development of sociology into the conflict–consensus dichotomy is Randall Collins's (b. 1941) *Conflict Sociology: Toward an Explanatory Science* of 1975.

Collins accepts and builds on Dahrendorf's revision of Marx, but he tries to proceed mainly by using Goffman, ethnomethodology, and symbolic interactionism (see chapter 12). Those were the traditions that Collins himself came from. His explicit ambition was to "put everything together in one book" (Collins in Ritzer 1992: 559), but it is not clear whether he means everything he had learned and thought until then, or if he aims at a total framework for the study of society and history. Nevertheless it is a violently ambitious work; he wants to solve the problem of subjective and objective factors in explaining human action (Collins 1975: 73), and he seeks to mediate between the micro and macro level, mainly by reducing all structure to action on the micro level, to the concrete experience of individuals (Collins 1975: 90).

Even the conflict perspective is defined into a perspective of the individual use of resources for strategic action (Collins 1975: 89), in arenas like the class and stratification system, formal organizations, and politics. Contrary to Dahrendorf, he investigates the micro level; he wants to do a scientific study of small-scale manifestations of social conflicts.

It is not easy to see whether Collins's "conflict sociology" is contributing to the traditions we have sought to identify here (the conflict–consensus dichotomy), or if he uses the term conflict sociology for his own theoretical project. It really seems as though he is doing the latter. The social sciences will always be concerned with integration and coercion, with power, societal conflict, and consensus, but all sociology treating "conflict" and "power" is not necessarily relevant to our perspective.

It seems correct to maintain the view that conflict theory is best treated as two different, simultaneous reactions to Parsons, and to structural functionalist hegemony: Dahrendorf's and Mills's are two types of criticism that mingled with the political left–right dimension in the sixties. In this view the conflict–consensus debate is situated in a certain political and historical epoch, even if Dahrendorf in particular brings in a classical philosophical discourse. Because of this it is quite confusing when this dichotomy is projected into other situations. Since the sixties, no theory and no perspective has gained the kind of hegemony in sociology that structural functionalism used to have, and the opposition between coercion and integration since then has to be played out in different ways.

Bibliography

Primary:

Collins, Randall. 1975: *Conflict Sociology. Toward an Explanatory Science*. New York: Academic Press.
Dahrendorf, Ralf. 1959/1972: *Class and Class Conflict in an Industrial Society*. London: Routledge & Kegan Paul.
—— 1968: *Essays on the Theory of Society*. London: Routledge & Kegan Paul.
—— 1973: *Homo Sociologicus*. London: Routledge & Kegan Paul.
—— 1975: *The New Liberty*. London: Routledge & Kegan Paul.
—— 1983: *Die Chancen der Krise*. Stuttgart: Deutsche Verlagsanstalt.
—— 1987: *Fragmente eines neuen Liberalismus*. Stuttgart: Deutsche Verlagsanstalt.
Mills, C. Wright (with Schneider, Helen) 1948: *The New Men of Power: America's Labor Leaders*. New York: Harcourt, Brace & Co.
Mills, C. Wright (with Senior, Clarence, and Goldsen, Rose K.) 1950: *The Puerto Rican Journey: New York's Newest Migrants*. New York: Harper Bros.
Mills, C. Wright. 1951: *White Collar: The American Middle Classes*. New York: Oxford University Press.
Mills, C. Wright, and Gerth, Hans H. 1953: *Character and Social Structure: The Psychology of Social Institutions*. New York: Harcourt, Brace.
Mills, C. Wright. 1956: *The Power Elite*. New York: Oxford University Press.
—— 1958: *The Causes of World War Three*. New York: Simon & Schuster.

—— 1959/1980: *The Sociological Imagination*. New York: Oxford University Press.

Secondary:

Faris, Robert E. L. 1970: *Chicago Sociology 1920–1932*. Chicago: Rand McNally.

Gerth, Hans H., and Mills, C. Wright (eds) 1946: *From Max Weber: Essays in Sociology*. New York: Oxford University Press.

Gouldner, Alvin W. 1970: *The Coming Crisis of Western Sociology*. London: Heinemann Educational Books.

Homans, George C. 1961: *Social Behaviour: Its Elementary Forms*. New York: Harcourt, Brace and World.

—— 1964: Bringing Men Back In. *American Sociological Review*, 29, 809–18.

Horowitz, Irving L. 1983: *C. Wright Mills: An American Utopian*. New York: Free Press.

Lipset, S. M., and Smelser, N. 1961: Change and Controversy in Recent American Sociology. *British Journal of Sociology,* 12/1, 50.

Merton, Robert K. 1949/1967: *On Theoretical Sociology. Five Essays, Old and New*. New York: Free Press.

Parsons, Talcott. 1937/1949: *The Structure of Social Action*. New York: Free Press.

—— 1951: *The Social System*. Glencoe, IL: Free Press.

—— 1966: *Societies*. Englewood Cliffs, NJ: Prentice-Hall.

—— 1971: *The System of Modern Societies*. Englewood Cliffs, NJ: Prentice-Hall.

—— 1977: *The Evolution of Societies*, ed. and introd. by Jackson Toby. Englewood Cliffs, NJ: Prentice-Hall.

Ritzer, George. 1992: *Contemporary Sociological Theory*. New York: MacGraw-Hill.

Thomas, W. I., and Znaniecki, F. 1918/1974: *The Polish Peasant in Europe and America*. 2 vols. New York: Octagon.

Veblen, Thorstein B. 1921/1963: *The Engineers and the Price System*. New York: Harcourt Brace Jovanovich.

chapter 17

Jean-Paul Sartre

Dag Østerberg

Key Concepts

ALIENATION – a distortion of praxis. The active person does not recognize himself in his own work, but confronts it as a stranger. Alienation was first described by Hegel and later developed by Marx, who regarded wage labor, indeed capitalism in general, as being inherently alienating.

EXISTENTIAL FREEDOM – the experience of being responsible for one's actions and one's lifestyle. As external circumstances condition but never entirely decide one's choice, the individual must in the final instance always choose what he or she will become. Kierkegaard was the first one to describe this in his book, *The Concept of Anguish.*

INAUTHENTIC EXISTENCE – to conceal one's existential freedom from oneself through various forms of self-deception – "bad faith." The opposite is authentic existence, living in clear consciousness of being free and responsible for one's actions.

INERT FIELD OF ACTION – when the situation makes *demands* upon us, which stem from material scarcity (e.g., the car has to be treated for rust), this is experienced as an inert field of activity. Our praxis is unfree and alienated, because it obeys the demands of the inert field of action. Here our actions are impotent, "we act as someone other than ourselves."

PRAXIS – man's active relationship to his material world, whereby this is shaped through work and struggle with others. Praxis was a basic concept in Marx's teaching about man: Through praxis man realizes his being.

SERIALITY – a special form of impotence in the inert field of action, which is due to the fact that material establishments and the built environment have led to mutual schisms and impotence. Each individual must act as he or she does, because of the others, who again act as they do because of the others, in a continuous chain or "series."

Biography: *Jean-Paul Sartre*

Jean-Paul Sartre (1905-80) was the son of a French naval officer who belonged to the French bourgeoisie. His father died early and the son grew up in his grandparents' home in Paris with Albert Schweitzer's brother, Charles Schweitzer, a language teacher, and here he became fascinated by the world of books. He wanted to become an author. He studied philosophy at the elite Ecole Normale Supérieure and taught until 1944.

He made his début as a fiction author in 1938 with a novel entitled *Nausea*, which brought him to the fore. He took part in military action in the spring of 1940 and was imprisoned for a year by the Germans. These experiences changed him from a nonpolitical to a political person. In 1943 he published his great work, *Being and Nothingness*, an existential situation philosophy which made him world-famous as a thinker. Together with the philosopher Maurice Merleau-Ponty, he established the periodical *Les Temps Modernes*, which has played an important role on the political left-wing. He wrote a number of plays, among them, *Closed Doors* and *Dirty Hands*, which are found regularly in the repertoires of Western theatres.

Apart from biographical works, he wrote a great number of political essays and commentaries based on the Marxist point of view. Relations between Sartre and the French communist party were hostile, apart from the years 1952 to 1956. When the Soviet Union crushed the Hungarian uprising, he broke off relations for ever with the French communists. In 1960 his second treatise of situational philosophy, the *Critique of Dialectical Reason*, was published, a grandiose attempt to show a third alternative in the ideological war between the West and the East Bloc.

Sartre was awarded the Nobel Prize for literature in 1964, but refused to accept it, the only person to have done so up till now. He became in time one of the world leaders of political opinion and, together with Bertrand Russell, the philosopher, he led the Vietnam tribunal in Roskilde in 1968. From his student days he was closely connected with Simone de Beauvoir (1908–86), who like him was a philosopher and writer of fiction, and in addition a leading figure within the new feminist movement in the eighties.

Sartre presented his theories regarding action and interaction in two works, *Being and Nothingness* (1943) and *Critique of Dialectic Reason* (1960). The general background for the first work is the philosophy of existence, Søren Kierkegaard's (1813–55) philosophy of existence, but first and foremost that of Martin Heidegger (1899–1976). The basic existential thinking of man's anxiety-filled freedom, as a project in a world into which one is thrown, is linked in Sartre's philosophy to the principles of the psychology of perception, imagination, drives, and desires (psychoanalysis). The theory of action and the social psychology in *Being and Nothingness* stands out as an ahistorical description of man's existence, regardless of time and place.

The other work's general background is Karl Marx's (see chapter 2) materialist conception of history. He described mankind as active creatures which through their metabolism with nature transform both the world around them and themselves and thus create history. Moreover, he showed how ownership of the means of production forms the basis for the class struggle, which he claims to be the driving force of history. Sartre wishes to give this social and historical science a new basis and at the same time to integrate his first, timeless theory from *Being and Nothingness* into history. "It [Marxism] remains, therefore, the philosophy of our time," he claims (Sartre 1968: 30). It is valid for our time, and its purpose is to make itself superfluous. "As soon as a margin of 'real' freedom beyond production exists for everyone, Marxism will have run its course; a philosophy of freedom will then take its place" (Sartre 1969: 34).

As is well known, Marx's work may be interpreted both humanistically and technologically deterministic, in which his early publications support the first interpretation and his later works the other one. The official state philosophy in the "East Bloc" countries, Marxism-Leninism or dialectical materialism, definitely had a deterministic tinge. Sartre perceives Marxism as humanism and is therefore affiliated with the Marxist tradition from the German, Karl Korsch, the Hungarian, Georg Lukács, the Italian, Antonio Gramsci (see chapter 9) and the Frenchman, Henri Lefèbvre, and others. In his immediate surroundings it was Maurice Merleau-Ponty (1908–61), who influenced him in this direction through his interpretation of Marxism in *Humanism and Terror* (1947) and *Sense and Non Sense* (1948).

Sartre wrote *Critique of Dialectical Reason* in the cold war period. His starting point is that the Marxism which characterizes the communists, and particularly the French communist party, has become rigid, and that Marxism will be reduced to a skeleton, if it does not accept psychoanalysis and sociology (Sartre 1969: 71). At the same time he claims that non-Marxist social research needs a better foundation for its ad hoc approaches to problems. Through his basic reflections on mankind's material *praxis*, Sartre wished to overcome the clash during the fifties between rigid (dogmatic) Marxism and unprincipled empiricism and positivism.

Situated (Contextual) Freedom

Man is "condemned to be free." He has a consciousness of or is always in a position to (either prereflectively or reflectively) choose his relationship to his surroundings, which therefore cannot determine what a person does. Man also chooses how he will relate to his own body, his own talents and inclinations, his own past.

Neither heredity nor milieu can determine a person's actions. But conversely a person cannot act without heredity and environment. He necessarily relates to a definite, special *situation*. Freedom is *situational*, or in more ordinary language within sociology, *contextual*. Sartre's situationism is extreme – freedom is nothing but relating to and revealing aspects of the situation.

Existential interaction

In *Being and Nothingness* Sartre treats social interaction from the point of view of existential, situational freedom. What happens when one freedom meets another? That this encounter can be shocking, Sartre demonstrates by imagining how it feels to be under the scrutiny of the Other Person. When I feel that the Other Person is looking at me, I become aware that I have an exterior side, a being for the Other Person which escapes me. I cannot grasp what I am for the Other, since the Other uncovers my exterior through his freedom. To the Other's stare I am an object. A feeling of shame (or vanity) is, according to Sartre, an expression of this objective experience as opposed to a situational freedom, which is a subjective experience. The one who is being looked at by Another may choose to look back and assert his subjectivity proudly. Then the Other becomes the object of the look. I never meet the Other's look. A look cannot be looked at. The one who wants to look at the look meets only two eyes, two objects in the world. This first investigation leads to the conclusion that, in the meeting between two freedoms, it is not possible for both to assert themselves as subject at the same time.

Another series of investigations comes to another result, where the division between authentic and inauthentic behavior is decisive. Freedom is inauthentic when it denies itself and strives to be both the object and the subject at the same time (the impossible synthesis "being-in-itself-for-itself"). Freedom is authentic when it affirms itself without foundation and at the same time unconditionally ("absolute"), that is, it is a choice of itself and the way a situation is disclosed.

The encounter with the Other becomes inauthentic when one or both sides seeks to make an object of the other or to make itself into an object for the Other, with the intention that the two consciousnesses or freedoms should constitute a subject–object. Further it becomes inauthentic when one or both sides remain indifferent to the other and assume a calculating or strategic attitude, for that is the same as hiding the other's freedom for oneself (a form of self-delusion or "bad faith").

Authentic forms for social interaction can be certain situations of help. The person who does not demand, but who requests or appeals for help, keeps his freedom at the same time as he or she communicates with the other's freedom. The one who helps also has the other person's freedom as an aim, without giving up his own. Love can also be authentic, when the one who loves seeks to protect the other's situated freedom and confirms this freedom in all its bodily vulnerability (Sartre 1983: 524).

From existential freedom to praxis in the inert field of action

In the *existential* situation freedom is situated and absolute. One cannot shove the blame onto circumstances, because it is inherent in our situation that circumstances exist. We are not free in spite of or by lifting ourselves above the situation, but only in and through the situation. Our task is to choose our relation to the situation, to extend it in one direction or the other through our project. To represent it for oneself, even if circumstances force one to do so, is to be in "bad faith," to fall victim to self-delusion. This is most obvious in the case of a person who takes the game seriously, for the importance of the game is precisely to demonstrate freedom. The playful action is not a goal in itself, nor is it the expressed purpose of the action, which represents its aim or deeper meaning; the function of action is to reveal and make present absolute freedom *for itself*, the absolute freedom which is the person's real existence (Sartre 1943: 670).

In the *practical* situation freedom is still unconditional, but it is alienated or distorted and becomes unfree. This is because material scarcity changes the situation into an *inert field of action* and the project and the action into a *praxis* in this field. Here necessity takes over. Instead of a free, situational existence, each one is now an organism in threatening surroundings. Human "metabolism with nature," which Marx speaks about, is in its most abstract form the organism's absorption of nourishment and digestion. At this level the organism experiences scarcity as the deciding factor; there is not enough for everyone.

This experience of scarcity is *internalized* in different ways, for example, as miserliness or anxiety, but most often as aggression. In the inert field of action each one "in principle" is one too many, one person too many, because just by his very presence he constitutes a demand on some of the scarce resources. The presence of *the Others* in the inert field of action threatens me and I them; I am also Another in relation to myself, in that I realize this mutual threat of superfluity.

Hate as a social relationship leads Sartre back to scarcity and not to any inherent evil in man's being as such. Humans affected by scarcity hate, are violent, even gruesome; therefore Sartre speaks of the inert field of action as a "hell". It is simply not possible to escape, there is no room anywhere, or there is a scarcity of land and other resources.

Methodological Individualism

Sartre presented his sociology – or rather his foundation of sociology – as a renewal and continuation of Marx's materialist conception of history. He therefore does not stress the statements in Marx's writing which deal with iron-clad laws for historical development, or that the formation of society changes itself in ways that evade man's consciousness. On the contrary, Marxism is interpreted as a theory of action of a quite different type, a theory concerning the individual's freedom and action in a situation. Sartre refers here to *The 18th Brumaire of Louis Bonaparte*, where Marx writes that men create their own history, but on terms they themselves have not made, that is, based on their situation (see chapter 2).

The starting point is methodological individualism which is to say that the basis for *all* understanding of social life and history must be the single person's or individual's action or praxis. Hence Sartre rejects any thought of supra-individual or collective consciousness, whether it stems from conservative, romantic-organic thinkers or from the classical French sociologist, Emile Durkheim (see chapter 5). Thereby he becomes like so many others, a spokesman for a methodological individualism.

This can be easily misunderstood. Most methodological individuals combine their individualism with a utilitarian or instrumental concept of action, while Sartre operates with a dialectical action concept. The individual – the practical organism – is a negation of the existing material situation, which is transcended through praxis. Man changes his surroundings and himself through work and other forms of praxis by answering challenges from the inert field of action. The dialectical action is a totalizing movement which is constantly producing something new.

Sartre also agrees with the assertion that "class struggle is the driving force in history," as stated in *The Communist Manifesto*, and also with the idea that the clash between productive forces and relations of production are fundamental in the course of history. What he wants to contribute is to make understandable how clashes between individuals can exist and how these antagonisms produce social formations which are *dialectical* totalities, that is, totalities that constitute negations.

Alienation, Counter-Finality, Reification

Through his transcending praxis man leaves his mark on his surroundings, which appears as "worked matter". But the worked matter eludes the agent and acquires an independent existence. It can turn against its origin and thereby bring about *alienation*. The worked matter appears as something else than the praxis which produced it. One of Sartre's simpler examples is deforestation in old China. Each individual farmer cut down trees independent of the others, and altogether these operations led to overcutting in huge areas, which resulted in soil sliding into the rivers, which in turn produced recurring floods. The inert material field of action totalized individual actions into one great destructive praxis. The individual's action is alienated by the Other's presence and activity.

Another example is the Spanish king's import of gold from America in the sixteenth century. The gold was minted and, when this was put into circulation, it led to a general rise in prices, to an inflation which contributed strongly to Spain's downfall as a great power. The example is more complex because it implies the people of that time were dazzled by the power of gold. They were incapable of understanding that the reason for the inflation was the amount of gold in circulation. Man's praxis, which was the basis for all value, was estranged in relation to gold. Riches were estranged and contorted into their opposite, a "dialectical reversal." A third example is the way in which material production appears as capital, as a foreign and hostile power, as shown by Marx in his works.

Counter-finality (a finality which counter-strikes) is a special form of alienation. When the chimneys in English industrial cities belched noxious smoke, or when the use of private cars spread a layer of exhaust gas, smog, over city areas, this was a result of human praxis, a counter-praxis which is registered in materiality and turns against human beings with hostile intention (counter-finality).

Sartre's notions of alienation are not at all the same as the "unintended consequences of action," as the American Robert K. Merton (see chapter 14) and the Austrian-British philosopher, Karl Popper, and others have emphazized. Sartre bases his work on the German philosopher G. W. F. Hegel's and Marx's philosophy of action, which signifies here that the materialized praxis is not a purely instrumental condition; it is the acting person himself in objectified form. Because there is an inner relation between praxis and its product, the product's distortion of the intention becomes a suffering; we suffer under alienation because we recognize ourselves in our creation, at the same time as we *are* this creation.

> Each one spends his life engraving his malicious picture on things which fascinate him and lead him astray, if he wants to understand himself in this picture, although he is nothing but this totalising movement which leads to *this* objectivation (Sartre 1960a: 336).

Reification, especially as it was described by Georg Lukács, is a kind of alienation. The mode of being of things is the opposite of that of the active person, it is concluded, inert, calculable, while praxis is open to the future, transcending and incalculable. The inert field of action can be structured in such a way that it forces us to conduct ourselves as things. In the daily hurly-burly we repeat ourselves, as we also do in the routines of working life. A thing cannot be reified. Reification is a suffering, exactly because it exploits and presupposes man's freedom.

Collectives and series

An important socialization form in the inert field of action is *serialization*, which corresponds to the kind of social-material objects Sartre calls *collectives*. An example is collective means of transportation, as we know them in our liberal-democratic society. Everyone uses them as another than oneself, and fellow-passengers are also others. Here there is no reciprocity, even if everyone is identical to the others with respect to use. The ticket, a month's card, or the like makes me a link in an endless series of passengers, who are external and indifferent in their relations to one another. This is most obvious at rush hour when each person wishes that the others weren't there. The private use of cars constitutes a collective with its serial mode of being. Each car-driver in general wishes to be alone on the road. The road makes everyone into a seriality; it forces everyone to drive according to the rules and to pay attention to others. This can be seen most clearly in traffic bottlenecks, where the car-driver's freedom consists solely of following the regulations of the inert action field's worked matter.

Other forms of collectives are the media, that is, a newspaper or a radio channel. They shape the readers and the listeners into series in relation to the newspaper and the programs. They read and listen serially, like persons apart from themselves and conscious of the fact that the others are reading and listening in the same way. These media develop reciprocal feeling of impotence in their users. This can be clearly seen if a reader or a listener gets annoyed and wants to oppose the message processed by the media. He realizes that the message has gone out to an indefinite series of readers and listeners, which he himself cannot reach (without himself controlling a collective or getting a column or program time in the medium which annoys him). He would be forced to take them one by one – a hopeless task which gives rise to a peculiar bitterness.

A liberal or free market, for example, the real-estate market is also a collective with a serial mode of being and logic. Every buyer experiences the Others contributing to pushing housing prices upward, indeed he contributes himself, as simply by his presence in the market he increases the demand. The same is true on the seller's side. Both buyers and sellers have to act in accordance with the Others, whom they do not know. The Others force me to demand a high price for my home, because I myself have to buy from others who will also demand at least as high a price from me, etc. Everyone forces the Others, and in this way the market price is formed as a serial quantity. Other important forms of serialization are rumor – everyone hears and conveys the rumor as Another than himself; panic – every-one jams the exit door and hinders free exit as Another than himself, everyone presses forward because all the others do it; the bestseller which everyone gives as a present or reads as another than oneself, because the Others are reading it.

The series and serialization constitute, as it were, a social form according to Georg Simmel's reasoning, but one which Simmel himself forgot to include in his general morphology of 1908, *Soziologie* (see chapter 7).

The fighting group

In the inert field of action each person can only experience his fellow beings as the others, who alienate and reify, and cannot do anything but acquire and subject himself to analytical reasoning. However, there exists a negation of alterity (otherness) and serialization, namely the fighting group. This springs up as an answer to a threat, in that a number of people find themselves in a sociomaterial situation, which they experience alike, and which makes possible a joint attack. The serial impotence which marked everyone changes to a group praxis. All of a sudden the otherness is overcome. While previously each one was Another for the Others and for himself, each one now experiences the other as the *Same* as himself or herself. The group consists of a number of individual praxes, which totalize the field of action through their project. That which the individual member does conveys and creates the common project. The one who keeps watch on his side sees the other group members as doubles of himself as they keep their positions or advance on their side. This being in the group constitutes an independent form of socializing in relation to individual praxis and alterity. Each individual changes from being a serial individual to being a *common individual*.

Sartre differs in relation to the group concept from the sociologists who describe the group as a "we-solidarity." Even though each one experiences the others as the same as himself, this is not experienced as any "we" or as a group consciousness. Sartre stays aloof from Durkheim's thought that there is a collective consciousness as such. His alternative consists in emphasizing the group's three-dimensional or ternary structure: Each participant in the group alternates with the others in being the third person in relation to the others. This is done by making oneself into a semi-spectator and seeing the group with the regard of a spectator. Thereby it appears as a totality. Afterwards he makes himself again into a participant, whereupon another of the members of the group makes himself the third. In this way there is an exchange between an internal and external relationship to the group, the group is formed as a group. However, it is still not substance; it consists solely of praxis in a given situation.

Sartre draws attention to the fact that the formation of the group can easily be interpreted from the point of view of utility, that the individual's only chance is that everyone joins together against the enemy. "However this rationalism is not dialectic, and we see clearly . . . its analytical and positivistic origin" (Sartre 1960a: 471). Sartre wishes by means of the group concept to describe a social situation beyond egoism and altruism, where each one as a third person does not distinguish between his own rescue and the other person's, and where each one experiences his possibility of being killed or taken prisoner as a "specification of the common danger." Being in the group is a new irreducible form of socializing.

Analytical Reason and Dialectical Reason

The general thought or form of understanding of alienation, reification, and serialization is *analytical reason*, as opposed to *dialectical reason* which is the logic of inner contradictions, totalities, and syntheses. Analysis – as performed by the French philosopher, René Descartes, and the tradition after him – consists of splitting experience and its themes into single, independent components and establishing exterior connections between them or calculable laws for their reciprocal relationships. Each single person, each "individual," is treated separately and confronts other individuals in an external relationship; they are experienced as the Others.

Analytical reason thus has its validity domain. When, for example, a traffic plan is drawn up for collective traffic, analytical reasoning is required. Social statistics are altogether analytical. Analytical thinking can form a part of, be transcended by, and be supplemented by synthetic, dialectic thinking, which is the logic of nonalienated praxis and nonalienated reciprocity between people. When analytical reason is made absolute, it is an aspect of domination which is the correlate of impotence. The usual investigation methods within empirical, social research must always be integrated into a dialectical, totalizing "perspective."

Sartre's dialectical sociology becomes therefore a variety of critical theory. It will go beyond all *data*, all that is *given* to contribute to a transcending, liberating process.

Typology of Organizations

When the fighting group is in the making, during fusion, it is pure praxis without inertia, without any trace of alienation or reification. As such it is transitory. In order that it should not disappear at once, the members of the group can set in motion a preserving praxis: they swear that they will keep together. This oath may be given through rituals or be implied tacitly. In both cases it means that each one -in a borderline case – will kill the one who betrays, and conversely desires that the others should kill him or her, if he or she betrays them. Each person will protect himself against his own possible weakening, will stiffen himself. In this way the group inflicts upon itself a certain *inertia*, by each one swearing that he will remain the same tomorrow as he is today, he swears that he will not change. This is the structure of the *sworn* group.

Such a group is homogeneous, all the members take on any task whatsoever, the praxis of each one is simply an answer to the demands of the situation. There is therefore an increase of inertia when the group differentiates by dividing the tasks between them. A structure of functions arises, then of reciprocal rights and duties: I have my duties and my rights as well as the right to do my duty and to see that others do not prevent me from doing so, by themselves neglecting their duties, etc. It is on this plane of social life that Sartre finds structure, such as is described by the French anthropologist, Claude Lévi-Strauss (see chapter 18) in *Les Structures élémentaires de la parenté* (The Elementary Forms of Kinship, 1949) and other works. The reciprocal obligations have become a network of relationships to which each one conforms as something comparatively external, as a set of rules. The group has now not only given its oath, it has become an organized group, an organization.

This group form is considered by Sartre to be the most effective; its inertia is not yet alienating, everyone recognizes himself in the others' praxis.

Alienation first occurs when a leader and leadership come into the picture, an authority. Since man is a sovereign being according to Sartre, this entails complying with another person's commands and orders; that one becomes another than oneself, that one becomes a stranger to oneself. The reason for leadership arising may be a certain structural lack of clarity in the situation, chance features in the inert field of action, which results in one of the members ending in a leading position, that is, praxis with regard to the others turns into orders which they must obey. That they have to obey is because of impotence. All authority is in the last instance due to impotence. *Divide et impera*, divide and rule, is the basis of all dominion.

Sartre calls a directed organization an institution. It is characterized by alienation and inertia. The participants experience the institution as something apart from themselves, something external that they must relate to as their alienated exterior. The rules and routines of the institution force them to repeat themselves. This occurs in a reification of their transcending praxis. This alienation is additionally sharpened from the outside: The institution's employee is perceived by his surroundings to be the embodiment of the institution's presence. The postal employee stands for the customers as the postal service itself, and this being for the customers is internalized by the postal service employee. He or she *is* the institution (or "service") although in an alienated mode.

When inertia and leadership go to extremes, Sartre speaks of bureaucracy. While Max Weber (see chapter 6) interprets bureaucracy as a well-functioning machinery or apparatus, Sartre describes it as an almost completely paralyzed group. Every level in the leader hierarchy alienates the level below, which feels impotence both toward the leader and toward those to be found on the same level. The alienation also affects the leader or leaders, who feel impotent regarding the bureaucratic organization, which barely lets itself be led. Everyone feels that it is others who decide, and that what is done or what happens is something else than what they themselves would have wanted through their praxis. On the strength of this general impotence, the bureaucratized group moves toward the serial state and the circle is complete. The fighting group emerges as a negation of the impotence of the serialization; through increasing leadership, alienation, and reification it falls back into serialization.

Class Struggle

Classes in society are in themselves serial collections of people, situated in and connected with each other through some of the collectives of the inert field of action, for example, the bourgeois cities' "workers' districts," the "East End" with its tenements, their meeting-places of a "proletarian" stamp, with their own tone and jargon, etc. And correspondingly the opposite side, the "West End" with more "elegant" residential districts, their private homes, their "fashionable" restaurants, and their bourgeois public places (the galleries, theatres with their foyers, the opera, etc). These different "environments" are serial, in that everyone takes part in them and confirms them as another than himself. Their ways of speaking, their ways of acting circulate and make everyone identical with the others, without there being a group formed for this reason. Joint impotence underlies this class identity and their difference from the other class. Up to this point Sartre simply carries on Marx's concept of class *an sich*.

However, instead of the concept class *für sich*, Sartre uses the concept of fighting groups. They arise in the midst of the class society's sea of seriality, for example, in the form of wildcat strikes, and crystallize as organized group struggles in the way described above. Trade-union movements and labor parties are the main forms of these kinds of groups. Even in their most paralyzed forms they cannot comprise the entire class of wage-earners, which remains serial and as such is manipulated by the class groups. How, then, can a social class become a whole, be totalized?

Externally, by being totalized by the other hostile group. Thus, the French proletariat interprets the violence which the bourgeois state exerts over French wage-earners as violence on behalf of the entire bourgeoisie; all members of this class are made "collectively responsible." Correspondingly, the bourgeoisie makes every French wage-earner collectively responsible for the violent actions certain fighting groups might commit. Each class in society has its attitude toward the other class, which it must assume (almost in the same way that every tourist in the poor part of the world, in the eyes of its inhabitants, appears as a "rich American" and must accept this as his exterior).

Through this mutual totalization from the outer side, the relationship between the two classes becomes a dialectical, negative totality.

The problem of mediation

Even though class struggle is the driving force and the crux of the inert field of action, everything which happens in society cannot be reduced to the conflict between labor and capital. On the contrary, this basic conflict is *mediated* in a number of ways in a number of fields. The "problem of mediation" arises: to understand how the conflict of interests at the base of society's formation appears, for example, as political, cultural, religious antagonisms, in which each has its special way of being. Thus, *sports* are a field with its own problematic. A sociologist investigating sport as a social institution has also to be engaged by sport as such, its distinctive form of excitement and beauty. In other words: to reduce one aspect of the "superstructure" to the "base" and its class differences is after Marx an important, but not particularly demanding task. What is demanding is to show what is distinctive with respect to sport, e.g., in relation to other cultural activities.

Sartre therefore calls his procedure a *progressive-regressive method*: Faced with a given social situation or a social phenomenon the task is both to accomplish a regression to the fundamental abstract class relationships and then undertake a progression toward the concrete phenomena in their fullness.

Sartre himself investigated the field of fiction from this point of view, especially the transition from romantic literature to realism and *l'art pour l'art* (art for art's sake). These forms of art certainly express class conflicts, but they also pose special artistic problems which the artist attempts to solve. *L'art pour l'art* is a *distinguished* art form which is suited for and recognized by people with a *distinguished* lifestyle, a lifestyle which becomes one aspect of an oppressing class praxis, However, *l'art pour l'art* also implies special attention to the question of form, for example, a preoccupation with language which in itself is important, and which appears again in the avant-garde art of our time.

A fully elaborated example of how great structural conflicts in social formation are experienced by the individual, and how social history and biography are woven together, is given by Sartre in his three-volume biography of the author Gustave Flaubert (1821–80), *L'Idiot de la famille* (The Idiot of the Family, 1971–2). Flaubert's "pathetic" project developed as an answer to the contrasts between his parents' class background and made him poorly adapted to the demands the middle-class situation confronted him with; he didn't have the right "achievement orientation." The educational system's mediation of class antagonisms brought his maladjustment to a crisis which made him into a neurotic and a modern artist, who wrote fiction which his contemporaries mistook for "realism."

Sociology and History

Sociology must in the final instance be encompassed by and superseded by historical understanding and action. The leitmotif of history, according to Sartre, is scarcity and the struggle to overcome it. This struggle is mediated through class struggles and other social conflicts. If scarcity can be overcome, a new historical era will occur and thereby a different kind of man, unlike the beings of scarcity we all are today.

Can history really be understood as a dialectical course, as a totalizing movement set in motion and furthered by man's actions? Sartre did not complete his work by showing the rationality of history (see the second volume of *Critique of Dialectical Reason*, published posthumously in 1985). However, he completed a couple of analyses or rather syntheses of two partial historical processes which contribute to answering the question of whether dialectical reason is valid for history.

One investigation concerns class struggles in France. Sartre first shows how the revolution in 1830 and the development of productive forces prepared the ground for the February and June revolutions in 1848, which resulted in antagonism between the bourgeoisie and the proletariat becoming hateful, a matter of life and death. Next he shows how this antagonism resulted in the bourgeoisie giving up their belief in good human nature and becoming misanthropic. The bloody suppression of the Paris commune sharpened the conflict even more. Sartre shows how the bourgeoisie adopted an economic policy which weakened the wage-earning class: Productivity increases, but not production; whereupon unemployment increases, more wage-earners become superfluous; which is again reflected in the increase of abortions among the women of the proletariat.

Class suppression develops as "Malthusianism," the number of inhabitants in France sinks or stagnates. Economy, politics, family relations, and cultural relations become susceptible here to a dialectical, totalizing, synthetic interpretation. The main aim is to show that even though the bourgeoisie refer to economic laws which determine development, and even though capital is an overwhelming power, in the last instance it is individuals who act; it is through individual praxis that history is in progress.

The second investigation concerns the civil war in the Soviet Union during the twenties and thirties. Here the problem is to make it understandable, how a project for the joint liberation of everyone and the abolishing of the old power structures could be contorted and develop into a new powerful elite's hard-handed rule with an ensuing civil war and purges, etc. The saying goes that revolution consumes its own children. Sartre, however, rejects such an interpretation, because it makes revolution into either a supra-individualistic proc-

ess or a nature-like course of events, which in both cases implies a break with the methodological individualism, that mankind's world must be understood from the point of view of
mankind's actions.

Sartre shows how the difference between Joseph Stalin and Leo Trotsky goes back to the
difference between the backward country town and the intellectual élite, who were partly
driven into exile by the czar's suppressive rule. Stalin personified the country town and the
majority of Russian society, while Trotsky was the cosmopolitan, accustomed to universalistic thinking. The internal antagonisms of the former czar's rule are recreated and take
on a new form through the conflict between the two. The violence of the struggle is an expression of how dangerous the situation is. Shortages call forth immediate need, which is
answered by hate and violence; external menaces against the new republic call forth the
same responses.

That the "modernization" of the Soviet Union followed a course full of conflicts and
violence is understandable as a material, dialectical process. The revolution takes place in
an inert field of action with extreme shortages. It is also understandable how impotence,
which spreads serially, forms the basis for a new political leadership, and the top political
leader becoming a monster. Stalin is not a "product" of the situation, he becomes it by
virtue of his praxis. However, he is not just a chance figure. As he gradually develops a
"persecution mania" this is because he amplifies personal characteristics which were already answers to former situations in his life. Another leader than Stalin is possible, but he
would have developed other "morbid" inclinations. When the situation is so dreadful, the
leader himself must be or become dreadful – in one way or another. Freedom is always
freedom in one situation, in an inert field of action. This situation also totalizes the historical course of events and shows how we create history on the basis of given conditions.

Conclusion

Sartre is an outsider in sociology, within the Marxist branch as well. His theory of action is
little known and has not been used very much. However, certain influences are evident.
This applies primarily for the American Peter Berger's and the German-American Thomas
Luckmann's well-known joint work *The Social Construction of Reality* (see chapter 12),
and subsequently the Frenchman Alain Touraine's (b. 1925) and the Italian Francesco
Alberoni's (b. 1930) theories concerning social movements; the latter's theory concerning
the group *in statu nascendi* (in embryo) definitely is based on Sartre's group theory, even
though Alberoni frames his theory in another direction. The Frenchman Pierre Bourdieu's
theory of structuration (which antedates that of Giddens), habitus, and distinction as a form
of power (see chapter 20) furthers several of Sartre's contributions, just as Michel Foucault's
(see chapter 19) book on "the medical look" furthers Sartre's interpretation of the look. In
his general sociology, the Englishman Anthony Giddens (see chapter 24) has worked in
Sartre's concept of seriality, albeit in a modified form. The Norwegian Dag Østerberg has
similarly in several publications based his work on Sartre's concept world, especially with
respect to "the inert field of action" and the way it results in impotence.

Sartre's theory of action in *Critique of Dialectical Reason* contributes to the solution of
several basic problems within general sociology. In the first place it contributes to clarify
the "macro-micro link," that is, how sociology can connect descriptions of social interac-

tion in small groups, in face-to-face contexts, with descriptions of encompassing social institutions such as the economy, politics, etc. Sartre wishes to show how one can maintain that members of society are free, active beings -"actors"- without society and history for this reason disintegrating into individual actions or into a stream of small "episodes" and "encounters" (as has been objected to the phenomenological sociology of Alfred Schutz; see chapter 12).

Secondly it contributes to a clarification of the concept of action. By differentiating between dialectical and analytical reason the basis is established for a specification of the concept of action, which makes means-end oriented and strategic action one – alienated, reified – form of transcending action, which produces something new: the dialectical action. The opposition between feeling and reason is overcome, in that feelings according to Sartre have intentionality; they are directed toward situations and are part of every praxis.

Thirdly it contributes to a clarification between action and society as meaningful and as material entities. Through his concepts of the worked-up matter and the inert field of action, an intermediary layer or mediation is established between idea and matter. Earlier praxis has formed layers or inscribed itself into the matter as a field of solidified meanings. The worked-up matter is therefore marked both by the project and by materiality. Much of the research which has been done during the seventies concerning space and society could with advantage be based upon Sartre's theory of praxis in the inert field of action.

Bibliography

Primary:

Bibliography:

A complete bibliography of Sartre's works until 1969 can be found in Michel Contat and Michel Rybalka: *Les Écrits de Sartre*. Paris: Gallimard, 1970. A supplement to this is *Obliques* (1979). Another bibliography is Robert Wilcok, *Jean-Paul Sartre, A Bibliography of International Criticism*. Edmonton: University of Alberta Press, 1975.

Sartre, Jean-Paul. 1943: *L'Etre et le Néant*. Paris: Gallimard. (Translated as *Being and Nothingness*. New York: Philosophical Library, 1956).
—— 1946: *L'Existentialisme est un humanisme*. Paris: Nagel.
—— 1947: *The Age of Reason*. London: Hamish Hamilton.
—— 1960: *Critique de la raison dialectique, précédé de Questions de méthode*. Paris: Gallimard. (Translated as *Critique of Dialectical Reason*. London: New Left Books 1976).
—— 1963a [1960]: *The Problem of Method*. (Introduction to *Critique of Dialectical Reason*). London: Methuen.
—— 1963b: *Les Mots*. Paris: Gallimard.
—— 1966: *Of Human Freedom*. New York: Philosophical Library.
—— 1968: *Search for a Method*. New York: Vintage Books.
—— 1945–70: *Situations I–X*. Paris: Gallimard.
—— 1971a [1939]: *Sketch for a Theory of the Emotions*. London: Methuen.
—— 1971b: *L'Idiot de la famille, I–III*. Paris: Gallimard. (Translated as *On the Idiot of the Family. In Life-Situations*. New York: Pantheon, 1977).
—— 1972: *Plaidoyer pour les intellectuels*. Paris: Gallimard.
—— 1978: *Sartre in the Seventies: Interviews and Essays*. London: Andre Deutsch.
—— 1983a [1962]: *Between Existentialism and Marxism. Sartre on Philosophy, Politics, Psychol-

ogy, and the Arts. New York: Pantheon Books.

—— 1983b: *Les cahiers pour une morale.* Paris: Gallimard.

—— 1985: *Critique de la raison dialectique, II.* Paris: Gallimard.

—— 1992 [1989]: *Truth and Existence.* Chicago: University of Chicago Press.

—— 1995 [1940]: *The Psychology of Imagination.* London: Routledge.

Secondary:

Alberoni, Francesco. 1984 [1981]: *Movement and Institution.* New York: Columbia University Press.

Berger, Peter, and Luckmann, Thomas. 1967: *The Social Construction of Reality.* New York: Anchor Books.

Bourdieu, Pierre. 1984 [1979]: *Distinction. A Social Critique of the Judgement of Taste.* London: Routledge & Kegan Paul.

Cohen-Solal, Annie. 1985: *Sartre 1905–1980.* Paris: Gallimard.

—— 1987: *Sartre: A Life.* New York: Pantheon Books.

Craib, Ian. 1976: *Existentialism and Sociology. A Study in Jean-Paul Sartre.* Cambridge: Cambridge University Press.

Flynn, Thomas R. 1997: *Sartre, Foucault, and Historical Reason.* Chicago and London: University of Chicago Press.

Foucault, Michel. 1973 [1963]: *The Birth of the Clinic.* New York: Vintage.

—— 1977 [1975]: *Discipline and Punish.* New York: Pantheon.

Fourny, Jean-François, and Minahen, Charles D. 1997: *Situating Sartre in Twentieth-Century Thought and Culture.* Basingstoke: Macmillan.

Giddens, Anthony. 1984: *The Constitution of Society.* Cambridge: Polity Press.

Hayim, Gila J. 1996: *Existentialism and Sociology: The Contribution of Jean-Paul Sartre.* New Brunswick: Transaction Publishers.

Krogh, Thomas. 1998: *Technology and Rationality.* Aldershot: Ashgate.

Lévi-Strauss, Claude. 1977 [1949]: *Les Structures élémentaires de la parenté.* Paris: Mouton. (Translated as *The Elementary Structures of Kinship.* Boston: Beacon Press, 1969).

Merleau-Ponty, Maurice. 1966 [1948]: *Sens et non-sens.* Paris: Nagel. (Translated as *Sense and Non-Sense.* Evanston, IL: Northwestern University Press, 1968).

—— 1972 [1947]: *Humanisme et terreur.* Paris: Gallimard. (Translated as *Humanisn and Terror.* Boston: Beacon Press, 1969).

Østerberg, Dag. 1981: Notes on the Concept of Matérial. *International Journal of Sociology.*

—— 1989: *Metasociology : An Inquiry into the Origins and Validity of Social Thought.* Oslo: Norwegian University Press.

—— 1997: The Urban Region's Mediation of the Class Structure. In O. Källtorp, J. Elander, and O. Ericsson (eds), *Cities in Transformation – Transformation in Cities: Social and Symbolic Change of Urban Space.* Aldershot: Avebury.

Touraine, Alain. 1973: *Production de la societé.* Paris: Seuil. (Translated as *The Self-Production of Society.* Chicago: University of Chicago Press, 1977).

chapter 18

Structuralism

Tom Broch

KEY CONCEPTS

The principle of **IMMANENCE**, the principle of **OPPOSITION**, and the practice of **SUBSTITUTIONAL ANALYSIS** are interconnected concepts, in such a way that they form a conceptual structure. The component elements of a structure are defined by their relationships with one another, i.e., they have an immanent (innate) existence in relation to the structure, in which they become manifest as distinct elements of mutually oppositional relationships. The oppositional relationship can be studied by means of substitutional analysis. We can imagine two hammers in a woodworking environment. They are somewhat different, but are used interchangeably. The two hammers represent in this case a single component element within a larger structure. However, in another woodworking environment, the two hammers have distinct uses, thereby forming two mutually opposed structural elements. Substitutional analysis, in which one example is replaced by another, can have one of two results: either the two items are variant forms of a single structural element, or they are distinct elements in an oppositional relationship.

LANGUE//PAROLE – language as a social institution, as against the speech of an individual.

SYNTAGM//PARADIGM – syntagm represents consecutive events, paradigm a set of alternatives within the train of events. The word "paradigm" originally denoted the grammatical declensions of language, which is precisely a set of alternatives, in which the language structure itself sometimes constitutes the determining element (e.g., the question of which grammatical case is governed by a given preposition), while at other times it is the social actor that makes the choice (e.g., for the positive as against the superlative form of adjective).

There is one factor that makes the definition of sociological structuralism both difficult and almost intangible. This is the fact that structuralism, as generally understood, has its origin outside the field of sociology – in linguistics and in the generalized science of signs, semiology or semiotics – while also turning up in concepts and forms of analysis that lie at the heart of sociological theory. We thus encounter "structuralism" in two senses: The first is as an exclusively semiologically inspired sociology, and the second is as the totality of all the concepts and approaches that can be identified as structuralist.

How, then, can we identify an approach, a theory, or a conceptual system as structuralist? Two principles can be indicated: first, invariability through variations, meaning that there is something (something important) that is held constant, while something else varies, and second, that the individual element is defined by the whole of which it is a part. The relation of these two principles is not accidental, in that it is precisely invariability which binds the individual element to the whole.

We can illustrate the features of structuralism by a game, for example, the game of chess (following the example of the "founder" of structuralism, Ferdinand de Saussure). Obviously, no element in chess (piece, square, or rule) is arbitrary in relation to the game as a whole. The invariable, structure-defining elements here are the two opposing sides (identified by colour), a board with 64 squares (in alternate colours), 32 pieces (divided between the two sides and the six different kinds of chess pieces), and certain given, defining rules regarding the properties of the pieces and the conduct of the game. Seen in relation to the enormous complexity of chess and to the astronomical number of possible chess games, the rules which define the game itself are amazingly simple. We now observe that the size of the board and of the pieces may vary, as may the material of which they are constructed. The pieces can take the form of pure works of art or be quite simple, and their colours may also vary. But the structure of the game of chess is independent of all these variations. Invariable, on the other hand, are the properties of the pieces and their role in the game, whose object is to defeat one's opponent's king.

All this seems obvious. One could say that everyone is more or less a structuralist when it comes to chess, or to other games. But can we transfer this approach to society and to social relations? Perhaps this is most easily achieved with regard to language, inasmuch as it is in the linguistic sciences that structuralist approaches have been particularly prominent.

If one wishes to capture the "essence" of a particular theoretical tendency, it can be worthwhile to ask why this tendency has succeeded in attracting representatives from differing professional fields. What is it that has exercised this fascination? As far as structuralism is concerned, it is necessary, in order to answer this question, to examine the state of research in the relevant disciplines – first and foremost in linguistics – at the time of structuralism's breakthrough. At the beginning of the century, linguistics – in common with nascent sociology – was marked by a contradiction at the basic level of theory and method. On one hand, there was the traditional, humanistic (philological) tradition, and on the other hand, the natural scientific approach. It was against this background that the French-Swiss linguist, Ferdinand de Saussure (1857–1913), formulated a methodological and theoretical programme for linguistics which was radically different from that of both natural science and traditional humanism (Saussure 1916).

The Principle of Opposition

For Saussure, language is first and foremost a series of "negative" stipulations, that is, a system of opposites, which play a role both in a language's expression and in its content. If English, for example, contains a pair of complementary expressive elements "n//m," it is because one can, via this opposition, derive differing words such as "night" as against "might." Phonetic variations which cannot be used to create differing words (for example, the considerable variations in the pronounciation of "r," depending on its position within the word), such as "read" as against "dear," do not constitute a part of the language's structure. *The distinctive character of the expressive elements of a language consists in their ability to differentiate content.*

Not all languages, however, contain the same expressive oppositions. The distinction, for example, between "voiced" and "unvoiced" elements is not found in every language. A sound in the range "d" to "t" in a language without this distinction will merely indicate variations in the language's physical material. There are corresponding oppositions on the content side, such as size in plate//dish and wood//forest or gender in girl//boy and cow//bull – but variations in mental connotations, which are not manifested as differing words, are not part of the language's structure either. *The distinctive character of the content elements of a language consists in their ability to differentiate expression.* This relationship has, since Saussure, been more precisely defined by later linguists, notably the Dane Louis Hjelmslev (1899–1965) (Hjelmslev 1943). One should, however, note that the analysis of language content structure is more problematic than the analysis of its expressive structure, although this question will not be discussed here.

From Linguistics to Other Sign Systems – a New Kind of Science

The principle of oppositional analysis has been applied to other sign systems and to other social and cultural phenomena. It is of course obvious that other sign systems do not consist of distinct elements in the same manner as natural languages. The structuralist approach has, however, brought to communications theory an awareness of the fact that even in media where the imaging relationship is of a technical-physical quality, distinctive elements are implied – for example, the choice of camera angle in a photograph.

While we can state that structuralism in its specific form arises from linguistics, we can conversely state that generalized linguistics, the universal science of signs known as semiology or semiotics, arises out of structuralism. The fascination of structuralism apparently lies in the fact that the idea of oppositional analysis transforms the generalized science of signs into a particular form of knowledge, stringent and open to formalization, but radically different from physics and the sciences derived from physics. Durkheim termed sociology a science sui generis. We can surely with as much right state the same of the science that received its breakthrough with Saussure. We could even say that with structuralist linguistics and semiology, a new kind of science arises.

Structuralism and Sociology

Structuralism in its specific form, with its roots in semiology, plays a significant role today at the periphery of sociology, with the formation of meaning as its object of study, partly in opposition to, and partly complementing, other communications-theory approaches. The question then becomes, to what degree is this structuralism in accordance with the structuralism that is integral to certain central concepts of sociological theory, such as the concept of roles or of institutions, in which theory is based on invariant forms that have an autonomous existence, while varying in their concrete manifestations: that is, actual persons and organizations can be replaced, while roles and institutionally defined functions are maintained.

Much is often made of the distinction between structuralism and structuralist functionalism (see chapter 14). In reality, however, all structuralism is in some sense structuralist functionalism, inasmuch as structural change comes about via changes in the function of component parts. A structure is not altered by John taking over George's job, but by some of George's responsibilities being delegated to a new post or being transferred to Peter's area. The institutional network of which a society is made up is an exceedingly complex structure in comparison with, for example, the phonemic system of a language, but in both instances, structural change implies the functional redefinition of component elements.

Ferdinand de Saussure and Emile Durkheim (see chapter 5), the linguist and sociologist, Francophone theorists and contemporaries, have both, in their separate ways, made important contributions to what is now termed "structuralism" in the fields of sociology and anthropology, Saussure as the founder of specific, semiotically oriented structuralism (semiology), Durkheim as the originator of structuralist thinking within sociology.

The influence of the Saussurian tradition in anthropology and sociology makes itself felt in particular via certain fundamental concepts. First, we find the following pairs of oppositional concepts: signifier//signified (expression//content), syntagm//paradigm (axis of combination//axis of association, for example, pizza and ice cream as elements of a meal with several courses [syntagm], as opposed to pizza and pasta as alternative main courses [paradigm]), and language system (*langue*)//language use (*parole*). To this may be added the oppositional conceptual pair: form//substance.

In recent structuralist linguistics, the theme of form//substance has come to occupy a central role. This pair of concepts possesses a kind of "borderline" status within structuralism, in that, although structuralist analysis by definition is concerned with form, the concept of form, like all concepts of structuralist analysis, derives its meaning from its opposite, the concept of substance.

On a more practical level, this interplay between form and substance gives rise to a number of interesting philosophical speculations and questions. Why, for example, is the color spectrum divided up (in non-European languages) in so many different ways? The question of the range of variation of form also turns up in the sociological arena, for example, with regard to roles; from the extremely rigid to the very loosely defined, in the order: Hindu priest//Christian priest at the altar//Christian priest in the pulpit//comedian.

Fundamental Concepts

Syntagm//Paradigm

If one were to select one of the above pairs of concepts as being the most significant, it would have to be syntagm//paradigm, consecutive events as opposed to alternatives, in that this set of concepts captures the essence of the principle of oppositional analysis: something acquires meaning, by virtue of the fact that something else could have occupied its position. Paradigmatic relations refer to replaceable items. A meal is a structure in which pizza and pasta can replace each other as the main course. Syntagmatic relations refer to combinatory relations between signs. For example "I love" can be followed by "you," "flying," "pulp fiction," "Copenhagen," etc. It cannot be followed by "she," "undermined," etc. Thus we find a group of words which according to the rules of syntagmatic relations, can follow "I love."

The choices of the paradigm are partly exercised by the individual social actor – the choice of words in a conversation, the choice of a particular film or of meals in a restaurant – and partly by the social collectivity: which grammatical case is controlled by a particular preposition, or what kind of behavior is prescribed for a particular role.

The principle of immanence

Briefly put, the message of structuralism can be said to be that a particular reality (whether textual, social, or something else entirely) can be regarded as a system of relations, whose elements are determined by the relations they enter into, whether in combination (table and chair), or as alternatives (office chair or armchair).

From this we can derive an important analytical principle, namely the principle of immanence. This principle means quite simply that all stipulations are made with regard to the current system, that is, systems of analysis derived from other systems or from earlier historical conditions cannot be applied to the system under study (the languages of the North American Indians, for example, cannot be analyzed via a grammatical schema derived from Latin).

The central point is that a system such as the language system is not an aggregate of signs, nor does the system derive its meaning from outside the system itself. A specific sign such as the colour green cannot be conceived as an independent isolated sign which creates meaning in itself. First, in the moment green is contrasted to other signs, for example, red the sign gets a meaning. In a traffic light it is not the colour green which permits you to "go" but the difference between green, yellow, and red in the traffic-light system which creates the meaning of the three colors.

Langue//Parole

Saussure distinguished between *langue* and *parole*. *La parole* refers to the "executive side of language" with actual utterances – the individual speech act. *Langue* – the independent language system – refers to a shared set of structural properties underlying language usage. Saussure's point of departure in order to study languages is the language system – *la langue*. According to Saussure, the language system is the precondition of the individual person's communication with other people. People can only speak and write because of the presence of a pre-existent language which is a shared social experience.

The theme of "langue"//"parole" has played a central role in structuralist thinking, as well as in attempts to extend structuralism from linguistic analysis to other fields. It is possible, however, that in this instance there may have been some influence in the opposite direction. It is unknown to what degree there may have been contact and mutual influence between Durkheim and Saussure, as contemporaries and as Francophone academics, but it is tempting to see the inspiration of Durkheim in the concept of "langue," which can in the context of sociology be regarded as a social institution – as opposed to "parole," which applies to individual behavior.

Meanwhile, the theme of "langue"//"parole" has been subjected to critical analysis by recent generations of linguists. It has been demonstrated that not only the language usage of a particular group (sociolect), but also the language pattern of an individual (idiolect) can be analyzed as a system. This implies a radical relativizing of the theme language system// speech act.

Systemic Analysis

The recognition of the language system as an irreducible whole is inextricably bound up with the recognition of language as a system of oppositions. This oppositional analysis has a methodological side, substitutional analysis, which can be most easily demonstrated on the level of phonetics. As an example, we can take the two d's in the Danish word *død* ("dead"). Despite considerable variations in pronunciation, these constitute a single phoneme; we cannot establish new words by replacing one variant with another. The radical aspect of this approach is that the claim that two phenomena are distinct, rather than the claim that they are equivalent, is the qualified one. Transferred to sociology, we might ask to what extent a change in patterns of behavior will change the social structure in question.

We begin with a short overview of the arenas in which structuralist theory has found expression: Russia around the time of the revolution and in the twenties (before Stalinism silenced the tendency), Czechoslovakia between the wars, the USA during World War II, where various European intellectuals sought a haven from Nazi persecution, and France in the postwar period. Here we will focus on Roman Jakobson's significance for Russian formalism, and on Claude Lévi-Strauss and French structuralism.

Roman Jakobson and Russian Formalism

> **Biography:** *Roman Jakobson*
>
> Roman Jakobson (1896–1982) began his academic career in pre-revolutionary Russia. Jakobson spent many of the interwar years in Czechoslovakia, where he became a driving force in Czech structuralism, which, on the basis of linguistic analysis, extended the structuralist perspective to encompass all sign phenomena (as in postwar French structuralism). Nazi aggression forced Jakobson once again into exile, and after short periods in Norway and Sweden, he arrived in the USA in 1941, where he rapidly became a source of inspiration for other exiles (among them Lévi-Strauss). His extremely eclectic work ranges from the periphery of medicine (aphasia) to literary analysis, centered on linguistic subjects of every variety.

More than any other individual, it was Roman Jakobson who contributed most to the formation of structuralist linguistics and general semiology (semiotics) in accordance with the intentions of Saussure, through the development of the basis of structuralist analysis in the study of forms of language expression (phonology), but also by the application of the principles of structuralist analysis to other fields, for example, literary analysis (Jakobson 1962). As a prolific and active debater, Jakobson had a decisive influence on a large number of theorists who have since contributed to the development of the structuralist perspective, first and foremost, Claude Lévi-Strauss. It may well be that Jakobson also influenced the sociologist Talcott Parsons (see chapter 14), in that his description of pattern variables shows striking similarities with the thinking of Jakobson.

Among other representatives of Russian formalism, we can mention Vladimir Propp (1895–1970), who, through his analyses of fairy tales, revealed general narrative structures (narratology) (Propp 1971 [1928]). The subject of universal narrative structures was later adopted by French structuralism.

Claude Lévi-Strauss

> **Biography:** *Claude Lévi-Strauss*
>
> Claude Lévi-Strauss (b.1908) began his anthropological career as a field researcher in the Brazil of the 1930s. From 1935 Lévi-Strauss was a professor of anthropology at Sao Paulo. He resided in the USA during the war years, and from 1950 he was a professor in Paris.
>
> There are two strands in the writings of Lévi-Strauss. One is logical analysis, uncovering structures in social organizations and in patterns of thought. The other is active participation

in the cultures he studies. Without being antipathetic toward civilization, Lévi-Strauss continually points out how the modern world destroys existing cultures and rips away the foundations of diverse ways of life. That the "primitive" way of thinking is far from primitive in the everyday sense can be said to be his chief message.

Lévi-Strauss (b.1908) occupies an absolutely central position within structuralism. He continued a tradition extending from Durkheim through Marcel Mauss (1872–1950), Durkheim's nephew and assistant. Mauss's and Durkheim's joint work on primitive classifications, and Mauss's essay on gifts, exhibit moreover an amazing likeness to structuralist work. Against this background, Lévi-Strauss was, via Roman Jakobson, decisively influenced by semiotic structuralism. By synthesizing these two traditions, Lévi-Strauss created genuine structuralist anthropology (Lévi-Strauss 1968 [1958]).

The analysis of kinship structures

Lévi-Strauss received his breakthrough via a major work on kinship structures, *The Elementary Structures of Kinship* (1969[1949]). Kinship systems are a necessary and universal aspect of all societies. According to Lévi-Strauss, the traditional research on kinship had not produced convincing theories which could explain differences between kinship systems. Is kinship a cultural or a biological matter?

Lévi-Strauss argued that the presence of rules indicates that we are dealing with cultural matters. In all kinship systems we find one fundamental rule: incest taboo. This rule heralds the emergence of the social and cultural on earth.

The incest taboo requires a mechanism of exchange. When one cannot marry one's own siblings one needs to find a spouse from another family. Lévi-Strauss reached this conclusion by conceiving the kinship system as relations of signs. When these signs are contrasted with each other they have a meaning. Each element of the kinship system is an element of meaning. The meaning of one element, for instance, the mother, depends on how that element (the mother) can be distinguished form the other elements in the system (father, son, uncle, etc.). The system is a collective unconscious creation. The point of departure is the incest taboo. When this rule is established as the foundation of the system the rest follows automatically. You are compelled to exchange to avoid marrying someone from your own family. Thus the kinship system becomes a system of exchange.

The kinship system is a subject which is particularly well suited to structuralist analysis, in that it concerns a system possessing clearly distinctive qualities: gender, generations (up/ /down), and a number of degrees of lateral kinship. But the point is that against this universal background, archaic types of society form different kinds of kinship structure by endowing particular relations with a marked level of distinctiveness. From this are derived classificatory kinship systems, that is, systems in which individuals belong to different classes of kinship, and where marriages take place between persons from particular kinship classes.

Such kinship systems can be matrilineal (the man marries into the woman's line) or patrilineal (the woman marries into the man's line), but can also be bilineal (the female and male lines cross each other, with some relations being inherited matrilineally, others patrilineally). A kinship structure can be viewed as a kind of "grammar," and for Lévi-Strauss, kinship and language are parallel phenomena. *The Elementary Structures of Kinship* (1969[1949]) is filled with formal depictions of kinship structures, which remind one of formalized linguistics.

For Lévi-Strauss exchange is fundamental in every social relation. He operates with three different forms of exchange: exchange of articles for everyday use, exchange of messages (linguistic communication), and exchange of women between groups of kinship. Lévi-Strauss's theory of exchange enables him to provide a new explanation of the incest taboo. According to Lévi-Strauss, this cannot be explained by biology but is a social (cultural) matter. When incest takes place there is no exchange between social groups.

The central and connecting element in Lévi-Strauss's study of kinship organization is the clarification of the structural transformations between the different kinship systems.

Myths and patterns of thought

But in what follows, Lévi-Strauss changes his area of interest. He continues to focus on archaic societies, but his subject now becomes myths and patterns of thought. His analyses of patterns of thought in archaic cultures can, in brief, be described as an underlining of the importance of the principle of opposition. The central principle of structuralist linguistic analysis, distinctiveness, the definition of phenomena via their mutual opposition, is for Lévi-Strauss particularly relevant to the understanding of patterns of thought in archaic societies.

For Lévi-Strauss, there is also a connection between these two topics, in that the study of patterns of thought begins with totemistic societies, in which the organization of kinship is connected to the cognitive organization of the world, that is, a perspective through which all kinds of natural objects are seen as being related to one another and to the society in question. A minor work on totemism (Lévi-Strauss 1963) was the first to be published on this subject, but was followed by what is perhaps Lévi-Strauss's best-known book, *The Savage Mind* (Lévi-Strauss 1972). It is often said that Lévi-Strauss dismisses totemism as an illusion, but another way of looking at it would be to say that totemism represents the most complex form of a universal institution, by which groups and individuals base their sense of identity on an oppositional relationship with other groups and individuals.

Following the publication of *The Savage Mind*, Lévi-Strauss worked for many years on a massive project on the subject of mythology, which was published in four volumes (Lévi-Strauss 1973–81). He describes in this work fundamental structural similarities between the myths of different cultures, and concludes that myths possess universal, basic structures. These structures are presented as oppositional themes, of which the themes of nature//culture predominate. The myths thematize the action of humankind upon nature.

French Structuralism

Compared with Russian formalism in the twenties and Czech structuralism of the thirties, postwar French structuralism is very heterogeneous, and the degree to which we can speak of a single tendency is an open question. Lévi-Strauss and his disciples naturally belong under the heading "French structuralism," but Lévi-Strauss will only to a minor degree acknowledge a relationship with the other tendencies.

The Lithuanian-French semiotician and narratologist, A. J. Greimas (1917–92), and the psychoanalyst Jacques Lacan (1901–81) are located, as regards subject matter, at the periphery of the social sciences.

Within French structuralism, Greimas has the closest connection with Russian formalism, primarily because he continues, generalizes, and makes abstract the narratology of Propp (Greimas and Cortés 1982). Through this work, he arrives at a set of actants, structural points in the narrative, which, at the level of the text, parallel the phrase at the level of the sentence. Greimas can appear verbose, but he excels in concise and rigorous argumentation.

Lacan is by far the least accessible of the French structuralists. His main project is a reconstruction of Freud, where the subconscious is structured like a language (Lacan 1977). Among those occupying a more central position with regard to questions of social science are Louis Althusser (see chapter 9), Michel Foucault (see chapter 19), and Roland Barthes.

Roland Barthes

Barthes (1915–80) is the theorist most closely related to Saussure, in that he contributes to the realization of Saussure's dream of a universal science of signs (semiology) (Barthes 1992 [1964]). His most famous book is undoubtedly *Mythologies* (Barthes 1973), in which he propounds a concept of myth for modern societies, which closely resembles the concept of ideology. The modern ideological myth is not told directly, but reveals itself through the substitutional relationship that exists between its manifestations. The strength of the ideology (or myth) lies precisely in the fact that its ideological (mythic) content remains constant, while its manifestations vary. The myth of the excellence of the French Empire (in a period when it was threatened by various liberation movements), for example, could be communicated via a picture of a bold black soldier saluting the flag of France, but also via a picture of a French nurse tending a wounded Arab. Here Barthes undertakes an expansion of the sign model. The primary textual or pictorial sign possesses a specific expression and content. This sign, however, can function as the expression of a secondary sign, the mythic sign, for which various primary signs can stand as variants, in order to communicate a myth. The transition from the primary to the secondary level of signs is for Barthes a mechanism of meaning, and it is through this mechanism that the mythic content sneaks, so to speak, into the subject.

Other Schools of Structuralist Thought and Analysis

A fundamental premise of structuralist analysis is that culture and society organize the varying features of nature into distinctive, functional oppositions. Against this background, one could imagine a complementary relationship between the natural sciences and a structuralist analysis of culture.

This scenario is also the one sketched by the American linguist, Kenneth Pike, who introduced the terms "etics//emics," derived from phonetics (the study of physical sound qualities) as against phonemics (the study of distinctive sound qualities) (Pike, 1967). (Compare "The Principal of Opposition," above.) The idea was that this complementary relationship could form the basis of a unitary social science.

The relationship of an interaction to its surrounding space, and the formation of meaning in this context, is the theme of several analytical approaches of a semiotic character. Here we could mention Kevin Lynch with his "reading the city" (Lynch 1960) and Edward T. Hall's "proxemics" (Hall 1969), in which Lynch analyzes the city with the aid of distinctive factors such as traffic arteries, junctions, landmarks and borders (e.g. rivers), while Hall analyzes contiguous space transformed into discontiguous qualities, from intimate distance to formal distance in assemblies of people. The cultural phenomena of modern society too (e.g. subcultures) have been, to varying degrees, studied using the structuralist approach. A prominent example is the so-called "Birmingham School" (Hebdige 1979).

Fundamental Problems

In conclusion, we can observe that there are three fundamental problems that characterize the discussion of the foundation of structuralism, all of which are unresolved, in the sense that they have no generally accepted solutions. These concern the problem of universal laws, the problem of realism and the problem of consciousness.

1 Does structuralism aim at uncovering universal laws – i.e., does it follow the nomothetic ideal of natural science – or is it (in accordance with the principle of immanence) concerned with individual systems – which is to say, is it, at bottom, idiographic in nature, like traditional humanism?
2 Where does structuralism stand in the traditional debate between realism and nominalism? Do its concepts and models directly correspond to phenomena in observable reality, or are its categories merely tools to aid philosophical analysis?
3 Does structuralist analysis reflect a content which is manifest for the social actors concerned, or are there objective categories which are independent of the the actors' subjectivity?

It seems possible to suggest some solutions here which will "cut through the middle" of each of these three questions.

At their roots, all social and cultural "laws" are local in nature, in that they are based on specific historical structures. This, however, does not preclude the existence of more or less universal factors, in that differing structures can have component structures in common. The incest taboo, for example, is a universal feature of kinship structures. Lévi-Strauss derives this from the exchange of women between exogamous kinship groups, which can vary, but which possess kinship relations regulated by the incest taboo as a common core.

With regard to the question of the degree to which structures pertain to the reality under study, or are merely implements at the service of the theorist, it is clear (as most structuralists would agree) that while the analytic delineation of structures is created by theorists, this delineation must necessarily reflect distinctions within the system under study, if the analysis is to be a valid delineation of that system.

With respect to the problem of consciousness, it may be convenient to regard Durkheim's "collective consciousness" (see chapter 5), Lévi-Strauss's "unconsciousness," and Giddens's "practical consciousness" (see chapter 24) as being essentially the same phenomenon. The practical, collective, or "unconscious" consciousness is then the nonreflective consciousness forming the backdrop to routine actions. This background consciousness then gives way to a reflective consciousness (called by Giddens the discursive conscious) if something unusual happens, or if one wants to change something. The interesting thing is that the practical, background consciousness often is more "sophisticated" than the discursive conscious. A language user can, for example, utilize a very complicated grammatical structure, without ever being able to explain its grammatical rules via the discursive conscious. This practical or collective consciousness occupies a central position within structuralism's field of study. One could perhaps go so far as to say that structuralism's overall task is to reconstruct the rules followed by the social actor. From this perspective, the task of structuralism complements that of phenomenology and hermeneutics (see chapter 12), which focus on the intentional center, that is, the social actor's discursive conscious.

Does structuralism play a lesser role today than it did in the seventies? It is obviously less talked about. But one could say the same of functionalism (see chapter 14), existentialism (see chapter 17), phenomenology (see chapter 12), and other tendencies. There are those who, from a "postmodern" perspective, declare that the "great histories" are in decline (see chapter 26). It is hard to say whether they are right. But a more important question is the degree to which structuralism is now utilized. What position does structuralist theory and method occupy in the sociology of the nineties? Not many years ago, there was a sharp division within sociology between the supporters of quantitative as against qualitative method. It is now generally accepted that these are complementary approaches. It is not unlikely that yesterday's "schools" and "tendencies" are beginning to be integrated into a standard sociological science. In that case, the place of structuralism within that standard science will become a question for the sociology of science.

Bibliography

Primary:

Collected works:

Roland Barthes's collected works are being published. So far one volume has been published:
Barthes, Roland. 1993: *Oeuvres completes*. 1: 1942–1965. Paris: Seuil.
Nordquist, Joan. 1994: *Roland Barthes: A Bibliography*. Santa Cruz, CA: Reference and Research Services.

Works:

Barthes, Roland. 1972 [1971]: *Critical Essays*. Evanston, IL: Northwestern University Press.
—— 1973 [1957]: *Mythologies*. St Albans, Herts.: Paladin.
—— 1974a [1970]: *S/Z*. New York: Hill & Wang.
—— 1974b: *Structural Analysis and Biblical Exegies: Interpretational Essays*. Pittsburgh: Pickwick Press.

—— 1976a [1971]: *Sade, Fourier, Loyola*. New York: Hill & Wang.
—— 1976b [1973]: *The Pleasure of the Text*. London: Cape.
—— 1977a [1975]: *Roland Barthes by Roland Barthes*. New York: Hill & Wang.
—— 1977b [1959]: *Writing Degree Zero*. New York: Hill & Wang.
—— 1981 [1985]: *The Grain of the Voice: Interviews 1962–1980*. New York: Hill & Wang.
—— 1982: *A Barthes Reader* (ed. Susan Sontag). London: Cape.
—— 1983a [1981]: *The Fashion System*. New York: Hill & Wang.
—— 1983b [1963]: *On Racine*. New York: Hill & Wang.
—— 1984 [1977]: *A Lover's Discourse: Fragments*. New York: Hill & Wang.
—— 1985 [1982]: *The Responsibility of Forms*. New York: Hill & Wang.
—— 1986 [1970]: *The Empire of Signs*. New York: Hill & Wang.
—— 1987a [1966]: *Criticism and Truth*. Minneapolis: University of Minnesota Press.
—— 1987b [1979]: *Sollers, Writer*. London: Athlone.
—— 1987c [1954]: *Michelet*. Oxford: Blackwell.
—— 1988 [1985]: *The Semiotic Challenge*. Oxford: Blackwell.
—— 1992a [1964]: *Elements of Semiology*. New York: Hill and Wang.
—— 1992b [1987]: *Incidents*. Berkeley: University of California Press.
—— 1993 [1980]: *Camera Lucida: Reflections on Photography*. London: Vintage.
—— 1996: *Image, Music, Text: Essays*. New York: Hill & Wang.
—— 1997: *The Eiffel Tower, and Other Mythologies*. Berkeley: University of California Press.
Greimas, Algirdas J. 1970: *Du sens: essais sémiotiques*. Paris: Larousse.
—— 1972: *Essais de sémiotique poetique*. Paris: Larousse.
—— 1983a [1966]: *Structural Semantics: An Attempt at a Method*. Lincoln: University of Nebraska Press.
—— 1983b: *Du sens II: essais sémiotiques*. Paris: Seuil.
—— 1987: *On Meaning: Selected Writings in Semiotic Theory*. Minneapolis: University of Minnesota Press.
—— 1988 [1976]: *Maupassant: The Semiotics of the Text*. Amsterdam and Phila delphia: John Benjamin.
—— 1990a [1976]: *The Social Sciences, a Semiotic View*. Minneapolis: University of Minnesota Press.
—— 1990b: *Narrative Semiotics and Cognitive Discourses*. London: Pinter.
Greimas, Algirdas J., and Courtés, J. 1982 [1979]: *Semiotics and Language: An Analytic Dictionary*. Bloomington: Indiana University Press.
Greimas, Algirdas J., and Fontanille, J. 1991: *The Semiotics of Passion*. Minneapolis: University of Minnesota Press.
Jakobson, Roman. 1962: *Selected Writings*. 6 vols. The Hague: Mouton.
—— 1978: *Six Lectures on Sound and Meaning*. Cambridge, MA: MIT Press.
—— 1979: *The Sound Shape of Language* (with Linda Waugh). Bloomington: Indiana University Press.
—— 1980: *The Framework of Language*. Ann Arbor, MI: Michigan Slavic Publications.
—— 1985: *Verbal Art, Verbal Sign, Verbal Time*. Oxford: Blackwell.
Jakobson, Roman, and Halle, Morris. 1956: *Fundamentals of Language*. The Hague: Mouton.
Lacan, Jacques. 1975a: *Livre XX, Encore*. Paris: Seuil.
—— 1977 [1966]: *Ecrits: A Selection*. London: Tavistock.
—— 1978 [1973]: *Book XI, Four Fundamental Concepts of Psychoanalysis*. New York: Norton.
—— 1981a: *Livre III, Structures freudiennes dans les psychoses*. Paris: Seuil.
—— 1981b: *Speech and Language in Psychoanalysis*. Baltimore: Johns Hopkins University Press.
(Previously published as: *The Language of the Self: The Function of Language in Psychoanalysis*. Baltimore, MD: Johns Hopkins University Press, 1968).

—— 1982: *Feminine Sexuality: Jacques Lacan and the Ecole Freudienne.* London: Macmillan.

—— 1986: *Livre VII, L'ethique de la psychanalyse.* Paris: Seuil.

—— 1988a [1975]: *Book I, Freud's Writings on Technique, 1953–1954.* New York: Norton.

—— 1988b [1978]: *Book II: The Ego in Freud's Theory and in the Technique of Psychoanalysis, 1954–55.* New York: Norton.

—— 1988c: *The Seminars of Jacques Lacan. Books 1, 2, 3, 7.* Cambridge: Cambridge University Press.

—— 1990 [1974]: *Television: A Challenge to the Psychoanalytic Establishment.* New York: Norton.

—— 1991a: *Livre XVII, L'envers de la psychanalyse.* Paris: Seuil.

—— 1991b: *Livres VIII, Le transfert.* Paris: Seuil.

—— 1993: *The Psychoses.* New York: Norton.

—— 1998: *Le séminaire de Jacques Lacan; Livre 5.* Paris: Seuil.

Lévi-Strauss, Claude. 1948: *La vie familiale et sociale des indiens Nambikwara.* Paris: Société des Americanistes.

—— 1952: *Race and History.* Paris: Unesco.

—— 1963 [1962]: *Totemism Today.* Boston: Beacon Press.

—— 1967 [1960]: *The Scope of Anthropology.* London: Cape.

—— 1969 [1949]: *The Elementary Structures of Kinship.* Boston: Beacon Press.

—— 1969–78 [1958]: *Structural Anthropology.* Vol. I. London: Doubleday; *Structural Anthropology.* Vol. II. Harmondsworth, Middlesex: Penguin Books.

—— 1972 [1962]: *The Savage Mind.* London: Weidenfeld and Nicolson.

—— 1972: The Bear and the Barber. Offprint from W. Lessa and E. Z. Vogt (eds), *Reader in Comparative Religion.* New York: Harper & Row, 1963.

—— 1973–81 [1964–71]: *Introduction to a Science of Mythology.* 4 vols. London: Jonathan Cape.

—— 1974 [1955]: *Tristes tropiques.* New York: Atheneum.

—— 1977: *L'identité: séminaire interdisciplinaire.* Paris: Grasset.

—— 1982 [1979]: *The Way of Masks.* Seattle: University of Washington Press.

—— 1985 [1983]: *The View From Afar.* New York: Basic Books.

—— 1987 [1984]: *Anthropology and Myth: Lectures 1951–1982.* Oxford: Basil Blackwell.

—— 1987: *Introduction to the Work of Marcel Mauss.* London: Routledge & Kegan Paul.

—— 1988 [1985]: *The Jealous Potter.* Chicago: Chicago University Press.

—— 1991 [1988]: *Conversations with Claude Lévi-Strauss*, interviewed by Didier Eribon. Chicago: University of Chicago Press.

—— 1989: *Des symboles et leurs doubles.* Paris: Plon.

—— 1995 [1991]: *The Story of Lynx.* Chicago: University of Chicago Press.

—— 1995: *Myth and Meaning.* New York: Schocken Books.

—— 1997 [1993]: *Look, Listen, Read.* New York: Basic Books.

—— 1998: *Myth and Meaning: Five Talks for Radio.* Ann Arbor: UMI.

Lévi-Strauss, Claude, and Backes-Clement, C. 1974: *Levi-Strauss: ou la stucture et le malheur.*

Other structuralists:

Hall, Edward T. 1969: *The Hidden Dimension. Man's Use of Space in Public and Private.* New York: Doubleday.

Hebdige, Dick. 1979: *Subculture – the Meaning of Style.* London: Methuen.

Hjelmslev, Louis. 1961 [1943]: *Prolegomera to a Theory of Language.* Madison: University of Wisconsin Press.

Lynch, Kevin. 1960: *The Image of the City.* Cambridge, MA: MIT Press.

Pike, Kenneth L. 1967: *Language in Relation to a Unified Theory of Human Beha vior.* The Hague: Mouton.

Propp, Vladimir. 1971 [1928]: *Morphology of the Folk Tale*. Bloomington: Indiana University, Folklore and Linguistics.
Saussure, Ferdinand de. 1986 [1916]: *Course in General Linguistics*. La Salle, IL: Open Court.

Secondary:

*Badcock, C. R. 1975: *Lévi-Strauss: Structuralism and Sociological Theory*. London: Hutchinson.
Brachner, Mark. 1994: *Lacanian Theory of Discourse*. New York: New York Univer sity Press.
Burke, Sean. 1998: *The Death and Return of the Author: Criticism and Subjectivity in Barthes, Foucault and Derrida*. Edinburgh: Edinburgh University Press.
Caudill, David Stanley. 1997: *Lacan and the Subject of Law*. Atlantic Highlands, NJ: Humanities Press.
Chaitin, Gilbert D. 1996: *Rhetoric and Culture in Lacan*. Cambridge: Cambridge University Press.
Culler, Jonathan. 1983: *Roland Barthes*. New York: Oxford University Press.
Dor, Joel, Gurewich, Judith Feher, and Fairfield, Susan. 1997: *Introduction to the Reading of Lacan: The Unconscious Structured Like a Language*. London: Jason Aronson.
—— 1997: *The Clinical Lacan*. London: Jason Aronson.
Dosse, François. 1997: *History of Structurlism*. Minneapolis: University of Minnesota Press.
Ehrman, Jaques (ed.) 1970: *Structuralism*. New York: Doubleday.
Flower MacCannell, Juliet. 1986: *Figuring Lacan: Criticism and the Cultural Unconscious*. London and Sydney: Croom Helm.
Gurewich, Judith Feher, Tort, Michel, and Fairfield, Susan. 1996: *The Subject and the Self: Lacan and American Psychoanalysis*. London: Jason Aronson.
Holenstein, Elmar. 1974: *Roman Jakobson's Approach to Language*. Bloomington: Indiana University Press.
Julien, Philippe. 1994: *Jacques Lacan's Return to Freud*. New York: New York University Press.
Knight, Diana. 1997: *Barthes and Utopia: Space, Travel, Writing*. Oxford: Clarendon Press.
Kurzweil, Edith. 1996 [1980]: *The Age of Structuralism: From Lévi-Strauss to Foucault*. New York: Columbia University Press.
Lavers, Annette. 1982: *Roland Barthes: Structuralism and After*. Cambridge, MA: Harvard University Press.
Leach, Edmund R. 1970: *Claude Lévi-Strauss*. London: Fontana/Collins.
Lechte, John. 1994: *Fifty Key Contemporary Thinkers: From Structuralism to Postmodernity*. London: Routledge.
Moriarty, Michael. 1991: *Roland Barthes*. Cambridge: Polity Press.
Muller, John P., and Richardson, William J. 1982: *Lacan: A Reader's Guide to Ecrits*. New York: International Universities Press.
Nasio, Juan-David. 1998: *Five Lessons on the Psychoanalytic Theory of Jacques Lacan*. Albany: State University of New York Press.
Pace, David. 1983: *Claude Lévi-Strauss, The Bearer of Ashes*. Boston: Routledge & Kegan Paul.
Rabaté, Jean-Michel. 1997: *Writing the Image after Roland Barthes*. Philadelphia: University of Pennsylvania Press.
Ragland-Sullivan, Ellie. 1986: *Jacques Lacan and the Philosophy of Psychoanalysis*. Urbana and Chicago: University of Illinois Press.
Robey, David (ed.) 1973: *Structuralism. An Introduction*. Oxford: Clarendon Press.
Roudinesco, Elisabeth. 1997: *Jacques Lacan*. Cambridge: Polity Press.
Rylance, Rick. 1994: *Roland Barthes*. London: Harvester Wheatsheaf.
Schleifer, Ronald. 1987: *A.J. Greimas and the Nature of Meaning: Linguistic Semio tics and Discourse Theory*. London: Croom Helm.
Sorensen, Dolf. 1987: *Theory Formation and the Study of Literature*. Amsterdam: Rodopi.

Stafford, Andy. 1998: *Roland Barthes, Phenomenon and Myth*. Edinburgh: Edinburgh University Press.

Steiner, Peter. 1984: *Russian Formalism: A Metapoetics*. Ithaca, NY: Cornell University Press.

*Sturrock, John (ed.) 1979: *Structuralism and Since, from Lévi-Strauss to Derrida*. Oxford: Oxford University Press.

Waugh, Linda. 1976: *Roman Jakobson's Science of Language*. Erdenheim: John Benjamins North America.

Wulf, Catharina. 1997: *The Imperative of Narration: Beckett, Bernhard, Schopenhauer, Lacan*. Brighton: Sussex Academic Press.

Zizek, Slavoj. 1997: *Looking Awry: An Introduction to Lacan through Popular Culture*. London: MIT.

chapter 19

Michel Foucault

Sven-Åke Lindgren

KEY CONCEPTS

ARCHAEOLOGY – a method of historical research aimed at the statements of discourses and statement processes (practices) whose primary purpose is to reveal the discursive rules that constitute various fields of knowledge.

BIOPOWER – a kind of power that has developed since the seventeenth century, which operates by disciplining individuals and regulating the population.

DISCOURSE – usually explained as a "regulated order of talk," but here it includes the concept of chains of statements, institutionalized statement processes (practices), and the historically and culturally determined rules that regulate the form and content of the order of talk.

EPISTEME – a structured field of knowledge or the unreflected conditions, the historical and cultural patterns, that determine what is thought and what is conceivable during various periods.

GENEALOGY – a method of historical research aimed at the discovery and derivation of power relationships for the purpose of creating a foundation for criticizing contemporary phenomena.

PANOPTIC – an all-seeing form of surveillance that can be traced back to Jeremy Bentham's idea of an "inspection house," where from a central point it is possible to see and monitor what is going on all around.

POWER ANALYTICS – the inductive approach to a more complex power analysis that is used to study biopower.

PRACTICES – rule-controlled actions, conduct, procedures, methods, etc. that have to do with discourses, but also institutions and systems. A *discursive practice* can be, for example, the specific procedure of social science for developing and reproducing knowledge about an object of knowledge (e.g. unemployment). A *nondiscursive practice* can correspond to political events within an institutional field, an economic state of the market, a technological invention, etc. *Non-discursive practices* are in Foucault's epistemology elements which are taken up and transformed by *discursive practices*, rather than "background factors" causing or determining these practices.

Biography: *Michel Foucault*

Paul-Michel Foucault was born in Poiters on October 15, 1926. When the war ended in 1945, he came to Paris and entered the elite university, the Ecole Normale Supérieure in 1946, where he received his basic degrees in philosophy and psychology. Foucault was in Uppsala in Sweden from 1955 to 1958, where he was a lecturer in French and director of the Maison de France. He returned to France in 1960, following brief sojourns in Warsaw and Hamburg, and began teaching psychology at Clermont-Ferrand University. A year later Foucault received the highest French doctoral degree with *Madness and Civilization* as his main dissertation. In 1962 he became professor of philosophy at Clermont-Ferrand University and during the following years he was a visiting professor in Tunis, during which time he published *The Birth of the Clinic* (1973 [1963]) and *The Order of Things* (1970 [1966]). The latter brought him renown outside French academic circles as well. In 1968 Foucault was appointed professor and head of the Department of Philosophy at the newly established university in Vincennes, Paris. Thus he landed in the conflicts and open battles that challenged university life that year. Foucault's notoriety grew even more in 1969, when he was elected to the Collège de France as professor of the History of Systems of Thought. He spent the following year teaching, doing research, and becoming more involved in politics. In 1971 he formed le Groupe d'Information sur les Prisons (Group for Information on Prisons) and this initiative was followed by active work in various working groups. In 1975 he published *Discipline and Punish* (English translation 1997), a study that marked a heightened interest in the disciplining effects of power. The analysis of power is also at the center of his next work, the first part of *The History of Sexuality*, which was published in 1976 (English translation 1978). The second and third parts of this work were not published until 1984. Meanwhile Foucault reconsidered the direction of his project, which was initially intended to include six different parts. The two later parts included a more active individual actor, which many believed Foucault had made far too strictly parenthetical in his earlier works. Michel Foucault died in Paris on June 25, 1984.

A Transgressor

Esbern Krause-Jensen (1985) used the expression "nomad philosophy" to describe various tendencies in recent French philosophy. By that he means departing, going beyond, and further developing existing forms of Marxism and psychoanalysis. The metaphor of no-madic life is quite useful for beginning a discussion of Michel Foucault. He was among those who departed from the dominant traditions of thought in his time. In his case, this was primarily a departure from hermeneutics (the theory of interpretation) and the idea of an underlying truth, as well as phenomenology and emphasis on the subject's intentions. But he is also a nomad with respect to his own work. He changes topics, empirical fields, meth-ods, and emphases, frequently, without comment or explanation. This changeability is am-plified by the absence of any explicit feedback or reference to his own previous studies. The nomadic aspect also comes through in another regard: in Foucault's stubborn resistance against all efforts to label him and to place him in some direction or -ism.

Foucault was not out to develop general theories of man and society. On the contrary, all his work was aimed at demonstrating that it is unreasonable and harmful to develop thought and theory structures with universal claims. Instead, he tried to demonstrate the usefulness of concrete research in limited empirical fields. He was a philosopher by trade, but his work is far too extensive and interdisciplinary to be confined by this limited academic field of endeavor. Based on the topics and depth of his studies, he can also be seen as a social or ideological historian, a scientific, literary, and cultural theoretician, or a sociologist. In ad-dition, he worked extensively in arenas other than academia. In his capacity as an intellec-tual, he contributed analysis and commentary to the public social debate and, in his role as an activist, he was involved in work toward practical social and political change. What we have said so far implies that Foucault can be read and understood through various interpre-tations. This chapter will concentrate on his studies involving the exercise and functions of power. This means it will concentrate on Foucault's "middle period," that is, the books *Discipline and Punish* (1977 [1975]) and *The History of Sexuality. Vol. 1: An Introduction* (1978 [1976]). This delimitation and emphasis will bring out the sociological aspects of Foucault's work. Finally, his influence on developments within sociology today will be examined. First, however, we will outline Foucault's earlier work.

The Asylum and the Clinic

Madness and Civilization (1989 [1961]) describes how the insane were singled out as a separate category from among the heterogeneous mass of beggars, vagabonds, whores, robbers, cripples, invalids, etc., who a hundred years before had been the objects of the "great incarceration" in hospitals, workhouses, and correctional facilities throughout Eu-rope. Toward the end of the eighteenth century, lunatics were given their own institutions: the asylums. Here it was possible to study insanity. However, the scientific ambition was limited to observation and classification. It was never a matter of dialogue with those who represented insanity. According to current historical research, the French physician Philippe Pinel was a great humanist. It was he who freed the lunatics from their chains in the Bicêtre Hospital in 1794. Foucault, however, hardly sees this event as a crucial break with the past or a victory for humanism and enlightenment. He believes such an interpretation is more an expression of empty idealization. The lunatic that Pinel liberates encounters a freedom that consists of new and different chains. There are normative judgements and labelings that require something in return in the form of affirmative self-accusation. Without this stigmatizing consent you remain a captive of the asylum. Thus, psychiatry arises from a morally infected ground. Psychiatric knowledge is coordinated with power, whose purpose is to correct and normalize under the guidance of rational reason. This is a reason whose bounds are set by talk about and the practical distinction from its diametric opposite – insanity.

In *The Birth of the Clinic* (1973 [1963]) Foucault deals with the development of medical practice during the period 1760 to 1810. This is a period in which a new kind of view, clinical observation, revealed domains that had previously been invisible. Both the body (life) and death become objects of this new, explanatory view. Diseases are no longer interpreted in terms of the metaphysics of evil, but in relation to experience-based knowledge that developed when autopsies became common. Foucault believes that this incorporation of death into medical thinking gave birth to a new kind of medicine in the form of a science of the living individual. In an astonishingly short period of time a new scientific discourse (theoretical and conceptual system) and an anatomical/clinical order were established. Foucault points to certain specific thought models, power relationships, and practices as building blocks in this process of coming into being: a medical profession defined on the basis of competence criteria, a physician supported by an institution and having power to make decisions, a new relationship between doctor and patient based on observation and questioning, and a clinical view that evaluates and calculates, constantly looking for the pathological.

Foucault credits medical science with playing an extremely important role in the growth of the human sciences. It serves an exemplary function in establishing human existence as an object of positive knowledge. It is also from medical science's new view of life and death that both a fundamental and general anthropology (a view of man), essential to all human sciences, emerges.

"The Death of Man"

The Order of Things (Foucault 1970 [1966]) is a profound reflection on the patterns that order experiences and conceptions into a distinct system of knowledge and how various patterns give knowledge its specific meaning. These patterns are called *episteme* (Greek: knowledge). Foucault unearths these spontaneous conditions of our knowledge, from the Middle Ages to modern times. This presentation deals with the areas of language, nature, and economics, and the problem he raises is how knowledge in these areas was shaped during the Renaissance, the classical period, and since the beginning of the nineteenth century. At this time the modern *episteme* emerges, which, according to Foucault, is characterized by the fact that life, language, and work become domains with their own historicity and that it is given a pronounced anthropological foundation. In a new way, man becomes the center of the field of knowledge. It is from him that the order of things emanates.

Foucault's uncovering of the foundations of European knowledge leads him to a perspective that questions the Enlightenment's ideal of knowledge. According to Foucault, knowledge is contextually bound in history and culture, and not universal. The movement of history is discontinuous – not cumulative in general – and man's position and significance in this context is not at all as crucial as humanism would have us believe. The fact is, Foucault concludes, that man is a recent "invention" – an "invention" that in a future episteme could well "be erased like a face drawn in the sand at the edge of the sea" (Foucault 1970: 387).

The Order of Things was a great success and Foucault became a celebrity, at least in France. This popularity was certainly a result of the stormy debate sparked by the book. The proclamation of the "death of man" (note the parallel with Friedrich Nietzsche [1844–1900] and his proclamation that "God is dead"), a parenthetic subject, and a historical account based on structures, caused a great stir among many people. It added additional fuel to the fire in the so-called structuralism battle, the issue that drew the battle lines, initiated by Claude Lévi-Strauss (see chapter 18) several years earlier. The structuralists attempted to bypass the question of meaning and the meaning-giving subject by focusing on structures as decisive for human action. For Foucault it is the concept and the system that are stressed, and when asked when he stopped believing in "meaning" he answered:

> The break came the day that Lévi-Strauss demonstrated – about societies – and Lacan demonstrated – about the unconscious – that "meaning" was probably only a sort of surface effect, a shimmer, a foam, and that what ran through us, underlay us, and was before us, what sustained us in time and space, was the system. (Foucault, in Eribon 1991: 161)

Even though Foucault cannot be seen as an orthodox structuralist, he has been identified with that camp. It was a label he tried to escape, in part by clarifying his project and his method.

The Statement in Focus

In *The Archaeology of Knowledge* (1989 [1969]) Foucault develops a special method: archaeology directed at discourses. It deals with an investigation of what has already been said on the discursive level. Archaeology attempts to define the actual statements as practices that are subject to certain rules, historically and culturally determined rules that determine what statements are produced and in what way this is done. The primary analytical element of archaeology is the statement, which is seen as an irreducible element. According to Foucault, the statement is one object among others that man produces, uses, changes, and exchanges. As stated before, he is not looking for some underlying meaning (truth) or, for that matter, an understanding derived from the subject's properties and intentions. The subject's place has been taken over by the composite circumstances that make room for a speaking subject.

This discourse is also a recurring theme in his inaugural lecture, *The Order of Discourse* (1982 [1971]). It is a summary of Foucault's archaeological project, with a discussion of the procedures and principles that regulate, control, organize, and distribute the dissemination and effects of the discourse. There are also indications here of projects in the making and Foucault introduces the genealogy (analysis of descent) as an approach that complements archaeology.

At this point it may be a good time to summarize the main features of Foucault's early production. With the archaeological discourse analysis he uncovers the rise of a positive knowledge that has man and human life as its primary object of knowledge. This objectification of man produces a new rationality of that which is human, which is then reversed toward the subject in order to elucidate boundaries and bring about change. This creates a new and different self-consciousness and man as subject is changed. It is this process of subjectivation that Foucault gives as his primary theme: "to create a history of the different modes by which, in our culture, human beings are made subjects" (Foucault, in Dreyfus and Rabinow 1986: 208). It is important to note in this context that the term "subject" means "human being," "person," "individual," but "subservient," "subordinate," and "vulnerable" are also understood (Beronius 1991: 82). It is submission that results from being subjected to a historically new knowledge and the accompanying social practices that shape modern man. Thus, subjectivation and knowledge are truly the major items in Foucault's early work. Power and its significance have not yet emerged as the third component in the triangular drama – power, knowledge, and the subject – that forms the recurring theme of Foucault's work during the 1970s.

The Generalized Prison

In the late eighteenth century a change occurred in the perspective on penal law. The soul (conscience) and not the body became the primary object of punishment. Of course, the tradition of the great incarceration of the seventeenth century played an important role in the new order of incarceration that developed. Another significant factor was the classical theories of punishment that were formulated around the mid-eighteenth century. Cesare Beccaria (1738–94) and other legal philosophers objected to the arbitrariness and brutality of authorities and called for a penal system that was rational with respect to changed economic, social, and political conditions in a society that was increasingly dominated by the growing bourgeoisie. In 1791 the English philosopher Jeremy Bentham (1748–1832) presented his idea of a *panopticon* or "inspection house." This was a prison built around an inner tower and having an outer ring of cells, all of which could be observed from the tower in the middle. Bentham presented his creation as a universal model for all buildings involved in activities that required supervision: hospitals, asylums, workhouses, schools, factories, etc. His model provided an answer to the question of how the few could watch the many and how this surveillance could be made more efficient, so that those who were watched could always be observed and thus must live their lives knowing there was a risk that they could always be seen.

But how could imprisonment become so universally prevalent and popular in such a short time? How could it take over as the sole alternative to the differentiated scale of corporal punishment and humiliation that had been used for centuries? In *Discipline and Punish* (1977 [1975]) Foucault stresses one circumstance that may explain the rapid triumph of the prison system: the thorough disciplining process that comprises an inseparable part of the emergent capitalist society.

According to Foucault, incarceration is more than a legal deprivation of freedom. It is not just a punishment, but also a process for converting the incarcerated individuals. Punishment is not primarily repayment for an incurred injury, but more a supervised penance emanating from the individual, his biography, and causal connections derived therefrom. Thus, the execution of the sentence is separated from the offence against the law per se. Even though the prison is part of a larger legal context, on the inside it is a system that judges and treats the inmates in accordance with moral standards. On the outside the legal system prevails, but inside the walls the system of norms rules. It is a system that constructs a specific biographical unit: the criminal unit, which is characterized by all manner of short-comings and dangers that represent a deviation from what is perceived as normal.

The advance of the prison system forms an outer framework for Foucault's presentation. But the modern prison is merely an extreme manifestation of a more general process of conversion in the emergent capitalist society. There is an all-encompassing disciplinary power that permeates the entire "social body." This power does not operate solely behind prison walls, but also on military bases, in the new factory buildings, in schoolrooms, and in hospitals. Foucault sees new spatial creations everywhere in which individuals are sepa-rated out of the collective and subjected to various disciplinary techniques. Typical of this disciplinary power is its hierarchical supervision, normalizing sanctions, and integration of these into various examination processes (examination in the sense of scrutiny and testing).

Foucault likens the new disciplinary formation of society to a generalized prison, but he points out that discipline cannot be reduced solely to a negative, destructive force. It is highly positive. It produces not only the criminal as a new type of person, but also the obedient soldier, the useful worker, and the educated and trained child. Regardless of its institutional ties, the goal of this disciplinary technology is to mould docile bodies: compe-tent individuals who can be used, changed, and developed. In his history of discipline and punishment, Foucault develops for the first time the theme of power/knowledge in an ex-plicit manner and he links this new form of supervisory social control to the emergence of capitalism. These techniques precede modern capitalism. According to Foucault, while they do not cause its emergence, they are essential preconditions for the success of capitalism.

Speaking of Sex

In *The History of Sexuality, volume 1: An Introduction* (1978 [1976]) Foucault turns up-side down the traditional notion that since the seventeenth century we have been in an epoch that has imposed an oppressive silence around sex. On the contrary, he says, we live in a time that is characterized by a veritable explosion of talk on and around sex. At least since the eighteenth century, when the population problem began to be an issue, discourses have been developed incessantly concerning human lust and bodily pleasure. These are discourses based on analysis, statistics, classification, and specification, a quantitative and causal study centered around sex. This analysis of sexual behavior, its causes and effects, ushered in an era with countless power centers that observe sexuality in a unique manner.

Historically, according to Foucault, there are two procedures for revealing the truth about sex. On one hand, we have societies that have created an *ars erotica* (China, Japan, India, Rome, etc.), an art of love that presents a truth from the pleasure itself. On the other hand, we have a *scientia sexualis* in which Western civilization is unique. Here the truth about sex is expressed in a language that is based on power/knowledge and that has confession as its primary expression. It is a truth ritual that goes back to Christian penance and confession and the accompanying admission of the practice of pleasure. This is an order that can be

traced back to the thirthteenth century, after which Foucault says that "we have since become a singularly confessing society" (Foucault 1978: 59). Of course, confession has changed
since it left the former penance procedures, developed by way of eighteenth-century pedagogy and nineteenth-century medical science, and ended up in totally different contexts. In
the past, one spoke to a priest, schoolteacher, or physician, but now it may be a social
worker, family counsellor, or therapist, or, for that matter, it may be some other kind of
professional adviser whose job it is to guide people down the difficult path of life.

Discipline and Regulation

In the latter two works mentioned above, the issue of power comes to the fore. Foucault calls
this concentration on power *power analytics*. This is not a theory or elucidating analysis with
a certain direction, but rather preparations that can lay the groundwork for a more complex
power analysis. In focus for these analytics is *biopower*, a type of power that has developed
since the seventeenth century and whose highest function is not to kill, "but to invest life
through and through" (Foucault 1978: 139). This is a power that works in two directions: first
disciplining of the individual and secondly control of the population. Foucault is not interested in the nature of power or the intentions of those who have it, but rather in its exercise
and effects on the level of those subjugated by it. He speaks of *micropower*, power that permeates the "capillaries" of people in their concrete situation on an everyday social level.

To grasp this power, which is exercised by administrative techniques, such as control and
normalization, rather than by legislated principles and rights, we must free ourselves of
certain deeply rooted ideas that localize power within the legal sphere of the state. We
should avoid reducing power by deducing all power as emanating from one phenomenon,
such as the domination of the bourgeoisie and, instead, examine how the mechanisms of
power actually operate and note both their intended and their unintended consequences.
Power relationships are never simple projections of class relationships or political relationships. Relationships between the genders, between generations, between natives and immigrants, relations within existing institutions, etc., make possible the existence and functioning
of the state. But they are not projections of the state's power. Every network of relationships has its own power pattern and relative autonomy.

An important part of this *power analytic* is the identification of detailed power rituals and
the identification of the place of these rituals within the social field (Dreyfus and Rabinow
1986: 110). Through his analysis of the origin of the prison system and the discourse of sex,
Foucault identifies and localizes two key power rituals (power principles): the all-seeing
surveillance (panoptic) and the confession. Without question, they comprise two key components in the social control that permeates modern Western social formation.

A basic force

How, then, are we to understand Foucault's concept of power? The simplest way is to begin
with a negative definition, that is, to try and clarify what it is not. It is not a resource or an
ability that someone possesses, nor a possession that can be exchanged, nor is it synonymous
with an institution or structure, and power has no specific form or localization. Power is not

something that is primarily destructive and negative (Deleuze 1988; Brenner 1994: 679). Foucault's power refers rather to an elementary force that is primary with respect to social formations and essentially a basic constituent of every social relationship. Thus, every relationship is a power relationship, although this must be understood as an open and variable play of forces. Consequently, Foucault conceptualizes power using clear physical analogies and he speaks of the *microphysics* of power as the term for how it works (Dreyfus and Rabinow 1986: 114). Power, or force, has no separate being. It is a neutral capacity to affect, to influence, and to change. Like force, power is operational in nature – and it is the mechanisms and effects, power and the exercise thereof, that his analysis focuses upon. This is an emphasis that prompted Gilles Deleuze to speak of a *new functionalism* (Deleuze 1988; Brenner 1994).

There are three original aspects of Foucault's concept of power that should be stressed. They are the relationship between power and institutions, the mutual dependence between power and knowledge, and his view of the subject with respect to power. As we have seen, Foucault rejects the idea that power is synonymous with specific institutions. He believes that power precedes institutions. The latter represent power, but do not produce it. In Foucault's view, institutions are operational instances that integrate and reproduce existing power relationships. The state, the family, religion, science, the market, etc. comprise points of concentration that absorb, coordinate, and disperse power.

Another characteristic is the mutual dependence between power and knowledge. This refers to modern knowledge that examines and evaluates in the search for truth, where man himself is the primary object of knowledge. The process is generative and results in a constant production of new experience and insights, which are reversed onto the knowing subject. It is knowledge that constantly oscillates between these poles: man as both the subject and the object of the knowledge process; it is knowledge directed both outwardly and inwardly, a process that puts into motion, touches, and affects. Thus, knowledge is an inseparable part of power in the sense of the force, or capacity to affect, that operates between the various entities of the social field (individuals, groups, organizations, systems, etc.). Power and knowledge imply and presuppose each other and in every social situation we find a dynamic interplay between these two aspects.

Foucault's way of conceptualizing and illustrating power and its effects also includes an indirect criticism of the assumption in the liberal (humanistic) tradition of thought of a presocial subject and of Marxism's assumption of authentic (objective) human interests as something external to power relationships (Sawicki 1991: 22). In Foucault's presentation, man in his capacity as a self-conscious individual is a social and cultural product. There is no void outside power/knowledge relationships, no entry and exit to an original, natural, or true dimension, from which man comes and to which he can return.

Thus, Foucault's presentation differs from the power that usually takes shape in the area of political theory. This distinction can be made clear with the help of Jana Sawicki (1991: 20–1) in the following table:

The juridico-discursive model:	*Foucault's model:*
– Power is possessed.	– Power is exercised rather than possessed.
– Power flows from a centralized source from top to bottom.	– Power is analyzed as coming from the bottom up.
– Power is primarily repressive in its exercise.	– Power is not primarily repressive, but productive.

Foucault's analysis of power has been subjected to extensive criticism (Hoy 1986; Habermas 1987; Fraser 1989; McNay 1992; Brenner 1994). One of the goals of this criticism is the issue of the normative motives and practical possibilities of resistance. Foucault's perspective, with its emphasis on subordination and discipline, tends to present the subject as far too determined, compliant, and passive. Why and how is this "minimal actor" to offer resistance? On what normative foundation can resistance be built if human rights and general legal principles are made relative and reduced to control mechanisms and disciplinary techniques? Foucault believes that there is always resistance where there is power (Foucault 1978: 95–6). It is not on the outside with respect to power. Resistance too must be thought of in terms of *microphysics*. Resistance comprises the various obstacles and impediments that power or force meets in its motion.

By analogy to the fact that power cannot be reduced to an overriding principle, this means there is no resistance with a capital R, that there is no specific rebellion or revolt center, and that there is no one pattern into which all resistance can be placed. Instead, according to Foucault, we have many different types of resistance: spontaneous, concerted, solitary, violent, selfish, altruistic, compromising, unrelenting, etc. But does this not mean that power embraces resistance, that power and thus oppression are inevitable? After all, with Foucault's conceptualization of power and resistance there is no external position with respect to power, from which resistance can rise. This critical slant ignores the fact that, for Foucault, power per se is always relational and that the relations are not asymmetrical and hierarchical in advance. Relational power can be seen as a strategic game and the outcome of this game is open, since the power relationships are changeable, fluid, and reciprocal. Foucault makes a distinction between power per se and the dominant conditions that arise when power relationships are fixed in asymmetrical and hierarchical conditions of dominance (Beronius 1991: 116). For Foucault, these conditions are examples of a certain power constellation, but they are not the same as power in general.

A Synthesis Suggested

The question is whether, in his last two works, *The History of Sexuality, volume 2: The Use of Pleasure* (1985 [1984]) and *The History of Sexuality, volume 3: The Care of the Self* (1986 [1984]), he does not open up his perspective of power as something that disciplines and makes compliant, conceding more room for action to the subject. In these two works, in which the empirical material comprises the discourse of sexuality in the form of numerous texts from ancient Greece and imperial Rome, it is not disciplinary control and confessions that form the background for the presentation. Instead, Foucault focuses on the voluntary processes through which people attempt to transform themselves. This attitude is associated with an ethics-oriented moral concept, which means that:

> the individual delimits that part of himself that will form the object of his moral practice, defines his position relative to the precept he will follow, and decides on a certain mode of being that will serve as his moral goal. And this requires him to act upon himself, to monitor, test, improve, and transform himself. (Foucault 1985: 28)

It is an ethics-oriented moral understanding that Foucault contrasts to the law-oriented moral understanding he previously emphasized, that is, the system of social control and confession that can be traced to legalized ethics that work through regulative and controlling institutions. This opening toward more room for a reflecting subject who acts on the basis of his own deliberation can be seen, at least in part, as a new direction. At the same time, however, it must be stressed that this is not a question of re-establishing a subject in the sense of an individual with original and genuine properties or, for that matter, an awakening of universal values. The individual shapes and improves himself in relation to the discourses that encompass and fill the social field.

Of course, one might think that Foucault's concentration on self-constructing practices are simply a result of the fact that ancient Greece and imperial Rome lacked a social infrastructure with disciplinary control and regulatory confessional systems. Such an objection can be countered, however, by saying that in his last series of lectures and in his final seminars Foucault suggests a synthesis of different ways in which people become subjects. The topic of these final comments was self-constructing and the "governmental rationality" (Martin et al. 1988; Bernauer and Rasmussen 1988; Gordon 1991: 1–49). In these lectures he studies social control at various social levels: care and shaping of oneself, intimate interpersonal relationships, relations between institutions and societies, and relations with relevance to the exercise of political power. He deals with various historical epochs: Antiquity and the early Christian period, seventeenth-century Europe, the eighteenth century and the rise of liberalism, and the late twentieth century with its neoliberal thinking. Foucault sees a characteristic feature of control practice in the development of the Western world, namely a strong tendency toward political control in the form of regulating each and every person. In the modern welfare state, with its sanction-based control of social threats and modeling of desirable individual careers that are disseminated by the mass media, historically different forms of subject genesis flow together. It is a form of control that is anxious both to totalize and to individualize. We can say that it is a formula for control that makes us confuse the vestments of normality with individual freedom.

Genealogy, or the History of Today

In the 1970s, when Foucault concentrated his studies on power and the exercise thereof, this also resulted in a change of method. He did not abandon archaeology, but genealogy was given a clear precedence. This is an analytical form that takes into account the relatedness of phenomena, their origin and transformation, in contrast to traditional history that is primarily narrative interested in a beginning, an identity, a cause, and a development. It is not hidden meaning and stated intentions that interest the genealogist, but relationships among forces that are expressed in various historical situations. In Foucault's version, genealogy is a de-psychologized perspective. Psychological motives are never a source of historical events, but rather a result of "strategies without strategists" (Dreyfus and Rabinow 1986: 109). For the genealogist there is no subject, individually or collectively, which enters the political scene and puts it into motion. The subjects emerge on a delimited field, where they participate in a network of dynamic power relationships. They play their roles and it is in this capacity that they interest the genealogist.

Compared to the archaeologist, the genealogist has a more interpretive method. According to Beronius (1991: 60), genealogy belongs to the same family tree as hermeneutics, but it rejects interpretative work that seeks deeper meaning and critical truth. Dreyfus and

Rabinow (1986) call Foucault's version of genealogy an *interpretive analytic* beyond structuralism and hermeneutics. Flyvbjerg (1997: 95) uses the expression *decipherment* (Foucault's term in French is *déchiffrement*) to stress the method's originality and he points out that it is a method that encompasses both interpretation (knowledge from within) and historical analysis (explanation from without).

The "Foucault Effect"

Foucault's work has had, and continues to have, a great influence. In some areas, the so-called Foucault effect is almost overwhelming. The social history of psychiatry and medicine, the social control of modern society, the social construction of identities, the history of sexuality, the exercise and effects of power are examples of areas and topics in which no well-informed presentation can proceed without relating to Foucault. At this point, we should also add the increased interest regarding the body in what has been somewhat vaguely called postmodern sociology and cultural studies (see chapter 26). This is a problematization that, to a great extent, can be traced back to Foucault's studies on biopower and the strategy of creating docile bodies (Turner 1991: 1–35). We also see new interest in Foucault's work and historical method among historians (Goldstein 1994) and attempts to incorporate an "effective history" into historical sociology (Dean 1994). Foucault's influence can also be detected in what Swidler and Arditi (1994) call the new sociology of knowledge, which stresses institutional production of knowledge rather than knowledge in relation to the individual's localization and interests.

Even though Foucault's world is a male world, his work has also had considerable significance in the development of feminist theory (Hekman 1996). According to Sawicki (1991, 1994), this is because both feminism (chapter 29) and Foucault have attempted to "emancipate" power from the traditional conceptualization of political theory. Thus, to many his works appear as an alternative to liberal and Marxist emancipation theories. This is particularly true of feminists who reject a gender concept based on essential categories of inherent (true) qualities and who distrust the idea of a universal global sisterhood based on a uniform notion of femininity. Of course, there are also feminists who are considerably more negative and who believe he has had a harmful influence. There is criticism aimed at the perceived relativism, nihilism, and pessimism in the work of Foucault (Fraser 1989, Hartsock 1990) a criticism that has been articulated outside feminism as well.

The examples above indicate something of the scope and penetrating power that characterizes the "Foucault effect." It is an effect that can be traced to a man of uncommon curiosity and keen insight who opposed the framework surrounding the thinking of his time and began to cross boundaries. Or perhaps it was the case that for several decades in France there existed the precise combination of circumstances that made room for a mobile subject in the borderland between certain systems of thought and certain discursive practices.

Bibliography

Primary:

Bibliography:

Nordquist, Joan. 1986: *Michel Foucault: A Bibliography*. Santa Cruz: Reference & Research Service.

Foucault, Michel. 1954: *Maladie mentale et personnalité*. Paris: Presses Universitaires de France.
—— 1970 [1966]: *The Order of Things: An Archaeology of the Human Sciences*. New York: Random House.
—— 1973 [1963]: *The Birth of the Clinic*. New York: Vintage.
—— 1976 [1962]: *Mental Illness and Psychology*. New York: Harper & Row.
—— 1977 [1975]: *Discipline and Punish*. New York: Pantheon.
—— 1978 [1976]: *The History of Sexuality. Vol. 1: An Introduction*. New York: Pantheon.
—— 1979: *Les machines a guerir: aux origines de l'hospital moderne*. Brussels: P. Mardaga.
—— 1980: *Herculine Barbin*. New York: Pantheon Books.
—— 1982a [1971]: *The Archeology of Knowledge and the Discourse on Language*. New York: Pantheon Books; also published 1971 in *Social Science Information*, 10/2.
—— 1982b: *I, Pierre Riviere, Having Slaughtered my Mother, my Sister, and my Brother – : A Case of Parricide in the 19th Century*. Lincoln: University of Nebraska Press.
—— 1983: *This is Not a Pipe*. Berkeley: University of California Press.
—— 1985 [1984]: *The Use of Pleasure: History of Sexuality, Vol. 2*. New York: Pantheon.
—— 1986a [1984]: *The Care of the Self. The History of Sexuality, Vol. 3*. New York: Pantheon.
—— 1986b [1963]: *Death and the Labyrinth; World of Raymond Roussel*. New York: Doubleday.
—— 1987 [1986]: *Foucault, Blanchot*. New York: Zone.
—— 1989a [1961]: *Madness and Civilization: A History of Insanity in the Age of Reason*. London: Routledge.
—— 1989b [1969]: *The Archeology of Knowledge*. London: Routledge.
—— 1993: *Dream and Existence*, ed. Ludwig Binswanger. Atlantic Highlands, NJ: Humanities Press.
—— 1997: *The Politics of Truth*, ed. Sylvère Lotringer, and Lysa Hochroth. New York: Semiotext(e).
—— 1998: *Aesthetics: Method and Epistemology. The Essential Works of Michel Foucault, vol. 2*, ed. James F. Faubion. New York: New Press.
—— 2000: *Power. Essential Works of Michel Foucault, vol. 3*, ed. James F. Faubion, and Colin Gordon. New York: New Press.

Collections of articles, notes, and interviews with Michel Foucault:

Bouchard, Donald Fernand, and Simon, Sherry (eds) 1980: *Language, Counter-Memory, Practice: Selected Essays and Interviews*. Ithaca, NY: Cornell University Press.
Burchell, Graham, Gordon, Colin, and Miller, Peter (eds) 1991: *The Focault Effect: Studies in Governmentality: With Two Lectures by and an Interview with Michel Foucault*. London: Harvester Wheatsheaf.
Defert, Daniel, and Ewald, François (eds) 1994: *Dits et écrits: 1954–1988*. 4 vols. Paris: Gallimard.
*Gordon, Colin (ed.) 1980: *Power/Knowledge: Selected Interviews and Other Writings 1972–1977 by Michel Foucault*. New York: Pantheon Books.
*Kritzman, Lawrence D. (ed.) 1988: *Michel Foucault, Politics, Philosophy, Culture. Interviews and Other Writings 1977–1984*. London: Routledge.
Lotringer, Sylvère (ed.) 1989: *Foucault Live (Interviews 1966–84)*. New York: Semiotext(e) Foreign Agents Series.

*Rabinow, Paul (ed.) 1984: *The Foucault Reader*. New York: Pantheon Books.

——— 1997: *Ethics, Subjectivity and Truth. The Essential Works of Michel Foucault 1954–1984, vol. 1*. New York: New Press. [Selections from *Dits et Ecrits*.]

Trombadori, Duccio (ed.) 1991: *Remarks on Marx: Conversations with Duccio Trombadori*. New York: Semiotext(e).

Secondary:

Arac, Jonathan (ed.) 1988: *After Foucault: Humanistic Knowledge, Postmodern Challenges*. New Brunswick, NJ: Rutgers University Press.

Barker, Philip. 1998: *Michel Foucault: An Introduction*. Edinburgh: Edinburgh University Press.

Barry, Andrew, Osborne, Thomas, and Rose, Nikolas. 1996: *Foucault and Political Reason: Liberalism, Neo-liberalism, and Rationalities of Government*. London: UCL Press.

Bernauer, James, and Rasmussen, David (eds) 1988: *The Final Foucault*. Cambridge, MA: MIT Press.

Beronius, Mats. 1991: *Genealogi och sociologi. Nietzsche, Foucault och den sociala analysen*. Kungshult: Brutus Östlings Bokförlag Symposion.

Brenner, Neil. 1994: Foucault's New Functionalism. *Theory and Society*, 23, 679–709.

Burchell, Graham, Gordon, Colin, and Miller, Peter (eds) 1991: *The Foucault Effect: Studies in Governmentality. With two Lectures by and an Interview with Michel Foucault*. London: Harvester Wheatsheaf.

Dant, Tim. 1991: *Knowledge, Ideology & Discourse. A Sociological Perspective*. London and New York: Routledge.

Dean, Mitchell. 1994: *Critical and Effective Histories. Foucault's Methods and Historical Sociology*. London and New York: Routledge.

Deleuze, Gilles. 1988: *Foucault*. Minneapolis: University of Minnesota Press.

Dreyfus, Hubert, and Rabinow, Paul. 1986: *Michel Foucault: Beyond Structuralism and Hermeneutics. With an Afterword by Michel Foucault*. Brighton: Harvester Press.

Dumm, Thomas L. 1996: *Michel Foucault and the Politics of Freedom*. Thousand Oaks, CA: Sage.

*Eribon, Didier. 1991: *Michel Foucault (1926–1984)*. London: Faber.

Flyvbjerg, Bent. 1997: *Rationality and Power, Democracy in Practice*. Chicago: University of Chicago Press.

Fraser, Nancy. 1989: *Unruly Practices: Power, Discourse and Gender in Contemporary Social Theory*. Cambridge: Polity Press.

Goldstein, Jan (ed.) 1994: *Foucault and the Writing of History*. Oxford: Blackwell.

Gordon, Colin. 1991: Governmental Rationality: An Introduction. In Graham Burchell, Colin Gordon, and Peter Miller (eds), *The Foucault Effect. Studies in Governmentality*, London: Harvester Wheatsheaf.

Gutting, Gary (ed.) 1989: *Michel Foucault's Archaeology of Scientific Reason*. New York: Cambridge University Press.

*——— 1994: *The Cambridge Companion to Foucault*. New York: Cambridge University Press.

Habermas, Jürgen. 1987: *Philosophical Discourse of Modernity*. Cambridge: Polity Press.

Hartsock, Nancy. 1990: Foucault on Power: A Theory for Women? In Linda J. Nicholson (ed.), *Feminism/Postmodernism*, London and New York: Routledge.

Hekman, Susan J. (ed.) 1996: *Feminist Interpretations of Michel Foucault*. University Park, PA: Pennsylvania State University Press.

Hoy, David Couzens (ed.) 1986: *Foucault: A Critical Reader*. Oxford: Blackwell.

Hunt, Alan, and Wickham, Gary. 1994: *Foucault and Law: Towards a Sociology of Law as Governance*. London and Boulder, CO: Pluto Press.

Kelly, Michael (ed.) 1994: *Critique and Power: Recasting the Foucault/ Habermas Debate*. Cambridge, MA: MIT Press.

Krause-Jensen, Esbern. 1985: *Nomadfilosofi: Aktuella tendenser i franskt tänkande*. Gothenburg: Daidalos.

Lemert, Charles, and Gillian, Garth (eds) 1982: *Michel Foucault: Social Theory as Transgression*. New York: Columbia University Press.

Lloyd, Moya, and Thacker, Andrew. 1997: *The Impact of Foucault on the Social Sciences and Humanities*. Basingstoke and New York: Macmillan Press and St. Martin's Press.

Martin, Luther H., Gutman, Huck, and Hutton, Patric H. (eds) 1988: *Technologies of the Self. A Seminar with Michel Foucault*. London: Tavistock Publications.

McHoul, A. W., and Grace, Wendy. 1995: *A Foucault Primer: Discourse, Power and the Subject*. London: UCL Press.

*McNay, Lois. 1992: *Foucault and Feminism: Power, Gender and the Self*. Cambridge: Polity Press.

—— 1994: *Foucault: A Critical Introduction*. Cambridge: Polity Press.

*Merquior, J. G. 1985: *Foucault*. London: Fontana Press/Collins.

Moss, Jeremy. 1998: *The Later Foucault: Politics and Philosophy*. London: Sage.

Petersen, Alan R., and Bunton, Robin. 1997: *Foucault, Health and Medicine*. London: Routledge.

Poster, Mark. 1984: *Foucault, Marxism, and History*. Cambridge: Polity Press.

—— 1993: Foucault and the Problem of Self-Constitution. In John Caputo and Mark Yount (eds), *Foucault and the Critique of Institutions*, University Park, PA: Pennsylvania State University Press.

Prado, C. G. 1995: *Starting with Foucault: An Introduction to Genealogy*. Boulder, CO, and Oxford: Westview Press.

Rajchman, John. 1985: *Michel Foucault: The Freedom of Philosophy*. New York: Columbia University Press.

Ransom, John S. 1997: *Foucault's Discipline: The Politics of Subjectivity*. Durham, NC and London: Duke University Press.

Sawicki, Jana. 1991: *Disciplining Foucault. Feminism, Power and the Body*. London and New York: Routledge.

—— 1994: Foucault, Feminism and the Question of Identity. In Gary Gutting (ed.), *The Cambridge Companion to Foucault*. New York: Cambridge University Press.

*Simons, Jon. 1995: *Foucault and the Political*. London and New York: Routledge.

Smart, Barry (ed.) 1994–5: *Michel Foucault: Critical Assesements*. 7 vols. London: Routledge.

Swidler, Ann, and Arditi, Jorge. 1994: The New Sociology of Knowledge. *Annual Review of Sociology*, 20, 305–29.

Turner, Bryan S. 1991: Recent Developments in the Theory of the Body. In Mike Featherstone, Mike Hepworth, and Bryan S. Turner (eds), *The Body. Social Process and Cultural Theory,* London: Sage.

Visker, Rudi. 1995: *Michel Foucault: Genealogy as Critique*. London and New York: Verso.

chapter **20**

Pierre Bourdieu

Staf Callewaert

KEY CONCEPTS

CAPITAL – in Bourdieu's terms capital does not have the same technical meaning it has in bourgeois or Marxist economics, nor the meaning it has in everyday language. It is a conceptual construction which denotes the material and social-cultural inheritance which forms the basis on which various social agents act in various fields in social space. Not everything can be called capital, only that which is saleable in a market within a field is capital.

ECONOMIC, SOCIAL, AND CULTURAL CAPITAL – Bourdieu distinguishes between many different forms of capital, but the most prevalent concepts are economic capital (material riches), social capital (influential relations), or cultural capital (symbolic capacities). As regards the concept of cultural capital, a distinction is made between symbolic capacities or benefits in objectified form (books, paradigms, methods), in a personified form (like a habitus or a collection of dispositions), or in an institutionalized form (titles, diplomas, identification papers).

FIELD – this concept indicates separate spaces within the social space, which can be constructed as soon as it is possible to ascertain that certain positions, relations, and activities have been differentiated and follow a particular subject-matter logic, for example, the religious field, the literary field, the state field. Then, for example, the issue of abortion will consist of religious, moral, legal, medical, psychological, and social aspects which cannot be reduced to each other, and we are dealing with a differentiated society that the concept of field tries to encompass.

HABITUS – a concept which encompasses the fact that the individual – and many individuals together – over a period of time develop realistic, cognitive orientations and strategies of action, which are not rooted in consciously premeditated and fully negotiated projects, but rather in a tacitly acquired readiness to act, which has internalized the mutual objectified conditions of life and the practically possible ways of meeting them. Habitus designates the fact that social life is played like a jam session: without a score and without a conductor.

REPRODUCTION – this concept includes all aspects of innate inertia in social dynamics. Everything which prevents life from being lived according to intention and will, everything which causes change to be something which must be conquered from an innate tendency to reproduce. The concept of capital denotes that the history of society is not an entrepreneur's project: not only does the entrepreneur invest capital, but capital also invests the entrepreneur.

SOCIAL SPACE – this concept replaces the intuitive experience of society and social classes with the concept of a multidimensional, geometric space, which is defined by positions which are related to each other and the distance between them.

SYMBOLIC CAPITAL – the concept of symbolic capital is in a class of its own: a person with considerable economic, social, and cultural capital can, if the occasion should arise, look forward to a large amount of symbolic capital if all of these forms of capital pay off in excess because everyone not only succumbs to the power behind the words as a superior force but believes with all their hearts in deceptive appearances: that an honorable man is rich, well-liked, and wise because he is a man of honor and not vice versa. The impact of the purely symbolic is superimposed upon the real yet not recognized field-specific impact, which in turn is dependent upon an unrecognized worldly impact. If everyone believes that it is honor, intelligence, or merit that make the difference and not various forms of capital, then capital makes an even bigger difference.

SYMBOLIC VIOLENCE – the differentiation into fields of worldly power and symbolic signs respectively in modern society is what gives specific scope to what Bourdieu calls symbolic violence. When one basically assumes that all societies are based on some form of oppression or exploitation and that these conditions reproduce with time, not only because of physical violence or worldly power, but also because of a consensus, then there is a proper contribution to the upholding of order made by the symbolic representation of reality. These contribution is "violent" to the extent that it is arbitrary. This symbolic violence operates according to specific different principles in the various fields of modern society. Bourdieu's thesis is that since these fields have relative autonomy, they appear as completely detached from internal power structures and from worldly conditions. Thus they can contribute greatly to legitimate worldly conditions, which are actually arbitrary, as being well-founded. In any case it is about arbitrariness, and in that sense about violence: but violence can be symbolic.

> **Biography:** *Pierre Bourdieu*
>
> Pierre Bourdieu was born in 1930 in a village in the *département* of Beárn in southwestern France. He is descended from a family of farmers, but his father was an employee of the state and held a modest job in the local community. Bourdieu attended a secondary school in Pau as a boarder but was then accepted at one of the elitist schools in Paris, the Lyceé Louis-le-Grand. From 1951 to 1954 he continued his studies at the famous École Normale Supérieure in Rue d'Ulm. He finished his formal education with a degree in philosophy, but without presenting the obligatory thesis as a demonstration against internal conditions at the institute. Bourdieu was now qualified to teach in higher education and in the following year he worked as a college teacher in the provinces.
>
> In 1956 and the following two years he did military service in the French army in Algeria during the war of independence. After his military service Bourdieu remained in Algeria, working as an instructor at the University of Algiers. During this time he did anthropological studies on the Berbers in Kabylie and sociological studies on the transformation of the agricultural proletariat in the period of transition from traditional society and the colonial regime to the society which emerged during the decolonization.
>
> In 1960 Bourdieu returned to France and worked as an instructor and then associate professor in Lille and Paris. In 1964 he was appointed director of research at the Ecole des Hautes Etudes en Sciences Sociales (EHESS) under Raymond Aron (1905–83), and director of the Centre de sociologie européenne. At the same time he lectured at the Ecole Normale Supérieure in subjects like the sociology of art and literature. During this time he gained recognition for his books on cultural sociology and the sociology of education and as the editor of the periodical *Actes de la Recherche en Sciences Sociales*.
>
> In 1981 he was appointed professor of sociology at the Collège de France, where he still lectures and works with a group of researchers.

The Sociological Consequences of a Biography

The most noticeable things about Bourdieu's career is that, first, he came to research as an upstart and an outsider and, second, that he constantly moved within elitist institutions and submitted to academic rituals only to a minimal degree. Furthermore he left philosophy in favour of a combination of anthropology and sociology, yet did so at a time in which these subjects had not yet constituted themselves and therefore his studies were predominantly of himself. His experiences in the Algerian war and his upbringing among poor farmers played a decisive role in his switch from philosophy to social science, from the method of academic work to using sociology as socioanalysis and self-analysis. Thus Bourdieu personifies the tension between growing up outside the academic world and having a career within it, between the general university career and the more autonomous elitist institutions, between integration in the world of research and his breach with it. He has consciously made use of these biographical qualifications as a theoretical and methodical tool in forming his own particular theories in social science.

Bourdieu's Position in the Fields of Philosophy and Sociology

If one were briefly to characterize the intellectual area in which Bourdieu found his feet, the philosophical climate in postwar Paris would be a suitable place to start. The arena was characterized by classical French rationalism, which was on the wane; by Husserl's legacy, phenomenology (see chapter 12); by existentialism, in which Sartre was the principal character (see chapter 17); and by Marxism (see chapters 2 and 9), Bourdieu was immediately influenced by phenomenology, but he was mainly inspired by a peripheral group of specialists in the philosophy of science, for example, Bachelard, who considered philosophy to be pure science rather than a complete philosophy of life.

Bourdieu took a crucial step when he switched from the area of philosophy to that of empirical social science, which uses philosophy to reflect on its epistemological presuppositions . In terms of prestige he took a step down the ladder while at the same time being able to contribute to social developments through his scientific work.

In France the field of sociology was at that point in time characterized by, on the one hand, the lingering legacies of Durkheim (see chapter 5) and Weber (see chapter 6), and on the other hand, the massive input from the empirical and structural-functionalistic American sociology (see chapter 14), which was almost obsessed by methodology. In opposition to all this Lévi-Strauss (see chapter 18) was establishing his structuralist anthropology as a deviant yet attractive paradigm, while studies of Hegel and Marx competed with more ideologically oriented Marxism. Bourdieu was strongly influenced by structuralism in the field of linguistics (see chapter 18) and by anthropology before the structuralistic wave set in. Likewise he was inspired by Marx before Althusser started the wave of structural Marxism. He had already been influenced by phenomenology and this led to an interest in ethnomethodology (see chapter 12). He also reverted to the original Durkheim tradition and Weber's sociology of religion.

This is a portrayal of a somewhat original position firmly rooted in classics like Marx, Weber, and Durkheim, which were a stronghold against Sartre's existentialism. On top of this comes a mediation of phenomenology and structuralism as the two extremes, which are played against each other to contend a third position. This results in a strong criticism of the main streams in American sociology, yet still upholding empirical studies on the condition that they are theoretically and metatheoretically well-founded.

One can compare Bourdieu with his contemporary French colleagues by, on one hand, setting him up against the conflict between Boudon (the American tradition) and Touraine (action research), and on the other hand, the conflict between Lévi-Strauss's symbolic and Althusserian behavioral structuralism. Bourdieu takes his place in the cross section of these two contrasting pairs. Moreover his position defines itself as pure science and is thus in constant opposition to the more charismatic role which Sartre had taken upon himself.

This position also claims to integrate and transcend many "-isms." Its main concern is to abolish the well-established and mutually exclusive oppositions between qualitative and quantitative, individualistic and collectivistic, meaningful action and determined behavior, symbolic systems and worldly power structure, conflict and consensus, reproduction and change.

Politically Bourdieu belongs to the noncommunist left-wing socialism, although his attempt in recent years to contribute to an alliance between social science and the established Social Democrats has only given rise to disappointment.

In the recent debate among European intellectuals, Bourdieu is exceptional in that he has contributed to maintaining a forum for research and debate independent of national bodies, the mass media, the academic establishment, and initiatives sponsored by industry.

A Brief Account of Bourdieu's Work

Bourdieu and his colleagues have published an amazing amount. His first books are about Algeria in our time and premodern Kabylie.

These social and cultural anthropological studies are still strongly influenced by structuralist thought. Central to them all is an attempt to grasp the correlation between the mundane and the symbolic in a society which has not yet begun a process of differentiation which would make it possible to discuss the mundane and the symbolic separately. These studies are about being a man of honor, about the symbolic arrangement of the house, about kinship, etc.

The core of his studies on Algeria as a society in transition is a critique of the classic theories of modernization. These theories implicitly perceive the spirit of capitalism as universally human and consider different forms of society to be more or less pathologically deviant, although this can be rectified by inculcating the correct view in people. In contrast to this Bourdieu sets up his habitus theory and a theory of practice, which is formulated here for the first time: in times of upheaval the material conditions determine whether one needs one's old or new self.

His anthropological studies and theory of science are published under the title *Esquisse d'une théorie de la pratique, précédée de trois études d'ethnologie kabyle* (1972), published in English in a different version as *Outline of a Theory of Practice* (1977), and in a later version as *The Logic of Practice* (1990). The core of Bourdieu's theory of practice is that the practitioner's practical sense is not applied theory, but that the scientist tends to project his own impractical relationship to the practice into the mind of the practitioner, thus giving us an incorrect theory of the theoretical and the practical practice, an incorrect theory of science and scientific practice.

Earlier Bourdieu and his colleagues had published a book on the theory of science and method, *The Craft of Sociology: Epistemological Preliminaries* (1991 [1968]). Bourdieu's main idea in regard to method is that all methods are relatively crude and mute, and that they can all be applied if they are part of an act of construction. As regards the theory of science, the central idea is that science is construction work which first breaks with the spontaneous home-made theory and then with the scientific construction work too, as purely theoretical work.

Next in line are numerous cultural sociological studies and studies in the sociology of education of which the best-known is *Reproduction in Education: Society and Culture* (1977 [1970]). In all Bourdieu's studies of modern formal public education systems, he has attempted to show that these systems, neither in relation to societal conditions, their internal way of functioning, nor in their external effects on society, can be seen in the way they portray themselves, namely as meritocratic-based institutions for the democratic advancement of universally valid knowledge.

Through his empirical studies of the recruitment to education and of pedagogical forms of communication, particularly at universities and elitist schools, he shows that what is going on is mainly a state-guaranteed social distribution of cultural capital. Bourdieu returned to the subjects of the university and elitist education in *Homo Academicus* (1988 [1984]) and *State Nobility* (1995 [1989]). The first work attracted much attention as a professor's carefully thought out attempt to write a professor's sociology and to expose the qualitative differences between the five faculties as a manifestation of different combinations of mundane and symbolic power, of cultural and socioeconomic capital.

Bourdieu's analysis of the relationship between the social structure of society and the lifestyle and taste of different classes' is found in *Distinction: A Social Critique of the Judgement of Taste* (1984 [1979]). This work contains not only the most thorough account of Bourdieu's alternative to Marxist class analysis and to a functionalistic theory of stratification as a basis for an analysis of socially conditioned lifestyles, but also a critique of modern aesthetics, which has either reduced lifestyle to signify its economic conditions or has proclaimed, ultimately, the radical autonomy of the judgement of taste. In opposition to the economic explanation, Bourdieu claims that one first must compare one lifestyle or taste to another, and not each of them individually to their group of social bearers. Yet in opposition to humanistic aesthetics Bourdieu claims that the aesthetic difference of taste is the result of and brings about its effect through mundane differences. He returned to this subject in a large-scale theory on art and literature as social phenomena in *The Rules of Art: Genesis and Structure of the Literary Field* (1996 [1992]).

The huge volume *La Misère du monde* (The Misery of the World) (1993a) is an in-depth interview-based inquiry on outcasts from "two-thirds society." This work is methodologically important as an example of the constructivistic use of an interview technique based on a theory which is suspicious of immediate experiences and confessions. In regard to theory, the work is important as an analysis of the modern state's retreat from public responsibility for the dynamics of social reality.

The Social World and Knowledge of this World

Spontaneous everyday consciousness and homemade theories

In everyday life, knowledge operates like a flashlight in the dark. When we act, our knowledge sheds a light in front of us and in this light we see the reality we are in. We do not act blindly. We know what we are doing and the realm in which we are acting. And in a kind of second-degree consciousness we also know where we are placed within this realm even though our consciousness is primarily focused on the world, that is, the realm in which we are placed.

The flashlight is our practical sense. At one and the same time it is readiness to act and orientation. It is united in a basic orientation which then divides into very different orientations which can come to the fore in different fields in the social space with which one is familiar. On top of this, many other forms of impetus and knowledge settle, ultimately including professional technologies and basic sciences. However, they are all subsequent rationalizations of the practical sense, even when they question it and break it down. Within this context Bourdieu has theoretically reconstructed his concept of habitus.

In this way we all act in a realm which has the designation: our society, for example, Denmark. That is the part of the globe which is found on a map in which all the inhabitants who live there have a Danish passport, speak Danish, have a residence and a right to a retirement pension, have a family and an affinity to a municipality to which they pay tax. Some are members of a trade union and spend a significant amount of time in protesting against the Maastricht Treaty, but have not resigned membership of the Danish National Church. Others have parents who own a small farm, but have striven to send their children to college. Still others have an academic degree and are employed by the state, but their children go to a business school and are counting on a career in the private sector, which today affords a better chance of maintaining the income, status, and standard of living to which they are accustomed.

Society is experienced as a limited number of concrete individuals who are organized in various unions, each with their own system of rules, which ultimately fit into an order which limits all these individuals' efforts to get as much as possible of the good things in life. Thus we understand from just a glance at a map of the world that there are many societies like this, divided into unions, continents and somewhat loosely united by an organization called the United Nations.

Science as a break with immediate experience

Social science constructs itself from and breaks with this perception of society which is experienced in practice. Bourdieu's theory is a theoretical construction which traverses the experienced spontaneous perception of society which home-made sociology fabricates. Instead the theory works with concepts like social space, fields within this space, dimensions within social space and social fields. Various incorporated, objectified, and institutionalized capitals are distributed among positions. These positions are occupied by agents with corresponding dispositions and a tendency for corresponding attitudes and behavior.

So what is social science? If we are to believe Bourdieu, it is a completely different kind of flashlight invented 200 years ago, in which a small corps of experts are very proficient and work on a full-time basis in special institutions. But ordinary people, who usually get by with their everyday flashlights, do use, much more than they realize, batteries which are partly charged with energy from the flashlights of social science. Even in everyday life reality appears in a form colored by the light of popular science.

Bourdieu is a sociologist and anthropologist, roughly speaking. He is an expert in two disciplines in social science and, among other subjects, in political economy and law. In actual fact he does not work in a way which respects these divisions, but rather in a way which constantly transverses these disciplines. He works in areas which belong to the subjects of economics or law, but also the science of religion, literary history, etc.

Bourdieu's interdisciplinary social science is, according to himself, about creating a flashlight in whose light aspects of our everyday life become visible; aspects which we repress and fail to appreciate in order to manage everyday life on the established premises – premises which we have already recognized beforehand in practice, before we are aware of it. But social science is also about – and this is perhaps highly typical of Bourdieu's work – creating a flashlight in whose light aspects of the scientist's work become visible, and which the scientist represses in order to manage science on the established premises. The light which is produced by social science neither presumes to replace the everyday flashlight nor to be the only true light. It does presume to be a light which reduces the number of blind spots.

Yet it is through everyday activities that we must reinvent life after having had our batteries recharged during an illuminating recess.

Can practical sense be scientific?

Social science in general, sociology, and the works of Bourdieu are thus part of the rather particular world that was created by Western civilization in the past 200 years: a world which, among other things, is built up around a systematic combination of an everyday life with confidence in everyday common sense on one hand, and a coordinate suspicion of any form of common sense which is just an afterthought, not a different belief. The flashlight of afterthought does not replace the simple-minded flashlight; the practical sense which guides everyday life is not an applied scientific theory, but a sense in its own right which is the decisive impetus behind actions. Certainly this practical sense may have been subjected to X-rays in certain aspects and this may have left its mark. Yet this is a far cry from establishing a picture of history in which the world is transformed into a "rational clinic," that is where no one does anything that cannot be justified by the results of scientific research.

The modern rationalistic utopia of the Age of Enlightenment, which actually lives on in spite of postmodern critiques of "the great legends," at least as a reflection of professional technologies in nursing, social services, and various arts of engineering, does not have anything to do with the combination of practical sense and social science. Yet even a more humble combination of practical sense and science did not exist in other civilizations in time and space, for example, in the oral civilizations of the old Europe and the Africa of today. Perhaps it will not remain this way, even in modern Western civilization. Perhaps science will follow.

Science breaks with science

Now we have indicated a few of the most basic characteristics of Bourdieu's work as a social theorist. This does not offer a systematic description of the world we live in, it does not substantiate an account of the true meaning of our world, history, and our lives. It does not indicate how individuals, who are united beneath a national flag, should be organized in a perfect world. Its goal is to find the spots which are still blind in the light of the flashlights of science and the everyday in such a way that a new basis comes to light – out of the countless ones we use to orient ourselves practically, so we have a greater knowledge, albeit hypothetical, in the recess of afterthought, of what it is we are doing. Yet only providing what is produced in a specialized workshop meets social conditions allowing it to be generally active.

Hence a theory about society is a conceptual construction, not only in the sense that reality is replaced by words and concepts which represent it, so we no longer are dealing with reality but with concepts. It is not only a matter of verbalizing things or orienting oneself in thought, it is about working with material made up of concepts and with tools which are concepts, in order to do a piece of work which results in concepts.

The material for this construction consists of all the words, tales, and explanations, all the skills, practices, and sets of rules, all the experiences and expressions, all the desires and efforts with which we already have ordered our world in everyday life, be it spontaneously and privately, but also officially and organizationally.

The method aims to organize a way in which all the words, tales, explanations, practices, sets of rules, etc. can come to experience one more time with a predisposition which refuses to listen to the spontaneous experience and its way of designating, classifying, interpreting, and managing. This predisposition is suspicious of everything which seems to be what meets the eye. But it is also suspicious of the theorist's particular way of taking for granted that one can explicate silence, that one can reconstruct the system of rules behind ingrained practice, that one can place things in a wider and deeper perspective than everyday practice can take in or has the scope to acknowledge, that one can think of explanations that one had not yet thought of or dared to consider.

This suspicion is directed at conceiving of a choice of partner as a love affair, but also at the table in the scientific report which shows the system of rules which prescribes marriage between cousins as an explanation of how X was married to Y. None of these are taken for granted.

This way of producing knowledge is of course circular. That is to say that it works on the assumption that the very nature of social life gives good reason for this double suspicion, for this double hesitation to build upon what one takes for granted at the very beginning. The investigation must validate whether this assumption was justified. In other words, the very need to work with a theory arises from the fact that, even for everyday experience, things do not appear as they should, if everything were to fall into place. The basic assumption is not that reality makes sense, but that one can figure it out, that everything has a reason/cause, although it may not be the reason/cause one thought it would be in the beginning.

To be more specific, the basic assumption is that the putty that unites the inhabitants of a country consists of social magic as well as organization. One can say that the opportunity for research stems from a critical interest in knowledge. Just as the natural sciences are based on a desire to master and make use of the physical world and thereby find how our world is put together, social science is based on a desire to know the reason why we can participate in establishing and maintaining an arrangement which is neither random nor necessary, but arbitrary, that is to say, not as it is expected to be according to the experienced assumptions which everyone takes for granted. Therefore, because even the practical sense lies to itself, a science of the practical sense is possible and necessary (see *The Craft of Sociology: An Invitation to Reflexive Sociology*,1991 [1968]).

Social Space, the Autonomous Field, Dispositions and Positions, Symbolic Violence, and Habitus

It is rather misleading to consider Bourdieu a cultural sociologist because most of his empirical-theoretical studies are about culture perceived as systems of symbols. What interests Bourdieu is the way in which the representation of reality makes reality more real than nature. What interests him is the way the symbolic contributes to establishing and maintaining or changing the order of things, whether it has not yet been differentiated into a relatively independent area of social practice (for example, in so-called oral cultures) or whether it has been differentiated to a great degree from nonsymbolic domains, such as landscapes, the distribution of control over resources and power (in the so-called modern societies). The point is not only that the symbolic systems (mother tongue, lifestyle, myths and rites, religion and morals, customs and law, art and professional technologies and sciences) – just like any operation – also uses economic resources and has a power base: for example, the Church has an economy and a situation in relation to the government. But it is more important that in their own field the symbolic systems have a symbolic structure, which in a transformed form reproduces the distribution of resources and power from the nonsymbolic mundane field. In their own religious field the positions of ministers and laymen corresponds to the positions of capital and labor in the economic field, and so do the positions of the expert and the client in service fields, etc . However, most important of all is that this homology between the various fields ultimately reinforces conditions in the mundane field. It is the agents' basic habitus, which lies deeper than the differentiated fields, which brings about this homology: the agents' dispositions, which are a wide range of orientations, which are specific for each field and each position within a field (ministers and laymen, respectively in the religious field), are collected in the agents' basic habitus, which corresponds to their position in the global social space (cf. *The Field of Cultural Production: Essays on Art and Literature*, 1993b; *Genèse et structure du champ religieux* (The Genesis and Structure of the Religious Field, 1971).

Let us take an example: The Church not only has an economy and a setting as part of the temporal authorities. It also has its own internal symbolic economy and power structure which juxtaposes, for example, ministers and laymen. But above all, the training and practice of religious faith, like a form of symbolic violence, contributes to the maintenance of the nonsymbolic violence found in the mundane relations between the rulers and the ruled as regards economy and political power. The relatively independent religious field, which evidently functions as an independent economy of religious practices of a nonmundane character, has a symbolic economy, which is not completely detached from the mundane economy in its origin or its effects. And this is so no matter whether a religious life and the composition of the congregation preach brotherly solidarity or justify individual profit, submission, or rebelling against authority. The latter can act as a reinforcement or an undermining of the prevailing mundane order. But it does not function as "symbolic violence."

Bourdieu speaks of symbolic violence only when a symbolic system appears to be a religious, artistic, linguistic truism, which obtains the participants' natural acceptance and participation in the arbitrary, but not random, organization of the of religious salvation, aesthetic experience, etc. It is perceived as a religious truism and at the same time is not recognized as arbitrary, that is, not necessary from a religious point of view, but conditional to the mundane. On one hand symbolic violence means violence, that is, an infliction of something arbitrary as if it were necessary, and on the other hand symbolic, that is something invested with a higher sublimated legitimacy, which is acknowledged as a necessity from a higher order: God has decided to relinquish the economy of salvation to his messengers.

Necessity is not meant in the sense of natural necessity or logical necessity, but rather as a consequence of what one considers to be right in a given situation, in this case the religious economy of salvation. If the enchantment were broken and the question asked whether religious faith entails the laymen's submission to the minister's supremacy, the defenders of the true faith (orthodoxy) would claim that the minister's role does not have and must not be allowed to have anything to do with supremacy, although anyone can see that that is the case, if one takes a step back and looks at it. Nonetheless, the religious economy functions so the orthodoxy, the truistic faith, counts on the minister's intervention.

Hence there is a connection between the theory of social space, the theory of symbolic fields, and the theory of symbolic violence. The crucial thing about the concept of symbolic violence (in contrast to physical violence) is that symbolic violence works through a faith in something which does not even enter one's field of vision as something which could be different or problematic, and therefore it is neither voluntarily accepted, nor chosen, nor forced on one. It is experienced just like the air we breathe. Symbolic violence lives on the previously established harmony between dispositions and the social world's structures, between the individual's willingness to see and manage the world and the way it works. Put even more strongly, it is not so much about faith but about a way of doing things which is ingrained in the body. The exclusion of women from men's serious games like war, economics, and politics in a male-dominated society is ingrained in her inculcated way of not crossing the square but walking along the safety of its walls (Bourdieu and Wacquant 1992: 168–72; Bourdieu 1990a). A lack of acknowledgement of this fact or a suppression of it is not something one does consciously; that is the flipside of what one does, namely to recognize fully and experience the order of things. In this sense the word "violence" can be misleading: it is violence only in the objectified view. Here violence stands for everything which cannot be legitimated by what one believes, that is, by what is random (arbitrary). Therefore it does not make any sense to romanticize the practical sense in the same way that craftsmanship, family ties, primitive societies, and the like are romanticized.

The practical sense has the upper hand because it is first and last and because it seems infallible as long as a pre-established harmony is intact. It is sufficiently fluid and polyvalent to be like a cat which always lands on its feet, but since it doesn't objectify on its own behalf, it is neither critical, analytical, nor technological in a reflexive way. But it is rational in its own way. But different forms of objectification and afterthought arising from the practical sense can contribute to critical or technological elaboration. The mistake arises, however, when one has the idea that social practices, for example, in the professions, are and must *only* be based upon applied science, which can, as it were, hop over its own shadow, the practical sense. This obviously cannot be done (see *The Logie of Practice*, 1990).

It is also a mistake to suppose that, through controlled experiments, science develops technologies which in turn supply a form of knowledge which replaces the practical sense. This is a modernist project, gradually to replace the mooring of the life-world in the symbolic order with the professional expert's monopoly on prescribing criterion-rational actions to which everyone has learned to submit. Then one has crossed from the general competence of the purely oral to the general incompetence of the literate by means of a rationalization process which is also a disciplinary process. Bourdieu's analysis of higher education and the state-guaranteed legitimating of examinations, titles, and professions elucidates the underlying mechanisms in this social magic.

Society is not only held together by the control of power and resources, but also by the putty which we all contribute by playing the game as if it were a law of nature. When one begins to question this – that is, if one has power behind one's words – then the spell is broken and the system is in motion. Now the fight begins for the very prerequisites for playing the game, which, in turn, means that a new game is in the making . . .

The State and the Education System: On Symbolic, Economic, Social, and Cultural Capital

This theoretical construction work can be illustrated by briefly referring to what it leads to when we talk about the formal education system, which is rooted in and has an effect on the class structure in society and economy. (We refer to Bourdieu's latest account in *Practical Reason* (1998 [1994]).

The school, as an institution under the auspices or supervision of the government, takes part in the reproduction of the distribution of cultural capital and thus in the reproduction of the distribution of positions within social space. Social space is divided into two dimensions: the vertical dimension, which is all about ownership of capital (the rulers and the ruled) and the horizontal dimension, which is all about the type of capital (predominantly economic-political versus predominantly cultural capital). A society's means of reproduction combines these two dimensions. The reproduction of the distribution of cultural capital takes place in the relation between the family's reproduction strategies and the school's intrinsic logic as an institution.

The family's reproduction strategies – that is, striving to maintain or improve its position within the relational field of positions – are numerous: the number of children, the children's marriages, the way of letting all forms of capital be transferred from one generation to the next, and finally, formal education. How great a role formal education plays compared to the other strategies is determined by the whole field, the whole social space, and the various relative positions which indicate a formal education's rate of return for this particular class or faction.

In passing we may note that these concepts are radically different from other paradigms in the sociology of education, which in a simplified form see the role of the formal educational system as:

- an organ for the transmission of culture between the generations (Habermas);
- an organ for the production and distribution of the labor force's technical and social qualifications (Neo-Marxist qualification theory);
- an organ for society's and the individual's investment in the most productive and thus most highly paid formal competence (human capital theory);
- an organ for the equalization of class differences (equality theory).

Bourdieu's construction must also leave room for these aspects, but it takes its starting point from a completely different basic concept.

With this basic concept the theory can account for the fact that today even the economical-political capital's agents are banking on a formal education alongside other resources. Thus more than ever before, higher elitist education has become monopolized by the privileged classes in contrast to all the talk about mobility, equality, and democratization.

The strength of Bourdieu's theory is not to point out these facts in a descriptive manner once more, although one tends to forget them (even though he was one of the first people to point them out). The strength of the theory lies rather in the construction of an explanation of why it is so and how it is done (cf. *Reproduction in Education, Society and Culture*, 1977; *State Nobility*, 1995).

The Relationistic Way of Constructing Theory

In this construction every single utterance, agent, position, and institution is not seen as an occurrence in a world which is in equilibrium, whether by chance or as created by a conscious will, but is seen as determined by its relational difference to all other possible realizations and relevant realized occurrences within the same field. When one compares single utterances, agents, positions, and institutions from different fields in social space, then one does not compare them on a one-to-one basis, but only by means of the relative setting of a single utterance, etc. in the same field. One cannot understand the school strategies of the working class by linking them to the workers' position in the economic field, but only by comparing their differential position in the distribution of cultural capital to their differential position in social space (cf. the analysis of lifestyle and taste in relation to social classes in *Distinction*, 1984).

In his book *Practical Reasons* (1998) Bourdieu gives the following example. Japanese female farm workers with little education have the highest voting percentage in general elections of all social groups. The opposite is true of French women. With a theory which relates social position to voting behavior, this phenomenon becomes inexplicable and the theory false. With a theory which begins with the reconstruction of the farm workers' client relationship to the landowners and the subsequent instilled submission to paternalistic supremacy as a cultural differential position (one does what one is told instead of being left to one's destiny), and on the basis of a social differential position, one can understand why participating in an election and voting for the landowners and not participating in the election are two variants of the same pattern.

Thus one can defend the Japanese case with the same explanation given for the French one. That is to say that one can defend a "strong theory" in spite of the fact that it would appear to be falsified by the Japanese conditions. In my opinion, this theory is particularly relevant for the analysis of the idea that the democratization of developing countries must take place by means of general elections, which has lately become some kind of new hegemonic political ideology all over the world.

But Bourdieu also gives some more trivial examples: There no longer exists a necessary inner correlation between the aristocracy and riding or playing golf. The correlation evaporates as soon as other societal groups begin to play golf or go riding. In itself riding has no importance as a social identity or a judgement of taste, but only to the degree that – and as long as – it makes a difference. The significance of riding depends, on one hand, on what others do in their leisure time compared to those who have nothing but leisure time and those who hardly have any at all. Nonetheless this does not prevent the aristocracy and its onlookers – not to mention the theory of aesthetics – claiming vehemently that riding in itself is indeed something special and cultured, etc.

Because Bourdieu gives a high priority to this relationalistic thinking, he has also systematically given a high priority to a special technique of processing quantified empirical data, namely the so-called correspondence analysis. He prefers this method, which, on one hand, allows one to include variables with completely different qualities, and which, on the other hand, is based on measuring the distance between positions in multidimensional space. The so-called correspondence analysis leads in Bourdieu's books to the well-known, but somewhat mysterious, diagrams of social space or its individual fields, which visualize the starting point of construction work. The diagram is not an explanation of the results, but a tool to be used in the subsequent interpretation.

Bourdieu and his Critics

The work of Bourdieu has not been subjected to much critical scrutiny in France or internationally. There has been much controversy, which has underlined that orthodox Marxists and Neo-Marxists, supporters of critical theory, neofunctionalists, and rationalists disagree with Bourdieu because they all have different starting points. But this is so obvious that the reader is none the wiser on being told this. Others have dismissed his books as French works about French conditions, and so recondite that they are of no interest to anyone outside France.

There has also been quite a bit of controversy based on a misinterpretation of Bourdieu and it has been so simplistic that it is no longer interesting. For example, this is how innumerable education scholars have attributed the so-called reproduction theory to Bourdieu. This theory states that schools maintain, without exception and without resistance, the socioeconomic oppression of the working classes. Then these scholars replace this mistaken theory with a better one, which at best is a pale copy of Bourdieu's theory, which they have misunderstood. (J. Giroux and M. Apple are the latest to do so. See H. Giroux, *Theory and Resistance in Education*, 1986, and M. Apple, *Education and Power*, 1985.)

In some cases these misinterpretations smack clearly of an ideological and political intervention, the purpose of which is to stem Bourdieu's increasing influence. An example of this is the book by Parsons's successor in the United States, Professor Jeffrey Alexander, who discloses the fact that Bourdieu is a communist (cf. Jeffrey C. Alexander, *The Reality of Reduction: The Failed Synthesis of Pierre Bourdieu*, 1993), but in the proper analysis of Bourdieu's work more or less consciously leaves out half the argument. Wacquant confronted Bourdieu with more substantial critics and gave him an opportunity to dispel certain misunderstandings.

The question in most need of close scientific scrutiny is whether or not Bourdieu's entire construction has a sociologistic bias. That is to say, Bourdieu answers the question of what a phenomenon is by indicating the conditions of its social origin and survival, and this is normal for a sociologist. But thereby he is possibly suggesting that that's all there is to it, and that would be a sociologism. Bourdieu himself carefully tries to avoid this, but the question is whether he succeeds.

It has taken some time for the works of Bourdieu to be translated and they have not been done in the order in which they were originally published. This has in turn contributed to some misunderstandings in the way in which they were received in various cultural and linguistic areas. In the past few years there has been a great amount of secondary literature (cf. Bourdieu and Wacquant 1992). But there is still a great need for an in-depth critique and discussion of his works and one that is not based on misinterpretation. This need is all the greater now since his influence has suddenly spread like a worldwide fashion.

Bourdieu in Scandinavia and the United Kingdom

Compared to the rest of the world, Bourdieu's work became relatively quickly known in parts of Scandinavia. Much attention was drawn to Bourdieu's educational sociology by

Bengt Gesser's group at the Sociologiska Institutionen in Lund, Sweden, in the late sixties. In the seventies this interest spread to major areas of pedagogical research in Sweden and Denmark with input from Staf Callewaert's and Bengt Nilsson's research papers and also from Swedish and Danish translations led by Jens Bjerg from Roskilde, Denmark. In Finland J. P. Roos's group primarily worked with Bourdieu's work in the field of cultural sociology. A new wave of works emerged in the eighties, namely works influenced by Bourdieu, translations, and monographs; these were initiated by Donald Broady and Michael Palme at Lärarhögskolan in Stockholm, and they attracted scholars from nearly every department of social science and humanistic subjects in Sweden.

Meanwhile Callewaert had taken part in creating a new Bourdieu-inspired environment at the Institute for Pedagogics at the University of Copenhagen and had done so in the dynamic development of the field of welfare and nursing (cf. Karin Petersen (ed.) 1995). The Department of Social Anthropology in Århus, Denmark has always had close ties to Bourdieu's work.

In the nineties in Scandinavia, as well as in the rest of the Western world, it has become a must to refer to Bourdieu's work. In future it will be more important for many new research projects in the areas mentioned above to refer to Bourdieu's work.

Bourdieu's work was well-known in the United Kingdom from the days of the not very productive dialogue between Bourdieu and Basil Bernstein during the 1960s. A landmark was the publication of two papers in the reader edited by Michael F. D. Young, *Knowledge and Control* (1971), and naturally the English version of *Outline of a Theory of Practice* (1977). Later on the scientific and editorial environment created by Giddens promoted both the editing of the complete works in English and scientific discussion of it. The story of this reception, with its North American correspondent, would need a monograph of its own .

Bibliography

Primary:

Joan Nordquist. 1997: *Pierre Bourdieu: A Bibliography*. Santa Cruz: Reference and Research Services.

Bourdieu, P. 1962 [1958]: *The Algerians*. Boston: Beacon Press.
—— 1967a: Systems of Education and Systems of Thought. *International Social Science Journal*, 19/3.
—— 1967b: Postface. In Erwin Panofsky (ed.), *Architecture gothique et pensée scolastique*. Paris: Éditions de Minuit.
—— 1968: Structuralism and Theory of Sociological Knowledge. *Social Research*, 35/4, 681–706.
Bourdieu, P. 1971 [1966]: Intellectual Field and Creative Project. In Michael Young: *Knowledge and Control. New Directions for the Sociology of Education*. London: Collier-Macmillan.
—— 1973: The Three Forms of Theoretical Knowledge. *Social Science Information*, 12, 53–80.
—— 1976: Le champ scientifique. *Actes de la recherche en sciences sociales*, 2–3.
—— 1977b [1972]: *Outline of a Theory of Practice*. Cambridge: Cambridge University Press.
—— 1979a [1977]: *Algeria 60*. Cambridge: Cambridge University Press.
—— 1982: *Leçon sur la leçon*. Paris: Minuit.
—— 1983–4: *La lecture*. Strasbourg: Centre de Documentation en Histore de la Philosophie.
—— 1984 [1979]: *Distinction. A Social Critique of the Judgement of Taste*. London: Routledge & Kegan Paul.
—— 1985a: *Propositions pour l'enseignement de l'avenir, élaborées à la demande de Monsieur le*

Président de la République par les professeurs du Collège de France. Paris.

—— 1985b: Vernuft ist eine historische Errungenschaft, wie die Sozialversicherung. *Neue Sammlung*, 25/3, 376–94.

—— 1986a: L´illusion biographique. *Actes de la recherche en sciences sociales*, nos. 62–3, 69–72.

—— 1986b: Der Kampf um die symbolische Ordnung. *Ästhetik und Kommunikation*, 16, 142–64.

—— 1988 [1984]: *Homo Academicus*. Cambridge: Polity Press.

—— 1989: *Les Enjeux philosophiques des années 50*. Paris: Centre Pompidou.

—— 1990b: La Domination Masculine. *Actes de la recherche en sciences sociales*, 84, 2–31.

—— 1990c: Principles for Reflecting on the Curriculum. *Curriculum Journal*, 1/3, 307–14.

—— 1990d [1980]: *The Logic of Practice*. Cambridge: Polity Press.

—— 1990e [1987]: *In Other Words: Essays Towards a Reflexive Sociology*. London: Polity Press.

—— 1991a [1975]: *The Political Ontology of Martin Heidegger*. Oxford: Polity.

—— 1991b [1982]: *Language and Symbolic Power*. Cambridge: Polity Press.

—— 1991c [1971]: Genesis and Structure of the Religious Field. *Comparative Social Research*, 13/1, 43.

—— 1993a [1984]: *Sociology in Question*. London: Sage.

—— 1993b: *Field of Cultural Production: Essays on Art and Literature*, ed. R. Johnson. Cambridge: Polity Press.

Bourdieu, P. et al. 1993c: *La Misère du monde*. Paris: Seuil.

—— 1995a [1989]: *State Nobility: Grandes écoles and esprit de corps*. Cambridge: Polity Press.

—— 1995b [1992]: *The Rules of Art. Genesis and Structure of the Literary Field*. Cambridge: Polity Press.

—— 1997d: *Méditations pascaliennes*. Paris: Seuil.

—— 1998a [1996]: *On Television*. New York: New Press.

—— 1998b: *Acts of Resistance: Against the Tyranny of the Market*. Cambridge: Polity Press.

—— 1998c [1994]: *Practical Reason*. Oxford: Polity Press.

—— 1998d: *La domination masculine*. Paris: Seuil.

Bourdieu, P. 1999: *The Weight of the World; Social Suffering in Contemporary Society*. Cambridge: Polity Press.

Bourdieu, P., Darbel, A., Rivet, J.-P., and Seibel, C. 1963: *Travail et travailleurs en Algérie*. Paris and The Hague: Mouton.

Bourdieu, P., and Abdelmalek, S. 1964a: *Le Déracinement. La crise de l´agriculture traditionelle en Algérie*. Paris: Éditions de Minuit.

Bourdieu, P. with Éliard, Michel. 1964b: *Les étudiants et leurs études*. Paris.

Bourdieu, P., and Isambert-Jamati, Viviane. 1967–8: *Sociologie de l'éducation*. Paris.

Bourdieu, P., and Passeron, J.-C. 1977a [1970]: *Reproduction in Education, Society and Culture*. London: Sage.

Bourdieu, P., and Passeron, J.-C. 1979b [1964]: *The Inheritors. French Students and Their Relation to Culture*. Chicago and London: University of Chicago Press.

Bourdieu, P., Boltanski, L., Castel, R., and Chamboredon, J.-C. 1990a [1965]: *Photography: A Middle-Brow Art*. Cambridge: Polity Press.

Bourdieu, P., and Coleman, J. S. 1991d: *Social Theory for a Changing Society*. boulder, CO: Westview Press.

Bourdieu, P., Darbel, A., and Schnapper, D. 1991e [1966]: *The Love of Art*. Cambridge: Polity Press.

Bourdieu, P., Chamboredon, J.-C., and Passeron, J.-C. 1991f [1968]: *The Craft of Sociology. Epistemological Preliminaries*. Berlin and New York: Walter de Gruyter.

Bourdieu, P., and Wacquant, L. J. D. 1992: *An Invitation to Reflexive Sociology*. Chicago: University of Chicago Press.

Bourdieu, P., Passeron, J.-C., and Saint Martin, M. de (eds) 1994 [1965]: *Academic Discourse: Linguistic Misunderstanding and Professional Power*. Cambridge: Polity Press.

Bourdieu, P., and Haacke, Hans. 1995c [1994]: *Free Exchange*. Cambridge: Polity Press.

Bourdieu, P., and Alford, Wiliam P. 1997a: *To Steal a Book is an Elegant Offence: Intellectual Property Law in Chinese Civilization*. Stanford, CA: Stanford University Press.

Bourdieu, P., Stewart, M., and Comaroff, J. 1997c: *The Time of the Gypsies*. Boulder, CO: Westview Press.

Chartier, Roger, with Bourdieu, P. 1985: *Practiques de la lecture*. Marseilles: Rivages.

Secondary:

Alexander, J. C. 1995: *The Reality of Reduction: The Failed Synthesis of Pierre Bourdieu*. In J. C. Alexander, *Fin de Siècle Social Theory: Relativism, Reductionism, and the Problem of Reason*. New York: Verso.

Ansart, P. 1990: *Les sociologies contemporaines*. Paris: Éditions du Seuil.

Apple, M. W. 1985: *Education and Power*. London: Routledge & Kegan Paul.

Bohn, C. 1990: *Habitus und Kontext: ein kritischen Beitrag zur Social Theorie Bourdieus*. Opladen: Westdeutscher Verlag.

Calhoun, C., LiPuma, E., and Postoen, M. (eds) 1993: *Bourdieu: Critical Perspectives*. Chicago: University of Chicago Press and Cambridge: Polity Press.

*Derrek, R. 1990: *The Work of Pierre Bourdieu: Recognizing Society*. Milton Keynes: Open University Press.

Fowler, Bridget. 1997: *Pierre Bourdieu and Cultural Theory*. London: Sage.

Gebauer, G., and Wulf, C. (eds) 1993: *Ästhetik: Neue Perspektiven im Denken Pierre Bourdieus*. Frankfurt am Main: Suhrkamp Verlag.

Giroux, H. 1986: *Theory and Resistance in Education*. South Hadley, MA: Bergin & Garvey.

Herker, R., Mahar, C., and Wilkes, C. (eds) 1990: *An Introduction to the Work of Pierre Bourdieu: The Practice of Theory*. London: Macmillan.

Janning, Frank. 1991: *Pierre Bourdieus Theorie der Praxis: Analyse und Kritik der Konzeptionellen Grundlegung einer Praxeologischen Soziologie*. Opladen: Westdeutscher Verlag.

Jenkins, R. 1992: *Pierre Bourdieu. Key Sociologists*. London: Routledge.

Lamont, M. 1990: *Power and Culture: Pierre Bourdieu and Contemporary French Sociology*. Cambridge: Polity Press.

Ledeneva, Alena V. 1994: *Language as an Instrument of Power in the Works of Pierre Bourdieu*. Occasional Paper no. 41, University of Manchester, Department of Sociology.

Liebau, Eckhard. 1987: *Gesellschaftlichen Subjekt un Erziehung. Zur pädagogischen Bedeutung der Sozialisation. Theorien von Pierre Bourdieu und Ulrich Oevermann*. Weineheim: Juventa.

Petersen, Karin Anna (ed.) 1995: *Praktikteori i sundhedsvidenskab*. Copenhagen: Akademisk Forlag.

Robbins, D. 1991: *The Work of Pierre Bourdieu; Recognizing Society*. Milton Keynes: Open University Press.

Swartz, David. 1997: *Culture and Power: The Sociology of Pierre Bourdieu*. Chicago: Chicago University Press.

Thomson, J. B. 1984: *Symbolic Violence: Language and Power in the Sociology of Pierre Bourdieu. Studies in the Theory of Ideology*. Cambridge: Polity Press.

Windolf, P. 1987: *Berufliche Sozialisation. Zur Produktion des beruflichen Habitus*. Stuttgart: F. Enke Verlag.

Young, Michael. 1971: *Knowledge and Control. New Directions for the Sociology of Education*. London: Collier-Macmillan.

chapter 21

Jürgen Habermas

Heine Andersen

KEY CONCEPTS

COMMUNICATIVE ACTION – action oriented toward understanding, that is, action based on a consensus of definitions regarding situations dependent upon the mutual recognition of perceptions of the environment, social norms, and the identities of individuals.

DISCOURSE ETHICS – a theory of morality, claiming that moral norms concerning justice can be tested rationally in an argumentative dialogue; the ideal (counterfactual) precondition is that dialogue should be free of domination.

FORMAL PRAGMATICS – a theory of the basic principles of rational communication oriented toward understanding. Habermas applies a rational reconstruction of these principles in order to demonstrate that rational communication can include three types of validity questions: truth, rightness, and truthfulness.

KNOWLEDGE-CONSTITUTIVE INTERESTS – these express the perspectives and cognitive strategies on which human beings base their cognition of reality; knowledge is tied to fundamental interests in the history of the human species: the technical, the practical, and the emancipatory.

LIFE-WORLD – a stock of meaning patterns constituting the basis for communicative action; life-world is reproduced and organized linguistically. It can be perceived as the worldview from the participant perspective comprising culture, the social world, and personality.

STRATEGIC ACTION – Social action based on egocentric, purposive, rational calculations to determine which actions best fulfil goals stipulated a priori. The calculations include the influence of decisions taken by other actors.

SYSTEM – social systems of action on which purposive rational action is organized and coordinated through the institutionalized steering media of money and power. The system functions relatively independent of mutual understanding and of communication on situational definitions and social norms.

Biography: *Jürgen Habermas*

Jürgen Habermas was born in Düsseldorf on June 18, 1929, and grew up in Gummersbach, where his father was director of the chamber of commerce. He described the surroundings of his childhood years during the Nazi regime as bourgeois, conformist, and fairly unpolitical. In his youth and during his studies, he experienced the shocking disclosures of the Nuremberg trials and the gradual postwar reconstruction of democracy.

From 1949 to 1954 he studied philosophy, history, psychology, and German literature at universities in Göttingen, Zurich, and Bonn. In 1961 he obtained a doctoral degree at the university of Marburg. His academic career has been a conspicuous one. First, he was appointed professor of philosophy and sociology at Heidelberg and Frankfurt am Main. From 1971 to 1982 he was director of the Max Planck Institute in Starnberg, and in 1982 he returned to his professorship in Frankfurt. Since 1994 he has been an emeritus professor there. He has also been a visiting professor at several prominent universities throughout the world and has received numerous academic awards. In 1987 he was given the Sonning Prize in Copenhagen.

Habermas is the most important heir to critical theory and the older Frankfurt School, especially Theodor Adorno and Max Horkheimer. It is evident that Habermas's life and experiential background has taken a different course. The former developed their ideas under Nazism, exile, impotence, and desperation. In contrast, Habermas's project for a critical social theory has been carried by persistent optimism about the institutions and rationality of modern society. His project is a continuation of modernity as an unfinished project, neither transgressing nor rejecting it.

Habermas has introduced his ideas energetically into the public political debate. He was one of the intellectual resources for the students' movement, but he soon came into conflict with its most militant and activist elements. The democratic potential for grassroots movements requires that these express universal human values. He has no faith in protest movements which are not based on values that can be made universal.

In the mid-sixties, Jürgen Habermas became known as one of the young generation of proponents of so-called critical theory, which is associated with the Frankfurt School (see chapter 10). Today he is one of the most far-reaching and discussed philosophers and social theorists of the twentieth century. The complex of problems characterizing Habermas's texts concerns the conditions for free and democratic dialogue in the modern industrial society, dominated by a technical-scientific culture with power concentrated in large, anonymous, bureaucratic and financial systems of control. The critical task of the social sciences as participants in collective self-reflection is tied internally to this engagement. Habermas's project rests on the pillar that such a dialogue and reflection can and must build on rational arguments. He refers to his project as "a theory on the pathology of modernity from the viewpoint of the realization – the deformed realization – of reason of history" (Habermas 1992a: 98).

Being raised intellectually in the German tradition of learning, combined with a very great openness, especially toward Anglo-Saxon philosophy and sociology, Habermas included and reconstructed a wide variety of theories. The influence in his younger years from the leading figures of the Frankfurt School, Theodor Adorno and Max Horkheimer, is reflected in his critical attitude toward the dominance of the one-dimensional, instrumental rationality of modern technical scientific culture and capitalist society (see chapter 10). This attitude is again rooted in both German idealist philosophy, from Immanuel Kant and G. W. F. Hegel to Edmund Husserl, in Max Weber's theory about the "iron cage" of purposive rationality (see chapter 6), and in Karl Marx's theory about alienation (see chapter 2), especially as imparted by Georg Lukács (see chapter 9). However, Habermas does not share Adorno's and Horkheimer's pessimism (as expressed in for example, *The Dialectic of Enlightenment* of 1947) about whether it is possible for reason to liberate itself from this "iron cage."

Therefore Habermas attempted to develop a more comprehensive, universal concept of reason, which not only covered instrumental and purposive rationality, but also morality and solidarity. Thus he followed in the steps of Enlightenment thinking and critical rationalism, but rather than basing his theory on idealist transcendental philosophy, he wanted to develop it from a rational reconstruction of studies and theories within sociology, psychology, and philosophy in order to uncover any potential which developments in social institutions, culture, language, and personalities might offer for extending the rational, argumentative dialogue and communication in modern society.

The Public Sphere and Knowledge-Constitutive Interests

One of Habermas's goals was to clarify the prospect of a rational consensus between free citizens with autonomy and responsibility (*Mündigkeit*) in modern societies. In his book, *The Structural Transformation of the Public Sphere* (1962, English translation 1989a), he addresses this theme historically by examining the creation and development of the public sphere for political opinion-forming among citizens from the eighteenth century to our own time. It is no coincidence that the creation of such a public sphere coincided with the development of capitalist market economies and bourgeois constitutional states. This development implied a growing separation of civil society from the state, and Habermas tied the development of frameworks for public debate to the ideas of early, liberal capitalism about enlightened, autonomous, and responsible citizens, private persons with independent reasoning and powers of judgement, who wanted to establish a public space for mutual opinion-forming as a critical body of control over the state. This differs from the feudal society of the Middle Ages, when the public was primarily a "representative public" that did not provide political communication, but simply created an aura of authority and glory around feudal rulers.

Habermas followed the structural changes in the public sphere since that time, and found these to have been subjected to a kind of "refeudalization" connected with the transition from a liberal to a regulated type of capitalism, organized with interaction between state bureaucracies, parties, large interest organizations, and powerful private firms. Thus, to an increasing extent, the public sphere has become an acclamation forum for the administrators of power, rather than a platform for open, mutual reasoning and opinion-forming. However, there is no idealization of earlier conditions underlying this diagnosis. Naturally, Habermas is fully aware of the serious hindrances that have always existed to access in participatory opinion-forming, including the early liberalist phase, primarily conditioned by economics, class, and gender. But he did not find this to be an expression of limitations in the very project of the public sphere, rather a deformation caused by the capitalist setting under which this has taken place.

The positivist dispute: knowledge and human interests

But these restraints from participation have other roots as well, reflected in the role science and technology play in the economic and political control of modern society and culture. In the early 1960s, the so-called positivist dispute arose between Theodor Adorno and Karl Popper, which is where Habermas began to play a central role. According to positivist thinking, the social sciences should proceed like the natural sciences, searching for objective, universal laws which are testable through observation (see chapters 1 and 5). Habermas's major point was that positivism had come to express a "bifurcated rationalism" (Habermas 1963, 1964), which itself becomes in practice a form of ideology by legitimizing instrumental ways of thinking and technical-rational control disguised as scientific neutrality. In this way, questions regarding collective goals and morality can be classified as purely subjective and irrational, thus inappropriate for rational debate (Habermas 1964; 1974: 253–82). This corresponds to a tendency to turn all political problems into technical problems of control, even though these are tied to questions of moral connotation, such as power, democratic influence, and equal and just distribution of life prospects. Thus, science and technical expert knowledge are given the highest authority, leaving public debate as a forum for the collective formation of will to become impoverished and fragmented. Scientism has thus developed into an ideology.

Habermas claimed that the takeover by this disguised ideological role was due to positivism, a theory of knowledge, or epistemology, incapable of comprehending the basic connection between theory and practice. Alternatively, he attempted to develop an epistemology based on philosophical anthropology, meaning a philosophical theory of what is basic for human beings. The basics would be those forms of practice, or media as Habermas called them, through which man could realize his life. These media again would encompass certain knowledge-constitutive interests (Habermas 1972).

This approach resulted in the definition of a typology of different media (forms of practice), types of knowledge, and knowledge-constitutive interests. "Knowledge-constitutive interests take form in the medium of work, language, and power" (translated from Habermas 1969: 14). One of the forms included in this typology is empirical-analytical knowledge. The ideal of positivism is nomothetic, to disclose universal laws in nature and the social life. Knowledge of such laws makes it possible to predict the effects of certain interventions into nature and the objectified social world. Therefore the practical importance of empirical-analytical knowledge is that it can be transformed into technical knowledge, which is effective in relation to given objectives. It enhances our technical domination over nature and society.

This knowledge is tied to the type of practice of performing work. Thus, Habermas views work as a purposive-rational practice, the inherent logic of which is to manipulate nature into serving human needs in order to liberate man from the constraints of nature. This is governed by the technical knowledge-constitutive interest. In this sense, empirical-analytical knowledge does play an emancipatory role, but to assume that this is the only form of knowledge, and work the only mode of action or behavior, is erroneous. Social life, the interrelationship between individuals, cannot be understood utilizing the work concept. Social life involves relationships of power, and relationships oriented toward legitimizing norms and collective morality. Therefore linguistic communication plays a decisive role in sustaining and developing social relationships, and linguistic communication cannot be understood by applying the purposive-rational logic of work.

Thus, in addition to work Habermas introduced the practice forms – or media – of language and power. Language is what fundamentally distinguishes man from the rest of nature and justifies an interest in autonomy: "Through its structure [the language's] autonomy and responsibility [*Mündigkeit*] are posited for us. Our first sentence expresses unequivocally the intention of universal and unconstrained consensus" (Habermas 1972: 314).

The idea is that the history of mankind can only be seen as a dialogue, but an imperfect and distorted dialogue due to oppression and power relations. Social interaction takes place within institutional frameworks and norms, the meanings and legitimation of which are communicated linguistically. This form of knowledge, which interprets and expands knowledge about culture and traditional values, is historical-hermeneutic knowledge, which Habermas connects with a practical knowledge-constitutive interest ("practical" in the traditional philosophical sense of that which concerns what we ought to do).

Language also facilitates reflection and critique. The task of critical social science is to examine if consensus about ideas, beliefs, and norms is justified rationally and is in keeping with universal interests, or if it is an expression of open or covert coercion, deceit, or manipulation, and thus revealed as the result of illegitimate power relations. The idea is that some forms of power can be functional, a means for effective organizing in the pursuit of common goals, whereas others can be oppressive and expressions of class interests or other particular goals. The regulative principle behind such critical social-science research is the idea of the domination-free dialogue, a discourse where consensus builds exclusively on mutual recognition of the strength of arguments, and where knowledge-constitutive interest is emancipatory. Consequently, critical theory is given the leading role as a medium for collective self-reflection and emancipation.

This philosophical-anthropological typology of knowledge is summarized in figure 21.1. This conceptual development takes place through extensive discussions and critical dia-

Medium	Work	Language	Power
Form of Knowledge	Empirical-analytical	Hermeneutic	Critical Theory
Knowledge-constitutive interests	Technical	Practical	Emancipatory

Figure 21.1   Media, forms of knowledge and knowledge-constitutive interests

logues with several philosophical and social-theoretical schools. In distinguishing between work and interaction, Habermas takes as his point of departure Hegel, but also builds on Marx's anthropology and theory of history (see chapter 2), Weber's (see chapter 6) and Talcott Parsons's theories of action (see chapter 14), pragmatism (see chapter 8), and hermeneutics (see chapter 12). This distinction implies a fundamental dualism characterizing all Habermas's thinking. This is also at the bottom of his major critique of Marx and historical materialism: Marx tends to reduce all action to that of work, implying that social life, class struggle, and historical development should be perceived as means toward achieving labor efficiency, a question of what furthers or impedes the development of productive forces.

But building such a theory of knowledge, based on a philosophical theory of forms of practice and the role of knowledge throughout the evolution of mankind, implies having to confront many serious problems. In the early 1970s such problems made Habermas modify the idea of knowledge-constitutive interests as basic epistemological concepts. Instead, he now emphasized the development of a sociological theory on system and life-world as determining the conditions for rational communication in modern society. But the distinction between purposive-rational action (work) and communicative action (linguistically mediated action) is still essential.

System and Life-World

Habermas first introduced his distinction between system and life-world in *The Legitimation Crisis* (1973, translation 1988b), and the theory was later fully developed in his two-volume work, *The Theory of Communicative Action* (1981, translated 1984a [volume 1] and 1987a [volume 2]). According to Habermas, society and social life as such can be viewed from two perspectives, each characterized by their own organizational principles, forms of rationality, and action orientations.

System and egocentric rationality

The system, both economic and political-administrative, is governed by the steering media of money and power, based on demands for functionality and efficiency, and characterized by the actors' strategic rationality. Steering media function are anonymous media, which, under favorable conditions, can coordinate and organize large, complex systems of action, bringing them to work as relatively stable and efficient. Through market mechanisms, the money medium coordinates activities between millions of firms, consumers, and banks, etc., with minimal communication and mutual understanding. Even if actors behave as ego-centrically rational in order to maximize their own individually determined objectives of utility or economic profit, a certain degree of integration and stability can be created. Here Habermas talks about system integration.

Likewise, the power medium, which is based on hierarchies of positions and posts in bureaucracies and the political system, is capable of coordinating actions vis-à-vis system requirements. Habermas adopted the concept of system from modern sociological system theory, especially the work of Talcott Parsons and Niklas Luhmann, which he had studied since the 1960s (Habermas 1970a, translation 1988a; Habermas and Luhmann 1971). He borrowed the concept of steering media from Parsons.

It is a characteristic of media that they function relatively independently of any rationally justified consensus on action goals, norms, and situational interpretations. By that they actually reduce communication, which is one of the preconditions for their efficiency. Actors take a strategic and rational stand on the actions of others when subjected to steering media. They estimate how the choices of others may affect the achievement of their own goals, and then make their decision on this basis. This typically applies to economics, when firms, for example, attempt to influence consumer behavior through product design, price, and advertising, expecting consumers to choose what satisfies their own needs. Firm strategies are to a great extent based on sales figures and financial statements, which again reflect actual consumers' buying behavior.

In this way, steering media function on the basis of expectations of the reward or punishment the actual behavior will result in. This involves a minimum degree of communication, and implicit agreement on norms, intentions, action goals, and personal motives, and these are not subject to communicative reflection and evaluation in the interaction.

Life-world and communicative rationality

Habermas accepted that certain aspects of social life can be described and analyzed as objective, self-regulating systems which form part of a relationship of exchange with natural and social surroundings. Yet he criticized system theory for reducing everything human and social to systems subjected to steering media. Meaning, solidarity, and personal identity cannot be evoked commercially or administratively but only through verbal communication within a life-world. Accordingly, Habermas felt that system theory suffered from one serious deficiency in that it potentially let the individual become absorbed by system roles, being subjected to the systems, demand for functional efficiency (Habermas and Luhmann 1971; Habermas 1987a: 261–82).

Life-world, culture, social norms, morality, and the personal identity of human beings are tied to principles for action, action coordination and action integration, which are fundamentally different from those of the system and its steering media. Life-world is the world viewed from a participant perspective, and it is structured by meaningful symbols, communicated through verbal action that is oriented toward understanding. This coordination and integration of action builds on consensus established communicatively through recognizing the validity of verbal statements. Therefore content can be subjected to rational reflection and critique in a dialogue. This implies social integration (as opposed to system integration). Action is based on implicit agreement on situational interpretations, action goals, morals, and self-understanding. Consensus is based on linguistic communication, which can always, in principle, be contested and made the object of discursive, argumentative, later tests. Mutual understanding rests on voluntary recognition of the validity of arguments for truth, moral rightness, and truthfulness (Habermas 1987a: 119–52).

Habermas borrowed the concept of life-world from the phenomenological tradition, specially Edmund Husserl, and from the sociologist Alfred Schütz, who developed the concept further (see chapter 12). Hermeneutics is also an important source. But Habermas doubts the ability of phenomenology to comprehend the life-world as an intersubjective world, a collective phenomenon which can form part of a sociological theory of culture and social integration. The philosophy of consciousness takes as its point of departure the subjectivity of the individual. Habermas wants to make a paradigm shift from the philosophy of consciousness to a theory of communication.

Formal pragmatics

In order to do so, Habermas developed a theory of what linguistic communication entails when understood as rational, argumentative dialogue. His goal was to disclose the possibilities of rationality in the dialogue, viewed in relation to the life-world. He introduced so-called formal pragmatics (which he had earlier named "universal pragmatics"), utilizing results from the modern philosophy of language (especially Ludwig Wittgenstein (1889–1951), John L. Austin (1911–60), John R. Searle (b. 1932), Karl Bühler (1879–1963), Karl-Otto Apel (b. 1922). The idea is that speech is a form of social action, and if it is to be rational, the validity of what is said must be substantiated with arguments. Habermas distinguishes between three forms of speech acts: constative (what is), regulative (how one ought to act), and expressive (what one feels, wishes, experiences). Correspondingly, there are three types of rationally motivated validity: truth, rightness (moral), and truthfulness. Habermas's typology of "pure types of linguistically mediated interaction" is summarized in figure 21.2.

This typology of validity forms and types of linguistically mediated interaction represents the core of Habermas's formal pragmatics, as well as his theory of communicative rationality. Even though it may seem fairly simple and clear, it actually consists of some of the most profound concepts and differentiations in philosophy, which are also tied to an understanding of modern society and enlightenment, containing several controversial and debated assumptions.

To begin with, the differentiation between truth, rightness, and truthfulness corresponds to the traditional differentiation between "the true," "the good," and "the beautiful," which can be traced back (at least) to Immanuel Kant. Habermas also found, based on Max Weber's analysis of the evolution of Western rationality, that further differentiating these forms of validity and turning them into independent value spheres, specializing in modern institutions for science, ethics, and art, is a feature particularly characteristic of rational and enlightened thinking in modern societies (Habermas 1984a: 157–242).

The very ontological (ontology: study of the nature of existence or being as such) distinction between the objective world, the social world, and the subjective world is also a feature

Type of speech act	Constatives	Regulatives	Expressives
Orientation of action	Oriented to reaching understanding	Oriented to reaching understanding	Oriented to reaching understanding
World relations	Objective world	Social world	Subjective world
Validity claims	Truth	Rightness	Truthfulness
Function of speech	Representation of states of affairs	Establishment of interpersonal relations	Self-representation

Figure 21.2   Formal pragmatics and pure types of linguistically mediated interaction. (Habermas 1984a, vol. 1: 328)

of modern worldviews. The division into three, and the related theory of rationality, implies commitment toward modern rational thinking. This commitment requires an account of how the various forms of validity are justifiable through rational argumentation oriented toward reaching understanding.

Habermas has accordingly worked with developing discourse theories about both truth and rightness, issues traditionally addressed by epistemology and moral philosophy. However, the validity type of truthfulness occupies a somewhat different position in that the individual always has privileged access to his or her subjective world. Therefore utterances about the subjective cannot be treated with intersubjective, rational validation. Regarding truth and rightness, the strategy, based on formal pragmatics, is to justify the conditions for how rational consensus can be achieved in a free dialogue based on the acceptance of valid arguments.

Discourse ethics

Most interesting (and controversial) is Habermas's moral theory. His claim that moral rightness can be justified rationally implies a break with the dominant view in this century that moral judgements are based on what is irrational, emotional, or purely subjective. In contrast, Habermas attempts to show that some of what is called morality in everyday life can be justified rationally. This concerns principles of justice as opposed to the good (a distinction dating back to Aristotle; see Habermas 1990a: 104ff; 1993: 2–17). It is characteristic of ideas of justice that they typically refer to universal principles which must apply to everyone in situations which are identical in all relevant aspects. This is not identical with the good, with what offers a valuable and happy life. Habermas called this formulation the universalization principle:

> Thus every valid norm has to fulfill the following condition (U): All affected can accept the consequences and the side effects [which] its general observance can be anticipated to have for the satisfaction of everyone's interests. (Habermas 1990a: 65)

First, notice what this principle does not mean. First of all, it does not determine what is good for individual persons, and it does not claim that universal agreement on what makes life valuable should be morally desirable. On the contrary, universalization concerning basic moral principles, for example, human rights, is a necessary precondition for mutual respect when it comes to differentiation of subcultures, forms of life, and individual values (this is discussed extensively in Habermas 1998b: 3–46).

Secondly, the principle does not require everyone to be subjected to the same norms, since some norms or rights may presuppose differentiating between various categories of persons (for example, children and adults, rich and poor). Likewise, the principle does not imply universal consensus about every single norm, only norms so general and abstract that they can be said to have consequences for everyone.

The point now is to show that an acceptance of this types of norm is justifiable rationally, and to account for the conditions for this. Habermas's reasoning does not require final proof. On the whole, Habermas distanced himself from "final proofs" and foundationalism, and instead subscribed to a fallibilistic position – the possibility that a theory may prove imperfect always exists. This argumentation is indirect, Habermas attempts to demonstrate that denying the possibility for arguing rationally in favor of moral principles will lead to contradiction, thereby meaning this is not valid.

Habermas use the concept of performative contradiction (inspired by the philosophers Jaako Hintikka (b. 1929) and Karl-Otto Apel). As opposed to traditional logical contradiction, performative contradiction lies between the very fact that you say something and the content of what you have said (one example is the statement: "I do not exist"). Habermas's reasoning aims to demonstrate that anyone entering into an argument must presume the existence of certain valid rules for argumentative discourse, including social norms. He then demonstrates that these rules imply the validity of the principle of discourse ethics: "Only those norms can claim to be valid that meet (or could meet) with the approval of all affected in their capacity as participants in a practical discourse" (Habermas 1990a: 66).

Habermas takes as a point of departure that anyone attempting to justify an action norm using argumentative speech must implicitly presuppose the validity of the universalization principle (Habermas 1990: 80). He then claims that argumentative discourse necessarily presumes the validity of certain general and necessary conditions for communication. These are rules for utilizing logic and semantics, procedural rules, and rules for the setting and process of the discourse itself. The latter category makes the assumptions that: (1) everyone is allowed to participate in the discussion; (2) everyone is allowed to introduce and problematize any assertion; (3) everyone is allowed to express attitudes, desires, and needs; and (4) no one may be prevented from exercising these rights through coercion. This summarizes Habermas's notion of the ideal speech situation (the domination-free dialogue).

Habermas's fundamental assertions are the following: everyone who pretends to be conducting an argumentative discourse must accept these rules; and these rules imply the principle of discourse ethics. A person who attempts to argue against these rules, for example by arguing for the legitimacy of using coercion in an argumentative discourse, commits a performative contradiction. Such a person would not be able to make any justifiable claim to having proven the validity of his or her assertion through argumentation. Naturally, this does not prevent him or her from choosing to stick to his or her viewpoint, but it would not rest upon an argumentative discourse. Thus, an important property of discourse ethics is that it is a form of procedural ethics (as opposed to substantive ethics). It does not a priori prescribe the contents of ethics, but merely states a formal procedure by which concrete proposals for moral norms, emanating from the life-world, can be tested in an argumentative discourse among the persons involved.

The Rationalization of Life-World and System Colonization

If the theory of discourse ethics is right, it proves in principle the capacity that exists for social order within norms and institutions, basically resting on communicative rationality. The idea is that the very ability to communicate linguistically implies the potential for rational argumentation, and that mutual recognition of valid arguments has an action motivating and coordinating force. However, although the potential exists, this is not to say that it will become reality. Economic inequality, suffering, and violent oppression throughout history have constantly prevented free communication. It therefore became imperative for Habermas to develop his sociological theory in order to identify the conditions necessary to liberate rational communication. Habermas addressed this problem in part by looking back into history, and in part by studying the dynamics and tendencies of contemporary modern societies.

Developmental Logic

Habermas calls his review of history a developmental logic (Habermas 1979: 95–177; 1987a: 153–97), by which he means a reconstruction of historical developments, which have led to modern society, viewed in the perspective of rational communication, meaning history viewed as a kind of learning process. His theory is that history can be read backwards as a process in which system and life-world are gradually decoupled, implying that the life-world, with its conceptions of reality, identity, and moral norms, becomes increasingly autonomous in relation to the functional claims induced by the struggle for survival. For example, in earlier societies, family institutions and religions were, to a higher degree, tied to their roles in organizing material production and politics. Decoupling is also accompanied by increasing linguistification of the life-world, not the least of which is religion. This is illustrated by the increasing importance of a theological religion communicated linguistically and in writing at the expense of religious worship based primarily on performing rituals.

This linguistification increases possibilities for reflection on and rational critique of the validity of traditional elements in the life-world. The material condition for this decoupling is growing economic production, which again is conditional on the gradual development of system-steering media, that is, the formation of a money economy and large political and administrative organizations in the form of modern, bureaucratic, constitutional states. On one hand, this development leads to increasing differentiation, not only between system and life-world, but also between various subsystems (economic and political), and between world pictures and value spheres. In context, this particularly applies to the gradual separation of the objective, the social, and the subjective worlds, which Habermas (referring to Max Weber, among others) finds characteristic of modern world pictures, and which is fundamental to his formal pragmatics. Thus, according to Habermas, this differentiation reflects a progressive communicative rationality.

This theory is not about which mechanisms have caused the development. History is not "suitable for theory" (Habermas 1979: 142), because it is not determined by any evolutionary laws. But retrospectively, viewed from the perspective of modern times, it can be interpreted this way.

System colonization of the life-world

It is obvious that this reconstruction signifies a belief in the basic elements of modern social institutions and culture, as regards the unfolding of reason and freedom. But Habermas views the modern as an "unfinished project" (Habermas 1981b: 444), which contains potentials and promises that have not yet unfolded, owing to intrinsic defects and conflicts in modern societies. This is reflected in his thesis about the system colonization of the life-world, and his diagnosis of pathologies in modern societies, such as the weakened legitimacy of existing institutions, weakening solidarity, and personal identity crises (Habermas 1987a: 301–73).

Colonization occurs when the system, thanks to intrinsic dysfunctions and tendencies toward crisis, is forced continuously to expand its purposive-rational steering capacity at the expense of the communicative rationality of the life-world. For example, competition compels firms to attempt to influence consumer "needs" and identity perceptions through intensive marketing and advertising, resulting in increasing needs being catered for by consuming goods and commercial services. Likewise, the state is forced to compensate for failing markets (economic crises, unemployment, ecological problems) by expanding public steering instruments and introducing compensatory subsidies that may threaten the self-esteem and personal autonomy and responsibility of groups within the population which may be left in the lurch by the logic of the market.

All of these steering instruments function according to the logic of strategic rationality and thus suspend communicative rationality. The outcome is crises in the life-world, reflected in loss of meaning, weakening belief in the legitimacy of political institutions, the undermining of solidarity, and uncertainty about personal identity and belonging. These are elements of the life-world that can only be produced communicatively.

Despite the basic belief in a modern society, the thesis about colonization leaves a predominantly pessimistic impression. Liberating the life-world and communication requires extended system efficiency, which will then colonize the life-world to the extent that it will be left with its "frustrated validity claims" (Giddens 1985: 121). There is no doubt that Habermas finds this a real danger in modern society. Nevertheless the insidious fatalism is unintended, a flaw in the theory rather than an assertion about determinism. The theory demonstrates, not quite intentionally, a serious asymmetry between the system's roots in powerful economic and political-administrative institutions and the life-world, which is not viewed as receiving equal support by certain institutions or social forces.

Democracy and the Constitutional State: Facticity and Validity

The reason for this is a notable absence of an elaborated theory on politics, especially regarding the relationship between the political system and communicative rationality. Since the political-administrative domain is classed with system and strategic rationality, it becomes difficult to understand how consensus, obtained communicatively, is to be transformed into political action. Here, Habermas's theory of the role of law in the modern constitutional state becomes central. Habermas develops this theory in his book of 1992, *Between Facts and Norms (Faktizität und Geltung)*. His basic premise is that there is an internal connection between democracy and the development of law, and that law is the medium which can transform communicative power (the power stemming from motivation for collective action based on free communication in the life-world), into political-administrative steering power (Habermas 1997a: 150). (Habermas has borrowed the key concept of "communicative power" from Hannah Arendt, who described it as a "freedom instituting power," exemplified by democratic revolutions. It stems from the ability "not only to act, but to act in concert," as opposed to violent and oppressive power.)

The very title of the book alludes to the same ambivalence we encountered earlier, such as the relationship between coercive, false consensus, and consensus based solely on the recognition of rational arguments. Facticity is the given condition at the given time, whereas validity is that which can be substantiated in a rational discourse. Habermas's major thesis is that, above all, the law, which originates from a democratic process in a constitutional state, is the medium which mediates between facticity and validity. In itself, the law is a duality: in order to function, it must appear as both an objective reality, which actually regulates behaviour in a system functional way, and it must possess an intersubjective legitimacy, which creates social integration. This corresponds to citizens perceiving themselves as being both authors and subject to the law. The law occupies a position of tension between expectations of moral legitimacy and functional efficiency.

Habermas finds the explanation for how the law can mediate this tense situation by explaining, based on discourse ethics, the normative content of the idea of citizenship in democratic constitutional states. But discourse ethics is not to be used for justifying concrete judicial laws in and of themselves, but, on the contrary, to legitimize law as a form as well as a certain form of democratic procedure, both of which institutionalize the necessary conditions for discursive political autonomy. This includes guarantees of basic rights concerning personal and political freedom, rights to participate in the democratic process, and equal (material) opportunities, all of which ensure citizens status as equal members in a community of law. Thus the moral discourse cannot directly validate concrete political decisions, but indicates a critical normative measure, and guidance for the framework within which they are made.

Therefore Habermas is critical of system-theoretical and functionalist views of democracy, because these only place emphasis on the system's ability in crisis management and to compromise interest conflicts, thus neglecting the normative aspects. Instead, the task becomes one of explaining the preconditions for participation in democratic processes in modern, complex societies characterized by extensive state control fulfilling basic normative ideals. Strengthening a free and open reasoning public, whose opinions can be canalized into the political decision-making system, means that a living, pluralistic, civil society becomes imperative (Habermas 1997a: 329–87). This requires that institutions exist to ensure autonomy and equality between different life forms, opportunities for access to the public (media), and an open and critical public administration of justice.

Habermas views the social movements which have emerged over the last couple of decades as indicators of the role and potential of civil society. These movements have forced important issues into the political arena. But he also points out certain threatening inclina-tions toward big brotherhood in modern welfare states as a result of growing legislation. Such propensities are reactions against growing demands for control in modern, highly complex societies, but need not lead to fatalism. The normative task should be, through the use of institutional reforms, to revitalize the channels connecting the various spheres of civil society to the political system. Under certain circumstances, Habermas's normative view of democracy even allows for extreme forms of pressure from civil society itself, civil disobedience, and considers it a legitimate means for affecting or changing an otherwise impenetrable political structure (Habermas 1997a: 382ff).

The importance of this type of problem is also shown by the increasing number of con-flicts in the world involving problems concerning equal rights and opportunities for the preservation of cultural identities, national identities, and forms of life, at both national and transnational levels. They reveal latent problems in liberal, individualistic principles be-hind modern democracy, and have invoked communitarian ideas of collective rights to guarantee cultural survival. To this Habermas argues that respect of persons' autonomy must include recognition and protection of the collectively shared cultural and historical background of which the person is part (Habermas 1998b: 215–20). Contrary to a narrow interpretation of liberalism, autonomy means private *and* public autonomy. Relying on his procedural theory of democracy, Habermas says that mutual recognition of collective iden-tities and forms of life must build on universalistic principles of law, reflected in consensus on democratic procedures.

Influence and Critique

The scope and synthesized thinking of Habermas makes him one of the most influential and often quoted contemporary social theorists and philosophers. In the seventies, when he was introduced to the Anglo-Saxon world, his influence further increased throughout a broad spectrum of disciplines, especially the social sciences and the humanities. Precisely due to the scope of his thinking, and naturally also because of his profound and controversial theses, Habermas's works have been subjected to equally far-reaching and comprehensive criticisms, advanced from widely different positions and based on often conflicting ideas. One such objection, raised both by one of his major critics, Niklas Luhmann (see chapter 22) and by postmodern-oriented theorists (Jean-François Lyotard [1924–98], Richard Rorty [b. 1931]; see chapter 26), concerns his basic view of modern society and of its role and potential for reason. He is accused of "old European" ethnocentrism, of wanting to see one particular culture, delimited historically and geographically, as an expression of a new uni-versal epoch in history, as a homogeneous whole, rather than as one culture among several.

A related but more specific objection is that the ideal of rational consensus neglects the multiplicity and incompatibility of values and life forms. The possibility of ever being able to explain morality, at least on the basis of any belief in universal rationality, is contested. In this regard, Habermas is also accused of neglecting, or at least underplaying, nonrationality in history, and the destructive elements of rationality itself.

System and life-world, as well as the concepts of strategic and communicative rational-ity, which are the basis of his structure, have been subjected to criticism. Some have claimed that he has not succeeded in combining an objectivist system theory with hermeneutically inspired theory about the life-world as a subjective meaning universe. Marxists have especially criticized Habermas for abandoning Marx's idea of man's self-realization through practice in the sense of working in a social community. He is also accused of neglecting class conflicts as the basic driving force of history. He merely reduces these to one form of interest conflict among several.

Habermas has continuously engaged in dialogues with his critics, and the revisions and elaborations he has made of his theories over the years are in part the result of these dialogues. Viewed through the framework of Habermas's own theory, those criticisms and counter-arguments confirm, in a way, his own belief in the argumentative discourse.

Bibliography

Primary:

Görtzen, René. 1982: *Jürgen Habermas: Eine Bibliographie seiner Schriften und der Sekundärliteratur 1952–1981*. Frankfurt am Main: Suhrkamp.
Rasmussen, David. 1990: *Reading Habermas*. Oxford: Basil Blackwell.

Habermas, Jürgen. 1954: *Das Absolute und die Geschichte. Von der Zwiespältigkeit in Schellings Denken*. Inaugural-Dissertation Philosophie. Bonn.
—— 1961: *Student und Politik. Eine soziologische Untersuchung zum politischen Bewusstsein Frankfurter Studenten* [with Ludwig von Friedeburg, Christoph Oehler, Friedrich Weltz]. Neuwied and Berlin: Luchterhand.
—— 1963: Analytische Wissenschaftsteorie und Dialektik. In Max Horkheimer (ed.): *Zeugnisse. Festchrift für Theodor W. Adorno*. Frankfurt am Main: Europäische Verlagsanstalt.
—— 1964: Gegen einen positivistisch halbierten Rationalismus. *Kölner Zeitschrift für Soziologie und Sozialpsychologie,* 16, 635–59.
—— 1969 [1968]: *Technik und Wissenschaft als 'Ideologie'*. Frankfurt am Main: Suhrkamp.
—— 1971: *Toward a Rational Society. Student Protest, Science and Politics*. London: Heinemann.
—— 1972 [1968]: *Knowledge and Human Interests*. Boston: Beacon Press and London: Heinemann.
—— 1973: *Kultur und Kritik*. Rev. edn. Frankfurt am Main: Suhrkamp.
—— 1974 [1963]: *Theory and Practice*. London: Heinemann.
—— 1976: *Zur Rekonstruktion des historischen Materialismus*. Frankfurt am Main: Suhrkamp.
—— 1978: *Politik, Kunst, Religion. Essays über zeitgenössische Philosophen*. Frankfurt am Main: Suhrkamp.
—— 1979: *Communication and the Evolution of Society*. Boston: Beacon Press.
—— 1981: *Kleine Politische Schriften (I–IV)*. Frankfurt am Main: Suhrkamp.
—— 1982: A Reply to my Critics. In John B. Thompson and David Held (eds), *Habermas, Critical Debates*. London: Macmillan.
—— 1983a [1971]: *Philosophical-Political Profiles*. London: Heinemann.
—— 1983b: *Moralbewusstsein und kommunikatives Handeln*. Frankfurt am Main: Suhrkamp.
—— 1984a [1981]: *Theory of Communicative Action*. Vol. I. Boston: Beacon Press and Cambridge: Polity Press.
—— 1984b [1979]: *Observations on "The Spiritual Situation of the Age"*. Cambridge, MA: MIT Press.
—— 1984c: *Vorstudien und Ergänzungen zur Theorie des kommunikativen Handlens*. Frankfurt am Main: Suhrkamp.
—— 1985: *Die Neue Unübersichtlichkeit. Kleine Politische Schriften V*. Frankfurt am Main: Suhrkamp.
—— 1987a [1981]: *Theory of Communicative Action*. Vol. II. Boston: Beacon Press and Cambridge:

Polity Press.

—— 1987b [1985]: *The Philosophical Discourse of Modernity. Twelve Lectures.* Cambridge, MA: MIT Press.

—— 1987c: *Eine Art Schadensabwicklung. Kleine Politische Schriften VI.* Frankfurt am Main: Suhrkamp.

—— 1988a [1967]: *On the Logic of the Social Sciences.* Cambridge, MA: MIT Press and Cambridge: Polity Press.

—— 1988b [1973]: *Legitimation Crisis.* Cambridge: Polity Press.

—— 1989a [1962]: *The Structural Transformation of the Public Sphere.* Cambridge: Polity Press.

—— 1989b: *The New Conservatism.* Cambridge: Polity Press.

—— 1990a: *Moral Consciousness and Communicative Action.* Cambridge, MA: MIT Press.

—— 1990b: *Die deutsche Geist der Gegenwart.* Bonn: Bouvier.

—— 1990c: *Die nachholende Revolution. Kleine politische Schriften VII.* Frankfurt am Main.: Suhrkamp.

—— 1991a [1986]: A Reply. In Axel Honneth and Hans Joas (eds), *Communicative Action,* Cambridge: Polity Press, 214–64.

—— 1991b: *Texte und Kontexte.* Frankfurt am Main: Suhrkamp.

—— 1991c: *Staatsbürgerschaft und nationale Identität.* St. Gallen: Erker.

—— 1992a: *Autonomy and Solidarity. Interviews,* ed. and introd. by Peter Dews. London: Verso.

—— 1992b [1988]: *Post-Metaphysical Thinking: Philosophical Essays.* Oxford: Polity Press.

—— 1992c: *Die Moderne, ein unvollendetes Projekt.* Leipzig: Reclam.

—— 1992d: Yet Again: German Identity - A Unified Nation of Angry DM-Burghers? In Harold James and Maria Stone (eds), *When the Wall Came Down.* London: Routledge.

—— 1993 [1991]: *Justification and Application: Remarks on Discourse Ethics.* Cambridge: Polity Press.

—— 1994 [1991]: *The Past as Future.* Cambridge: Polity Press.

—— 1997a [1992]: *Between Facts and Norms: Contributions to a Discourse Theory of Law and Democracy.* Cambridge: Polity Press.

—— 1997b: *Vom sinnlichen Eindruck zum symbolischen Ausdruk: philosophische Essays.* Frankfurt am Main: Suhrkamp.

—— 1997c: *Die befriende Kraft der symbolische Formgebung.* Berlin: Akademie Verlag.

—— 1998a [1995]: *A Berlin Republic.* Cambridge: Polity Press.

—— 1998b [1996]: *The Inclusion of the Other.* Cambridge, MA: MIT Press.

—— 1998c: *Die postnationale Konstellation.* Frankfurt am Main: Suhrkamp.

—— 1998d: *Philosophie und Politik. 3: Jürgen Habermas und Gerhard Schröder über die "Einbeziehung des Anderen".* Essen: Klartext-Verlag.

—— 1998e: *On the Pragmatics of Communication,* ed. Maeve Cooke. Cambridge, MA: MIT Press.

Habermas, Jürgen, and Schmidt, Alfred. 1968: *Antworten auf Herbert Marcuse.* Frankfurt am Main: Suhrkamp.

Habermas, Jürgen, and Luhmann, Niklas. 1971: *Theorie der Gesellschaft oder Sozialtechnologie. Was leistet die Systemforschung.* Frankfurt am Main: Suhrkamp.

Habermas, Jürgen, and Henrich, Dieter. 1974: *Zwei Reden. Aus Anlass der Verleihung des He gel-Preises 1973 der Stadt Stuttgart an Jürgen Habermas am 19. Januar 1974.* Frankfurt am Main: Suhrkamp.

Habermas, Jürgen, and Gadamer, Hans-Georg. 1979: *Das Erbe Hegels. Zwei Reden aus Anlass der Verleihung des Hegel-Preises 1979 der Stadt Stuttgard an Hans-Georg Gadamer am 13. Juni 1979.* Frankfurt am Main: Suhrkamp.

Habermas, Jürgen, and Friedeburg, Ludwig von. 1983: *Adorno-Konferenz.* Franfurt am Main: Suhrkamp.

Secondary:

Adorno, Theodor W. et. al. 1976 [1969]: *The Positivist Dispute in German Sociology*. London: Heinemann.

Andersen, Heine. 1990: Morality in Three Social Theories: Parsons, Analytical Marxism and Habermas. *Acta Sociologica*, 33/4, 321–39.

—— 1994: Review Essay: Jürgen Habermas, Faktizität und Geltung. *Acta Sociologica*, 37/1, 93–9.

Benhabib, Seyla, and Cornell, Drucilla. 1990: *The Communicative Ethics Controversy*. Cambridge, MA: MIT Press.

Bernstein, Richard J. (ed.) 1985: *Habermas and Modernity*. Cambridge: Polity Press.

—— 1995: *Recovering Ethical Life: Jürgen Habermas and the Future of Critical Theory*. London and New York: Routledge.

Braaten, Jane. 1991: *Habermas' Critical Theory of Society*. Albany, NY: SUNY Press.

Brand, Arie. 1989: *The Force of Reason. An Introduction to the Work of Jürgen Habermas*. Sydney and London: Allen & Unwin.

Calhoun, Craig (ed.) 1992: *Habermas and the Public Sphere*. Cambridge, MA: MIT Press.

Chambers, Simone. 1996: *Reasonable Democracy: Jürgen Habermas and the Politics of Discourse*. Ithaca, NY, and London: Cornell University Press.

Cooke, Maeve. 1997: *Language and Reason: A Study of Habermas's Pragmatics*. Cambridge, MA, and London: MIT Press.

Deflem, Mathieu. 1996: *Habermas, Modernity and Law*. London: Sage.

Fleming, Marie. 1997: *Emancipation and Illusion: Rationality and Gender in Habermas's Theory of Modernity*. University Park, PA: Pennsylvania State University Press.

Frank, Manfred. 1988: *Die Grenzen der Verständigung. Ein Geistergespräch zwischen Lyotard und Habermas*. Frankfurt am Main: Suhrkamp.

Geiss, Imanuel. 1988: *Die Habermas-Kontroverse. Ein deutscher Streit*. Berlin: Siedler Verlag.

Geuss, Raymond. 1981: *The Idea of a Critical Theory. Habermas and the Frankfurt School*. Cambridge: Cambridge University Press.

Giddens, Anthony. 1985: Reason Without Revolution? In Richard J. Bernstein (ed.), *Habermas and Modernity*, Cambridge, MA: MIT Press.

Gripp, Helga. 1984: *Jürgen Habermas. Und es gibt sie doch – Zur kommunikations theoretischen Begründung von Vernunft bei Jürgen Habermas*. Paderborn: F. Schöningh.

Held, David. 1980: *Introduction to Critical Theory. Horkheimer to Habermas*. London: Hutchinson.

Honneth, Axel. 1985: *Kritik der Macht. Reflexionsstufen einer kritischen Gesellschaftstheorie*. Frankfurt am Main: Suhrkamp.

Honneth, Axel, and Joas, Hans (eds) 1991 [1986]: *Communicative Action*. Cambridge: Polity Press.

Honneth, Axel, McCarthy, Thomas, Offe, Claus, and Wellmer, Albrecht (eds) 1989: *Zwischenbetrachtungen. Im Prozess der Aufklärung. Jürgen Habermas zum 60. Geburtstag*. Frankfurt am Main: Suhrkamp.

Ingram, David. 1987: *Habermas and the Dialectic of Reason*. New Haven and London: Yale University Press.

Kelly, Michael (ed.) 1994: *Critique and Power. Recasting the Foucault/ Habermas Debate*. Cambridge, MA: MIT Press.

Lalonde, Marc P. 1999: *Critical Theology and the Challenge of Jürgen Habermas*. New York: Peter Lang.

McCarthy, Thomas A. 1978: *The Critical Theory of Jürgen Habermas*. Cambridge, MA: MIT Press.

Maciejewski, Franz (ed.) 1973: *Theorie der Gesellschaft oder Sozialtechnologie. Beiträge zur Habermas-Luhmann-Diskussion*. Supplement I. Frankfurt am Main: Suhrkamp.

Maciejewski, Franz (ed.) 1974: *Theorie der Gesellschaft oder Sozialtechnologie. Neue Beiträge zur Habermas-Luhmann-Diskussion*. Supplement II. Frankfurt am Main: Suhrkamp.

Meehan, Joanna (ed.) 1995: *Feminists Reading Habermas: Gendering the Subject of Discourse*. New York: Routledge.

Negt, Oskar (ed.) 1968: *Die Linke antwortet Jürgen Habermas*. Frankfurt am Main: Europäische Verlagsanstalt.

New German Critique 1985: 35, Spring–Summer. [Special Issue on Jürgen Habermas.]

Outhwaite, William. 1994: *Habermas: a Critical Introduction*. Cambridge: Polity Press.

—— (ed.) 1996: *The Habermas Reader*. Oxford: Polity Press.

Passerin d'Entreves, Maurizio, and Benhabib, Seyla. 1997: *Habermas and the Unfinished Project of Modernity*. Cambridge, MA: MIT Press.

Philosophy and Social Criticism 1994: 20/4 Special Issue: Habermas, Modernity and Law.

Pusey, Michael. 1987: *Jürgen Habermas*. New York: Routledge.

Rasmussen, David M. 1990: *Reading Habermas*. Oxford: Basil Blackwell.

Rehg, William. 1994: *Insight and Solidarity: A Study in the Discourse Ethics of Jurgen Habermas*. Berkeley and London: University of California Press.

Roderick, Rick. 1986: *Habermas and the Foundations of Critical Theory*. Basingstoke and London: Macmillan.

Thompson, John B., and Held, David (eds) 1982: *Habermas. Critical Debates*. London and Basingstoke: Macmillan.

Wellmer, Albrecht. 1971: *Critical Theory of Society*. New York: Herder and Herder.

White, Stephen K. (ed.) 1995: *The Cambridge Companion to Habermas*. Cambridge: Cambridge University Press.

chapter 22

Niklas Luhmann

Roar Hagen

KEY CONCEPTS

(A more comprehensive list of concepts can be found in Luhmann's *Ecological Communication* [1989])

ACTION – acceptance or rejection of a communicative event in accordance with ego's evaluation of whether it is to his or her benefit or detriment – where interest also arises in communication as a result of communication.

AUTOPOIETIC SYSTEM – a system that creates itself, that is, all the parts it consists of, both elements and relations, through a network of such elements and relations, whereby it distinguishes itself from an environment.

COMMUNICATION – describes not only an utterance that "transfers" information, but an independent autopoietic operation combining three different selections – information, utterance, and understanding – into an emergent unity, which can serve as the basis for further communication.

COMPLEXITY – a situation is complex when it comprises so many elements that these can only be combined selectively. Complexity therefore always presupposes procedures that establish models for the selection of relations, thus excluding others as merely latent linking elements.

DIFFERENTIATION, FUNCTIONAL – refers to the establishment of system/environment distinctions within systems. Differentiation is functional to the extent that the subsystem acquires its identity through fulfillment of a function for the entire system.

MEANING – focused attention on one of many possibilities that cannot be pursued simultaneously; a surplus of potential experience and action.

OBSERVATION – designates the unity of an operation that makes distinctions in order to indicate one or the other side of this distinction. Its mode of operation can be life, consciousness, or communication.

SELF-REFERENCE – designates an operation that refers to something beyond itself and through this back to itself. Pure self-reference which does not take this detour through what is external to itself would amount to a tautology. Real operations or systems are dependent on an "unfolding" or clarification of this tautology because only then can they grasp that they are possible in real environments only in a restricted, nonarbitrary way.

SOCIAL SYSTEMS – arise by means of autopoietic linking of communications which distinguish themselves from their environment by limiting further potential communications. Accordingly, a social system does not consist of persons and actions, but of communications.

Biography: *Niklas Luhmann*

Niklas Luhmann was born in 1927 in Lüneburg, Germany. He trained as a lawyer and worked at first in public administration. In 1960–1 he studied public administration and sociology at Harvard University, where Talcott Parsons had a prominent position. In 1966 Luhmann took his doctorate in sociology, and in 1968 he was appointed professor of sociology at the University of Bielefeld, where he stayed until retirement and then as an emeritus professor. He died in 1998.

Niklas Luhmann was one of the most creative sociologists of our time, with regard both to the scope and originality of his production. In 35 years he published about 70 books and more than 450 articles covering a broad spectrum of subjects. While Luhmann's early work focused on organizational studies and the sociology of law, from the late 1960s his interest was directed toward a theory of society.

The core concepts are introduced and developed in his major theoretical work, *Soziale Systeme* (1984). In 1997 Luhmann completed thirty years of research into a theory of society with his two-volume *Die Gesellschaft der Gesellschaft*. A series of Luhmann's longer monographs is dedicated to the various *functional systems* of modern society: the family, the economic system, the political system, the legal system, science, art, the educational system, and religion. Many of his articles are collected in a series, currently comprising six volumes, entitled *Soziologische Aufklärung*. In spite of the title, the texts are not to be understood as a contribution to a clarification of reason. On the contrary, they are concerned with the light shed on the world when it is examined in the light of a distinction between *system* and *environment*. Another series deals with the relationship between *Gesellschaftsstruktur und Semantik* through case studies.

Niklas Luhmann worked on two major interrelated projects. On the one hand, Luhmann wanted to develop a general theory of social systems. In his view, sociology is facing a theoretical crisis. As an academic discipline develops and the empirical knowledge at its disposal becomes more specialized, it becomes more and more difficult to develop concepts that are both sufficiently general and scientifically defensible. Scientific progress threatens to disappear in a cloud of disconnected detail. What is required is a unified sociological theory that can guide and integrate empirical and theoretical research. What normally passes as sociological theorizing is, for Luhmann, too strongly oriented toward interpreting the classics. Luhmann begins his own attempt at theorizing with Parsons's concept of double contingency and makes use of suggestions from *interdisciplinary systems theory*, *communication theory*, and *evolutionary theory*.

On the other hand, Luhmann was working on a comprehensive theory of modern society. The modern cannot be defined with regard to only one of its functional domains. It cannot be described as a civil society with dichotomies like capitalism versus socialism, or as a technological-scientific system. Modern society is a *functionally differentiated* system.

Luhmann's general theory of social systems is very abstract and complex. We will therefore look first more closely at his theory of society, and especially modern society.

System Differentiation

In contrast to earlier forms of differentiation, modern society is differentiated by Luhmann with respect to functions. It consists of a series of subsystems such as the economy, politics, science, law, the family, education, religion, and so forth. Each system is organized around its own criteria or a *code* that sets up two alternatives: to have property or money/not to have property or money, to have governmental power/to be in opposition, true/false, legal/illegal, being loved/not being loved, good marks/bad marks, etc. The codes have a built-in preference structure with positive and negative sides. People marry in our society for love, rather than money or political power. And when people divorce, we say it is because their love has died.

Each system serves a special function for society. The political system supplies society with collectively binding decisions, while science produces new knowledge for society. Functional differentiation implies that each function system is autonomous and operates independently of the others. It is the juridical system that distinguish between legal and illegal, and the medical system decides between sick and healthy as a basis for further operations of the system. One system, for example, the political cannot control and regulate the operations of other systems, and use its power to instruct science to establish certain findings as true and others as false. Thus the subsystems of modern society do not form a hierarchy with the political system at the top, or with the economy as an even more impor-tant base. Modern society is centerless and polycontextual; it does not have a single or dominant perspective.

Since Luhmann emphazises social differentiation, he continues along lines laid down by Herbert Spencer (see chapter 3), Georg Simmel (see chapter 7), Emile Durkheim (see chap-ter 5), Max Weber (see chapter 6), and Talcott Parsons (see chapter 14). Luhmann differs from these, however, in his understanding of integration.

Integration

How do the many differences and autonomous function systems of modern society com-bine into a whole, an all-compassing social system? By and large sociologists base their theories about society on the methodological assumption that society consists of concrete individuals and relationships between individuals. Integration of society can then be thought of in terms of a consensus among the individuals that make up society. This explains the weight placed by sociologists on shared values and norms, and on morality. But according to Luhmann the different codes are not integrated through morals as a super-code, as the codes themselves are amoral. It is not morally better to govern rather than to be in opposi-tion, and to have money is no indication of moral superiority. Morals though, have a place in the subsystems when the codes themselves are displaced, as in cheating with data in science and doping in sport.

The idea that society could be integrated at the level of individuals becomes less likely as society becomes more complex and actions connect to increasingly larger networks or sys-tems. The economy is today a global system, as is the system of scientific publications. The political system lags behind, but even at the national level those who want to make them-selves politically influential must take the number of votes necessary to gain political power into account, and cannot simply act out their value commitments. Sociology has reacted to this "disintegration" by distinguishing between social integration and system integration, between the orderly or conflicting relationships between actors, and relationships between the subsystems of society. By this step sociology can continue to believe in a human core beneath the systemic level, supposedly with the potential to check and limit system opera-tions to what is concomitant with human needs.

Luhmann undercuts this distinction between human and systemic integration with the suggestion that the last or smallest social element is not the individual or an action, but communication. Society does not consist of human beings, but solely of communication, whereas psychic systems and human bodies belong to the environment of society. On this basis Luhmann makes his own distinction between system to system relationships and re-lations between social systems and persons (1997b: 601).

Differentiation implies increasing independence and dependence at the same time; every system that specializes into one function becomes dependent on the operations of other systems for its own functioning. If the law disintegrates it will have severe consequences for other systems, and modern society could hardly do without money. Through social evolution function systems develop a sensitivity to operations of other function systems that is especially important to its own operations, or what Luhmann calls *structural cou-plings*. Politics and the economy are coupled through taxes, politics and law by the constitution, and science and education through university organization. Thus coupled the systems remain separated in their operations. To teach is different from doing scientific research, even if it is undertaken by the same organization.

When it comes to relations between social systems and persons, human beings with stomachs, backbones, and a mental life can, of course, not literally enter into society. Social integration of persons is a question of whether individuals are *included* or *excluded* from the communication of the different function systems. Functional differentiation implies that each system should be open to all; some cannot be working all the time while others just educate themselves. The development of fundamental rights to life, freedom, property, the franchise, economic and social justice, is based on the differentiation of functions (Luhmann 1965). Rights are valued, not because they reflect natural rights, or some intrinsic, mystical essence of the individual, but because they contribute to and protect functional differentiation.

Forms of differentiation

Generally, Luhmann's view is that integration, order, or unity is achieved through difference. It is not as though first there are differences, which then have to be integrated, but differences as distinctions in the process of communication limit what is possible, and thus structure the communication of society. Society is not a place populated by people, a territorial unit like the nation-state, but a form of differentiation. Luhmann divides social evolution into four major stages: *segmentary* societies, societies differentiated into *center and periphery, stratified* societies, and *functionally differentiated* societies. Archaic society consisted of settlements that existed one beside the other, where communication was structured according to characteristics of kin and residence. People recognized each other as coming from a certain place and belonging to a family or a tribe.

In the next stage the village identified itself as a periphery of the nearby town. In towns a social group might develop that distinguished itself from others, for instance, by intermarriage, and slowly came to dominate other strata and the surrounding countryside. Stratified societies are structured hierarchically, and the ruling functions are served by an upper class. Consequently, this dominant group could count as the center of society, and speak for or represent society as a whole. In modern, functionally differentiated society there is no longer any such representation of society within society, and no overall social rationality, but only the rationalities of the different subsystems.

Forms of communication that contradict the overall structure of society cannot take place, but anything goes that is compatible with it. The often-mentioned crisis of modern society caused by the breakdown of norms has no basis in reality itself, but is the result of the fact that sociologists describe the modern in terms of antiquated concepts. In Luhmann's view, Parsons, for instance, overestimated both the existence of and the need for shared, superordinate value obligations. Instead of indulging in nostalgia, we ought to understand modernity's own norm-free mechanisms of integration. What is required is for individuals to manipulate the codes; use money, recognize the difference between yours and mine, respect the fact that the party that wins the election takes power, etc.

Differentiation simplifies communication, and therefore paves the way for complex interactions. When we use money to purchase goods, we are indifferent to the seller's morality or personal qualities. Thus superficial, frictionless contact between large numbers of people, even between strangers, becomes possible. Similarly, teachers are supposed to ignore social differences and award grades according to how much of the syllabus their pupils have learned. Distinguishing between systems can create stability, because crises in one sphere, for instance, in the economy, are not easily transferred to the family system, whose economic independence is ensured by a welfare state.

Modern society is acentric. Because of, rather than in spite of this, it has the potential for ordered development and change. It can combine integration, complexity, and equal rights with variation in types of work and lifestyles. But it is also faced with problems particular to its structure. Autonomous systems define their own problems. The educational system responds to problems by offering more education. The result is that young people remain longer and longer in surroundings that do not necessarily equip them better for life outside the system. The causes of ecological problems are rooted in several systems, and their solution perhaps requires a holistic orientation or collective action. But ecological threats have no clear address in a society in which subsystems can only react in accordance with their own codes (Luhmann 1986a).

Likewise, modern society creates its own forms of exclusion. An individual that is excluded from one system is likely also to fall out of others. To get a job one must have an education, and without money one cannot do much. This process is witnessed at the fringes of the system, among the homeless and destitute, first and foremost in Third World countries, but also in the urban centers of Europe and the United States. To the extent that today's world society is differentiated into social strata or center and periphery, this is also a result of the operations of function systems. The primacy of functional differentiation does not imply that segmentary differentiation and social inequalities disappear. On the contrary, they might increase, because function systems like the economy and the educational system exploit and thereby enhance inequalities as an element of the rationality of their own operations. Society reacts to this by new forms of differentiation and function systems, for instance, by social policy and development aid.

On the personal level, participation in many subsystems can be frustrating when there is a lack of socially accepted models of how to combine all the roles in a functioning life history. We are forced to shape our own lives, obliged to choose freedom and individuality.

System and Environment

What a social sciences is able to observe and explain depends on the vocabulary at its disposal. Logically therefore, Luhmann's general theory preceded his theory of society. His theoretical system, as presented in *Social Systems* (1995a [1984]), is organized around a series of concepts like *system and environment, complexity, meaning, autopoiesis, communication,* etc. which are defined in relation to each other. By focusing on the concept of a system Luhmann links up with the systems theoretical tradition in sociology, but more important are the connections to the interdisciplinary field of *general systems theory*.

In older thinking about systems, a distinction was drawn between *part* and *whole*, presenting the system as a whole made up of parts. This makes it difficult to imagine anything beyond the system. New observations always had to be integrated into the system to form a new whole, and the system became universal and boundless. Luhmann instead employs a distinction between *system* and *environment*, developed within general systems theory. A central notion is that not every situation in the system corresponds to a situation in the environment of the system. The system is always simpler than its environment. The legal system deals with criminal actions, rather than the economic, religious, or political consequences of its decisions. Any system or any order is therefore a *selection*, a choice among many possibilities. Closely associated with the distinction between system and environment is therefore the concept of complexity.

Complexity

We often give the impression that the complex can or should be reduced to something simple, but the natural sciences have taught us that the world is infinitely complex. Atoms are not the smallest building blocks of the universe; they break down into "quarks" and goodness knows what else. There is no foundation upon which everything rests, no place from which to see the world in its total complexity. Any observation becomes possible only by relating something to something else, that is, by way of a system that reduces complexity. We must thus distinguish between the unstructured complexity of the world and the structured complexity of a system. And we may say that an interconnected collection of elements, or a system, is complex when it is no longer possible at any moment to relate every element to every other element.

Not only the natural sciences must deal with complexity; the core problem of the human sciences is how to understand *meaning*, and, with reference to Edmund Husserl, Luhmann argues (1990a) that *meaning is a form of complexity*. Meaning is attention focused on one possibility among many. There is always a core which is taken for granted, surrounded by references to other possibilities, which cannot be pursued simultaneously.

Luhmann's concept of complexity occupies the same position as the concept of rationality in other theories. A system, for example, an actor, can never gain an overall view of all possible alternatives in order to subsequently make a rational choice among them. Systems theory tackles the information problem encountered by rational choice theory (see chapter 13). Luhmann also distances himself from Jürgen Habermas's theory of communicative rationality (see chapter 21). For Habermas, communicative action presupposes an ideal speech situation or discourse. But debates are, according to Luhmann, subject to limitations and are therefore systems (Habermas and Luhmann 1971). As a rule, not all the affected parties are present; participants must focus their contributions on the theme; only one may speak at a time; and the more participants there are, the more difficult it is to maintain the focus of attention. According to Luhmann (1992a), a mere consideration of what we ourselves say suffices to make us aware of how carefully we must select to say what can be said, how little of what we mean is actually expressed, and how much a word used is not what was thought or intended.

It is impossible to communicate about everything at the same time, and every actual communication is a selection that reduces complexity. But any selection or choice is, in the light of the unrealized possibilities, *contingent* – it could always have been different. Contingency entails the necessity of choosing, and choices are risky, in that they are not based on a complete overview of alternatives and consequences. It is nevertheless impossible *not* to make choices. Some basis is always being laid, and thus a systemic network of closer and more distant possibilities is constituted. We decide to move the sofa and must also make a decision as to where to put the lamp, where the picture over the sofa should now hang, etc. As soon as something happens or is decided, simultaneously a limit is set as to what fits in with this, and so begins a history of adaptation to the possibilities that remain open.

Autopoiesis

Social systems are not creations of the environment, but self-producing or autopoietic. Autopoiesis is a compound of the Greek words *auto* and *poiesis*, which respectively mean "self" and "creation." It was developed by the Chilean biologists Humberto Maturana and Francisco Varela (1980, 1987) as a response to questions like "what is life?" and "what is perception?" Their model is the living cell which produces itself. However, there are also *nonliving* autopoietic systems, and Luhmann abstracts away from life, defining autopoiesis as a general form of systems formation, more specifically as *self-referential closure*. Furthermore, he distinguishes between a general theory of self-referential autopoietic systems and a more concrete level in which we can identify living, psychological and social systems respectively as different *types* of autopoietic systems (figure 22.1).

Autopoiesis touches on the *relationship* between the system and the environment. In the history of systems theory, there is an important division between open and closed systems. Closed systems were without contact with the environment, while open systems were thought to be able to interact with their environment. The relationship between system and environment is described as an exchange relation, in which the system is capable of maintaining a complex order by means of input and output. In this view, the autonomy of the system lay exclusively in its guiding principles, while it took its components in a sense readymade from its environment.

In the theory of self-referential and self-producing systems, the concepts of open and closed have another meaning. Systems boundaries are not physical limits or territorial divisions which exclude or channel elements from the environment into the system. Autopoietic

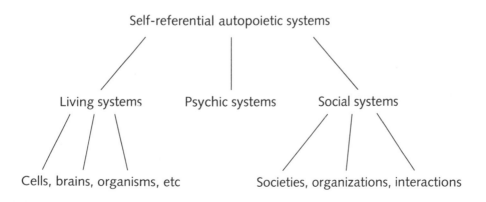

Figure 22.1 Types of autopoietic systems

systems are *closed* systems. Nothing from the environment is admitted into the system. The concept of autopoiesis shifts the self-referential principle from the structural to the operational level. Now a system consists of nothing but self-produced elements. Everything that functions in the system as a unit is produced within the system.

We should therefore not imagine systems in material or physical terms. The boundaries of a university organization are not the doors and gates of its buildings, but the criteria for admission and employment. Its self-produced elements are syllabuses, examinations, candidates, regulations, and the rules for making rules. In order to be able to produce itself, the system must observe itself and the environment; it must be able to distinguish between what belongs to the system and what belongs to the environment, and not confuse the environment with itself. The distinction between system and environment is an *internal* division within the system, which the system "uses" to maintain a boundary with the environment. We might therefore also say that the environment is system-relative, and that each system lives in its own environment.

Nor does the fact that the system is closed therefore entail that it exists in isolation from, and independent of, the environment. Social systems cannot exist without consciousness; consciousness cannot exist without a brain; and the brain requires a body, which can only maintain itself under certain clinical conditions. The concept of *structural coupling* has been developed to acknowledge that dependence on the environment is compatible with autopoiesis and operational closure, and to explain how this is so. The environment does not contribute to the operations of the system, but it can disturb, irritate, or, in Maturana's terms, "perturb" the operations of the system. The system cannot intervene in the environment, and the environment cannot intervene in the system, but that does not preclude an observer seeing how the system is affected by the environment, or how it systematically affects other systems in the environment. The differentiation of systems makes possible certain forms of contact with the environment. A university organization can react to increased student numbers by changing its admission criteria, or by asking the political system for more resources. Earthquakes may rock the economy and send currency exchange rates up and down. *Because the system is closed, it is also open*; it relates to the environment by means of its own codes.

Communication

Sociology that takes as its basic assumption that society consists of individuals brings into itself a paradox that hampers theoretical development. The impression is created that society is made up of individuals and something else. On second thoughts one finds that a concept of society as something separate, outside and "above" the individual human body, is untenable, and that society consists only of individuals. But this reductionist interpretation is also unsatisfactory; from where does the individual gets his ideas, the values and norms that motivate his actions, if not from society? There are ongoing controversies concerning the extent to which action or system – individualism or holism – is the correct approach to social reality. But, according to Luhmann (1986b), there is no serious ongoing conceptual discussion concerning the *relationship between communication and action*.

Luhmann replaces the dichotomy of individual and society with the distinction between psychic and social systems. If they are autopoietic, social systems cannot consist of individuals, since the human body obviously is not among its self-produced elements. The human being is not one system, but comprises several operationally closed systems, and should not be reduced to any single one of them, like the organism or the psychic system. Social systems, in Luhmann's view, consist of communication and nothing but communication, not of individuals and not even of actions understood as substances produced by the organic-psychological structure of human beings, existing in and of themselves outside the communication process. As social phenomena, actions, indeed even human beings, are also communications, that is, distinctions in the communication of social systems.

This concept of communication is different from the traditional one. In the perspective of action theory, communication is presented as the *transmission* of thoughts from one individual to another via sound and light waves, or modern telecommunications. However, Luhmann points out the obvious fact that it is not possible to transfer thoughts and meanings in the same way as we might send a letter in the post, or electronic messages via the internet. Consciousness and communication are self-referential autopoietic systems which produce their own impassable and impenetrable boundaries. One consciousness does not come into "contact" with another except through communication, that is, by imagining a receiver or communication partner. Alter is therefore a construction of ego, and to the extent that this construction of alter comes to determine ego's dispositions, Luhmann (1995a) characterizes this as communication.

Communication is not, as in the exchange model of action theory, a two-stage operation involving a sender and receiver, but a three-stage process of selection which distinguishes between *information, utterance, and understanding.* Information is not a thing or a message which ego receives from alter, but a selection ego makes when communicating with alter. Unlike perception, communication presupposes that information is observed as utterances. Ego observes, for instance, not only that the weather is good, but that alter has made an utterance about the weather; he or she *says* that "the weather is good."

The difference between information and utterance lies to begin with in alter's observation by ego. Ego distinguishes between *communicative behavior* and *that which is communicated.* This need not correspond to relevant operations on alter's side – think, for instance, of cases where you have broken the rules of etiquette without realizing you were doing so. Luhmann therefore inverts the usual relationship between ego and alter. Information does not flow from alter to ego. Rather, alter is constituted through ego's observations. When alter then feels he or she is being observed, he or she can accept the distinction between information and utterance, and use it more or less successfully to steer the process of communication.

On the basis of the distinction between information and utterance, *understanding* is introduced as a necessary third selection. Ego must assess the informational content of alter's utterance. The understanding concludes the communication as a unity of three selections.

Communication and Action

With his concept of communication, Luhmann links up with distinctions introduced by Karl Bühler and developed into a theory of *speech acts* by John L. Austin and John R. Searle. Jürgen Habermas has added to this a typology of validity claims that are implicit in the communication. All of this begins, however, with an understanding of communication as action, and thus views the communication process as the successful or unsuccessful *transmission* of messages, information, or understanding expectations. In a systems-theoretical approach it is the very *emergence of communication* that is emphasized. Nothing is transmitted (Luhmann 1992a: 254).

The difference between Habermas and Luhmann relates in particular to the last of the three differences in the communication process. For Habermas, it is intersubjective understanding that can oblige actors to cooperate. According to Luhmann, understanding cannot bind actions. Communication always creates an open situation of acceptance or rejection. To the extent that ego distinguishes between information and utterance, he or she must also choose whether to accept or reject the communicated meaning. Communication is the *unity* of the three differences. Action is thus a fourth selection. One must distinguish the addressee's understanding of the selection of meaning that has taken place from acceptance or rejection of that selection as a premise of the addressee's own behavior. The communicative content can be rejected, even if it is understood, indeed perhaps precisely *because* it is understood.

The communication process proceeds, then, via this type of communicative action.

> When one communicative action follows another, it tests whether the preceding communication was understood. However surprising the connecting communication may turn out to be, it is also used to indicate and observe how it rests on an understanding of the preceding communication. (Luhmann 1995a: 143)

Regardless of whether the communicative content is rejected or accepted, it is informative as the basis for further communication, for example, *reflexively*, as communication about communication. The communication process in a sense includes its own comprehension test: It checks itself by referring to itself. In this relationship Luhmann sees the basis for the thesis that communication is a *closed, autopoietic system*. Communication does not mediate between the understandings of psychic systems, but confirms understanding internally in the communication process. Ego does not observe alter's thoughts, but understands through communicative acts of acceptance or rejection. Thus communication cannot be reduced to ego and alter respectively – to their thoughts or motives – but represents some *emergent* reality, which they both observe when communicating, and by means of which they understand one another.

This concept of communication enables us to solve the problem of *double contingency*, as formulated by Parsons, in a new way. The problem of double contingency arises when ego makes his or her action dependent on alter's reaction, and alter makes his or her reactions dependent on ego's action. The relationship is indefinite and overcomplex, and the interaction cannot proceed. Parsons saw the solution to this problem in an already existing normative order which determines actors' expectations of one another in such a way that the problem does not arise. Luhmann sees other possibilities, for instance, in the *time dimension*. Ego can feel his or her way with a smile or a present, and then evaluate alter's reaction as the basis for the next step. The expectation ego reveals restricts alter's freedom of movement (if this is taken into consideration), and leads to the formation of systems through mutual adjustments.

Social systems consist of *communication* as a unity of the differences between information, utterance, and understanding. Why, then, is this not immediately obvious? Why does communication show itself as action rather than communication? According to Luhmann, this is because communication cannot be observed directly, but only *inferred*. In order to be observed, or in Luhmann's terms, *in order to be able to observe itself*, a communicative system must define itself as an action system. The process of communication focuses on the question of the extent to which communication is understood – on the third selection – and observes this as action.

The function of the attribution of actions in the system is to simplify the communication process. Communication is symmetrical, the way is open to pursue each of the three selections, for instance, in an eternal hunt for further information. Action renders communication asymmetrical, as a relationship in which ego transmits something to alter. Focusing on action also leads to synchronization. Actions are time-bound events which thus create experiential simultaneity among participants in communication. Actions are easier to recognize and process than communication; therefore they have communicative value. Luhmann also understands the wholly unrealistic attribution of actions to *individuals* in the light of the same need to reduce complexity.

Epistemological Constructivism

The theory of self-referential systems has epistemological premises and consequences. Autopoietic systems are observing systems, but they do not see the environment as it is in and of itself (Foerster 1981). They do not operate with a copy of the environment in the system, but develop their own internal description. Nor can information cross the boundaries of systems. How, then, can we perceive reality when it cannot be represented or described as it is?

Observation becomes in this respect the central concept. Knowing is not a mirroring of some outer reality, but refers to an observer who sees, regards, or understands something. How, then, do we observe? We observe, says Luhmann (1990b, c, d) – referring to Maturana and Varela (1987), and more particularly to G. Spencer Brown (1969) – by means of an *act of distinction*, that is, we "draw a distinction" and thus mark something off from its environment. To observe is to apply to the world distinctions that were not there before. Making distinctions entails dividing and separating, and to see something we must characterize or indicate one side of the distinction. Observation, in other words, entails making distinctions and indications, and thus giving and creating meaning.

By this means, Luhmann is not advocating a new form of idealism. He takes as his epistemological starting point the fact that a reality exists independent of our observations, but we do not have any direct access to it. The observer cannot access the environment without perception; the process of knowing stands in a sense between the observer and reality. Knowledge is therefore not a copy, reflection, or representation, but the construction of reality. Luhmann's constructivism is one *based in a theory of knowledge,* and is not to be confused with the social construction of reality through the actions and interpretations of members of society, as in symbolic interactionism (see chapter 12).

Observers do not see the distinction they employ to make the distinction; they see in a sense only what they have indicated. The other side of the distinction, which remains unmarked, is also excluded; the same applies to all the other distinctions observers might have based themselves on. All observations have a blind spot; we cannot both see and simultaneously see what we see with. This blindness is not a problem that can or should be resolved in the usual sense. On the contrary, it is the observers' blindness that ensures contact with reality. Criminality and lack of educational opportunities are, as we are aware, real *and* system- dependent phenomena.

The distinction used in observation first becomes visible through *observation of the observation*. This Luhmann calls reflexivity. A constructivist theory of knowledge understands itself as an observation of observation. Traditionally, observation of observation has been directed toward the *object*, toward what the observer observes. We have distinguished between subject and object, or perception and object, and primarily been interested in the object, that is, in how the subject arrives at a correct understanding of the object. The constructivist instead directs interest toward the observer, or rather, toward the *observation*, that is, *how* the observer observes.

Only on this level of *second-order observation* does reality come into view, but on the other hand, from this vantage point we can see everything, both what observers see – the object – and what they do not see – that is, the distinctions they employ to make distinctions and indicate objects. For this type of second-order observation too, we may say that observers themselves cannot see the distinctions they use to observe observations. All of the above, of course, also applies to scientific observations. Scientific truths are also constructions of the system, rather than accounts of "the way things are." It is the theoretical concept of a system that makes social systems empirically observable.

Evolutionary Theory

Social development does not have a goal, nor is it guided by rationality; rather, it is subject to the mechanisms of evolution: *variation, selection, and stabilization*. Luhmann employs a modified Darwinist explanatory model in his analysis of social development. The first societies were systems of *interaction*, communication occurred face-to-face, and the system necessarily comprised few individuals. Also oral conversation has a limited capacity to store and process information. The transition from segmentary to hierarchical and functionally differentiated societies assumes that communication exceeds the boundaries of the system of interaction. This happens through the development of so-called media of dissemination – writing, printing, and modern mass media like newspapers, radio, and television.

However, the expansion of the number of participants in communication means that ego's acceptance of alter's communicative message becomes less likely. New mechanisms for the integration of communication are required. Luhmann here makes a link with Talcott Parsons's concept of *symbolically generalized media*. Media like money, power, tokens of love, scientific knowledge and grades, symbolize the connection between motive and action. When money is tied to a communicative message, the likelihood increases that it will be accepted as a basis for further communication. And it is likely that students attend lectures and read the syllabus because it may have a bearing on their grades. The development of media, and the differentiation of functional systems, are two sides of the same coin.

Within mediated communication, *organizations* develop. Organizations are social systems that regulate communication through membership rules. One works for the organization not because the task in itself is rewarding, but because of the utilities connected to the membership.

Rejection and Acceptance

Luhmann's sociology has been the object of increasing interest, but its position nonetheless remains marginal. Established sociologists reject it or treat it with caution. Only a small part of his work has been translated into English, and his major 1984 book was not published in America until 1995.

Luhmann has had his greatest impact within Germany. He first became known to the broader scientific public as a relentless critic of Jürgen Habermas. Their controversies appeared in a joint publication in 1971 under the title *Theory of Society or Social Technology: What Does Systems Research Accomplish?* In the political and radical climate of the seventies Luhmann's ideas found little support. In the mid-eighties the reception was more favorable and his now more voluminous work became the focus of serious attention and scientific debate. Today research along Luhmann's lines is conducted on a broad scale and in many different fields, for example, "risk research " by Baecker (1991), sociology of law by Teubner (1993), political sociology by Willke (1992), sociology of knowledge by Stichweh (1991, 1994). As of 1995 there is also a particular journal, *Soziale Systeme*, dedicated to discussions with and within systems theory.

Luhmann was constructing a new "grand theory," and after Parsons, people have been skeptical of this. Moreover, many find it difficult to abandon the notion of integration as shared understanding. And if society lacks social norms, it should be possible to establish new ones through public debate, as Habermas has pointed out, also with critical reference to Luhmann (e.g., Luhmann and Habermas 1971; Habermas 1981; 1985; 1992). Luhmann, however, makes the point that we cannot send five thousand million human beings out hunting for consensus.

Is Luhmann, then, more closely aligned with the so-called postmodernists (see chapter 26)? What is called postmodernism is, for Luhmann (1992b), a rather shallow treatment of modern society's self-observation. In no way does reflexivity lead to "anything goes," in either science or society; the development of systems is an essential quality of communication. Dag Østerberg (1988) suggests that Luhmann is presenting a neo-anarchistic doctrine. Others claim that systems theory, in its insistence on the autonomy of systems and lack of opportunities for control, is more akin to liberalism (Zolo 1992).

When one reads the critics and compares theoretical positions it is important to bear in mind that traditional concepts have been redefined and acquire new meaning in Luhmann's theoretical system. Even if the words are the same, system, communication, action and structure have a precise and different meaning than, for instance, in the work of Parsons, Habermas, and Giddens. By founding his general theory in a concept of meaning as reduction of complexity, Luhmann annuls the distinction between system and a life-world of shared understandings that plays such an important role in traditional action-theoretical approaches. With his concept of communication Luhmann claims to solve the problem of the hermeneutic tradition; how understanding can take place despite the fact that consciousnesses remain closed to each other, by turning it on its head. It is the untransparency of consciousness that makes communication necessary and possible. Luhmann is able not only to uphold the sociological claim that the social is a reality on its own, sui generis, but also to say what it is. With the concept of autopoiesis that subordinates the schemata of cause and effect to that of self-reference, he explains how society reproduces itself. And by placing the individual in the environment man is no longer simply a continuation of the social, and the individuality of the individual can be taken seriously.

Besides supplying sociology with a new theory of modern society as functionally differentiated, his greatest contribution might be that Luhmann rids sociology of some of its epistemological obstacles and thus opens up new venues for theoretical and empirical research.

Bibliography

Primary:

Luhmann, Niklas. 1965: *Grundrechte als Institution: Ein Beitrag zur politischen Soziologie.* Berlin: Duncker und Humblot.
—— 1968a: *Zweckbegriff und Systemrationalität: Über die Funktion von Zwecken in sozialen Systemen.* Tübingen: Suhrkamp.
—— 1968b: *Vertrauen: ein Mechanismus der Reduktion sozialer Komplexität.* Stuttgart: F. Enke.
—— 1969: *Legitimation durch Verfarhren.* Neuwied am Rhein.
—— 1970: *Soziologische Aufklärung: Aufsätze zur Theorie sozialer Systeme.* Cologne and Opladen: Westdeutscher Verlag.
—— 1971: *Politische Planung: Aufsätze zur Sociologie von Politik und Verwaltung.* Opladen: Westdeutscher Verlag.
—— 1975: *Soziologische Aufklärung, Bd. 2: Aufsätze zur Theorie der Gesellschaft.* Opladen: Westdeutscher Verlag.
—— 1976: Generalized Media and the Problem of Contingency. In J. J. Loubster et al. (eds), *Explorations in General Theory in Social Science 1–2.* New York: Free Press.
—— 1978: *Organisation und Entscheidung.* Opladen: Westdeutscher Verlag.
—— 1979 [1975]: *Trust and Power: Two Works.* Chichester: Wiley.
—— 1980: *Gesellschaftsstruktur und Semantik. Studien zur Wissenssoziologie der modernen Gesellschaft, bd. 1.* Frankfurt am Main: Suhrkamp.
—— 1981a: *Soziologische Aufklärung, Bd. 3: Soziales System, Gesellschaft, Organisation.* Opladen: Westdeutscher Verlag.
—— 1981b: *Gesellschaftsstruktur und Semantik. Studien zur Wissenssoziologie der modernen Gesellschaft, Bd. 2.* Frankfurt am Main: Suhrkamp.
—— 1982: *The Differentiation of Society.* New York: Colombia University Press.
—— 1984 [1977]: *Religious Dogmatics and the Evolution of Societies.* New York and Toronto: Edwin Mellen Press.
—— 1986a: *Ökologische Kommunikation. Kann die moderne Gesellschaft sich auf Ökologische Gefährdungen einstellen?* Opladen: Westdeutscher Verlag. (Translated as *Ecological Communication.* Cambridge: Polity Press, 1989).
—— 1986b: The Autopoiesis of Social Systems. In F. Geyer and J. van der Zouwen, *Sociocybernetic Paradoxes,* London: Sage.
—— 1987a: *Soziologische Aufklärung, Bd. 4: Beiträge zur funktionalen Differenzierung der Gesellschaft.* Opladen: Westdeutscher Verlag.
—— 1987b: The Evolutionary Differentiation Between Society and Interaction. In Jeffrey C. Alexander (ed.), *The Micro-Macro Link,* Berkeley: University of California Press.
—— 1988a: Wie ist Bewusstsein an Kommunikation beteiligt? In Hans U. Gumbrecht and K. Ludwig Pfeiffer (eds), *Materialität der Kommunikation,* Frankfurt am Main: Suhrkamp.
—— 1988b: *Die Wirtschaft der Gesellschaft.* Frankfurt am Main: Suhrkamp.
—— 1989: *Gesellschaftsstruktur und Semantik: Studien zur Wissenssoziologie der modernen Gesellschaft, Band 3.* Frankfurt am Main: Suhrkamp.

—— 1990a: *Essays on Self-Reference*. New York: Columbia University Press.

—— 1990b: *Die Wissenschaft der Gesellschaft*. Frankfurt am Main: Suhrkamp.

—— 1990c: *Soziologische Aufklärung, Band 5: Konstruktvistische Perspektiven*. Opladen: Westdeutscher Verlag.

—— 1990d: The Cognitive Program of Constructivism and a Reality that Remains Unknown. In W. G. Krohn and H. Novotny (eds), *Portrait of a Scientific Revolution,* London: Kluwer Academic Publishers.

—— 1990e: *Paradigm lost: Über die ethische Reflexion der Moral*. Frankfurt am Main: Suhrkamp. (Translated as 1991: Paradigm Lost. *Thesis Eleven*, 29, 82–94).

—— 1990f [1981]: *Political Theory in the Welfare State*. Berlin: Walter de Gruyter.

—— 1990g [1982]: *Love as Passion*. Cambridge: Polity Press.

—— 1992a: What is Communication? *Communication Theory*, 2, 251–90.

—— 1992b: *Beobachtungen der Moderne*. Opladen: Westdeutscher Verlag. (Translated as *Observations on Modernity*. Stanford, CA: Stanford University Press, 1998).

—— 1993a: *Das Recht der Gesellschaft*. Frankfurt am Main: Suhrkamp.

—— 1993b [1991]: *Risk: A Sociological Theory*. Berlin: Walter de Gruyter.

—— 1995a [1984]: *Social Systems*. Stanford, CA: Stanford University Press.

—— 1995b: *Die Kunst der Gesellschaft*. Frankfurt am Main: Suhrkamp.

—— 1995c: *Soziologische Aufklärung 6. Die Soziologie und der Mensch*. Opladen: Westdeutscher Verlag.

—— 1995d [1964]: *Funktionen und Folgen formaler Organisation*. Berlin: Duncker & Humblot.

—— 1995e: *Die Realität der Massenmedien*. Opladen: Westdeutscher Verlag.

—— 1996: On the Scientific Context of the Concept of Communication. *Social Science Information*, 35, 257–67.

—— 1997a: *Recht und Automation in der offentlichen Verwaltung*. Berlin: Duncker & Humblot.

—— 1997b: *Die Gesellschaft der Gesellschaft*. 2 vols. Frankfurt am Main: Suhrkamp.

—— 1997c: Globalization or World Society: How to Conceive of Modern Society? *International Review of Sociology*, 7, 67–97.

Luhmann, Niklas, and Habermas, Jürgen. 1971: *Theorie der Gesellschaft oder Sozialtechnologie - Was leistet die Systemforschung?* Frankfurt am Main: Suhrkamp.

Luhmann, Niklas, and Albrow, Martin. 1983: *Rechtssoziologie*. Opladen: Westdeutscher Verlag. (Translated as *A Sociological Theory of Law*. London: Routledge and Kegan Paul, 1985).

Luhmann, Niklas, and Fuchs, Peter. 1989: *Reden und Schweigen*. Frankfurt am Main: Suhrkamp.

Luhmann, Niklas, and Hellmann, Kai-Uwe. 1996: *Protest: Systemtheorie und Soziale Bewegungen*. Frankfurt am Main: Suhrkamp.

Interviews:

Baecker, Dirk, Luhman, Niklas, and Stanitzek, Georg. 1987: *Archimedes und wir: Interviews*. Berlin: Merve Verlag.

Secondary:

Acta Sociologica, 23/1, 2000: Special Issue on Luhmann.

Baecker, Dirk. 1991: *Womit handeln Banken?* Frankfurt am Main: Suhrkamp.

Bråten, Stein. 1986: The Third Position: Beyond Artificial and Autopoietic Reduction. In F. Geyer, and J. van der Zouwen, *Sociocybernetic Paradoxes,* London: Sage.

Foerster, Heinz von. 1981: *Observing Systems*. Seaside, CA: Intersystems.

Habermas, Jürgen. 1981: *Theorie des kommunikativen Handelns*. 2 vols. Frankfurt am Main: Suhrkamp. (Translated as *The Theory of Communicative Action*. 2 vols. 1984–7. Boston: Beacon Press and

Cambridge: Polity Press).

—— 1985: *Der Philosophische Diskurs der Moderne*. Frankfurt am Main: Suhrkamp. (Translated as *The Philosophical Discourse of Modernity*. Cambridge: Polity Press, 1987).

—— 1992: *Faktizität und Geltung*. Frankfurt am Main: Suhrkamp.

Maturana, Humberto R., and Varela, Francisco J. 1980: *Autopoiesis and Cognition*. Boston: Reidel.

—— 1987: *The Tree of Knowledge*. Boston: Shambala.

New German Critique, 1994, no. 1: Special Issue on Niklas Luhmann.

Østerberg, Dag. 1988: *Metasociology*. Oslo: Universitsforlaget. (Chap. 11).

Spencer Brown, George. 1969: *Laws of Form*. London: Allen & Unwin.

Stichweh, Rudolf. 1991: *Der frühmoderne Staat und die europäische Universität: zur Interaktion von Politik und Erziehungssystem im Prozess ihrer Ausdifferenzierung (16.-18. Jarhhundert)*. Frankfurt am Main: Suhrkamp.

—— 1994: *Wissenschaft, Universität, Profession: soziologische Analysen*. Frankfurt am Main: Suhrkamp.

Teubner, Gunther. 1993: *Law as an Autopoietic System*. Oxford, UK and Cambridge, MA: Blackwell.

Wilke, Helmuth. 1992: *Ironie des States*. Frankfurt am Main: Suhrkamp.

Zolo, Daniel. 1992: The Epistemological Status of the Theory of Autopoiesis and its Application to the Social Sciences. In G. Teubner and A. Febbrajo, *State, Law and Economy as Autopoietic Systems*, Milano: Dott. A. Giuffré Editore.

chapter 23

Norbert Elias

Gunnar Olofsson

KEY CONCEPTS

CIVILIZING PROCESS – the theory of "the civilizing process" is a comprehensive term for Elias's social theory. The centralization of power and containment of violence in the state and modulations in the codes of conduct of individuals and groups are two aspects of the same process of social change, the civilizing process.

ESTABLISHED–OUTSIDER – is a figuration that is present in many social contexts. The dominant position of the established is usually indicated by a moral polarization in the groups so that the "good" and well-adjusted segment of the established group and the "bad" and aberrant segment of the outsider group are made to represent both groups' evaluation of both themselves and the other group.

FIGURATION – a basic category in Elias's theory. "Figurations" can be defined as "networks of inter-dependent, i.e. reciprocally dependent individuals and groups, with shifting and asymmetrical power balances between them."

HOMO CLAUSUS – Elias's term for the socially autonomous individual of classical epistemology who, incorrectly according to Elias, is made into the subject for the acquisition of knowledge.

INTERDEPENDENCE – denotes the reciprocally dependent relationship between individuals and/or groups, communities, etc. Processes that increase interdependence in a society are, for example, a developed division of labor, increased differentiation of state institutions, etc.

PROCESS REDUCTION – Elias's term for the tendency of many philosophers and sociologists to dissolve a *process* – which is the starting point for sociological analysis in Elias's view – into a combination of a static condition and an external changing force.

SOCIAL RELATIONSHIPS – the starting point for sociological analysis is, according to Elias, the *relationships* between groups and individuals; "the individual" is a social and conceptual construction. Groups, not individuals, and above all, the power relations between them are the basic unit in sociology. Groups are the "survival units" of society.

Biography: *Norbert Elias*

Norbert Elias (1897–1990) was born in Breslau in a Jewish bourgeois environment; his father managed a textile factory. Elias was shaped by the classical and philosophical orientation of the German humanist tradition. He received a doctorate in philosophy at Breslau University. Subsequently he studied sociology, in Heidelberg (with Alfred Weber) and later on in Frankfurt, where he was the assistent of Karl Mannheim.

After the Nazi putsch in 1933 Elias moved to Paris and then to England. There he received his first position as an academic teacher of sociology, at Leicester in 1954. From the mid-sixties he was a visiting scholar at several universities and he worked in Amsterdam during his last decade, in the eighties.

The central work of Elias is *The Civilizing Process* (1994 [1939]). A number of other studies are related to this work, for example, the study of court society, *The Court Society* (1983), its sequel, *The Society of Individuals* (1991), and an analysis of the development of sports in *The Quest for Excitement* (1986). *Mozart: The Sociology of a Genius* (1994) applies

Elias's theory of the interaction between social change and individuality in an attempt to explain Mozart's "individual" destiny in sociological terms.

Elias accounts for his view of sociology in *What is Sociology?* (1970). He argues that sociology should transcend the tendency to apply dichotomies like individual–society. *Involvement and Detachment* (1987) stresses that the capacity for detachment determines whether sociology can reach beyond a stance of personal engagement. *Established and Outsiders* (new edition 1994) is an inventive analysis of power relationships, thought patterns, and self-images in a local community.

Late works like *Time* (1984) and *The Germans* (1996) are variations on material in the study of court society and *The Civilizing Process*. *The Symbol Theory* (1991) links this theory with work on the sociology of science. Stephen Mennell's study, *Norbert Elias: An Introduction* (1992) discusses Elias's work and his links to other sociologists. Elias's autobiography can be found in *Reflections on a Life (1994)*.

Norbert Elias (1897–1990) is today an important and central figure in European sociology. His work has been translated into several languages. A number of sociologists pursue the lines of enquiry in Elias's work, above all in the Netherlands, Germany, and Great Britain. Pierre Bourdieu has pointed to Elias as a model. A central textbook in the eighties, Philip Abrams's *Historical Sociology* (1982), is strongly influenced by the work of Elias.

Elias wrote his main work, *The Civilizing Process*, during his years of exile in England in the thirties. It was published in two volumes in Switzerland in 1937 and 1939 but remained unknown in wider circles for many years. In the late sixties it was reissued in Germany. This initiated Elias's fame. During the seventies and eighties a number of his books were published and he kept working intensively until his death in 1990.

The Theory of the Civilizing Process

The Civilizing Process (Elias 1994a [1939]) is a broadly structured, historically vast and theoretically ambitious study of the emergence of the European nation-state and modern forms of sociability, social behavior, and interaction. It consists of two parts. The first part deals with "the history of manners." Through a study of conduct books and other rules for behavior, changes in norms and standards of normality are described. Elias examines how and why the "civilizing" of behavior proceeds as it does. The second part analyzes the process of establishing nation-states in Western Europe from the twelfth century onward. The analytical ambition of Elias is to view changes in conduct and the centralization of the state as two aspects of the same historical process, called the civilizing process in Elias's terminology. It links the monopolization of taxation and the means of violence, that is, the development of a state, with changes in human manners and emotional life. The central idea of the work is the transformation of social discipline into self-discipline, from *Fremdzwänge* to *Selbstzwänge*.

Accordingly, the formation of the state and the individuality are, to Elias, simultaneous, tightly linked, and complementary social processes. In the concluding chapter of *The Civilizing Process* it is stated that

> The peculiar stability of the apparatus of mental self-restraint which emerges as a decisive trait built into the habits of every civilized human being, stands in the closest relationship to the monopolization of physical force and the growing stability of the central organs of society. (Elias 1994a: 447)

> The controlling agency forming itself as part of the individual´s personality strcuture corresponds to the controlling agency forming itself in society at large. (Elias 1994a: 451)

How is the link between the changes in personality structure and social structure explained by Elias? Are the changes temporally simultaneous only, causally linked, or are they more intimately related, results of the same fundamental processes? Elias's theory argues for the third alternative.

Processes of social change have, according to Elias, two main forms: increasing and decreasing differentiation and integration. Furthermore, Elias argues, the regulation of emotions and the system of social control evolve in the same direction, as a long process of evolution, a *civilizing process* in other words. It is a special kind of process as it is a "process without a subject." This means that it can be analyzed without having to presuppose the will of an agent or subject that gives the process its forward momentum. The process is not initiated by a certain social stratum or class – it gets underway as a result of tensions *between* different functional groups in a social field and *between* groups that compete within such fields.

Central concepts in the theory of the civilizing process

Elias's central theoretical concepts are *functional differentiation, interdependence, figuration, power differences,* and *self-control. Functional differentiation* is, according to Elias, the primary force resulting in decisive social change. He shares this point of departure with classical social science and its analysis of the social consequences of the division of labor (cf. Adam Smith, Karl Marx, and Emile Durkheim). In a society shaped by differentiation and division of labor, social relations become more complex. Increasingly long and complicated chains of interdependence are created. The differentiation of labor and institutions extends this chain of relationships of interdepence. The concept used by Elias to cover this successive aspect of reciprocal dependence is *interdependence*.

The core of the theory of the civilizing process is that the extension of the chains of interdependence leads to a transformation of society which affects the forms of both state and individuality. When "state control" is condensed and consolidated in social life, stable central (state) organs arise. This long process of historical development also affects the process of mental control, so that psychological drives, emotions, and self-discipline assume a more regularized form.

This twofold rationalization of social life is not a result of rational planning, since it takes place, Elias says, "without planning but with a unique kind of order." Social developments are seen by Elias as independent processes, the outcome of which is not planned or possible to foresee. Nevertheless, they have their *own developmental logic* which is called, in a different terminology, "emergent properties."

The sociological enigma to Elias is how it is possible that something can be created in the human world which no single human being has *intended* to create. A specific coercive order arises out of the interdependent relationships between human beings. The basis for the civilizing process is this *dependence* between human beings that is created by the tightly knit order of interdependence. The dynamic of this linking process is inexorable. "Civilization . . . is set in motion blindly, and kept in motion by the autonomous dynamics of a web of relationships, by specific changes in the way people are bound to live together" (Elias 1994a: 445). The basis for this internal dynamic is the *differentiation of functions*. More and more functions and individuals become increasingly dependent on each other. The consequence is that "As more and more people must attune their conduct to that of others, the web of actions must be organized more and more strictly and accurately, if each individual action is to fulfil its social functions" (Elias 1994a: 445). The increasingly differentiated regulation of the mental complex is determined by the development in social differentiation, the progressing differentiation of functions, and the extending chains of interdependence, in which every action of the individual is embedded.

An example: the hazards of travel

Elias's line of thought can be illustrated by one of his own examples – the differences between travelers of the past and of our time. What risks and problems were faced by travelers at the end of the Middle Ages? It was not only the condition of the road, its mud and unevenness, that constituted a problem. A greater problem was the risk of being surprised by highwaymen. On the freeways of our time it is rather the heavy traffic and unpredictability of other drivers that produce dangers. The differences between these two situations require different attitudes to action. In the former case, the ability to take action and defend oneself is required. In the case of the modern driver, however, the required abilities are mental and physical concentration, range of vision, ability to foresee the actions of other drivers, and impulse control. We have proceeded from the ability to handle a surprise attack to the demands of the complexities of modern traffic on range of vision and self-control.

The example of the traveler is a simple illustration of the essentially very complex relationships in a society. The chains of actions in which individuals are embedded become increasingly long and individuals become increasingly dependent on each other. The individual who falls prey to spontaneous impulses and drives is socially disadvantaged in comparison to individuals who are able to impose self-control.

Why do changes in conduct and manners take place? Changes in self-control are enforced by the less visible and more impersonal coercion that is created by social interdependence (chains of social dependence). The control mechanisms become automatic, unconscious, and internalized (as they are gradually and increasingly a result of education). It is the significance of change in the complexities of social relationships and altered forms of interdependence that leads to Elias's analysis of court life and court society.

The Strategic Role of the Courts for the Civilizing Process: The Aristocracy's Progress from Rapier to Intrigue

Elias's thesis is that modern civilized and calculating conduct started in court society. Calculation is not only related to the merchant class and a result of the increasing complexity of economic networks in trade capitalism.

When do self-discipline and self-control become adequate responses? For individuals whose functions interrelate several different chains of action and interdependence it becomes mandatory, on account of this coordinating role, to control how time is being used. The merchant bourgeoisie, especially the group involved in long-distance trade, became tied to long and increasingly complex chains of action. This particular group has also been cast in the role of a modern social stratum, for example, by Weber, and it is the norms of conduct of this stratum, its rationality, which have been seen as typically modern. Elias, however, argues that it was not only this group's engagement with business and economic calculations that led to modern codes of conduct. The codes of conduct and self-image of the modern age arose, according to Elias, in the government circles of the state and, not least, in the stratum of the nobility. This was as important a source of modern conduct as the merchant bourgeoisie. Through emphasizing the coordinating functions in managing the economic and political sphere, Elias seeks the explanation in general social factors like interdependence and patterns of social relations.

The role of the court as the center of the state was determined by the king's relationship to the aristocracy. Throughout a long period in Europe – notably in France, which is Elias's key example – the balance of power between the king and the nobility gradually shifted to the king. This was due to the progress of arms technology, more efficient taxation, the possibility of the king to hiring mercenaries, and the relative decrease in land revenue for the nobility.

The court evolved into an instrument through which the aristocracy could be both controlled and supported. The position of the individual nobleman in the power game of court life was determined by his standing with the king. The ability to gain confidence, to show aptitude as a courtier, and to handle conflicts and intrigues became significant personal assets (and finally personality traits). Conversation and intrigue replaced courage and the rapier as instruments through which power and influence could be gained. Elias asserts that it is in court culture that a psychological view of man is first developed. Literature and accounts of human behavior, for example, in the memoir, are first developed in court culture. The court decisively influenced the development of modern forms of advanced music (cf. Elias's analysis of Mozart, 1994b).

The rationality of court society

Court life had a unique kind of rationality. Rational predictability and calculation became increasingly necessary. But the rivalry and competition was not about money and markets but about people and prestige. The complex dependence of individuals was determined by the actions and judgements of others. The division of power between the king and the aristocracy made the situation increasingly unpredictable and complex. The coercive form of court intrigue made certain types of conduct more advantageous. Rules of conduct were, on one hand, a way to distribute royal grace and prestige to the subordinate players. On the other hand, the combination of manners and complex machinations resulted in a special kind of power-game rationality which corresponded with the new type of personality. Out of this analysis Elias derives his thesis that the relationships between human beings are the circumstances that transform the human psyche. This conclusion makes clear the parallels to G. H. Mead (see chapter 8).

In contrast to lower strata, the merchant and the court aristocrat both had functions which led to and enforced conduct based on long-term impulse control and calculation. Which part of the conduct code becomes most refined and differentiated? Elias argues that this is determined by the area that is of the greatest importance to the social stratum in question. This area becomes a distinguishing trait and instrument in the competition. For the aristocracy this area turned out to be the refinement of social interaction which becomes an instrument for gaining respect and, as a consequence, influence. For the bourgeoisie impulse control is shaped by functional virtues like saving, prescience, and planning – all virtues important to becoming a successful businessman.

A function which coordinates several different chains of interdependence increases the demands on control of the self and the process. The number of actions which are dependent on others increases, as do the length and density of the chains in which the actions are interwoven. The network of interdependent relationships is kept in motion by power relations in the form of competitive rivalry. Elias asserts that self-disciplined conduct increases when the chains of interdependence of which the agents are a part become longer, denser, and more complex.

The relationship between the king and the court aristocracy in court society is an important *figuration*, which is one of Elias's central categories. *Figurations* can be defined as "networks of reciprocally [interdependent] individuals, which are shaped by shifting asymmetrical power relations" (Benthem van den Bergh as quoted in Mennell 1992: 252). *Relations between individuals* are both the object of study and the analytical point of departure in Elias's research agenda. Consequently, court society cannot be understood in terms of the personality of the more or less absolute monarch – it is the complex power relations between king and nobility, and to other social strata, above all the bourgeoisie, that make up the character and dynamic of this society.

Games as Models for Social Relationships, Interdependence, and Sociability

In order to elaborate Elias's concept of figuration I will discuss his use of game metaphors and his analysis of the "established–outsider" figuration.

Games are determined by rules but they are also combats. Strength is not an absolute quality in the players but an aspect of the relations between them. These two aspects of games are the reason why Elias employs game metaphors to illustrate social processes. Games possess different degrees of social complexity, from chess with two participants to team sports like soccer. Analyses of games can, according to Elias, provide illuminating perspectives on other social phenomena, for example, processes of state formation and democratization.

If there is a considerable difference in skill between two chess players the stronger will be able to direct the sequence of the game. He will not only win but also determine *how* he will win, that is, he determines both the outcome and the sequence of play. If the skill is more evenly balanced between the players the sequence of play will not be so uniformly directed. The outcome and sequence of play will depend on the moves and strategies of each player. Through the web of moves of the two players a unique sequence of play develops, which none of the players had planned or foreseen. This is what sociologists call "emergent properties," that is, relationships that arise out of social processes.

As more players are included in a game it will be more difficult to foresee the sequence of play and the outcome. In a game with teams of several different players each individual action will not only be hard to place in relation to the strategy of the individual team but will also be dependent on the sequence of the game as a whole.

From game analysis to analyses of power relations between the bourgeoisie and the working class

Following Elias's lead, it is possible to transfer the analysis of complex games to the power relations between social groups. The analysis focuses on *power differences*, the complexity of the "teams," and the complex character of the "game." The aim is to identify the patterns that emerge out of the sequence of the game. In "games" with several "players" and an increasing number of links between them it is difficult to survey and foresee the sequence. Each "team" may become increasingly specialized and new "fields of play" may be established.

The relations between the social classes in the emerging modern industrial society are an example of this. As the power differences between upper and lower strata diminish, the sequence and outcome of the "game" will become increasingly hard to predict. This is illustrated by the relationship between the working class and the bourgeoisie in modern societies. As the interdependence between the two groups increases, another situation than that of a simple upper and lower order will emerge. Increasingly long and complex chains of interdependence will lead to a situation of reciprocal control between different social strata. Changes in the power relations and increasing interdependence between different groups are seen by Elias as central elements in the long civilizing process of Europe and the emerging "functional democratization."

The working class aimed for a levelling of the power balance through confrontations and negotiations in various areas ("fields of play"). Increasing their degree of organization was one of its instruments of power, but it also led to a far-reaching division of labor within the "team." The focus on negotiation, like the differentiation of leaders and members, resulted in new forms of conduct and self-control. Loyalty and solidarity became important elements. But these normative systems were not derived from the upper strata but were developed within the working class itself. A Swedish historian of ideas, Ronny Ambjörnsson, shows in his work *Den skötsamme arbetaren* (The Disciplined Worker, 1988), how a focus on acquiring knowledge and personal discipline came to play an important role in the shaping of self-confidence in the Swedish labor movement and its later success in the new arenas of power that arose out of negotiations between unions and employers as well as political ones. In these arenas a certain type of competence and ability in politics and discourse were required and these abilities coincided with the ideals of self-discipline which emerged.

Power Difference and Figuration: The Dynamics between the Established and Outsiders

In *The Established and the Outsiders* (1965, revised edition 1994), a study of three areas in an English suburb, in the study named Winston Parva, is presented by Elias and his colleague, John Scotson. One of the areas was regarded as having a higher ratio of youth criminality than the other two – and this difference was the problem that led to the study being commissioned. However, during the period in which the study was undertaken the small difference in the crime rate between the three areas disappeared, but the *image* of the stigmatized area remained. It was still seen as a bad area and the inhabitants were regarded as people of less value.

Winston Parva indicates, in Elias's view, a phenomenon of general applicability. Differences in power between two interdependent and interacting groups will give rise to notions of different moral value in the two groups. The group in power will regard itself as better than the others. The dominant group will be able to force its view of itself and the others on the other group. Power differences between groups will be followed by differences in moral status.

In all established power relations, be it the relation between estate owner and tenant farmer, white and black, Christians and Jews, men and women, or, as in the study of Winston Parva, between an old and established working-class group and a new proletarian area:

> In all these cases the more powerful groups look upon themselves as the *better people*, as endowed with a kind of group charisma, with a specific virtue shared by all its members and lacked by others. What is more, in all these cases the "superior" people may make the less powerful people themselves feel that they lack virtue – that they are inferior in human terms. (Elias and Scotson 1994: xvi)

How is this brought about? To begin with, the established group avoided all contact with the outsiders, apart from the necessary interaction in work-places, and looked down upon them as a group. The distance was maintained through social control, with gossip as a key mechanism ("what are people going to say?") and a ban on all social intercourse. The established group ascribed superior qualities to itself, which motivated the social exclusion of the other group.

In Winston Parva there was, to the outside observer, nothing to distinguish the two areas in terms of order, class, or ethnicity. No differences could be found that could be identified as socially distinguishing traits. The only difference between the two areas was the different capacity of the two groups for integration and cohesion within the group (for example, knowledge of the identities of the members). Power was maintained by the established group through its greater capacity for cohesion and ability to use social control mechanisms. The cohesion of the group is its power base.

Moral differentiation

The conclusions to be drawn from the study of Winston Parva led Elias to the assertion that moral differentiation plays an important role in how differences in power are established and maintained. The established group ascribes the "bad" traits of the "worst" segment of an outsider group to the group as a whole, that is, an aberrant minority is made to represent the whole group. Inversely, the self-image of the established group is based on its most exemplary and proper segment, that is, the segment from which its norms are derived. A part of the group is made to stand for the whole group and the dynamic in the established–outsider figuration distils the representative elements for each group from the "minority of the best" of the established group and the "minority of the worst" of the outsider group. This systematic distortion makes it possible for the established group to prove its valuation of the outsiders to itself and to others – there will always be examples to support this mechanism.

This process of evaluation and stigmatization is, according to Elias, not an individual problem, as the category "prejudice" might suggest, but a group problem. The ability of one group to assert the inferiority of another group is due to the power relations between the two groups. The fact that an individual in one group views a member of another group as inferior is not related to individual traits or qualities. Members of a stigmatized group or category are collectively viewed as separate from and inferior to their own group.

Elias argues that a model based on his analysis of Winston Parva's study is widely applicable and can serve as an "empirical model" also for relations between other social groups and even states. What is the central element in the established–outsider figuration? The answer is the unequal power balance and the tensions this gives rise to. The form of the stigmatization is a result of the power difference. The situation of untouchables in India or slaves in the USA denotes an extremely unequal power balance. To label one group as "less valuable" is an instrument in the struggle between groups whereby the established group can maintain its social superiority. What makes this instrument so effective is that the label also affects the self-image and identity of the other group and, as a consequence, makes it weaker.

The newcomers in Winston Parva were seen as a threat to established norms and values, the lifestyle and manners of the established group. By exclusivist measures the established group confirmed its own identity, created differences in the way in which the two groups were viewed, at the same time as group cohesion was the power instrument that made it possible to maintain the differences.

The relative similarity between the two areas in the study of Winston Parva made it possible for Elias to discover that it was the form and intensity of the cohesion of a group that determined the power difference; the difference in cohesion is a source of power differences.

An important aspect for Elias is the complementary relationship between the charisma of the individual's own group and the disgrace of the other. This is the basis for the emotional barrier to contact between the two groups. The mechanism in question can be more sharply observed in the distance established by high-caste groups in India towards the untouchables. Similarly, the discriminatory attitudes of whites in the USA are reflected in the blacks' evaluation of themselves as inferior.

In order to become a member of the established group, and partake in its superiority, the individual has to pay the price of submitting to the norms of the group. All intercourse with the outsider group threatens the position within the established group – there is a risk of "contagious infection" as the outsider group by definition is seen as of inferior moral status. The terms for describing the outsider group are in themselves powerful expressions of subordination and stigmatization. An outsider group, on the other hand, cannot stigmatize an established group by denigrating appellations.

Power differences and conflicts between groups

There are recurring elements in the stigmatization of outsiders. Examples of these are notions of unreliability, lack of discipline, and lawlessness. Why are the degrading characteristics seemingly universal? Elias's point is that the symptoms of human inferiority a dominant, established group tends to observe in a subordinated outsider group are exactly those modes of conduct and traits that are created by the very state of being an outsider and the subordination that is a consequence of this. Power differences, accordingly, tend to become socially and conceptually self-legitimizing.

Elias explores how groups are formed and how cohesion within the group is established and works. Cohesion is based on memories, shared values, a long-term, intimate amity or hostility. It is this custom-based, nontheorized, and nonexplicit web of cohesion and interaction that creates the power relation between established and outsiders. The network of the old families in Winston Parva's study illustrated these characteristics in exemplary fashion. Their internal cohesion was not visible to the newcomers, who perceived the old inhabitants as similar to themselves and never understood why they were excluded from social intercourse and were stigmatized as "lesser people."

The stigmatization that is the outcome of the established–outsider figuration has a strong impact on the self-image. The self-image of individuals in the outsider group is affected by the sense of belonging to a stigmatized and excluded group. Whenever the established-outsider figuration is present so are these emotions.

The figuration of established–outsider arises in the junction and interaction of different groups. It emerges when formerly independent groups become increasingly reciprocally dependent. It is the conflict between groups and not between individuals that, in Elias's view, plays the decisive role in social change. In a characteristic formulation, Elias states that groups and not individuals make up survival units.

Relationships as a Fundamental Sociological Category: Elias's Critique of Dualism

Unlike many other sociologists, Elias does not attempt to establish firm and discrete units and categories, in the form of dichotomies like ego–alter, individual–society, in order to construct relationships based on them. In contrast, Elias sees patterns of relations to be of greater significance. "The individual" is not the point of departure or epistemological foundation for sociology. *Social relationships* should, according to Elias, be the analytical starting point for sociology as a study of how societies work. The object of sociology should not be how already established individuals consciously and rationally construct their social relationships. They exist and are recreated, reconstructed, and shaped in various different ways. Individuals – as bodies, as persons – of course exist but are viewed analytically as necessary conduits for these relationships.

The solution to the problem of the individual and society, the chicken and egg problem of sociology, is not to construct a *Homo economicus, Homo sociologicus*, etc. Rather, the solution is to be found in regarding "bondings between people" as just as real as the individuals themselves: *the category of relationships is the point of departure.*

The critique of the conceptual dichotomies of sociology

The sociologically relevant aspects of individuals are products of society. But how is it possible for us as sociologists to see another object than the individual or society, that is, to focus on the *relationship* between individual and society as the basic analytical unit? In order to do this we need to problematize the apparent truisms of received notions and thought patterns and to emancipate ourselves from the idea that individuals are separable from society or that the individual and society constitute two different realities. Rather, they should be seen as aspects or phases in a unitary human reality. The significance of individualism – and the category of the individual – in Western philosophical and political thought is obvious. This thought pattern was first expressed in Descartes's subject philosophy but subsequently also appeared in the ideas of individual action, utility, and consequent rational interaction in economic theory.

The revolutionary impact of sociology was its (re)discovery of the social sphere as something more than a side-effect of agreements and transactions between independently acting individuals. But sociology initially also added to the problem by assigning a dualistic form to the relationship between individual and society. This very dualism between individual and society is what, according to Elias, has to be "unthought" – deconceptualized. It is, however, problematic to conceptualize the unity between individual and society in a discourse that had been designed to define their separateness. Elias's concept of figuration stresses this unitary character.

Process reduction

Elias criticizes the tendency of *process reduction* of sociologists and philosophers. The basic mode of process reduction is to reduce a process to a combination of a static condition and a changing force. An example is that "blowing" is construed as "the wind is blowing." Similarly, "activity" is construed as "agent plus action." In more general terms relationships are reformulated so that different objects are separated in order to be subsequently set in relation to each other. Individual and society are construed as two separate worlds. The separation that a dualistic set of concepts has created is supposed to be painstakingly rejoined.

From the individual–society model to figuration

In his critique of dualism Elias employs two conceptual models, one an ego-centered individual–society model and one a figurational model. The first model is the egocentric worldview with the "self" in the center, surrounded by rows of concentric circles. It is an image that presents itself naturally to spontaneous reflection. It produces an understanding of the world in terms of a *dualistic, reciprocally objectifying* view and externalizes two separate objects, ego and system, agent, and the structure with which he comes into contact. It is an image of an individual "I" and its environment. This corresponds to the construction of *wirlose Ich* ("we-less I's") in subject philosophy.

In the figurational model individuals are seen as nodes in long and complex chains of dependence and interaction, constituting chains of interdependence between human beings. In this construction individuals are joined and related to each other and there are power relations between them. They make up "figurations" of various kinds, for example, families, schools, cities, etc. The figurational model is also applicable to the relations between social groups like social classes and even states.

The figurational concept: the "heliocentric" worldview of the social sciences

Elias's suggested program for the social sciences can be compared to the transition from the geocentric to the heliocentric worldview in astronomy and the natural sciences. In the latter view we regard nature at a distance as a chain of interdependence with no concomitant idea of an animated or natural center. This is, in Elias's view, a basic condition for scientific enquiry. This condition can, according to Elias, never be achieved and reach general consensus unless human beings refrain from unreflecting and spontaneous attempts to construe everything they experience as having an aim and meaning for themselves.

The conception of the *agent* as an independently acting or choosing individual was a decisive step in the history of philosophy and the social sciences. The problem for sociology is that the models and constructions of this theory assume an independent life of their own; the category of the individual is reified and we get what Elias terms the idea of the *Homo clausus*. Through the construction of *Homo clausus* the idea is created that the self is contained inside the individual human beings, isolated both from other people and external reality. The interior is perceived as separated by a wall from others. This isolation has been conceptualized in the view of the acting self and the idea that we meet other people as "the other." This view permeates subject-oriented philosophy and the traditions of social science which originate in this philosophy, for example, neoclassical economics. Elias argues that this conception is useless for sociology.

This idea of *Homo clausus* leads to a conception of the adult, rational individual as, Elias states, "a philosopher who has never been a child." The fact that self-consciousness is an extremely creative instrument for reflection gives rise to the idea that consciousness is an independent entity and that reflection is not a social phenomenon.

Conclusion

Norbert Elias's main contribution to modern sociology is that he, through the theory of the civilizing process, has demonstrated *one* possible solution to the macro–micro problem in sociology. The solution consists in Elias's linking of the development of the external discipline and changes in the state with the changes in self-control and inner discipline in the individual, the mechanism of internal coercion. This link is established by relating both processes to changes in the social relationships between individuals, groups, and states. Changes in these relationships are in their turn affected by the development of social differentiation and power relations. Elias analyzes historical processes in terms of development but from a non-teleological point of view. His conception of the process stresses the unintended, unplanned outcome as a consequence of the interaction between the changes in interdependence and power relations.

Elias's analysis of the relationship between established and outsider as a power relation between groups is an important and useful example of his figurational analysis. In the figuration established–outsider the power difference between the groups leads to a moralizing and evaluative polarization of "good" and "bad" which explains how power is created and how communal self-images are created.

The general methodological and theoretical contribution of Elias to modern sociology is his part in dismantling conceptual dichotomies and reaching beyond the reductive binaries that still play a significant role in sociological enquiry: individual–society, agent–structure, etc. Instead he stresses process, relations, and interdependence as elemental categories of sociology.

Elias's views have been disseminated in sociology through, for example, Philip Abrams's introductory work *Historical Sociology* (1982). There is an obvious similarity between Elias and Pierre Bourdieu but also with some of Giddens's categories (for example, the concept of structuration). Elias's study of Mozart has clear affinities with the sociology of Bourdieu (the concepts of field and habitus).

Bibliography

Primary:

Elias, Norbert. 1978: *What is Sociology?* London: Hutchinson.
—— 1983 [1969]: *The Court Society*, Oxford: Blackwell.
—— 1985: *The Loneliness of the Dying*. Oxford: Blackwell.
—— 1987a: *Involvement and Detachment*. Oxford: Blackwell.
—— 1987b: *Los der Menschen: Gedichte, Nachdichtungen*. Frankfurt am Main: Suhrkamp.
—— 1991a: *The Symbol Theory*. London: Sage.
—— 1991b: *The Society of Individuals*. Oxford: Blackwell
—— 1992: *Time. An Essay*. London: Sage.
—— 1994a [1939]: *The Civilizing Process*. Oxford: Blackwell.
—— 1994b: *Reflections on a Life*. Cambridge: Polity Press.
—— 1996: *The Germans*. Cambridge: Polity Press.
Elias, N., Whitley, R., and Martins, H. G. (eds) 1982: *Scientific Establishments and Hierarchies*. Dordrecht: Reidel.
Elias, N., and Dunning, E. 1986: *Quest for Excitement. Sport and Leisure in the Civilizing Process*. Oxford: Blackwell.
Elias, N., and Schroter, Michael. 1994c: *Mozart. Portrait of a Genius*. Cambridge: Polity Press.
Elias, N., and Scotson, J. L. 1994d [1965]: *The Established and the Outsiders*. London: Sage.
Elias, Norbert, Mennell, Stephen, and Goudsblom, Johan. 1998: *Norbert Elias on Civilization, Power, and Knowledge: Selected Writings*. Chicago and London: University of Chicago Press.

Secondary:

Abrams, Philip. 1982: *Historical Sociology*. Shepton Mallet: Open Books.

Ambjörnsson, R. 1988: *Den skötsamme arbetaren*. Stockholm: Carlssons Förlag.

Duindam, Jeroen. 1995: *Myths of Power: Norbert Elias and the Early Modern European Court*. Amsterdam: Amsterdam University Press.

Elias, Norbert, Mennell, Stephen, and Goudsblom, Johan. 1998: *The Norbert Elias Reader: A Bibliographical Selection*. Oxford: Blackwell.

Fletcher, Jonathan. 1997: *Violence and Civilization*. Cambridge: Polity Press.

Gleichmann, P. R., Gouldsblom, J., and Korte, H. (eds) 1977: *Human Figurations: Essays for Norbert Elias*. Amsterdam: Stichting Amsterdams Sociologisch Tijdshrift.

Korte, Hermann. 1988: *Über Norbert Elias: Vom Werden eines Menschenwissenschaftlers*. Frankfurt am Main: Suhrkamp.

Lepenies, Wolf. 1978: Norbert Elias: An Outsider Full of Unprejudiced Insight. *New German Critique*, 15, 57–64.

*Mennell, Stephen. 1992: *Norbert Elias. An Introduction*. Oxford: Blackwell.

Mouzelis, Nicos. 1995: *Sociological Theory – What Went Wrong? Diagnosis and Remedies*. London: Routledge.

Theory, Culture and Society 1987: Special Issue: Norbert Elias and Figurational Sociology, 4/2–3.

*Van Krieken, Robert. 1998: *Norbert Elias*. London and New York: Routledge.

chapter 24

Anthony Giddens

Lars Bo Kaspersen

KEY CONCEPTS

DUALITY OF STRUCTURE – the mediating concept that transcends the actor–structure dualism. Structure is both the medium for and the outcome of the actor's actions.

PLASTIC SEXUALITY – when sexuality is no longer synonymous with reproduction, it can be shaped and used to further our process of self-identity.

PURE RELATION – a relation between two persons who enter a relationship for their own sake and who stay together only as long as it is satisfactory for them to do so.

SELF-IDENTITY – not a given entity but a process. It is constantly produced and reproduced via the actor's actions.

SOCIAL ONTOLOGY – structuration theory is an attempt to describe the social reality and is therefore Giddens's social ontology.

SOCIAL PRACTICE – society does not consist of a predetermined universe of objects. Society is constantly produced and reproduced by actively acting agents in their social practice. Social practice constitutes us as actors and simultaneously realizes and embodies structures.

Biography: *Anthony Giddens*

Anthony Giddens, born in 1938, was educated at the University of Hull, where he got a BA degree with honours in sociology. At the London School of Economics (LSE), a thesis about the development of soccer in the 1800s earned him a master's degree. Initially, he planned a career as a civil servant, but after 18 months at LSE, he was offered a lectureship at Leicester University, where he stayed from 1961 to 1969. At Leicester he worked with leading English and European sociologists, among others, Norbert Elias and Ilya Neustadt. During the same period, he was also a guest lecturer at Simon Fraser University near Vancouver and at the University of California, Los Angeles. From 1970 to 1985, he was a lecturer at the University of Cambridge, and in 1985 he became a professor there and a fellow of King's College. He has also been a guest lecturer at the University of California, Santa Barbara. He is also a director of Polity Press, one of the leading publishers within social sciences and humanities. In addition to his teaching, research, and publishing activities, he travels the world as a guest lecturer. In 1996 he left Cambridge and became the director of the London School of Economics.

In recent years Giddens has joined the political debate in England and is a member of one of the Labour Party's think tanks. He is also one of the advisers of the Prime Minister, Tony Blair.

The British sociologist Anthony Giddens is today regarded as one of the leading social theorists. His work can be divided into two periods. In the first, from the early 1970s until the mid-1980s, he developed his so-called theory of structuration. The main focus of the second period, from the mid-1980s until today, is a sociological analysis of modern society. Giddens's work in the two periods is related, since he first worked on developing a theoretical perspective that could form the basis for the work in the second period: a concrete analysis of contemporary society.

Giddens as Critic and Structuration Theorist

Giddens's basic opinion is that it is necessary for modern social sciences to reread the classical sociologists to gather inspiration for a modern and more contemporary sociological theory (Giddens 1971a). This is an attempt to break with structural functionalism (see chapter 14) and action sociology, including social interactionism (see chapter 6 and 12) which have dominated postwar sociological debates. At the same time, Giddens emphasizes that it takes more than Karl Marx (see chapter 2), Max Weber (see chapter 6), and Emile Durkheim (see chapter 5) to create a foundation for a theory that wants to highlight the special character of modern society. It takes a different and new type of sociological theory that transcends the foundational problems in classical sociology.

According to Giddens, classical and modern contributions to the social sciences share a number of problems. They all contain seemingly incompatible conceptions of society. Is society made up of the sum of individuals' actions? Or is society more than the sum of these actions and is there a social structure that is independent of each individual's actions?

Agent–structure dualism

In very simple terms, sociological theory can be divided into two groups: a group of theories that view society from a system or structure perspective and that, often unintentionally, ignore the significance of the acting actor. Functionalism, structuralism, and parts of Marxism belong to this group. The other group takes its point of departure in actors and their actions. The actors and the sum of their actions make up society and there are no structures or systems that are independent of the actors. The strong emphasis on the individual and its actions in action sociological theories leads to a neglect of an adequate understanding of social institutions. As exponents of this approach, Giddens mentions Weber (see chapter 6), theories of social interaction (George Herbert Mead, Erving Goffman, Harold Garfinkel, Alfred Schutz; see chapters 8 and 12), rational choice theory (see chapter 13), and parts of Marxism (including analytical Marxism; see chapter 11).

A system/structure-based analysis of the education system would see society as a structure (or system) in which a number of needs must be satisfied for the system to reproduce itself: A society requires that individuals are socialized into certain types of norm sets and that skills are passed on from generation to generation. This requires institutions that carry out certain functions, and the main function of the educational system is to head this socialization process. However, Giddens finds such a theory about the educational system problematic because individual actors are not seen as independent, reflecting individuals. They are assigned different roles and positions in the system as teachers or students and are "forced" to take on certain norms and skills that are already embedded in the system.

If the educational system is conceived via action sociology, the point of departure is the individual actors, their actions and motives. Winchester College exists not because British society needs this school, but because the actions of a number of individual actors, such as politicians, civil servants, teachers, and students, make it possible. Their motivations may be different, but the sum of their actions make it possible for Winchester College to exist. Action sociological theories run into problems when they have to explain the presence of rules and norms available to be used by each actor in order to act. Apparently, certain societal conditions exist before the single actor.

In other words, the two sociological theories come up with very different answers to questions such as: To what degree can we as individuals create our own lives and frames for our lives, and to what degree are we already constrained by society and its structures when we are born?

Giddens describes this conflict between individual and society as a dualism between actor (the acting individual) and structure (society), and he claims that this dualism must be transcended if sociology wants to comprehend more adequately the complexity of modern society.

Giddens's solution: theory of structuration

Structuration theory, Giddens's own contribution to overcoming this dualism, was developed as a result of a critical dialogue with the major schools of social theory: sociological theories of action (see chapters 6, 8, 12, and 13), functionalism (see chapters 5, 14, and 15), structuralism (see chapters 18 and 19), and Marxism (see chapters 2 and 9). This dialogue has been developed in several publications since the 1970s (Giddens 1976, 1977, 1979,1981, 1982b).

The Constitution of Society (Giddens 1984) gives the most coherent presentation of structuration theory. According to Giddens, it is a severe mistake that sociology for the most part uses *either* actor *or* structure as its point of departure. Instead, he claims that the actor–structure relation fundamentally must be seen as a *duality of structure*, by which he means a coherent relation in which structure is both the medium and the outcome of the actors' actions. When I get on a bus, I produce and reproduce a structure, the public bus system, which is connected with a number of rules and routines: I have to buy a ticket, know when the bus leaves, refrain from smoking on the bus, etc. When I take the bus, I use existing structures and simultaneously I create these structures the minute I step on the bus. This way, society is constantly created in a continuous structuration process. Giddens also calls this process social practice.

In the books *Central Problems in Social Theory* (1979) and *The Constitution of Society* (1984), Giddens defines social practice, which, as the mediator between action and structure, is a central concept for him. In his definition, he uses core concepts from classical and modern sociology and philosophy, such as agent, action, structure, system, and power. He redefines and reformulates the concepts in such a way that they become mutually dependent and combine to constitute social practice. Let us take a closer look at some of the individual elements that are combined to make up social practice.

Social Practice

The concept of agent

Giddens claims that a society consists of social practices that are produced and reproduced across time and space. Consequently, Giddens finds it necessary to define social practice by using concepts that do not favor the action perspective over the structure perspective, or vice versa.

He starts his attempt to pin down social practice with a definition of the concept of agent.

Agents are knowledgeable about most of their actions. This wealth of knowledge is primarily expressed as *practical consciousness*. I know how to play soccer, but I do not have to
account for how it is physically possible for me to kick the ball. Giddens points out that we
possess enough knowledge to carry out these actions, but that this knowledge is rarely
formulated discursively. We often know how to act. We know the rules of conduct and we
know the sequence of actions. When we get to work, we say hello to the receptionist, hang
up our coats, turn on the coffee machine, etc., etc. These actions are routinized and take
place at a practical level of consciousness.

Our *discursive consciousness* is different from the practical level of consciousness, which
includes knowledge we cannot immediately account for. A discursive explanation implies
that we explicitly express why and/or how we play soccer, and it may take place at several
levels. For example, I may answer that I am practicing for an important game, give an
anatomical or physical explanation, or claim that I play soccer to get some exercise.

By highlighting the knowledge of the agent, Giddens emphasizes that systems and structures do not act "behind the actor's back." Besides enabling us to formulate explanations,
discursive reflexivity on an action gives us the opportunity to change our patterns of action
(see figure 24.1). Not all motives for action are found at a "conscious" level. So in contrast
to many action sociologists (see chapters 8 and 12), Giddens employs an *unconscious level*,
which comprises actions spurred by unconscious motives. The unconscious comprises repressed or distorted knowledge.

The transition from discursive to practical knowledge may be diffuse, but there is a "bar"
between these two types of knowledge and unconscious motives which, for example, because of repression, cannot immediately turn into conscious knowledge (Giddens 1984: 49).

All three levels are important, but practical knowledge seems to be most decisive for an
understanding of social life. The significance of this concept, compared to the two others, is
to rehabilitate the large amount of tacit knowledge which is often ignored by social theory.
This tacit knowledge and experience that agents possess are very important for the maintenance and reproduction of social life.

Discursive consciouness

Practical consciousness

Unconscious motives/cognition

Figure 24.1 The agent and its reflexive form of knowledgeability.

Agency

In contrast to many classical sociologists, Giddens does not see actions as isolated phenomena. He sees action as a flow of events, pervading society in a never-ending process that is analogous to the processes of thought and cognition that constantly pervade our minds. Action is a flow without start or finish, in short, a structuration process.

Agency takes place with knowledge and, most often, practical consciousness. To Giddens, actions are purposive and intentional, but it is important to point out that the agent is not practically or discursively conscious of all consequences of his actions. On the contrary, Giddens stresses that these repeated actions often have unintended consequences. For example, I speak English with the intention that those who listen will understand me. The unintended consequence of this action is that I simultaneously reproduce the English language. The concept of "unintended consequences," which is taken from R. K. Merton (see chapter 14), is important, because it introduces the reproductive character of actions and because Giddens with this concept approaches the dimension of structure.

The unintended consequences of our actions become conditions for new actions, and this makes it clear that actions in Giddens's sense are not rationally considered, isolated actions with anticipated results. Therefore, history is not a rational, progressive process with a specific goal. The course of history changes constantly and often in unpredictable ways, precisely because our actions have unintended consequences which again become the conditions of future actions. An agent's knowledge is always bound by the unacknowledged conditions and the unintended consequences of action.

Structure, system, and structuration

Like "agent" and "action," the concept of structure also needs to be redefined. Giddens distinguishes between *structure* and *system*. Every day of the year, city buses drive along the same routes, passengers get on, buy tickets, sit down, get off. These actions are constantly repeated and reproduced in a social pattern that Giddens calls a *social system*. Social systems consist of relations between actors or collectivities that are reproduced across time and space, that is, actions that are repeated and therefore extend beyond one single action. Social systems are social practice reproduced, thus creating a pattern of social relations.

In contrast, *structures* are characterized by the absence of acting subjects and exist only "virtually." Accordingly, structures are present only as options that have not manifested themselves actively. This indicates that Giddens's concept of structure is to a large extent inspired by structuralism (see chapter 18).

Structures exist only in practice itself and in our human memory, which we use when we act. Giddens does not use his concept of structure as an external frame. Structures emerge in our memory traces only when we reflect discursively on a previous action. In other words: Structure does not exist, it is continuously produced via agents who draw on this very structure (or rather structural properties) when they act.

To avoid the conception of structure as an external frame that determines and thus constrains our actions, it is stressed that structures are both enabling and constraining. Structure or structural properties, as Giddens prefers to call it, consist of *rules* and *re-*

sources which agents draw upon in their production and reproduction of social life and thus also structure. In accordance with the philosopher of language, Wittgenstein, rules should be understood very broadly as those techniques and formulas that, anchored in our tacit practical consciousness, are employed in action. Giddens's concept of rule refers to procedures of action – aspects of practice – and they work as formulas telling us "how to go on in social life" (Wittgenstein) (Giddens 1984). The concept of resource is closely related to power as the medium through which agents can perform their "transformative capacity".

Thus agent, action, and structure are connected, and therefore structure in Giddens's terms cannot be conceived as something external or "outside of" the agent. The traditional concept of structure is dissolved and simultaneously becomes the medium for and outcome of the social practice of the agent.

The duality of structure

This brings us to the key concept, namely *duality of structure*, the very core of structuration theory and the concept of practice. "Structure is both the medium and outcome of the practices which constitute social systems" (Giddens 1981: 27). In other words, the structure–actor relation is no longer conceived as a dualism, but as a duality. The concept of duality of structure connects the production of social interaction, performed by knowledgeable agents, with the reproduction of social systems across time and space.

The fact that the traditional concept of structure has been replaced by a conception of structure as structural properties consisting of rules and resources means that to Giddens structure is no longer deterministic, but both enabling and constraining. Language is one example. When I speak English, I use certain rules to make myself understood. At the same time, I reproduce these rules and thus the structure of the language. Language is enabling because it allows me to express my wishes and intentions, but the moment my motives or wishes cannot be expressed in words, language becomes constraining. Likewise, English can be constraining for me if I meet someone who does not know this language. In fact, structuralism and functionalism have often been criticized for being deterministic as a consequence of the concept of structure and system embedded in these theories.

(Structural) functionalism – especially Parsons – is often trapped by this problem, but Giddens avoids this by maintaining that structure is rules and resources that are used in all actions. According to Giddens, values and norms (rules and resources) are embedded in the agent (Giddens 1984: 17–28), whereas Parsons embeds values and norms in the structure or system, thus placing them outside the agent, and consequently they guide and constrain the agent's possibilities of action.

The duality of structure is the core of Giddens's conception of social practice and thus also of his social ontology, that is, his conception of the nature of society. Society is seen as social practice, constantly creating and recreating society in a structuration process. The duality of structure is Giddens's solution to the actor–structure dualism and thus the basis of an adequate analysis of modern society.

Analysis of Modernity

Giddens outlined an analysis of modernity in his book *Nation-State and Violence* (Giddens 1985), but only in the 1990s has he presented a more coherent analysis of contemporary society (*Zeitdiagnose*) that includes an analysis of the characteristics of institutions in modern society and the specific characteristics of modern people, our self-identity and mutual relations. This analysis of contemporary society is found in the books *The Consequences of Modernity* (1990), *Modernity and Self-Identity* (1991), and *The Transformation of Intimacy* (1992a).

What is modernity?

Giddens claims that the social forms of organization that developed in Europe from the start of the 1600s, and that have since become global, are unique in relation to earlier forms of society. These forms of organization and thus "modernity" developed in the interplay of a number of institutional dimensions, namely capitalism, industrialism, the surveillance and information control of the nation-state, and the development of military power. According to Giddens, grasping the complexity of this interplay is essential for a new sociological theory that wants to comprehend our society.

What distinguishes premodern from modern types of society? First and foremost, Giddens emphasizes the dynamic character of modern society, the pace, intensity, and scope of change. Another important feature is the type and nature of modern institutions. Characteristic of our civilization are the nation-state, the modern political system, hyper-mechanized and hyper-technological production methods, wage labor, commodification of all relations, including the work force, and urbanization.

What is the source of these dynamics? The most dynamic aspects of modernity can be boiled down to three aspects that run through Giddens's entire analysis of modernity: separation of time and space; disembedding mechanisms; and the reflexive character of modernity.

Time–space separation

For the most part, everyday social interaction no longer takes place at the same time or in the same space. Unlike earlier times, when the home and the village were the central places (locale), families are now scattered in time and space. Dad sells furniture to Germany via phone, fax, and e-mail. Mom, who works as a health visitor, drives around to her patients but is in contact with her superior via mobile phone. Their son is in the sixth grade and in geography class he gathers information on Ghana's infrastructure from a database. His older sister is an au pair in California but communicates frequently with her family by phone, air mail, or e-mail. This is a pretty typical modern family, but it would have been science fiction just a few decades ago. Standardization and globalization of time enables the family members to interact with each other and the surrounding world without problems.

Not only the concept of time but also the concept of space is changing and undergoing a process of "emptying." Each new technological development expands our space significantly. The fact that we can be in the same space but not necessarily the same locale (Giddens 1990: 18–19) is one of the driving forces behind the modern rational organization. If a modern corporation wants to function optimally, it must be able to coordinate the actions of large numbers of persons who may be separated in time and space.

Disembedding of social systems

In previous societies, before time–space separation, institutions and actions were embedded in local communities. This has changed because now social relations are no longer limited to local communities but have been "lifted out" from a local context of interaction by disembedding mechanisms (Giddens 1990: 21). Giddens distinguishes between two types of disembedding mechanisms, *symbolic tokens* and *expert systems*. Combined, they make up *abstract systems*. Symbolic tokens are media of exchange that "can be passed around" among individuals and institutions, for example, money (see also Parsons, chapter 14, and Luhmann, chapter 22). As a form of credit, money is a means of bracketing time. It represents a value that can later be spent on the purchase of new goods. Due to their standardized value, symbolic tokens disturb the perception of space as agents who never actually meet each other can carry out transactions with each other. In other words, symbolic tokens lift transactions out of their "particular milieux of exchange" and produce new patterns of transactions across time and space.

Expert systems that surround us in our daily lives are an example of an abstract system that is also a disembedding mechanism. When I take the bus, I enter a huge network of expert systems that enable the construction of buses and roads and the development of traffic systems. Without knowing anything about the codes of knowledge used to develop these systems, I can take the bus as long as I have money for the ticket and know my destination. Due to expert systems, social relations move from one context to another, and expert systems and symbolic tokens increase my radius of movement.

Time–space separation and disembedding mechanisms are mutually dependent. Abstract systems increase the time–space distanciation.

The reflexivity of modern society

Reflexivity is in a fundamental sense a defining characteristic of all human action. However, reflexivity also has a different character which is specific to modernity (Giddens 1990: 36ff). Modern society is undergoing a reflexivity process that exists at an institutional as well as a personal level, and which is crucial to creating and changing modern systems and forms of social organization.

Giddens defines reflexivity as the regular use of knowledge which institutions and individuals continuously collect and apply to organize and change society. Corporations perform market surveys to help them devise sales strategies. States take censuses to figure out their tax base.

This increased reflexivity is facilitated not least by the development of mass communication. Writing started the process, but the development of other means of communication enabled societies to collect and store large amounts of information and thus raised the level of reflexivity compared to earlier times. In modernity our actions are only rarely guided by tradition, and we act according to tradition only if it seems justified and rational. Marriage is a good example: Earlier, people would get married because it was a natural part of tradition. Today, people still get married, not because tradition says they have to, but more as part of a reflexive process. The fact that some people choose not to get married forces us into a process of reflexivity in which we have to be able to justify our own actions.

Increased reflexivity should not be mistaken for increased and better knowledge which has enabled us to "control" life. This is far from reality, because this increased reflexivity creates a fundamental doubt about the certitude of new knowledge. We can no longer be sure that this knowledge will not be revised, and therefore the knowledge claim can no longer be certainty and truth. We constantly experience how scientific discoveries are challenged by new research, and this creates a doubt that has become an existential feature of modern human beings, with consequences for our identity.

These changes in the nature of reflexivity and the role of tradition have moved society towards what Giddens calls a post-traditional order. Tradition has become evacuated and problematized. This has implications for our ontological security.

The consequences of modernity for ontological security

The increased reflexivity of modernity helps to create a radical doubt at both the institutional and the personal or existential levels. This doubt influences our perception of trust and risk. Facing insecurity and several choices, trust in a person or a system is crucial for the choice that has to be made. Relations of trust are crucial to a person's development and possibilities of action, and consequently the concept of trust is crucial to Giddens (Giddens 1990: 79ff; 1991: 36ff).

Giddens sees trust as being closely related to so-called ontological security. An infant develops the basis for ontological security in relation to its mother and father. If an infant experiences many strong, positive, and primarily predictable routines in relation to its mother, it develops a strong ontological security system. Trust developed between mother and child is a kind of vaccine that protects the child against unnecessary dangers and threats. Trust shields the self so that it can handle the many choices that constantly surface.

Trust in systems and the risks connected with this trust are crucial for the ontological security which constitutes the basis of our own identity and a confidence in the social and material world we live in. Trust in abstract systems creates trust in our daily lives, but it cannot replace the reciprocity or intimacy of personal relations. Trust in impersonal principles and anonymous "others" becomes an inevitable and necessary part of our lives and creates a new kind of psychological vulnerability.

The self as a reflexive project

In the last 20 to 30 years, our relations of trust, risk profile, and thus ontological security system have changed radically with consequences for our identity. Institutionalized radical doubt, insecurity, and many constant choices we face affect the development of self and identity, and vice versa. Ontological security is fundamental to a person's self-identity. Only strong ontological security can help a person develop a self-identity that enables him or her to accept the reality of things and of others.

Self-identity is, in Giddens's sense, a reflexive project, since reflexivity, so characteristic of modernity and its institutions, also penetrates the core of the self. In premodern societies kinship, gender, and social status determined a person's identity at birth. A child born among peasants in the 1770s would not even consider other "career paths" since its identity was already determined by external relations and tradition. This has changed with high modernity where self-identity is a reflexive project and everybody is responsible for their own identity. We are what we make ourselves, and therefore life is a matter of choosing and making the right decisions so that we can keep going our own particular narrative of the self.

The transformation of intimacy

The radical and rapid changes of high-modern society have freed the self and self-identity. The self is not something given, but a reflexive project. To create a self-identity, we must continually make choices, also in the sphere of intimacy, where the destruction of the bonds of tradition has created an opening which means that everybody is now more or less forced to actively choose and shape their intimate relations.

An individual develops parts of its self-identity in close and intimate relations in what Giddens calls *the pure relationship*. The pure relationship emerges because the significance of external factors for the relation is dissolved. The term "the pure relationship" refers to a situation,

> where a social relation is entered into for its own sake, for what can be derived by each person from a sustained association with another; and which is continued only in so far as it is thought by both parties to deliver enough satisfactions for each individual to stay within it. (Giddens 1992a: 58)

Close relations of trust that are significant for our ontological security are developed in social contexts where the pure relationship is the ideal type. We participate in a number of necessary intimate relations, for example, sexual relations, marriage, and friendships. Earlier, such relations were subject to the precise rules of tradition, but this is no longer the case, and therefore the participants must constantly and reflexively negotiate the conditions of a relationship. Today, we choose not only a partner but also rules for relationships.

In earlier times, marriage was subject to external conditions. It was often arranged by parents and/or was entered for economic reasons. The division of labor with the husband as the breadwinner and the wife as the homemaker determined the frames of the marriage. These external conditions have disappeared, and modern marriage or cohabitation understood as a pure relationship (which of course has nothing to do with sexual purity!) have become contracts between two equal parties. If either party feels that they no longer obtain the desired satisfaction (emotionally, sexually, etc.), they may leave the relationship and start over with someone else.

Relationships, marriage, and friendship are examples of pure relationships. Mutual trust between the parties is a condition for the stability and development of such relationships, which requires that the parties open up and disclose themselves and their intimacy. This process of disclosure can become the foundation of strong, intimate relations of trust. However, this process is also risky for a fragile self. The self can be badly bruised if it experiences rejection after having revealed itself emotionally.

Plastic sexuality

Sexuality is also subject to the reflexive project of the self. *Plastic sexuality* – a sexuality that is no longer synonymous with reproduction – gives us the opportunity to use and shape our sexuality in the development of our self-identity process. Sexuality in itself becomes an important part of our self-realization and thus the development of our identity. It can be an important factor when we choose a partner.

With the concept of plastic sexuality, Giddens also points out that our sexuality is no longer determined once and for all. Since it is much more fluid than we previously assumed, we are more free to challenge sexual boundaries. These new developments confront the individual with even more choices.

Giddens concludes that modernity is synonymous with fundamental changes in institutions and individuals at both a local and a global level. These processes of changes force individuals to create their own identities and lives and consequently, many people attempt in their everyday lives to influence and make demands on life and also of those institutions that have an impact on our lives.

Giddens and politics

Giddens has often been criticized for not taking part in the public political debate. He answers this criticism in his book *Beyond Left and Right* (Giddens 1994a) which is a study, based on his analysis of the post-traditional society, of the consequences for practical politics. Most recently he has published *The Third Way: A Renewal of Social Democracy* (Giddens 1998a), which more or less attempts, with *Beyond Left and Right* as a point of departure, to provide a new foundation for social democracy. Globalization and related processes of change weaken the conditions for the dominating ideologies, especially socialism, liberalism, and conservatism. Therefore it is necessary to develop a political program that encompasses local, national, and global dimensions. Modern welfare institutions must be restructured so that they further a democratic dialogue instead of turning citizens into clients. The potential for democratic dialogue is present both in intimate relations and in global relations. The main goal must be to develop institutions that enable this dialogue within and between all levels.

Giddens's Sociology: Final Comments

Giddens's sociology, a wide-ranging project based on more than 30 years of research, includes a dialogue and critique of classical and modern social theory, the development of his own theoretical contribution, and modernity analysis. Different aspects of the project have recently been debated and criticized (see, e.g., Bryant and Jary 1991; Clark et al. 1990; Cohen 1989; Craib 1992; Held and Thompson 1989; Mestrovic 1998; Tucker 1998; Kaspersen 2000).

Two points of criticism in relation to structuration theory stand out. One group of critics, among them Thompson (1984, 1989), Archer (1982; 1990), Layder (1985), and Livesay (1989), points out that Giddens puts too much emphasis on the actor and the enabling side of the agent at the expense of the constraining element, that is, the structural frames. Giddens does not specify how enabling or constraining structures are. The other point of criticism concerns the applicability of the theory in relation to empirical analyses. Gregson (1986; 1987; 1989), Bertilsson (1984), and Thrift (1983, 1985) claim that, although structuration theory is interesting and perhaps transcends some dualistic problems at a theoretic level, it is less fruitful in empirical research. The abstract level of the theory weakens its fruitfulness.

Other social theorists also discuss his modernity analysis (see Beck 1992; Turner 1992; Robertson 1992). Turner claims that Giddens's points are already contained in Max Weber's sociology. Beck criticizes the way that Giddens uses the concept of reflexivity. Giddens equates reflexivity with knowledge, a definition Beck claims is too narrow and vague (Beck 1992: 166–7).

Bibliography

Primary:

Beck, U., Giddens, A., and Lash, S. 1994: *Reflexive Modernization*. Cambridge: Polity Press.
Giddens, Anthony. 1971a: *Capitalism and Modern Social Theory*. Cambridge: Cambridge University Press.
—— (ed.) 1971b: *The Sociology of the Suicide*. London: Cassel.
—— 1972a: *Politics and Sociology in the Thought of Max Weber*. London: Macmillan.
—— (ed.) 1972b: *Emile Durkheim: Selected Writings*. Cambridge: Cambridge University Press.
—— 1973/1981: *The Class Structure of the Advanced Societies*. London: Hutchinson.
—— (ed.) 1974: *Positivism and Sociology*. London: Heinemann.
—— 1976: *New Rules of Sociological Method*. London: Hutchinson.
—— 1977: *Studies in Social and Political Theory*. London: Hutchinson.
—— 1978: *Durkheim – Modern Masters*. London: Fontana.
—— 1979: *Central Problems in Social Theory*. London: Macmillan.
—— 1981: *A Contemporary Critique of Historical Materialism*. London: Macmillan.
—— 1982a/1986: *Sociology – A Brief but Critical Introduction*. London: Macmillan.
—— 1982b: *Profiles and Critique in Social Theory*. London: Macmillan.
—— 1984: *The Constitution of Society*. Cambridge: Polity Press.
—— 1985: *The Nation-State and Violence*. Cambridge: Polity Press.
—— (ed.) 1986: *Durkheim on Politics and The State*. Cambridge: Polity Press.
—— 1987: *Social Theory and Modern Sociology*. Cambridge: Polity Press.
—— 1989: *Sociology*. Cambridge: Polity Press.
—— 1990: *The Consequences of Modernity*. Cambridge: Polity Press and Stanford, CA: Stanford University Press.
—— 1991: *Modernity and Self-Identity*. Cambridge: Polity Press.
—— 1992a: *Transformation of Intimacy*. Cambridge: Polity Press.
—— (ed.) 1992b: *Human Societies*. Cambridge: Polity Press.

—— 1993: *The Giddens Reader*, ed. P. Cassell. London: Macmillan.

—— 1994a: *Beyond Left and Right: The Future of Radical Politics*. Cambridge: Polity Press.

—— 1995a: *Politics, Sociology and Social Theory*. Cambridge: Polity Press.

—— 1995b: *Politics, Sociology and Social Theory; Encounters with Classical and Contemporary Social Thought*. Stanford, CA: Stanford University Press.

—— 1996: *In Defence of Sociology; Essays, Interpretations, and Rejoinders*. Cambridge: Polity Press.

—— 1998: *The Third Way: A Renewal of Social Democracy*. Cambridge: Polity Press.

—— 1999: *Runaway World*. London: Profile Books.

—— 2000: *The Third Way and its Critics*. Cambridge: Polity Press.

Giddens, A., and Stanworth, P. (eds) 1974: *Elites and Power in the British Society*. Cambridge: Cambridge University Press.

Giddens, A., and Mackenzie, G. (eds) 1982: *Social Class and the Division of Labour, Essays in honour of Ilya Neustadt*. Cambridge: Cambridge University Press.

Giddens, A., and Held, D. (eds) 1982: *Classes, Power, and Conflict*. London: Macmillan.

Giddens, A., and Turner, J. (eds) 1987: *Social Theory Today*. Cambridge: Polity Press.

Giddens, A., and Pierson, C. 1998: *Conversations with Anthony Giddens. Making Sense of Modernity*. Cambridge: Polity Press.

Giddens, A., and Hutton, W. (eds) 2000: *The Edge*. London: Jonathan Cape.

Secondary:

Archer, M. S. 1982: Morphogenesis versus Structuration: On Combining Structure and Action. *British Journal of Sociology*, 33/4, 455–83.

—— 1990: Human Agency and Social Structure: A Critique of Giddens. In J. Clark, C. Modgil, and S. Modgil (eds), *Consensus and Controversy: Anthony Giddens,* London: Falmer Press.

Beck, U. 1992: How Modern is Modern Society? *Theory, Culture & Society*, 9/2 (May), 163–9.

Bertilsson, M. 1984: The Theory of Structuration: Prospects and Problems. *Acta Sociologica*, 27/4, 339–53.

Bryant, C. G. A., and Jary, D. 1991: *Giddens' Theory of Structuration: A Critical Appreciation*. London: Routledge.

Clark, J., Modgil, C., and Modgil, S. 1990: *Consensus and Controversy: Anthony Giddens*. London: Falmer Press.

Cohen, I. J. 1989: *Structuration Theory: Anthony Giddens and the Constitution of Social Life*. London: Macmillan.

Craib, I. 1992: *Anthony Giddens*. London: Routledge.

Fontana, B. 1994: Plastic Sex and the Sociologist: A Comment on The Transformation of Intimacy by A. Giddens. *Economy and Society*, 23/3, 374–83.

Franzén, Mats. 1992: Anthony Giddens and his Critics. *Acta Sociologica*, 35/2, 151–6.

Gregson, N. 1986: On Duality and Dualism: The Case of Structuration and Time Geography. *Progress in Human Geography*, 10, 184–205.

—— 1987: Structuration Theory: Some Thoughts on the Possibilities for Empirical Research. *Environment and Planning D: Society and Space*, 5, 73–91.

—— 1989: On the (Ir)relevance of Structuration Theory to Empirical Research. In D. Held and J. Thompson, *Social Theory of Modern Societies: Anthony Giddens and his Critics,* Cambridge: Cambridge University Press.

Held, D., and Thompson, J. 1989: *Social Theory of Modern Societies: Anthony Giddens and his Critics*. Cambridge: Cambridge University Press.

Jary, David, and Jary, Julia. 1995: The Transformations of Anthony Giddens: The Continuing Story of Structuration Theory. *Theory, Culture & Society*, 12/2, 141–60.

Kaspersen, L. B. 2000: *Anthony Giddens: An Introduction to a Social Theorist*. Oxford: Blackwell.

Layder, D. 1985: Power, Structure and Agency. *Journal for the Theory of Social Behavior*, 15/2, 131–49.

Livesay, J. 1989: Structuration Theory and the Unacknowledged Conditions of Action. *Theory, Culture and Society*, 6, 263–92.

May, Carl, and Cooper, Andrew. 1995: Personal Identity and Social Change: Some Theoretical Considerations. *Acta Sociologica*, 38/1, 75–85.

Mestrovic, Stjepan G. 1998: *Anthony Giddens*. London: Sage.

Mouzelis, N. 1997: Social and System Integration: Lockwood, Habermas and Giddens. *Sociology*, 31/1, 111–19.

O'Brian, M., Penna, S., and Hay, C. (eds) 1998: *Theorizing Modernity; Reflexivity, Environment, and Identity in Giddens' Social Theory*. New York: Longman.

Robertson, P. 1992: Globality and Modernity. *Theory, Culture & Society*, 9/2, 153–61.

Shilling, C., and Mellor, P. A. 1996: Embodyment, Structuration Theory and Modernity: Mind/Body Dualism and the Repression of Sensuality. *Body and Society,* 2/4, 1–15.

Thompson, J. B. 1984: The Theory of Structuration: An Assessment of the Contribution of Anthony Giddens. In J. B. Thompson, *Studies in the Theory of Ideology,* Cambridge: Polity Press.

—— 1989: The Theory of Structuration. In D. Held and J. Thompson, *Social Theory of Modern Societies: Anthony Giddens and his Critics,* Cambridge: Cambridge University Press.

Thrift, N. J. 1983: On the Determination of Social Action in Space and Time. *Environment and Planning D: Society and Space*, 1, 23–57.

—— 1985: Bear and Mouse or Bear and Tree? Anthony Giddens's Reconstitution of Social Theory. *Sociology*, 19/4, 609–23.

*Tucker, K. H., Jr. 1998: *Anthony Giddens and the Modern Social Theory*. London: Sage.

Turner, Bryan S. 1992: Weber, Giddens and Modernity. *Theory, Culture and Society*, 9/2, 141–6.

part III

Contemporary Challenges to Classical and Modern Social Theory

chapter **25**

Post-industrialism, Cultural Criticism and Risk Society

Gorm Harste

Biography: *Daniel Bell*

Daniel Bell was born in 1919. He was a professor at Harvard University for a number of years and has written books and articles which have obtained a special status on the agenda of the sociological debate. After four books about right and left opposition, he published the eloquently titled *The End of Ideology* in 1960, a book that left its mark on the debate about harmony and convergence in industrial societies. Bell's main works intensely analyze significant contemporary trends. Both as a person and as a researcher, he puts remarkable effort into keeping abreast of his topics. It is probably this strength that has created the vast interest in Bell's books, rather than their systematic theoretical form which, almost antithetically, is influenced by his opinion that politics, economics, and culture are separated in modern society. Bell has been very influential in the Democratic Party in the US and has been chairman of the Commission Toward Year 2000.

The American sociologist, Daniel Bell, has been one of the most influential figures in discussions during the last couple of decades about what tendencies characterize modern society. He has pointed out that, since the end of the 1950s, it has been an intellectual challenge to come up with concepts about the type of society that is developing. Most observers have a more or less clear idea that the type of society that existed, at least until the end of the 1950s, differs in many ways from the type of society we are entering. Many concepts have been proposed as adequate in order to grasp the new structures of contemporary and future society, but just a few of them can be sustained and verified after more rigid sociological analyses. The reason is that the significance of new trends can be judged only according to more "grand theories" describing all the more important developments of society. This chapter will concentrate mainly on theories about "post-industrial society," about cultural trends, and about "risk society."

These general social concepts serve at least three purposes: First, concepts like "industrial society" and "modernity" describe *historical eras*. Second, they describe or express certain *trends*. And third, they describe how *contemporary time* and society are experienced and perceived. It is important to keep in mind that the object of analysis is the society one lives in. Thus, in order to create a distance from the contingent fashionable ways of self-description of society, the systems theoretician Niklas Luhmann pays attention to the methodological way sociologists recognize "observations of their own way to observe society" (see chapter 22).

An evaluation of how successfully the three aspects are treated in theory can be based on different criteria. For example, theories that attempt to map social development from one era's social formation or principle of organization to a subsequent era are constructed with a considerable empirical ambition in mind. These theories must include many different phenomena and at the same time keep track of developments in religion, law, politics, art, science, military, production, trade, cities, agriculture, etc. Thus, for Daniel Bell, analytically, society can be divided into three parts: the social structure, the polity, and the culture. The social structure comprises the economy, technology, and the occupational system. The polity regulates the distribution of power and adjudicates the conflicting claims and demands of individuals and groups. The culture is the realm of expressive symbolism and meanings. It is useful to divide society in this way because each aspect is ruled by a different axial principle (Bell 1976: 12).

We could say that, methodologically, theories about industrial society, the information society, and post-industrial society generally adhere to *macro-sociological objectivistic* analyses and descriptions of developments related to production. Another type of cultural diagnostic analysis mostly keeps to analyses of how social order is experienced. This, in turn, could be analyzed *subjectively* or from the *micro-sociological* point of view of the individual and the social meaning of the order. Some of these analyses of culture discuss risk structures of social order according to the ways the order is *reflected*. This methodological difference structures the three main sections of this chapter.

Theories about Post-Industrial Society

The concept of post-industrialism emphasizes that industrial mass production is not the only important thing in economic development. Standardized, manual labor will not dominate the economy. Instead, production of knowledge will be decisive, as it can be used in the manufacture of products and in the service sector. According to those who claim that we are about to enter the post-industrial era, the transition from industrial society to post-industrial society should be just as significant as the transition to industrial society. "The concept of a post-industrial society gains meaning by comparing its attributes with those of an industrial society and pre-industrial society" (Bell 1976: 126).

For Bell, "the concept of post-industrial society deals primarily with changes in the social structure" and to a lesser extent with the polity and the culture (Bell 1976: 13). Bell starts out by challenging a number of Karl Marx's generalizations about the significance of labor for the social order. According to Bell, other phenomena besides a pre-industrial "game against nature" and an industrial "game against fabricated nature" could become significant. Therefore the social structure is different in different eras. First, people lived in a natural world and reality, then in a technical reality, and in the future "reality is primarily the social world" (Bell 1976: 488). Bell's thoughts are summed up in table 25.1.

The point in Bell's table is that the different factors in, for example, the post-industrial structure are intrinsically connected. Accordingly, people who work with knowledge production exchange information, not energy. Bell thinks that conditions that existed in pre-industrial Europe and the US now exist in Asia, Africa, and Latin America, where farmers and fishermen exchange raw materials with nature rather than information. The table mentions Bell's own claim about what he himself is doing, namely "social forecasting" (Bell 1976: 3). This is the way time is observed in post-industrial society, whereas predictions and projections were more typical of industrial society.

The idea of industrial society

Before describing post-industrial society in more detail, it is necessary to analyze what the idea of industrial society actually is. What is the substance of this talk about transition from industrial society? Right here we run into several problems, because it turns out that it is not clear what is meant by the statement that modern societies have been industrial societies.

Table 25.1 From industrial to post-industrial society: a general scheme of social change

	Pre-industrial	Industrial	Post-Industrial	
Regions:	Asia	Western Europe	United States	
	Africa	Soviet Union		
	Latin America	Japan		
Economic sector:	Primary Extractive:	Secondary goods:	Tertiary:	Quinary:
	Agriculture	Manufacturing	Transportation	Health
	Mining	Processing	Quaternary:	Research
	Fishing		Trade	Government
	Timber		Finance	Recreation
			Insurance	
Occupational slope:	Farmer	Semi-skilled worker	Professional and	
	Miner	Engineer	technical scientists	
	Fisherman			
	Unskilled worker			
Technology:	Raw materials	Energy	Information	
Design:	Game against nature	Game against fabricated nature	Game between persons	
Methodology:	Common-sense experience	Empiricism Experimentation	Abstract theory: models, simulation, decision theory, systems analysis	
Time perspective:	Orientation to the past Ad hoc responses	Ad hoc adaptiveness Projections	Future orientation Forecasting	
Axial principle:	Traditionalism: Land/resource limitation	Economic growth: State or private control of investment decisions	Centrality and codification of theoretical knowledge	

(Bell 1976: 117)

This is a problem, because attaching the term "post-" to a specific social form is like admitting that you are not sure about a new concept which does not have its own description. Bell says that "the term *post* is relevant in all this, not because it is a definition of the new social form, but because it signifies a transition" (Bell 1976: 112). In other words, it is important to have a precise understanding of industrialism in relation to post-industrialism. Oddly enough, Bell is critical of the theory of industrial society.

A distinction is often made between the first, second, and third industrial revolutions, depending on which technology the development of industrial production is based on. An industrial revolution can be described as having created totally new opportunities to avoid manual or organic-physiological work being the only source of energy. The first Industrial Revolution is synonymous with the steam engine and its significance for weaving mills and coal mining. The second industrial revolution occurred with the invention of electronics and gasoline engines around the turn of the century. The third revolution is the micro-electronic development which is related to the concept of the information society.

Industrial societies are often seen as standardized and conformist societies. According to this view,

> there are some common characteristics for all industrial societies: the technology is every-where the same; the kind of technical and engineering knowledge (and the schooling to provide these) is the same; classification of jobs and skills is roughly the same . . . the spread of wages is roughly the same (so are the prestige hierarchies); and . . . management is primarily a techni-cal skill. (Bell 1976: 75)

Bell also discusses whether it is empirically correct to say that modern societies have pre-dominantly been industrial societies. Only in England was a majority of the working-age population, for a short period in the 1800s, employed in industry. Therefore, Bell says that "the most important social change in Western society of the last hundred years has been not simply the diffusion of industrial work but the concomitant disappearance of the farmer" (Bell 1976: 124).

It is possible that industrial production has had a great impact on the social order. The influential French sociologist, Raymond Aron (1905–83), is perhaps the most prominent advocate of the concept of industrial society. In 1962, he wrote *Dix-huit leçons sur la societé industrielle* (Eighteen Lectures on Industrial Society) which is almost entirely dedicated to economic problems related to growth, profit, and distribution in industry. However, it is impossible to know the importance of industry unless other possible, perhaps equally im-portant and decisive, dynamics are examined, such as religion, law, the military, communi-cation, and urbanity.

Bell really makes an effort to demonstrate that the modern social order may very well be a result of what Max Weber called rationalization and what Emile Durkheim called differ-entiation (see chapters 5 and 6). Modern society was thus dominated by bureaucrats long before industrial technology became a serious factor in modern societies.

Accordingly, the idea of the industrial mass production of goods seems to be contingent on phenomena that are not really caused by technical inventions. Instead, decisive phenom-ena came about because it was possible to connect and coordinate the advantages of large-scale production, division of labor, marketing, product development, financing, infrastructure (railroads), etc. (Chandler 1990). Equally important was the coupling of the development of mass production and the advantages of large-scale production and price minimization, a development that was self-reinforcing. Therefore, Bell claims that the so-called "manage-ment revolution" is just as old as industrialism.

The meaning of "industrial society" has thus in many ways been misleading. The reason it has not been completely rejected is that it has been a conceptual umbrella for socialist and capitalist countries. Terms like industrial society, post-industrial society, and also informa-tion society aim at characteristics that appear homogeneous for societies that otherwise seem different and that may even be adversaries or engaged in exploitative relations.

In sum, Bell describes industrial society in order to be able to define post-industrial soci-ety. But according to his analysis, the term "industrial society" is not so much an expression of a coherent and clear *description* of an objective state as it is an image of our *idea* of society. Therefore Bell's purpose is to make a forecast, not to describe or predict the future.

The conception of post-industrial society

Post-industrial society in Bell's sense has the significance of knowledge as a background for production, the changed role of knowledge producers, the political consequences of this, the expansion of service functions, and the growth in knowledge technology (Bell 1976: 14). These five items will be discussed below.

Knowledge production

Daniel Bell points out that we often associate certain images without conceptions of an industrial society or a feudal agricultural society. We see this on television, where industrial society is depicted by assembly-line production, while feudal agricultural society is depicted by old villages. Similarly, we also associate certain images with post-industrial society. Bell mentions the lab technician dressed in white. Today the researcher in front of a computer is a common media prototype of a post-industrial employee. Knowledge of research especially has become very common: more has been written about research in the last ten years than in the entire history of the world, and there are more researchers now than all previous and deceased researchers combined.

In addition, the image of the typical employee has become diversified: it could be a female designer. Most often, the typical employee is well spoken and highly educated, and thanks to the explosion in higher education, not just engineers, but also economists and psychologists who work as corporate consultants or in information systems become representatives of post-industrial society. This image rarely gives a clear impression of *what* these jobs are actually all about. The productive value that comes from new knowledge cannot simply be measured by how many hours of work go into creating this knowledge. And Bell interestingly notes that it is not the work of post-industrial employees, but their communication, which is central in the image or picture that is communicated:

> what is central to the new relationship is encounter or communication, and the response of ego to alter, and back . . . the fact that individuals now talk to other individuals, rather than interact with a machine, is the fundamental fact about work in the post-industrial society. (Bell 1976: 163)

However, the importance of organizing knowledge in a less instrumental way did not become clear until after 1968, when youth and student revolts created demands for decentralization and participation.

The role of knowledge producers

In his book of 1969, *Post-Industrial Society*, the French sociologist Alain Touraine pointed out that organized welfare-state planning and industrial programs had to learn from the student movements. Bell has expressed similar thoughts:

> The post-industrial society, thus, is also a "communal" society in which the social unit is the community rather than the individual, and one has to achieve a "social decision" as against,

> simply, the sum total of individual decisions which, when aggregated, end up as nightmares, on the model of the individual automobile and collective traffic congestion. But cooperation between men is more difficult than the management of things. Participation becomes a condition of community. (Bell 1976: 128)

Bell's vision of post-industrialism is thus related to a development in what could be called a "post-hierarchical" direction. In Bell's vision, knowledge production of know-how, service production, and the hi-tech production of information are more decentralized, and the hierarchic control therefore demands a democratization of organizations from within. In connection with organizational changes, several experts pronounce their verdicts, each within their special field, about the benefits of such changes. Similarly, there are now a lot more "generalist" experts on *how* to organize than on *what* to organize. For example, the number of people who graduate in social sciences has grown enormously.

But Bell also demonstrates new trends toward what he calls meritocracy. One of the most important merits is higher education, which has also become the most important mechanism in social mobility. According to Bell, this could lead to more equality in connection with developments in the welfare state, but he mentions a number of opposing phenomena, like social heritage. Bell demonstrates that earlier in the modern period, education was used as a means to destroy the old, established order and then create new opportunities for equality. Now, however,

> The post-industrial society . . . is the logical extension of the meritocracy; it is the codification of a new social order based, in principle, on the priority of educated talent. In social fact, the meritocracy is thus the displacement of one principle of stratification by another. (Bell 1976: 426)

And this creates new inequalities.

Political consequences

Specialization in and among organizations and corporations leads to democratization as well as new, distinct, professional groups and subcultures. It also implies social disintegration and unions lose many of their old functions. Social order turns into disorder. Here, the disintegration thesis seems to be supported by Bell's cultural analysis, which he otherwise keeps separate from his more economically oriented structure analysis (Bell 1979). In Bell's view, modern culture, with its modernism and hedonism, creates individualism and fragmentation of the social and political life.

Bell's argumentation is in many ways correct, but the growth in unemployment since he wrote his book has undoubtedly meant more employee discipline and even demands that employees "identify with their jobs." This has strengthened management, contributed to centralization, and led to new conformity and new types of adherence to community. But disciplining has probably also increased productivity in service production and productivity in connection with organizational improvements far more than Bell forecasted, as he stated, "the simple and obvious fact that productivity and output grow much faster in goods than in services" (Bell 1976: 155).

Still, he seems to be right that professional expertise has obtained a new and more complex significance in social development.

> If the struggle between capitalist and worker, in the locus of the factory, was the hallmark of
> industrial society, the clash between the professional and the populace, in the organization and
> in the community, is the hallmark of conflict in the post-industrial society. (Bell 1976: 129)

There have been many examples of these new conflicts during the last 25 years, for example in connection with European Union referendums in European politics.

Bell uses the argument that active and passive union membership is declining in most countries and therefore unions are less and less able to control conflicts to support his claim. The focus on expertise, communication and "know-how" instead of "know what" creates new conflict dimensions. Just like Bell, but in a French background, the Marxist André Gorz, in his famous book, *Farewell to the Working Class* (Gorz 1982), argued that work and the "productivistic rationality" in a post-industrial society can be pushed aside in favor of cultural orientations that originate outside the work sphere. In this way cultural movements would thrive at the expense of the labor movement.

The development in service production

Bell emphasizes that we are only dealing with trends. Obviously, we do not have empirical knowledge about the future. And since this is about creating a new society, his arguments can only be primarily theoretical (Poster 1990: 25ff). Therefore we might expect Bell to perform a penetrating theoretical analysis like Luhmann or Habermas. However, he tries to show the trend by statistical indications of the growth in the five dimensions, for example, the growth in the number of persons in the service sector, the number of persons with a higher education, the number of computers, etc. Bell's book dates from 1973, and his information is old. Instead of repeating Bell's figures, it is far more interesting to check if his predictions are correct so far, if we include more recent numbers. His analysis seems to be confirmed by findings from North America, Western Europe, and Japan.

However, the national statistics do not include developments in newly industrialized countries where many classical industrial jobs are established and to which many jobs in the secondary sector are transferred, among other things because of post-industrial developments in management. Of course, hi-tech production is also rising in several areas in countries like India, Brazil, and some Southeast Asian countries.

Furthermore, the growth in several areas cannot be said to represent anything new. Several people have pointed out that many service jobs have just been transferred from the hidden work of civil society and home life (Kumar 1978; Loftager 1985).

Knowledge technology

On the fifth point, growth in knowledge technology, it is common knowledge that the sale of computers has exploded, especially since the beginning of the 1980s. Automation and robot components often replace standard industrial work, but computers also replace a lot of information work in the service sector, for example, in banks. Technological progress has a very broad meaning to Bell: "all the better methods and organization that improve the efficiency (i.e., the utilization) of both old capital and new" (Bell 1976: 191). Technological developments thus consist of changes that concern machines as well as sociological suggestions for new divisions of labor. Growth in productivity, technical aids, formal knowledge production, the speed with which innovations are disseminated can all be proven statistically, but it is hard to document their complex interrelations and development.

It is still a question whether the technologically based part of service and knowledge development has changed more things in society than, for example, paved roads or telephones, cars, airplanes, or, above all, railroads did when they were introduced (Bell 1976: 192). Here, Bell himself says that even exponential developments follow S-shaped growth curves.

Bell's cultural diagnosis

Bell did not want to present a "total image" of society, rather what Weber called an "ideal type" (see chapter 6), with

> three components: in the economic sector, it is a shift from manufacturing to services; in technology, it is the centrality of the new science-based industries; in sociological terms, it is the rise of new technical elites and the advent of a new principle of stratification. (Bell 1976: 487)

But on several points it is hard for Bell to keep up his otherwise ideal-typical separation of structural and cultural development, and already in his book about post-industrialism, he mentions that "culture has replaced technology as a source of change in the society" (Bell 1976: 115). Despite such announcements, as well as the many cultural enlightened comments in his book on post-industrialism, his analysis was attacked for economic determinism by several commentators (Floud 1971; Janowitz 1974; Stearns 1974; Poster 1990).

In his book *The Cultural Contradictions of Capitalism* (1979), he presented an almost opposite analysis. From the beginning, he attempts to demonstrate that cultivation and cultural development have their own dynamic, and that:

> culture has become the most dynamic component of our civilization, outreaching the dynamism of technology itself. There is now in art – as there has increasingly been for the past 100 years – a dominant impulse toward the new and original, a self-conscious search for future forms . . .
> It is true, of course, that the idea of change dominates the modern economy and modern technology as well. But changes in the economy and technology are constrained by available resources and financial cost. In politics, too, innovation is limited by existing institutional structures . . . But the changes in expressive symbols and forms . . . meet no resistance in the realm of culture itself. (Bell 1979: 33–4)

Bell's cultural analysis shows how intellectual developments in art and art perception have spread far beyond narrow art circles. He shows that modern art and culture are influenced by demands to transcend barriers, genres, and forms of perception and by demands for self-realization, experience, and pleasure. In his structure analysis of post-industrial economy as well as in his cultural analysis, Bell emphasizes that innovations come from reflexive knowledge. Paradoxically, however, he nominates both knowledge technology innovation *and* cultural innovation as dominating factors in social development, which has created some confusion in the debates about his books as to what Bell really means, not least because Bell himself is critical of cultural innovation and defends cultural conservatism.

In sum, we can say that in his post-industrial vision, technology will enable "social reality" and its cultural forms to dominate in the future. To the extent that organizational "know-how" marks a post-industrial break rather than a technical "know that," it seems that phenomena such as organization, communication, and culture should be the focus of contemporary social and cultural diagnosis.

Cultural Diagnosis

The 1970s were a period of rapid development of sociological theory in connection with the so-called "communicative turn in social theory." *Interpreting* intersubjective and communicative relations became the decisive factor instead of *explaining* instrumental subject–object relations. Concepts like work, production, and instrumental domination of nature lost some of their significance in sociological theory and became more delimited by concepts and ideas that are more related to linguistic and communicative experiences. Also the "subject" and the individual became central concepts.

Already in 1961, David Riesman's book *The Lonely Crowd* signaled that the subject had to find a new way to focus on itself in what he called "service society." And despite a long tradition of diagnosis of our contemporary society (Weber's *Zeitdiagnosis*; see chapters 6, 7, and 10), his book became a model for many subsequent analyses. Towards the end of the 1970s, a "new subjectivism" led to a number of important analyses of the development of individualism. Those by Richard Sennett, Christopher Lasch, and Thomas Ziehe demonstrated the significance of individualism and made individuality the center of their cultural sociology. We will consider the sociological diagnosis of Sennett, Lasch, and Ziehe.

Sennett: the tyranny of intimacy

Richard Sennett (b. 1943) is an American sociologist who is deeply influenced by European cultural history. He is a professor not only in New York but also in London. Since his early writings, *The Uses of Disorder: Personal Identity and City Life* (1970) and *The Hidden Injuries of Class* (1972, with Jonathan Cobb), he has been occupied with the social forms that create space *and* time for individuals. Accordingly, his writings cover a range of analyses concerning the social ordering of space in cities and of time in work and leisure activities. Thus, Sennett questions how it is possible to obtain a social order in which individuals have trust in themselves. How is social tolerance possible in cities, in family life, in work-places, in public life and mass media? And how can modern individuals resist the capitalist commodification of individual activity?

Sennett praises the reservations of individuality necessary to the development of human character. Individuality is matured only if life can be narrated in some kind of order. However, the clarity of the public realm is getting obscure under capitalist pressure for smooth and high performance: capitalist work deregulates time, first in the classic control of work by stopwatch, then by the disruptions of family life when distinctions between work and leisure are blown up as well as lifetime jobs and settings. Mature personalities can trust themselves only when they can trust their own life story, but skills and competence are easily outmoded under the claims of new so-called cultural management. In Sennett, we therefore see a commitment to criticize abuses of culture and individuality.

In his main work, *The Fall of Public Man* (1979), Richard Sennett described the paradoxical, historical origin of individuality and personality: From the beginning of the eighteenth century, a number of public roles developed in the thousands of cafés, salons, clubs, and theaters in the new urban centers. Public life and the people who lived there were astonishingly theatrical. It was literally in fashion to make a scene: In Paris, a theater audience demanded nine replays of a particularly sad and tragic scene until they felt they had cried and wailed enough. These public theatrical displays of excessive and competing gestures and courtesy turned out to be a gain for human freedom, because the many social conventions created civilized rules for interaction detached from recently achieved individual positions. Sennett defines civility as "the activity which protects people from each other and yet allows them to enjoy each other's company" (Sennett 1979: 264). Hence, urbanity is the way tolerant civilized interaction is learned.

Sennett now thinks that those conventions, forms, and norms that allow this civilized interaction in modern society are breaking down, not so much because they are disappearing, but because public life is made more subjective and intimate. One example is American politics. Mass media concentrate almost exclusively on statements by presidential candidates that concern their private lives. Questions about "how you really feel" dominate public life as well as the private life of individuals. What people "think they feel" – which before Freud was a completely meaningless and tautological question – now determines guidance in significant parts of modern life and modern social order. According to Sennett, emotion has become tyranny instead of freedom. Artistic and cultural demands for authenticity and genuineness become commercial, professional production of images, relaxation and closeness, typically seen on TV and in other mass media.

From an economic point of view, Sennett is, like Bell, a socialist in the sense of being very critical of the costs of capitalist dynamics; politically, both are liberals, but in their analysis of social and cultural forms, Bell tends to be more conservative than Sennett. Sennett's historical orientation should not be misunderstood as a conservative longing for a revival of communities obliging individuals to be totally included as members of their social bodies. On the contrary, in his book *The Corrosion of Character* (1998), Sennett criticizes the ethos of those organizational cultures that try to exploit the flexibility of modern individuals. The hope that work could be self-realization is used as justification for an overburdening ethos of performance. The virtues of teamwork could be more democratic and decentralized than classical Weberian bureaucracy (see chapter 6); however, what often happens in the recent post-hierarchical forms of management is that individuals are stressed because they have to demonstrate a happy and flexible performance which never guarantees them any time or any territory protected from the team. The team members are asked to be obsessed with motivation. A certain kind of "Teamwork takes us into that domain of demeaning superficiality which besets the modern workplace. Indeed, teamwork exits the realm of tragedy to enact human relations as a farce" (Sennett 1998: 106).

The teams function on the surface of human life and corrode not only the safety of those people, who might have known that they were all right; the team also destroys the basic trust of all those employed who are not included among the dominating performers. The most basic values are dissolved under the banners of dynamism, quality of life, and flexitime in the discourse of managerial culture:

> We imagine being open to change, being adaptable, as qualities of character of change. In our own time, however, the new political economy betrays this personal desire for freedom. Revulsion against bureaucratic routine and pursuit of flexibility has produced new structures of power and control, rather than created the conditions which set us free. (Sennett 1998: 47)

Sennett's analysis argues for a society in which different spheres, for example, public and private, can be distinguished, and is not that far from Habermas's less and less skeptical analyses of interconnections between the public sphere and the liberal society (see chapter 21; Habermas 1990). Ever since his first writings, Sennett – like Habermas – has criticized "the myth of the purified community" in corporations, in city quarters, and in public life. This endeavor is quite opposite to Christopher Lasch's.

Lasch: the culture of narcissism

Christopher Lasch (1932–94) carried out what might look like a similar, but more pessimistic analysis in the cult book, *The Culture of Narcissism* (1979). Lasch has no models that explain how to create a rational separation of private and public spheres. Such a model could counter a new glorification of subjective emotion.

Against such endeavors, Lasch wanted to defend the community, not the individual. Freud analyzed narcissism as an individual, neurotic disorder (Freud 1982: 325–39), but to Lasch it is an entire era that promotes neurotic traits. A "narcissist" is someone who only sees himself as the center of his universe, and who therefore never breaks away from his childhood's ego-centered interpretation of the world. Narcissism is more subjective than egoism, since egoism after all is based on a separation of ego and surroundings.

Not only are the many conventions and norms of the constitutional state and the public sphere disappearing, but in addition, says Lasch, the subjectivization of public life is reinforced by welfare states, private corporations, and nations. The cult of corporate culture turns corporations into families you have to identify with. Likewise, a nation can be called "one big family." Also welfare states have a tendency to undermine demands on the super-ego of individuals. Individuals in the narcissistic culture thus never encounter what Freud called the principle of reality; the individual lives in a world of pleasure and greed, engaged in an endless quest to "find oneself." Finding oneself and realizing oneself constitute the most important activities, and whereas the egoist sees it as an obstacle that the world is not arranged accordingly, the narcissist sees it as morally wrong. An example is education, where a complex lecture or textbook is blamed on poor or faulty pedagogy and not on the nature of the subject.

Lasch makes many interesting observations in his essay, and in his later books he criticizes the corporate elites in their striving for a new but superficial individualism. He points out contemporary trends, but does not really present a coherent theory about a new era. Against his analysis and equal to the criticism against Bell, there are several indications of new claims to self-discipline superposed by too strong corporate duties. Many norms and conventions that were earlier clear objective markers of the previous modern social order have not disappeared but have become omnipresent and implied in disciplined corporate interaction.

Ziehe: unusual learning processes

Whereas Lasch claims that many common norms and conventions are disappearing, the German professor of pedagogics, Thomas Ziehe, says that there are more types of norms than ever before. Ziehe (b. 1947) elaborates Sennett's and Lasch's analyses, but he combines them with some of the complex, especially German, theories of communication, for example, Jürgen Habermas and Niklas Luhmann (Ziehe 1991). As a social psychologist in Hanover, Ziehe studies cultural trends, partly because his approach to the contemporary diagnosis of culture is research of "unusual learning processes" of new youth cultures (Ziehe et al. 1982). He belongs to the tradition of critical theory and to the tradition of cultural diagnosis known from the old Frankfurt School (especially Adorno; see chapter 10). In contrast to, or perhaps rather in culmination of, the critical analyses of reification and "cold technological trends," Ziehe claims that the new subjectivization constitutes a kind of "superheated trend." He talks about three cultural trends that influence subjectivization and its significance.

First, subjectivization is linked to *increased reflexivity*. We're not becoming more and more oriented toward "subjectivity" and "sincerity" without knowing what these terms really mean. Rather, as a matter of fact, we have an all too precise and differentiated awareness when we and others have had a "correct feeling" as opposed to a "wrong feeling." We cannot escape the bombardment of descriptions of how important it is to feel good about oneself and one's emotional life. Consultants create courses on how to find yourself, and millions of people follow these almost identical courses, while thousands of corporations through the same consultants try to find their unique image and "corporate identity." Ziehe here draws on Niklas Luhmann, who acutely describes this as "insincere agreement about sincerity."

The second trend is *increased abstraction*. Labor- and function-divided societies are made coherent by norms, rules, and interpretations which themselves are disconnected more and more from the concrete life forms they are part of. Already in 1893, Emile Durkheim described how differentiated societies presuppose integration at a certain level of abstraction (see chapter 5). Individuals in modern societies are thus able to communicate with people who are completely alien to them, simply because the modern development of common frames of reference, cultural codes, and figures has become so vast that it can create links between even the most different subcultures and life forms.

Cultural spaces in modern cities are places where people can experiment with their behavior and find out how much they can deviate and still be recognized, integrated, and absorbed in social normality. They are therefore also laboratories, not only for technical innovations in corporations and organizations, but also for linking subdivided and highly specialized organizations, despite previous problems with communication between people from different classes, estates, professional cultures, urban or rural districts, nationalities, etc.

The third trend is a *contingency or context expansion*, consisting of the endless number of possibilities offered. The degrees of freedom seem endless, compared to earlier times when there were very few or no possibilities of, for example, choice in careers, shopping, marriage, housing, travel, entertainment, TV shows, computer programs, books, films, music, etc. The same goes for corporations that not only produce basic needs, but will do anything and are forced to invent needs that never existed before.

According to Ziehe, this is fortunate, but it also creates new problems, some of which might be related to a phenomenon described by Bell and Sennett: You have to sell yourself, and this is your way of communicating, rather than your labor.

This is the basis of a renewed search, which Ziehe describes in three dimensions: objective, intersubjective, and intrasubjective. In the objective dimension we experience a deprivation of understanding and a devaluation of our own existence. We now "anticipate a self-relating unambiguous stability of world views." Intersubjectively, we experience "atmospheric coldness and anticipate warmth, likemindedness and intuitive certainty." Subjectively, we experience "inner ambivalence and anticipate upgrading psychic intimacy and stability in our self-image" (Ziehe 1989: 21f).

The consequence of this demand for closeness and easily accessible meaning is a subjective fear of, instead of fascination with, the unknown and the incomprehensible, and, in addition, a loss of the possibility of guidance, because we stick to what we know. In modern society, however, we will learn to swim only if we dare take the plunge.

However, Ziehe does see other possibilities for a new type of self-limitation, new reservations, and a new respect for anonymity and for the Other with capital O. In other words, a new distance and reflexivity, which dares to accept that not everything must be communicated; that not everything must be turned into products and goods; that not all cultural knowledge must be subject to demands for marketability and commodification.

Bell's cultural diagnosis and Sennett's, Lasch's, and Ziehe's analyses seem to add a new type of analysis to the production of knowledge from the industrial or post-industrial societies, a type that shows that reflexive knowledge cannot be reduced to a new technical rationality. In addition, new phenomena have emerged in modern societies, whether we call them industrial societies, post-industrial societies, or information societies. The concept of the "risk society" is an attempt to capture these new phenomena.

Theories About Risk Society

Biography: *Ulrich Beck*

Ulrich Beck (b. 1944) has been professor of sociology at the University of Munich since 1982 and publishes the periodical *Soziale Welt*. In 1972, he wrote a Ph.D. thesis about *Objektivität und Normativität*, which placed him in the neighborhood of critical theory. Later in the 1970s he wrote another doctoral thesis about labour sociology. His book about *Risk Society* of 1986 became his breakthrough. The book was published shortly after the Chernobyl disaster, which is analyzed briefly in the introduction. Beck's books are characterized by a strong social sensitivity and by an ability to find new conceptual angles. He attempts to create a new paradigm for understanding society, which, however, seems to be more prominent in some of his radical reformulations and in his view of the reverse side of society than in a theoretical and empirical breakthrough. Beck is also the author of *Gegengifte. Die organisierte Unverantwortlichkeit* (1989) (*Counterpoison*, 1991), *Politik in der Risikogesellschaft* (1991), *Die Erfindung des Politischen* (articles, 1993), and *Die feindlose Demokratie* (1995).

Ulrich Beck's analysis

A German sociologist, Ulrich Beck, invented the concept of risk society, described in his book *Risk Society* (1986), in which he claims that modern society not only systematically produces products, goods, and wealth, but also risks. Welfare societies redistribute wealth, whereas risk societies redistribute risks. Through this analytical section, Beck gives a coherent perspective that focuses on the flipside of modern society. He mainly speaks about ecological risks, but also about military risks and about new types of poverty and new types of exclusion of groups in developed and underdeveloped countries. Even the concept of development and the assumption that what sociologists call the modernization process will lead to progress are no longer given, because the risks produced by modern society are far too systematic. Thus, we can observe tendencies toward diminishing returns of technological development. The struggle for daily bread has been replaced by a struggle to avoid certain risky future scenarios. "We do not yet live in a risk society, but we also no longer live only within the distribution conflicts of scarcity societies" (Beck 1986: 27).

In fact, we could add a concept of complex "enfoldment" to the concept of development. An astonishing amount of the incessant industrial and social developments in modern society carry with them new, complex compensations and side effects, which must be alleviated by new remedies. Development creates complexity, and it no longer means unilinear progress, rather a complex process enfolded in complex implications. Likewise, actions performed in modern society have become more reflexive. They must be thematized, explained, and explained away, related to consequences and other possibilities to an extent where the emphasis is often on the processing and interpretation of these reflexive phenomena (Beck et al. 1994; Lash and Urry 1994). The problem here is strongly related to the inherent risks in the irreversible damage we cause to our surroundings. It is wrong to claim that earlier societies did not develop irreversibly, but now they implicate themselves irreversibly in changes that cannot be undone by simply replanting rain forest that has been destroyed.

Instead of just focusing on the productive forces of modern society, its destructive forces must also be analyzed, especially since an "overproduction" of destruction is created because the waves of it are interconnected in ecological cycles.

Basically, the concept of risk society is linked to the fact that risks are no longer limited to natural disasters like earthquakes. Natural disasters are no longer "acts of God," but are often caused by man's interference with nature. For example, when the Yangtze, the Mississippi, or the Rhine rivers flood large areas of land, it is, of course, partly because of heavy rain, but also because streams have been straightened, and wetlands which used to absorb large amounts of rainwater have been drained and perhaps even paved. Agricultural development as deforestation and draining consequently implies new reflexive research in meteorology, dikes, and dams.

According to Beck, the concept of risk is related to the desire to avoid problems in the future, which also makes risk society dependent on reflexive knowledge. Here, Beck's arguments are stronger than Bell's: Since we do not know the future, socially argued and scientifically produced knowledge is, in reality, the basis for understanding risks and the struggles about them in the risk society. Therefore, it is important to understand which kind of social rationality is a foundation for technical rationalities.

The production of risks thus depends on decisions, and all decisions lead to large or small risks. But in contrast to "real" natural disasters (acts of God), manmade ecological disasters have become dependent on decisions.

The connection between reflection and risks arose during the 1980s when so-called risk research made it clear that risks are not only objective. Risks are subject to interpretation, and risks are first and foremost risks if we cannot accept them. Thus, social legitimation and acceptance of risk have become decisive for understanding the significance of risks for the social order (Douglas 1986). In this "turn" in risk research, conflicts about risks thus, to a large extent, become knowledge struggles, for example, "definition struggles." These struggles give politics new content and new meaning, because politics become far more dependent on knowledge, even more focused on technocratic problem avoidance. Accordingly, politics turn into what Beck calls "sub-politics," that is, institutional arrangements of researchers, corporate delegates, and governmental experts who reveal concerted agreements about standards and options to follow.

However, politics in risk society are also more vulnerable to spontaneous rumors. One may disagree with the details of the alarming image displayed by Beck, but his central insight is probably exactly the often metaphorical way he describes the structure of the fears of risk society: The reflexive construction of our experiences of security and of dangers leads us to mythical cognitions about what will happen, open to rumors and to frightening stories narrated by the reporters of the mass media competing for the best pictures of the worst scandal.

These phenomena shake the position the political system has had in the classic social order of modernity. In addition, risk society is transnational and its structure may literally blow with the wind, to take the example of the radioactive rain after the Chernobyl nuclear disaster. Beck talks about "removing the equation between industrial society and national state" (Beck 1991: 44).

Beck's analyses have become very influential, first, because of the radical fantasy of his argumentation, and because he unequivocally points out that the new ecological consciousness marks something radically new. Second, he writes very well, in an indignant, emphatic style. However, he often piles new insights on top of his analyses, which may be interesting, but they lack a basic empirical background and a systematic, theoretic consideration of the basic concepts.

Luhmann's analysis

Another German sociologist, Niklas Luhmann, considers these things more thoroughly. Compared to Beck's analyses, Luhmann's are much more theoretically nuanced, and they belong completely to the so-called communicative turn in social theory. Luhmann's total production is immense and contains a comprehensive theory about communication and differentiation in social systems (see chapter 22). Luhmann has written a couple of books related to Beck's, *Ecological Communication* (1986) and *Risk Sociology* (1991), and in addition a number of articles. Luhmann's analyses of risks are theoretically much more interesting, acute, and imaginative than Beck's, but their tone is far from the indignant commitment expressed by Beck.

Luhmann's thesis is that risks are inevitable and total security is an illusion. His basic distinction is not between risk and stability, but between risk and danger. The problem with risks is not so much the future, but the present. All observations are made in the present, and the future is observed and interpreted through codes of the present time.

The economic subsystem allows us to look at the future through the present time lens of interest rates, profitability, and depreciation. For the reality of the economic system it is therefore unrealistic to plan 50 or 100 years ahead, although our grandchildren will be alive in 50 and even 120 years. The subsystem of family and love can have a much longer time horizon than the economic subsystem, just as a plantation owner who plants oak trees may operate with a time horizon of 200 or 400 years! Thus, each subsystem has its own temporal bonds.

Each subsystem thus refers to itself. They constitute so-called "self-referential systems," and, according to Luhmann, we cannot get rid of them and we should not try. Our ability to observe, for example, ecological risks and react to them is based on systems refined over 300 years for scientific, legal, artistic, and political communication, each of which observes and reacts to risks in its own way. Above all, says Luhmann, ethics will not help us find out what to do about these risks, because ethics have been separated from justice, art, love, etc. Equally, the political system can only be alarmed in a political way according to standards which are political and not in their own sense biological.

Risk in the risk society is therefore that with the systems we have, these systems follow their own pace and makes their own observations. Risk in the risk society lies in the fact that it is next to impossible to change current social systems from the outside. Whereas theories about the industrial society spoke of "convergence" in social development, the risk society entails new types of fragmentation.

Luhmann's analysis of the future is consequently skeptical, but not unambiguously so, because he also points out that social systems contain an inner complexity in that they must constantly operate with codes for their surroundings. They also have to accept criticism and opposition from their surroundings so that they can maintain their self-organization. The fact that social systems actually do change may also contain a moderate optimism.

Summary

There are both theoretical and empirical reasons why sociological analysis of society has removed itself more and more from objectivistic analyses of industrial society, information society, and post-industrial society. The primary reason is a methodological and theoretical paradigm shift. Diagnoses of communication and culture are analyzed in new ways. The new methods are less occupied with explanation and description and more with interpretation; and other phenomena are relevant for these interpretations. Bell's analysis of post-industrial trends was thus characteristically based on large amounts of statistical data, while his cultural diagnosis three years later contained only one table (in a note). The secondary reason is that social theory has moved from an overall optimistic vision of the future to a more moderate or even skeptical vision. In the rich part of the world, the scarcities are not instrumental but much more subjective and symbolic.

Poverty, exclusion, conflict, wars, and crises have not disappeared. There is, however, some discussion about whether service production and service goods can pollute less than material production. Global interdependencies, population growth, food shortages, and the greenhouse effect will undoubtedly be prominent in the development of future diagnoses.

Bell's analysis of post-industrialism was written at a time when these problems were only beginning to be recognized, unemployment in Western countries was almost nonexistent, and class differences were smaller.

Bibliography

Aron, Raymond 1962: *Dix-huit leçons sur la société industrielle*. Paris: Gallimard.
Beck, Ulrich (ed.) 1982: *Soziologie und Praxis*. Göttingen: Schwartz.
—— 1986: *Risikogesellschaft*. Frankfurt am Main: Suhrkamp. (Translated as *Risk Society*. London: Sage, 1992).
—— 1991: *Politik in der Risikogesellschaft*. Frankfurt am Main: Suhrkamp.
—— 1992: From Industrial Society to the Risk Society. *Theory, Culture and Society,* 9, 97–123.
—— 1993: *Die Erfindung des Politischen: zu einer Theorie reflexiver Modernisierung*. Frankfurt am Main: Suhrkamp.
—— 1995: *Ecological Enlightenment*. Atlantic Highlands, NJ: Humanities Press.
—— 1997: *The Reinvention of Politics*. Cambridge: Polity Press.
Beck, Ulrich, and Beck-Gernsheim, Elisabeth. 1990: *Der ganz normale Chaos der Liebe*. Frankfurt am Main: Suhrkamp.
Beck, Ulrich, and Fucks, Ralf. 1991: *Sind die Grünen noch zu retten?* Reinbek bei Hamburg: Rowohlt Taschenbuch Verlag.
Beck, Ulrich, Giddens, Anthony, and Lash, Scott. 1994: *Reflexive Modernization*. Cambridge: Blackwell.
Beck, Ulrich, and Beck-Gernsheim, Elisabeth. 1994: *Riskante Freiheiten: Individualisierung in moderne Gesellschaften*. Frankfurt am Main: Suhrkamp.
Bell, Daniel. 1960: *The End of Ideology*. Glencoe, IL: Free Press.
—— 1968: *Toward the Year 2000*. Boston: Beacon Press.
—— 1976: *The Coming of Post-industrial Society*. New York: Basic Books.
—— 1979: *The Cultural Contradictions of Capitalism*. London: Heinemann.
—— 1980: *The Winding Passage*. Cambridge, MA: Abt Books.
—— 1995a: *Communitarianism and its Critics*. Oxford: Clarendon Press.
—— 1995b: *Towards Illiberal Democracy in Pacific Asia*. Oxford; New York: Macmillan.
Chandler, Alfred, Jr. 1990: *Scale and Scope. The Dynamics of Industrial Capitalism*. Cambridge, MA: Harvard University Press.
Dahrendorf, Ralf. 1959: *Class and Class Conflict in an Industrial Society*. London: Routledge & Kegan Paul.
Douglas, Mary. 1986: *Risk Acceptability According to the Social Sciences*. London: Routledge & Kegan Paul.
Floud, Jean. 1971: A Critique of Bell. *Survey,* 17 (Winter): 25–37.
Freud, Sigmund. 1982: *Psykoanalyse*. Copenhagen: Hans Reitzels Forlag.
Gorz, André. 1982: *Farewell to the Working Class: An Essay on Post-industrial Socialism*. London: Pluto.
Janowitz, Morris. 1974: Review Symposium. *American Journal of Sociology,* 80, 230–6.
Kumar, Krishan. 1978: *Prophecy and Progress. The Sociology of Industrial and Post-Industrial Society*. Harmondsworth, Middlesex: Penguin Books.
Lasch, Christopher. 1979: *The Culture of Narcissism*. New York: Warner Books.
Lash, Scott, and Urry, John. 1994: *Economies of Signs and Space*. London: Sage.
Loftager, Jørn. 1985: Post- eller super-industrialisme. *Politica,* 17/3, 359–80.
Luhmann, Niklas. 1986: *Ökologische Kommunikation*. Opladen: Westdeutscher Verlag.
—— 1991: *Soziologie des Risikos*. Berlin: Walter de Gruyter.
Poster, Mark. 1990: *The Mode of Information*. Oxford: Polity Press.

Riesman, David. 1961: *The Lonely Crowd: A Study of the Changing American Character*. New Haven: Yale University Press.

Sennett, Richard. 1970: *The Uses of Disorder*. New York: Vintage.

—— 1979: *The Fall of Public Man*. New York: Vintage.

—— 1993a: *Authority*. London; Boston: Faber.

—— 1993b: *The Conscience of the Eye*. London: Faber and Faber.

—— 1996: *Flesh and Stone*. New York; London: Faber and Faber.

—— 1998: *The Corrosion of Character: The Personal Consequences of Work in the New Capitalism*. New York: W. W. Norton.

Sennett, Richard, and Cobb, Jonathan. 1993: *The Hidden Injuries of Class*. London: Faber.

Stearns, Peter M. 1974: Is There a Post-industrial Society? *Society*, 11, 10–22.

Touraine, Alain. 1969: *La Société post-industrielle*. Paris: Denoël.

Ziehe, Thomas. 1975: *Pubertät und Narzißmus*. Frankfurt am Main: Europäische Verlagsanstalt.

—— 1982: *Plädoyer für ungewöhnliches Lernen. Ideen zur Jugendsituation*. Reinbek: Rowohlt.

—— 1985: Vorwärts in die 50er-Jahre? Lebensentwürfe Jugendlicher im Spannungsfeld von Postmoderne und Neokonservatismus. In D. Baacke and W. Heitmeier (eds), *Neue Widersprüche*. Weinham and Munich: Juventa.

—— 1989: Die unablässige Suche nach Nähe und Gewissheit. *Ästhetik & Kommunikation*, 70/71, 19–25.

—— 1991: *Zeitvergleiche. Jugend in Kulturellen Modernisierungen*. Weinham and Munich: Juventa.

—— 1992: Cultural Modernity and Individualization. In J. Fornäs and G. Bolin (eds), *Moves in Modernity*. Stockholm, Sweden: Almqvist & Wiksell International.

—— 1995: Good Enough Strangeness in Education. In T. Aitolla et al. (eds), *Confronting Strangeness*. Jyväskulä, Finland: Jyväskylän yliopisto.

—— 1998: English translation of: Adieu, 70er Jahre! Jugendliche und Schule in der zweiten Modernisierung. In E. Prescod (ed.), *Zapping Through Wonderland*. Amsterdam, Netherlands: Royal Tropical Institute.

chapter 26

Our Present: Postmodern?

Poul Poder Pedersen

KEY CONCEPTS

DIFFERENTIATION – a pivotal sociological concept applied mainly in theories of social change which refer to a process whereby something unified is divided up. Differentiation is a sign of increasing specialization and heterogeneity among society's constituent parts. An example is the traditional family, which used to take care of reproductive, productive, and educational activities. Today productive and educational functions are handled in institutions of work and education.

INTEGRATION – the creation of coherence among the various elements and agents within society. Sociologists usually regard integration as based on universally acknowledged values, on mutual interdependence among different social groups, given society's specialized division of labor, or on relations of domination.

CONTINGENCY – derived from the Latin verb *contingere*, to touch or occur. Contingency is a pivotal concept in postmodern thought, and has numerous applications: as opposed to necessity and universality, contingency refers to variability and particularity; unlike constancy and certainty, contingency refers to mutability and uncertainty; unlike things resting in themselves and causing effects, contingency relates to things that are dependent upon and are affected by others; unlike regularity, contingency designates irregularity; unlike safety and security, contingency refers to danger and uncontrollability.

THE ENLIGHTENMENT – a certain school of thought and movement emanating from the "scientific revolution" at the end of the sixteenth century. Enlightenment thought focuses on humankind and its knowledge by underlining the possibility of an infinite expansion of knowledge and at the same time rejects traditional metaphysical and religious worldviews.

LEGITIMACY – social processes whereby power is institutionalized and given a moral justification. When a stable distribution of power is acknowledged as proper it has legitimacy.

MODERNISM – a term from cultural history referring to various artistic departures from European realistic tradition from around the mid-nineteenth century onward. A certain aesthetic movement breaking with ingrown habits and experimenting with new modes of expression.

PLURALISM – refers to a multiplicity of perceptions and views. In modern sociology, pluralism refers particularly to social organizations or entire societies where power is not centralized but distributed among multiple groups or agents struggling with each other.

During the past few decades, almost anything has been termed postmodern – in May 1993 the *New York Times* even announced the arrival of "the postmodern sandwich." Yet this ubiquitous concept is no spring chicken. The historian Arnold Toynbee (1889–1975) and the sociologist C. Wright Mills (see chapter 16) both employed this term in the 1950s to describe a new era in history (Smart 1993: 24). In American literary criticism of the 1960s, the term once referred to extreme modes of expression in the arts such as avant-gardism, deconstruction, and minimalism (Jencks 1991: 20). But "the postmodern" did not really enjoy widespread usage until it was employed in reference to a specific architectural movement (Kellner 1995: 46).

This is evidenced by the architectural historian Charles Jencks (b. 1939) in his influential *The Language of Post-Modern Architecture* (1977). Jencks points out that postmodern architecture is preoccupied with mixing styles from past eras, thus allowing buildings to coalesce "organically" with the local environment in which they are placed. Stressing complexity, stylistic eclecticism, and the spirit of place, Jencks's notion has exerted considerable influence on discussion of "the postmodern" within various artistic and intellectual disciplines.

One book in particular, *The Post-Modern Condition* (1984 [1979]), firmly ensconced "the postmodern" within the European intellectual agenda (Smart 1992: 169); partly as a normative or philosophical debate about concepts such as reason and enlightenment (Lyotard 1984, 1992; Habermas 1987); partly as a polemic concerning the character and role of science, with postmodern science seeking to avoid the untenable endeavor toward comprehensive, value-neutral, and objectivistic theories (see *Sociological Theory*, the special issue devoted to "Postmodernism" 1991; Denzin 1986; Murphy 1988). Furthermore, analyses of social changes and conditions are permeated by visions of new circumstances prevailing after "the modern." This chapter is devoted to such visions as expressed in a number of analyses concerning trends and changes occurring in *modern* Western societies.

Before we can speak of the *post*modern, that is, of something different from, or something following "after" the modern, we must delineate what is meant by "the modern" or by modernity. Modernity is a very broad concept characterizing the predominant societal type in Western countries over the past two centuries. The meaning of the concept varies, but in the social sciences the usage often encompasses a meaning dating back to the Enlightenment of the eighteenth century. In the Enlightenment way of thinking "the modern" is tantamount to any society hailing all things new, be it the eighteenth or the twentieth century (Kumar 1993). In an elementary sense, embracing all that is new is what separates modern from premodern or traditional (medieval, ancient, etc.) societies. In a more tangible sense, the modern societal type may also be described as a conglomeration of widespread phenomena and circumstances such as urbanization, parliamentary systems, visual mass media, tourism, problematization of gender, and endeavors to create a rationally directed and organized society (Bech 1994, 1995; Bauman 1987, 1991a).

This broad delineation of "the modern" will be expanded by examining various postmodern visions, because the specific meanings of "the modern" depend on the specific postmodern theory in which the term is used.

The concept or, more properly, conceptions of the postmodern are not particularly well defined. This is because they primarily derive their meaning from "negating" specific modern circumstances and phenomena. Thus, they adumbrate incipient states that by their very nature display no clear tangibility (Featherstone 1988: 197). This chapter will investigate the question of our postmodern present age by reviewing a series of key concepts describing new conditions and trends that could all be called "after the modern," in a number of specified senses of that word.

The first part of the chapter sketches a theory concerning a new condition prevailing in regards to society's way of legitimizing or justifying scientific and technological development. The second part describes a postmodern form of culture and a cultural set of conditions in which hitherto impassable cultural distinctions and boundaries are dissolved. The third part concerns a new, postmodern condition for integration, identity, community, and morality. In conclusion, this chapter provides a selective assessment of what postmodern arguments have contributed to the social sciences and to their understanding of the present era.

Knowledge in a Postmodern Condition?

Bibliography: *Jean-François Lyotard*

Born in France in 1924, Lyotard was a secondary-school teacher in Algeria from 1950 to 1952, and earned his Ph.D. in 1971. For two decades he has been a professor of philosophy at institutions like the Sorbonne, Nanterre, CNRS, and Vincennes University in Paris. He has been director of the Collège International de Philosophie, and was associated with the University of California in the United States. Lyotard was a prominent and active figure in international as well as French philosophical debate right through the 1980s and 1990s. He has published several books on ethical and aesthetic problems viewed from the postmodern perspective. He died in 1998.

One prominent instigator of the postmodern debate was the French philosopher, Jean-François Lyotard, with his report (*The Postmodern Condition,* 1984 [1979]) to the Canadian Council of Universities on the post-industrial nature of highly developed societies (see chapter 25) and on the postmodern condition of knowledge; as well as the book *The Postmodern Explained to Children* (1992 [1986]) (Smart 1992: 169; Giddens 1990). In these two books, Lyotard explicates and discusses a thesis for which he is renowned, the thesis of "the dissolution of the great narratives."

For Lyotard, postmodernism does not mean an entirely new, historical epoch or a new society; it means a new way of understanding science, technology, and development as they are already evolving in modern society. The target he is aiming at is our modern perception of scientific and technological development as being the "driving force" of our steadily increasing societal progress, as well as being a lever for the universal emancipation of humankind. Doubts have been raised regarding such a progress-adoring legitimizing of science and technology right from the beginnings of modern society (Lyotard 1992). However, for Lyotard, the point is that nowadays these doubts have become predominant in the public sphere not because technological development has come to a halt, but on the contrary, because it continues to be successful. Thus the postmodern perspective has to do with whether or not scientific and technological development can be legitimized in another manner.

Modern narratives of emancipation

Modern society is characterized by the fact that scientific and technological development is embedded in a philosophy of history with a metanarrative concerning the continued onward march of humanity toward a benevolent, utopian society, thanks to the results of science and technology. These are different overarching narratives or ideologies legitimizing scientific and technological developments. One example is the Marxist narrative about how developments will lead to a communist realm where everybody will contribute to the best of their ability and receive according to their needs. Like myths, these modern "great narratives" legitimize institutions as well as legislative, social, and political measures, etc. But unlike myths, they do not lay claim to legitimacy because of one pivotal, primordial act in the past. On the contrary, the legitimacy of these narratives is supposedly derived from a future yet to come.

Modern legitimacy is thus founded upon an idea that we can strive toward realizing. And the idea has a comprehensive (universal) legitimizing value insofar as it extends to all fields of human endeavor and conceptions of reality. This form of legitimacy, based on an idea, is what imbues the modern attitude to life with its characteristic *project nature*, meaning that the will is focused upon a goal (Lyotard 1992).

Modern existence as a project is given specific expression through several political ideologies within modern society; ideologies that may be described as emancipatory projects aimed at realizing utopian and allegedly universal ideas of freedom, enlightenment, socialism, and welfare for all; ideologies that have functioned as crucial legitimacy values throughout the history of modern society. Despite the discord prevailing between political liberalism, economic liberalism, the different forms of Marxism and anarchism, and the third republic's radicalism and socialism, these ideologies agree upon one and the same goal: the universal liberation of humankind.

"Liquidating" modern legitimacy

Modern human beings are not likely to forget or to forswear the modern legitimacy given to scientific and technological developments. Rather, the big emancipatory narratives have been rendered invalid – "liquidated" – during the past 50 years: "Auschwitz" repudiates the speculative idea of the Spirit's (reason's) self-fulfillment as envisioned by modern philosophy. The doctrine propagated by historical materialism – "Everything which is proletarian is communist; everything which is communist is proletarian" – is disavowed by the workers' (the proletariat's) revolts against the party in Berlin (1953), in Budapest (1956), in Czechoslovakia (1968), in Poland (1980), etc. The doctrine upheld by parliamentary liberalism turns problematic as evidenced by *les événements* of May 1968; these French student rebellions showed that ordinary, everyday life opposes the formal, representative form of democracy. And the economic crises of 1911, 1929, and 1974–9 repudiate the doctrine upheld by economic liberalism affirming that whatever benefits market freedom is also beneficial to universal prosperity, and vice versa (Lyotard 1992).

The very notion of prosperity inherent in the modern "progress" project serves to confirm a well-known truth, that is, that scientific and technological discoveries have never been subject to demands rooted in human needs; and this precisely constitutes the most important reason for the "liquidation" already mentioned. Techno-scientific development strengthens the feeling that the more we know, the more powerless we become, and heightens a following despondency over this fact, rather than assuaging such emotions. Along with scientific developments we see a rise in the level of complexity until it reaches a degree where "the modern project" – which is essentially about controlling the world, nature and society – loses its credibility. Development within science and technology can no longer be thought of as progress in a situation in which it has become blatantly obvious that they will not fulfill the promise of a universal liberation of humanity – the promise made by modern narratives of emancipation.

The reason that this promise cannot be kept is rooted in the very nature of that development, since it entails a new illiteracy, Third World deprivation, widespread unemployment, the rule of media-generated prejudice, and the precept that whatever is efficient is also implicitly good. Science and technology may allow us to obtain a limited degree of control over our endeavors and to manipulate the facts of reality; but science and technology do not – as was once believed – lead to increased freedom and to the distribution of wealth to the benefit of everyone. The most important aspect regarding the defeat of the modern project, which in principle concerns all humanity, is possibly the division of humankind into two groups: one group able to face the present and future challenge of increased complexity, and another group left to face the "terrible" challenge of stark survival.

The postmodern stance, which, as described, consists in widespread doubt concerning modern narratives of legitimacy, does not herald the dissolution of society, but augurs an increased societal complexity. Alongside the description of the weakening of this modern project, there is no agreement about which road society will or should take from now on. Thus Lyotard asks what means of legitimacy we can invoke for continuing the present state of development. Is it acceptable from a moral point of view that development within science and technology today is justified by its ability to increase pure efficiency for economic, political, and technocratic systems of action? The postmodern state of knowledge is a state of incalculability and it is precisely this indeterminacy as to how you legitimize developments anew that constitutes one of the reasons behind the many contradictory ways in which the term postmodernity is used (Lyotard 1992).

Lyotard's theory affords a new, postmodern perspective on how to understand scientific and technological development in modern society. Science and technology in themselves do not change character with the transition to a post-industrial society, just as the economy continues to be capitalist (Lyotard 1992; Smart 1992). But with his thesis delineating a new, postmodern perspective, Lyotard is proposing a fundamental discussion about modern society's values and where it is heading.

A Postmodern Culture?

Whether or not culture is turning postmodern is a question concerning more than just the fragmentation of modern narratives of emancipation (Turner 1990; Smart 1990, 1992, 1993; Featherstone 1991). Using "the postmodern" as a concept is an important beginning when coming to terms with an array of social transformations instigated by global processes in and between societies (Featherstone 1991: 11–12). According to the English sociologist Mike Featherstone (b. 1945), "the postmodern" is really about changes in the artistic and intellectual domain when the balance of power between different groups shifts, and when, as a result, the production, consumption, and circulation of symbolic merchandise also change. Furthermore, the debate is about more widespread cultural changes since the evolving practices of everyday life entail new patterns of orientation and identity.

Pluralism

Pluralism is one of the key concepts in discussing postmodern culture. It is used in connection with art and culture, where postmodernism stands for a softening of the demarcation lines that have hitherto placed highbrow or avant-garde culture in opposition to lowbrow or mass culture (Huyssen 1986; Turner 1990: 3). Postmodern culture is described as expressing an "anti-authoritarian populism" and an extremely mobile and border- crossing culture (Lash and Urry 1987). The postmodern stress on pluralism is linked to a radical invocation of freedom, entailing a steady rejection of hierarchy in any form.

This anti-hierarchical conception is nurtured by a "postcultural" state of affairs prevailing in our present age, "postcultural" in the sense that this cultural climate is not characterized by clear and normative delineations and demarcations, that is, it is not "cultural" if that word is defined as the cultivation of certain values and things. In other words, this cultural state is not distinguished by projects of cultural construction such as, say, the nationalism prevalent when modern nation-states were being established. On the contrary, it is characterized by undemanding "cultural offerings," small enclaves of arbitrating cultural connoisseurs, a mounting glut of signifiers, and perennial change (Bauman 1992a). Examples illustrating this free and "horizontalized" cultural situation are the ubiquitous popular games and quizzes where knowledge of World War II ranks no higher (nor any lower) than knowing the year of an actor's demise; as well as the way the mass media treat all things as if they were on the same level.

The concept of pluralism is also used to characterize how Western societies see themselves in relation to the rest of the world today. In general, postmodernism expresses a mode of questioning the authority of Western European culture, even if its symptoms are described in different ways (Owens 1983). The prevailing self-understanding of Western societies, seeing themselves as beacons of humankind's true, scientific, and steadily progressing culture, is no longer taken for granted. The cultural authority previously vested in Western societies as purveyors of progress and affluence is attacked and doubted.

Hitherto, human rights were about modernizing (and thus "civilizing") the world outside of Europe; today, they are about the right to cultural diversity and autonomy (Bauman 1995: 22, 253). Today, other societies on the planet want to preserve their own culture and not just copy that of the West. And in this sense, global culture is pluralistic.

Bibliography: *Scott Lash*

Born in the USA; 1945, and educated at the University of Michigan, Northwestern University, and the London School of Economics (Ph.D., 1980), Scott Lash has been based in England since 1977, first as a professor of sociology at Lancaster University, and since 1997 professor of cultural studies at Goldsmiths College, University of London. Lash is well known for the book *The End of Organized Capitalism* (written with John Urry and published in 1987), and several articles on postmodernism as a cultural and social theoretical phenomenon. In 1990 he published *Sociology of Postmodernism*, one of the first attempts at a sociological understanding of postmodern culture. Since then he has developed the theory of "aesthetic reflexivity" - which, according to Lash, has become a burgeoning trait of the culture industry. The "aesthetic" form of reflexivity or mediation is based on "mimetic" (reproductive) symbols and images, not on cognitive concepts, as in the theory of reflexivity and modern life proposed by Anthony Giddens and Ulrich Beck (Lash and Urry 1994a; Lash, Beck and Giddens 1994b).

"Figural" culture

The sociologist Scott Lash offers a theory about the unique character of postmodern culture and its significance for culture in general. Postmodern culture is dubbed "figural" because it creates meaning by juxtaposing signs from the commonplace and variegated contexts of everyday life. In the figural culture, the effect of cultural products is more important than their meaning or significance. By contrast, in the modernist, "discursive" constitution of meaning, words and concepts take precedence over images. Modernist cultural artefacts focus the attention of the spectators on hidden conventions determining how each artefact generates meaning. The crucial aspect is the qualities of meaning and form of the cultural artifact. On a conscious, intellectual level, the aesthetic product is scrutinized for its ability to represent (replicate) reality.

Lash illustrates these two types of constitution of meaning by distinguishing between postmodern, "figural" films on one hand, and modernist, "discursive" films on the other. According to Lash, modernist films attach prime importance to displaying a "logical" coherent story line. And when taking in a modernist picture, viewers identify with the main character of the film, who thus functions as an "edifying" role model for the spectator ego. This does not apply to postmodern films. On the contrary, postmodern films are much more prone to exult in dramatic, erratic, and glaring images at the expense of a coherent narrative. Unlike the modernist film, in which the intentional narrative dominates, the spectacle on display holds sway in postmodern pictures such as *Blue Velvet*, *Diva*, and the popular Spielberg, Rambo, and Schwarzenegger epics. The "figural," postmodern film entices audiences to become captivated merely by the images in an immediate and intense emotional fascination. Viewing postmodern films, audiences are not particularly urged to engage analytically in dissecting the "story" behind them, as is the case with modernist pictures.

Postmodern films draw the attention of the audience to the immediate reality engendered by the film itself. Therefore, audiences are not invited to scrutinize the film as aesthetic per se, as material following specific conventions governing how you should and should not portray reality. Each film may seem "real" in and of itself, abstaining from attempts at describing and referring to any reality outside the film's own reality. But then again – in a film like, say, *Blue Velvet*, the celluloid reality is exposed as artificial when, in its closing shot, the camera focuses on a flower that turns out not to be a genuine (real) flower, but papier-mâché. Thus, the end suggests the conclusion that reality is not what it seems to be and is therefore unreliable (Lash 1990: 192).

Behind the "figural" as an art form, lies the urge to investigate how real "down-to-earth reality" in fact is, and whether all reality is "really" real in the sense that it is permanent and stable. The figural culture inquires into the very nature of reality, using visual and multiple signifiers where the generation of meaning by images questions the seemingly monolithic reality based on unambiguous concepts. "Discursive" form centers on whether each cultural artifact unveils reality convincingly, using words and concepts. This form presupposes a certain cultural differentiation or separation – since it separates reality on one side and representations (portrayals) of it on the other. The signification process is divorced from reality and a marked distance prevails between cultural products and reality (Lash 1990: 191).

The crucial difference between modernism and postmodernism as cultural movements thus consists in that postmodernism sees reality itself as its main problem, while the problem for modernism lies in how to depict reality in a truthful manner (Lash 1990: 13; Bauman 1992a; Mchale 1987).

The "de-differentiation" of culture

As understood by Lash, postmodern culture is seen as an inquiry into the fluctuating reality of our present day and age, as well as an attempt at orientation within this chaos. It constitutes an attempt at finding out the consequences for us, now that our reality has been dispersed by the endless torrent of images and signs with which we are inundated (Lash 1990: 14). Figural culture examines the opaque and ephemeral nature of reality by surveying our present surface reality, consisting of images and signs that often merely refer to other representations and not to "real" things.

The larger-scale cultural significance of figural culture is that it leads to a de-differentiation, whereby ingrained (modern) cultural boundaries and distinctions tend to dissolve. Thus, in figural generation of meaning, the separation between reality and representation (the autonomy of the cultural sphere – Weber, see chapter 6) disappears in the sense that images no longer acquire their meaning through resemblance to the "real" world. They are less removed from the real phenomena (the referents) than the linguistic signs of language; the reason being that nowadays, more and more real objects ("referents" – say, a chair) actually function as signs or representations. Thus, daily life today is dominated by a reality mixing signs upon signs, as when the individual perceives the world of signs made up by TV, adverts, video, computerization, the Walkman, the CD, the CD-ROM, and multimedia.

Another aspect associated with de-differentiation is that the cultural sphere is losing its privileged aura, that is, the surrounding glow formerly making it something entirely special and a cut above ordinary, everyday life. "Cultural" life is no longer clearly separated from (ordinary) social life – in principle, anything and everything can be "culture." When the tendency is that nothing is pure art, art itself ceases to be something special. The dissolution of the former boundaries separating highbrow culture from popular, mass culture and the ensuing development of a mass audience for highbrow cultural artifacts is partly to blame for the evaporation of a unique aura of culture – artifacts can no longer be "highbrow" when they are possessed or may be possessed by everybody.

Lash locates postmodern culture in a socio-economic context, maintaining that especially members of the "new" middle class are producers and consumers of postmodern culture. Individuals employed in the sectors of services or informatics, as well as university students with malleable identities, may use postmodern culture to set themselves apart compared to members of the old middle class, who primarily adhere to modernistic culture. (For comparable studies linking postmodern culture to actors of the middle class, see Featherstone 1991; Betz 1992).

Through the concept of the "figural generation of meaning" Lash delineates the specific characteristics of postmodern culture and explains its de-differentiating effect on the culture of modern society in a broad sense. According to Lash, postmodern culture is preoccupied with the question of what constitutes reality or realities. This leaves open the possibility of our getting a (better?) grasp of it.

Simulation – hyperreality

According to the famous French writer, Jean Baudrillard, the question of reality has now become obsolete because we are now living in an age of "simulation" and "hyperreality" as the following section will seek to explain.

Baudrillard has written a lot on social theoretical and philosophical questions, but also on themes such as consumption, seduction, the Gulf War, America. Often his ideas cause controversy – original, fascinating, and provocative as they are. Baudrillard is trained as a sociologist but does not write as most sociologists do (Rojek and Turner 1993). His often radical ideas have circulated and still circulate widely in the debate about postmodernity. Baudrillard has been regarded *the* theorist of postmodernity but he himself does not consider the debate concerning postmodernity particularly fruitful or important (Baudrillard in Gane (ed.) 1993). But nevertheless he has used the notion of postmodern and postmodernity in some of his texts. His texts often involve the idea of ruptures, which might be one reason why they are easily interpreted as dealing with a new (postmodern?) state of affairs.

In this context the focus will be solely on the theme of simulation and hyperreality – a main theme in the discussion of our postmodern present. According to Baudrillard, we are now living in a new historical period, in which we do not make any attempt to fight against simulation and seek the truth behind it. Instead, we cannot do otherwise than live in our world where simulations become hyperreal, that is, more real than reality.

In today's world of simulation we lose our sense of some things being more real than others. "Simulation is the generation by models of a real without origin or reality: a hyperreal" (Baudrillard 1983c: 2). This new kind of constructed "reality" is more than real since it exceeds our ordinary, realist(ic) thinking in terms of signs referring to the real reality behind the signs. It goes beyond the real(istic) world since it implies a world where the search for the (real) reality is becoming futile.

This world of simulated hyperreality is produced by the ever-increasing presence and significance of mediatizing technologies – computers, television, etc. It comes about as an unintended consequence of the crucial and generalized role of media and communication. Communication as such becomes more important than the exchange of a certain message or content. Living in such a media-dominated world of endlessly circulating images and signs pointing to other images and signs without ever ending, we can no longer ascertain anything as the (real) referent to which signs or images refer.

The historical actuality of events gets lost in this world of hyperreality, where a communication principle rules out the reality principle and you can no longer interrogate the truth or falsity of something (Baudrillard in Gane (ed.) 1993: 146). We can no longer master reality by grasping it. Reality vanishes in the infinite flux of mediatized images and signs. Simulation is no longer about cheating in the sense of hiding the true things, in the sense of covering up. Today's simulation means signs referring to signs that refer to signs that refer to signs . . . Simulation is the name of the game – a game we cannot escape.

Baudrillard illustrates the notion of simulation by discussing the phenomenon of public opinion. Today's public opinion is no longer produced as a result of a political discussion between people or social groups. Instead it is reproduced exclusively through the working of the tests of the polling game which refer to nothing but itself, that is, its ways of asking questions which determine their own answers. Tests are perfect forms of simulation since their questions induce the answers. Tests are *design-ated* in advance (Baudrillard 1993: 62). This makes public opinion as we now confront it "a hyperreal political substance, the fantastic hyperreality which survives only by editing and manipulation by the test" (Baudrillard 1993: 64). On a personal level the world of simulation means that the idea of expressing a hidden but authentic subjectivity loses its significance. According to Baudrillard, individuals of today are occupied by their acts of appearance, not worrying themselves about overcoming alienation, since they live without the modern idea of being alienated (Baudrillard in Gane (ed.) 1993: 41). Compared to Lash's diagnosis, our condition is far more transformed if we listen to a selective but important part of the far-reaching diagnosis of Baudrillard.

A Postmodern Condition?

The question of whether or not we are living in postmodern times is also about envisioning a new social condition concerning integration, identity, community, and morality. One sociologist in particular, Zygmunt Bauman, has developed a theory of postmodernity that takes this comprehensive approach.

Bibliography: *Zygmunt Bauman*

Born in Poland in 1925 and educated at the University of Warsaw, where he attained a Ph.D. in 1956 and received tenure in 1960, teaching general sociology there from 1962 to 1968. As a result of political and antisemitic pressure, he subsequently moved to Israel where he taught sociology until 1971. He was a professor of sociology at Leeds University, United Kingdom, from 1971 to 1990 (and is now professor emeritus). He has written, among other things, about the working class, culture and hermeneutics. Received the European Amalfi prize for Sociology and Social Theory for his book *Modernity and the Holocaust* (1989), in which he examines what the holocaust experiences may teach us about modern society. Bauman also enjoys international renown for his extensive inquiries into modernity-postmodernity seen from the perspective of the nation-state, the intellectuals, ethics, culture and power. In September 1998 Bauman received the honour of the Theodor W. Adorno Prize.

According to him, work no longer comprises *the* integrating mechanism in postmodern society. The postmodern social contract is based on a seductive and privatized consumerist liberation which the majority of the population values so highly that this very majority perpetuates society's fundamental structure by democratically held elections. The minority population which does not function properly as "healthy" consumers with purchasing power are integrated through the intervention of various state-run surveillance and controlling agencies (Bauman 1988). This displacement shift in social integration becomes prevalent in the USA and Western Europe from the 1950s onward.

In order to comprehend a society where the freedom of the consumer is all-important and all-determining, Bauman relinquishes concepts such as structure and system, since these terms presuppose a mechanical and determinist order which society does not in fact possess (Bauman 1992b). As a means of describing postmodern societal totality, he prefers to speak about "habitat," referring to a latitude described by historically defined ends and means with which, and within which, the agents of society act. Habitat is nothing more than the total life context in which actions and meanings are possible, and inside which the freedom and dependency of the agents are constituted. The habitat concept is meant to refer to the postmodern societal totality in an open and nondeterministic manner.

The changes constantly taking place in the habitat cannot be objectively explained; that is to say, they are inexplicable without involving the (subjective) actions undertaken by the participating agents. Had some of the agents chosen different courses of action, the surroundings too would have been different. The appearances taken on by the habitat imply no inner necessity or, to use a postmodern keyword, they are *contingent*. For each individual agent the habitat is thus a chaotic or ambiguous framework in which to exist and to act. But the most free and therefore powerful agents are, of course, the best equipped to influence the chaotic habitat according to their wishes (Bauman 1992a).

A farewell to modern illusions

What postmodern art depicts is the postmodern world in its contingency; by being pluralistic and by rejecting hierarchies, postmodern art alludes to the existential mode of reality as it is found outside the world of art (Bauman 1992a: 30). In this way, postmodern art reveals that reality does not rest on a fixed basis independent of human practices. Reality is not based on an unchanging foundation; on the contrary, its "foundation" is made up of the variegated practices of its agents. Not being bound by a common and neutral foundation, the agents construct separate realities for themselves. And the mutability of social practices makes it impossible to arrive at *one truth* about reality (that is, about its *foundation*) – and, as a consequence, the postmodern perspective has relinquished any broader claim to an absolute truth.

Postmodern art and culture constitute a new cultural experience finding its expression in a postmodern worldview in which reality is seen as a self-creating process determined only by the strength and dynamics of the process itself. According to this *Weltanschauung*, the world is not realizing modern ideals of an "increasing universalizing of the human condition" and a "rationalizing of human actions/behavior." Viewed from this postmodern perspective, reality cannot be described as one definite object since our human universe is composed of innumerable more or less self-sustained and meaning-generating agencies (Bauman 1992a: 35–9).

The Italian philosopher Gianni Vattimo (b. 1936) also understands our postmodern present as a corollary of the disappearance of an objective perspective on reality. The incessant expansion and trading of information concerning multitudinous facsimiles of reality makes it impossible to conceive of just one *single* reality. To the extent that a present-day conception of reality does exist, it cannot be perceived as an objective, established truth unaffected by the images of reality gleaned from the media. Rather, reality is a construct emanating from a conglomeration of images, interpretations, and reconstructions permeating the media in mutual competition without any "central" coordination (Vattimo 1992: 7).

Given this condition, where reality is not a given fixture but is dependent on ever-changing perspectives incessantly being foisted upon us, the modern understanding of emancipation cannot be sustained, for modern liberation revolves around achieving a clear self-understanding and a perfect – that is, a non-ideological – knowledge of the status quo, which is impossible in our present "media society." Instead of pursuing an insight regarding the inherent structure of reality and adapting accordingly, postmodern emancipation will more likely strive to undermine the reality principle itself. Postmodern emancipation means being able to shift gears between multiple perspectives and thus to live with the "disorientation" which emancipation in a pluralistic world necessarily entails (Vattimo 1992: 8).

Pursuing a modern way of thinking, science strove to demystify the world by unveiling the objective, fundamental order of things. The goal was to subjugate nature, society, and the world at large, thus eliminating the vagaries of chance. The postmodern condition has meant that modern ideals extolling order, transparency, universality, and unambiguity have lost their appeal and their allure. To the extent that they have come to realize that these modern ideals are not viable, all human beings of the present have become postmodern.

What is new – postmodern – is thus the concession that we cannot get rid of chaos, contingency, and ambiguity. These phenomena, however, are not in and of themselves new; they have proliferated incessantly in modern society. The postmodern condition, therefore, implies becoming reconciled to the disturbing tendency toward dissolution of traditions and institutions that is endemic in modern society. Thus, modern society is evolving in a *new* and more self-critical phase that has relinquished the dreams cherished by modern Enlightenment philosophy; the dreams of an orderly, rational, and transparent society (Weber, see chapter 6) (Bauman 1991a).

Identity?

Modern society's increased pace and complexity leads to a gradual erosion of identity. Thus, in our postmodern culture, the individual human being is no longer a subject or a well-defined ego, but has dissolved into a torrential flow of intense yet disconnected experiences (Jameson 1991: 16). Depth, substance, and coherence are, consequently, neither ideals nor realities for the postmodern individual, as they once were for the modern one (Kellner 1995: 233).

A professor of literature, Fredric Jameson (b. 1934), identifies "the death of the subject," considered by many to be a particularly postmodern thesis, as manifest in postmodern culture's use of pastiche as a contemporary mode of expression, that is, a poignant emulation of previous styles; and in the absence of "personality" in a more traditional, fixed sense, which is observable in present-day Hollywood stars – as is evident when comparing William Hurt to an older star such as, say, Steve McQueen (Jameson 1991: 16, 20).

Sometimes, postmodern arguments concerning identity focus on the transformation rather than the dissolution of identity; so the dissolution of the grand modern narratives of emancipation does not make identities dissolve. As emphasized by Lyotard, even though people become enmeshed in ever more complex relations and communications networks compared to earlier times, they are never completely without power over the messages passing through them (Lyotard 1984). Postmodern identity is weaker, but not dissolved.

The American philosopher Douglas Kellner (b. 1943) regards the difference between identities modern and postmodern as a difference of degree. Modern identity is formed through the conglomeration of a series of different social roles and norms governing how to be a father, a worker, and so forth. These roles and norms converge to create a relatively stable modern identity. In comparison, postmodern identity is *more* unstable since it is chiefly created from a set of socially more ephemeral (symbolic, transitory) choices of lifestyle, and the consumption of status-conferring designer labels, knowledge, etc. (Kellner 1992; 1995: 257).

Modern society has undermined identity formation related to certain social contexts (work, for instance). Therefore, it has now become only too easy to pick and choose an identity, while holding on to one is impossible (Bauman 1995: chapter 3). Thus Bauman sees a fundamental difference between the modern and the postmodern forms of identity; modern people seek a stable identity, while postmodern people wish to keep their possibilities, and thus their identities, open. Modern identity is carefully constructed with a view to a certain target in life. The fulfillment of such a "life project" is based on the premise that you are living in an environment possessing a stability extending beyond an individual life span, so that individuals may actually experience whether or not their actions bring them to their life goals, or at least approximate this achievement.

In a world undergoing constant, fundamental change, retaining a set of lifetime goals becomes meaningless. In such an environment you must continually revise your personal goals and therefore it does not make sense to describe identity formation as a progressing realization of a preset and fixed life project (Bauman 1992a).

Postmodern identity formation involves an ongoing "constitution of self;" meaning that while you are creating and developing one side of your life or personality, you are at the same time forfeiting others. Thus, postmodern identity cannot be likened to building a house, stone upon stone, until it eventually stands finished with well-defined rooms and solid walls.

Another predominant concept in the discussion of postmodern identity is the idea of the "decentering of the self." This means that people no longer believe that the self contains an inner, true core which determines identity. As a result, people are no longer preoccupied with searching for and "actualizing" the so-called authentic core of the self, as prescribed by the modern personality ideal (Gergen 1991; Bech 1997). Nor does the decentered individual elevate the inner self to become the seat of residence for the truth about the entire personality.

The decentering of the self means that the appearances of the self are to be understood in relation to their specific contexts and not in terms of expressing some kind of truth of the self (Tseëlon 1992: 123). A postmodern self is an "open-ended" and "relational" one, meaning that the individual is acutely aware that its ambigious identity is constructed by social, as opposed to private, relations in which it is placed (Tseëlon 1992; Gergen 1991; Molin 1989). The decentered self is a multifaceted self whose identity is formed in a conversational and experimental mode, as opposed to the introspective mode of "self-realization." When the name of the game is no longer "to find your own true self" it seems more obvious to construct an identity, guided by aesthetic and ethical notions concerning what is beautiful, attractive, and desirable (Cohen and Taylor 1992). Such identity formation, then, is not tantamount to an idolatry of superficiality, since the self is characterized precisely by its lack of any true core which could be used to distinguish authentic actions from nonauthentic ones.

Responsibility

Often, postmodern theory has been equated with a relinquishment of values and morality, but a sizable part of these theories do in fact deal with the change in morality, not with its demise.

An American psychologist, Kenneth Gergen (b. 1934), characterizes the postmodern world as a world "where everything which can be negotiated is also permitted" (Gergen 1991: 7). In his inquiry into "the twilight hour of duty and the painless ethics in the new democracies," the French sociologist, Gilles Lipovetsky (b. 1944), describes modern morality as "post-moralist" morals (Lipovetsky 1992). By this he is referring to a postmodern, flexible morality based on negotiation and compromise. The only "absolute" requirement laid down by "post-moralistic" morals is that we should parley and negotiate our way towards an adequate measure of regulation (Hansen 1994). Such a morality constitutes an "individualism of responsibility," as opposed to the prior "individualism of transgression." Individualists of today see respect and caring for others as a cherished and inevitable aspect of their personal self-expression, and do not strive toward transcending all social boundaries and considerations (Christensen 1993).

Lipovetsky claims that since modern morality based on duty is no longer valid, morality boils down to a question of personal conscience and responsibility. Because of a general crisis of morals in the sense of abstract principles and rights, and because of the dissolution of widely acknowledged and therefore "objective" moral standards, morality is nowadays anchored to individual feelings and personal conscience (Bauman 1995: 43). The postmodern world is resonant with moral voices all contradicting one another. Thus it dawns upon individuals that they themselves are left to choose which rules to follow and which not to follow. It is therefore no longer really possible to be a "conformist" – following certain rules does not make you exempt from responsibility.

The present-day dissolution of traditions and institutions entails an existential insecurity that keeps individuals mindful of the inescapable fact that *their* particular choice is crucial in determining events. Any moral responsibility for actions taken will end up with the actual owner of that responsibility, to wit, the individual behind the action (Bauman 1991a: 51). So the autonomous individuals of today must cope with situations of choice where they are incapable of saying that if they had only known more (been more rational) then the choice would have been self-evident. They must live without the "guidance" of modern attempts at scientific and supposedly unambiguous organization (Bauman 1990, 1991b). And they no longer trust large institutions – for example, the Church, trade unions, political parties, academic institutions – to tell them what to do (Bauman 1992b).

Thus they find themselves in a predicament without correct solutions. Instead they are faced with the full responsibility with which complex moral choices are fraught. Moral life becomes an extremely difficult pursuit since the postmodern condition neither comes equipped with nor seems about to acquire any ironclad principles to guide people in their individual and collective choices. Individuals must negotiate whenever dealing with their significant other, children, parents, colleagues, or sexual partners, and the moral responsibility for the outcome of those negotiations rests firmly on the shoulders of the individual (Bauman 1993a).

Ephemeral tribes of taste

The task of acquiring an identity and living a meaningful life is left to each individual as a private person. In postmodern society, individuals must seek to chart their course in a chaotic market where innumerable experts compete with each other, trying to convince consumers that they offer the right worldview, the right lifestyle. In the postmodern, pluralistic society each individual stands alone and isolated with the fear of facing up to the arbitrary futility of life. This fact is also the reason that the postmodern era has become a time in which individuals are assiduously seeking communities; by being a part of a community, the individual may assuage his or her existential unrest and anxiety.

Yet, postmodern communities are not solid, institutionalized communities like, say, modern trade unions. Bauman describes postmodern communities as ephemeral tribal communities without the sturdiness and weight achieved by traditional tribes through their hierarchical structure and ritualized practices. Postmodern "neo-tribes" are founded upon individual identification with something that has also been chosen by others as a focal point of congregation. In other words, they are communities without authorized persons with the endowment and the legitimate right to decide who belongs and who does not. As examples of "neo-tribes" based on individual tastes, witness the communities that evolve as people indulge in a specific trend, a particular lifestyle, or admiration of a certain idol (Bauman 1992a, 1992c; Maffesoli 1988, 1996).

A More Critical Understanding of Modern Society

Initially, the controversies concerning "the postmodern" were often either overstated in their assurances that we are now in the midst of a completely new epoch, or understated in their dismissals of "postmodern" as being "really just modern." In its entirety the debate was, and still is, quite immense and complex, and it is constantly evolving along new lines. Thus, it cannot be airily dismissed by labeling it an insignificant 1980s fad or with a few peremptory conclusions. This said, many commentators now do agree that postmodern changes are best understood as closely connected to modern society and its dynamic nature (Smart 1992, 1993).

In other words, certain postmodern changes have rather a quantitative character. Modern phenomena, which previously only enjoyed marginal incidence and significance can now, having become more widespread, be said to have acquired such a marked significance that a new state arises. An example of this is Lash's pointing out how the sheer *multitude* of images and signs leads to a new figural culture, and its corollary, the de-differentiation of culture. Other aspects of the postmodern development amount to something qualitatively new. Thus, the past few decades have brought on decidedly *new* phenomena such as television- and computer-based communication, constituting, according to Vattimo, the essential background for the new "media society" which dissolves the objective perspective of reality.

Postmodern theories invite new questions, new lines of inquiry. Thus they make it possible to uncover new phenomena and relations whereby we may gain insight into the present that is ours. In other words, the challenge lies in the fact that the changes and problems hypothesized as postmodern are insufficiently elucidated by existing social theory (Smart 1990). And since the more moderate postmodern theories seem to provide the most convincing responses to that challenge, this chapter has focused on them.

Today's mass-media spectacles can truly be so overwhelmingly present that their simulations (of reality) become more real than reality and Baudrillard's analyses of such circumstances are intriguing and compelling (Wakefield 1990; Crook, Pakulski, and Waters 1992). Nevertheless, part of the postmodern theorizing – often inspired by Baudrillard's writings – tends to overemphasize the significance of the media world. Still there is more to present social existence than media and simulations. And even if the significance of simulations increases, it gives us no reason to downplay the multifarious layers of reality and experience embedded in our complex social life. When such downplaying happens or is believed to happen, postmodern theorizing has been dismissed as defeatist nonsense of the emphatic "anything goes" variety.

But such a rejecting reaction is superficial. Lyotard, as we have seen, poses the profound and impassioned question of whether or not our scientific and technological rate of development could be legitimized in a new and more trustworthy way, taking into account a number of critical thoughts prompted by the historical mistakes made by modern societies. Postmodern pluralism is not tantamount to a despondent quandary devoid of morals and values; more to the point, it offers individual and moral responsibility a positive opportunity for playing a more prominent role in the organization of social existence. As described previously, Bauman is of the opinion that this pluralist state of affairs really adds up to a new chance for morality (see also Bauman 1997).

In conclusion, based on this explanation of a series of postmodern key concepts and ideas, we may say the ongoing postmodern debate urges a more critical understanding of modern society and a heightened sensitivity toward tendencies reaching beyond modern society.

Bibliography

Primary:

Bibliographies:

Nordquist, Joan. 1991: *Jean Baudrillard: A Bibliography*. Santa Cruz, CA: Reference and Research Services.
—— 1991: *Jean-Francois Lyotard: A Bibliography*. Santa Cruz, CA: Reference and Research Services.

Baudrillard, Jean. 1975: *The Mirror of Production*. St. Louis, MO: Telos Press.
—— 1983a: *Les strategies fatale*. Paris: Editions Grasset & Fasquelle.
—— 1983b: *In the Shadow of the Silent Majorities, or, The End of the Social, and Other Essays*. New York: Semiotext(e).
—— 1983c: *Simulations*. New York: Semiotext(e).
—— 1987: *Forget Foucault; & Forget Baudrillard: an Interview with Sylvère Lotringer*. New York: Semiotext(e).
—— 1988 [1987]: *The Ecstasy of Communication*. New York: Autonomedia.
—— 1989 [1986]: *America*. London: Verso Books.
—— 1990a: *Seduction*. Basingstoke: Macmillan Education.
—— 1990b: *Cool Memories*. London; New York: Verso.

—— 1990c/1999: *Fatal Strategies*. London: Pluto and New York: Semiotext(e).

—— 1991 [1986]: *For a Critique of the Political Economy of the Sign*. St. Louis, MO: Telos Press.

—— 1993a [1976]: *Symbolic Exchange and Death*. London: Sage.

—— 1993b [1990]: *The Transparency of Evil*. London: Verso.

—— 1994 [1992]: *The Illusion of the End*. Oxford: Polity Press.

—— 1995: *The Gulf War Did Not Take Place*. Bloomington: Indiane University Press.

—— 1996a [1995]: *The Perfect Crime*. London: Verso.

—— 1996b: *The System of Objects*. London: Verso.

—— 1998 [1997]: *The Cool Provocateur: Jean Baudrillard Interviewed by Philippe Petit*. London: Verso.

—— 1998 [1986]: *The Consumer Society*. London: Sage.

Baudrillard, Jean, and Breerette, Geneviéve. 1997: *Entrevues á propos du "complot de l'art"*. Paris: Sens & Tonka.

Bauman, Zygmunt 1987: *Legislators and Interpreters: On Modernity, Postmodernity and the Intellectuals*. Cambridge: Polity Press.

—— 1988: *Freedom*. Milton Keynes: Open University Press.

—— 1989: *Modernity and the Holocaust*. Cambridge: Polity Press.

—— 1990: Effacing the Face: On the Social Management of Moral Proximity. *Theory, Culture and Society*, 7 (1), 5–38.

—— 1991a: *Modernity and Ambivalence*. Cambridge: Polity Press.

—— 1991b: The Social Manipulation of Morality: Moralizing Actors, Adiaphorizing Action. *Theory, Culture and Society*, 8/1, 137–51.

—— 1991c: A Sociological Theory of Postmodernity. *Thesis Eleven*, 29, 33–46.

*—— 1992a: *Intimations of Postmodernity*. London: Routledge.

—— 1992b: *Mortality, Immortality and Other Life Strategies*. Cambridge: Polity Press.

—— 1992c: Modernity, Postmodernity and Ethics: An Interview with Zygmunt Bauman (with Timo Cantell and Poul Poder Pedersen). *TELOS*, 93, 133–44.

—— 1993a: *Postmodern Ethics*. Oxford: Blackwell

—— 1994a: Morality without Ethics. *Theory, Culture and Society*, 11/4, 1–34.

—— 1994b: *Alone Again*. London: Demos (paper no. 9).

—— 1995: *Life in Fragments*. Oxford: Blackwell.

—— 1996: From Pilgrim to Tourist. In Stuart Hall and Paul du Gay (eds), *Questions of Cultural Identity,* London: Sage.

—— 1997: *Postmodernity and its Discontents*. Cambridge: Polity Press.

—— 1998a: *Globalization: The Human Consequences*. Cambridge: Polity Press.

—— 1998b: *Work, Consumerism and the New Poor*. Milton Keynes: Open University.

—— 1999a [1973]: *Culture as Praxis*, New edn. London: Sage.

—— 1999b: *In Search of Politics*. Cambridge: Polity Press.

Gane, Mike (ed.) 1993: *Baudrillard Live: Selected Interviews*. London: Routledge.

Habermas, Jürgen. 1987: *The Philosophical Discourse of Modernity. Twelve Lectures*. Cambridge, MA: MIT Press.

Lash, Scott. 1985: Postmodernity and Desire. *Theory and Society,* 1, 1–33.

—— 1988: Discourse or Figure? Postmodernism as a 'Regime of Signification'. *Theory, Culture and Society*, 5/2–3, 311–36.

—— 1990: *Sociology of Postmodernism*. London: Routledge.

—— (ed.) 1991: *Post-Structuralist and Post-Modernist Sociology*. Aldershot: Edward Elgar.

Lash, Scott, and Urry, John. 1987: *The End of Organized Capitalism*. Cambridge: Polity Press.

Lash, Scott, and Friedman, Jonathan. 1992: *Modernity and Identity*. Conference. Oxford, UK and Cambridge, MA: Blackwell.

Lash, Scott, and Urry, John. 1994a: *The Economies of Signs and Space*. London: Sage.

Lash, Scott, Giddens, Anthony, and Beck, Ulrich. 1994b: *Reflexive Modernization*. Cambridge: Polity Press.

Lash, Scott, Heelas, Paul, and Morris, Paul. 1996a: *Detraditionalization: Critical Reflections on Authority and Identity*. Conference. Cambridge, MA and Oxford, UK: Blackwell.

Lash, Scott, Szerszynski, Bronislaw, and Wynne, Brian. 1996b: *Risk, Environment and Modernity*. London: Sage.

Lyotard, Jean-François. 1984a [1979]: *The Postmodern Condition. A Report on Knowledge*. Manchester: Manchester University Press.

—— 1988b: *Peregrinations: Law, Form, Event*. New York: Columbia University Press.

—— 1989 [1983]: *The Differend: Phrases in Dispute*. Manchester: Manchester University Press.

—— 1992a [1986]: *The Postmodern Explained to Children*. Sydney: Power.

—— 1992b [1988]: *The Inhuman – Reflections on Time*. Cambridge: Polity Press.

—— 1993a: *Moralités postmodernes*. Paris: Galilee.

—— 1993b: *Libidinal Economy*. London: Athlone Press.

—— 1996: *Signe Mairaux: biographie*. Paris: Grasset.

Lyotard, Jean-François, and McKeon, Roger 1984b: *Driftworks*. New York: Semiotext(e).

Lyotard, Jean-François, and Thébaud, Jean-Loup. 1985 [1979]: *Just Gaming*. Minneapolis: University of Minnesota Press.

Lyotard, Jean-François, and Boone, Bruce. 1990: *Pacific Wall*. Venice, CA: Lapis Press.

Lyotard, Jean-Francois, Roberts, Mark S., and Harvey, Robert. 1993: *Toward the Postmodern*. Atlantic Highlands, NJ and London: Humanities Press International.

Lyotard, Jean-François, Geiman, Kevin Paul, and Readings, Bill. 1993: *Political Writings*. London: UCL Press.

Poster, Mark (ed.) 1988: *Selected Writings*. Stanford, CA: Stanford University Press.

Secondary:

Bech, Henning. 1994: Er 90'ernes sociologi postmoderne? In Allan Madsen, Signe Ejersbo, and Søren Damkjær (eds), *Den kultursociologiske omtanke*. Copenhagen: Akademisk Forlag.

—— 1995: Citysex. Die öffentliche Darstellung der Begierden. *Soziale Welt: Zeitschrift für sozialwissenschaftliche Forschung und Praxis*, 46/1, 5–26.

—— 1997: *When Men Meet. Homosexuality and Modernity*. Cambridge: Polity Press.

Betz, Hans-Georg. 1992: Postmodernism and the New Middle Class. *Theory, Culture and Society*, 9/2, 93–114.

Christensen, Søren. 1993: Moralens diskrete genkomst. *Tendens*, 5/1, 9–18.

Cohen, Stanley, and Taylor, Laurie. 1992: *Escape Attemps: The Theory and Practice of Resistance to Everyday Life*. London: Routledge.

*Crook, Stephen, Pakulski, Jan, and Waters, Malcolm. 1992: *Postmodernization: Change in Advanced Society*. London: Sage.

Denzin, Norman K. 1986: Postmodern Social Theory. *Sociological Theory*, 4/2, 194–204.

Diacritics, 1984, 14/3. Special Issue on the Work of Jean-François Lyotard.

Featherstone, Mike. 1988: In the Pursuit of the Postmodern. *Theory, Culture and Society*, 5/2–3, 195–215.

—— 1991: *Postmodernism and Consumption Culture*. London: Sage.

Gane, Mike. 1991: *Baudrillard's Bestiary – Baudrillard and Culture*. London: Routledge.

Genesko, Gary. 1994: *Baudrillard and Signs*. London; New York: Routledge.

Gergen, Kenneth. 1991: *The Saturated Self: Dilemmas of Contemporary Self*. New York: Basic Books.

Giddens, Anthony. 1990: *The Consequences of Modernity*. Oxford: Polity Press.

Habermas, Jürgen. 1985: *Die neue Unübersichtlichkeit*. Frankfurt am Main: Suhrkamp. [A selection from this title and the following collection, *Kleine Politische Schriften VI*, has been published in

English: Shierry W. Nicholson (ed) 1989: *The New Conservatism: Cultural Criticisms and the Historians' Debate*. Cambridge, MA: MIT Press.]

——— 1987: *The Philosophical Discourse of Modernity. Twelve Lectures*. Cambridge, MA: MIT Press.

Harvey, David. 1989: *The Condition of Postmodernity*. Oxford: Blackwell.

Hebdige, Dick. 1988: *Hiding in the Light*. London: Routledge.

Huyssen, Andreas. 1986: *After the Great Divide – Modernism, Mass Culture, Postmodernism*. London: Macmillan Press.

Jameson, Fredric. 1991: *Postmodernism or the Cultural Logic of Late Capitalism*. London: Verso.

Jencks, Charles. 1991 (1977): *The Language of Postmodern Architecture*. London: Academy Editions.

Kellner, Douglas. 1989: *Jean Baudrillard: From Marxism to Postmodernism and Beyond*. Cambridge: Polity Press.

——— 1992: Popular Culture and the Construction of Postmodern Identities. In Scott Lash and Jonathan Friedman (eds), *Modernity and Identity*, Oxford: Blackwell.

——— 1994: *Baudrillard: A Critical Reader*. Cambridge, MA: Blackwell.

*——— 1995: *Media Culture: Cultural Studies, Identity and Politics between the Modern and the Postmodern*. London: Routledge.

Kilminster, Richard, and Varcoe, Ian. 1996: *Culture, Modernity, and Revolution: Essays in Honour of Zygmunt Bauman*. London and New York: Routledge.

Kumar, Krishan. 1993: Modernity. In William Outhwaite and Tom Bottomore (eds), *The Blackwell Dictionary of Twentieth-Century Social Thought*. Oxford: Blackwell.

Levin, Charles. 1995: *Jean Baudrillard. A Study in Cultural Metaphysics*. London: Prentice Hall/Harvester Wheatsheaf.

Lipovetsky, Gilles. 1992: *Le Crépuscule du devoir – L'éthique indolore des nouveaux temps démocratiques*. Paris: Gallimard.

Maffesoli, Michel. 1988: The Ethic of Aesthetics. *Theory, Culture & Society*, 8/1, 7–20.

——— 1996: *The Individual and Mass Society*. London: Sage.

Mchale, Brian. 1987: *Postmodernist Fiction*. London: Methuen.

Molin, Jan. 1989: Duggen på spejlet. In Jan Molin and Majken Schultz (eds), *Kalejdoskopiske fortællinger fra en videnskabelig verden*. Copenhagen: Akademisk Forlag.

Murphy, John W. 1988: Making Sense of Postmodern Sociology. *British Journal of Sociology*, 39, 600–14.

Owens, Craig. 1983: The Discourse of Others: Feminists and Postmodernism. In Hal Foster (ed.), *The Anti-Aesthetic*, Seattle, WA: Bay Press.

Poster, Mark 1988: *Jean Baudrillard: Selected Writings*. Cambridge: Polity Press.

Rojek, Chris. 1998: *The Politics of Jean-Françcois Lyotard*. London: Routledge.

Rojek, Chris, and Turner, Bryan S. (eds) 1993: Introduction: Regret Baudrillard? In Rojek, Chris, and Turner, Bryan S. (eds), *Forget Baudrillard?*, London and New York: Routledge.

Sim, Stuart. 1996: *Jean-François Lyotard*. New York and London: Prentice Hall/Harvester Wheatsheaf.

Smart, Barry. 1990: Modernity, Postmodernity and the Present. In Bryan Turner (ed.), *Theories of Modernity and Postmodernity*, London: Sage.

*——— 1992: *Modern Conditions, Postmodern Controversies*. London: Routledge.

*——— 1993: *Postmodernity*. London: Routledge.

Sociological Theory 1991: 9/2 Special issue about Postmodernity.

Tseëlon, Efrat. 1992: Is the Presented Self Sincere? Goffman, Impression Management and the Postmodern Self. *Theory, Culture and Society*, 9/2, 115–28.

Turner, Bryan S. 1990: Periodization and Politics in the Postmodern. In Bryan S. Turner (ed.), *Theories of Modernity and Postmodernity*, London: Sage.

Vattimo, Gianni. 1992: *The Transparent Society*. Cambridge: Polity Press.

*Wakefield, Neville. 1990: *Postmodernism: The Twilight of the Real*. London: Pluto Press.

chapter 27

Social Theory, Morality, and the Civil Society

Heine Andersen

Historically, there has always been a connection between social theory and moral understandings of the good life and justice. From Antiquity till our own time, philosophers and thinkers have been preoccupied with discovering how man could realize a good life, and how the ideal society should be organized. However, ideas about the connection between social theory and moral understanding have varied considerably. One fundamental question has been about the relationship between knowing how man is created and actually lives, and the moral norms and ideals about the good life and justice advanced by philosophers, theologians, and just people in general.

Experience clearly shows that moral perceptions vary greatly. As early as the fifth century B.C., the Greek historian Herodotus (approximately 485–425 B.C.) pointed out that what one people regarded as best practice, such as devouring their dead parents, others viewed as barbarian and blasphemous. Can this type of observation prove that no universally valid moral principles exist? Are some born to be slaves? Are divisions of social position, class, and inequality a given part of a natural or divine order or the result of organic balance? If so, does this prove that such social formations are morally right?

Since the emergence of the modern, science-based world picture, scientific theory and thought about moral-normative judgements and ideals have gradually been dissociated. Taking into consideration the theories presented in this book, it will become conspicuously apparent that ideas about what should characterize a good and just society occur only spo-radically throughout history, and in most cases are not confronted directly or openly. This reflects a shift, emerging around the year 1500 during the Renaissance, at which time the Florentine diplomat, historian, and philosopher, Niccolò Machiavelli (1469–1527), formu-lated his epoch-making ideas about state and princely power, based on a foundation which he considered to be above the realm of ethics (Machiavelli 1985 [1532]). This shift in per-ception continued and gradually gained ground over the following 300 to 400 years, in which by the end of the nineteenth century, modern, academic, social-science disciplines were established, separate from theology, moral philosophy, and normative political theory. Since at least the beginning of the twentieth century, the predominant perception has been that social science (and science in general) must be confined to describing and explaining factual conditions, and refrain from judging whether these are more or less morally right and from advancing moral precepts.

It is evident, however, that the total separation of scientific description and explanation from moral judgement is yet to be achieved. In practice, there is still an intimate connection, and the principle itself is routinely contested. In recent years, there have been examples of social scientists ascribing explicitly moral-normative tasks to social theory. In this context, the idea of *the civil society* or similar concepts have often played an important role.

In the remaining part of this chapter, we will discuss the background of the separation of social science from normative ethics. Then we will address the difficulties confronted when attempting to sustain this separation in practice, and we will respond to positions claiming that, in principle, social science will always be dependent on values and interests. Finally, we will present new examples of social theories which explicitly incorporate moral-norma-tive aspects and make use of the idea of civil society.

The Separation of Social Science from Normative Morality

Taking into consideration the roles of science and morality in modern society and predom-inant thinking about these, it is evident that the two domains differ tremendously. Science appears as a very professional activity in which people, selected on the basis of specialized, higher education, attempt to produce new knowledge, the validity of which is tested by apply-ing criteria and methods determined by themselves. This takes place at universities and re-search institutions, which are often fairly closed, elitist, and shielded from external interference (on the creation of modern scientific institutions, see Ben-David 1971; Whitley 1984).

Whether or not scientific results may be valid is usually not considered as something to be decided in parliaments or by popular vote. Within its domain, social science is normally granted autonomy or expert authority, giving it precedence over not only lay people, but also political authorities and all other social institutions. Since the Enlightenment, the ideal has been to simply announce the findings of science to the population, as the results which

constitute the basis for learning in modern societies; if one does not master these sufficiently well, one fails examinations.

It is different with moral issues. Today it is difficult to find any specific institutions or
categories of individuals, whose authoritative precedence is generally accepted, as was the
case in former times with the Church and the priest, the monarch and the patriarch. Tendencies to leave it to experts to judge moral questions are usually received with skepticism. In
modern societies, morality is relatively autonomous in relation to political and other institutions, but unlike science, it is not embedded in specialized or professionalized institutions
designed for this purpose. Morality is, to a much higher degree, considered to be a subjective and personal matter.

This development is a specific feature of differentiation in modern society. Many of the
theories addressed in this book analyze differentiation as a general sociological phenomenon (see Herbert Spencer, chapter 3; Emil Durkheim, chapter 5; Max Weber, chapter 6,
functionalism, chapter 14; Niklas Luhmann, chapter 22). When it comes to the separation
of morality from social theory, three sets of philosophical assumptions are of fundamental
importance to modern culture: (1) the epistemological distinction between recognition of
reality and moral judgements; (2) the distinction between positive, existing law and morality; and (3) the development of ideas about the social world being governed by regularities
or universalities analogous with natural laws.

The separation of "is" from "ought"

In his major work, *A Treatise of Human Nature* (1739–40), the Scottish philosopher David
Hume (1711–76) told of an observation he had made while reading about moral systems:
"instead of the usual copulations of propositions, *is*, and *is not*, I meet with no proposition
that is not connected with an *ought*, or an *ought not*" (Hume 1990: 469). Hume found totally
incomprehensible how it was possible to deduce formulations with "ought" from formulations with "is," and advised caution in this matter; he was persuaded that "this small attention would subvert all the vulgar systems of morality" (Hume 1990: 470).

It is no exaggeration to say that this logical distinction, which has been referred to as "the
gulf doctrine," concerns central and fundamental features of the world picture that is part of
modern societies and which has developed from the time of the Enlightenment. It has both
epistemological and moral philosophical aspects. David Hume was one of the founders of
modern empiricism, the idea that all recognition must build on sensuous experience. But
such observations could not be used to differentiate between good and evil. Nor could they
offer rational explanations or logical arguments. In Hume's opinion, moral judgements
could only be based on feelings, a particular moral sense, which he believed all human
beings to possess.

The German philosopher Immanuel Kant (1724–1804) was an antipode to Hume's empiricism in the Enlightenment. Being a critical rationalist, Kant found that basic moral principles could only be explained rationally. Possessing reason and free will, man is his own
legislator in moral matters. His own, most fundamental moral law is the *categorical imperative*: "Act only according to that maxim by which you can at the same time will that it
should become a universal law" (Kant 1959: 39). But even though Kant found moral laws
justifiable rationally, this did not imply that he wanted to abolish the logical distinction

between "is" and "ought." Both statements about objective reality and moral commands and judgements can be explained rationally, but they belong in two different spheres. Together with a third sphere, the beautiful, the true and the good constitute distinct realms, the internal autonomy of which is fundamental to Kant's philosophy of enlightenment and to modern culture as a whole.

Despite these fundamentally different philosophies, the conclusion was that a distinction between "is" and "ought" was necessary. This had far-reaching implications for social thought, even though it only gradually gained acceptance. Social science in a modern sense was not established until later, but in relationship to the thinking of that time, this distinction became especially important for moral philosophy and political thinking. One of the most important outcomes was that it helped change basic ideas about the relationship between nature and society. This is illustrated by the contribution that distinction made toward the abandonment of the idea of *natural rights*.

Natural law had had a very long tradition, but the assumption that humans were by nature independent of the state and equipped with inalienable civil rights played a particularly important role in the fight against absolutism and the foundation of modern constitutional states with liberal-democratic forms of government. This was, among others, formulated by the British philosopher John Locke (1632–1704) in "the bible of liberalism," *Two Treatises of Government* (1690). The phrases "laws of nature" and "natural rights" were used in the American Declaration of Independence in 1776 and in the Declaration of the Rights of Man in 1789. Now, contemporary thought and language often equate rights with being natural or inborn, for example, in the United Nation's Declaration of Human Rights. One often encounters this phrase in everyday locutions (such as when justifying something by referring to it as "natural"). This demonstrates how established the idea about natural rights is.

Of course, the idea that moral rights are justifiable according to what is natural does not stand up to any consistent enforcement of the distinction between "is" and "ought." Nature cannot be judged morally, as opposed to political forms of government or other social institutions. Therefore, most people today, based on a moral philosophy, are prone to understanding the phrase "natural rights" metaphorically, a phrase stressing the universal and basic status of these rights. Yet, despite numerous debates over the years about the basis for and validity of this distinction between "is" and "ought," it is still widely accepted in its logical sense. It is considered a logical fallacy to pretend to draw conclusions from assertions about the nature of reality for how one ought to act and vice versa. In his book, *Principia Ethica* (1903), the British philosopher G. E. Moore (1873–1958) called this approach *the naturalist fallacy* (Blegvad 1959).

The demand for value-free social sciences

The consequences of this logical distinction gradually became part of the self-understanding and basis of the social sciences. The interplay between moral ideas and social theory is far more multifaceted and complex than this logical relation is capable of describing. Most classical social theorists continued to adhere to the perception that social science should contribute toward uncovering or developing ideas about good and bad ways of organizing society. Thus classical economics, founded by the end of the eighteenth century, referred to itself in its first 100 years as "political economy," and the founder of the science of economics, Adam Smith, was also a moral philosopher. Political economy was occupied with the problems of economic wealth and poverty, population growth, and class relations, and wanted to judge whether conditions were good or bad in a moral sense.

Many themes in classical sociology included moral aspects. Does industrialism imply moral evolution (see Herbert Spencer, chapter 3)? Is the division of labor and individualism compatible with solidarity and moral community? (See Ferninand Tönnies, chapter 4; Emile Durkheim, chapter 5.) Is it possible for the metropolitan to maintain personal identity and moral responsibility when being exposed to the value levelling of money? (See George Simmel, chapter 7.) At the same time, social theorists increasingly tried to consolidate the same autonomy and authority in the social sciences as that in the natural sciences. But the institutionalization of social science as an academic discipline did not take place until the end of the nineteenth century (Wagner 1990; Ross 1991), and only at that time were serious attempts made to separate morality from social science.

Here, Max Weber's formulation of the demand for value freedom was of great importance. In several writings from the early twentieth century, Weber fought intensively against the inclination to produce value judgements based on a "scientific worldview," an approach he found widely accepted among social scientists. Instead, he defended the viewpoint "that it can never be the task of the empirical science to discover binding norms and ideals and from these deduce directions for practice" (translated from Weber 1985 [1922]: 149). This was primarily a methodological requirement, but Weber also stressed that researchers and university teachers should not use their scientific positions to promote certain sets of values (Weber 1985 [1922]: 524ff).

A similar tendency was predominant in several other countries where the social sciences struggled for academic recognition and scientific status (Wagner 1990; Ross 1991), and by the end of World War I, the claim for value freedom was fully accepted within the social sciences. This was further emphasized by the emergence of *logical positivism* in the late 1920s (Radnitzky 1968), which gradually came to dominate the philosophy of knowledge within social science. In view of this position, moral judgements were simply perceived as meaningless pseudo-propositions that could be neither true nor false (Ayer 1978: 144–83). Evidently, they had to be abandoned by science, which searches only for truths.

Descriptive and normative analysis of morality

Logical empiricism perceives morality as a form of meaningless proposition, a position called *meta-ethical noncognitivism*. Meta-ethics are theories about moral analysis, and *noncognitivism* claims that one can never know, in the literal sense of the word, what is morally right. When expressing moral judgements, such as finding the Holocaust reprehensible, these are considered to merely reflect subjective feelings or personal choices. They cannot be validated as objective knowledge. The noncognitivist perception of morality has definitely dominated this century (apart from Ayer, other prominent noncognitivists are Richard M. Hare and Charles L. Stevenson).

On the other hand, meta-ethical cognitivists claim that moral judgements are indeed justifiable as true or false. Some of these, such as natural law theorists, believe that judgement builds on propositions about factual conditions. Other cognitivists, such as Kant, find moral judgements to be verifiable rationally, while yet others (e.g. Moore) assume the existence of a particular moral intuition. Jürgen Habermas's discourse ethics (see chapter 21) is an example of the cognitivist understanding of morality, though only in a formal sense.

Within contemporary moral philosophy, noncognitivism has been almost universal. However, the postulates for neither value freedom nor noncognitivism mean that social science cannot, or will not, address questions of morality in practice. Social science may take on studies of morality, describe and analyze various perceptions of morality, and theorize as to their variations and roles in social life. Thus, a distinction must be made between *descriptive* and *normative* analysis of morality.

The aim of descriptive analysis is to describe and possibly explain morality as a sociological, psychological, and historical phenomenon, as the conceptions and norms of a given population or group. Naturally, the claim for value freedom will not exclude this as a task for social science. By comparison, the normative analysis of morality attempts to prescribe what true morality is, and to judge whether or not certain actions are morally right. It is this kind of normative analysis of morality that supporters of value freedom have abandoned. Yet, even if the argument for value freedom were to gain ground theoretically, this does not necessarily imply that it would be realizable (see below).

Positive law and the separation of law and morality

Another part of the distinction between social science and normative morality is the separation of morality from law. Historically, law had been closely linked to religious and cosmological systems of ideas, which had tied it to an inner legitimacy, rather than being based on the mere fact that it existed and was enforced by a prince, an emperor, or some other sovereign. The idea that the law expressed a more fundamental justice, including a moral sense, was deeply rooted in, and formed part of, the natural law mentioned before.

The Enlightenment and the formation of modern, constitutional states changed this perception toward what has been called the *positive understanding of law*. The actual law, referring to that law which is enforced by the legal system of society, does not deduce its validity from inner moral principles. Legal positivism and legal realism, represented, among others, by legal philosophers such as the Austrian-American Hans Kelsen (1881–1973), the British Herbert Hart (1907–92), and the Scandinavians Axel Hägerström (1868–1939) and Alf Ross (1899–1979), has further developed this perception in keeping with the empiricist view of science. The narrow positivist understanding of law claims that no other sources of prevailing law exist other than what the legal system and other written sources state positively as such. It is of no importance if this is in conflict with any moral norms. However, a broader, realist understanding, such as the one Alf Ross subscribed to, includes the notion that enforcement of law should build on cultural traditions, etc., (Ross 1953: 119ff).

This liberation of rules of law from morality has helped to clear the way for a more value neutral, formalistic, and technocratic understanding of law. This can be viewed as an element of the penetration of purposive rationality and bureaucracy in modern society. Laws and rules can be introduced, changed, and abolished with relative autonomy from personal conceptions of morality, based on the need for efficiency and control. Law becomes to a much higher degree an instrument for organizing and controlling, a designed construction which can be adapted dynamically to the functional needs of society. In consequence, the coupling of law to conceptions of morality is reduced, though not eliminated totally. The law is transformed into an external fact, an objective reality, which appears as a given framework for action, in itself devoid of moral value, and on which one can take a purposive, rational stance.

The separation of morality from law is also reflected in the development of social theories, that is, in the separation of normative, legal, politically oriented analyses of legal systems and jurisprudence from the sociology of law as value-free disciplines. Therefore, pronouncements for value freedom or legal positivism can be viewed as phases in the cultural liberation and subjectivization of morality in modern society. Morality becomes an internal, private, and subjective matter, something everyone must settle with their own convictions, as opposed to the external, factual world around us at any given time – which can be observed and described by the social sciences.

The social sphere as nature and system

Few will consider it to be morally either right or wrong that the earth goes around the sun, or morally reprehensible that the fox eats the hare, because this is according to nature. If we took a similar view of social norms and viewed these exclusively as pure fact in line with nature, as something exogenous controlled by natural laws, it would render judgements of social morality meaningless. In practice, few social theorists have attempted any literal application of this mechanical and fatalistic view of society. Nevertheless, tendencies toward that end have been fairly predominant during certain extensive periods in the history of social science in connection with the cultivation of natural science as an ideal, using a fundamental idea about the ontology of the social world.

From the time of the establishment of the social sciences onward, the natural sciences have been the predominant, though not universal, ideal for all scientific knowledge. The ultimate goal was to find explanations for and to predict events, based on knowledge about laws. August Comte (see chapters 1 and 5) formulated the task of sociology as "to predict in order to be able to control," Karl Marx (see chapter 2) wanted "to find the law of motion of society" with "the precision of natural science," and Herbert Spencer (see chapter 3) worked from the hypothesis that universal laws existed, governing all development in the universe. The most perfect laws were purely deterministic, like Newton's laws. In our century, this understanding has been supported by strong advocates, basing their arguments on logical empiricism with the so-called *unified science program*, and the ideal of reductionism (Radnitzky 1968: 72– 93). Reductionism implies that all universal laws, including those governing sociology, economics, and psychology, must be derived ultimately from the theories of physics.

This epistemological ideal has often been tied to a naturalistic, mechanical, or organic picture of the society. Naturalism can be understood in a stronger or weaker sense. In the strong sense, naturalism implies that everything in existence is reducible to a physical-material level. The weaker sense does not imply reductionism, but merely views society as pure fact, analogous with physical-material nature. Both Spencer and Durkheim talked about different aspects of society as "things" in order to emphasize this analogy. Metaphorical expressions were used to illustrate this analogy, such as social mechanisms, systems mechanisms, social forces, equilibrium, mechanical, and organic solidarity.

Many consider the search for universal laws, reductionism, and naturalism to be an imperative condition for social science. Compared to the understanding of morality based on a subjective, free choice, this must clearly produce a schism. One would have to claim any moral choice as illusory, a purely subjective self-deception, or at least having no influence on those actions the social sciences attempt to explain. This schism does not disappear, even if one tempers one's assumption that universal laws must be deterministic and confined to stochastic laws (statistical laws). To act and judge morally is not to act and judge fortuitously. In neither the strong nor the weak sense has naturalism been predominant, though it has contributed profoundly to the separation of normative morality and social theory.

The Claim for Value Freedom in Practice

These central ideas, which have gradually settled in over a period of more than 200 years since Hume propounded his gulf doctrine, all point in the direction of the impossibility of including moral, normative judgements in social-science theories. What does reality reveal? At a superficial glance, *total* separation has not been achieved. For some theories, the connection is evident and explicit. Diagnostic concepts from classical sociology, such as exploitation and alienation (Marx), evolution and progress (Spencer), solidarity and anomie (Durkheim), loss of meaning and freedom, and the iron cage of rationality (Weber) indicate normative judgements. Several recent theories also contain clear references to normative understandings of morality, such as analytical Marxism's concept of exploitation (see chapter 11), Jean-Paul Sartre's concept of alienation (see chapter 17), Jürgen Habermas's concept of domination-free dialogue and systems colonization (see chapter 21), and Michel Foucault's concept of disciplining (see chapter 19).

In other, later theories, this connection is more subtle and complex. One instructive example is functionalism (see chapter 14). Talcott Parsons's functionalism has often been criticized for expressing a normative defence of value consensus, stability, and the status quo, building on political and economic institutions in modern, Western societies (cf. chapter 16). These theories have been said to be conservatively biased. In short, the reason for this is a functionalist claim that the maintenance of a common value system is a functional necessity in order to be able to maintain a norm system, which again is imperative for keeping social order and societal efficiency. Institutions supporting this value consensus thereby become functional necessities, as in the case of the nuclear family, the legal system, educational institutions, and the Church.

The participating role of the social sciences

Though this example demonstrates some kind of connection with normative morality, this connection is more complex than what Hume, with his "gulf doctrine," and Weber with his demand for value freedom were striving to get at. It is not a question of Parsons having been able to deduce from "is" to "ought," or that he wanted explicitly to produce value judgements. He is not guilty of the naturalistic fallacy. This would be the case if one deduced that based on the functional societal necessity of an institution (for example, the nuclear family), the given institution "ought to" be preserved. Evidently, this would be untenable, because without arguments, one introduces the premise that the existing society "ought to" be preserved. One the other hand, claiming that an institution is functionally necessary for a given society, while simultaneously advocating its abolition, is not inconsistent logically.

The connection with normative morality is therefore of a different nature than purely formal logic, due to the different societal roles of natural science and social science. Social scientists are communicative participants in the social life they study (Andersen 1990: 321ff). The theories of social science are disseminated with scientific authority through education and media, and thus become part of the population's understanding of social conditions and their own role in these. Presumably, a broad spectrum of political conceptions have, in fact, adopted the functionalist understanding of society with two types of effects (naturally there are many other sources than Parsons). One effect is a tendency to promote moral understandings oriented toward utility and calculation of consequences. Moral theory distinguishes between *consequentialist morality* and *deontological morality*. According to consequentialism, the moral rightness of actions or norms must be judged solely on the basis of their consequences. For example, the act of speaking the truth has no true moral value in itself, but the good or bad consequences of telling the truth do (one can easily imagine situations where this may harm others – for example, the activities of informers). Utilitarianism is a classical example of consequentialism: one is to act according to what yields the greatest possible utility. In contrast, deontology claims the very principle underlying an act to be the determining factor, no matter what the consequences are. Kant's categorical imperative reflects a deontological understanding of morality: the act maxim must be followed irrespective of the consequences.

Functionalism tends to predispose consequence-oriented thinking if it is used as the basis for decisions in practical life ("predispose" is used in order to avoid the impression of a strictly logical implication). And much seems to indicate that this type of functionalist thinking has become widespread in political and economic spheres. There is a broad tendency to assess institutions, norms, and rules based on their efficiency in relation to certain overall goals. Certain types of functionalism are related to *rule utilitarian* morality, the perception that one ought to comply with rules of action which yield the highest possible total utility (Van Parijs 1981: 148ff; Andersen 1990: 324ff). But this does not apply to Parsons's version of functionalism. It may be related to consequentialism, but the steering objective is not maximizing utility. Parsons operates with a system of "ultimate values," which he has not specified in detail, but which at least contain more than utility in the traditional, one-dimensional sense of utilitarianism. Thus, normative implications of functionalism are to predispose consequence morality in general at the expense of other perceptions of morality. The more people that are convinced that functionalism is a scientifically correct theory, the more difficult life will become for a confirmed adherent of deontological morality, which itself is not supported by any scientific authority.

The other effect is what has provided the background for accusations that functionalism has a conservative bias. It occurs when consensus exists, at least in general, that present society is worth preserving, but when there is also disagreement about the value of maintaining certain institutions, such as the traditional family pattern. This has undoubtedly been a prevailing condition in many societies. If functionalism claims the latter to be imperative functionally in order to maintain the first, and if, furthermore, there is consensus about functionalism being a correct theory, supporters of the traditional family pattern will have a solid argument. In this sense, the theory can be said to be partial and have a "conservative bias." But two things should be borne in mind. First, the value premise is presumed independently of the theory. Second, partiality in itself says nothing about whether or not the theory is correct. Thus, in many instances, the normative role of functionalism is to demonstrate the *consequences* of various components of the social structure, compared to given objectives.

Mannheim, Myrdal, and the argument of the sociology of knowledge

From the 1930s, the Swedish economist Gunnar Myrdal (1898–1987) criticized social science for being biased toward certain sets of values. He especially used American social science as an example, and claimed it was biased by white middle-class values, but biased in a totally different sense from the one mentioned above. Here, biased means that values appear as a kind of source of error, the outcome of which is distorted or biased results. Myrdal claimed social researchers (like human beings in general) tend to think opportunistically, that they are inclined to interpret observations and design descriptions and theories in a way which confirms their preconceived values. In a study of the African-American situation in American society in the 1930s, Myrdal found a widespread tendency among whites in the South to employ existing knowledge in a selective and distorted way, while simultaneously concealing their own value premises. According to Myrdal's analyses, such values among researchers, which are typically traditional middle-class values, saturate large parts of social research. Words such as equilibrium, balance, stable, normal, adjustment, lag, or function express hidden value premises, which "have in all social sciences have served as a bridge between presumably objective analysis and political prescription" (Myrdal 1969: 52).

Myrdal was of the opinion that psychological and sociological mechanisms, those influences researchers are subject to during their upbringing, will always make value biases unavoidable. His answer to dealing with this was to attempt a disclosure of the implicit values as absent, but logically necessary premises for the conclusions advanced, and then to make these explicit, facilitating a conscious stand. However, this solution raised another problem, which traditionally has been central to the sociology of knowledge, the problem of knowledge relativism. Karl Mannheim (1893–1947), one of the founders of the sociology of knowledge, addressed this problem in detail.

Mannheim (1968) started from the concept of ideology and its relationship to science. His understanding of ideology was influenced by Karl Marx: ideologies are systems of beliefs and ideas originating from the life forms, experiences, worldviews, and interests within a certain class or social group. The political ideologies of the nineteenth century were liberalism, conservatism, and socialism. Stigmatizing an opponent's conception as an ideology is in itself part of the ideological struggle, thus reducing the conception to an expression of particular interests containing no universal validity.

The problem of knowledge relativism

The problem with knowledge relativism is whether the consequential implementation of the sociology of knowledge thesis will ultimately lead to all knowledge having to be understood as ideology in the above sense. If so, this means that no universally valid knowledge exists at all, only different systems of collective beliefs conditioned by the interests and living conditions of specific classes or groups. Relativism implies that no foundation exists on the basis of which one can determine whether one belief system has greater validity than another.

There are positions which argue for this relativism, or at least accept it. In modern times, this has been influenced especially by Wittgenstein's philosophy of language (Wittgenstein 1953), Kuhn's paradigm theory, and the so-called "sociology of scientific knowledge" (Sismondo (1993) and Restivo (1994) have an introduction to the latter), but relativism is also an inherent consequence in Myrdal's conception. For lack of space, comprehensive epistemological theoretical discussions are not addressed here. But one classical argument should be mentioned, which begins with the so-called self-reference problem: self-reference may lead to assertions dissolving their own validity. Self-reference occurs if that which one claims in a given sentence also must be true for the sentence itself. If one claims all knowledge to be relative to certain social conditions or values, then this must also be true of the claim itself. But then, relativism must also apply to the claim itself, meaning that, in itself, it is not universally valid, so it is false.

Mannheim would not accept relativism, and his suggestion for a solution had three components. First, for epistemological theoretical reasons, he exempted the exact sciences from the problem of the sociology of knowledge. Second, for the social sciences, he introduced the assumption that it would be possible for categories of individuals in specific positions to liberate themselves from class interests and other social influences which might distort or limit recognition. Here, he operated with the concept of "free-floating intelligentsia" (adopted from Alfred Weber; Mannheim 1968: 136–46) characterizing an enlightened group of intellectuals who were claimed to be above the societal class structure. Third, in consequence, he suggested the concept of *relationism* rather than relativism. Though the former is a relation between social position and views, the very insight into this relation will lead to a more universally valid recognition, a possibility he did not refuse.

If we compare how the sociology of knowledge treats the interrelationship of social theories with the assertion of bias discussed above, using functionalism as an example and referring to the participatory role of social research, there is one important difference. The sociology of knowledge is interested in social determinants of bias in research, whereas the participatory role perspective is interested in the *consequences* of research on normative conceptions in society. And even though it is obvious to assume there exists a possible relationship, this does not have to be the case at all, at least not in a simple way. Even if one imagines research being able to free itself from ideologies and biases in the Myrdalian sense, it may have moral-normative consequences in that it produces interpretations of social life (Andersen 1990).

This discussion demonstrates that, despite serious reasons for separating social science theories from normative morality (cf. the previous section), this has not been realized in practice. Neither has consensus been achieved about whether this separation is realistic or desirable. In the concluding section, recent examples of theories are discussed, which explicitly attempt to reintroduce a normative perspective.

The Civil Society and Morality

Such examples have occurred within sociology and economic theory within the last couple of decades. Moral philosophers have advanced remarkable theories, building a bridge to social-science theories. A few of these are addressed below, their common trait being that they couple the normative perspective with a concept deeply rooted in the history of ideas, namely *the civil society* (or other concepts addressing nearly identical issues) which has once again become topical.

In its long history, this concept has had several connotations (Keane 1988: 1–72; Cohen and Arato 1992). Derivations of the word civil, such as civilization or civilized, demonstrate that it is meant to capture the socially shaped, cultivated, refined, and urban aspects of social life, as opposed to the brute and barbarian, or those determined by nature. In modern times, this has played a vital role since the time of the Enlightenment, when thinkers of liberalism emphasized civil society as being an independent source of morality from the state.

In his book of 1767, *An Essay on the History of Civil Society,* the Scottish philosopher Adam Ferguson portrayed the evolution of civil society from its early brute, barbarian, and wild life forms. A civil society presupposes the existence of refinements, such as industry, trade, culture, art, and morality. It is the task of the state to create peaceful and orderly settings to facilitate this development.

In Hegel's more conservative conception of society, the *bourgeois society* (*bürgerlische Gesellschaft*) became a link between the state and the private sphere of the family. In his historical materialism, Marx conceived of the bourgeois society as being identical with the material conditions of capitalist modes of production, which again determined ideological, legal, and political conditions. It is well-known that Marx did not have much confidence in bourgeois society.

It is characteristic of these early definitions that, across differences in general, civil or bourgeois society is perceived as a sphere either opposite, or primary, to the state. After a period, the concept almost disappeared from social thinking until it was taken up again by the Italian Marxist, Antonio Gramsci (see chapter 9). He employed the term in the sense of a social sphere relatively independent of both the state and the economy. He viewed it as a political resource basis from which democratic potential could be developed as a counterweight to economic and political class power.

It is also from this political perspective that the idea about civil society being a relatively autonomous sphere between economy and state has acquired its current influence. In Eastern Europe, it has been used by the Polish Solidarity Movement, by Charter 77 in the former Czechoslovakia, and by dissident movements in the former USSR, in the struggle against totalitarian regimes. The concept was advanced in Scandinavia in the early 1980s (Berntson 1983; Nielsen 1984). In Western countries in general, the concept of civil society has probably been promoted by increasing popular skepticism over the state's and the market's ability to cope with threats of economic stagnation and unemployment, environmental problems, ethnic conflicts, and threats of war, as illustrated by the emergence of new grassroots movements (Keane 1988; Cohen and Arato 1992).

Thus, ideas about civil society are clearly linked to normative, moral, and political ideas about democracy, good, and justice. Therefore different perceptions exist on how the ideal civil society ought to be organized, corresponding to different concepts about politics and morality. Conservatives would be more inclined to place an emphasis on institutions, such as the family and the Church, whereas socialists would probably emphasize unions and social movements. Together with Andrew Arato, Jean Cohen has written one of the most profound recent books about the subject, *Civil Society and Political Theories* (1992), and according to Jean Cohen, "in the end, it is all a matter of words which we attempt to infuse with meaning" (Larsen 1994: 32).

Despite differences, the various perceptions of civil society view it as a sphere for relatively spontaneously organized social life, building on voluntariness and opinion-forming, which in turn is based on open and free communication. This comprises voluntary societies (non-governmental organizations), social movements, local communities, interest groups, religious communities, and groups and movements within art and culture, etc. This points toward some of the central concepts from earlier sociological traditions, which are applicable when giving civil society a more theoretical form. Ferdinand Tönnies's *Gemeinschaft*, Emile Durkheim's collective consciousness, George Herbert Mead's generalized other, and Talcot Parsons's societal community are examples which all contain connotations about moral communities.

The social sciences as moral guides?

The American sociologist Alan Wolfe has actually claimed that sociology offers a sort of moral codex for civil society, just as the science of economics does for the market and political science for the state. He has said that the modern social sciences "remain the most common guideposts for moral obligation" in our time (Wolfe 1989: 7). This perspective on the role of sociology resembles that described earlier as the participant role perspective. This states that the central task of sociology is to develop "a perspective on moral agency different from those of the market and the state, in short, allows us to view moral obligation as a socially constructed practice negotiated between learning agents capable of growth on the one hand and a culture capable of change on the other" (Wolfe 1989: 220). By this, Wolfe want to construct a concept of moral action which is neither purely individualist nor purely collectivist, as determined by culture. Civil society is an open ground where individuals jointly construct, develop, and change moral norms, and hence also transform their cultural heritage.

The same intention governs Amitai Etzioni's "I-we paradigm" in his book *The Moral Dimension* (1988). Etzioni is strongly critical of both the very individualistic, egocentric, utility-oriented perception of man in modern economic theory, and the oversocialized perception of man in functionalist sociology, where man is easily reduced to merely an actor playing a predefined role in conformity with given norms. Instead, he wants to construct a paradigm containing both considerations for each individual's maximizing utility, as well as collectively binding morality.

Although both Wolfe's and Etzioni's objectives are clearly normative, their moral sociology is incapable of answering the eternal question of normative moral theory: Which moral requirements are the right ones? The civil society has produced racism, intolerance, terrorism, and egoism, as well as tolerance, altruism, and solidarity. Evidently, the fact that a norm or a judgement emanates from spontaneous organizing in civil society is not in itself a criterion for its moral rightness (which Wolfe and Etzioni naturally recognize). This requires a theory of civil society which can be anchored in a cognitivist theory of morality.

This is what Jürgen Habermas has attempted in his book *Between Facts and Norms* (1997; chapter 21). He starts with his own discourse ethics, which deduces what is morally right from what is acceptable by everyone affected in a domination-free dialogue. This provides the basis for formulating which frames must be present in civil society in order for this ideal to unfold in the best possible way. (Civil society must not be mistaken for what Habermas calls the life-world. An open civil society and the life-world are interdependent, but not identical.)

Drawing on Cohen's and Arato's 1992 analysis, Habermas claims the necessity of four components: (1) pluralism: family forms, informal groups and associations, etc., which make room for variations in life-forms; (2) a public sphere with open institutions for culture and communication; (3) a private sphere in which self-realization and individual moral choices can take place without interference from others; and (4) legality: laws and basic rights ensuring the delimitation of pluralism, the private sphere, and the public sphere from state and economy. It concerns basic political and personal rights, such as the freedom of opinion and expression, freedom of assembly and association, the right to vote, and the right to personal property, etc.

This clarification makes it possible to diagnose threatening tendencies and mechanisms in economic and political systems, as well as in civil society itself. According to Habermas's analysis, these are not caused by governance problems of the public sector, as claimed by neo-liberalists, but are rather structural in nature, connected with too much independence and closedness in public administration, political parties, and interest organizations, not to mention the concentration of financial power in the hands of large firms, and the impoverishment of the public due to commercialization and the concentration of media, etc. The means to counteract these threats are radical-democratic reforms, involving the citizens more in political-administrative decisions, in critical and open communication forums involving administration in general and the administration of justice, and by creating a more open and critical legal profession, more ombudsman institutions, and public hearing institutions, etc.

Conclusion: A Schism of Multiple Aspects

The question regarding connections between social theory and morality has multiple aspects, and only a few of these can be considered as clarified. But the answer to the classical question seems fairly plain: Can descriptions of reality verify normative morality? They cannot. Moral rightness is different from scientific truth.

Other aspects are still unclear. Do the social sciences as participants in public discourses contribute toward creating certain perceptions of morality? If so, which perceptions are right? Are social sciences biased toward certain interests? Will the participant role lead to expert moralism and scientific paternalism in questions of morality? If so, should political conclusions be drawn concerning the organization and control of research? Is it unavoidable that values and interests will affect the contents of theories? If so, does this imply knowledge relativism? Only the future will show whether it is possible to clarify these fundamental, epistemological, moral philosophical, and political questions.

Bibliography

Andersen, Heine. 1990: Morality in Three Social Theories: Parsons, Analytical Marxism and Habermas. *Acta Sociologica*, 33/4, 321–39.

Ayer, Alfred J. 1978 [1936]: *Language, Truth and Logic*. Harmondsworth, Middlesex: Penguin Books.

Ben-David, Joseph. 1971: *The Scientist's Role in Society*. Englewood Cliffs, NJ: Prentice-Hall.

Berntson, Lennart. 1983: Från Aristoteles till Gramsci. Teorier om det civile samhället. *Zenit*, 81, 5–18.

Blegvad, Mogens. 1959: *Den naturalistiske fejlslutning*. Copenhagen: Gyldendal.

Cohen, Jean L., and Arato, Andrew. 1992: *Civil Society and Political Theory*. Cambridge, MA: MIT Press.

Etzioni, Amitai. 1988: *The Moral Dimension*. New York: Free Press.

Habermas, Jürgen. 1997: *Between Facts and Norms. Contribution to a Discourse Theory of Law and Democracy*. Cambridge: Polity Press.

Hume, David. 1990 [1739–40]: *A Treatise of Human Nature*. Oxford: Clarendon Press.

Kant, Immanuel. 1959 [1785]: *Foundations of the Metaphysics of Morals*. Indianapolis: Bobbs-Merrill.

Keane, John (ed.) 1988: *Civil Society and the State*. London and New York: Verso.

Kuhn, Thomas S. 1962: *The Structure of Scientific Revolutions*. Chicago: University of Chicago Press.

Larsen, Øjvind. 1994: Interview med Jean Cohen. *Social Kritik*, 29, 29–34.

Machiavelli, Niccolò. *c.*1985: *The Prince*, a new translation, with an introduction, by Harvey C. Mansfield Jr. London: University of Chicago Press.

Macpherson, C. B. 1985: *Rise and Fall of Economic Justice and other Papers*. Oxford: Oxford University Press.

Mannheim, Karl. 1968 [1929]: *Ideology and Utopia*. London: Routledge & Kegan Paul.

Moore, George E. 1971 [1903]: *Principia Ethica*. Cambridge: Cambridge University Press.

Myrdal, Gunnar. 1944: *An American Dilemma: The Negro Problem and Modern Democracy*. New York: Harpens.

—— 1958: *Value in Social Theory*. London: Routledge & Kegan Paul.

—— 1969: *Objectivity in Social Research*. New York: Pantheon Books.

Nielsen, Torben Hviid. 1984: Stat, civilt samfund og marked som organisationsformer. *Samfundsøkonomen*, 3, 4–11.

Radnitzky, Gerard. 1968: *Contemporary Schools of Metascience*. Vol. I. Lund: Scandinavian University Press.

Restivo, Sal. 1994: The Theory Landscape. In Sheila Jasanoff (ed.), *Handbook of Science and Technology Studies*. Thousand Oak, CA: Sage.

Ross, Alf. 1953: *Ret og retfærdighed*. Copenhagen: Nyt Nordisk Forlag, Arnold Busck.

Ross, Dorothy. 1991: *The Origins of American Social Science*. Cambridge: Cambridge University Press.

Sismondo, Sergio. 1993: Some Social Constructions. *Social Studies of Science*, 23, 513–53.

Van Parijs, Philip. 1981: *Evolutionary Explanation in the Social Sciences*. Totowa, NJ: Rowman and Littlefield.

Wagner, Peter. 1990: *Sozialwissenschaft und Staat*. Frankfurt am Main: Campus Verlag.

Weber, Max. 1985 [1922]: *Wissenschaftslehre*. Tübingen: J.C.B. Mohr.

Whitley, Richard. 1984: *Intellectual and Social Organization of the Sciences*. Oxford: Clarendon Press.

Wittgenstein, Ludwig. 1953: *Philosophical Investigations*. Oxford: Blackwell.

Wolfe, Alan. 1989: *Whose Keeper? Social Science and Moral Obligation*. Berkeley: University of California Press.

chapter 28

State, Nation and National Identity

Uffe Østergaard

At the outset it is important to distinguish between "nationalism" and "national identity" or "ethnic identity." Of course, there are certain points of contact between nationalism as ideology and the reality it tries to conceptualize. Nationalism designates those movements which at the political level seek to realize the ideas of what is common to people, while nationality or national identity is that "something" upon which they base their mobilization. The most dangerous thing a nationality researcher can do, however, is to take for granted nationalist myths about the nature and antiquity of the common origin. They are precisely that: myths, often established in the last century, but similar processes are constantly taking place. Today we see a typical example of such mythmaking taking place among members of the Kurdish minority in Turkey. After finally succeeding in capturing the world's attention, Kurdish intellectuals have begun to write a common "national" past for themselves, so that they can appear as a respectable "nation" when the international borders are redrawn. To allow research on such consciously constructed myths to be done by nationalist partisans is just as distorted as allowing the study of railroads to be done by railroad enthusiasts, as the historian Eric Hobsbawm (b. 1917) put it so masterfully (Hobsbawm 1972).

Historically speaking, there is more truth in the Czech-British anthropologist and philosopher, Ernest Gellner's (1925–95) acutely functionalist assertion that national movements and ideologies emerged first; when established these movements then constructed suitable national identities for themselves equipped with an invented history. Not quite freely invented, of course, but alternative national constructions than the ones existing today could have been possible. We may comfort ourselves on this point by investigating some of the constructions which failed; these are in fact just as interesting as those which have succeeded in making an impact but they are obviously difficult to analyze as they lost the competition and left few traces.

National identity, understood as a people's notion of having several specific features in common, is largely a result of conscious political choices and actions which have often taken place so recently that we have sources to follow the process. No modern national identity without a precursor nationalist movement exists. The problem is what to call the collective identities which preceded the modern national states.

Eric Hobsbawm in 1988 compromised with his earlier, more consistent formulations, when introducing the notion of "proto-nationalism" (Hobsbawm 1990: 46–7). Yet this concept hardly solves the problem, but simply moves it in time. This is no fundamental help aside from also creating terminological confusion. We can, for example, certainly encounter the term "nation" in the Middle Ages, but the word meant something completely different than in the age of nationalism, where it was inextricably linked with the effort to create an associated state. In the medieval universities, students were organized into "nations" coming from the same geographical area. The label entails a notion of a common origin, but a nation could include groups within the same Latin-language, Catholic culture. The individual "nations" were not defined by their specific local language, and they had no meaning outside the universities, that is, these "homelands" were not identical with the modern nation-states of similar names. Hence, the "French nation" at the university in Paris included all students speaking Romance languages, and the "German nation" included Germans and English, Scandinavians, Czechs, Poles, etc. (Østerud 1994: 16).

The problem with the study of national identity is that we are now relegated to studying the process with the help of modern and therefore anachronistic concepts which are necessarily colored by the fact that we know what happened afterwards. We are today caged by the nation-builders' own ideological formulations and their conscious reinterpretations of past and present.

Nationalism

Nationalism, as an "ism," i.e., as an ideology, is a modern phenomenon. In 1944 the godfather of nationalism research, Hans Kohn (1891–1971), reaffirmed that nationalism in the word's current sense emerged at the end of the 1700s. The first great impact of this new ideology was the French Revolution, which in turn diffused the new idea throughout Europe on the tips of French bayonets (Kohn 1944: 3).

This national idea has since been victorious and has become the state-bearing principle throughout the entire globe, to such a degree that today the existence of a single common national identity in independent states is viewed as the decisive precondition for successful democracies. In nationalism's first epoch, from the end of the eighteenth century to the 1950s, the concept of "national identity" was not used, the key term being instead "national character." For various reasons, this latter expression was discredited by the beginning of the 1950s, giving way to concepts as "national identity " and "ethnic identity." Today the two words are often used interchangeably, though their origin and content is logically quite different.

Ethnic identity

In logical terms, "ethnic identity" can be juxtaposed to "national identity" in four ways: (1) as a subcategory in relation to national identity; (2) as a historical predecessor, the raw material from which the national identity is created in modern times; (3) as a competing identity, which is the case in many new states where tribal affiliations compete with state or national affiliations; or (4) as a superordinate category such that "national identity" is simply a special case of "ethnic identity." These four meanings are inconveniently mixed together in most of the generalizing literature on the subject. Without making the necessary distinctions, researchers generalize on the basis of relatively few known cases. They think either of nationalism in the new states, or of ethnic groups in mixed cultures, or of regional movements in old states such as the Basques, Bretons, or Northern Ireland. While there are similarities between these types of identity creation, they are certainly not identical.

Because of American dominance in the field of research on nationalism, the predominant view is to see national identity as a special case of ethnicity. The situation does not appear this way, however, if one studies the phenomenon on the basis of European experience, where the state played a decisive role in the creation of national identities. In Europe, the Nordic countries represent a further special historical experience. In Denmark, Sweden, Norway, Iceland, and Finland, state, society, and nation overlap with each other in a totally unique way. This is primarily due to the fact that these states have shrunk in size after military defeats; nevertheless they survived, primarily because their survival as relatively weak powers around the Baltic Sea was in the interest of Great Powers. The Nordic countries constitute an exception, but other countries as well have experienced a national identity at the state level which has existed for so long that it has developed into an almost preconscious mentality. This makes it difficult and especially necessary for Scandinavians to clarify precisely the distinctions between state, national, ethnic, and regional identity.

Nation and people

In most of the European languages, the words of "nation" and "people" (or *folk/Volk*) come from the Latin words *natio* and *populus*. *Natio* derives from the verb *nascor* (to be born), and refers to belief in a common origin. In the Middle Ages the word *natio* meant tribe or clan, but was at times also used to refer to people who were born in the same geographical area, referred to as land. In the seventeenth and eighteenth centuries, "nation" gradually came to connote the inhabitants of a more or less precisely defined territorial state.

Common language was usually linked to notions of a common ancestry, but along with the development of the first classical, territorial states in Western Europe, the kingdoms of France, England (which later subdued the rest of the British Isles and became the United Kingdom of Great Britain and [Northern] Ireland), Denmark (with Norway) and Sweden (with Finland), language was something new connected with the state.

Before the French Revolution, sovereignty had been derived from absolutist kings who administered God's will on their people. With the French (and American) revolutions sovereignty was transferred to the people, and with this development "nations" changed their subject. They no longer referred to a dynastic territorial realm but to a politically defined collective, which logically, and gradually also historically, was assumed to have existed prior to the state. For the Enlightenment thinkers, only the "people," as bearers of sovereignty, could delegate this collective sovereignty to an elected, representative assembly (Kemiläinen, 1984: 33–4). The nation is thus a relatively modern phenomenon. Or more correctly, what is new is the identification of state, people, and the new shared political concept of nation, in short the nation-states of the modern epoch.

In the early nineteenth century, Britain and France appeared as archetypes of the national state, even though they had achieved this status by two very different paths. The existence of these two nation-states stimulated similar developments in several other European countries. First the German and Italian liberals, followed by the Slav, Scandinavian, and South American liberals made it their program to achieve a status equal to that of Britain and France. The German *Volk*, the Russian *narod*, the Italian *nazione*, and the rest asserted their demands on the legacy of state power which their rulers had created.

National Identity

Herder

The notion of national identity was promulgated in the 1770s by the German Lutheran thinker, Johann Gottfried von Herder (1744–1803). Herder did not generally believe that national character could be inherited, only learned. During the intensive debate on heredity versus environment which took place during the eighteenth century, Herder took the side of those who spoke out for the significance of the environment.

Herder's nonaggressive nationalism constitutes the point of departure for both the most influential views of national identity in the nineteenth and twentieth centuries, the Romantic or objective definition and the political affective disposition of the nation. The problem is that the objective definition emerged victorious and, with the Versailles Treaty of 1920, became the basis for the reordering of Europe in so-called nation-states after World War I. During the Cold War era, this well-intentioned order functioned rather well, but after 1989 we have undeniably become aware of the immense problems it created in the form of dissatisfied national minorities. In reality, as shown by the political scientist Walker Connor (b. 1926), it is difficult to identify more than a dozen countries in the world which live up to the demand of identity between state and nation. As a consequence we see increasing demands for more and ever smaller "national" or "ethnically cleansed" states, even in apparently well-established West European states (Connor 1978, 1994).

"What is a nation?"

The problem with the objective definition of the nation which emerged victorious is that it builds upon some untenable views regarding the association between language, "race," and political attitudes. Despite innumerable attempts, it has proven impossible to agree upon an "objective" definition of the nation. In fact, most wars, from the French Revolution to to-day's "ethnic cleansing," have been fought in the name of competing definitions of national and historical "right." It is therefore necessary to accept that every ethnic group which defines itself as a nation, or is viewed as such by others, is in fact a nation. This view was argued by the French historian of religion, Joseph Ernest Renan (1823–92), in a speech entitled "What is a nation?" (1882). Renan's task was to prove that the French population in Alsace-Lorraine had the right to its own, French nationality, even after the provinces had been ceded to Germany in 1871.

Renan asked, rhetorically but very precisely, "But what is a nation then? Why are the Netherlands a nation, while Hannover or the Grand Duchy of Parma is not? How is it that France continues to be a nation, when the principle which created it (the monarchy) has disappeared? Why is Switzerland, with its three languages, two religions and three or four races, one nation, while Tuscany, for example, which is so homogeneous, is not? Why is Austria a state and not a nation?" (Renan 1882).

The occasion for Renan's consideration was that well-respected liberal, German historians had made their contribution to the German war effort and the unification of the German Reich in 1871 by justifying the conquest of Alsace-Lorraine (in French) or Elsass-Lothringen (in German) by reference to the fact that the population, objectively speaking, belonged to the German *Volksgeist*. German historians thus referred to unconscious forces which control the individuals behind their backs as expressions of their "true essence": language, race, and the historical tradition. People in Alsace spoke German and were of German culture; hence the conquest was legitimate.

French scholars responded to this challenge by "proving" the Alsatians' right to remain French. The most convincing response in this debate was provided by Renan. After a thorough testing of the arguments for and against the different definitions, he ceased referring to the population's "age old Celtic roots," its "race." On the contrary, while acknowledging without reservation that the Alsatians were of German language and race, he argued that they were nevertheless French in their preferences.

This was not always the case. At the outbreak of the 1789 Revolution, France's borders were neither logical nor necessary. In the century after the Peace of Westphalia in 1648, the French monarchy had conquered considerable land areas in the northeast which had earlier

belonged to the German Roman empire. The connection between the provinces was constituted only by a common affiliation to the French Crown. After 1789, the French nation
defined itself as a political community, a nation with all the strengths and weaknesses entailed in such a voluntaristic definition. In contrast to those German-speakers residing in the
Rheinland, the majority of Alsace's German-speaking inhabitants joined the new, revolutionary community during the wars in the 1790s. Renan emphasized that the Alsatians felt
no desire to be a part of the German Reich, where they felt themselves repressed, and apparently preferred the French political community symbolized by the Republican tricolor, the
Marseillaise, and the image of Marianne.

  This observation led him to the following famous definition of national affiliation: "A
customs union is no fatherland. A nation is a soul, a spiritual principle. A nation is a great
solidarity, formed by experience with the victims it has brought into the past, and those it is
willing to bring in the future. A nation's existence is a daily referendum" (Renan 1882).
This definition of national identity emphasizes volition, solidarity, and sentiments in the
population and, what in this context is most important, the organized political framework
within which this subjectivity is expressed, the state. The logical consequence of Renan's
subjective national view was to accept cultural autonomy within the existing states, regardless of whether or not these were in national terms.

  Basing oneself on the political definition of national identity, it is possible to draw two
opposing conclusions regarding the question of the extent to which states must be ethnically homogeneous, or whether multinational states can function. In 1861 the philosopher
John Stuart Mill (1806–73) affirmed that "the general will is a precondition for free institutions, that the government's limits overlap with the limits of nationality" (Mill 1861). Mill
argued that the public opinion on which a representative government is based cannot exist
in a people if there is no feeling of community and a common language. Distance and
isolation prevent the necessary formulation of public opinion. Mill's main argument, however, is that a multinational state lacks the guarantees against dictatorship which he thought
existed in nation-states. While a national community in itself does not ensure free institutions, such free institutions, Mill argued, cannot exist without a such a community. Nationality is a necessary but not a sufficient condition for democracy.

  In contrast to this radical liberal point of view, another Englishman, the conservative
historian Lord Acton (1834–1902), asserted that "the combination of different nations in a
state is just as necessary a prerequisite for civilized life as is the combination of people for
society" (Acton 1862). According to Acton, multinationality gives vitality and tensions to
society and acts as a challenge and as education. The nationality principle means isolation,
stagnation, and decline. In Acton's view, the nationality principle is a step backwards which
suffocates vitality, progress, and development.

Social Scientific Theories of Nationalism and Nationality

Serious research on nationalism and national identity which does not take the phenomenon
as a natural given is recent. Only in 1931 did the American historian Carlton J. Hayes publish a work which forged a new path for comparative, typologizing nationalism research. A
Catholic, Hayes was profoundly skeptical of the ignorant, popular nationalism he had encountered in his own country, which had just made its entry into the international arena as an

equal Great Power. Hayes saw nationalism as requiring a doctrine of popular sovereignty, and he differentiated between two main types, a so-called "original" and a "derived" version of nationalism. The "original" nationalism characterizes, according to Hayes, nationalities who struggled for their freedom or unification, while the "derived" could only evolve when a people had obtained their own state. He divided nationalisms into five types, which he called "humanitarian," "Jacobin," "traditional," "liberal," and "integral."

Another prominent figure in this predominantly intellectual study of the roots of nationalism was the German-Czech Jew, Hans Kohn (1891–1971), born in Prague. Kohn authored the still unsurpassed classic in the study of nationalism, *The Idea of Nationalism*, in 1944.

Like Hayes, Kohn operates with two basic forms of nationalism, which he calls "Western" and "Eastern." Western nationalism, based on political liberalism, in his view emerged in states which were already territorially consolidated prior to the era of nationalism. After 1800, these so-called "state-nations" changed into "nation-states." Eastern nationalisms emerged in Eastern and Central Europe, but here the movements first had to create "their" own states and therefore often oriented themselves in a cultural direction. This led them in the direction of what Kohn saw as political irrationality because of the lack of a bourgeoisie with sufficient strength to moderate the intellectuals' excesses. In Eastern Europe, asserted Kohn, national independence became more important than Western ideals of freedom. In this observation Kohn built on his own experiences as a German-speaker in Prague under the flowering of Czech nationalism (Kohn 1964).

National identity

So much for the tradition of research into the intellectual roots of the ideology of nationalism. What about national identity? A mixture of suspicion toward nationalism – which Hayes called integral – and general methodological hesitations caused most historians to shy away from dealing with the subject, even after many began to distance themselves from the nationalism of the nineteenth century. This process was that much more difficult inasmuch as professional historiography owed its existence to precisely the formation of the national states. This hesitant attitude toward the phenomenon appears with exemplary clarity in the first authoritative social-science reference book, the *Encyclopedia of the Social Sciences,* of 1933. Hayes's colleague, the historian Max Boehm, who dealt with the theoretical aspects of nationalism, observed in the entry on "Nationalism" that it is especially "travelers, poets, participants in military expeditions and tourists" who dare express themselves in a generalizing way about people's national character (Boehm 1933: 232). Perhaps a "national character" can be found, but it changes over time and is extremely difficult to define, says Boehm. Such a reservation was absent among representatives from the rising behavioral sciences represented in the same dictionary. In the entry on "Personality," the anthropologist Edward Sapir concluded self-confidently that it is possible to outline cultural identities on a scientifically solid foundation (Sapir 1933: 87).

In a short-term perspective, Sapir was right. When the old nationalist historiography became totally discredited by the excesses of fascism and Nazism, the American anthropologists Gregory Bateson (1904–80), Ruth Benedict (1887–1948), and Margaret Mead (1901–78) continued the study of what they too called "national character." This research took place during and immediately after World War II and applied the entire gamut of social, psychological, and behavioral science conceptual apparatus. Even though their methods later came under attack, preoccupation with collective identity did not cease. Instead, researchers preferred to speak of "ethnic" or "national" identity.

The Study of National Character and National Identity

Under the leadership of Margaret Mead, a comprehensive comparative study of national differences was initiated and conducted by the project group on Research in Contemporary Cultures. Mead started the project in 1942 with a mobilizing book, *And Keep Your Powder Dry*, which used anthropological methods to describe uniquely American values and discussed the circumstances under which Americans would be willing to fight. Mead insisted that she was seeking to do what no anthropologist had dared to do earlier, namely to write about larger, complex cultures with the help of the model for entire cultures which had evolved through studies of small primitive societies; one of these was the Samoa which Mead herself had made famous in the 1920s (Mead 1928).

According to Mead, the goal of the postwar project was to use experiences from hundreds of cultures to create a single international culture which could collect the best from all of them (Howard 1984: 236). In 1946, Mead's friend and mentor Ruth Benedict published an anthropological analysis of Japan, *The Chrysanthemum and the Sword*, a work which won greater notoriety than her earlier *Patterns of Culture* of 1934. Without ever having set foot in Japan, Benedict attempted to analyze the basic features of Japanese culture, using data collected by the Office of War Information during the war. Benedict distinguished "shame cultures" such as Japan's from the "guilt culture" of the West. This method is paradigmatic for their new cultural research project, which went under changing designations such as "Cultures at a Distance," "The Study of National Character," and "Research on Contemporary Cultures" (Mead and Metraux 1953).

This combination of ethnographic observation and psychological assumptions in the study of how group norms and attitudes come to characterize members of various societies gave inspiration to the Freudian-oriented Danish-German-born psychoanalyst, Erik H. Erikson. With his *Childhood and Society* (1950). Erikson exerted a fundamental influence on the view of childhood's decisive significance for the creation of individuals, and with his biographies of Luther and Gandhi subsequently gave impetus to the establishment of what now is known as "psychohistory." During the war, Erikson had helped elaborate memoranda for the Committee for National Morale on the effects of prolonged duty on board submarines. He interrogated German war prisoners and undertook psychological studies of interned war prisoners. Erikson's most important contribution to the war effort was to demonstrate how Hitler had impressed German youth by personifying the anxieties and fantasies of an entire generation who had experienced national humiliation, cultural crisis, and economic collapse.

Political Science Theories of National Political Culture

The respected American historian David Potter still placed high hopes in the psychological and psychoanalytic approach as late as 1954. But in reality Potter stood quite alone with his newly converted excitement and faith in the explanatory power of this research orientation. Instead, the torch was passed to some courageous political scientists who, armed with quantitative methods, dared enter the historians' territory.

Leading the pack of these practitioners of comparative historical sociology was Seymour Martin Lipset. Lipset was well equipped to do so, with experiences from the study of various areas such as Canada in the 1930s and 1940s and Nazi Germany (Lipset 1950, 1960). As a good political scientist, Lipset insisted on a distinction between the "historical" and the "comparative" methods. Despite this he made a valuable contribution to our historical understanding of the revolutionary origins of American political culture, because he did not exaggerate his rejection of the historical perspective like later political scientists of functionalist persuasions (Lipset 1963: 9–10).

The work of Lipset and others opened an entirely new field of study which came to be called "political culture." The most prominent practitioners of the genre were Gabriel Almond and Sidney Verba (1963). However, they did not follow Lipset's good advice from 1963 to emphasize the historical specificity of their results. Almond and Verba achieved extremely valuable insights concerning political behavior and political values in various countries but, as is so often the case in comparative studies, they failed to clarify the unstated value premises on which they had based their comparison. In their case, the ideal on which all other democracies were measured was the Anglo-Saxon two-party system with majority voting in individual districts and oscillation in power-holding between a clearly defined "government" and an "opposition." The Anglo-Saxon system was for them the only form of a viable and "normal" democracy, and from this they gave largely negative evaluations to all other political systems.

All this came to an end in the 1960s under the influence of the student revolts and demands for an increased sophistication of quantitative methods. Back in 1953, Karl W. Deutsch in his influential *Nationalism and Social Communication*, had attempted to collect quantitative data which could support impressionistic descriptions of the behavior of various nations. The demands for methodological sophistication combined with the student revolts, the women's movement, and general sympathy for oppressed minorities resulted in a praiseworthy dissolution of the ideas of permanent and unproblematic entities which could be studied under single headings. Out went all talk of national identity and in came race, class, and gender. The sociolinguists even dropped the very idea of "national" language, since they could only define national languages as dialects with armies and navies. Ultimately, the conventional wisdom stated that each single individual has his or her own identity and own language and basically could not be sure whether they shared a culture with others.

Renaissance of nationalism research

Within the past 20 years, interest in nationalism and national identity has re-emerged on a global scale. This is due partly to political events in East, West and South. Old books are being republished with new prefaces, and new ones appear as if on an assembly line.

In the mid-1980s, the American sociologist Robert Bellah collected a small team of psychologists and sociologists in order to revive the type of research which Riesman had rejected in 1958. In the attempt to break out of the rigid distinction between "is" and "ought" in social-science research, Bellah returned to the unsurpassed French, aristocratic, political sociologist, and politician, Alexis de Tocqueville (1805–59). Tocqueville has given us one of the most ground-breaking and comprehensive analyses of the relationship between a political system and political culture/national character ever written. In *Democracy in America* (1835– 40) Tocqueville defined the use of the classical concept of "mores" (French *moeurs*) in a section entitled "The Significance of Custom for the Maintenance of the Democratic Republic in the United States of America."

Tocqueville's "mores," or "habits of the heart," come very close to what subsequent researchers have called "national political culture" or "mentality." Bellah's group has taken the English translation of Tocqueville's expression as the title of their very exciting book on what is uniquely American in American political culture and morality today, *Habits of the Heart*. On the basis of in-depth interviews with a few hundred representative Americans, Bellah and his colleagues succeeded in identifying four dominant social characters which they then correlated with the four dominant political traditions in the United States. In this way they succeeded in achieving a satisfactory description of the major features in the political culture and mentality in the major part of the America's white middle class.

The Nation-State in Historical Sociology

The postwar era's most interesting investigations of national differences, however, come from macrosociological studies of those features which have been decisive for the various developments between states. Themes such as the organization of work, political traditions, democratic and authoritarian regimes, have been treated by researchers who derived their inspiration from a combination of Max Weber (see chapter 6) and Karl Marx (see chapter 2).

In the case of national identity, the main emphasis has been on studies of the planned "integration from above" of European peasant populations at the end of the nineteenth century by means of school systems, general conscription, and the mass media. This process has been baptized "the nationalization of the masses" by the American historian of German origins, George Mosse (1975), or "peasants into Frenchmen" by the American historian of Romanian origin, Eugen Weber (1978).

The problem with these works emphasizing integration from above, linguistic homogenization, and the like is that this process did not build exclusively on coercion. Some historians of mentality emphasize that it also builds upon one or another degree of receptivity, somewhat different dispositions in broad popular cultures outside the elite cultures, even though there is general agreement that the popular cultures in Europe had far greater common features before 1800 than after, when the elites invented the concept of "people." As already indicated, there was "something" the elites could utilize when constructing an association between national feelings and state identity. That such a potential was necessary for the establishment of national identity appears solely from the fact that attempts to create new national identities, from above or from below, sometimes failed. Nations are created by "historical coincidences" (or accidents) but are not random coincidences. "Historical coincidence" means that the outcome can be described afterwards but cannot be predicted with any form of certainty.

The absent state

Since the emergence of behaviorism and functionalism in the 1930s and 1950s, the state has played a relatively modest role in the dominant social-science paradigm. As a consequence of the behavioral science breakthrough, the state was viewed as a legacy of the social sciences' historical juridical past. The study of state and power was replaced by the study of interest groups, organizations, leadership, parties, and bureaucratic organs. This applies, paradoxically enough, even to the field which in Denmark is called *statskundskab* (literally "statecraft") and in Norway and Sweden to what is called *statsvidenskab* (literally state science). This approach underlies the authoritative summary of the field of 1968, by the first Danish professor of political science, Erik Rasmussen. Here the concept of state is conspicuous by its absence in favor of political systems and the like. In both contexts the state is viewed as a juridical fiction.

Nation-building studies

It was only historical macrosociology, with its study of nation-building, which paid attention to state formation and nation-building. In the 1950s it entered into a general modernization syndrome as the political counterpart of the industrialization which the economists were researching. This took place on the basis of very heavy-handed assumptions regarding the direct positive association between economic growth and political "modernization." In the 1960s this dominant modernization paradigm was revolutionized by researchers such as Reinhard Bendix (1916–91), Stein Rokkan (1921–79) and Seymour Martin Lipset (b. 1922). Inspired by Max Weber, they added a historical dimension to the quantitative, comparative procedures hitherto at the forefront of social science for a generation or two.

As early as 1956, Bendix had presented a comparative study of the various definitions of work and authority in Russia and England. In this context, his most important work is *Nation-Building and Citizenship* (1964). Bendix follows two axes in the historical development: on one hand, the extension of public authority with the resulting state penetration into new areas of social life, and on the other the development of political civil rights, that is, "citizenship." Political legitimacy, understood as the degree of support around central political institutions and political rules of the game, depends on how these two processes relate to each other. From around 1500 nation-building in Western Europe became a strategy for the dominant elites, aimed at forging direct links between the territorial state and its individual subjects. This required that dominant local bonds of solidarity be broken down via the development of universal citizenship and its complex of rights and obligations. In this way, nation-building became a pattern of territorial integration constructed upon three main elements: new forms of public authority, development of a national community across subnational affiliations, and mobilization of new social groups according to universal criteria for participation.

In the introduction to his standard work, *The Formation of National States in Western Europe* (1975), the historical sociologist Charles Tilly emphasizes the historically unique character of West European state formation in the period after 1500. The national state which evolved here generally controlled a well-defined, cohesive area of territory. It was relatively centralized, distinguished itself clearly from other organizations, and ensured itself a gradual monopoly over the means of physical coercion within its own borders. This state expanded with the help of war; but because of the cultural homogeneity in Europe it was often possible to incorporate populations from the conquered areas, as when Sweden, in the latter part of the 1600s, succeeded in "Swedisizing" the Danish population of Scania (Skaana) within just one-and-a-half generations, a population which as late as the 1670s had revolted en masse against their new masters. The existence of a relatively homogenized peasant economy and a small but widely dispersed class of estate owners also promoted integration possibilities in Europe. On the other hand, there were also such great variations that a host of power centers could continue to coexist. At no time did any single institution succeed in consolidating power in a single hand, as occurred in China.

According to the British historian and sociologist Perry Anderson, this situation of permanently competing power centers, where no one alone could outcompete all the others, was the precondition for capitalism as an economic system in Europe (Anderson 1974). In China a capitalist process had been well underway, but when the political organs felt their power monopoly to be threatened, one Ming dynasty emperor, in 1436, decided to strangle the rising merchant class at the outset by burning their junks, forbidding foreign trade, and bringing up the merchants' sons to be officials of the classical school, Mandarins.

The most systematic model for understanding nation-building was developed by the doyen of quantitative, comparative macrosociology, the Norwegian Stein Rokkan. In the years prior to his untimely death in 1979, Rokkan placed increasingly stronger emphasis on the significance of historical state formation for differences in political behavior. He formulated a program to combine his quantitative political sociology with traditional political history. The most important innovation in his model was the two-dimensional, four-field scheme consisting of economy, power, legality, and culture, traversed by a center–periphery axis for each of the functional elements. The four main functions thereby become four different components in a center–periphery relationship: the military-administrative coercive power, the economic, the cultural, and the legislative-juridical. The creation of centers in a national system can vary with the degree of homogeneity and degree of geographical overlap of various functions, while the periphery, on the other hand, can be integrated into the system via various organizations for control or articulation of resistance. All this has shown itself an extremely fruitful research strategy, not yet fully realized.

"Bringing the state back in"

Evidence for the whole change in the political and social sciences is an anthology entitled *Bringing the State Back In* (1985), edited by one of the main initiators of a historiographical challenge to structural-functionalism in history and social science, the American historical sociologist Theda Skocpol. Her point of departure was Barrington Moore's groundbreaking work, *Social Origins of Dictatorship and Democracy* (1967). From here Skocpol extended Barrington Moore's perspective of internal class constellations to include the state as an independent actor, including competition among states in the international system of states. The challenge has had an enormous impact, and today the incorporation of the state into sociological analyses represents the dominating tendency in modern history research and social science, in any case, among those working at the macro level.

Evidence of the strength of this new turn is the fact that the British sociologist, Anthony Giddens, has dedicated an entire volume to the state and its monopoly of the legalized exercise of power. In his comprehensive and ambitious revision of historical materialism, *The Nation-State and Violence* (subtitled *Volume Two of A Contemporary Critique of Historical Materialism*, 1985). As a critique of the concept of state in Marxist terms he offers this defense:

> The nation-state, which exists in a complex of other nation-states, is a set of institutional forms of governance maintaining an administrative monopoly over a territory with demarcated boundaries (borders), its rule being sanctioned by law and direct control of the means of internal and external violence. (Giddens 1985: 121)

In accordance with Max Weber, Giddens draws attention to the significance of the legitimate monopoly of violence for the state's existence; but it should be noted that it is *legitimate* violence, not any kind of violence he investigates. Giddens fails to sufficiently highlight the sources of this legitimacy (this is elaborated much better by the Weberian, Reinhard Bendix), but Giddens must be praised for his systematic attempt to expand narrow class-focused historical materialism. The same critique applies to Michael Mann's magnum opus, *The Sources of Social Power*, two thick volumes of which have appeared (1986 and 1993).

Current Theories of Nationality

Ernest Gellner: industrialization and modernization

One must go to the Czech-British anthropologist and philosopher, Ernest Gellner (1925–95), to find a methodological and theoretically coherent analysis of the significance of national identity for state formation and industrialization. For Gellner it has no meaning to speak of national identity and nationalism in premodern, "agrarian-literary" societies (those we normally call "high cultures"). The elites and the food-producing masses always led completely separate cultural lives, and no ideology proved able to transcend this fundamental difference, not even the great religions, which had this as their explicit intention and existential justification. For Gellner, nations and nationalism are exclusively the result and a condition of the industrial society. Modern industry demands a mobile, literate, and technologically educated population, and the modern state is the only organ capable of delivering this commodity via its public, coercive, omnipotent, and standardized educational system. The cultural homogeneity demanded by modern society has been created via the national ideologies. These nationalisms, in contrast, have invented nations, which did not exist before as anything other than nationalist myths. Nations and nationalisms are basically arbitrary phenomena, regardless of how much they assert their antiquity and unbroken continuity.

While traditional society was determined by structures, modern society is determined by culture. Hence, the borders of the modern state extend as far as their monopoly of the issuing of diplomas extends. But Gellner's modernist functionalism and instrumentalist analysis does not explain why certain identities have been successful in creating their own states and others have not. This shortcoming of the functional analysis has provoked several alternative explanations, known as "perennialist" or "primordialist." In their extreme form, as we encounter them among various national movements, such views of certain nations' eternal existence are easy to reject as naive falsifications of history. The primordialists are opposed by the circumstantialists or "optionalists," as the sociologist Philip Gleason prefers to call them, in order to emphasize the element of choice which lies in the acknowledgement of ethnic identity (Gleason 1983: 919). The two explanations correspond respectively to the psychoanalytical definition of identity, which was promoted by Erikson, while the second group corresponds to the more sociological one, which emphasizes roles and reference groups. Common to both explanations, however, is that they emphasize the significance of continuity in the formation of identity. The disagreements consist in the degree to which we are in the hands of such preformed structures, thus giving us a new variant of the well-known interplay between structural determinism and actor freedom which has characterized sociology and political science from their very beginnings.

Smith and Armstrong: ethnic identity

As with most things in life, the truth is surely somewhere in between. But where? The American political scientist John Armstrong and the British sociologist Anthony Smith have, independently of each other, formulated attempts to mediate between the historical and the functionalist explanations of ethnic identity. Their focus is on the socalled "etnies" which existed prior to the modern national states. In the introduction to his book, *The Ethnic Origins of Nations* (1986), Smith criticizes the dominant positions. None of them meets his demands, and this leads Smith to develop an alternative understanding of the origins of nations. On one hand he dismisses the modernists, who assert that nations build on a radical break with the organizations and mentality of premodern societies. On the other hand, he attempts to avoid the perennialist camp, which claims that nations always have been there. In order to do this, Smith introduces the concept of *etnie*.

In contrast to John Armstrong, Smith seeks to retain a distinction between ethnic group and nation and between ethnicity and nationality. His intention is to identify the ethnic roots of modern nations in order to explain why some etnies became nations and others not. The point of departure is the nationalist hypothesis that every ethnic group is a potential nation. This is disputed by functionalists such as Gellner, who see political nations as results of modern political and economic processes. Only when they are well on their way to political existence as nations, these etnies "invent" or "construct" a past for themselves. This process is currently occurring among the Kurds, and has been underway for well over twenty years among the Palestinians in the Arab village societies and clans on the West Bank and in Gaza, as a response to the presence of a Jewish state.

Smith places special emphasis on the complex of myths and symbols in the form of "mythomoteur," that is, the constitutive myth for the ethnic community. The concept of "mythomoteur" stems from John Armstrong, who again adapted it from a Spanish study of the Visigoths on the Iberian peninsula in the sixth century. Smith and Armstrong both emphasize the central role played by myths and symbols as the embodiment of ethnicity, such that it can be transferred from one generation to the next. According to Smith, the unique feature of an etnie is not its ecological location, class constellation, or political and military condition, but the complex of myths and symbols regardless of their historical veracity.

Anderson and the "imagined community"

Deep down, the majority of "ordinary" men and women now believe that national differences have become constant properties, even though they prefer not to talk about this too openly. One can say that they/we think in categories from "primitive ethnography." In contrast to this, most scholars view identity as a discursive phenomenon which has been constructed at specific times for specific purposes. National identity is what we say it is, not an observable essence. National myths are real only in the sense that people believe in them and act upon them. For this notion of reality, it is totally unimportant whether the myths' content is historically true.

This important distinction between reality as effects and reality as absolute truth or essence has not been sufficiently emphasized by Anthony Smith in his otherwise highly praiseworthy discussion of the various ways of investigating national identities. Rather, this has been the project of the political scientist and Indonesia specialist, Benedict Anderson, in his brilliant book entitled *Imagined Communities* (1983, slightly revised 1991). Anderson seeks to mediate between the functionlist and primordialist positions in a manner different from Smith, because he places the main emphasis on communication. He explains the emergence of these so-called "imagined communities" as a result of the new printing technology, "print capitalism," as he has termed the phenomenon. In conjunction with the retreat of religions and the victory of the printed word, it became possible to imagine communities which are at the same time sovereign and limited, communities through which the individuals' immortality can be ensured, and through which otherwise anonymous individuals could identify themselves. Via the printed word, persons who otherwise do not know each other feel that they live in the same homogeneous and empty time and space dimensions and imagine that they have something in common with people they never will meet, people who are already dead or not yet even born. These "imagined societies," that is, nations, filled important psychological as well as economic functions under the special circumstances of moden secular capitalism.

The other new element in Anderson's theory is his refinement of the exact significance of the metaphor "construction" or "invention." According to Anderson, the underside of such formulations, what Gellner has demonstrated so efficiently, is that nationalisms tend to embellish themselves with borrowed or, more correctly, freely invented feathers. For Gellner "invention" means "fabrication" and falsification, whereas Anderson interprets it more positively as "imagination" or "creation." Anderson's definition of national identity is therefore less functionalist than Gellner's. Moreover, the social psychological factors are included and expanded through specific social and technological conditions instead of argued on the basis of vague assumptions about individuals' psychological needs.

National identity as mutual recognition

But it is possible to go further than Anderson. In a highly original analysis of Danish national characteristics, the anthropologist Michael Harbsmeier has further developed Anderson's explanation by emphasizing that national identity, in contrast to all other possible forms of social identities, is totally dependent on being acknowledged as national otherness by other nations (Harbsmeier 1986: 52). This national discourse entails that nations do not view themselves as universal phenomena, as do some religions, and do not derive their legitimacy from sources beyond this world, as do many empires. Nevertheless, there is a universal element in modern national discourse which distinguishes it clearly from the imaginations of collective identity we find in Greco-Roman Antiquity and early Christianity. When the Greeks called other peoples "Barbarians," when the Christians classified non-Christians as "Heathens," and when "civilized" Chinese or Europeans of the eighteenth century called other peoples "uncivilized," they did so in an effort to get them to acknowledge their subordinate status. Basically, it was an asymmetrical relation. Modern national identities, according to Harbsmeier, are quite different:

> When one calls oneself a Dane, German, Englishman or Frenchman, one does not make the others into barbarians, heathens, savages or infidels, but assumes that the others can correspondingly put a name on their own nationality . . . Nations . . . seduce each other into recognizing each other in the other's images. Not so as to then become something other than oneself, but in order to become that which one has in reality always been. Nations force the others to tell the truth about themselves. In religions and empires, truth is bound to a place, a language, a writing system, a book, or to specific groups of people. In nations the truth has been spread to all the winds: in principle we all possess the truth about both ourselves and about the others. (Harbsmeier 1986: 53)

Nationalities thus implicitly acknowledge the other nationalities as belonging to a comparable category. As is most often the case, we assume that our own identity is best, but normally we will not contest others' rights to belong to another national group, even though one would only exceptionally share one's own privileges with these others. This univeralism, however, does not change the fact that the whole point of modern nationalism is the discrimination of entire groups of people. The positive definition of a national identity ultimately rests on exclusion and negative characteristics. "Danish" is defined as "non-German," French as "non-German and non-British," and so on.

But even though one's own national identity is thus often assumed to be superior, it logically follows from the implicit or explicit comparison with other nationalities, that they belong to the same category. Modern national identities thus distinguish themselves from the distinctions of classical cultures between civilized and uncivilized. Normally national stereotypes are used as if they denote actually existing relations in the "real world." Even the methodologically most sophisticated researcher, who in a professional context would never dream of using such imprecise concepts as "national identity" or "national character" can be heard to make observations from the excesses of primitive ethnography when talk settles on his own experiences from learned conferences or vacations. Everyone knows about "French" rhetoric, "American" aggressiveness, or "Scandinavian" reserve, regardless of how many times such categories have been denied. The national stereotypes belong to a world which is not disrupted by empirical observations. So why not try to take these stereotypes as a point of departure for one's perspectives and see where they lead us instead of wasting time trying to deny their content in the best historical source-critical tradition? This can be called a discourse approach. It is here that the debate about national identity stands today.

National boundaries and symbolic boundaries

National boundaries are about attitudes and exist primarily in human consciousness. Symbolical boundary-making mechanisms are often words. They are traffic lights which mark out that one is now approaching a barrier which separates one group form another. National symbolic communication is communication over time, and very long time at that. Hence, a symbol's duration is more important that its precise origin. Seen over the long term, the legitimating power of individual mythical structures is promoted by fusion with other myths in a "myth machine" (mythomoteur) whereby their content is defined in relation to a specific social and political unit (Armstrong 1982: 8–9, 129–67, 293).

To characterize these complex structures as "mythic" does not imply that they are false, just as the study of the origin of religious myths does not negate their theological value. One of the most important effects of myths is the evocation of an intense feeling of belonging and common destiny among a group of people. From the perspective of myth and symbol theory, the common destiny is simply the degree of affect which emphasis on the community imbues into the individual member. It follows that it is the symbolic rather than the material aspects of the shared destiny which are decisive for the maintenance of collective identity. In short, the national discourse is at the same time a vehicle for and the very content of national or ethnic identity. As in so many other situations, the medium is the message, as Marshall McLuhan formulated it in 1962. The ancient Greeks denied this, as do nationalists and primitive ethnographers of our own day. But this does not make the modern social scientific insight into the relative and positional character of national and ethnic identity any less true. On the other hand, one must not conclude that any sort of identity could be formulated by anyone. In current times, it is associated with the identification of collective identities and national territories in the concept of nation-states. It still remains to be seen whether efforts to link identification with entities other than existing states will have any chance of success.

Bibliography

Acton, John, and Dalberg, E. E. 1967 [1862]: Nationality. [*Home and Foreign Review*, July.] In Lord Acton: *Essays in the Liberal Interpretation of History*. Chicago: Phoenix Books.

Almond, Gabriel, and Verba, Sidney. 1963: *The Civic Culture: Political Attitudes and Democracy in Five Nations*. Princeton, NJ: Princeton University Press.

Almond, Gabriel, and Pye, L. (eds) 1965: *Comparative Political Culture*. Princeton, NJ: Princeton University Press.

Anderson, Benedict. 1983: *Imagined Communities*. London: Verso.

Anderson, Perry. 1974: *Lineages of the Absolutist State*. London: NLB.

Armstrong, J. 1982: *Nations before Nationalism*. Chapel Hill, NC: University of North Carolina Press.

Bateson, Gregory. 1972 [1942]: Morale and National Character. In *Steps to an Ecology of Mind*. New York: Ballantine Books.

Bellah, Robert, et al. 1985: *Habits of the Heart. Individualism and Commitment in American Life*. Berkeley: University of California Press.

Bendix, Reinhard. 1956: *Work and Authority in Industry: Ideologies of Management in the Course of Industrialization*. Berkeley: University of California Press.

—— 1964: *Nation-Building and Citizenship*. Berkeley: University of California Press.

—— 1980: *Kings or People. Power and the Mandate to Rule.* Berkeley: University of California Press.

Benedict, Ruth. 1934: *Patterns of Culture.* Boston: Houghton Mifflin.

—— 1967 [1946]: *The Chrysanthemum and the Sword: Patterns of Japanese Culture.* London: Routledge & Kegan Paul.

Boehm, Max Hildebert. 1933: Nationalism. Theoretical Aspects. In E. R. A. Seligman (ed.), *Encyclopedia of the Social Sciences*, vol. XI. New York: Macmillan & Free Press.

Carrèrre d'Encausse, Hélène. 1990: *La Gloire des nations ou la fin de l'Empire soviétique.* Paris: Fayard.

Connor, Walker. 1972: Nation-building or Nation-destroying? *World Politics*, 24.

—— 1973: The Polititics of Ethnonationalism. *Journal of International Affairs*, 27/1.

—— 1978: "A nation is a nation, is a state, is an ethnic group, is a . . .". *Ethnic and Racial Studies*, 1/4.

—— 1984: Eco- or Ethno-nationalism? *Ethnic and Racial Studies*, 7/3.

—— 1994: *Ethnonationalism. The Quest for Understanding.* Princeton NJ: Princeton University Press.

Deutsch, Karl W. 1953: *Nationalism and Social Communication. An Inquiry into the Foundations of Nationality.* Cambridge, MA and New York: Technology Press of MIT and J. Wiley.

Erikson, Erik H. 1945: Childhood and Tradition in Two American Indian Tribes. *Psychoanalytical Study of the Child*, 1.

—— 1950: *Childhood and Society.* New York: W.W. Norton.

—— 1958: *Young Man Luther. A Study in Psychoanalysis and History.* New York: W. W. Norton.

Gellner, Ernest. 1964: Nationalism. In Ernest Gellner, *Thought and Change.* London: Weidenfeld & Nicolson.

—— 1973: Scale and Nation. *Philosophy of the Social Sciences*, 3.

—— 1983: *Nations and Nationalism.* Oxford: Blackwell.

—— 1994: *Encounters with Nationalism.* Oxford: Blackwell.

Giddens, Anthony. 1985: *The Nation-State and Violence.* (Vol. 2 of *A Contemporary Critique of Historical Materialism*). Cambridge: Polity Press.

Gleason, Philip. 1983: Identifying Identity: A Semantic History. *Journal of American History*, 69/4.

Harbsmeier, Michael. 1986: Danmark: Nation, kultur og køn. *Stofskifte*, 13.

Hayes, C. J. 1926: *Essays on Nationalism.* New York: Macmillan.

—— 1968 [1931]: *The Historical Evolution of Modern Nationalism.* New York: Russell & Russell.

—— 1933: Nationalism. Historical Development. In E. R. A. Seligman (ed), *Encyclopedia of the Social Sciences*, vol. XI.

—— 1960: *Nationalism: A Religion.* New York: Macmillan.

Herder, J. G. von. 1967 [1774]: *Auch eine Philosophie der Geschichte.* Frankfurt am Main: Suhrkamp.

Hobsbawm, E. J. 1962: *The Age of Revolution 1789–1848.* London: Weidenfeld and Nicolson.

—— 1972: Some reflections on Nationalism. In T. J. Nossiter, A. H. Hanson, and S. Rokkan (eds), *Imagination and Precision in the Social Sciences: Essays in Memory of Peter Nettl.* London: Faber & Faber.

—— 1975: *The Age of Capital 1848–1875.* London: Weidenfeld & Nicolson.

—— 1987: *The Age of Empire 1875–1914.* London: Weidenfeld & Nicolson.

—— 1990: *Nations and Nationalism since 1780.* Cambridge: Cambridge University Press.

Hobsbawm, E., and Ranger, T. (eds) 1983: *The Invention of Tradition.* Cambridge: Cambridge University Press.

Howard, Jane. 1984: *Margaret Mead. A Life.* New York: Simon and Schuster.

Kemiläinen, Aira. 1984: The Idea of Nationalism. *Scandinavian Journal of History*, 9.

Knudsen, Anne. 1989: *Identiteter i Europa.* Copenhagen: Chr. Ejlers Forlag.

—— 1992: Folkevandring eller Middelalder. *Udenrigs*, 2, 15–26.

Knudsen, Anne, and Wilken, Lisanne 1994: *Kulturelle verdener: kultur og kulturkonflikter i Europa.*

Copenhagen: Columbus.

Kohn, Hans. 1944: *The Idea of Nationalism. A Study in its Origins and Background.* New York: Macmillan.

—— 1962: *The Age of Nationalism. The First Era of Global History.* New York: Harper & Harper.

—— 1964: *Living in a World Revolution. My Encounters wih History.* New York: Trident.

Lipset, S. M. 1950: *Agrarian Socialism.* Berkeley: University of California Press.

—— 1960: *Political Man.* London: Mercury Books.

—— 1963: *The First New Nation. The United States in Historical and Comparative Perspective.* London: Heinemann.

McLuhan, Marshall. 1962: *The Gutenberg Galaxy: The Making of Typographic Man.* London: Routledge.

Mann, Michael. 1986: *The Sources of Social Power.* Vol. I: *A History of Power from the Beginnings to A.D. 1760.* Cambridge: Cambridge University Press.

—— 1993: *The Sources of Social Power.* Vol. II: *The Rise of Classes and Nation-states 1760–1914.* Cambridge: Cambridge University Press.

Mead, Margaret. 1943 [1928]: *Coming of Age in Samoa: A Psychological Study of Primitive Youth for Western Civilization.* Harmondsworth, Middlesex: Penguin Books.

—— 1930: *Growing Up in New Guinea: A Comparative Study of Primitive Education.* London: Routledge.

—— 1942: *And Keep Your Powder Dry: An Anthropologist Looks at America.* New York: Morrow.

Mead, Margaret, and Métraux, Rhoda (eds) 1953: *The Study of Culture at a Distance.* Chicago: University of Chicago Press.

Mill, John Stuart. 1861: *Considerations on Representative Government.* London: Longmans, Green.

Moore, Barrington. 1967: *Social Origins of Dictatorship and Democracy.* Harmondsworth, Middlesex: Penguin Books.

Mosse, George L. 1975: *The Nationalization of the Masses. Political Symbolism and Mass Movements in Germany from the Napoleonic Wars Through the Third Reich.* New York: New American Library.

Østergård, Uffe 1988: Er republikanske dyder det egentligt "amerikanske" ved amerikanerne? In S. Zetterholm (ed.), *Alexis de Tocqueville.* Copenhagen: Nyt fra Samfundsvidenskaberne.

—— 1990: Begrundelser for nationalitet. To definitioner af nationen i det 19. århundredes tænkning. *Scandia,* 56/1.

—— 1991a: Feinbilder und Vorurteile in der dänischen Öffentlichkeit. In G. Trautmann (ed.), *Die hässlichen Deutschen.* Darmstadt: Wissenschaftlice Buchgesellschaft.

—— 1991b: Etnisk og national identitet. In H. Fink (ed.), *Identiteter i forandring,* Aarhus: Århus Universitetsforlag.

—— 1992: *Europas ansigter.* Copenhagen: Munksgaard.

—— 1995: The Return of Empires? In B. Hansen (ed.), *European Security - 2000,* Copenhagen: Politiske Studier.

Østerud, Øyvind 1978: *Utviklingsteori og historisk endring.* Oslo: Norsk Gyldendal.

—— 1987a: *Det moderne statssystem og andre politisk-historiske studier.* Oslo: Norsk Gyldendal.

—— 1987b: *Nationalism och modernitet. I Lycksalighetetens halvö. Sverige och Europa.* Stockholm.

—— 1994: *Hva er nasjonalisme?* Oslo: Universitetsforlaget.

Poggi, Gianfranco. 1978: *The Development of the Modern State. A Sociological Introduction.* Stanford, CA: Stanford University Press.

Rasmussen, Erik. 1968: *Komparativ Politik I–II.* Copenhagen: Gyldendal.

Renan, Ernest. 1947 [1882]: Qu'est-ce qu'une nation? In *Oeuvres Complètes I.* Paris: Calman-Lévy.

Rokkan, Stein. 1987: *Stat, nasjon, klasse.* Oslo: Universitetsforlaget.

Said, Edward. 1978: *Orientalism.* London: Routledge & Kegan Paul.

Sapir, Edward. 1933: Personality. In E. R. A. Seligman (ed.), *Encyclopedia of the Social Sciences,* vol. XII.

Skocpol, Theda. 1979: *States and Social Revolutions*. Cambridge: Cambridge University Press.

Skocpol, T., Evans, P., and Ruschmeyer, D. (eds) 1985: *Bringing the State Back In*. New York: Cambridge University Press.

Smith, Anthony. 1971: *Theories of Nationalism*. London: Duckworth.

—— 1986: *The Ethnic Origins of Nations*. Oxford: Blackwell.

—— 1991: *National Identity*. Harmondsworth, Middlesex: Penguin Books.

Tilly, Charles (ed.) 1975: *The Formation of National States in Western Europe*. Princeton, NJ: Princeton University Press.

—— 1990: *Coercion, Capital and European States, A.D. 990–1990*. Oxford: Blackwell.

Tocqueville, Alexis de. 1969 [1835–40]: *Democracy in America*. New York: Anchor Books.

Weber, Eugen. 1978: *Peasants into Frenchmen. The Modernization of Rural France 1870–1914*. London: Chatto & Windus.

chapter 29

Gender and Society

Karin Widerberg

Key Concepts

Gender – originally a grammatical concept that was taken over by feminist researchers in the beginning of the seventies, to emphasize an understanding of sex as socially constructed, that is "the social sex" (in contrast to biological sex). Gender is made and not something as which we are born (Simone de Beauvoir). The concept of gender is most often used to define or characterize systems or structures (gender systems and gender structures).

Gender as Variable – expresses an understanding of gender as one of several other possible qualities, all independent of each other (for example, age independent of gender and vice versa). In contrast, gender as perspective, emphasizes that qualities are gendered and that gender is the very result or sum of the qualities. Our understanding of age, for example, is gendered ("older women" are younger than "older men"), which in its turn influences our understanding of gender.

Patriarchy – a system of male dominance and female subordination. It is used to characterize systems of different kinds, for example, a society, an institution, or an organization. The purpose is to stress structural principles or processes that result in oppression of women and not primarily the role of the singular man in this process.

Sex-Role (old concept) or **Gender-Role** (new concept) – gender is understood in terms of the position to which expectations and norms are attached. Accordingly, it is a "role" one can step into (or out of) and play more or less well.

Women-Focused – here the emphasis is on "visiblizing" (making visible) women's situations, conditions, activities, and so forth on "their own premises," that is, without having a comparison with men as a starting point or norm.

Our understanding of gender – our theories of gender – have a history. Each period produces its own understanding of gender, based on cultural imagination and representation and intellectual debates, as well as the actual organization of gender which permeates the structure and functioning of societies. All understanding of society – theories of society – are therefore at the same time also theories of gender, and vice versa. Societies have gender, in a double sense: They are permeated by gender and are gendered as well as engendering.

This implies that, when trying to tell the story of the development of understanding of gender, it will always be a "situated" story: a story told from a certain site. Giving another impression – that there is one story valid for us all – would be wrong. And yet, today, through the internalization of knowledge and the dominance of the English language as its mediator, we are made to share understanding to a higher degree than we are made to share actual social arrangements. That is, we might live in quite differently organized countries and cultures but our intellectual tools are very much the same. So, when this story of the development of understanding of gender is to be told, it will be from the site of the Scandinavian context, a context which is also strongly influenced internationally (from the US and Europe in particular).

Without eliminating this site, and the differences that might be news to the reader and as such contribute to productive reflections, I have tried to focus on aspects considered vital in the Western world. Here we all share the political idea and ideal of equality and this has been the foundation for the development of our understanding of gender. In countries with formal inequality, the history of the understanding of gender will, of course, be very different from the one I am now about to tell.

We start in the seventies and try to illuminate the intellectual context which the new women's research both emanated from and revolted against. Here I will use women´s research as a more general term for the first periods decribed and then gender research for the present period. The two terms include feminist research, in which the political and liberating means and goals of research are more strongly underlined. In this phase, starting in the seventies – "the phase of theory critique" (the naming of the phases, as well as part of the content, are from Widerberg 1992) – the sociological classics were given such rough treatment that there is little left at the entrance of the next phase in the understanding of gender: the phase of making visible or "visiblizing." Visiblizing might be a new word in the English language, but it was also a new word in the Scandinavian languages when the feminists started to use it to stress that one is always actively either "visiblizing" or "unvisiblizing" gender. It is a word well worth exporting. In the theoretical and empirical effort to make women's lives visible, the women researchers accordingly had to start more or less from scratch. Today, in the middle of "the phase of reflectivity" – when we are trying to grasp the understanding of gender the women and gender researchers themselves have produced – the classics, as well as the so-called poststructuralists, are actively debated.

The purpose of this exposé of understanding of gender and society is to demonstrate the immense development of knowledge that has taken place in the Western world during a relatively short time span. It is a development in which the understanding of gender and society of today is not the end of the journey, but rather a ticket to the future where sociologists – men as well as women – can and ought to have a say regarding the direction.

The Phase of Theory Critique

The women's research and the women's movement that evolved in the seventies indicated their difference from those of previous generations, by naming themselves as "the new women's research" and "the new women's movement." They were both children of the revolution of 1968, which in itself was a revolt of intellectuals against predominant theories of society as well as its actual organization. The "new" left reclaimed the acquaintance with Karl Marx's theories on society, redeveloping these to account for the society of the seventies.

With one foot in

The production of knowledge, and its institutions (not least the universities), were also caught in the stream, resulting in the so-called "critique of positivism." With the concept of "interest" as a tool, ideas of value-neutrality and objective knowledge were slaughtered and with them the model of production of knowledge which till then had dominated the social sciences. In its place the concepts of power and interest were introduced and made relevant to all stages in the research process, resulting in discussions of alternative research practices too. The issue was not only *what* (which themes) to research, but also *how,* and by *whom.* These questions (what, how, and who) were also the central ones within women's research and were given different answers – resulting in different understanding of gender – in the phases described below.

And one foot out

After unsuccessful efforts in trying to engage the leftist movement in a discussion of the gender aspect – and not only of that of class – of concepts of power and interest, the women started to organize on their own. This was in the late sixties. The "new" women's movement soon spread to the universities, giving rise there to the new women's research.

Influences from the leftist movement were still strong and its understanding of society, production of knowledge as well as alternative forms of praxis, permeated the understanding of gender produced in the seventies by the women's researchers. But the influences were not unequivocal. Critique as well as alternatives was also formulated. A characteristic of the women's research has always been this very position: one foot is always kept out of dominant theoretical traditions. This balancing act reflects the fact that understanding of gender has never been at the center in theories of society – nor, for that matter, in theories of production of knowledge – making it impossible for women researchers to settle down theoretically. Instead, they have had to be open to all fruitful understanding of gender, regardless of theoretical or disciplinary boundaries. In the seventies, all the "other" understanding came from the US.

The white, West, and middle-class-dominated debate from the US also became decisive for the direction of women's research in other parts of the world. Within the Scandinavian countries, for example, women's research turned out to be quite similar, in spite of the great variety of actual organization of gender relations among the countries. There, the few apparent differences regarding direction of research reflected the type of Marxist school that dominated each country rather than the actual organization of gender relations.

Enlivened by the feminist movement and stored with the intellectual impulses mentioned above, a critique of the implicit understanding of gender of different theories and methods, was formulated. The first man out – within sociology – was Talcott Parsons (see chapter 14) and his concept of sex-roles.

The Concept of Sex-Roles

The concept of sex-roles captured all the understandings of gender that had dominated sociology and the social sciences the decade before. It emanated from Talcott Parsons but was put forward and used in a slightly different way by the "mothers" of the "new" women's research.

To understand gender in terms of positions, norms, and expectations was, at the time the concept of sex-roles was introduced, an immense sociological – and political! – progress. Here gender was no longer conceived of as something natural or supernatural. Gender was neither biology, a quality nor "spirit," but something socially produced. Roles, defined as expectations and norms linked to positions, were social products and, as such, changeable. We – women and men – were not to blame, but the sex-roles. And it was the "mothers"of the new women's research who pointed out what the problems with sex-roles were all about.

Harriet Holter – the "mother" of Scandinavian women's research – used the concept of sex-roles to disclose how they are used as a tool for the distribution of "benefits and burdens" within society, resulting in the discrimination of women (Holter 1970). Parsons's understanding of the male and female roles as equal and complementary was transcended. Through the aspect of power, a wedge was driven into the Parsonian foundation, which later – in the new women's research – was used as a crowbar.

Among the new women researchers, with their roots in the leftist movement, the role concept was considered quite problematic, to say the least. Roles as a concept connote freedom of choice: they are something you can choose to step in or out of. But one cannot choose not to be treated as "the gender," and then again, not to be "the other gender" (paraphrasing Simone de Beauvoir), that is, the subordinated and less valued gender. In this perspective, sex-roles are just an ideological expression of the power and oppression that "unvisiblizes" what gender is all about. To understand gender in terms of power, other concepts on other – structural – levels, were called for. And in this search Marx was used as a guide.

Marxist Understandings of Gender

Since Karl Marx himself had not written much about gender and gender relations, the idea was to interpret the implicit understanding of gender embedded in his understanding of society, as well as to further develop his theorizing on gender relations. Let us have a brief look at some of the issues, the targets for criticism or theoretical development.

Production and reproduction – a true Marxist couple

Production and reproduction are central concepts within Marxism and, as can be understood by the very words, one is primary and the other is secondary. The fact that each sphere is dominated by one gender – at least during capitalism – naturally raises questions as to the definitions of the concepts, as well as the relation between the spheres, in a gender perspective. To Marx, it was the relations of the capitalist mode of production that were to be focused. And in his time, these were relations between men, as a result of the *historically* gendered division of labor, between production and so-called reproduction. Women bearing and caring for children and doing domestic work were preconditions for the men to enter the scene of production as "the naked workers." This precondition, that is, the social and gendered organization of reproduction, was not problematized by Marx and accordingly interpreted as something more or less natural. The relation between the spheres, as well as the content of the so-called women's sphere, are thus made more or less invisible. To "visiblize" the sphere of reproduction in terms of work, as well as the relation between the two spheres, therefore became an important task for the women researchers.

The gender of the class concept

The Marxist class concept takes the relations of production as its starting point. This implies, first of all, that those outside production – for example, domestic workers – are not situated in a class position of their own. Women and children without a class position of their own are categorized in that of their husband or father. Second, men's domination within production has influenced the very class definitions. It is men's work, their conditions and relations which have been the points of departure of traditional class analysis. Within production, typical women's work – when increasing – has been defined as an addition "to the classes-affiliated groups." The gender division within production has accordingly not affected the way class is defined; relations between men are still the script. The gender relations of production are hereby made invisible. In other words, how the relations of production – the class relations – are being gendered, as well as engendering the participants, is not made visible. Armed by empirical investigations, women researchers have even questioned if it is not the case that the differences between the genders within the same class are actually bigger than those between men – or between women – belonging to different classes.

A debate is still going on about whether gender and class are to be understood in terms of one or two relations and how these relations are then to be defined, although not as intensively as during the eighties (the debate within British sociology was particularly extensive; see the journal *Sociology*).

Simultaneously with this critique of Marxism and the Marxist heritage – which is far from being finished, although less influential during the nineties, at least in our part of the world – much women's research was also enacted in its spirit, making use of the theory or developing it further. For example, the family as well as domestic work was investigated and analyzed in a Marxist perspective. The "domestic labor debate," taking place in the seventies, can be looked upon as the final great effort to try to interpret and expand Marxist concepts to include the "women's domains" (Coulson, Magas, and Wainwright 1975; Dalla Costa and James 1973; Seacombe 1974).

In the domestic labor debate the focus was on the relation between domestic labor and capitalism, and *not* on the relation between the genders. The question raised was whether domestic labor gave rise to surplus value or just use value. To the understanding of women's subordination or the politics needed for their liberation, these analyses had little to contribute. So when the women researchers – in the phase of "visiblizing" – approached the theme of domestic work again, Marxist tools were not used. This is a conscious and stated choice. Marxist concepts appear to be of limited use when the aim is to see and understand women's situations on "women's terms."

Theorizing Patriarchy

A structural explanation of the oppression of women

The theory of patriarchy is a child of Marxism although born out of wedlock. It is a theoretical approach that underlines the totality and the structural aspects, just like Marxism. And here too, the founding cause is searched for but the foundation and the forces are now stated to be gender relations and not relations of production. The "debate on how to theorize patriarchy," taking place more or less intensively from the mid-seventies until the mid-eighties, concerned how patriarchy – as a concept of a system or structure of male dominance and female subordination – was to be analytically defined. Different theoretical definitions implied different understandings of the oppression of women and its causes.

The debate was the epicenter in the understanding of gender at that time. All feminist perspectives were represented here. They can be roughly sorted into three distinctly different approaches; first of all the "dual system-approach," enclosing all those in favor of using two different theories – one to explain the development of society and another to explain the oppression of women. Heidi Hartmann, as one of its best-known spokeswomen, stated that men's control of women's sexuality and work was the cause of women's oppression (Hartmann 1981). Second, there were the "radical feminists" (with, among others, Al Hibri [1981] as one of its representatives) who said that the organization of gender – and the gender division of labor that comes with it – was the first and most basic organizing principle of every society. And the root of it all was to be found in reproduction. Men "had to" control women, for only through them could a man establish a relationship to a child: the guarantee of old age and immortality. Finally, the third approach, the "materialist feminist"(among others, represented by Young [1981]), propagated a joint theory on the development of society and the oppression of women. Here the division of labor was taken as the starting point, while claiming that the division between men and women was the very first one.

Theorizing patriarchy – a blind alley?

Contributions within each approach were of course both many and varied, and the debates were just as intense here as those between different approaches, that is, over "the frontiers." When the debate – rather suddenly – died out, it was probably due to lack of progress. Most of the theorizing was abstract, ahistorical, and universal (Carlsson et al. 1983). The step from the dawn of history to the men's society of today was just too much. But of course the attraction of the big question – *why* oppression of women – as well as the search for one single cause and answer, still remains with many women.

Entering the phase of "visiblizing," the pressure to concentrate efforts on describing and analyzing the men's society of today was also more explicit. Consequently, the concept of patriarchy disappears from the theoretical vocabulary. Instead many variations within, as well as between, gender, cultures, and historical periods, are highlighted. This is an approach that gave rise to a far more complex understanding of gender and which, in its turn during the next phase within women's research (the phase of reflexivity) is the foundation of the development of new approaches even further away from those of the patriarchy debate. Little response is therefore given to those single voices that still try to brush up the concept of patriarchy (Walby 1989). Dual-system theory and universalistic claims of knowledge seem definitely passé. But even if our intellectual understanding of gender has made immense progress, the question of *why* still lurks in the shadows.

Who, what, and how?

During this period it was the women who had been working with understandings of gender, with the exception of a few men, scattered all over the world. But it had also been an explicit precondition that women – for the first time in history – should not be only objects but also subjects in the research process. Women were to be understood from a women's or feminist perspective, from the situation and interests women were assumed to share. Gender as such was actually not much talked about; it was rather the women – as gender and vice versa – that were in focus. And yet, there was no intention of producing a complementary perspective. The explicit aim was quite on the contrary, to develop a perspective that would revolutionize our understanding of society. And this was the reason for engagement in the theoretical debate about large and basic issues and questions.

How to do research and how to develop theoretical critique and alternatives, were, however, less articulated, that is, within academia. Outside its walls, where much of the women's research during this period was actually done – in contexts marked by the praxis forms of the women's movement (flat structure, etc.) – alternatives were explored. During the phase of "visiblizing," methodological approaches were developed and explored, even within academia. This, which might be labeled as "the second stage in the critique of positivism," is further developed and pronounced in the third phase – the phase of reflectivity – within women's research and accordingly in today's understanding of gender.

The Phase of "Visiblizing"

Empirical work to make women's lives and situations visible got started parallel to the theoretical investigations described above. At the end of the seventies and in the beginning of the eighties, the empirical research had increased to such proportions that we can talk of a new phase within women's research, the phase of "visiblizing." This does not imply that theoretical critique stopped, only that the focus shifted from the critique to the construction of concepts and theories. This was also the explicit aim of the empirical studies undertaken, particularly the qualitative ones, dominating the women's research during the period. Empirical research on women's lives and situations would be the foundation for conceptualizing, giving rise to new understanding of gender as well as society. And so it was.

What was made visible, however, varied from one country and cultural context to the other, and consequently so did the understanding of gender. In countries dominated by the ideology of paid labor, for example, England and the Scandinavian countries, gender was primarily investigated and understood in terms of labor.

Gender = labor

While the well-known sociologist Erik Allardt (1975) proclaimed "to have, to love and to be," to be the central dimensions within modern welfare states, women researchers stressed "doing" as the central dimension in women's lives even in these societies (Leira 1992). Women's research is actually about work and the division of work, to such an extent that work is made the dominant metaphor. All human activity – and of course gender – is understood in terms of division of labor and the social regulations linked to it. Consequently, the labor concept is expanded to include, not only paid labor, but also unpaid labor.

The concept of "unpaid labor" and "care work/caring work" made all the work done by women visible, work for which they were not economically justified. The labor concept was also used to make connections between the two (gender) spheres more visible, between the productive and the reproductive, the paid and the unpaid, and the private and the public. It was demonstrated how women, through their unpaid labor, made it possible for men to work full time and over time, a precondition for economic rights (pensions, unemployment subsidies, and so forth) and political power. The organization of the care/caring work is accordingly a precondition for the organization of paid labor, and vice versa. And this organization is both gendered and engendering.

The gender of the paid labor

Studies giving rise to a redefinition of the concept of labor took everyday life as its starting point. And everyday life, besides qualitative methods, is what most people connect with women's research of this period. It is, however, important to stress that the effort to visiblize work also included the "gender of paid labor." Several extensive empirical studies have highlighted the division of paid labor in a gender perspective. Detailed qualitative as well as quantitative analyses have been made of how jobs and work tasks – for example, work conditions and salaries – are constructed from ideas of gender, and how these in turn catch on to the subjects and the surroundings. Studies like these have served as a foundation for theoretical organization analyses from a feminist perspective, in which understanding of "the hidden hierarchy" (Ressner 1985) and "hierarchy as gender" (Kvande and Rasmussen 1990) are some of the results.

Even the forms of rationality of paid labor were made a topic in a gender perspective. The concept of "responsibility rationality" and "caring rationality" (Sørensen 1982), a further development of Max Weber's (see chapter 6) concepts on instrumental and value rationality, covered the forms of rationality connected to women's caring work and responsibility. Indirectly, this made the gender of the technical and economical form of rationality of the paid labor visible. Rationality forms could no longer be talked of in gender-neutral terms.

The gender of sexuality

I have tried to argue and illustrate how the development of concepts connected to the making of women's work visible resulted in a constructive critique of "general" concepts (for example, the concepts of labor and rationality) and perspectives (for example, those of organization theory) within sociology. And that making women's situation visible is to make gender and gender relations visible and, accordingly, the gender of the society. In this "work of making visible," labor has been used as the main tool, area, and approach. Sexuality, though, has been another important aspect. Our understanding of gender is also colored by extensive empirical research in this field. And just as in the field of labor, it has resulted in an impressive development of concepts.

It was not the difference between the sexuality of men and women – in spite of the gender differences highlighted by the Kinsey and Hite reports – that were focused, but the very relation – the sexual one – between men and women. The perspective of power, dominance, and subordination permeating women's research approaches in general – and thus their understandings of gender - is also used here when making sexual assault visible and understandable. It is a story of men as offenders and women as victims.

Sexualized violence – the back street of the gender relation

Sexualized violence was made a general concept for gender relations such as rape, incest, prostitution, pornography, woman battering, and sexual harassment. And each of these gender relations or "areas" was made the object of several studies, both quantitative and qualitative ones. The result was new meanings for old concepts. Prostitution was previously defined as "women selling sexual services." The new prostitution research, however, made the buyer – that is, the other part in this gender relation – visible, and that the services for sale were related to his, and not to her, sexuality (Høigård and Finstad 1986).

Woman battering was previously defined as "domestic violence." Uncovering a gender relation where men use violence to control and dominate women gave rise to this redefinition. The understanding of incest follows the same pattern. Incest was previously defined as sexual relations within a family – particularly between siblings – or among relatives. The fact that it was grown-up men who took advantage of the other partners dependent and subordinate position, and accordingly committed sexual "abuse," has shaken the very foundations of our understanding of gender, family, and society. The uncovering of sexual power relations within work life – "sexual harassment" – has perhaps not been that upsetting. Still, the analysis of the role of sexuality in the engendering process of jobs and work tasks, does present a totally new understanding of the gendered division of labor. For example, it has been demonstrated how ideas and expectations of "availability" are inscribed as formal or informal job qualifications and requirements, and how these in its turn are connected to subordinate positions, making women both economically and sexually vulnerable (MacKinnon 1979; Hearn & Parkin 1987; Brantsœter and Widerberg 1992).

Who, and what, actually is a man?

The examples given above, of research themes and the development of concepts, all started out as a wish to make the situation of the "other" part – that of the woman – visible. The use of dominance and subordination perspectives, however, made it quite clear that the position of the woman was dependent or even defined by the position of the man. Men and their situation were thus included, first only theoretically and in the abstract, but later also empirically. Men were also to be made visible, as men and as gender.

Men's research – quite often conducted by women – has focused on men who buy sex, violent men, men who rape, and men who abuse children. But men, not only as offenders, but also as victims of sexual assault, have also been highlighted. As a whole though, the so far tiny quantity of men's research – including research on men's role in unpaid domestic work – has been dominated by a perspective of "miserable" (in contrast to a perspective of "dignity," both labels deriving from the women's research). The challenge for the future – stated by leading researchers in the field, such as Michael Kimmel (US), David Morgan, Jeff Hearn, and Victor Seidler (England) – will be a combination of the knowledge already produced by women researchers with that of developing new knowledge and perspectives based on other aspects of men and masculinity that have so far been uncovered.

Understanding of gender as gender relations in the areas of labor/work and sexuality, and the connections between these areas, have also implied an understanding of the heterosexual determination and definition of sexuality. Sexuality is usually understood as heterosexuality, signalling that sexuality between persons of different sexes is both norm and praxis, to the extent that no further underlining or clarification is needed. This is clearly not the case with sexuality between persons of the same sex; the very concept of homosexuality is clear evidence. Heterosexuality as a concept, therefore, is often perceived as an offence, as a way to make "the natural sexuality" suspicious. The concept, however, makes it quite clear that it is a gender relation, implying a possibility of different sexualities or of a sexuality that is made into different ones in this gender relation. Sexuality as a concept works in quite a contrary way; besides veiling these issues, ideas of one (normal hetero)sexuality with a deviant one (homosexuality) are promoted. When the concept of "homosocial" is used for relations in working life, this is accordingly a way to "denaturalize" relations between men, through the use of sexual connotations.

The Phase of Reflectivity

Through "visiblizing" women's lives and situations and developing appropriate concepts, a foundation was laid for a new phase of theoretical critique. Dealing with the sociological classics, heavier dynamite could now be used. Moreover, the development within women's research had now been so comprehensive that this very research actually itself demanded an analysis. What understandings of gender had the women's research actually produced or given rise to? This phase – what I have chosen to label the phase of reflectivity – coincided with the so-called poststructuralism challenge. It should be stressed that even though poststructuralist influences have been vital, the women researchers have continued to keep one foot outside this paradigm, just as in previous paradigmatic debates.

Debating the approach

What understandings of gender can studies of women give rise to? The stated purpose with *women-centred* studies – dominating the women's research of previous decades – was primarily to make women's conditions and situation visible on their "own terms," that is, without comparisons to men or using the man as a starting point or norm. This was seen as a precondition to learn something new, and most of the knowledge we have today of women is a result of this very starting point. "Just" studying women when trying to understand gender was, however, now made an object of critical discussion.

A women-centred starting point does not in itself tell us what is *specific to women*, only that it is true for women. It does, however, give rise to ideas about "the typical female," no matter if this was the researchers' intention or not. Today we know a lot about women, with approaches and issues and areas that were never used or highlighted when studying men. We have, in other words, no corresponding knowledge of men. Conclusions as to what is specific to women or a typical female might accordingly prove wrong, and the knowledge of women, so far, a defective foundation for understanding gender.

"Just" studying women does not have to imply that gender is understood as something in itself, something static and a separate entity. Quite the opposite. A *relational perspective* might very well also be used within a women-centred approach. In a relational perspective gender is conceived of as a result of the interplay between the genders. In other words, gender is not a constant – something solid waiting to be discovered – but something produced in the interplay of gender.

When involved in a women-centred approach and making use of a relational perspective, women's situations are interpreted as expressions or results of gender relations. These relations, however, can be highlighted from the situation of women or from that of men. To do research "on men," is accordingly a logical response to the women research and a precondition for the understanding of gender.

A relational perspective might further imply that gender is neither used as a starting point – which the relation is to explain – nor focused upon as a result. Instead, the focus here is on *the very relation*. It is the relation or the relations that engender. Dorothy Smith, whose work will later be described more extensively, makes use of this approach when investigating how social relations engender the particular, local, and historical settings of women's and men's experiences. The focus then is on social relations and their engendering, not gender itself.

Are the genders "basically" (one and) the same?

Behind a women-centred approach, an *unproblematized relation to difference* has a tendency to lurk. Gender research within the social sciences has most often taken social differences between the genders as a starting point, while biology and biological differences have been given little attention. Gender and equality are thus indirectly expressed as "only" a matter of social organization.

In this aspect women's research follows a tradition within the social sciences. Here the human being has been considered a social and cultural entity, and as such changeable – of which history in itself is a proof – while her biology has been looked upon as a more or less stable item, although differently understood, that is, socially constructed and as such naturally of interest to social investigations.

The disinclination within women's research to take biology into account should also be understood as the background of the fact that women for centuries had been – and still are! – defined and oppressed with reference to biology. No wonder the women researchers tried to direct attention to the social aspects of gender! Yet, during the eighties, women's reproductive capacities are also focused within women's research. There are several reasons for this. The development within reproductive technology, the renewal of psychoanalysis, but not least the growing strength and amount of women's research, gave the women researchers the courage to confront biology and develop analysis on their own premises.

How to problematize biological difference?

Taking biological differences between genders as a starting point, women researchers within social sciences have focused on women's reproductive capacities. Womb and breast have been redefined as "productive forces" (making use of Marxist terminology) implying a redefinition also of the human nature as such. In her bodily ability to give birth and to breast-feed, women have an extra productive resource, besides the ones she shares with men. This biological difference accordingly implies a social difference. But it is stressed that this social difference does not have to implies social inequality. How we organize, make use of, and value productive forces is always a matter of social organization.

Besides being considered a productive force or advantage, women's reproductive capacities have also been understood in terms of implying a "psychological difference." Psychoanalytical perspectives were used here to explain how the fact that the mother–child relation was a gender relation (in which the boy is to be different and the girl is to be alike) resulted in gendered psychic structures. As the first object and subject of a child, the omnipotence of the mother stays with us all as a fear of and longing for the female, expressed individually and culturally.

Problematizing biological difference has, however, not only implied that it has been taken as a starting point for further analysis and investigation. Just as often – and just as important – there have been efforts to deconstruct the biological differences between the genders. Science has been proved to gender biology by over- or underestimating biological gender differences throughout history (Laqueur 1990; Haraway 1991). Scientific understanding of biology has accordingly been demonstrated as socially determined, and as such varying with gender ideas and ideologies.

This insight, that understanding of gender is produced both when we focus on differences and when differences are overlooked, is of course of general importance, and not restricted to problematizing biological differences in a gender perspective. Taking a starting point in differences (biological, social, or psychological) brings along just as many dilemmas as taking a starting point in no differences. The choice should, however, be a conscious one, where the one that will result in new understandings should be preferred. At a time, or on an issue, where differences have not been focused upon, this could prove to be the most fruitful strategy, while the opposite strategy should be preferred at another time or for another issue.

Differences between women – the end of gender as an analytical category?

Yet, when critically discussing the women-centred approach, as I've done above, it is important to keep in mind that this point of departure also implied a focus on differences between women. It was not the differences between the genders but within the genders – that is, among women – that were highlighted. During the phase of visiblizing, a foundation was laid for the further "deconstruction" of women, as an analytical category, taking place in the phase of reflectivity.

The fisherwoman, "the care-working farmer" (that is, women combining farming with care work), the working woman in industry, the nurse, the teacher, the lawyer, etc., they all have such different women's lives – especially when colour, ethnic, and religious differences are included – that one might question what they actually share as women. In the international debate of today, variations and differences are stressed to the extent that the fruitfulness of gender as a starting point is questioned. Some would claim that the only thing women have in common – besides the biological sex, which is also highly culturally defined and interpreted – is that their situation is second or different to that of men within each class, race, cultural or historical context, etc. Women-centred approaches have, in other words, resulted not only in an understanding of women as "special" or different from men but also as different from each other. Women are "plenty."

Gender, both variable and perspective?

The traditional understanding of *gender as variable* within sociology was early criticized and abandoned by the women researchers. Controlling for gender, that is, eliminating all differences between the genders (for example, regarding education, working hours, salaries, etc.) to find out what is left when you compare women and men that are socially alike, so as to state the importance of gender as a variable in its own right, was long the prevailing sociological tradition. As women researchers have underlined, this implies eliminating all the engendering conditions and processes, that is, the social context in which gender is being made. Gender, as they have stated, is the very sum of all these other variables, variables which in themselves are also gendered (women and men might, for example, have different types of education). The understanding of gender as a variable like any other easily give rise to the view that no gender differences equals no gender, genderless, or gender neutral. Contrary to this, *gender as a perspective* is an approach in which the world is viewed as fundamentally gender-structured, giving rise to a problematization of seemingly gender-neutral themes, areas, and actions. Gender and gender relations can accordingly be investigated also in areas or contexts where only one sex is present, for example, the army.

Sex or gender?

The discussion of gender as an analytical concept reflects several of the different approaches described above. In the English language there are now two words for gender: sex and gender. Gender, previously a concept referring primarily to grammatical and literary contexts, was conquered by the women researchers in the seventies to define the sex as social. Gender as a concept signalled that "one was not born a woman" (Simone de Beauvoir).

This conceptualization, of gender versus sex, implies introducing a separation between the biological and the social (sex). As social, gender is the "unnatural," the "un-natured" sex, while sex is the "natural," the "natured" gender. Thus sex is just as socially constructed as gender – what is nature or not nature is decided beforehand – a fact this very dichotomy makes invisible. As a dichotomy, they give each other meaning. Gender is understood as not sex, and sex as not gender.

Today when the body and sexuality, as social constructions, are at the core of women's research, the dichotomy of gender and sex becomes more and more problematic. The stories we need to write, criticize, and deconstruct are the stories of the connections between biological and social sex and sexuality. The defining away of one from the other – the implication of the dichotomy – is accordingly what should be focused and problematized.

In countries where English is not the native language, and where there might be one (for example, within the Scandinavian languages), several, or no (for example, in the French language) words for gender, different strategies have been chosen, reflecting the influence of the US as well as reaction to it by holding on to one's own cultural understandings of gender. In Scandinavia, for example, the effort to introduce the equivalent of gender, "genus," has not been very successful. Here the single Scandinavian word for gender and sex, *kön*, is still used and thought to be fruitful exactly because no distinctions between the biological and the social are made. As such it will always be open to contextual interpretation. And in France, the concept of difference is used instead of gender, signalizing a further nondistinction to other generated differences, such as class, race, and so forth. It is the differentiating processes and structures that are focused on here, resulting in gender-race-class. Translating research work from countries such as these into English, might accordingly prove highly problematic. Which word to chose – gender or sex – when one does not believe in this distinction and cannot subscribe to its implicit understandings of gender? The understanding of gender within other cultures can accordingly not be properly translated, it is made into something else, to the understanding of gender implicit in the English language. This is something some of us feel deeply, but it is hard to transmit. Yet it is of major importance for all of us to be aware of working in an international context where gender is so variably organized and understood, and expressed through the language of gender and the gender of language.

Individual, structural, and symbolic gender – a fruitful partition?

Sandra Harding's partitioning of gender as an analytical concept into three levels, individual, structural, and symbolic gender (Harding 1986), has made an impact within women's research at large. At the individual level, gender is made in the processes through which identity is formed, based on gender symbols and the gender division of labor. Structural gender is made when we organize and structure our social activities while making use of dualistic gender metaphors. Finally, symbolic gender is the result when dualistic gender metaphors are used as images of contradictions which have only a limited relation to real women and men. Examples of this are the connections of masculinity to intellect, mind and spirit, and activity, while femininity is connected to emotionality, body, subordination, and passivity. The level chosen to investigate "the construction of gender" is most often decided by one's disciplinary settings. But maybe an understanding of gender lies in the very relations between the levels, in what cuts through, keeps it together, and is the glue and pulse in social life?

Understandings of gender as products of academic traditions

It should be stressed that the approaches discussed here are the dominating ones within gender research in countries with – nowadays! – similar academic disciplinary boundaries and traditions (for example, Scandinavia, England, Germany, and the US). Countries with other academic traditions, particularly those with an interdisciplinary organization and approach, give rise to other ways of understanding gender. In France, for example, where the lines between the humanities and the social sciences are not so sharply drawn, gender is approached rather differently. There the connection of psychoanalytic theory to linguistics and philosophy has given rise to theories of the feminine as the founding point and frame of reference – the origin – in the production of meaning. Biological difference and heterosexuality are investigated here as social foundations, not only of the understanding of gender but of the social structure as such.

Understandings of Gender and the Gender of Modernity

Are the efforts to introduce gender as an analytical category an expression of how closely tied we are to academic traditions? Is this preoccupation with the understanding of gender a typical modern enterprise, that is, a characteristic of modernity? And to what extent is modernity then a gender(-ed) enterprise? The development within understanding of gender has made the women researchers re-address theories of society and production of knowledge. The theorists of modernity, as well as postmodernity, are now subjected to a scrutinizing rereading. In contrast to the previous "phase of theory critique," described above, the aim is now not only to uncover explicit or implicit understandings of gender but to analyze the theories as such, as expressions of gender. The focus has been removed from just understanding gender to understanding society from a gender perspective.

When reading Ferdinand Tönnies, for example, questions are raised as to the gender relations that are hidden behind the concepts of *Gemeinschaft* and *Gesellschaft* (see chapter 4). And today, are women the ones keeping up some form of *Gemeinschaft* and is this a precondition for *Gesellschaft*? Emile Durkheim´s theory (see chapter 5) on the division of labor and his concepts of *mechanical* and *organic solidarity* give rise to similar questions. Are the forms of solidarity presumably corresponding to the development of division of labor, only valid in men's work? What forms of solidarity are then related to women's work? And the gender division of labor, how is that to be understood within this perspective? Is mechanic solidarity a precondition to organic solidarity and to what extent is this a gendered division? Max Weber's understanding of bureaucracy (see chapter 6) and its related forms of *rationality*, have been subject to similar new perspectives through the means of gender.

Reading between the lines, these theories of the classics can be interpreted as an expression of a worry, a worry that the changing gender relations taking place would cause the dissolution of the family, maybe even the dissolution of society. The only sociological classic which has stated this quite openly, though, is Georg Simmel (see chapter 7 and Widerberg 1994). For the others, the workings of gender, in society as well as in their own way of thinking, is not an explicit topic.

The gender of postmodernity

What about the theoreticians influenced by poststructuralism? There are not too many sociologists in this "men's club," mainly due to the role given to text and meaning, here replacing the more traditional sociological focus of actual social arrangements. In a gender perspective this change of focus, in many ways challenging and fruitful, also proved problematic, causing a lively debate among women researchers. Making everything into an issue of text and discourse make the real power relations between the genders invisible. When Foucault (see chapter 19) writes about sexuality as discourse, the actual heterosexual relations are not made visible, neither is the discourse understood as a result of specific gender relations. And talk of "the Woman as that which is not" or as "the gender that can not be made represented within the symbolic order," might describe or explain some of the oppression of women and why she is positioned to be the other sex. As tools to grasp the ongoing changes of gender relations, they are, however, less suitable. Besides, there is a smell of essentialism and gender mysticism lingering in this kind of theorizing. Some women researchers have even questioned if it is a mere coincidence that postmodernism made such an intellectual hit when feminist theory – proving that women both exist and have things to say about gender and society – has finally gained some strength!

An Alternative Understanding of Gender and Society

The intention of the examples given above has been to illustrate how the periodization, structure, or functioning of a society can be understood as depending upon, as well as expressing and reproducing, certain gender relations. Sociological theories on society have a gender: they are a result of gender relations, they are gendered, and they engender our understanding of society and its understanding of gender. This is also what Dorothy Smith's critique of sociological traditions is all about. And with this as a background, she has formulated an alternative.

It was the split in her own life, between that of a woman – dominated by body and unmediated and actual activities – and that of a sociologist – dominated by texts and mediated and abstract labor, that made her problematize the sociological traditions. *Which* reality was made into sociology and *how* was this done?

Her first book (Smith 1987) is an attempt to answer the first part of the question – "which" reality is made into sociology – while in her later works (Smith 1990a, b) it is rather "how" the social is made into a (sociological) text on society that is focused. The change of emphasis – which can be seen as a result of a further development of one and the same approach she has used all along – has had the implication that her work is perceived now, even by male sociologists, as general sociological theory. Her focus on sociology as texts on and of society, also opens a dialogue with poststructuralists from a sociological perspective. Here I shall briefly present some of the main elements of her approach, focusing on both her earlier and later works.

Everyday life as a starting point

In "The Everyday World as Problematic – Towards a Sociology for Women" (Smith 1987), she presents and develops the claim that sociology as a discipline is developed from the position of men of a particular class. Class and men are understood as "material positions," where alienation in relation to body and actual labor are fundamental aspects. It is only from this position that society can be looked on and conceptualized the way sociologists have done. And it is only from "here" (up there) that everyday life appears to consist only of trivialities, which are being endlessly repeated in a chaotic manner. Thus understood, it is naturally "defined out" as an area for sociological investigations. Dorothy Smith claims that the sociological conceptual apparatus as a whole is developed out of this position, the position of men as rulers. Sociology is their map, made by and for men, as men and rulers.

Dorothy Smith has also criticized the women research within sociology for taking a similar position. Even though the women researchers have insisted upon studying the areas defined out by traditional sociology, their approach has still been influenced by a ruler perspective. Take women's activities in the home, for example. These activities and their content have been made visible through the concept of "unpaid housework." That is, however, a concept and a perspective that is not particularly well suited to these kinds of activities in which work, leisure, love, and service are so intertwined. No wonder we cannot agree politically when no concepts appropriate to women's activities have been developed!

What women do, when we "mother," has accordingly not been conceptualized within sociology. Sociology cannot supply the tools necessary to make us understand how the things women do hang together, to ourselves – as individuals – and between women as a collective. Reality and the scientific language – as a producer of meaning – fragment us, in relation to ourselves and in relation to each other. In this situation, it should be our aim as researchers to try to construct the connection that "reality" and the scientific language have so systematically deconstructed, and, in that aspect, taking a position radically contrary to the poststructuralist one.

The aim: understanding the structure and functioning of society

Dorothy Smith wants us to take women's activities and experiences as the starting point, in other words, we have to start where women are situated. This, however, does not imply that we are to study or understand women as "phenomena." The purpose is not to try to find out what women or men – or the daily life, for that matter – *are* as such. On the contrary, Smith states that it is the structure and functioning of a society that should be made visible, *but* from the position of everyday life. She argues in favor of a sociology that is situated in daily life but looks up and around, not a sociology from above, looking (down) at daily life.

By taking a starting point in daily life and by conceptualizing its relations, different analytical levels, for example, the macro and micro levels, are connected. By making the relations visible, the activities of the agents are made understandable to themselves and given a new or different meaning. That is the very purpose of the approach of Dorothy Smith. "Male-stream" sociology has little to say – at least to women – while she demands and expects the opposite of "her" sociology.

The Relations of the Sociological Text

In *The Conceptual Practices of Power: A Feminist Sociology of Knowledge* (Smith 1990a), Dorothy Smith applies the same approach when investigating the sociological text as such. To be a sociologist, she argues, is to be part of a social relation in which knowledge is separated from knowing. Research is made into a general capacity – everything can be researched – by specialists – only researchers can do research. As a sociologist one is by definition part of the ruling relations, where actual work is being separated from abstract and intellectual work and where the latter is being specialized. Dorothy Smith claims that it is this division of labor that is the foundation for the development of the sociological conventions of how the social is to be written, of how it is to be made into sociological texts.

The sociological conventions are characterized by establishing a position within the text where the social as written is separated from the social as lived and experienced. This results in position-less accounts; all subjects are either given the same position or are absent. It is as if the society could be understood in its totality, above, from the view of God, or rather, from the view of a bird without the bird. This basic convention for "how to do sociology," is labeled by Dorothy Smith as *objectifying*. The sociological text is, however, not only to be understood as a result of social relations, that is, of ruling relations. By placing the reader in a particular relation to the reality described in the text, the text is also made an active part in the ruling process. Through the objectifying convention, the reader takes the place of the ruler, she is offered "the view of God" where local positions, perspectives, and experiences are not only subordinated but also made invisible.

Alternative relations to sociological production of knowledge

The alternative, formulated by Dorothy Smith and others, for example, Donna Haraway (Haraway 1991), is *situated knowledge* (one always talks from a position) and *local claims of knowledge* (the talk is of something limited, something one can be held responsible for). The idea of a "privileged" position, from which a "superior" overview of the society can be given, is accordingly brushed aside. Instead, a systematic understanding of society from within, from the multitude of positions where we confront the social relations we are actively involved in, is sought. In the critique of a privileged position, this approach might seem to coincide with that of the poststructuralist approach. Dorothy Smith has, however, been explicitly critical toward poststructuralist proponents for their so-called "neglectance" of the social relations – both actual and abstract – of the text. The text is not to be understood only as "meaning" and its social relations as existing only within the text. The text is also a result of social relations as well as taking part in, and causing social relations. By problematizing sociology as text and the sociological text – from a feminist and materialist perspective – Dorothy Smith has provided a sociological answer to the poststructuralist challenge, a foundation for the further development of our understanding of gender and society.

Bibliography

Al-Hibri, Azizah. 1981: Capitalism is an Advanced Stage of Patriarchy: But Marxism is not Feminism. In L. Sargent (ed.): *Women and Revolution. The Unhappy Marriage of Marxism and Feminism*. London: Pluto Press.

Allardt, Erik. 1975: *Att ha, att älska, att vara*. Lund: Argos Förlag.

Åquist, Ann-Cathrine. 1989: Om patriarkatteori – en o-modern betraktelse. *Nordisk Samhällsgeografisk tidskrift*, 10.

Borg, Arne, et al. 1981: *Prostitution*. Stockholm: Liber.

Brantsœter, Marianne, and Widerberg, Karin (eds) 1992: *Sex i arbeid(et)*. Oslo: Tiden.

Carlsson, Christina, et al. 1983: Om patriarkatet: en kritisk granskning. *Kvinnovetenskapligt tidskrift*, no. 1.

Coulson, M., Magas, B., and Wainwright, H. 1975: Women and the Class Struggle. *New Left Review*, no. 89.

Dalla Costa, M., and James, S. 1973: *The Power of Women and the Subversion of the Community*. Bristol: Falling Wall Press.

Haraway, Donna J. 1991: *Simians, Cyborgs and Women*. London: Free Association Books.

Harding, Sandra. 1986: *The Science Question in Feminism*. Ithaca, NY, and London: Cornell University Press.

Hartmann, Heidi. 1981: The Unhappy Marriage of Marxism and Feminism: Towards a more Progressive Union. In L. Sargent (ed.): *Women and Revolution. The Unhappy Marriage of Marxism and Feminism*. London: Pluto Press.

Hearn, Jeff, and Parkin, Wendy. 1987: *"Sex" at "Work": The Power and Paradox of Organisation Sexuality*. Brighton: Wheatsheaf Books.

Høigård, Cecilie, and Finstad, Liv. 1986: *Bakgater*. Oslo: Pax.

Holter, Harriet. 1970: *Sex Roles and Social Structure*. Oslo: Universitetsforlaget.

Holter, Harriet. 1975: *Familien i klassesamfunnet*. Oslo: Pax.

Kvande, Elin, and Rasmussen, Bente. 1990: *Nye kvinneliv. Kvinner i menns organisasjoner*. Oslo: Ad Notam, Gyldendal.

Laqueur, Thomas. 1990: *Making Sex: Body and Gender from the Greeks to Freud*. Cambridge, MA: Harvard University Press.

Leira, Arnlaug. 1992: Hannkjøn, hunkjøn, intetkjøn – ? In A.Taksdal & K.Widerberg (eds), *Forståelser av kjønn i samfunnsvitenskapenes fag og kvinneforskning*, Oslo: Ad Notam, Gyldendal.

MacKinnon, Catharine A. 1979: *Sexual Harassment of Working Women*. New Haven: Yale University Press.

Ressner, Ulla. 1985: *Den dolda hierarkin. Om demokrati och jämställdhet*. Stockholm: Arbetslivscentrum.

Sargent, Lydia (ed.) 1981: *Women and Revolution. The Unhappy Marriage of Marxism and Feminism*. London: Pluto Press.

Secombe, W. 1974: The Housewife and her Labour under Capitalism. *New Left Review*, 83.

Smith, Dorothy. 1987: *The Everyday World as Problematic: Towards a Sociology for Women*. Boston: Northeastern University Press.

—— 1990a: *The conceptual Practices of Power: A Feminist Sociology of Knowledge*. Toronto: University of Toronto Press.

—— 1990b: *Texts Facts and Femininity: Exploring the Relations of Ruling*. London: Routledge.

Sørensen, Bjørg Aase. 1982: Ansvarsrationalitet – Om mål-middeltenkning blant kvinner. In H. Holter (ed.), *Kvinner i felleskap*. Oslo: Universitetsforlaget.

Walby, Sylvia. 1989: Theorising Patriarchy. *Sociology*, 23/2.

Widerberg, Karin. 1992: Teoretisk verktøyskasse. Angrepsmåter og metoder. In A. Taksdal and K.

Widerberg (eds), *Førståelser av kjønn i samfunnsvitenskapenes fag og kvinneforskning*. Oslo: Ad Notam, Gyldendal.

—— 1994: Simmel og det modernas kön. *Sosiologisk Tidskrift*, 2/2.

Young, Iris. 1981: Beyond the Unhappy Marriage: A Critique of the Dual Systems Theory. In L. Sargent (ed.), *Women and Revolution. The Unhappy Marriage of Marxism and Feminism,* London: Pluto Press.

chapter **30**

From Aristotle to Modern Social Theory

Margareta Bertilsson

It has been suggested that the modern social sciences were discovered, simultaneously in both France and Scotland, at the end of the eighteenth century (Eriksson 1988). For the first time observers then began to regard society as the unintended outcome of common people's efforts. This new approach broke with prevailing theories, from Antiquity and the Middle Ages, which proposed that society was the result of intentionality and will. This older philosophy was further supported by Christian notions of a supreme God, underpinning the entire world order. In its secular form, this theory of will found an echo in the numerous theories on princely power which became popular during the Renaissance. Niccolò Machiavelli is probably the best-known theorist of this genre. The same period also saw the beginnings of the modern nation-state. But these "modern" theories of the Renaissance were still shackled to ancient patterns of thinking: Society was still regarded as the product of a single ruler's will and actions.

The real breakthrough in social theory (and social science) came about only when large numbers of ordinary people became visible in scientific theory, it is their contribution which has created what we today call society. This contribution can be defined by a number of different types of activity such as physical labor, gift-giving, and communication. Modern theorists no longer look for a central controlling force or will behind what goes on in the visible world. It is a well-known fact, of course, that Adam Smith (1723–90), the father of modern economic theory, believed that the market (the relationship between demand and supply) was regulated by an "invisible hand" which he compared to divine providence. But providence, however one defines it, has proved to be notoriously difficult to investigate and understand.

The central task of the social sciences is to investigate patterns of social systems (speech, action, and labor) which people produce collectively. It is characteristic of modern societies to generate many reciprocally ordered systems, often in competition with each other. The uncontrolled growth of such systems could easily lead to chaos. The discovery of society, that is, that collective activities create ordered systems, which nobody had planned in advance, has had both positive and negative consequences. It has given some individuals a sense of freedom but it has also caused fear and disruption. Social scientists suffer from the same sense of anxiety which plagues many natural scientists when they see the consequences of their trail-blazing discoveries. Can we control the future of gene technology? Should we have halted research into atomic physics before it was too late? An uncertain future, which no one can control, can create anxiety within the community of social scientists. The central purpose of this chapter, on social theory, is to reveal the nature of this ambivalence with regard to the discovery of "the social" which in fact has characterized the social sciences since their inception. It is, however, in the light of the classical Aristotelian tradition that the discovery of the social realm can be regarded as epoch-making, as the basis of our own modern society.

On Aristotle and his Philosophy

The title of this chapter leads inevitably to the question; why start with Aristotle and not Plato? Alfred N. Whitehead (1861–1947) is supposed to have said that the history of philosophy is nothing more than footnotes to the works of Plato. Why should this not also apply to the social sciences? There is, however, good reason to regard Aristotle – who was Plato's pupil – as more interesting than his teacher when one investigates the development of the empirical (social) sciences. As far as Plato was concerned, the truth belonged to the realm of pure thought and as such was beyond the range of the human senses. All that is available to us, according to Plato, was a world of shadows.

Aristotle's (384–322 B.C.) great contribution to modern science is his work on the general foundations of scientific explanation, which even today is regarded as the foundation of "correct" methods of thinking. Aristotle's system of logic is called *Organon*, which means that it constitutes the tools of thought itself. In Aristotle's work one can also find a philosophy of nature (physics) which includes both nature and culture. This philosophy teaches us that "nature never does anything without a reason," a theory which has had wide-ranging consequences for both philosophy and science (Christensen et al. 1993: 11). Another difference between Plato and Aristotle is that Aristotelian teaching recognizes three equally valid areas for approaching understanding: theoretical, practical, and poietical knowledge. Medieval scholars characterized Plato's philosophy as an example of *vita contemplativa* while Aristole's philosophy was regarded as exemplifying *vita activa* (Arendt 1958: 31–41). The contemplative life concentrates on thought (*Logos*) while the active life focuses on action (*Praxis*). In this chapter I will touch on a number of key elements within Aristotelian teaching to show their significance with regard to the modern social sciences.

Logic

The introduction to a typical book on logic usually includes a sentence such as this: "The science of logic was founded by Aristotle more than two thousand years ago" (Marc-Wogau 1961: 7). Of course, logic has developed a great deal since Aristotle's time. Its concepts have been converted into mathematics and formalized. But the general foundations of logic have changed little since Aristotle laid them them down 2,400 years ago.

Logic involves the knowledge of inferences (syllogisms), something which for Aristotle and his contemporaries meant teachings about the process of thought itself. One of the laws which controls thinking, is the law of "the excluded middle" or what we would also call the principle of non-contradiction. It is impossible, at one and the same time, to propose A and not-A.

Logic plays an important role in all scientific activity because of what it tells us about inferences, that is, the necessity of drawing the correct conclusions from given premises. The classic form of conclusion is *deduction*, which can be formulated in the following way:

All men are mortal
Socrates is a man

Therefore Socrates is mortal

If the two premises are correct, then the conclusion – Socrates is mortal – will also be correct. Or in everyday speech: if one says A, one must also say B. But it is only in the world of pure thought that we encounter "pure truths." In the rough and tumble of everyday life, we usually operate with information garnered from experience (*empiri*). This type of knowledge normally includes events which cannot be inferred on a strictly deductive basis. Inductive thought processes start with simple statements such as "these women are intelligent" and "they are also ugly" and proceed to general observations, including possible connections, such as: Intelligent women are ugly. A conclusion like this is the result of previous observations, and excludes the results of future observations, which might contradict it. Induction is, in other words, a problematic method for reaching conclusions.

Aristotle created another even more problematic logical method than induction, and called it *abduction* (Peirce 1932: 182–205; Andersen 1994: 122–53). The following example, which is based on normal everyday experiences, explains how it works (Sacks 1974: 216–32):

> The child is crying
> The woman picks the child up
> _____
> The woman is the child's mother

As we can see from this example, abduction is, from a strictly logical standpoint, an invalid method for forming conclusions. Nonetheless, it has proved a fertile technique for providing us with meaningful connections in analyzing everyday events. It may also help create new unforeseen connections and force us to question those which we already take for granted. Why do we believe that the woman is the child's mother? Perhaps she is simply a passer-by who feels sorry for the child? She could even be attempting to kidnap the child. The question of observation is here put into an interpretive perspective. One sees something which one has not seen before or one becomes confused about something which is happening, but ought not to be happening. Abduction, as observation of events, has been called the engine of scientific thought. One of its most exciting properties is that it places the observer in the same situation as a detective who is in the process of solving a crime (Asplund 1976).

On cosmology and physics

Abductive operations – such as the one described in the above example, which, although often resorted to, are today considered highly problematic – can be explained within the Aristotelian tradition and its plural knowledge systems. Being (the universe) includes those things which are there by *necessity*, things which are there *by chance* as well as things which are in the state of *becoming*. Potential knowledge is a necessary part of Aristotle's epistemological theory and it has its counterpart in his cosmology and physics. The term cosmos includes both living things and non-living things in the natural world. The natural world as a whole is characterized by a strong teleological function: a means–end way of thinking (*telos* = aim). Everything which exists now and which will exist in the future fulfills a function or has an objective. The abductive inference draws our attention to new connections in Being, whose functions may only become apparent with further investigation. It is actually in the framework of a creation-perspective that the abductive inference has its telos: it can point out possibilities beyond those of simple existence within given phenomena.

Theories about possibilities and nonevents have been brushed aside as speculative and diffuse within positivist branches of epistemology. We have a tendency to bracket nonempirical reasoning as metaphysics, that is, experience outside a time–space framework. However, in Aristotle's day, metaphysics was not considered to be a negative term but rather an essential characteristic of Cosmos. One assumed that balance and order reigned within Cosmos. Everything had its allotted place within a holistic system, which only the gods fully understood. When surprising events (that is, which were not governed by rules) were observed, ancient thinkers believed such events to be properly understood when their position with regard to their functions within the greater whole was discovered. Then such events were assigned interpretive meaning.

Teleology in the Aristotelian tradition has played an important role in the development of the social sciences, especially their interpretation of concepts of truth. The truth may not be available today, but it will always remain a future possibility, depending on the effectiveness of our present actions. Marxism, pragmatism, and existentialism are notable for the way they place importance on human agency. Verification, which relies on human agency, is highly problematic from a strictly positivistic point of view, because such a standpoint operates with a much narrower observation horizon. But within the philosophical movements mentioned above, which stress the importance of human agency, the Aristotelian tradition is vividly manifest. Here verification is not only a concern of *Logos* (theoretical rationality) but is also dependent on the realm of practical actions and thereby on our ability to transform reality.

On patterns of explanation

Within the interwoven chain of relations between events, structures, and processes, which constitute the Aristotelian cosmic order, we also find a number of different causal relations: *causa materialis, causa formalis, causa efficiens, and causa finalis* (Lübcke 1983: 69–70). I will confine the present discussion to the last two causes as I consider the relationship between them to be central to an understanding of modern social theory.

Causa efficiens describes an exterior cause, for example, when a car runs over a dog, which in turn leads to a situation in which the dog dies. The collision between car and dog causes the dog's death. This event could not have been predicted. It simply occurred. The *causa finalis,* on the other hand, describes a force which is inherent within the phenomena themselves and which is realized in the course of development of a predetermined aim, for instance, when a young girl gradually develops into a woman and later becomes a mother. Final, or interior causes, reverse the temporal order of *efficient*, exterior causes; the state of womanhood temporally occurs after girlhood. The operative cause can be found in the future end while the *efficient* cause follows a regular scheme: x (cause) comes temporally before y (effect). The reversed temporal situation of the *final* construction (y–x–y) runs counter to the ideals of modern, experimental, epistemological thinking (x–y).

The modern, experimental, epistemological ideal – which insists that causes precede effects – required a completely different worldview (cosmology) to that contained within Aristotle's teleology. The modern view of the world was dominated by the idea of a universe as a giant piece of clockwork, a *perpetuum mobile*. The chief problem with this view was the question of who had originally set the clock in motion. The notion that the universe had spontaneously come into being and had then mutated over a long period of time into a stable, self-regulatory system was difficult for (late) medieval thinkers to accept. The teleological worldview of Antiquity – built upon the idea of *final* forces – existed for a long period side by side with the secularized idea of the universe as a mechanical piece of clockwork. Medieval science had no difficulty in including such diverse epistemological discourses as theology and the natural sciences.

Consequences of the new ideal

The new experimental, epistemological ideal was engendered in a series of powerful reactions to the natural philosophy of Antiquity and Christianity. The dispute centered on the question of the importance of *telos* and *causa finalis* in the world. The Italian monk, Giordano Bruno (1548–1600) was burnt at the stake by the Roman Catholic Church because he disputed the Church's thesis that the earth (and God) were the center of the universe (its final cause). The Italian mathematician and physicist, Galileo Galilei (1564–1642), officially broke away from the Catholic Church by insisting that the Copernican thesis – which proposed that the earth moved around the sun, rather than the opposite – was the only possible scientific truth. In 1633 the Catholic Church condemned Galilei's ideas as heretical, but thanks to a special pardon from the Pope, he did not share the same fate as the monk, Giordano Bruno (Butterfield 1951).

The development of new empirical sciences such as physics and chemistry necessitated a break with the old, dogmatic ideals as practiced within theology and law. Although exegetic disciplines such as law and theology were able to develop a certain amount of interpretative freedom within the framework of the Church's prescribed dogmas, it was the modern, empirical sciences which finally decided the battle as to which teaching was true. The truth could no longer be determined from above (by a single will), and had to be determined empirically via thousands of observations. The greatest advocate for the modern, empirical, scientific ideal is the founding father of classical physics, Isaac Newton (1642–1727). He is supposed to have stated that: "Hypotheses non fingo" ("I feign no hypothesis") unless proven through experimental means.

One of the theoretical consequences of this change in worldview and epistemological ideals was that the question of "why things came to be" became less interesting for science than the question of "how things operate." "Why" questions tend to suggest that occult forces – which cannot be tested experimentally – lie behind ordinary phenomena. However, if one poses the question "how something happens," an observer can manipulate causal relations through repeated experimentation to reveal which forces are at play. This (epistemological) displacement necessitates a distancing from the ideals of the Church and Antiquity: the observer becomes less speculative/theoretical and more experimental/active. The technical, knowledge-based ideal (see the section below on *Techne*) came to dominate all scientific activity. The Aristotelian teleology about immanent causes within phenomena gradually disappeared and the idea of a *telos* became more and more suspect within the worldview encapsulated by the modern theory of knowledge.

Do the Social Sciences need Final Cause Explanations?

It has long been a mystery why the social sciences – and especially sociology – have never really developed into a full-blown natural science of the social (Giddens 1976). One possible explanation for this apparent backwardness with regard to absorbing scientific methodology is perhaps that sociology (and several other functional and cultural disciplines) have had trouble releasing themselves from the thesis of final cause explanations. These types of explanations frequently occur as so-called "intentional" explanations at the micro-level and as "functional" explanations at the macro-level.

But such explanations, which present social and cultural scientists with special problems, have developed in tandem with the expansion of modern science having made significant inroads into what has been dubbed *Geisteswissenschaften*. This term, from the German, first came about as a reaction within the fields of the humanities and cultural sciences to the expansion of the experimental natural sciences to areas which had traditionally been guided by other cognitive ideals. The German philosopher and historian, Wilhelm Dilthey (see chapters 1 and 6), set himself the task of establishing an alternative epistemological foundation for the cultural sciences and the humanities. Hermeneutics (interpretation studies) developed into such an alternative foundation. As a result, there arose a conflict between two competing patterns of understanding – *Erklären* and *Verstehen* – and this conflict has played an important role within the social sciences. It was never made clear (and still has not been made clear) whether the social sciences ought to follow the example of the natural sciences or the cultural sciences. To *explain* a connection implies that one observes a causal relation and explains its law-like (*nomothetic*) course in accordance with prevailing theories. To *understand* a connection, however, implies that one applies an inferential course of a subjective meaning. Unlike explanation, understanding is ideographic: it requires, in other words, that one pays attention to concrete, historical connections (Habermas 1988: 17–65).

The conflict between these two epistemological ideals has been particularly fierce within the social sciences and can still be traced in the tension that exists between behavioral and intentional modes of explanation in social science. Those who believe that human actions must be understood in the light of the actors' intentions (consciousness, will, context) do not believe that the social sciences can be based upon the cognitive ideals of the natural sciences in contrast to the views of behaviorists, for instance (Winch 1958). This split between the exterior (observable) and the interior perspective of understanding has ensured that the language of the social sciences continues to be riddled by complexities.

But hermeneutics has not been the only epistemological system which has taken an oppositional stance toward the natural sciences and especially the paradigmatic dominance of physics in modern science. Functionalism too (see chapter 14) can be regarded as yet another reaction to the dominance in modern times of a materialistic and/or physics-based worldview (to explain a phenomenon by reducing it to its minimum physical parts).

Functionalism

The origin of functionalism is found in the biosciences, especially teachings about organisms. The function of the heart can only be understood by referring to its wider function for the whole system. In contrast to hermeneutics, a functional standpoint presupposes a number of generalizing intentions. Functionalism exists in a number of different versions. But they all share the Aristotelian postulate, that within nature (just as in culture), there exists an interior (necessary) context, a striving for balance. One could even go so far as to say that within the natural order, there exists an ideal state of balance (Lee and Newby 1989: 259–306). As a rule, functional properties are end-related properties. They do not necessarily exist in the here and now, but are postulated to exist as hypothetical suppositions.

Functionalism has played a key role in the genesis and development of the modern social sciences. This applies both to functionalism in its original manifestation as a superior theory of balance and in its later manifestation as an autopoietic theory of reproduction (Luhmann

1995; see chapter 22). Classic anthropology (Malinowski 1944; Radcliffe-Brown 1952) has heavily influenced contemporary functionalism: primitive rituals, for example, rain dances, were viewed within the framework of their functional meaning, their ability to create integration. The English sociologist, Herbert Spencer, utilized evolutionary thinking when he produced his theory of social development. Spencer assumed that social developments were "caused" by final forces of increased individualization, specialization and competetiveness between individual members of that society (see chapter 3). Spencer regarded capitalist society as a "natural order" brought about through (interior) sociobiological (system) forces. The most important task for sociology was to describe and explain the new forms of integration which appeared in modern society as a result of its far-reaching individualization.

The same type of challenge is also central to an understanding of Emile Durkheim's sociology (see chapter 5). To this can be added the present-day work of Jürgen Habermas (see chapter 21) and Niklas Luhmann (see chapter 22), who also make use of similar basic assumptions. However, modern functionalism has been forced to abandon, or radically revise, certain classical assumptions about society's immanent course of development. The large-scale final-cause explanations have gradually faded into the background in the social sciences. Instead, a new perspective is opening up, allowing chance and coincidence a much larger role in understanding development.

Marxism also regarded historical development as if it were a necessary result of an immanent class struggle (see chapter 2). Classical Marxism was characterized by strong teleological tendencies presupposing that the end of history would be heralded at the same time as the classless society came into being. Marxist explanations have consequently operated (and still operate) with a different (historical-functional) causal logic than the other empirical social sciences. An extensive theoretical discussion of different types of causal relations has also taken place within the Marxist tradition (Elster 1982: 453–539; see also other articles in this issue).

In today's (post)modern age, the social sciences are urged to break away from "the big stories" (Lyotard 1984; see chapter 26). But perhaps we are simply replacing the big stories with many small individual life-stories, thus preserving the need for meaning in human existence. Even if we abandon the idea that history contains *une grande finale* – a superior controlling principle and a realizable final aim – we cannot easily banish this idea at the micro-level among individuals. In the modern (post)-welfare state, individuals are forced to develop long-term plans for their own lives. Final causes continue to function at the micro-level as encroaching demands for self-realization among individuals.

On Intentional Explanations and Non-Intentional Consequences

As mentioned above, in an attempt to explain the emergence of modern social sciences, Björn Eriksson, made the following observations: The *modern* social sciences start emerging when explanations based on a great will are replaced by explanations based on the will and intentions of numerous ordinary individuals (Eriksson 1988). When he uses the term "great will," Eriksson is not thinking of divine will or an immanent force in nature (as Aristotle proposed) but rather the theories about contracts between more or less egoistical individuals, theories which laid down the basic tenets of the modern social sciences. Man was, as Thomas Hobbes saw it, for example, a creature controlled by his own selfish drives and lusts. To avoid a war of all against all, reason forced men to accept a peace pact with their fellow men. By entering into such a contract, human beings otherwise living in a natural state, handed over a large part of their sovereignty to the prince (Hobbes 1980). This contract between individuals represented the entrance of "society," a realm of thought where people were forced to recognize the existence of one another.

Björn Eriksson contends that state and legal philosophy, which are based on rational theories of contract and will, ought to be considered as "premodern" in relation to the social sciences proper. According to Eriksson, social science emerged when the market was discovered as a distinct self-regulatory system apart from the (exterior) state and the law. Society, he suggests, was suddenly regarded as much larger and more complicated as soon as it was realized that there existed a field which lay outside princely control. This new social realm gave rise to a completely different form of logic than that which postulated the hegemony of explanations, based on the will and intentions of princes or contracts. Monocentric thinking gave way to polycentric thinking. It was the accumulation of numerous individual actions and engagements which produced the conception of a society beyond the control of the state. The logic of the marketplace perverted the purposes and intentions of the prince in numerous non-intended directions.

Individual purposes – collective results

The study of non-intended consequences developed into a rich field of investigation within that branch of the social sciences which would now be called *empirical* in contrast to the *normative* disciplines of political and legal science. The study of the relationship between individual intentions (at the micro-level) and collective results (at the macro-level) would reveal itself to be a central problem in the development of the social sciences (see chapter 13). This can be summed up in the following classical expression: "Private vices, public benefits" (Mandeville in Elster 1978: 107).

The discovery of the social – of self-regulatory mechanisms within the marketplace and society – must be considered of crucial importance. In effect, this discovery helped to create the essence of the modern age. According to Eriksson, the discovery of the social within social science can be equated with the discoveries of Galileo and Newton within the natural sciences. The break with Aristotle's philosophy of nature and society was now completed and it became more and more difficult to resort to "final explanations." "Efficient" explanations survived at the level of human interaction – as human intentions, whose effects could not be predicted. Within this mental construction, there lay (and still lies) a duality. The interior is expressed in something exterior and the exterior traces its origins in the interior. Efficient and intentional explanations proved to be intimately intertwined.

It is here, in the dual nature of explanatory logic, that we discover the uniqueness of social science. Max Weber expressed this dual nature of social-science explanations by demanding that we understand human actions intentionally, while concentrating on their subsequent (exterior) progress in the form of causal connections (see chapter 6). At this conjunction, it is also worth mentioning two modern sociologists, Jürgen Habermas and Anthony Giddens. Habermas puts forward the idea that the nonlinguistic means of system-communication penetrate the intentionality of the life-world and vice versa. Giddens, on the other hand, postulates a reciprocal relationship between structure and action: structure constrains action while at the same time enabling it (Habermas 1981 and Giddens 1984; see chapters 21 and 24). The explanatory logic of the social sciences was also enriched by what C. Wright Mills regarded as the great challenge of sociology, that is, to trace the course of history through individual biographies and vice versa (Mills 1959; see chapter 16). In reality then, dual casuality constitutes the essence of social science.

This raises another difficult question for social science, namely which epistemological forms (or knowledge interests) are deemed valid?

Three (or Four?) Knowledge Interests: Theoretical, Practical, and Poietical (and Reproductive?) Knowledge

Aristotle's teachings include, by the standards of Antiquity, a general classification of knowledge forms: theoretical, practical, and poietical knowledge. In contrast to Plato, Aristotle places a high value on practical knowledge such as politics and ethics. Man is, he says, a political animal (*zoon politikos*).

I would like to discuss briefly the classical distinctions, to determine how they have developed and influenced discussion within social science. As I mentioned above, the modern social sciences have been characterized by a dual nature of causality. But in addition to this, social science includes non-causal cognitive claims (Habermas 1968).

Theoria: from spectator to power?

The Greek word *theoria* means "disinterested view." In Antiquity, this form of (passive) activity was reserved for philosophers. The ability to see was an act of appropriation. Its practioners – who were always men – were required to isolate themselves from the active life of society. The purpose of theoretical comprehension was to reflect the harmony and eternal cyclical nature of the cosmos. As mentioned before, Hannah Arendt (1906–75) called the act of theoretical comprehension the *vita contemplativa* – an apposite term since it brings to mind the concentration, stillness, and quietude which is necessary if one is to cultivate theoretical work. Theoretical comprehension resulted in *episteme*, true understanding.

Theoretical concepts are not treated in the same way by modern philosophies of science as they were in Antiquity. Passive observation has given way to active manipulation, and even to productive comprehension (*techne*).

It has been said that the modern scientific and experiment-oriented attitude represents a successful fusion of two previously separate activities, that is, the cultivation of Aristotle's logic within monastic communities and the ability of artisans to manufacture products (Zilsel 1976). Two social layers of society met, with the result that logic encountered crude experience (*empiri*).

The experimental design, which we recognize today, is an expression of this fusion. The sense of solitude and speculative observation which was an integral part of *theoria* in Antiquity (and which survived in monastic cultures) was consigned to oblivion while a completely new, empirically based concept of theory won acceptance: A "true theory" is now defined as a theory which can either be reduced, in its most minute constituents, to sense-observations (positivism), or as a theory which has shown itself to have consequences as far as action is concerned (pragmatism). As mentioned above, metaphysics has now been weeded out of scientific discourse and is often regarded as something occult. In this process, the Aristotelian elements of *causa finalis* have gradually been removed from scientific grammar. *Causa efficiens* has become the dominant form of causality: x is assumed to affect y as something exterior, and the relationship xy can be employed as a basis for calculation. The laboratory – and not the spectacular arena of Antiquity, or the monastic cell of the Middle ages – has become the new temple of knowledge, the place where science is cultivated.

Even though experiment-based epistemological models have become dominant, this does not mean that other epistemological models have completely disappeared. Alternative cognitive interests have acted as both a stimulant and an irritant when the modern sciences attempt to study humankind and its actions.

Praxis as form of knowledge and action

In contrast to the action concept, which I called *techne* above, and which represents humankind's ability to produce things, there exists another action dimension in ancient writings, the dimension of *praxis*. It is in fact through speech and action that human beings realize their inner selves. Unlike *techne*, *praxis* is focused on the life of the soul and the "products" created in the process of spiritual refinement. Praxis represents *internalized* actions while techne stands for *externalized* actions. But this is not to say that internalized actions must necessarily be private and subjective; in Antiquity, these actions were connected to the public sphere, and those areas of life which implied a common responsibility, within the *polis*. The concept of praxis has always been connected to ideas of virtue, to people's ability to maintain self-control and exercise moderation; in other words, what we would today define as control of ego. In G. H. Mead's approach to the development of the social individual as a result of communicative sociality (gesture and significant symbols; see chapter 8) one can clearly identify his debt to the Aristotelian tradition (Mead 1934).

In Antiquity, the form of understanding which is connected to the concept of praxis has nothing in common with the *theoria*. The main goal of *praxis* is not to produce a true understanding of the order of things based on exterior observations, but to promote man's moral character. *Phronesis* is a form of knowledge, which relates to humans' ability to form judgements and to make correct decisions. This type of decision-making has consequences for the surrounding environment. It is instrumental in either promoting or hindering the emergence of the good life. The good life, meanwhile, lacks the (theoretical) characteristics which allow us to describe it once and for all as a set of recommendations. *Phronesis* (the good judgement) is dependent on the situation: it involves the ability to determine which conditions apply in a given situation and then acting in accordance with them.

The idea of the good life, which is linked to the concept of praxis, has both an exterior and an interior side. For the individual, the good life implies a feeling of happiness while, for the group, it signifies collective harmony. Aristole's philosophy is characterized by a strong sense of political responsibility (Arendt 1958).

From praxis to techne

Much later, during the Renaissance period, philosophers revitalized the ancient concept of praxis; but they also altered its content (Lobkowicz 1967). When Niccolò Machiavelli advised the Italian prince on how power should be exercised, he underscored the importance of restraint and self-control (as Aristotle did). But the chief aim of these recommendations was that the prince should never show any signs of weakness in his dealings with others. The concept of praxis lost its classical communicative basis and instead became identified with the individual's ability to take advantage of, or even "seduce," his surroundings. As a functional concept *praxis* moved closer and closer to *techne*, toward the effectiveness of action and the ability to affect the exterior world. Machiavelli, and the philosophy which he encouraged (Thomas Hobbes et al.), reduced the conception of praxis to that of a technical model for arranging exterior objectified nature.

The outer natural world, or environment, can now be observed as "facts"(Macintyre 1981). At the same time as we externalize nature with the help of empirical facts, we internalize our own values as emotions. Human life is split up into a subject sphere and an object sphere, and this division also affects the ancient concept of praxis. Praxis becomes identified with an objective function – in speech and action the individual externalizes his or her inner life. However, when concepts of subject and object acquire their epistemological form (with Hobbes and Locke), praxis disappears from scientific discourse. Because of the lack of suitable measuring devices, the inner life of the subject remains beyond scientific observations. The division between facts and values is an important link in the modern process of increasing cognitive differentiation (for further discussion, see chapter 27).

The good life – or the concept of such a life – now loses its objectivity. It cannot be measured operationally, and the concept cannot easily be reconciled with modern science's demands for objective statements. The good life has therefore been subjectified along the level of individual preferences, which can then be measured as pure data and then related to factual statements. There exists, as Max Weber indicated, in the modern world of representations an extensive interaction between science and politics. It is the role of science to produce objective facts about, among other things, human relationships, and it is the role of politics to do something about the order of these things. Modern science has – and I include the science of action – become more and more theoretical and less and less practical (in the sense which the concept of praxis was used in Antiquity). Along with this cognitive transformation, we can also discern the influence of *techne*, because it is only by utilizing observations and predictions that we can come in contact with our (practical!) surroundings.

The dualism of facts and values, of object and subject and even of body and soul is deeply rooted in modern philosophy. Dualisms dominate the practical philosophy of Immanuel Kant, for instance. As body, the human being is subject to the same (*efficient*) causal laws which apply to the rest of nature. But the individual is also a spiritual being. We can thus control our activities in accordance with the modern principle of freedom (*Nein sagen können*; we can say no). But in Kant's work, we are also confronted with the desire to achieve (valid) knowledge in the practical realm of will and action. By subjecting our (value) acts to the "categorical imperative" we attempt, with the help of reason, to validate our actions in accordance with the "categorial imperative" (Kant 1998). Kant's strict demand for seeking valid understanding of the moral life resembles, in its universalizing aspiration, the demands for generalization within experimental analysis. This "operation of abstraction" has been criticized for applying the same claims of rationality to the practical world of values as apply to the theoretical (factual) sphere. Practical judgement thus breaks free from situational demands of the here-and-now and becomes theoretical! Ethics is subjugated to morality in Kant's practical philosophy.

Theory/praxis: the consequences for sociology

The influence of Kant and his division of the individual into body and will, has had far-reaching consequences as far as social science is concerned. We can trace the influence of Kant in the work of both Georg Simmel (see chapter 7) and Max Weber (see chapter 6). When Simmel, in his famous essay, answers the question *How is society possible* (Simmel 1968), he regards societal integration as the result of cooperative acts of will among individuals. The social order is therefore of a different character than the natural order: It is realized by individual acts that are interior rather than exterior. One could in fact characterize Simmel's view of society as an ongoing self-reproductive collective process of will-control, taking place among acting individuals. Externalized in the form of laws and monetary values, acts of will become alienated in relation to individual ends and purposes.

Perhaps one can also regard Emile Durkheim's concept of society in this way. Unlike Simmel, who clearly defines effective social power, Durkheim's concept is exterior and constraining. Kant's influence on Max Weber can best be discerned in Weber's demand for *Verstehen* in sociological analysis. The concept of *Verstehen* implies that we inquire into the subjective meaning (or will) which an individual places in his actions, which subsequently control their progress. Weber sought to combine the subjective and the objective in his sociology: in their aggregated form, acts of will become objectified facts. As objectified facts, acts are subject to the same demands of scientific objectivity as those applying to natural science. This means that social science becomes the bearer of cognitive claims which are complex in their duality, to unite the interior with the exterior and to unite the act of understanding with the explanatory power of theoretical (factual) analysis.

Regarding social science in this dual perspective, which stems from Kant and which was further developed by Weber, is still extant today, and is probably best represented in the writings of Jürgen Habermas. Our complex, modern society cannot be understood solely as a result of cognitive (will) acts. It must also be regarded as an non-intended, non-transparent system of objectified (efficient!) acts. The operations of the market are controlled by the demand for profit – whether short- or long-term yields – and this demand obscures individual meaning-claims. Habermas speaks, for instance, of nonlinguistic means of communication. He is referring to money and power, which as exterior means of control, usurp power and colonize the life-world of individuals. But the dual perspective – which combines both exterior and interior analysis – is just as important for Habermas as it once was for Weber, since it allows him to combine a practical-philosophical approach with a theoretical-sociological approach. However, it seems correct to suggest that the first approach has played a more important role in Habermas's work than in the writings of Weber.

Habermas can therefore, with full justification, present his sociology as "theoretical analysis" with "practical intentions" (Habermas 1971: 9).

A criticism of theoretical orientation

Both Weber and Habermas have through their characteristic use of theoretical (explanatory) analysis broken away from the old praxis philosophy of Antiquity. Their sociologies are not limited by situation-determined demands on understanding. But there have always been critical voices raised against sociology's penetration by the theoretical approach. One such critic is the German philosopher, Hans-Georg Gadamer (b. 1900), who has attacked modern science in general and social scientists and sociology in particular.

In his renowned work, *Wahrheit und Methode* (1962), Gadamer launched a fundamental attack on the modern, theorizing epistemological approach: the epistemology which seeks to achieve true knowledge (*episteme*). According to Gadamer, this theoretical approach is responsible for isolating knowledge from its required communicative function. Modern science includes a practical, communicative role, which is carried out by modern-day research teams (Kuhn 1972). When today's scientists develop their knowledge, the process takes place within the context of a limited historical time and space perspective, that is, within modern, institutionalized science. According to Gadamer, such verification claims are never universal. They are in fact dependent on a communicative understanding of meaning; on understanding something from a particular point of view. Communicative (hermeneutic) understanding is fundamental if one is to carry out a theoretical analysis, according to Gadamer. The problem with the (social) sciences of our own time is that they have forgotten the situation-determinedness of its own analysis. Science often serves outside power interests, which are then forgotten in the apparently universal form of its theoretical analysis.

In the later writings of Ludwig Wittgenstein – who influenced the hermeneutics of Gadamer – the same fundamental classical *praxis* approach comes to prominence again: to understand something is to see it through the linguistic prism of an already prevailing form of life (Winch 1958).

The same type of praxis-orientated criticism has been expressed recently within the area of the philosophy of morals and values. The movement known as communitarianism has strongly criticized notions of the individual as an abstracted being. This notion, which was first expressed by Kant, was later taken up by Weber and seems also to be present in Habermas (Bellah 1992; Benhabib 1994). The philosophy of values, cultivated by the communitarians, can be seen as a critical alarm clock ringing in the ears of the modern social sciences, as far as their technical construction of society is concerned (Macintyre 1981: 84–102). Critics feel that there is a risk that human dialogue will simply fade away under the factual demands of modern social science. By subjecting dialogue to the demands of technical processes it is emptied of its own function, that of producing morally valid judgements on our way of life.

Despite the return of modern *praxis* philosophy – as either a hermeneutic or a communitarian philosophy of values – discussions of *phronesis* do not dominate (post)modern social science. Instead, the postmodern cognitive ideal borrows the expressive artistic attitude: to create something new. The poietic or aesthetic ideal is different in both form and content than the distinction between theory and practice, as previously discussed.

Poietic-technical knowledge

Poietike is the Greek word for "productive activity." This epistemological concept applied to all artistic activity whether it was rhetoric, the visual arts, spear-throwing, dance, or song. It was primarily considered to be a homage to beauty. In the world of Antiquity, the artist held the privileged position of being a spokesman of the gods. *Techne* – which means to produce something, as a result of an activity – also included an aesthetic element. Today, the term productive activity is connected to the production of goods. The value of these goods, however, is rarely determined by their aesthetic properties. The original cognitive value of *techne* was to create beauty and harmony with the help of produced objects. An inferior value was linked to their "effective" purposes in rationalizing human energies. In modern times, however, values of efficiency have achieved dominance over the expense of aesthetics.

The technical knowledge interests, the production of objects (artifacts), is not confined to technology and the natural sciences but has also become a dominant ideal within social science. It has even been proposed that the very concept of the social is a brilliant artifact, created and supported by the new social scientists who came to prominence during the nineteenth century. The nineteenth century is also the period during which technical interests were acclaimed as the primary source of all science, including that of law (Anners 1980: 95–141). The French historian of sociology, Jacques Donzelot, has proposed that the concept of society as a modern construction (an artifact!), which has been developed to mediate in the economic and political conflict which came about as a result of industrialism and the French revolution (Donzelot 1988).

As we shall see later, it is this technical construction of the social against which Hannah Arendt, among others, has warned in her sharp criticism of modern social science (Arendt 1958). The idea of the good life loses its ethical power of social integration in a society, which consists of randomly connected individuals whose relations are external (*efficient*) rather than internal (*final*). In opposition to the views of Arendt – and of the aristocratic scare of mass society – it is worth noting that it is only in a modern, much criticized, mass society that one can talk about true freedom for individuals, namely the freedom to live one's own life as one wishes.

But the (Aristotelian) criticism of modern constructions in social theory is an important element in the ongoing discussion of concepts within social science, since it illustrates the displacement of cognitive interests and its wider consequences. The fact that *techne* has become the dominant cognitive value has led to both *episteme* and *praxis* becoming marginalized, and often considered irrational. In its most extreme form, the dominance of end-orientated technical rationalism has produced a situation in which *episteme* and *praxis* have been subsumed within *techne*. One can in fact propose that modern society has developed as a result of a narrowing of the more differentiated, cognitive horizon of Antiquity.

Even the postmodern discussion, which was put forward as a critique of modernity and its systems of knowledge, has tended to further the ideal of *techne* as the dominant cognitive interest. But *techne* has, in the latter case, taken on a more subtle form. The Protestant work ethic and the efficiency of engineering technology are no longer the centre of analysis, but rather the mechanisms of influence which human speech and actions contain in latent form. A performative speech act is a statement which affects human beings and makes them act. In a lecture hall, the command "open the window" will normally produce an effect, if a professor utters the words. Postmodern philosophers have discovered the mechanisms of suggestion innate in speech (Habermas 1981, vol. 1: 388ff). On the micro level – in interactions between people – *techne* can be experienced as impressions and subsequent seductions. The subject's manipulation of the object relation (that which the subject has created) leads to a situation where the privileged subject manipulates his or her surroundings. In this extraordinary creation scenario, the production process is aesthetisised as *poietike*. The postmodern movement can be characterized by the way it has transformed the ancient *techne* ideal to a dramatic *poietika*. By de-emphasizing ordinary, everyday experiences, antimodernism and postmodernism ironically overlap. One finds consistently, in both antipodes, a tendency to assume a critical, satirical attitude to the social as but a modern (superflous) construction.

Reproductive Understanding?

During Antiquity, the reproductive sphere was regarded as devoid of interest. No truth, goodness, or for that matter, beauty, could be ascribed to this private realm. The private realm consisted of activities such as housework and tending to others. The philosophers of Antiquity made a sharp distinction between the public sphere and the private sphere. They only regarded acts within the public sphere as being of cognitive interests. Outside the domain of public life, within the home and in the street, was the realm of unfree individuals: women and slaves. Merchants were also excluded from the public life of the city state. The knowledge produced within the private spheres, was exclusively aimed at re-establishing what was already in existence without contributing anything new.

It is in its attitude of this taken-for-granted approach, that modern (social) science most markedly diverges from the cognitive interests (action and understanding) of Antiquity. The upgrading of the material conditions of understanding is linked to modern cognitive attitudes and values and presumably to the changed position of women in modern society. In contrast to Antiquity's interest in the extraordinary, modernity includes a profound interest in the ordinary, that is, what promotes the material life-conditions of ordinary actors. The construction of a mass society, with boundaries which are potentially global, generates for that matter a very different view of life than what was obtained in the highly demarcated, strictly hierarchical city states of Antiquity (*polis*). Perhaps feminism's greatest contribution to social theory is the way it has upgraded cognitive processes. What was once considered to be merely private thought (intuition) is today an integral part of public debate (Pateman 1988; see chapter 29).

On Ambivalence with Regard to the Social Aspect

Despite the democratization of modern society, which has offered the masses such benefits as suffrage and guaranteed human rights, there have been scholars in social science, right from its inception, who were deeply critical of modernity and the dominance of *causa efficiens*, exterior relations between men. These scholars have opposed the view of society as a result of unintentional consequences. Since this debate has recently become newsworthy again, it seems appropriate to look a little more closely at the issues. The attack is directed at both the dominance of the market and its conjectured consequences on social life, that it produces solitary individuals in search of (or in flight from) casual relationships. In its most extreme consequence, the critique concerns mass society and the fear that it is morally debilitating. But it is also a criticism of the theoretical-technical character of social science, that it is *techne* and not *praxis* which dominates the epistemology of social science.

The discovery of the social as an anonymous field of action, outside the control and responsibility of any singular individual, implies, according to its critics, an alienation of the processes of thought and action themselves. One of the leading critics of modernity is the philosopher, Hannah Arendt. In her book *The Human Condition* (1958), Arendt points out that the role of anonymity in the construction of the social (as a modern invention) stands in sharp contrast to the fellow-community, which Aristotle considered to be the basis of public life in the city states of Antiquity. The innate irresponsibility of anonymous social relations in modern society tends to vulgarize public life. Communal life in modern society is not controlled by a higher sense of responsibility, with the aim of creating and administering the good society. Subjective politics, based only on selfish interests, creates a horde of politicians whose chief aim in life is to be re-elected.

The opposite of this form of interest-based, subjective politics can be found in the illusory objectivity of bureaucratic organizations. The banality of evil can be traced in the innocent individual member of bureaucratic organizations, an individual who simply follows the rules and does not take responsibility for the consequences of his actions. In her sharp criticism of modern mass society and of the construction of the social, Hannah Arendt has been the forerunner of a number of more recent antimodern works in sociology. In *Modernity and the Holocaust* (1989), Zygmunt Bauman puts forward the idea that modernity and the social are related to the anonymous mass society, whose discipline is guaranteed by the effectiveness of its bureaucratic regulations (see chapter 26.).

The same fear of construction of the social can be found in current discussions of *risk society* (Beck 1986; Luhmann 1991; see chapter 25). We do not know what consequences the sociotechnical system – which has broken free from the constraints of all human responsibility – will have in the future. We cannot ascertain which risks and dangers lie ahead, either within the realm of politics and the environment, or within ourselves. The image of Frankenstein's monster gives us an apt metaphor for this diffuse, rampant uneasiness about the future: the construction of an artifact in the shape of a free-floating social world with freely acting individuals has taken control of our lives. We do not know what long-term consequences this linking up between system and the life-world will have for humanity (Habermas 1981).

The break with the philosophy of Aristotle, that is, the discovery of a separate, aggregated social life, was a *sine qua non* (an essential requirement) for the creation of modern social science. But when the long-term consequences of this ground-breaking discovery finally sink in, a climate of horror and anxiety is spreading among the practitioners of that craft that Giambattista Vico (1688–1744) once dubbed *scientia nuovo*. Having a bad conscience about one's own discoveries is thus not restricted to the natural sciences, with the discovery of atomic power and gene technology. Qualms about one's own discipline and all the (unanticipated) changes its study has brought about, is also a common malaise among social scientists, and is perhaps most widespread among sociologists themselves.

Conclusion

In the preceeding pages, I have attempted to draw together the connecting lines, which link the cognitive traditions of Antiquity and modernity. I hope I have been successful in showing the clear connecting lines between different eras as well as the equally obvious points of disjuncture. The logical approach, which makes us demand clarity in statements we and others utter, is an attitude we have inherited from Aristotle. Ancient cosmology and ancient natural science are characterized by strong teleological tendencies. This chapter has aimed at discovering to what degree modern science has been able to release itself from the ideational ballast of Antiquity. As far as the human sciences are concerned, it seems that purposes are required for the understanding of both individual and collective actions as either intentions and/or functions. Investigating the relations between individual actions and their unanticipated consequences, on the collective level, must be considered to be one of the most important areas of study within modern social science. The ancients' view of the world, which was characterized by notions of harmony, balance, and moderation, could never envisage the concept of a split between individual and collective intentions. This split is just one of the "discoveries" made by modern social science.

The task of finding a moderate balance between Antiquity's three ideals for creating understanding, that is, *episteme, phronesis,* and *poietic-techne,* is, and will remain, a greater challenge for modern (social) science than it probably ever was for ancient philosophers. In ancient times, moderation (imposing restrictions) was a demand linked both to understanding and action. Imposing rules which can be applied to a global society is, however, significantly more difficult than breaking such rules. It is also easy to exaggerate one cognitive interest at the expense of the others. But awareness of the fact that there exists a plurality of cognitive forms might possibly inculcate in us a certain degree of humility with regard to the knowledge we already possess. It may also encourage respect for that knowledge which we do not possess, or which we simply have lost in the course of our historical development.

Bibliography

Andersen, Heine (ed.) 1994: *Videnskabsteori og metodelære. Bind I.* Introduktion. Copenhagen: Samfundslitteratur.

Anners, Erik. 1980: *Den europeiska rättens historia.* Vol 2. Stockholm: AWE/Gebers.

Arendt, Hannah. 1958/1989: *The Human Condition.* Chicago: University of Chicago Press.

—— 1978: *The Life of the Mind.* 2 vols. New York: Harcourt Brace Jovanovich.

Aristotle. 1998a: *The Nicomachean Ethics.* Oxford: Oxford Univ Press.

—— 1998b: *Politics.* Oxford: Oxford University Press.

Asplund, Johan. 1976: *Bertillon.* Gothenburg: Korpen.

Bauman, Zygmunt. 1989: *Modernity and the Holocaust.* Ithaca, NY: Cornell University Press.

Beck, Ulrich. 1986: *Risikogesellschaft. Auf dem Weg in eine andere Moderne.* Frankfurt am Main: Suhrkamp.

Bellah, Robert. 1992: *The Good Society.* New York: Alfred Knopf.

Benhabib, Seyla. 1994: *Situating the Self: Gender, Community and Postmodernism in Contemporary Ethics.* Cambridge: Polity Press.

Butterfield, Herbert. 1951: *The Origins of Modern Science 1300–1800.* London: G. Bell.

Christensen, Johnny (ed.) 1993: *Aristoteles om mennesket*. Copenhagen: Pantheon.

Donzelot, J. 1988: The Promotion of the Social. *Economy and Society*, 17/3, 395–426.

Elster, Jon. 1978: *Logic and Society*. New York: John Wiley.

—— 1982: Marxism, Functionalism and Game Theory. *Theory and Society*, 11/4, 453–82.

Eriksson, Björn. 1988: *Samhällsvetenskapens uppkomst. En tolkning ur den sociologiska traditionens perspektiv*. Uppsala: Halgren & Fallgren Förlag.

Gadamer, Hans-Georg. 1962: *Wahrheit und Methode*. Tübingen: J.C.B. Mohr.

Giddens, Anthony. 1976: *New Rules of Sociological Method*. London: Hutchinson.

—— 1984: *The Constitution of Society*. Cambridge: Polity Press.

Habermas, Jürgen. 1968: *Erkenntnis und Interesse*. Frankfurt am Main: Suhrkamp.

—— 1971: *Theorie und Praxis*. 4th edn. Frankfurt am Main: Suhrkamp.

—— 1981: *Theorie des kommunikativen Handelns*. 2 vols. Frankfurt am Main: Suhrkamp.

—— 1988: *Zur Logik der Sozialwissenschaften*. Frankfurt am Main: Suhrkamp.

Hobbes, Thomas. 1980 [1651]: *Leviathan*. Harmondsworth, Middlesex: Penguin Books.

Kant, Immanuel. 1998 [1785]: *Groundwork of the Metaphysics of Morals*, trans. and ed. by Mary Gregor; with an introduction by Christine M. Korsgaard. Cambridge: Cambridge University Press.

Kuhn, Thomas. 1972: *The Structure of Scientific Revolutions*. Chicago: Chicago University Press.

Lee, David, and Newby, Howard. 1989: *The Problem of Sociology*. London: Hutchinson.

Lobkowicz, Nicholas. 1967: *Theory and Practice. History of a Concept from Aristotle to Marx*. Notre Dame, IN: University of Notre Dame Press.

Luhmann, Niklas. 1991: *Soziologie des Risikos*. Berlin and New York: Walter de Gruyter.

Lübcke, Poul (ed.) 1983: *Politikens Filosofileksikon*. Copenhagen: Politikens Forlag.

Lyotard, Jean-François. 1984: *The Postmodern Condition. A Report on Knowledge*. Manchester: Manchester University Press.

MacIntyre, Alasdair. 1981: *After Virtue. A Study in Moral Theory*. London: Duckworth.

Malinowski, Bronislaw. 1944: *A Scientific Theory of Culture*. Chapel Hill, NC: Duke University of California Press.

Marc-Wogau, Konrad. 1961: *Modern Logik*. Stockholm: Liber.

Mead, G. H. 1934: *Mind, Self and Society. From the Standpoint of a Social Behaviorist*. Chicago: University of Chicago Press.

Mills, C. Wright. 1959: *The Sociological Imagination*. New York: Oxford University Press.

Newton, Isaac. 1967: [Anonymous article about I. N. in] *Encyclopedia of Philosophy,* vol. 5/6. New York: Macmillan.

Pateman, Carole. 1988: *The Sexual Contract*. Cambridge: Polity Press.

Peirce, Charles S. 1932: *Collected Papers*. Vol. 5, ed. Ch. Hawthorne and P. Weiss. Cambridge, MA: Belknap Press of Harvard University Press.

Radcliffe-Brown, A. R. 1952: *Structure and Function in a Primitive Society*. London: Oxford University Press.

Sacks, Harvey. 1974: On the Analysability of Stories by Children. In Roy Turner (ed.), *Ethno Methodology,* Harmondsworth, Middlesex: Penguin Books, 216–32.

Simmel, Georg. 1968 [1908]: Exkurs über das Problem: Wie ist Gesellschaft möglisch? *Soziologie. Untersuchungen über die Formen der Vergesellschaftung*: Berlin, 21–30.

Winch, Peter. 1958: *The Idea of a Social Science*. New York: Humanities Press.

Name Index

Subject Index